HISTORY BEHIND THE HEADLINES

HISTORY BEHIND THE HEADLINES

The Origins of Conflicts Worldwide

VOLUME 3

Nancy Matuszak, Editor

GALE GROUP
™
THOMSON LEARNING

Detroit • New York • San Diego • San Francisco
Boston • New Haven, Conn. • Waterville, Maine
London • Munich

Staff

Nancy Matuszak
Project Editor

Bernard Grunow, Contributing Editor; Jason M. Everett, Associate Contributing Editor;
Rita Runchock, Managing Editor.
Editorial

Maria Franklin, Permissions Manager; Margaret A. Chamberlain, Permissions Specialist.
Permissions

Mary Beth Trimper, Manager, Composition and Electronic Prepress;
Evi Seoud, Assistant Manager, Composition Purchasing and Electronic Prepress
Composition

Dorothy Maki, Manufacturing Manager; Rhonda A. Williams, Buyer.
Manufacturing

Barbara J. Yarrow, Imaging and Multimedia Content Manager; Randy Bassett, Imaging Supervisor;
Dean Dauphinais, Senior Editor, Imaging and Multimedia Content; Pamela A. Reed, Imaging Coordinator;
Luke Rademacker, Imaging Specialist; Christine O'Bryan, Graphics Specialist.
Imaging and Multimedia Content

Kenn J. Zorn, Product Design Manager; Pamela A. E. Galbreath, Senior Art Director.
Product Design

Library of Congress Cataloging-in-Publication Data

history behind the headlines
    p. cm.
        Includes bibliographical references and index.
        ISBN 0-7876-4953-8 (alk. paper)
            1. Civil rights—United States—History. I. Title.
JC599.U5S53 1988
323'.0973—dc21   98-13951
ISSN 1531-7307
ISBN 0-7876-4953-8

Printed in the United States
10 9 8 7 6 5 4 3 2 1

TABLE OF CONTENTS

More than twenty years after the violent Khmer Rouge
was ousted from government, the old leaders may finally face trial for their roles in perpetrating the "Killing
Fields."

The Canadian province of Québec maintains strong
ties to its French past, and the movement to separate
from the rest of Canada has grown in recent years.

The five nations bordering the Caspian Sea argue to
determine who has the rights to the sea and its resources.

China's far western province of Xinjiang struggles for
more recognition and rights from the Beijing government for its native ethnic populations.

With Laurent Kabila assassinated, his son Joseph
Kabila becomes the youngest president in Africa. Can
the young man be the strong leader his country needs?

D

De Beers' Central Selling Organization has controlled
the supply of diamonds on the market, and helped keep
prices high, for almost 100 years. Legal and ethical issues have risen to challenge the continued monopoly.

E

Sanctions have been increasingly used as an alternative
to violent persuasion, but are they an effective and valuable weapon or do they create a new set of problems?

In an attempt to stabilize its shaky economy, Ecuador
discarded its currency, the sucre, in exchange for the
U.S. dollar. A coup shortly followed, but the reforms
pushed forward.

The Cold War is over, but scars from the past remain.
Will granting the public access to secret files from Cold
War intelligence agencies open old wounds or help in
healing?

F

Human rights groups have spoken out against female
circumcision, but others claim the practice has cultural
roots.

Suffering three coups since 1987, Fiji's unique history
and culture does not exclude it from strong ethnic differences.

had prophesied. Were the dead religious believers or cult victims?

Prime Minister Tony Blair advocates the devolution of power for more regional and local control of government, but opponents protest changes to hundreds of years of history.

A civilian death during a U.S. military exercise gone awry prompted the public on Vieques, Puerto Rico, to clamor for an end to U.S. military presence on the island. It is a call that has also been raised at other ports around the world that host the U.S. military.

Y

Slobodan Milosevic struggled to keep his country together, by whatever means, and to maintain his grip on power, but when election time came and the results were counted, the public ousted this autocratic leader in favor of a new face.

CONTENTS BY SUBJECT

POLITICAL

RELIGIOUS

TERRITORIAL

ADVISORY BOARD

Jerry H. Bentley is Professor of History at the University of Hawaii and editor of the *Journal of World History*. His research on the religious, moral, and political writings of Renaissance humanists led to the publication of *Humanists and Holy Writ: New Testament Scholarship in the Renaissance and Politics and Culture in Renaissance Naples*. More recently, his research has concentrated on global history and particularly on processes of cross-cultural interaction. His book *Old World Encounters: Cross-Cultural Contacts and Exchanges in Pre-Modern Times* examines processes of cultural exchange and religious conversion before the modern era, and his pamphlet "Shapes of World History in Twentieth-Century Scholarship" discusses the historiography of world history. His current interests include processes of cross-cultural interaction and cultural exchanges in modern times.

Frank J. Coppa is Professor of History at St. John's University, Director of their doctoral program, and Chair of the University's Vatican Symposium. He is also an Associate in the Columbia University Seminar on Modern Italy, and editor of the Lang Series on Studies on Modern Europe. He has published biographies on a series of European figures, written and edited more than twelve volumes, as well as publishing in a series of journals including the *Journal of Modern History* and the *Journal of Economic History,* among others. He is editor of the *Dictionary of Modern Italian History* and the *Encyclopedia of the Vatican and Papacy.*

Paul Gootenberg is a Professor of Latin American History at SUNY-Stony Brook. A graduate of the University of Chicago and of Oxford University, he specializes in the economic, social, and intellectual history of the Andes and Mexico, and more recently, the global history of drugs. He has published *Between Silver and Guano* (1989), *Imagining Development* (1993) and *Cocaine: Global Histories* (1999). Gootenberg has held many fellowships: among them, Fulbright, SSRC, ACLS, Institute for Advanced Study, Russell Sage Foundation, the Rhodes Scholarship, and a Guggenheim. He lives in Brooklyn with his wife, Laura Sainz, and son, Danyal Natan.

Margaret Hallisey is a practicing high school library media specialist in Burlington, MA. She has a B.A. in English from Regis College and a M.S. in Library and Information Science from Simmons College. A member of Beta Phi Mu, the International Library Science Honor Society, she has served on the executive Boards of the American Association of School Librarians (AASL), the Massachusetts School Library Media Association (MSLMA) and the New England Educational Media Association (NEEMA).

Donna Maier has been with the Department of History at the University of Northern Iowa since 1986. Her research interests are in nineteenth century Asante (Ghana), African Islam, and traditional African medicine. Her extensive lists of publications include "The Military Acquisition of Slaves in Asante," in *West African Economic and Social History* (1990), "Islam and the Idea of Asylum in Asante" in *The Cloths of Many-Colored Silks* (1996), and *History and Life, the World and Its Peoples* (1977-90, with Wallbank and

Shrier). She is a joint editor of the journal *African Economic History*, and a member of the African Studies Association and the Ghana Studies Council. She is currently living in Tanzania.

Philip Yockey is Social Sciences Bibliographer and Assistant Chief Librarian for Staff Training and Development at the Humanities and Social Sciences Library at The New York Public Library.

ABOUT THE SERIES

In 1991 the Persian Gulf War was fought and won by a coalition of nations against Iraq. Since then the country has been subject to restrictive multilateral sanctions placed on it by the United Nations to encourage compliance with the war's ceasefire agreement and ensure that the country was incapable of producing biological or chemical weapons. Ten years later, the sanctions are still in place, but the once united international community is now divided. If the sanctions have not met with compliance by Iraq over the course of ten years, how effective are they? Should the Iraqi people continue to suffer from a shortage of goods and services brought about by the sanctions? Are there any alternatives that could better meet the goals the United Nations meant to achieve?

In 1960 the United States initiated unilateral sanctions against Cuba, a communist nation ninety miles from American soil. The intent was to discourage communism in the country and oust leader Fidel Castro. The result has been more than forty years of sanctions that have achieved no end. Castro remains in power, Cuba remains communist, and the rest of the world continues to have normal relations with the country, while the United States persists in limiting its business, cultural, and diplomatic contacts. Is the maintenance of unilateral sanctions against Cuba a refusal of the United States to admit defeat or does the U.S. government remain intent on ousting Castro? Are sanctions applied by one country against another, but not followed by the rest of the international community, merely a statement or might they have a chance of success?

History Behind the Headlines, an ongoing series from the Gale Group, strives to answer these and many other questions in a way that television broadcasts and newspapers can not. In order to keep reports both simple and short, it is difficult for these media to give the watcher or reader enough background information to fully understand what is happening around the world today. *HBH* provides just that background, giving the general public, student, and teacher an account of each contemporary conflict, from its start to its present and even its future. This thoroughness is accomplished not just by the in-depth material covered in the main body of each essay, but also by accompanying chronologies, textual and biographical sidebars, maps, statistics, and bibliographic sources.

Not only does *HBH* provide comprehensive information on all of the conflicts it covers, it also strives to present its readers with an unbiased and inclusive perspective. Each essay, many written by an expert with a detailed knowledge of the conflict at hand, avoids taking any particular side and instead seeks to explain each vantage point. Unlike television and newspaper reports, which may only have the time, space, or even inclination to show one side of a story, *HBH* essays equally detail all sides involved.

Given the number of conflicts that beg for such fuller accounts that *History Behind the Headlines* provides, an advisory board of school and library experts helps to guide the selection process and narrow down the selection for each volume. They balance the topic lists, making sure that a proper mix of economic, political, ethnic, and geographically diverse conflicts are chosen. One to two volumes, each written in an accessible, informative way, will be released each year.

PREFACE

Selection and Arrangement

This volume of *History Behind the Headlines* covers thirty conflicts—including ethnic, religious, economic, political, territorial, and environmental conflicts—and provides an essay exploring the background to today's events. For example, students wondering why more of the international community is turning against the continued use of sanctions in Iraq can explore where sanctions have been applied in the past, their effects, and alternatives. Each conflict covered in HBH is contemporary—it happened within the last several years—but the roots of today's headlines are of enduring interest.

The topics were chosen following an extensive review of the conflicts covered in newspapers, magazines, and on television. A large number of potential conflicts were identified. Advisors—including academic experts, high school social study teachers, and librarians—prioritized the list, identifying those conflicts that generate the most questions. Topics were then selected to provide a regional balance and to cover various types of conflicts.

The conflicts covered are complex. Each essay discusses multiple aspects of a conflict, including economic and social aspects, the interests of other countries, international organizations and businesses, and the international implication of a conflict. The entries are arranged alphabetically by a major country, region, organization, or person in the conflict. Where this might not be clear in the table of contents, the keyword is placed in parentheses in front of the title.

Content

Each essay begins with a brief summary of the current situation, as well as some of the major factors in the conflict and a list of terms used in the essay with which the reader may be unfamiliar. Each essay contains the following sections:

- **Summary of the headline event.** An overview of the contemporary conflict that has brought the issue to public attention. For example, Israel's admission of an official policy of assassination toward Palestinian "threats."

- **Historical Background.** The "Historical Background" is the heart of the essay. The author provides the historical context to the contemporary conflict, summarizing the arc of the conflict throughout history. Each essay tells the "story" of the history of the conflict, capturing important events, transfers of power, interventions, treaties, and more. The author summarizes the changes in the conflict over time, describes the role of major figures in the conflict, including individuals, political organizations, and religious organizations, and provides an overview of their positions now and in the past. Where appropriate the author may draw comparisons with similar situations in the country or region in the past. In addition, the author often attempts to put the conflict in the context of global politics and to describe the impacts the conflict has had on people around the world. Finally, the author may touch on how historians' understanding of the conflict has changed over time.

- **Recent History and the Future.** The final section brings the conflict up-to-date, and may offer some projections for future resolution.

Each essay is followed by a brief bibliography that offers some suggestions of resources for further research. In addition, brief biographies may accompany the essay, profiling major figures.

Sidebars may provide statistical information, a quote from a speech, a selection from a primary source document (such as a treaty), or a selection from a book or newspaper article that adds to the understanding of the conflict, or may explore an issue in greater depth (such as violence against aid workers in Indonesia or the rise of incidents of mass suicide like that suspected in Uganda).

Images may also accompany the essay, including one or more maps showing the area of conflict. A selected bibliography providing suggestions for background information and research on the nature of conflicts and a comprehensive index appear at the back of each volume.

History is to be Read Critically

Each of the talented writers (many academic authorities) in this volume has tried to provide an objective and comprehensive overview of the conflict and its historical context. The nature of conflict, however, involves positions strongly and passionately held; even if it were possible to write a completely objective overview of history, it would contradict with the view held by participants to the conflict. History—all history—should be read critically.

Acknowledgements

Many thanks for their help to the excellent advisors who guided this project—their ongoing attention and feedback was greatly appreciated. Thanks, also, to the thoughtful and dedicated writers who lent their expertise to help others understand the complex history behind sound bites on the news.

Comments on this volume and suggestions for future volumes are welcomed. Please direct all correspondence to:

Editor, *History Behind the Headlines*
Gale Group
27500 Drake Rd.
Farmington Hills, MI 48331-3535
(800) 877-4253

POL POT AND THE PROSECUTION OF THE KHMER ROUGE LEADERSHIP IN CAMBODIA

On January 2, 2001, after years of discussion and debate, the National Assembly of the Kingdom of Cambodia voted unanimously in favor of legislation to establish a tribunal to try former Khmer Rouge (KR) leaders for crimes against humanity and for killing millions of Cambodians during their time in power (April 1975 to December 1978). The Cambodian Senate approved the legislation on January 15 and the Constitutional Council gave its consent on February 12. It awaits only Cambodia's King Sihanouk's signature to become law. The King has indicated that he will sign the legislation. Sihanouk was in China for medical treatment when the legislation passed, and the acting head of state, Senate President Samdech Chea Sim, could have signed the bill for Sihanouk, but the final approval was left for the King.

The legislation, calling for a mixed tribunal with both Cambodian and international judges operating under the Cambodian judicial system, reflects the outcome of a long series of discussions and negotiations between the United Nations (UN) and the current government of Cambodia, led by Prime Minister Hun Sen, a former Khmer Rouge cadre, a member of a group that promotes the interests of a revolutionary party, in this case the Khmer Rouge. Basic elements in the process were agreed upon between the United Nations and Cambodia in July 2000. The process calls for a super-majority requirement to reach decisions. This means that any decision will require the approval of at least one of the international judges. A simple majority based only on the votes of Cambodian judges will not suffice. The United States, under the leadership of its ambassador to Cambodia, Kent Wiedemann, has played an effective role in helping broker the compromise. Assuming that

THE CONFLICT

With the deaths of perhaps one to two million Cambodian people at the hands of the Khmer Rouge leadership, survivors, both in Cambodia and abroad, have awaited the day when those responsible will be brought to justice. In 2001 legislation passed in Cambodia authorizing the establishment of a tribunal under which former Khmer Rouge leaders will be put to trial.

Political

- The Khmer Rouge leadership ruled Cambodia for a violent period from 1975 to 1978, contributing to the deaths of one to two million Cambodians.

- The Khmer Rouge attempted to create an economically independent, communist, utopian society with no religion, no family, no money, and no other "social evils." In the process, millions were dislocated and/or killed under the premise that the ends justified the means.

- The current Cambodian leadership voted to establish a tribunal to try former Khmer Rouge leaders, but how far the arm of justice will extend remains in question.

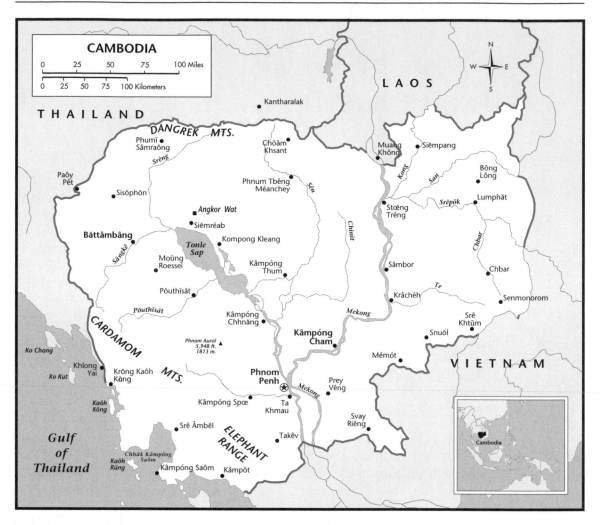

MAP OF CAMBODIA. *(Maryland Cartographics. Reproduced by permission.)*

the United States is satisfied with the tribunal's work in trying the former Khmer Rouge leaders for their crimes, there is the distinct possibility that the United States could provide major bilateral funding to Cambodia, which is desperately needed for diverse developmental needs.

HISTORICAL BACKGROUND

From the ninth to the fifteenth centuries the Khmer civilization was centered at Angkor in what is now northwest Cambodia. At the height of its strength and glory the Angkor Empire controlled what is now Cambodia and much of what is now Thailand, Laos, and the southern part of Vietnam. During the Angkor period advanced hydraulic irrigation systems were put in place allowing for multiple rice crops. The agricultural surpluses freed up labor to work on the religious monuments. Much of this labor was undoubtedly slave labor. The Angkor Empire eventually became overextended

and collapsed with the sacking of Angkor by the Siamese in 1430. The Khmer capital then shifted to Phnom Penh and Angkor fell into the oblivion of the jungle, to be rediscovered by the French in the nineteenth century.

With the capital shift to Phnom Penh the Khmer Kingdom became more commerce and trade oriented, linked to the South China Sea by the Mekong River. This period also saw the serious erosion of Khmer territory to Vietnamese and Siamese expansion, particularly in the eighteenth and nineteenth century. Vietnamese expansion to the south (*nam tien*) resulted in Cambodia losing the entire Mekong Delta, including Saigon (formerly known as Prey Nakor when it was part of Cambodia), to the Vietnamese. This led to deep resentment against the Vietnamese.

Cambodia became a French protectorate in 1863. It eventually became part of what was called French Indo-China, a colonial conglomerate in

CHRONOLOGY

March 1970 Neutralist Prince Sihanouk is ousted from his post as leader of Cambodia by General Lon Nol, who founds the Khmer Republic.

1969–73 The United States carries out bombings of rural Cambodia, which forces a tremendous influx of people into Phnom Penh and other cities. The bombing intensifies in 1973.

April 17, 1975 The Khmer Rouge comes to power with the fall, or liberation, of Phnom Penh. The urban population is forced into the countryside, causing widespread death and suffering. *Angka* (the organization) takes power, introducing radical measures such as the abolition of money and private property.

May 1975 Prince Sihanouk becomes a figurehead chief of state.

April 2, 1976 Sihanouk formally resigns as chief of state and spends the next 33 months under house arrest at the site of the Royal Palace in Phnom Penh. Pol Pot becomes prime minister.

December 25, 1978 Vietnam invades Cambodia and overthrows the Pol Pot regime. The Khmer Rouge leaders escape to the west and establish a new base for guerilla warfare in western and northwestern Cambodia.

January 9, 1979 Vietnamese troops reach Phnom Penh. A government under the People's Republic of Kampuchea (PRK) is installed by the Vietnamese.

August 17–19, 1979 A trial for genocide of the Pol Pot-Ieng Sary clique is held before a People's Revolutionary Tribunal in Phnom Penh. Pol Pot and Ieng Sary are sentenced to death *in absentia*.

1979–89 Civil war ensues in Cambodia between a coalition of Pol Pot's forces, forces loyal to Sihanouk, and forces loyal to the rightist politician Son Sann and the Vietnamese backed government (People's Republic of Kampuchea). The coalition against the Vietnamese-backed government receives diplomatic, logistical, economic, and military support from China, Thailand, the Association of Southeast Asian Nations, and the United States.

1989 Vietnamese troops withdraw from Cambodia, paving the way for a peace process and political reconciliation to begin.

1993 UN-supervised, free multi-party elections are won by Sihanouk's party, FUNCINPEC; in compromise, a government is formed with two prime ministers, including Sihanouk's son, Prince Renarridh, sharing power between FUNCINPEC and CPP.

August 1996 Khmer Rouge leader Ieng Sary and armies under his control defect to the Hun Sen government. Ieng Sary is granted amnesty by King Sihanouk.

June 10, 1997 Pol Pot's group murders Khmer Rouge leader Son Sen and 14 members of his family.

July 25, 1997 Pol Pot is purged and put on trial for treason of the Khmer Rouge before a People's Tribunal as a mass murderer of his own people.

April 16, 1998 Pol Pot dies in a Khmer Rouge camp near the Thai-Cambodian border.

July 2000 The UN and the Kingdom of Cambodia reach a compromise on the process of establishing a tribunal to try former Khmer Rouge leaders for their crimes against humanity.

January 2, 2001 The Cambodian National Assembly unanimously approves legislation to establish a mixed Cambodian/International tribunal to try former Khmer Rouge leaders for their crimes.

January 9, 2001 The Cambodian Senate approves the tribunal legislation.

February 2001 The Constitutional Court approves the tribunal legislation.

which local Vietnamese elite were given dominant administrative positions. The French, rather than abolishing the Khmer monarchy, decided to incorporate it into its system and favored royal rulers whose families became part of an elite local system. Over time the force of Khmer nationalism emerged especially with Japanese successes during World War II (1939–45). In the period following the war Prince Norodom Sihanouk played a key role in the peaceful attainment of Cambodian independence in 1953.

The Sihanouk Era, 1953–70

Prince Norodom Sihanouk was the dominant political figure during the political period from

1953 to 1970. He abdicated the throne as king to become a player in partisan politics. Though the regime was technically democratic, it was very much a one-man show dominated by Prince Sihanouk, as he had little tolerance for political dissent.

During the latter part of the French colonial period and the early Sihanouk period an elite corps of bright young Khmer—including Pol Pot, Ieng Sary, and Khieu Samphan—were sent abroad to study in France. There they became exposed to leftist radical politics. Pol Pot, Ieng Sary, and Khieu Samphan were later to assume important leadership positions in the local Cambodian communist movement, which Prince Sihanouk termed the Khmer Rouge. Upon their return to Cambodia many of the young Khmer were frustrated by Sihanouk's dominance of the political scene and by their inability to influence public policies or to bring about political change through peaceful means. They also were highly critical of Cambodia's feudalistic system. These factors contributed to the radicalization of such individuals and their eventual decision to defect and start a violent revolutionary movement in the jungles of Cambodia.

Despite the limited democracy of the period Cambodia, for the most part during Sihanouk's rule, remained a peaceful oasis in a sea of Cold War turmoil. Sihanouk was adamant in keeping Cambodia neutral and on friendly terms with all to preserve Cambodia's peace and national sovereignty. Though the country was materially poor, it was characterized by affluent subsistence, with most farmers owning their own land. Prince Sihanouk was particularly popular among rural peasants.

The Emergence of the Khmer Republic, 1970–75

While Prince Sihanouk was out of the country in Europe in March 1970, General Lon Nol led a coup against his government. It is said that the United States, engaged in the Vietnam War, was supportive of the coup in order to gain access to the country to pursue Vietnamese troops allegedly using sanctuaries in Cambodia. Sihanouk's political dominance as well as Lon Nol and his supporters concern about Sihanouk's unwillingness to confront North Vietnam about Viet Cong and North Vietnamese troops' use of Cambodian territory in their war with the United States, contributed to his downfall. The coup succeeded; the monarchy was abolished and Cambodia became the Khmer Republic.

Lon Nol's coup launched Cambodia into turmoil as the country was drawn into the conflict of U.S. involvement in Vietnam. Even prior to the coup, in 1969 the United States had launched a secret bombing campaign on Cambodia. It is estimated that 600,000 tons of bombs were dropped on Cambodia, a country the size of the U.S. state of Missouri, between 1969–73. The bombing intensified following the coup; many of the bombs were dropped on the most heavily populated areas of Cambodia. As a result, the Cambodian countryside was devastated, causing a tremendous influx of refugees into the cities to avoid the attacks. The population of Phnom Penh quickly grew from 600,000 to 3 million.

Primarily as the result of the overthrow of Sihanouk, who was extremely popular among the peasants, and because of the bombing and its disruption of life in rural Cambodia, the country's communist party, the Khmer Rouge, was dramatically strengthened. Prince Sihanouk subsequently joined with the Khmer Rouge in a civil war against Lon Nol. With the withdrawal of financial and military support by the U.S. Congress for Lon Nol's government in 1973, it was only a matter of time before the Lon Nol regime would collapse. This finally happened on April 17, 1975, when Khmer Rouge forces, led by Pol Pot, captured Phnom Penh and began their dramatic revolutionary experiment, perhaps the most dramatic form of social engineering ever attempted in human history.

Democratic Kampuchea (DK), April 1975 to December 1978

Upon taking Phnom Penh on April 17, 1975, the Khmer Rouge immediately called for the complete evacuation of the city, claiming that the city would be bombed by the United States. The actual reason for the evacuation was twofold, one practical and one theoretical. The practical reason was that there was inadequate food to support 3 million city dwellers. Thus, actually moving the people to where food could be produced may have had humanitarian dimensions, as mass starvation was a risk if all had remained in the cities. The theoretical reason for the evacuation was to move toward a utopian egalitarian society where everyone would work in the countryside and grow food, with no "parasites" in the city living off of the sweat and the toil of rural farmers. Dr. Khieu Samphan, the intellectual leader of the Khmer Rouge, articulated this philosophy. As a result of the mass exodus many feeble and sick Cambodians were not able to survive the journey to the countryside.

SALORTH SAR (POL POT)

1928–1998 Salorth Sar's rise to power as head of the Khmer Rouge and leader of a brutal regime is a story of paradoxes and a rather bizarre combination of influences. Salorth Sar, later known as Pol Pot, was born in 1928, the son of a prosperous farmer and a mother who was widely respected in her district for her piety and good works. At a young age he lived at the Royal Palace, where his cousin and sister were both members of the royal ballet and consorts of the king. Thus, Salorth Sar had a chance to observe feudalism first-hand. He also saw his sister and cousin exploited as sexual slaves. He spent several months as a Buddhist novice at a temple near the Royal Palace. Many years later he was awarded a scholarship to study in France, where he became exposed to radical Marxist-Leninist ideas.

In an article entitled "Monarchy or Democracy" in the Khmer students' magazine, *Khmer Nisut*, Salorth Sar adopted the pen name Pol Pot, which means, "Original Khmer." He viciously attacked the parasitic nature of the monarchy, which exploited the people. Also, while in Europe, he had the opportunity to spend time in a youth camp, where he was deeply impressed by the mobilization of the Yugoslav people as an enormous work collective, building factories, roads, and hydraulic centers.

In 1953 Pol Pot returned to Cambodia as a teacher. Eventually, as his politics became more radical and with Prince Sihanouk's repression of dissident elements, Pol Pot in 1963 became part of an emerging communist movement in the countryside. During this period as a revolutionary militant he had opportunities to visit and observe communism in both China and in Vietnam. These experiences later had an important influence on him. Toward the end of 1966 Pol Pot established new headquarters in the province of Ratanakiri in the remote northeast of Cambodia, an area inhabited largely by diverse non-Khmer ethnic nationalities. He was deeply impressed with these people, seeing them as uncorrupted by any social hierarchy or money.

As an individual, Pol Pot had impressive and fluid interpersonal skills. He was extremely smooth in dealing with diverse people. These qualities helped him to gain loyalty and to become an effective and persuasive leader. He was noted for being calm, soft-spoken, and gentle.

POL POT. *(AP/Wide World Photos. Reproduced by permission.)*

Given Pol Pot's life history of modest beginnings, exposure to the corruption of Cambodia's leadership, and indoctrination into communism, it is perhaps easier to understand his radical vision for a Cambodia free from feudalism, exploitation of the poor by the rich, and inequality. In Pol Pot's Democratic Kampuchea the extreme poor had the advantage over the formerly rich. This kind of extreme empowerment of the young and poor may account for the remarkable sustained loyalty toward Pol Pot, which enabled his guerilla army to fight on for almost 20 years after the 1978 Vietnamese invasion overthrew his regime. His intense Khmer nationalism also generated loyal support. During his time in power, however, violence reigned throughout the land, with an estimated one to two million Cambodians killed under the Khmer Rouge.

On July 25, 1997, Pol Pot was purged from the Khmer Rouge by his former supporters and put on trial. He was jailed by the Khmer Rouge after the trial and remained under guard until his death on April 16, 1998. Pol Pot's death allowed him to escape prosecution for crimes against humanity under the international tribunal approved by the Cambodian government in early 2001.

Those who moved to the countryside from the city were known as the "new people" or "April 17 People." Those who stayed in the countryside, and who had largely supported the Khmer Rouge, were known as the "base" or "old people" or "March 17 people" (the day of the overthrow of Prince Sihanouk and the real beginning of the war of liberation). The "new people" were treated more harshly by the Khmer Rouge than were the local "base people," who had been empowered by the revolution. The "base people" were considered superior since they had joined and supported the revolution early on, while many of the "new people" had fled to the city to avoid the U.S. bombings and were considered to have joined the "imperialists" and become "parasites."

From this point on, after the evacuation of Phnom Penh, Cambodia became a huge agricultural work camp. Most people labored to produce food or engaged in other agricultural work such as building irrigation canals. The vision underlying this "new utopia" was actually inspired by the past glory of Angkor. The idea was to dramatically increase food production to attain yields of three tons of rice per hectare. The all embracing presence of *Angka* (literally meaning "the organization") meant that the Cambodian people lost all of their individual rights and freedoms in pursuit of this idealized utopia. This type of society, with its almost total preoccupation with the collective "good" at the expense of individual rights, violated many of the provisions of the United Nation's (UN) Universal Declaration of Human Rights.

Khmer Rouge society, however, was relatively free from crime, rape, alcoholism, and other social evils during this period. With money having been eliminated as a medium of exchange, an almost absurdly high level of equality had been attained. In fact, the Khmer Rouge had dynamited what had formerly been the country's National Bank, and the former currency was worth nothing. In a fascinating and certainly romanticized account of egalitarian Democratic Kampuchea, Frenchwoman Laurence Picq, who lived under the Khmer Rouge, wrote in *Beyond the Horizon: Five Years with the Khmer Rouge* (1989):

> The time came for construction of a large work site. Neon lights were installed and loudspeakers connected. I joined in the work, and by five o'clock almost everyone was on the premises. In the dark of the night, the lights gave the paths of the garden the look of a large industrial site. It was magnificent. Everyone was in high spirits as they worked.
>
> For the intellectuals constructing the work site, this manual labor was not the work of peasants. Nor was

it a punishment or a sporting exercise. All of us equal, working together in the soil, intellectuals and combatants alike, we were transformed into companions, elevated by a feeling of pure joy. I was happy—insignificant and all-important at the same time, both a drop of water and the entire sea. . . .

Tuol Sleng (S-21)

Tuol Sleng was a central, but certainly not the only, source of much Cambodian suffering during the Khmer Rouge years. In fact, there were many "killing fields," this serving as only one. Once a secondary school named Tuol Svay Pray, the Khmer Rouge Security Police took it over in 1975, and ran it as a torture center and prison. Located in a southern area of Phnom Penh, Tuol Sleng was an interrogation center where enemies of the state were imprisoned, tortured, and then killed. Prisoners were forced to complete elaborate confessions. After the Vietnamese invasion and the establishment of the PRK, the site was turned into the Museum of Genocidal Crimes, documenting the atrocities of the Khmer Rouge reign.

Fourteen thousand men, women, and children were brought to Tuol Sleng, and only seven were said to have survived. However, the exact number of those killed is unknown. The director of S-21, Kang Kech Ieu, known as Duch, is likely to be one of the Khmer Rouge leaders to face the international tribunal. The deaths at Tuol Sleng primarily involved internal party purges of individual KR cadres accused of plotting against the regime. While the deaths there seem largely arbitrary, with no rights whatsoever accorded to individuals to defend themselves, it could well be that many of those killed were actually themselves perpetuators of crimes against humanity in their role as Khmer Rouge cadres. By the end of the Khmer Rouge's time in power Pol Pot allegedly had one-third of his own cabinet killed.

As an interrogation center under the Khmer Rouge, Tuol Sleng was surrounded with barbed wire and electrified fencing to keep prisoners from escape. Rooms that once served to educate children were turned into cramped prison cells. Prisoners, including entire families, were indiscriminately exterminated at Tuol Sleng. The museum opened in 1980 and contains hundreds of ID photos of the prison's victims. Bloodstains remain on the walls and floors. Shackles lie on the ground, and pictures and paintings document scenes of torture that may have occurred in the prison.

A YOUNG SURVIVOR FROM CAMBODIA'S "KILLING FIELDS." AS MANY AS TWO MILLION PEOPLE ARE THOUGHT TO HAVE BEEN KILLED AT THE HANDS OF THE KHMER ROUGE. *(AP/Wide World Photos. Reproduced by permission.)*

How Many Deaths?

There are some unusual dimensions in trying to understand the horrors that occurred in Cambodia during 1975–78, and specifically at Tuol Sleng. The Khmer Rouge was an agrarian revolution and did not support the use of much technology. Many people were killed with crude farm equipment. As many as two million people are thought to have died in this time period under the Khmer Rouge, and about 60 to 70 percent of Cambodian children lost their parents. Given such documentation of the horrors that occurred in Cambodia there still exists skepticism by many experts on the subject that such a genocide could occur. One major point of controversy includes the extensive amount of documentation itself and the large time span between its release and the actual occurrence. In fact, one major release of documents occurred only in 1995, 17 years after the Vietnamese invasion that overthrew the Khmer Rouge and ended the "killing fields." Extensive microfilming of the documents found at Tuol Sleng occurred 13 years after the discovery of its activities. Additionally, many of the documents released were carefully and neatly typed. Given that the Khmer Rouge were anti-technology and anti-intellectual, questions remain as to whether they would have kept such records, especially using the technology of a typewriter. Another significant point raised that brings the number of deaths committed at Tuol Sleng into question comes from villagers living near the site, who told a prominent Thai anthropologist that prior to its becoming a school, the site of Tuol Sleng was a cemetery.

Another point of controversy is the allegation of media exaggeration. One example is to attribute to the Khmer Rouge those deaths that would have occurred through normal mortality during the period in question. Another example is to count among the death toll those that fled the country, since these people are missing from Cambodia. Such variations make determining the true number of those killed due to Khmer Rouge policies a difficult task.

There is considerable controversy about the exact number and causes of death during the period. Since there were a large number of deaths during the 1970–75 period caused by the civil war and by extensive U.S. bombing, the situation is complicated. During the 1975–78 period, deaths were primarily caused by starvation, overwork, disease, and execution. Also, another cause of death almost never mentioned in media accounts was from landmines and unexploded ordnance (UXO) remaining from the 1970–75 civil war. With the majority of the population forced to engage in agricultural work, landmines were a major risk faced daily by many. Even in the present-day in the neighboring country of Laos people in rural areas die or are maimed frequently from UXO. As of the

INTERNATIONAL INVOLVEMENT: THE CASE OF THAILAND

Though Thailand and Cambodia share a number of important cultural influences, their political and historical relations have been strained for centuries, as they were major competitors over the control of mainland Southeast Asia. Over time the Khmer Empire suffered important territorial loses to the Siamese, a trend that continued through World War II, when Thailand was officially an ally of Japan. During the beginning phase of the Cold War and of the U.S. war in Vietnam, Thailand was a staunch anti-communist ally of the United States, while Cambodia under Prince Sihanouk remained neutral. When Cambodia eventually became communist in 1975, with Sihanouk's overthrow and Pol Pot's ascension to power, a serious threat was posed to Thailand, which had its own active insurgency led by the illegal Communist Party of Thailand. The playing out of the Killing Fields in Cambodia, however, resulted in powerful propaganda for Thailand against the "evils of communism."

The December 1979, invasion of Cambodia by Vietnam dramatically affected the Thai government's posture toward the Khmer Rouge, who retreated to the jungles near the Thai border. The Thais feared the presence of a powerful Vietnam Army near its borders and close to its capital. Thus, the Thai Prime Minister, General Kriangsak, cut a secret deal with the Chinese, who were also deeply concerned about Vietnamese expansionism (supported by the former Soviet Union). In exchange for the Chinese ending its support for Thailand's communist insurgency, the Thais would willingly become a conduit for Chinese military aid to the Khmer Rouge and provide a safe haven for Khmer Rouge guerillas. The end result of such strategies was highly successful for Thailand. Its own communist insurgency died, and in 1989 the Vietnamese withdrew their armed forces from Cambodia.

1990s an average of one person per week continued to fall victim to UXO in Cambodia.

Deaths from lack of food under the Khmer Rouge create somewhat of an anomaly since a major goal of the KR was to improve agriculture (to restore the glory of Angkor) and to achieve national economic self-sufficiency. There would appear to be three primary explanations for the food shortages. First, the Khmer Rouge began its move to the countryside at a time when the entire Cambodian countryside had been severely decimated by civil war and by extensive U.S. bombing. The second explanation for the food shortages was the agricul-

tural system's inefficiency. Many former urban dwellers were not accustomed to agricultural work and made inefficient farmers. The third and perhaps most telling explanation was that the KR leadership wanted to demonstrate that Kampuchea was capable of exporting food as a symbol of the success of its revolution. Also, Kampuchea desperately needed Chinese weapons, which it exchanged for food, to fight its enemy, Vietnam, and to provide military strength against any potential counterrevolution from enemies within. As a result of the KR focusing more on military might than food for its people, many workers suffered from malnutrition and starvation. Despite these obstacles, the Finish Inquiry Commission found that by the end of 1978 Democratic Kampuchea was gradually finding solutions to its basic problems regarding food supplies and was poised for an economic revival when the regime was ended. Consistent with this finding, some of the remaining KR agricultural infrastructure continues to be used into the twenty-first century.

Scholar Marek Sliwinski has done an extensive demographic analysis of Cambodia as a way to estimate the number of deaths during the Khmer Rouge period (see table entitled "Demographics of the Khmer Rouge Genocide"). During the period in question the Khmer population declined by 1,807,000, though this number includes deaths through normal mortality and those who fled to become refugees in Thailand or Vietnam, for example. Extensive research by Yale scholar Ben Kiernan provides the basis for estimated deaths by diverse social groups (see table entitled "Estimated Populations and Deaths of 'New' and 'Base' Peoples under the Khmer Rouge"). Interestingly, Kiernan's estimate of the total number who perished is strikingly consistent with Sliwinski's demographic analysis.

The extensive and diverse data on the Khmer Rouge, including accounts of refugees, do indicate that there were considerable local variations in conditions and with the behavior of Khmer Rouge cadres. Given the fragmentation within the Communist Party of Cambodia and given the regime's hostility toward modern technology, the enforcement and implementation of a monolithic uniform policy would have been difficult, if not impossible. Thus, conditions in various zones of the country differed considerably, dependent on local cadres and leadership. For example, the remote northeastern provinces of Ratanakiri and Mondukiri had a much smaller percent of population who were victims of the Khmer Rouge than other areas. There was, in fact, considerable variation among provinces.

A fundamental question must also be raised as to why the Khmer Rouge in general became so brutal compared to new communist regimes in Laos and Vietnam at the time. In fact, Laos and Cambodia shared a common Buddhist tradition and heritage. Different hypotheses and theories have been postulated. Cambodian writer Seanglim Bit argues that the Cambodian psyche involves a warrior heritage going back to the time of Angkor, when warriors were glorified. Both the Vietnamese and Thais historically have often perpetuated highly negative stereotypes of the Khmer as "less than human." Such views are both ethnocentric and highly biased. This author's view focuses on the massive and widescale bombing of Cambodia by the United States. Cambodians were exposed to a high level of violence on a continual basis during the U.S. bombing campaigns in Cambodia. While Laos also suffered from extensive U.S. bombing as well, most of it was concentrated in areas less populated by civilians. In contrast, U.S. bombing was widespread across the Cambodian countryside and affected many people. Thus, the bombing created anger against American capitalism and imperialism and those associated with it. When the Khmer Rouge took power away from the previous government, based on a U.S. system of capitalism, it reacted particularly negatively against any U.S. influences within the country and its government. The extreme radicalism of the Khmer Rouge vision and its commitment to its ambitious goal to achieve the highest level of genuine communism at any human cost was also a key factor in the brutality that resulted. The Khmer leadership, however, remained oblivious or perhaps indifferent to the violence it perpetrated. In a 1997 interview with Nate Thayer quoted in Kao Kim Hourn and Tania Theriault's *Skepticism, Outrage, and Hope: Reactions to the Death of Pol Pot* (1998), Pol Pot stated, "Look at me, am I a savage person? My conscience is clear."

The Establishment of the People's Republic of Kampuchea, 1979–89

On December 25, 1978, in a *blitzkrieg* type attack, Vietnam invaded Cambodia and overthrew the Khmer Rouge regime, forcing it to flee to the jungles along the Thai borders. By January 9, 1979, a new People's Republic of Kampuchea (PRK) regime was installed by the Vietnamese. Key leaders of this regime were Heng Samrin, Hun Sen, and Chea Sim, all former Khmer Rouge cadres who had earlier defected to Vietnam. The result was a

DEMOGRAPHICS OF THE KHMER ROUGE GENOCIDE

Year	Population
1962	5,760,000
1968	6,995,000
1972	7,796,000
1974	7,619,000
1975	7,230,000–7,566,000*
1978	5,759,000
1979	5,586,000
1981	5,715,000

Source: Marek Sliwinski. *Le Génocide Khmer Rouge: Une Analyse Démographique.* Paris: Editions L'Harmattan, 1995.

* Estimate by Sliwinski

THE EXACT NUMBER OF THOSE KILLED UNDER THE KHMER ROUGE IS NOT KNOWN, BUT ESTIMATES HAVE BEEN MADE THAT ARE SUPPORTED BY SIMILAR FINDINGS BY OTHERS. *(The Gale Group.)*

return to political normalcy and the end of the Khmer Rouge brutality.

Despite the return to political normalcy, an ensuing civil war began between the Vietnam-backed government in Phnom Penh and the Khmer Rouge, who were hiding in the countryside. The Vietnamese army remained in Cambodia for ten years to assist in this war and to support the PRK.

Ironically, during the civil war the Khmer Rouge were part of a coalition (Coalition of the Government of Democratic Kampuchea, CGDK) supported diplomatically and financially by China, Thailand, the Association of Southeast Asian Nations (ASEAN), and the United States. This coalition held Cambodia's seat at the United Nations. The United States actually asserted intense pressure to have this coalition established with Pol Pot, primarily because of Democratic Kampuchea's anti-Vietnam stance at the time. During this period Thailand provided a safe haven for Khmer Rouge guerillas. The KR allegedly had a secret headquarters in the Bangkhen area of Bangkok. Ieng Sary, a key Khmer Rouge leader, made frequent secret trips to Thailand.

ESTIMATED POPULATIONS AND DEATHS OF "NEW" AND "BASE" PEOPLES UNDER THE KHMER ROUGE

Social Group	Estimated 1975 population	Estimated Number Who Perished	Percentage, %
"New People"			
Urban Khmer	2,000,000	500,000	25%
Rural Khmer	600,000	150,000	25
Chinese (all urban)	430,000	215,000	50
Vietnamese (urban)	10,000	10,000	100
Lao (rural)	10,000	4,000	40
Total "New People"	3,050,000	879,000	29
"Base People"			
Rural Khmer	4,500,000	675,000	15
(Khmer Krom)	[5,000]	[2,000]	[40]
Cham (all rural)	250,000	90,000	36
Vietnamese (rural)	10,000	10,000	100
Thai (rural)	20,000	8,000	40
Upland minorities	60,000	9,000	15
Total "Base People"	4,840,000	792,000	16
Total Cambodia	7,890,000	1,671,000	21

Source: Ben Kiernan. *The Pol Pot Regime: Race, Power, and Genocide in Cambodia under the Khmer Rouge.* New Haven: Yale University Press, 1996.

ESTIMATES OF CAMBODIAN DEATHS DURING THE KHMER ROUGE PERIOD, ACROSS SOCIAL GROUPS. "BASE" PEOPLE LIVED MAINLY IN THE COUNTRYSIDE. MANY "NEW" PEOPLE FLED TO THE COUNTRYSIDE FROM THE CITY AND WERE TREATED MORE HARSHLY BY THE KHMER ROUGE. *(The Gale Group.)*

National Elections and a Coalition Government

The period from 1989–93 saw the largest ever UN peacekeeping mission in Cambodia to supervise the movement toward national democratic elections in 1993. A 22,000-member peacekeeping force was stationed in Cambodia and US$2 billion was spent on the operation. The United Nations Transitional Authority of Cambodia (UNTAC) played a major role in administering Cambodia during this period. The Khmer Rouge refused to participate in the national election of 1993 and continued its civil war against the existing government. Though Prince Rennarridh, the son of Prince Sihanouk, won the election, a two-headed coalition government was formed with two prime ministers, Prince Rennarridh and Hun Sen, the former Khmer Rouge cadre who defected in 1977.

Since the elections in 1993 both the monarchy and the democracy were restored in Cambodia, with Prince Sihanouk returning from exile to become King of Cambodia. His presence has represented an important stabilizing force. Factionalism within the coalition government continues, however, and the two-headed government proves rather unwieldy. When Prince Renarridh allegedly began some secret negotiations with his former allies, the Khmer Rouge, co-Prime Minister Hun Sen took preemptive violent action in July 1997. Political reconciliation took place rather quickly between competing factions, and new national elections were held one year later.

Hun Sen's ruling CPP won the national election in what international observers consider to be a fair election. In the interim the Khmer Rouge began to collapse. In 1997 Pol Pot ordered the murder of key Khmer Rouge leader Son Sen and his family, after becoming suspicious of him. He had 14 members of Son Sen's family killed to ensure that any resistance against him was eliminated. Also in 1997, the prominent Khmer Rouge leader Ieng Sary defected to the Hun Sen government. Later that year Pol Pot himself was purged and put on trial for treason by the Khmer Rouge, though not for his crimes against humanity but for his treason against the Khmer Rouge. He died on April 16, 1998, allegedly of heart failure and other ailments, though some suspicion exists about his cause of death. Had Pol Pot himself been forced to testify in an international tribunal, his testimony could have been extremely embarrassing, particularly to Thailand, China, and the United States, all of whom actively supported the CGDK for a number of years. With the deaths of Pol Pot and Son Sen; the defections of Ieng Sary, Khieu Samphan, and Nuon Chea; and the arrests of Ta Mok and Duch, the Khmer Rouge is dead as a political force in Cambodia. It is an "organ" with no head.

YOUK CHHANG, DIRECTOR OF THE DOCUMENTATION CENTER OF CAMBODIA, SHOWS DOCUMENTS RELATING TO THE CAMBODIAN GENOCIDE. MANY OF THESE DOCUMENTS ARE HOUSED IN CAMBODIA'S MUSEUM OF GENOCIDAL CRIMES. *(AP/Wide World Photos. Reproduced by permission.)*

RECENT HISTORY AND THE FUTURE

The Future Tribunal

With the legislation for a tribunal to try Khmer Rouge leaders having passed the National Assembly, the Senate, and the Constitutional Court in early 2001, the trial with a mix of Cambodian and international judges looks certain to occur. Since the Khmer Rouge atrocities involved thousands of leaders and cadres, many of whom have defected or were killed in purges, it is impossible to have a genuinely comprehensive trial. A likely scenario would be to have a showcase trial of 20 to 30 key leaders for whom good and reliable documentation exists for their perpetuation of atrocities. Prime targets for conviction are the "butcher" Ta Mok; Duch, the director of the Tuol Sleng torture prison where 14,000 or more "enemies" of the state were allegedly executed; and Ke Pauk, one of Pol Pot's most notorious generals. Ta Mok and Duch were captured while still in armed revolt against the current government and have been taken into custody.

There are many controversial and complex issues related to the tribunal. Various civil rights and human rights groups within Cambodia are strongly in support of the tribunal and are pleased to see that international judges will be involved. They and the large segment of the Cambodian population, having suffered at the hands of the Khmer Rouge, do not want these leaders to go unpunished and live comfortably into the future. Those in the Cambodian overseas communities in the United States, France, and other locales, who also suffered at the hands of the Khmer Rouge, are outspoken in their views that the Khmer Rouge leadership must be punished for its crimes against humanity.

Sam Rainsey, leader of the Democratic Opposition in the Cambodian Parliament, has a different view of the tribunal. He expressed these views in an address before the Council on Foreign Relations in Washington, DC, on March 6, 2001. Though he voted for the tribunal he has strong fears that it will become a charade, since the current government, under the Cambodian People's Party (CPP, a former communist party) has the power to appoint the Cambodian judges. Also, Prime Minister Hun Sen himself and several other prominent CPP leaders, such as acting head of state Samdech Chea Sim, had Khmer Rouge backgrounds prior to their defecting. Had Sam Rainsey not voted for the tribunal he would have been accused of not wanting to prosecute those responsible for Khmer Rouge atrocities. Thus, he was forced politically to vote for legislation which he felt was fundamentally flawed and he possessed reservations about how well the tribunal would perform in application.

The current government, which fought a war with the Khmer Rouge for almost 20 years, critically needs a successful tribunal process. This would further legitimate the regime, which was installed initially in 1979, after a Vietnamese invasion of Cambodia. It would also ensure that some of the worst perpetuators of Khmer Rouge atrocities such as the notorious Ta Mok (the Butcher) and Duch, the director of police security at Tuol Sleng Prison, would be brought to justice. The tribunal would definitely improve the country's human rights record and image.

It is clear, however, that Hun Sen and his party envision a more limited trial than many expect. He, for example, does not want to see Ieng Sary, the Khmer Rouge foreign minister, or Khieu Samphan, the intellectual leader of the Khmer Rouge, brought to trial. If they were convicted, Hun Sen feels this would rekindle renewed polarization, reactivate the Khmer Rouge as a political force, and destroy the important peace and reconciliation that has been achieved in recent years. Also, it is important to note that when Ieng Sary and Khieu Samphan peacefully defected in 1996, ending the civil war and bringing peace to Cambodia, King Sihanouk granted Ieng Sary amnesty as part of the deal to have the Khmer army surrender. Without that surrender, the civil war would have continued indefinitely. Thus, Hun Sen has a strong rationale for having a more limited trial to facilitate continued peace in Cambodia after years of turmoil.

Another view represented by a relatively small group both locally and internationally calls for Buddhist compassion. In fact, the new Cambodian constitution, reflecting Cambodia's Buddhist roots, forbids the death penalty. Such individuals emphasize peace and reconciliation perhaps along the lines associated with the Commission for Truth and Reconciliation in South Africa, inspired by the compassionate and visionary leadership of Nelson Mandela and Bishop Desmond Tutu. They emphasize the future, not the past and catharsis through compassion and kindness. Buddhist thinkers such as the Nobel laureate His Holiness the Dalai Lama and the monk Thich Nhat Hanh emphasize this type of loving kindness and compassion even toward those who have committed atrocities. This compassionate view is well articulated by Cambodia's leading monk who is active in the peace process, Maha Ghosananda: "I do not question that loving one's oppressors— Cambodians loving the Khmer Rouge—may be the most difficult attitude to achieve. But it is a law of the universe that retaliation, hatred, and revenge only continue the cycle and never stop it. . . ." (Ghosananda, *Step by Step*, 1992).

Still another view has been articulated by Dr. Caroline Hughes of the University of Notthingham in the United Kingdom. She has some serious reservations with the proposed tribunal involving international participation. She notes a major inconsistency in giving international judges the opportunity to judge on local crimes but then awarding immunity to international actors outside the limited time frame (1975–78) whose actions had severe and adverse impacts on Cambodia. She also fears that the ritual of justice could collapse into a spectacle. Finally, she feels that the mixed tribunal fosters continued international dependency and may marginalize and disempower Cambodian society.

Who's to Blame?

A key question facing the tribunal is which former Khmer Rouge leaders will remain exempt or immune from being put on trial. It seems clear that former lower level Khmer Rouge cadres who defected early (1977, for example), such as Prime Minister Hun Sen, will not be tried. These individuals would, in fact, argue that their defection was directly related to escaping the atrocities and the system creating them. The most complex cases will be that of Ieng Sary, former foreign minister of the Khmer Rouge; Khieu Samphan, the intellectual leader of the Khmer Rouge; and Nuon Chea (known as "Brother Number Two"), another key Khmer Rouge leader. They now live comfortably in their "special zone" in western Cambodia. Thus far, it appears that there are no "smoking guns," which would associate these leaders with direct orders to kill individuals. Additionally, considerable research indicates that Dr. Khieu Samphan had relatively little power in the Khmer Rouge power structure, with his position being largely in name only. If this is true, this could work in his favor during a trial, should he be indicted.

Should leaders such as Ieng Sary be put on trial, their lawyers certainly will bring up other individuals, especially international actors or Cambodians abroad who are also responsible for atrocities in Cambodia. Prime suspects would be General Lon Nol and his cronies, who orchestrated programs against Vietnamese living in Cambodia, and American Henry Kissinger, who orchestrated the secret bombing of Cambodia. Obviously these individuals will not be tried (Lon Nol passed away in 1985), but their important role in the Cambodian tragedy will certainly be highlighted by savvy defense lawyers for Khmer Rouge leaders on trial. Defense lawyers will also certainly bring a historical perspective to the trial, noting that for many world leaders the "ends have justified the means." They could bring up countless examples where prominent leaders have made decisions resulting in tremendous death and destruction to civilians, such as the Reign of Terror associated with the French revolution; the U.S. Civil War; the atomic bombs dropped on Hiroshima and Nagasaki, Japan, during World War II; the fire bombing of Tokyo; and more than 3 million Vietnamese killed during the U.S. war in Vietnam (1964–75), many of these civilians inadvertently bombed or killed. General Curtis LeMay, who orchestrated the fire bombing of Tokyo (killing mainly civilians), admitted that if the United States had lost the war, he would have been convicted of crimes against humanity. In contrast, defense lawyers for Khmer Rouge leaders could argue that whatever deaths occurred in Cambodia were associated with their clients' attempts to build an egalitarian, economically independent Cambodia, free of capitalistic social evils.

However savvy the Khmer Rouge lawyers may be, overwhelming evidence suggests that KR leaders such as Ta Mok and Duch would be found guilty of crimes against humanity and of perpetuating atrocities. This would likely bring a measure of relief to the millions who suffered at the hands of the Khmer Rouge; the result would provide valuable catharsis so that Cambodia could bring important closure to its tragic past and focus on a bright and peaceful future.

BIBLIOGRAPHY

Ablin, David A. and Marlowe Hood, eds. *The Cambodian Agony*. Armonk, NY: M.E. Sharpe, 1990.

Abrams, Floyd. *Kampuchea: After the Worst*. New York: Lawyers Committee for Human Rights, 1990.

Anderson, Jack and Bill Pronzini. *The Cambodia File*. London: Sphere Books, 1983.

Becker, Elizabeth. *When the War Was Over: The Voices of Cambodia's Revolution and Its People*. New York: Simon and Schuster, 1986.

Bit, Seanglim. *The Warrior Heritage: A Psychological Perspective of Cambodian Trauma*. El Cerrito, CA: Seanglim Bit, 1991.

Burchett, Wilfred. *The China Cambodia Vietnam Triangle*. Chicago, IL: Vanguard Books, 1981.

Carney, Timothy. *Kampuchea: Balance of Survival*. Bangkok, Thailand: DD Books, 1983.

Carrier, Scott. *Running After Antelope* Washington, DC: Counterpoint, 2001.

Chanda, Nanya. *Brother Enemy*. New York: Harcourt Brace, 1986.

Chandler, David P. *Brother Number One: A Political Biography of Pol Pot*. Boulder, CO: Westview Press, 1999a, rev. ed.

———. *Voices from S-21: Terror and History in Pol Pot's Secret Prison*. Berkeley, CA: University of California Press, 1999b.

———. *A History of Cambodia*. Chiang Mai, Thailand: Silkworm Books, 1998, 2nd ed.

———. *The Land and People of Cambodia*. New York: HarperCollins, 1991.

Chandler, David P., Ben Kiernan, and Chanthou Boua. *Pol Pot Plans the Future: Confidential Leadership Documents from Democratic Kampuchea, 1976–1977*. New Haven, CT: Yale University Southeast Asian Studies, Monograph Series 33, 1988.

Chomsky, Noam and Edward S. Herman. *After the Cataclysm: Postwar Indochina and the Reconstruction of Imperial Ideology*. Boston, MA: South End Press, 1979.

Deac, Wilfred P. *Road to the Killing Fields: The Cambodian War of 1970–1975*. College Station, TX: Texas A&M University Press, 1997.

Dudman, Richard. *Forty Days with the Enemy*. New York: Liveright, 1971.

Ghosananda, Maha. *Step by Step*. Berkeley, CA: Parallax Press, 1992.

Heder, Steven and Judy Ledgerwood, eds. *Propaganda, Politics, and Violence in Cambodia: Democratic Transition under United Nations Peace-Keeping*. Armonk, NY: M.E. Sharpe, 1996.

Hering, B. and Ernst Utrecht, eds. *Malcolm Caldwell's Southeast Asia*. Australia: James Cook University, 1979, pp. 27–137.

Him, Chanrithy. *When Broken Glass Floats: Growing Up under the Khmer Rouge*. New York: W.W. Norton, 2000.

Hitchens, Christopher. *The Trial of Henry Kissinger*. London: Verso, 2001, pp. 25–43.

Honda, Katsuichi. *Journey to Cambodia: Investigation into Massacre by Pol Pot Regime*. Tokyo, Japan: Committee of "Journey to Cambodia," 1981.

Hourn, Kao Kim and Tania Theriault, compilers. *Skepticsim, Outrage, Hope: Reactions to the Death of Pol Pot*. Phnom Penh, Cambodia: Cambodian Institute for Cooperation and Peace, 1998.

Hudson, Christopher. *The Killing Fields*. London: Pan Books, 1984.

Kaplan, Robert D. *The Ends of the Earth: From Togo to Turkmenistan, from Iran to Cambodia—A Journey to the Frontiers of Anarchy*. New York: Vintage Books, 1996, pp. 401–438.

Kiernan, Ben. *The Pol Pot Regime: Race, Power, and Genocide under the Khmer Rouge, 1975–1979*. New Haven, CT: Yale University Press, 1996.

———. *How Pol Pot Came to Power*. London: Verso, 1986.

Kiljunen, Kimmo, ed. *Kampuchea: Decade of the Genocide*. London: Zed Books, 1984.

Lafreniere, Bree. *Music through the Dark. A Tale of Survival in Cambodia*. Honolulu, HI: University of Hawai'i Press, 2000.

Locard, Henri and Moeung Sonn. *Prisonnier de L'Angkar.* Asnieres, France: Fayard, 1993.

Mehta, Harish C. and Julie B. Mehta. *Hun Sen: Strong Man of Cambodia.* Singapore: Graham Brash, 1999.

Morris, Stephen J. *Why Vietnam Invaded Cambodia: Political Cultures and the Causes of War.* Stanford, CT: Stanford University Press, 1999.

Ngor, Haing. *A Cambodian Odyssey.* New York: Macmillan, 1987.

Oeur, U Sam, translated from the Khmer by Ken McCullough. *Sacred Vows: Poetry by U Sam Oeur.* Minneapolis, MN: Coffee House Press, 1998.

Osborne, Milton. *The Mekong: Turbulent Past, Uncertain Future.* New York: Atlantic Monthly Press, 2000.

Picq, Laurence. *Beyond the Horizon: Five Years with the Khmer Rouge.* New York: St. Martin's Press, 1989 [translated from the French by Patricia Norland].

Ponchaud, François. *Cambodia Year Zero.* New York: Henry Holt, 1977.

Pran, Dith (compiler) and Kim DePaul, ed. *Children of Cambodia's Killing Fields.* New Haven, CT: Yale University Press, 1997.

Rivero, Miguel. *Infierno y Amanecer en Kampuchea.* Havana, Cuba: Ediciones Especiales, 1979.

Romero, Vicente. *Pol Pot: El Último Verdugo.* Barcelona, Spain: Editorial Paneta, 1998.

Samphân, Khieu. *Cambodia's Economy and Industrial Development.* Ithaca, New York: Southeast Asia Program, Department of Asian Studies, Cornell University, 1959. Data Paper No. 111 [translated by Laura Summers].

Schanberg, Sidney H. *The Death and Life of Dith Pran.* New York: Penguin, 1985.

Shawcross, William. *Side-Show: Kissinger, Nixon and the Destruction of Cambodia.* New York: Pocket Books, 1979.

Sihanouk, Prince Norodom. *War & Hope: The Case for Cambodia.* New York: Pantheon Books, 1980 [translated from the French by Mary Feeney].

Siv, Darina. *Never Come Back: A Cambodian Woman's Journey.* St. Paul, MN: The Writer Press, 2000.

Sliwinski, Marek. *Le Génocide Khmer Rouge: Une Analyse Démographique.* Paris, France: Editions L'Harmattan, 1995.

Stuart-Fox, Martin and Bunheang Ung. *The Murderous Revolution.* Bangkok, Thailand: Orchid Press, 1998.

Swain, Jon. *River of Time.* New York: St. Martin's Press, 1997.

Szymusiak, Molyda. *The Stones Cry Out: A Cambodian Childhood. 1975–1980.* New York: Hill and Wang, 1986 (Translated from the French by Linda Coverdale).

Thürk, Harry. *Der Reis und Das Blut.* Berlin, Germany: Bradencurgisches Verlagshaus, 1990.

Ung, Loung. *First They Killed My Father: A Daughter of Cambodia Remembers.* New York: HarperCollins, 2000.

Vickery, Michael T. *Cambodia 1975–1982.* Boston, MA: South End Press, 1984.

Y, Ly. *Heaven Becomes Hell: A Survivor's Story of Life under the Khmer Rouge.* New Haven, CT: Yale Southeast Asia Studies, Monograph 50, 2000.

—Gerald W. Fry

SPLITTING A NATION: QUÉBEC SEPARATISM IN CANADA

In the largest political rally in Canada's modern history an estimated 150,000 citizens gathered in Montréal on October 25, 1995, to show their opposition to a simple referendum question: *Do you agree that Québec should become sovereign?* At stake was nothing less than the nation's future as a united country, for if the referendum passed, negotiations over Québec's separation would begin in earnest. Adding to the urgency of the rally, pre-election polls showed that the referendum had the support of a majority of Québec's voters, few of whom were expected to change their minds at the last minute.

Québec Premier Jacques Parizeau and *Bloc Quebeçois* chief Lucien Bouchard, both leaders of the pro-referendum campaign, confidently expected its passage and derided the last-minute outpouring of sentiment toward Québec from across Canada as little more than political desperation. Their own campaign emphasized the benefits of Québec sovereignty in maintaining the cultural and linguistic heritage of the province's French-speaking majority and countered predictions of the province's economic devastation by pledging to keep Québec tied to Canada through mutually beneficial exchanges, possibly based on a common currency. The "Oui" group also questioned the grassroots nature of the Montréal rally, noting that Air Canada had cut its fares to Montréal from around the country by 90 percent to encourage attendance at the demonstration.

Over 93 percent of Québec's eligible voters went to the polls on October 30, and the referendum night results differed by only 54,000 votes of the 4,671,008 cast. By a bare 50.58 percent majority, the referendum went down to defeat. Averting a huge political loss over the referendum issue Prime Minister Jean Chrétien, himself a Québec

THE CONFLICT

Many sovereigntists claim that Canada has always been comprised as two separate and distinct nations, one French-speaking (Francophone) and one English-speaking (Anglophone). Some sovereigntists believe that declaring an independent Québec is the only way to protect the cultural, linguistic, and social equality rights of the majority-Francophone province. Those who believe in maintaining the status quo for Canada point out that bilingualism is the nation's official policy and that provincial rights are largely unencumbered by federal mandates. Further, as Québec entered the Canadian federation willingly, there is no historical basis for the "two nations" argument.

Historical

- Colonized by both England and France in the sixteenth century, competition over commerce set the foundation for rivalry between Anglophones and Francophones. Although the British triumphed over the French by 1763, Francophone society remained largely distinct in the ensuing centuries.

Political

- Canadian politics at the federal level has been dominated by the sovereignty issue in recent decades, which has made it difficult for any one party to gain favor on a nationwide basis. Currently, Canada's national parties are largely regionally based, with the Bloc Québécois holding sway in Québec, the Reform Party dominating the prairie provinces, and the Liberals holding a majority in Ontario.

Social and Economic

- French-Canadians point to the past domination of Québec's economic institutions by Anglophones as evidence of discrimination against French speakers. Sovereigntists argue that separation from Canada will allow Québec to enjoy a greater share of the benefits of economic development in the region.

CHRONOLOGY

1756–63 The French and Indian War ends with the Treaty of Paris, which results in the French ceding almost all of Canada to British control.

1774 The Quebec Act of the British Parliament grants legal and religious guarantees to French Canadians.

1867 The British North America Act establishes the Dominion of Canada with the provinces of New Brunswick, Nova Scotia, Ontario, and Québec. As of 2001, Canada consisted of ten provinces and three territories.

1939–45 Canada fights as a member of the British Commonwealth for the Allied Powers. As in World War I, many French-Canadians object to the military draft.

1960 The Quiet Revolution, or *Revolution Tranquille,* begins in Québec political, social, and economic affairs.

1967 Réne Lévesque leaves the Liberal Party and forms Parti Québecois the following year. French President General Charles de Gaulle visits Montréal and stirs up controversy with his declaration, *"Vive le Québec libre!"* His cancellation of a trip to Ottawa affronts many Canadians.

1969 French is recognized as an official language of Canada, along with English.

1970 Terrorist kidnappings are carried out by radical Front de Libération Québecois.

1976 Parti Québecois becomes the majority party in Québec.

1980 A provincial referendum on Québec independence is defeated by a 60 to 40 percent vote.

1982 The New Canadian Constitution creates a stronger federal governmental structure, which is perceived to take autonomy away from the provinces.

1987 The Meech Lake Accord attempts to recognize Québec's "distinct society" while retaining the Canadian federation. It is required to be passed by all ten provinces; the Accord dies in 1990 without being ratified.

1995 A referendum on Québec independence is defeated by narrow margin.

April **2001** Lucien Bouchard resigns as Premier of Québec and as leader of Bloc Québécois.

native, pledged to maintain the province's "distinct character" within Canada and pointed to the experience as a reaffirmation of the nation's basic values. "There are not many countries in the world where citizens can debate—peacefully, calmly, and without violence—the very existence of the country itself," he told the country in a speech October 30, 1995, after the results had been tallied, "Once again, we have shown the entire world our country's great values of tolerance, openness, and mutual respect."

The response from the losing side was less gracious. In a statement that shocked many Quebeckers, Parizeau blamed the defeat on "money and the ethnic vote," the latter a barbed reference to immigrants and Anglophones living in Québec who voted by a 90 percent majority against the referendum. Parizeau's attitude seemed to indicate that Québec's future under sovereignty would itself deny the distinct character of its diverse, non-Francophone communities. Following the uproar, Parizeau hastily resigned as premier of the province, but his statement left a bitter postscript to the campaign.

HISTORICAL BACKGROUND

The tensions between Québec's Francophone majority and the country's other provinces originated with Canada's colonial settlement by competing British and French explorers in the sixteenth century. John Cabot, in the employ of the British Crown, was among the first explorers to note the rich abundance of natural resources on the North American continent, especially for fishing and fur trapping. After Cabot's journey around the Maritime region in 1497, hundreds of commercial traders ventured to North America to fish, hunt, and trade with the indigenous people. Despite the profitable trade the region's harsh climate forestalled outright colonization efforts. The first land claims by the European powers did not arise until around 1534, when Jacques Cartier claimed an area around the mouth of the St. Lawrence River for France; in 1583 Sir Humphrey Gilbert followed suit and claimed Newfoundland for the British Crown. It was not until 1605, a full century after Cabot's arrival, that a permanent European settlement took shape under the French flag at Port Royal in what is now Nova Scotia. Samuel de Champlain founded another trade post on the St. Lawrence River in 1608, which eventually became Québec City.

Although other Europeans, including the Basques and the Scots, were active traders in the

MAP OF CANADA. *(Gale Research (Detroit). Reproduced by permission.)*

region, the two major colonial powers on the continent were Britain and France. As competition grew between the two powers for dominance, a series of wars disrupted colonial settlement throughout the seventeenth and eighteenth centuries. British forces captured Québec City in 1629 during one early conflict, although the settlement was handed back to the French three years later. King William's War (1689–97) involved another series of skirmishes between the rivals, although the subsequent Queen Anne's War (1702–13) had longer lasting consequences. The 1713 Peace of Utrecht, which ended Queen Anne's War, delivered much of the Maritime and Hudson Bay regions to the British, who now held a significant edge over the French. With the Treaty of Paris in 1763 this status was finalized, as France ceded almost all of its remaining colonial territory in Canada to Britain after losing the French and Indian (or Seven Years) War

(1754–63). British authorities now controlled the greater part of the North American continent.

After more than a century and a half of active settlement, however, British North America contained a diverse collection of European descendants, not to mention a host of indigenous peoples. There were legitimate fears on the part of Canada's French-speaking population that British rule would bring tyranny. In the most infamous example of their action against the Francophones British authorities had expelled the Acadians from Nova Scotia in 1755 over their refusal to take an oath of loyalty to the British King. More than 10,000 Acadians were forcibly removed from the region, and about one-third died during the deportations. After the expulsion orders were lifted in 1764, only 3,000 were able to return to Nova Scotia, where they found that much of their land had been taken by British settlers.

THE 1980 AND 1995 REFERENDUMS

Text of the 1980 Referendum:

The government of Québec has made public its proposal to negotiate a new agreement with the rest of Canada, based on the equality of nations; This agreement would enable Québec to acquire the exclusive power to make its laws, levy its taxes, and establish relations abroad—in other words, sovereignty—and, at the same time, to maintain with Canada an economic association including a common currency; No change in political status resulting from these negotiations will be effected without approval by the people through another referendum; On these terms, do you give the government of Québec the mandate to negotiate the proposed agreement between Québec and Canada?

Text of the 1995 Referendum:

Do you agree that Québec should become sovereign, after having made a formal offer to Canada for a new economic and political partnership, within the scope of the Bill respecting the future of Québec and of the agreement signed on June 12, 1995?

Fortunately, once the hostilities of the French and Indian War ceased in 1763, a more measured approach characterized British governance. Although the Anglican Church was nominally the official denomination under British rule, freedom of religious practice was observed, which allowed Roman Catholic institutions to continue their vital role in French-Canadian life. There were no reparations taken from Francophone civilians for the British losses in the French and Indian War, and French civil law was instituted for property matters under the Québec Act of 1774, which also specified that English common law would be used to decide criminal matters. The act also established an assembly appointed by the colonial governor to administer to the region, a move hotly contested by the Anglophone merchant class, which had demanded an assembly elected through a franchise limited solely to Protestant land owners. Finally, the act allowed the seigneurial system of land ownership to continue in Québec. Under the system, French *seigneurs*, or "lords," who had been given land grants by royal charter, leased lands to *habitant* settlers, who worked it and paid obligations back to the lord. As a quasi-feudal system in place until 1854, seigneurship kept most Québec settlers tied to the land while establishing the power of the

seigneurs, along with the Catholic Church, over the habitants. In contrast, the merchant class quickly became the leaders among Anglophone settlers.

The Constitutional Act of 1791 reiterated these differences. Establishing two separate administrative regions for British North America (in the wake of the American Revolution, 1775–83, no longer including the United States), the new constitution separated Lower Canada, or Québec, from Upper Canada, or Ontario. For Francophone Lower Canada, the seigneurial system was retained, while Anglophone Upper Canada allowed private property rights to be freely bought and sold, with the exception of lands set aside for the Anglican Church. The colonial governor would continue to oversee both colonies, with an appointed council and elected assembly forming the legislatures of Upper and Lower Canada. In practice, the assemblies lacked power, as they had no final authority over the laws of the land, although they could block the passage of new laws and budgetary expenditures. In Lower Canada, where most of the elected representatives were Francophones, the assembly quickly demonstrated its ability to counter the appointed council, comprised mostly of Anglophone merchants. French became the *de facto* language of governing Lower Canada, and by the 1830s, the Assembly demanded increased power over the province's affairs.

With open rebellion at hand in the colony Britain responded with the Act of Union in 1841, which reestablished a united government for Canada in the hope of diminishing the reformist impulse from the Lower Canada Assembly. Giving an equal portion of representatives to both provinces despite Lower Canada's larger population, the new legislature also diminished the proportional representation of the Francophone population. The merging of the two provinces' debts was also criticized in Québec, as Lower Canada had a far lower outstanding debt in comparison to Upper Canada. Finally, the act prescribed English as the colony's official language, although this rule was rescinded in 1848.

In contrast to the Act of Union's ostensible goal, the impact of the united legislature actually increased the impact of the reformers, as they united from both the Lower (or Canada East) and Upper (or Canada West) provinces to call for a greater role for elected officials. After 1848, with the support of a sympathetic governor, reformers had achieved their goal of colonial self-governance, as they were effectively able to pass legislation in

LUCIEN BOUCHARD

1938– Lucien Bouchard was born in 1938 in St. Couer-de-Marie in northern Québec and earned his law degree at Laval University in Québec City. Bouchard practiced law and served on government committees investigating corruption early in his career. He also worked as a legal advisor to the Parti Québecois from 1980–82, and served as ambassador to France from 1985–88. Bouchard served briefly in the Conservative administration as secretary of state and then as minister of the environment from 1988–90, when he resigned over the Party's handling of the Meech Lake Accord.

Bouchard also won elected office in 1988, although he switched party affiliation to the Bloc Québécois in 1993, a party that he had helped to found three years earlier. Because the Bloc Québécois earned the second-greatest number of seats in the House of Commons in 1993, Bouchard served as the official Opposition leader, a position he held until 1996, when he resigned to become Premier of Québec. Under pressure from Québec separatist hard-liners, Bouchard resigned as both Premier and Bloc Québécois leader in April 2001.

LUCIEN BOUCHARD. *(AP/Wide World Photos. Reproduced by permission.)*

their own right with the governor's tacit approval. Seeing little sense in continuing to guide Canada's internal affairs, the arrangement was soon endorsed by British authorities, thereby establishing Canadian sovereignty. Britain extended home rule to all of its other North American colonies, including Prince Edward Island, New Brunswick, and Newfoundland, in the 1850s.

Confederation

The introduction of home rule did not end the political stalemate that characterized political infighting in the united Assembly of Canada East and West. Anglophone Canadian West representatives, led by John A. Macdonald of the Conservative Party, were now dissatisfied with the equal number of assembly seats assigned to the two provinces. In the years between the Act of Union in 1841 and the Census of 1861, a population shift had given Canada West a majority of the population, 1.6 million citizens to Canada East's 1.1 million; consequently, Francophones were now proportionally over-represented in the assembly. In addition to diluting French-Canadian power in a national assembly by forming a federation of Britain's North American colonies, Macdonald and

other reformers hoped that the provincial government of Canada West would also gain more autonomy that it currently had in union with Canada East.

Enacted by Queen Victoria's signature in 1867, the British North America Act established the Dominion of Canada with the provinces of New Brunswick, Nova Scotia, Ontario, and Québec. The legislature retained an appointed body of representatives in the Senate, which reviewed laws passed by the elected officials in the House of Commons. Although Canada, as part of the British Empire, remained bound to England's directives on international relations and defense, a prime minister chosen by the majority (or coalition-majority) party would serve as the head of the government in Canada. Macdonald served as the first Prime Minister of the Dominion of Canada.

Confederation supporters also largely achieved their goal of strengthening the autonomy of the Canadian provinces, a platform that gained approval for confederation in Québec. Under the terms of confederation the federal government took responsibility for banking, defense, shipping, and criminal law, among other limited duties. The

JEAN CHRÉTIEN

1934– Born into a politically active family in Shawinigan, Québec, Jean Chrétien was a willful student who left—or was asked to leave—several boarding schools during his youth. Settling down after meeting his future wife, Aline Chaine, Chrétien completed his law degree in Québec City's Laval University. The young lawyer remained politically active and, after setting up a successful law practice in his hometown, ran successfully for the House of Commons in 1963. He was subsequently elected to six terms in office and served in several ministerial offices as an elected official in the areas of finance, native affairs, and industrial development.

From 1986 to 1990 Chrétien returned to private practice, but reentered public life as the leader of the Liberal Party in 1990, when he also regained his seat in the House of Commons. When the Liberals gained a majority in the Parliament in 1993, Chrétien assumed the office of Prime Minister. He has continued to hold the office since 1993, guiding the Liberals to a majority in three successive elections. Similar to Pierre Trudeau, another French-Canadian Prime Minister, Chrétien has worked to achieve a Canadian federation that includes Québec while acknowledging its distinctiveness.

provinces took control over matters of education, medicine, municipal governing, property rights, civil law, and natural resources. With this arrangement Québec could mandate its own laws over language and education as well as religion, and a majority of Canada East representatives voted in favor of confederation.

While the relatively weak federal government established by confederation abated some of the political tensions among the provinces, provincial prerogatives meant that French-Canadian language and cultural rights were not necessarily protected throughout the country. In 1912 Ontario enacted Regulation 17, which mandated English-language instruction in schools and severely limited language classes in French. Manitoba followed suit in 1916, although it had already eliminated French as an official provincial language in 1890. The onset of World War I (1914–18), however, revived tensions at the federal level, particularly over Prime Minister Robert Borden's decision to conscript soldiers to fight for the Allied forces. Borden's announcement was met with thunderous opposition from French-Canadians, most of whom viewed the

effort as an endorsement of Britain's imperial leadership. Consequently, when the Military Service Act came up for a vote in Parliament in 1917, every French-Canadian representative voted against it, although it nonetheless passed with a majority vote. The following year, when military authorities seized a suspected draft dodger in Québec City, a riot ensued over Easter weekend that resulted in four civilian deaths.

While World War I threatened national unity over the conscription issue, the industrialization of the era linked Québec more tightly with the rest of Canada. Here too, however, the results increased tension over charges of discrimination against French-Canadians. While the upsurge in manufacturing brought more Québec residents into the cities to earn their wages, it also brought them into contact with typically Anglophone factory owners and managers. It was difficult for French-Canadians to break into the managerial ranks, and almost impossible without fluency in the English language. Although a small middle class had emerged in Québec, decisions about the province's economic life were increasingly perceived as out of Quebeckers' control. During the prosperous 1920s, however, these charges were muted by the massive economic development of the pulpwood, minerals, and hydroelectric power industries in the province.

With the economic collapse of the Great Depression, French-Canadian resentment at Anglophone dominance helped the *Unione Nationale* under Maurice Duplessis come to power in Québec. Duplessis espoused an explicitly Québec-nationalist platform—most often based on fears of urbanization and modernization—and quickly turned his reign as provincial premier to eliminate political opposition through electoral corruption and outright intimidation. A favorite tactic was to label his adversaries communists, and with the help of the Roman Catholic Church Duplessis ushered in a distinctly anti-reform and anti-labor union era in Québec until his death in 1959. Duplessis was able to attract some foreign investment to Québec by promising to keep organized labor in check, but the results led Québec's wage-earning Francophones to receive 40 percent less in their paychecks than their Anglophone counterparts. By the end of the 1950s, under the sway of the *Unione Nationale* and the Roman Catholic Church, Québec seemed to be falling further behind its neighbors in economic development, educational attainment, and social reform.

La Revolution Tranquille

Ironically, Duplessis's conservative and corrupt regime paved the way for the most reform-minded period of Québec's history, known as *la Revolution Tranquille*, or the Quiet Revolution. After Duplessis's death in 1959 the *Unione Nationale*'s leadership fell apart. Seizing the opportunity for a political comeback the Québec Liberal Party, under Jean Lesage, triumphed in the 1960 provincial elections. For all of the *Unione Nationale*'s faults, it had nonetheless made Québec's provincial administration a formidable power, and Duplessis was always conservative with the province's finances. Therefore, Lesage inherited a strong, centralized provincial government with substantial financial reserves; immediately after taking office the new premier announced a new program almost every day in his first month in office.

Under the slogan *"Maitres chez nous,"* ("Masters of our own house"), the Quiet Revolution of the 1960s transformed Québec's social, political, and economic landscapes. The province's first Department of Education was established in 1964 to diminish the church's traditional influence on Québec's schools and to foster higher achievement in math, science, and engineering. In labor relations, the harsh repression of the *Unione Nationale* era abated, and the right to strike was extended to public employees. The Liberal government also reformed the province's electoral system, reaching a more equitable balance between urban and rural voting districts. Perhaps the most ambitious plans concerned the province's economic development. Under the leadership of the Minister of Natural Resources (and future *Parti Québécois* founder) Réne Lévesque, the province's privately held electricity producers were nationalized into *Hydro Québec*, which equalized its rates and sponsored industrial development across the province. Québec also established a pension plan for retired workers in 1965.

Although Lésage fought for more provincial control in government affairs—sometimes withdrawing Québec from federally sponsored programs—he was by no means a separatist. Yet other groups that wanted to go beyond mere reform shared his emphasis on French-Canadian nationalism at the heart of the Quiet Revolution. The *Front de libération du Québec* (FLQ) emerged in 1963 as a terrorist organization demanding Québec's immediate separation from Canada. During the rest of the decade, FLQ staged dozens of armed robberies to finance its operations, including over two hundred bombings that injured 40 people and killed six others. In 1970 the FLQ kidnapped

RÉNE LÉVESQUE

1922–1987 Réne Lévesque grew up in the Gaspe region of eastern Québec. Although he studied law at Laval University, he dropped out to work as a French-language correspondent for the U.S. Office of War Information in World War II. Lévesque continued working as a journalist, concentrating on international affairs, for the Canadian Broadcasting Corporation's Radio Canada, a French-language news service. In 1960, in the wake of a radio strike that embodied protest against anti-Québecois discrimination, Lévesque won a House of Commons seat as the Liberal Party candidate. However, Lévesque left the Liberals to form the Parti Québecois after he failed to gain the party's endorsement of sovereignty for Québec in 1968.

In 1976 the Parti Québecois replaced the Conservatives as the majority party in Québec and in 1980, Lévesque put a referendum on the ballot to decide Québec's independence. The move failed at the ballot box by a clear majority, gaining only forty percent approval in the province. Although his political reputation was diminished by the defeat, Lévesque remained a chief critic of Pierre Trudeau's position on Canadian federalism. Lévesque died in 1987.

British trade minister James Cross from his Montréal home and held him hostage for two months. Meanwhile, another FLQ cell abducted Pierre Laporte, Québec's minister of labor and immigration. In response to the kidnappings, Prime Minister Pierre Trudeau invoked the War Measures Act, which temporarily suspended some civil liberties. The act was duly passed by an overwhelming majority in Parliament, and soon hundreds of people were brought in for questioning. FLQ terrorists were rounded up within weeks, but not before they had executed Laporte. Despite the atrocity, FLQ members responsible for Laporte's kidnapping and murder served no more than 11 years in prison. However, the October Crisis, as the 1970 events would be labeled, marked the end of terrorist separatism in Canada.

Although Prime Minister Trudeau acted swiftly and decisively to smash FLQ, his efforts to maintain the Canadian federation typically took more bureaucratic and constitutional routes. During his first term in office Trudeau ushered in the Official Languages Act of 1969, which mandated the use of both French and English in Canada's government. Two years later, Trudeau was the

PIERRE TRUDEAU

1919–2000 Born into a wealthy Montréal family in 1919, Pierre Trudeau benefited from extensive travel and a private education during his youth. He completed his law degree at the University of Montréal in 1943, and subsequently studied for a Master's degree at Harvard University. After the conclusion of World War II (1939–45), Trudeau traveled to Europe, studying in Paris at the *Ecole des sciences politiques* and in London at the School of Economics. After a few of years of additional travel throughout Europe, the Middle East, and Asia, Trudeau returned to Canada, where he became involved in Liberal politics.

While teaching law at the University of Montréal in the 1960s, Trudeau was invited to run on the Liberal Party ticket. He won a seat in the House of Commons and was later appointed Minister of Justice in 1967. Trudeau became the Liberal Party head in 1968 and served as Prime Minister until 1979. After a brief departure from politics in the wake of a Conservative Party victory, Trudeau returned as Prime Minister from 1980–1984. During his terms in office, Trudeau supported a strong Canadian federation that also acknowledged Québec's distinct culture and language heritage. He died on September 28, 2000.

primary supporter of the Multicultural Act, which declared equality for all the nation's cultural and ethnic groups and provided funds for ethnic organizations and language instruction. The prime minister also used his office to speak out against the forces of separation, which he viewed as detrimental to the economic and social status of working Québec residents, not to mention the nation as a whole. In 1980 Trudeau faced the most direct challenge to the status quo when the *Parti Québecois* under Réne Lévesque called for a referendum on Québec sovereignty.

The 1980 and 1995 Referenda

Less than ten years after its founding Lévesque's *Parti Québecois* had become the majority party in the province, and it followed an ambitious program of protecting French-language rights in Québec. While the preceding administration had passed Bill 22 in 1974, declaring French the official language of Québec, Lévesque went even further three years later in his support of Bill 101, the "Charter of the French Language," which outlawed languages other than French on commercial signs

and restricted English-language instruction in the province's schools. Sensing that the time was right to ask voters to approve a call for Québec's separation from Canada, Lévesque put a "sovereignty-association" referendum on the ballot in 1980 that would allow Québec to begin negotiating its secession. Under the referendum's guidelines Québec would remain tied to Canada with a common currency and possibly a common market, but would otherwise become its own nation. As Lévesque had said in a 1977 speech to the French National Assembly, "For us Quebeckers, this is literally a question of our right to live."

After briefly stepping out of politics Pierre Trudeau resumed leadership of his party to chair the fight against the 1980 referendum. Trudeau reiterated his arguments against separation as detrimental to the welfare of the average Quebecker, and noted the protection to French language and culture that the Official Languages Act and Multicultural Act afforded to every Canadian. Indeed, many French-Canadians saw little need to undertake the drastic step of secession; as Bills 22 and 101 showed, Québec's government could act unilaterally to protect the French language in the province. Trudeau's personal magnetism and appeal to other French-Canadians also helped to stop the momentum of sovereignty's forces. In the end, the vote was a landslide for the anti-sovereignty side, which tallied 60 percent of the ballots.

Following his victory in the 1980 referendum Trudeau turned to a challenge that he perceived as his ultimate legacy to Canadian federation, the patriation of the country's constitution. Patriation is the process by which the power to amend the constitution is transferred from one country, in this case Britain, to another, Canada. As a legacy of the 1867 British North America Act, constitutional changes in Canada still had to be submitted to Britain for approval. In bringing the constitution back home, so to speak, Trudeau hoped to clarify the process of future constitutional changes—including secession of any of the country's provinces—as well as add a section of rights and freedoms guaranteed to all citizens. Knowing that Québec's separatist government under Réne Lévesque would block any such plans to patriate the constitution, however, Trudeau effectively cut Québec's premier out of the constitutional negotiations at the last minute. Although the 1982 constitution gave provinces the power to amend several of its provisions, in effect granting them veto power over many federal actions, Trudeau's compromise ensured that Lévesque would never accept the patriated constitution. Indeed, Lévesque immediately

SUPPORTERS OF QUEBEC'S SEPARATIST MOVEMENT REACT TO EARLY RESULTS OF THE INDEPENDENCE REFERENDUM VOTE IN OCTOBER 1995. *(AP/Wide World Photos. Reproduced by permission.)*

went on the attack, heaping accusations of betrayal on Trudeau and Minister of Justice and Attorney General Jean Chrétien, who oversaw the negotiations. Despite Lévesque's charges of treachery, however, the new constitution was signed into effect by Queen Elizabeth II on April 17, 1982.

Although Québec's voters had rejected Lévesque's dramatic nationalism in the 1980 referendum and for the most part ignored his bitterness over the 1982 constitution, the politics of nationalism dominated Québec and indeed, Canadian politics, in the decades to follow. Conservative Prime Minister Brian Mulroney drafted the Meech Lake Accord in 1987 to negotiate with the provincial premiers in an attempt to strengthen provincial powers and forestall further charges of the federal domination of Québec. Chief among its provisions was a section recognizing Québec as "a distinct society," which sparked criticism from many groups, including aboriginal associations, who viewed the accord as going too far in catering to

Québec's demands. Adding to the controversy, Québec Premier Robert Bourassa invoked a constitutional provision to nullify a Supreme Court decision overturning the province's restrictive, French-only language laws, and followed this announcement with plans to adopt even stricter standards. With public opinion turning against the accord in many parts of the country in the wake of Bourassa's actions, it died in 1990 without being ratified by all ten provinces, as specified in the agreement. Mulroney attempted a second set of negotiations in 1992, which resulted in the Charlottetown Accord. The second accord, like the first, attempted to extend provincial rights and declared "distinct status" for Québec, and added self-governing provisions for aboriginal groups. Unlike the Meech Lake Accord, however, the Charlottetown Accord was submitted to voters as a referendum measure. Despite the endorsement of every provincial premier and most political parties in Canada, the referendum was rejected by 54 percent of the voters.

Although he had served as an advisor in several key positions in Mulroney's Conservative administration, Lucien Bouchard emerged from the Accord negotiations as the leader of the opposition movement, a position he used to form a federal-level, separatist party in 1990, the *Bloc Québécois*. By 1993 the *Bloc Québécois* held the second-largest number of seats in Parliament to the Liberals under Jean Chrétien, making Bouchard the official Opposition Leader. After Québec Premier Jacques Parizeau moved for another referendum on the province's sovereignty in 1995, Bouchard quickly used his political skills and dynamic personality to lead the separatists into a commanding position in the weeks prior to the referendum vote. Chrétien, who had at first assumed that Québec's voters were simply tired of the separatist issue, fought back with the familiar arguments highlighting the danger of secession, along with a sentimental appeal to his fellow French-Canadians to preserve the nation. After a massive rally brought some 150,000 Canadians to Montréal to counter the separatist tide, the 1995 referendum went down to a narrow defeat.

RECENT HISTORY AND THE FUTURE

After the defeat of the 1995 sovereignty referendum Bouchard vowed that he would prepare the ground for another referendum on the issue, while Chrétien moved to prevent additional secessionist threats from paralyzing national politics. Public opinion in Québec on the matter remained hard to judge. On the one hand, a 1998 poll taken by *Maclean's* and the Canadian Broadcasting Corporation (CBC) showed that 56 percent of Quebeckers thought that the province would likely separate from Canada within 50 years. On the other hand, the Liberal Party received the most votes in the province's election that year (although the electoral distribution still has a majority of seats in the provincial legislature to the *Bloc Québécois*). As *Maclean's* Anthony Wilson-Smith commented, there seemed to be "a weary acknowledgement— reflected across the country—that Québec secession is a perpetual, barely changing blip on the political radar screen." Given the lack of consensus on the issue in Québec, Bouchard put aside plans for another referendum and focused on putting Québec's provincial finances in order. Acknowledged as the most capable Premier of Québec since the days of the Quiet Revolution, Bouchard erased the province's deficit and helped ease unemployment to the lowest figure in a generation.

While Bouchard waited for public opinion to coalesce around separatism, federalist forces prepared to set stricter terms for any future debate. Like Pierre Trudeau, Jean Chrétien viewed the preservation of the Canadian confederation as an important part of his political legacy and worked to ensure that any decisions over separatism would not be undertaken lightly. Following a Supreme Court decision authored in the wake of the 1995 referendum regarding the conditions for provincial secession, Chrétien sponsored the Clarity Act, which dictated that any separation questions submitted to voters must outline the specific conditions of separation. Enacted in 2000, the Clarity Act also mandated that all of the provinces would have to vote on secession, and that any provincial borders, including aboriginal lands, would have to be renegotiated as part of the process. In short, the referenda of 1980 and 1995 never would have been allowed to come to a vote under the terms imposed by the Clarity Act, a fact that led separatist forces to oppose its passage.

While the Clarity Act represented a serious obstacle to any future separatist efforts, the departure of Lucien Bouchard from office in early 2001 also diminished the political fortunes of the *Bloc Québécois* and *Parti Québécois*. Pressured into resigning by separatist hardliners, Bouchard was replaced by Bernard Landry, who was perceived as a political extremist with little appeal to those with ambivalent views on separatism. Landry also faced a ruling Liberal Party with renewed popularity from its key victory in the 2000 federal elections. Finally, in Jean Chrétien separatist forces also confronted a prime minister intent on preserving the confederation as a vital part of his political legacy. As Chrétien's skillful stewardship of the Clarity Act demonstrated, the conditions for Québec's sovereignty only became more problematic for separatists in the new century.

BIBLIOGRAPHY

"Apres Bouchard," *The Economist*, January 20, 2001.

April, Pierre. "Political Uncertainty Harming Québec Economy," *Canadian Press*, November 20, 1999.

Ayed, Nahlah. "Provinces to Get $1.8 Billion More in Payment, Québec Gets the Most," *Canadian Press*, February 27, 2001.

"Bouchard's Pragmatism Served Québec Well," *Toronto Star*, January 13, 2001.

Came, Barry. "A Man of the People," *Maclean's*, July 6, 1992.

Came, Barry, and John DeMont. "'Crusade for Canada,'" *Maclean's*, November 6, 1995.

Canada Country Report. "At a Glance: 2001–2002," *Economist Intelligence Unit*, February 2001.

———. "The Political Scene," *Economist Intelligence Unit*, February 2001.

Caragata, Warren. "Back from the Brink," *Maclean's*, November 6, 1995.

Chidley, Joe. "Vive le Canada Libre," *Canadian Business*, February 5, 2001.

Chrétien, Jean. "Statement by Prime Minister Jean Chrétien on Referendum Night, October 30, 1995." Available online at http://www.ccu-cuc.ca/. (cited May 14, 2001).

Collins, Michael. "Québec: Social Union or Separation?" *Contemporary Review*, March 1999.

"Day Urged to Crush Roots of Separatism," *Toronto Star*, February 15, 2001.

Doshi, Sameer. "Québec's Lesson: A Path of Peaceful Separatism," *Harvard International Review*, Summer 1999.

Dubuc, Alain. "Landry's Dilemma," *Time Canada*, April 2, 2001.

Dufour, Christian. *A Canadian Challenge*. Halifax: The Institute for Research on Public Policy, 1990.

Granatstein, J.L. "In Their Own Way, They All Fought for Reform," *Maclean's*, July 1, 1998.

Kierans, Eric. "Fondly Remembering Réne," *Maclean's*, January 1, 2000.

Lévesque, Réne. *My Québec*. Toronto: Methuen, 1979.

Martin, Lawrence. *Chrétien: The Will to Win*. Toronto: Lester Publishing, 1995.

McKenzie, Robert. "Bitter-sweet Tributes Bid Bouchard a Fond Goodbye," *Toronto Star*, February 23, 2001.

Morton, Desmond. *A Short History of Canada*. Fifth Revised Edition, McClelland & Stewart, Inc., 2000.

Nazareth, Linda. "Outlook for the Provinces," *CICB Observations*, September 1998.

Newman, Peter C. "Québec is Like Jane and Ted," *Maclean's*, February 7, 2000.

Riendeau, Roger. *A Brief History of Canada*. New York: Facts on File, Inc., 2000.

Royal Society of Canada. *Can Canada Survive? Under What Terms and Conditions?* Toronto: University of Toronto Press, 1997.

Rubin, Josh. "Hardliners Suffer the Wrath of Québec Media," *Toronto Star*, January 13, 2001.

Trudeau, Pierre. *Federalism and the French Canadians*. New York: St. Martin's Press, 1968.

Warwick, Liz. "The 'Ethnic' Shock," *Maclean's*, November 6, 1995.

Weaver, R. Kent, ed. *The Collapse of Canada?* Washington, DC: The Brookings Institute, 1992.

Wells, Paul. "What Can We Expect Now?" *Time Canada*, January 29, 2001.

Wilson-Smith, Anthony. "No 'Winning Conditions'," *Maclean's*, December 28, 1998-January 4, 1999.

—Timothy G. Borden

DISPUTED DRILLING RIGHTS IN THE CASPIAN SEA

THE CONFLICT

The Caspian Sea seabed contains many unexplored and undeveloped oil and gas reserves. These reserves are potentially worth billions of dollars to the nations and companies that develop them. Although some development is underway, legal wrangling by the five Caspian Sea border nations over who owns the reserves has held up production and led to intense negotiations over the sea's future.

Political

- High-level leaders and negotiators from the five nations bordering the Caspian Sea have met numerous times throughout the decades, but they have been unsuccessful in resolving the claims and territorial issues.

Economic

- Multi-billion dollar commitments are on the line as investors wait for the bordering nations to resolve the dispute.

Territorial

- Each nation brings different, and often shifting, views and opinions regarding how to mark the boundaries of the Caspian Sea.

The boundary-markings of the Caspian Sea—and thus ownership of the resources in the Sea—have long been debated by the five countries lining its coast: Azerbaijan, Iran, Kazakhstan, Russia, and Turkmenistan. In May 2001 a meeting was held between the deputy foreign ministers of Azerbaijan and Turkmenistan to set out the Caspian Sea's delimitation (boundary-marking) between their two countries. The meeting ended with mutual recriminations, illustrating the unresolved tensions that continue to stymie a solution. At the conclusion of the two-day talks in Turkmenistan's capital of Ashkhabad, the Turkmen Foreign Ministry denounced Azerbaijan for an alleged lack of good faith bargaining. According to the Foreign Broadcast Information Service (FBIS, Document No. CEP-261, May 3, 2001), Turkmenistan asserted that Azerbaijan's insistence on drawing a sectoral line closer to the coast of Turkmenistan than to its own "contradicts the principle of justice and equality." Turkmenistan demanded, pending the settlement of the dispute, that Azerbaijan and foreign energy firms "stop all projects connected with the exploration and extraction of hydrocarbons, including seismologic surveys . . . in zones of the Caspian Sea arguably between Turkmenistan and Azerbaijan." The Turkmen Foreign Ministry stated that it would appeal to international bodies for help in drawing the line and would protest Azerbaijan's alleged encroachment on Turkmen territory to the International Arbitration Court.

On the same day, Iran's Supreme Leader Ayatollah Ali Khamenei condemned the very holding of the Azerbaijani-Turkmen talks, stating the legal status of the Caspian Sea should be determined by each of the five coastal, or littoral, states surrounding the Sea. He underscored Iran's stance that "on the basis of international law, the Caspian Sea should be shared by all the five littoral states and no foreign power can interfere in affairs related to the sea." (FBIS, Document No. IAP-40, May 3, 2001)

The unresolved legal status of the Caspian Sea both contributes to and reflects wrangles over who owns major oil, natural gas, and other resources in the Sea, over fishing and navigation rights, and over responsibilities for environmental protection. Western private investors have made multi-billion dollar commitments to develop Caspian Sea oil and natural gas resources, but the uncertain legal ownership of oil and gas fields has held back some investment and has raised the costs of development. Increasing Caspian Sea pollution also remains an issue to be addressed. Pollution problems are highlighted by the 95 percent reduction in sturgeon catches in the Sea (the fish is the source of the famous Beluga caviar), by over-fishing and the destruction of spawning grounds, and by a recent major kill-off of seals.

Sea or Lake, What's at Stake?

In the popular mind the dispute over the legal status of the Caspian Sea has revolved around whether it is regarded as a sea or as a lake in international legal parlance. If it is a sea, these observers have supposed, then by international law and practice it should be divided among the littoral states. If it is a lake then its use could be jointly overseen by the littoral states in what is termed a condominium arrangement (joint sovereignty and joint rule). Neither of these suppositions is accurate. Those who support regarding the Caspian as an enclosed sea under the 1982 Law of the Sea convention point to general provisions that such a sea will be divided using equidistant lines, to include seabed resources. Legal scholars, however, point out that the Caspian is not really considered an enclosed sea as defined in the convention because it has no direct outlet to another sea or ocean, and because freedom of navigation by outsiders is not at issue. Iran is among those who have argued that the Caspian is a lake and should be ruled by a condominium arrangement. There are, however, no historical instances of common ownership of lakes or inland seas. Lakes shared by two or more countries have always been delimited using equidistant lines. This includes the delimitation of the Great Lakes in North America, Lake Tanganyika in Africa, and Lake Constance in Europe. Partial alterations from this principle have primarily been allowed only for historical or special circumstances,

such as to include or exclude a claimed island. In the case of the Caspian Sea, Iranian and Soviet claims that the Sea was a jointly shared "common sea" are not born out by the historical record.

Instead of arguing about whether the Caspian is legally a sea or a lake under international law, it is better to examine the resource or use of the Sea, according to lawyer Bernard Oxman. The states bordering the Caspian all agree that in the respect of its navigation and use the Caspian is a lake, and so only the bordering states should have say-so over these aspects. Regarding mineral resources, whether the Caspian is considered a lake or sea, an exclusive economic zone that will extend for 200 miles (320 kilometers) from the coastal lands is hoped to be established under international law. Both Azerbaijan and Kazakhstan have declared these 200-mile zones in a sea that is only 150 miles (240 kilometers) wide between them, clearly demonstrating the need for negotiations. The final status of the Caspian must be worked out by the littoral states, perhaps drawing from some Law of the Sea precedents for semi-enclosed marine seas or those worked out by countries sharing lake borders, and may involve a mix of partition and condominium features.

HISTORICAL BACKGROUND

During most of the 1990s Iran and Russia claimed that the Caspian was a "common sea" or lake under shared rule, as per provisions of 1921 and 1940 bilateral treaties. These treaties, however, were silent on seabed boundaries or energy rights. The 1921 Russia-Iran Treaty formalized Iran's border with the Soviet Union, which took control over Georgia, Armenia, and Azerbaijian, thus granting Russia access to ports on the Caspian Sea. The 1921 treaty referred to the Caspian Sea only in terms of where the land boundaries between the two countries began and ended. The 1940 Soviet-Iran Treaty granted each nation bordering the Sea exclusive fishing rights up to 10 miles (16 kilometers) from their coasts. Like the 1921 treaty before it, the 1940 agreement also did not address resources under the seabed, including oil and natural gas.

In 1994 Russia argued before the United Nations (UN) General Assembly that the Caspian Sea was a lake. As a body of water that is landlocked and not connected to a sea or ocean, Russia argued, it was therefore not subject to international navigation rights or to the delimitation of economic zones based on a continental shelf approach. It further insisted that the Caspian be subject to joint-

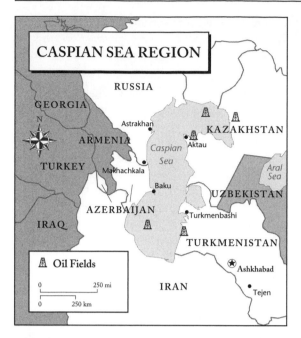

CASPIAN SEA REGION

THIS MAP ILLUSTRATES THE CASPIAN SEA REGION, NOTING MAJOR PORTS AND OILFIELDS. *(The Gale Group.)*

use agreements among the littoral states, as set forth in Soviet-Iranian treaties, which remain binding on the new states as successors to the treaties. (Armenia, Georgia, and Azerbaijan became independent nations after the collapse of the Soviet Union.) Legal scholars point out that Iran never challenged Soviet oil drilling in the Caspian Sea or other exploitation, nor did it claim a share of proceeds, although the Soviet-Iranian Treaty of 1940 spoke of the Caspian as belonging to the Soviet Union and Iran (beyond 10-mile fishing rights). Under this treaty Iran was entitled to a share of the proceeds. The lack of consultation between the two countries on this matter implies that Iran and the Soviet Union did not actually treat the Sea resources as shared. Legal scholar Scott Horton points out that Soviet-Iranian treaties dictating the status of the Caspian Sea have no validity under the Vienna Convention on the Law of Treaties, since those treaties cannot be binding on the new Caspian states, including Azerbaijan, unless they formally accept the treaties.

Among early efforts to resolve the legal status of the Caspian Sea after the Soviet collapse in 1991, Russia floated a draft treaty in late 1994 calling for a condominium of the Caspian Sea beyond a 20-mile (32 kilometers) coastal "zone of influence" by each littoral state, with a joint board to control the use of the rest of the Sea. In December 1996 Russia modified this proposal by enlarging the zone to 45 miles (72 kilometers) of exclusive control.

Azerbaijan in late 1996 reportedly rejected draft proposals prepared by Russia that called for the Caspian Sea to be held in common. At a November 1996 foreign ministerial meeting of the littoral states in Ashkhabad, the sides agreed to form a working group composed of deputy foreign ministers to draw up a convention on the Sea's legal status. The working group faced delays, but finally held its first meeting in Almaty in May 1997. It was, however, unsuccessful in drawing up anything but the preamble. Subsequent meetings held in December 1998 and February 2001 also failed to complete a draft convention. Azerbaijan and Turkmenistan clashed at the meetings over ownership of some oilfields, leading Turkmen President Saparamurad Niyazov to issue a decree unilaterally claiming the fields for Turkmenistan and ordering an international tender, or bid, to be held on developing these and other Turkmen fields.

Conflicting Positions

Beginning in the late 1990s halting forward movement was made toward agreement on delimiting the Caspian Sea. Of the states bordering the Caspian—Russia, Azerbaijan, Iran, Turkmenistan, and Kazakhstan—all except Iran appeared in 2001 to be ready to divide seabed resources, using a modified median line (equidistant or middle line) approach. Iran has been the slowest in developing its Caspian Sea resources and appears most interested in using the unresolved legal status of the Sea to discourage Western companies, particularly those of the United States, from assisting in energy development. Russia, during most of the 1990s, appeared to support Iran in calling for the basic retention of the legal status the Caspian possessed under Soviet-era treaties. In 1998, however, Russia embraced a modified median line approach to delimiting its own seabed borders with its bordering Caspian neighbor Kazakhstan, and in January 2001 it adopted the same approach with its other bordering neighbor, Azerbaijan.

The United States, an interested party in the resolution of the dispute due to the region's vast expanse of natural resources, has taken the position that Caspian Sea delimitation should be agreed upon by the littoral states, but that delimitation should permit the development of energy resources in line with existing contracts. Then-U.S. Caspian Envoy Richard Morningstar stated in early 1999 that, in practice, the division of the Sea into sectors would probably be the best method. In May 1999 he delivered suggestions to Azeri President Heydar Aliyev and Turkmen President Suparmurat

Niyazov for delimitating Caspian Sea borders between Azerbaijan and Turkmenistan. U.S. consultants to the Azerbaijani-Turkmen border commission developed the suggestions. On April 20, 2001, Russian Premier Mikhail Kasyanov rejected U.S. interest in the Caspian Sea and appealed to the 1921 and 1940 Soviet-Iranian treaties in asserting that non-littoral states have no role regarding the Sea. What role the United States could have had in the Caspian matter has thus been marginalized under these treaties.

Azerbaijan, as a nation bordering the Sea, has a vested interest in resolving the boundary and resource disputes. Since the early 1990s it has consistently called for all the Caspian—surface, water, and seabed—to be divided into national sectors. Azerbaijan maintains that the delimitation of the Caspian Sea worked out by the Soviet Ministry of Oil and Gas Industry in 1970 provides the legal basis to sectoral claims. Under this delimitation, Kyapaz (Azerbaijan's name for an oilfield; Turkmenistan calls it the Serder field) belongs to Azerbaijan. Azerbaijan has also claimed that, as the discoverer and developer of the Azeri and Chiraq fields, these oilfields should also belong to Azerbaijan.

Kazakhstan's stance in recent years has generally mirrored that of Azerbaijan. Kazakh President Nursultan Nazarbayev visited Baku, Azerbaijan's capitol, in September 1996. There, the two presidents issued a joint statement on the Caspian Sea, agreeing to work together to resolve legal issues, and supporting open navigation and the division of the seabed and waters into national sectors. Reporters asked Azeri President Aliyev if the joint statement was aimed against the stance taken by Russia and Iran on the Caspian Sea, which was that a coastal zone should be established and that the Sea's resources should be overseen jointly by the littoral states. Aliyev replied that the statement reflected the rights of coastal states to exploit Caspian resources.

Russia at first called the Caspian a "closed sea," a Soviet-era concept not recognized in international law. It also referred to the Caspian as a lake, not subject to the Law of the Sea, and stated that the 1921 and 1940 treaties remained in effect despite the dissolution of the Soviet Union and the independence of Azerbaijian, Armenia, and Georgia. Russia's position shifted slightly between 1994 and 1996, when it proposed a 20-mile (32 kilometers), and later a 45-mile (72 kilometers), coastal zone for each littoral state, outside of which there would be joint navigation rights, joint management

CHRONOLOGY

late-1860s Oil is formally extracted from on-shore wells near present-day Baku, Azerbaijan.

1921 The Russia-Iran Treaty of 1921 is signed between the Russian Federation and Iran. It formalizes the border between the two countries and gives control of Armenia, Georgia, and Azerbaijan to Russia.

1940 The Soviet-Iran Treaty of 1940 gives each nation bordering the sea exclusive fishing rights of up to ten miles from its coast. The treaty does not address resources found under the seabed.

1945 The first extraction of oil from the Caspian Sea takes place.

1991 Azerbaijan, Kazakhstan, and Turkmenistan declare independence from the Soviet Union.

July 1998 Russia and Kazakhstan agree to a median line approach to delimiting Russia's seabed borders.

September 1998 Iran proposes that the littoral states divide the coastal zones into national sectors so that each state receives 20 percent of the sea floor and surface.

November 2000 Russian envoy Viktor Kaluzhny states that Iran has become an impediment to the resolution of the Caspian Sea's status.

January 9, 2001 Russia and Azerbaijan agree to a modified median line approach to delimiting Russia's seabed borders. Iran responds harshly to the agreement.

February 2001 Deputy foreign ministers of the five littoral states meet in Tehran, Iran, in preparation for a March 2001 summit.

April 2001 The summit planned for March 2001 and to be attended by heads of the littoral states is rescheduled for April, and then postponed until October 2001.

May 2001 A meeting between the presidents of Azerbaijan and Turkmenistan ends with no resolution. The supreme leader of Iran condemns the meeting, voicing the opinion that all five littoral states need to be involved to discuss the legal status of the Caspian Sea.

of fishing and environmental protection, and joint resource exploitation. Despite a hard line by the Russian Foreign Ministry and presidential administration Russia's energy firms and its Fuel and Energy Ministry proceeded with energy development in the Caspian Sea. These internal clashes

THE NATIONAL EMBLEM OF AZERBAIJAN IS SEEN OVER OIL RIGS OFF THE SHORE OF THE CASPIAN SEA. BILLIONS OF BARRELS OF OIL MAY BE AVAILABLE FOR DEVELOPMENT BY THE FORMER SOVIET REPUBLIC IF THE MATTER OF RIGHTS TO CASPIAN RESOURCES CAN BE RESOLVED. *(AP/Wide World Photos. Reproduced by permission.)*

became more apparent after the Russian oil firm Lukoil was included in the Azerbaijan International Operating Company (AIOC), a consortium of major international oil companies. Lukoil joined the AIOC in early 1994, at the same time that the Russian Foreign Ministry was condemning the consortium for illegally seeking to exploit the Azeri, Chiraq, and Gunashli oilfields.

Russia's stance on the Caspian Sea shifted in 1997–98 once it became more apparent that it would gain substantial revenues from transporting Caspian Sea oil and gas through its pipelines. Turkmenistan's July 1997 protest that delimitation should be drawn according to equidistant, or median, lines, and not by joint arrangement, brought these internal tensions in Russia to a head. In July 1998 Russia signed an interim agreement with Kazakhstan to divide the north Caspian seabed using the median line principle, although Russia still maintained that the Soviet-Iran treaties governed the rest of the Sea under common agreement until a new system was agreed upon by the five littoral states. While Russia agreed with Kazakhstan and Azerbaijan on delimiting seabed borders for energy development—joint use of the central regions of the Sea—Russia and Iran continued to oppose the building of oil and gas pipelines on the Caspian seabed until the legal status of the Sea is settled. Critics view this stance as mainly designed to block energy development by Western firms and the construction of pipelines that would circumvent Iranian or Russian control. When the U.S. consortium PSG signed an accord in early 1999 with Turkmen President Niyazov on constructing a trans-Caspian gas pipeline, Russia warned that all the littoral states had to agree to such an ecologically dangerous project, especially given that the proposed pipeline would run through an earthquake zone. Iran called the contract "unacceptable" because all the states had not agreed to it and because the United States was involved.

While Russia's government has moved to embrace some aspects of sectoral delimitation, its legislature has been more reluctant. Russia's lower legislative chamber, the State Duma, held hearings on Caspian Sea delimitation in 1999 and concluded that the treaties of 1921 and 1940 should remain binding. The legislators stated that a system that held most of the Sea in common would permit Russia to exercise the most influence and gain more revenues from shared energy exploitation. One Russian energy expert who testified in the Duma implied that a final resolution of the Caspian Sea's status is not the top Russian concern, since Russia will probably not be a major offshore energy producer for the next few years. Instead, Russia's main concern will be helping to transport Caspian energy through its pipelines. Critics of this stance would point out, however, that Russia would have a stake in assuring the flow of oil by backing a stable Sea regime.

In agreement with Russia regarding continued adherence to the strictures set out in the 1921 and 1940 Soviet-Iran Treaties, Iran supported the treaties throughout the 1990s as a basis for settling legal disputes regarding the Caspian. Iran called for all littoral states to jointly agree on seabed exploitation of resources and to share in revenues. In 1993 it called in vain for the establishment of an organization of Caspian Sea littoral states to carry out joint decision-making on use issues. Due to a lack of consensus, however, such an organization did not emerge.

In September 1998 Iran was faced with opposition from Azerbaijan and Kazakhstan concerning Iran's support for a condominium arrangement, as well as a 1998 Russia-Kazakh understanding on dividing their seabed resources. Iran proposed as a replacement regime to the 1921 and 1940 treaties that the littoral states agree on dividing coastal zones equally into national sectors. In this way each state would receive 20 percent of the sea floor and surface. Division of the seabed by equidistant lines would give Iran only about 13–14 percent of the seabed, and at times it seemed that Iran was claiming 20 percent of offshore oil and gas reserves, contrary to the lines that would be drawn for its boundaries. Since Iran would get only 13–14 percent of the Sea under a modified median-line demarcation, its demand for 20 percent appears particularly threatening to neighboring Azerbaijan and Turkmenistan, rather than to the more distant Russia and Kazakhstan.

Unlike Iran, which has held fairly stable in its position regarding the Caspian, Turkmenistan has frequently and inconsistently changed positions on the Caspian Sea. At a November 1996 ministerial meeting in Ashkhabad, Turkmenistan agreed with Russia's proposal for a 45-mile (72 kilometers) coastal zone. It also joined with Iran and Russia in signing an accord to set up a joint-stock company to share profits from developing energy resources in the national zones of the three states. The accord, however, was never successfully implemented. A few months later, in February 1997, Turkmenistan's views appeared to shift when it agreed to divide its neighboring sectors with Kazakhstan on an interim basis until a final regime was determined. Then, one year later, in February 1998, tensions between Azerbaijan and Turkmenistan eased for a bit when the two states issued a statement calling for the division of resources under the equidistant line principle. This policy seemed to contradict the 1996 accord signed with Russia and Iran regarding the joint development and sharing of energy resources and profits. A 1998 statement by Turkmenistan and Azerbaijan declared that the two sides would set up a Turkmen-Azerbaijan Bilateral Commission on Defining the Coordinates of the Medial Line. The mediators, however, could not agree on where to draw a border regarding the Kyapaz/Serder oilfield, so a presidential meeting planned for November 1998 to formalize borders was called off. Reacting to the Russia-Kazakh Caspian delimitation agreement of July 1998, Turkmenistan again appeared to change its stance, agreeing with Iran's call to divide the sea and seabed equally, rather than equidistantly, and opposing bilateral agreements on the Sea, which it had just entered into a few months ago with Azerbaijan. At the deputy foreign ministerial meeting in Moscow in December 1998, however, Turkmenistan joined Azerbaijan in calling for the Caspian seabed and waters to be divided into national sectors.

Neighbors as Allies and Antagonists

Turkmenistan maintains that a Soviet-Iranian agreement of 1970, "On Median Lines in the Caspian Sea," calls for joint use of the central regions of the Caspian Sea, ostensibly including seabed resource exploitation. Turkmenistan also claims that the status of the Caspian Sea, including boundaries and resource use, is to be determined by negotiations by the littoral states and not by unilateral decisions. The matter of unilateral decisions appears aimed particularly at Azerbaijan, with whom Turkmenistan has unresolved disputes regarding ownership of oilfields, particularly the Kyapaz/Serder field. Turkmenistan demands a share of revenues Azerbaijan gains from exploiting the disputed fields. Analysts suggest that about one-fourth to one-third of the Kyapaz/Serder field may be in Turkmenistan's sector of the Caspian Sea, as determined by an equidistant line principle. Turkmenistan tried to include Serder in an international bidding process in September 1998, but received no bids for the disputed field. Turkmen President Niyazov has threatened to pursue Turkmenistan's claims to Kyapaz/Serder in international tribunals.

Meanwhile, Azerbaijan and Russia are aligned in dispute against Turkmenistan. Turkmenistan had been claiming the Azeri and part of the Chiraq oilfields, being developed by international

THE SEA AND ITS NEIGHBORS

The Caspian Sea lies at the eastern end of the Caucasian Mountains and marks what many regard as the southernmost edge of continental Europe. It is the world's largest inland body of water, covering an area of about 149,200 square miles (386,428 square kilometers). It is about 750 miles long (1,207 kilometers) and 270 miles wide (434.5 kilometers). It is saline, but is not connected directly to other seas, as is the Mediterranean. Geological evidence shows that the Caspian Sea was once much larger and was connected to the Sea of Azov, and thence to the Black and Mediterranean Seas. Its surface is about 90 feet (27 kilometers) below the level of the world's oceans, though water levels have been rising in recent years. The northern part of the Sea is shallow, averaging about 17 feet (5 meters), and freezes over in the winter. The southern part has a maximum depth of 3,200 feet (975 meters). The Sea is bordered by five states: Azerbaijan, Kazakhstan, Turkmenistan, Russia, and Iran. In Russia the Sea is bordered by the multi-ethnic Dagestan, historically Buddhist Kalmykia, and Muslim Astrakhan regions. Major ports include Makhachkala, Astrakhan, Aktau, Turkmenbashi, and Baku. During the Soviet period, treaties signed between Iran and the Soviet Union broadly governed rights in the sea. There was little political need to delimit the borders of the sea among the Soviet republics during the Soviet period, but some regulations were promulgated.

The 1921 Russia-Iran Treaty formalized the border between the Russian Federation and Iran and gave control of Armenia, Azerbaijan, and Georgia to Russia. It did not address resources in the Caspian Sea. In 1940 the Soviet-Iran Treaty was signed between what had become the Soviet Union (formerly the Russian Federation) and Iran. This treaty gave each nation bordering the Caspian Sea exclusive fishing rights up to 10 miles (16 kilometers) from the coast. Again, resources under the seabed, such as oil and natural gas, were not addressed. To support their positions regarding the Caspian Sea boundaries and resources, Russia and Iran have often referred to these treaties and maintained that they remain binding on the five littoral, or coastal, countries.

Just who has a right to what in the Caspian Sea is an important matter, as the Sea is rich in natural resources. Most oil and gas reserves in the Sea are undeveloped. The resources, however, provide energy for neighboring countries and could be a lucrative source of revenue on the international market. Proven oil reserves for the region are estimated at 18 to 35 billion barrels, while possible reserves may number 235 billion barrels or more. The region is also rich in natural gas.

The countries bordering the Caspian Sea have been embroiled in a merry-go-round of changing allegiances and contradictory policies. As of 2001, however, most had come to agree on at least a few points. Azerbaijan, Kazakhstan, and Turkmenistan are allied in their support for the division of the Caspian's surface, water, and seabed into national sectors, with open navigation of the Sea. Russia maintains its support for a 20 to 45 mile (6 to 14 kilometer) coastal zone. Beyond that point, it suggests joint navigation and management of fishing and environmental protection, and joint resource exploitation of the Sea between all five littoral states. The fifth littoral state, Iran, holds to a position different from both the Russian and the Azeri, Kazakh, and Turkmen stances. Iran proposes a condominium agreement, or joint rule, over the Caspian Sea, with a coastal zone divided into equal national sectors of 20 percent, to include the sea floor and surface. The finer points of these positions, and the various agreements between the littoral states, make determining the Caspian Sea's legal status and establishing clear standards for its use a difficult task.

consortia, and had notified energy firms in the consortia that it might take legal action against them. However, after Azeri President Aliyev visited Moscow in early July 1997, Turkmenistan reacted strongly to Azeri and Russian efforts to develop the Kyapaz/Serder field. At that time Azerbaijan's state-owned oil company, SOCAR, and Russia's Lukoil and Rosneft firms signed a contract on the main commercial principles of a production sharing arrangement to develop the Kyapaz/Serder field. Turkmenistan objected to this development, claiming that Serder fell under Turkmen control. It now also protested international development plans for the Azeri and Chiraq oilfields.

Turkmenistan immediately lodged a diplomatic protest with Moscow, demanding that the contract for the Chiraq fields be declared null and void. The Turkmen Ministry of Foreign Affairs released supporting materials, including maps,

CHEVRON OVERSEAS PRESIDENT RICHARD MATZKE SPEAKS AFTER A SYMBOLIC AGREEMENT MARKING THE BEGINNING OF THE BUILDING OF THE CASPIAN OIL PIPELINE IN 1998. *(AP/Wide World Photos. Reproduced by permission.)*

claiming complete ownership of not only the Kyapaz/Serder field but also of the Azeri field and partial ownership of the Chiraq field, which is also claimed by Azerbaijan. It asserted that all three fields were closer to Turkmenistan's shore than to Azerbaijan's, particularly the Kyapaz/Serder, which it insisted was about 100 km (about 63 miles) from Turkmenistan's shore and nearly double that (184 km, or about 116 miles) from Azerbaijan's shore. According to the FBIS (July 31, 1997) Turkmen Foreign Minister Boris Shikhmuradov argued that "the process of seeking agreement on the Caspian based on elaboration of its new legal status has been driven into a dead end by the so-called commercial agreement between Russia and Azerbaijan." Raising the stakes of its protest, Turkmenistan raised the issue of Russia's action at a mid-July 1997 meeting of the Organization for Security and Co-operation in Europe (OSCE), and Turkmen officials also complained that Russia's actions show that it did not play the role of "equal partner" in the Commonwealth of Independent States (CIS).

Besides the Turkmen Foreign Ministry protests, Turkmen President Saparmurat Niyazov sent a letter to Azeri President Heydar Aliyev asserting Turkmenistan's claims through a sectoral division of the Sea, including a "single definition of the status of both the sea floor and the sea itself. We believe that. . .a single national jurisdiction will be a more flexible tool for later agreements on shipping, fishing, and other human activities." (Yagmur Kochumov, *Caspian Crossroads*, Winter 1999) The letter was telling in that Niyazov pressed Turkmenistan's claims to Kyapaz/Serder, while clearly rejecting Iran's view that all the littoral states should share in exploiting resources.

Reacting to the Turkmen diplomatic protest, Russia dispatched a high-level delegation led by Vice Premier Valeriy Serov to Ashkhabad at the end of July 1997. Serov claimed that the Russian government had not been fully informed of the details of the commercial agreement drawn up by the Russian energy companies, but, according to some reports, he also initially tried to defend the merits of the deal. Turkmenistan, however, was adamant that Russia admit that the deal was illegal, and Niyazov rejected Vice Premier Serov's argument that the Russian government had not been closely involved in the deal making. Niyazov stated that Turkmenistan would not participate in negotiations on the legal status of the Caspian Sea until the deal was canceled. He also stated that Turkmenistan intended within a few days to offer a counter tender for the development of the disputed Kyapaz/Serder field. In the end Serov stated that Russia would soon make a public announcement about the Kyapaz/Serder oilfield deal. Niyazov quickly insisted on visiting Russia, where he met with then-Russian President Boris Yeltsin on August 7, 1997. At this meeting, the presidents issued a joint communiqué wherein Yeltsin repudiated the Russian contract.

At about the same time that Russia and Turkmenistan were switching from antagonists into allies, Russia and Kazakhstan went from allies to antagonists. Yeltsin had visited Kazakhstan in April 1996 and, with Kazakh President Nursultan Nazarbayev, signed an accord on the Caspian Sea calling for cooperation among the littoral states on use, pending the signing of a convention on the Caspian's status and use by the littoral states. A major disagreement developed between the two countries in late 1997, however. After the Russian Ministry of Natural Resources held an open bid for the exploration of fields in the northern Caspian, which were claimed by Kazakhstan, and awarded the proposal to the Russian firm Lukoil, Kazakhstan demanded that the bid be cancelled. This heightened tensions between the two countries. In early 1998 Russia and Kazakhstan focused on reaching an accord on sectoral delimitation that would permit uncontested exploitation of the fields.

OIL AND GAS RESERVES

Many parts of the Caspian Sea are not fully explored and most oil and gas reserves remain undeveloped. Most of Azerbaijan's oil resources, both proven and possible reserves, are located offshore, as are perhaps 30–40 percent of the total oil resources of Kazakhstan and Turkmenistan. Proven oil reserves for the entire Caspian Sea region (total country reserves, not just for the Caspian Sea itself) are estimated at 18–35 billion barrels (bbl), comparable to those in the United States (22 bbl) and the North Sea (17 bbl). Possible oil reserves are estimated at 235 bbl or higher. Preliminary drilling in Kazakhstan's Kashagan Field has indicated possible reserves of 40 bbl for this field, with 10 bbl recoverable. Natural gas reserves are large, accounting for almost two-thirds of the hydrocarbon reserves (proved, in addition to possible reserves) in the Caspian Sea region. Based upon proven reserves, Kazakhstan, Turkmenistan, and Uzbekistan each rank among the world's 20 largest natural gas countries. Proven gas reserves in the Caspian region are estimated at 236–337 trillion cubic feet (Tcf), comparable to North American reserves of 300 Tcf.

The Russian-Kazakh agreement of July 1998, "On the Delimitation of the Seabed of the Northern Part of the Caspian for the Purpose of Compliance with Sovereign Rights to the Exploitation of Minerals," called for dividing the north Caspian seabed along a "modified midpoint line" into national sectors, with the sides otherwise calling for cooperation on environmental, fishing, and navigation issues. The two sides agreed to open talks on exactly where to draw the line, based on points equidistant from the opposite shores closest to each of the countries and taking into account historical claims to some islands and "previously incurred geological expenditures." The two parties hailed the agreement as a basis for a general legal regime among the five states. Some contentious issues, however, have stymied final agreement on the modified midpoint line, including conflicting claims to islands and fields.

Despite these lingering issues, Russian President Vladimir Putin marked the two countries' continued cooperation in a mid-October 2000 visit to Kazakhstan. Although the two sides had agreed to a median line principle for dividing the seabed, they had not agreed on where to draw the line. In the meantime, Russia, in 2000, discovered an apparent large oilfield called Khvalynskoye in the north Caspian Sea. Seeking to avoid conflict, the two sides issued a declaration of cooperation in the Caspian which reiterated the principles of the July 1998 agreement, though many issues between Russia and Kazakhstan, indeed between all five littoral states, remain unresolved.

A sticking point in resolving some of these issues, Russia claims, is Iran. In November 2000, Viktor Kaluzhny, Putin's special envoy on Caspian Sea affairs, stated that Iran had become an impediment to the resolution of the problem of the Caspian Sea's status by its non-compromising stance. He noted that Russia had proposed holding a meeting of deputy foreign ministers from the five littoral states in August 2000, which had been turned down by Iran. Another meeting was scheduled in Moscow for December 2000. The newly appointed Iranian Caspian emissary visited Moscow and other capitals of the Caspian littoral states in December 2000. While repeating Iran's long-held position on delimitation, he announced that Iran would host a meeting of the deputy foreign ministers to discuss Caspian legal status in early 2001. This meeting took place in February 2001 in Tehran, and was mainly devoted to preparations for the planned March summit of heads of state.

RECENT HISTORY AND THE FUTURE

Azerbaijan and Kazakhstan have swung Russia around to their thinking on delimiting seabed resources into national sectors. Turkmenistan has also appeared to accept this position, resulting in Iran's isolation in calling for either joint rule or a delimitation giving it 20 percent of the Caspian Sea. Some analysts think that this recent agreement soon may pave the way to a convention among the littoral states on the legal status of the Caspian Sea, but other analysts note that various pronouncements of near settlement have been made by the states in the past to no avail. These analysts also point out that many issues dealing with exceptions to drawing an equidistant line remain contentious, including benchmarks, disputed oilfields, and islands, which stymie a comprehensive settlement of status. More likely than a grand, comprehensive settlement, these analysts suggest, piecemeal bilateral and other agreements dealing with seabed use and particular fields may gradually build a consensus among the littoral states. Iran's insistence on using equidistant lines to delimit seabed resources also remains an impediment to a multilateral settlement. The shaky ground of its position seems apparent to Iran, which itself has signed contracts with international energy companies to develop offshore resources.

Delimitation and use questions have slowed but not stopped energy development in the Caspian Sea. Some analysts warn that as the monetary stakes in the development of oil and gas fields grow higher and more obvious, the hopes of settling contentious ownership and use questions may lessen, and the chances of military conflict may grow.

Struggling to Reach Agreement

At the conclusion of Russian President Putin's visit to Azerbaijan on January 9, 2001, the two countries signed the Baku Declaration of their bilateral relations, terming their ties a "strategic partnership." On the status of the Caspian Sea the Declaration states that the two sides have come closer together on their thinking and that they would continue their consultations. A separate Joint Statement on the Principles for Cooperation on the Caspian Sea calls for drawing a median line, with each state having exclusive rights to develop its seabed resources. Iran responded harshly to the accord, harking back to the agreements it signed with the Russian Federation regarding the Caspian Sea in 1921, and with the Soviet Union in 1940, as still providing the only basis for dividing the Sea. The Azeri-Russian agreement effectively ended an almost seven-year dispute on Caspian Sea delimitation that emerged when Azerbaijan formed the first international oil consortium in 1994.

Trying to eliminate increasing Russo-Iranian tensions over Caspian Sea delimitation, Viktor Kaluzhny, Russian special envoy on Caspian Sea affairs, traveled to Iran in mid-January 2001. He described the talks with Iran as "difficult," but was optimistic that Iran would drop its demand that it receive 20 percent of the Sea if it is divided. He termed the 20 percent stance as unrealistic since Azerbaijan and Turkmenistan would be unlikely to relinquish parts of the Sea they would be allocated under an equidistant line delimitation. Iranian officials told Kaluzhny that they could not agree to bilateral agreements on Caspian delimitation that did not take Iran's interests into account.

All five countries did agree with Turkmen President Niyazov's proposal to hold a summit of the presidents of the littoral states in the port city of Turkmenbashi, Turkmenistan, to work out Caspian Sea demarcation and a comprehensive legal regime for shipping, fishing, and the environment. Trying to get Iran on board before the proposed March 8–9, 2001, Turkmenbashi summit, deputy foreign ministers from the littoral states traveled to Tehran in February to work out common positions on Caspian demarcation. At this meeting Iran continued to call for a condominium arrangement for the Sea, or for equal division of its resources (20 percent for each littoral state), and repeated its harsh call for all energy development to halt in the Sea pending the settlement of its status. Prior to the Tehran meeting Niyazov had stated that Turkmenistan now opposed common use of the waters and instead supported a comprehensive and complete settlement of Caspian Sea status, including the delimitation of both seabed and surface waters, the demilitarization of the Caspian, and agreement on environmental issues. Niyazov indicated that he would support Iran at the planned summit in criticizing Russia's agreements with Kazakhstan and Azerbaijan on delimitation. Turkmenistan's opposition to Russia's agreements with Kazakhstan and Azerbaijan appealed to Iran, as did the call for demilitarizing the Sea. However, Turkmenistan's call for comprehensive delimitation isolated Iran and may have contributed to Iran's request that Turkmenistan delay the March meeting until April. The summit was postponed again until October 2001, this time by Russia, when it became apparent that Iran would probably boycott a meeting in which it felt isolated.

In preparation for the planned March 8–9 summit Iranian President Kamal Kharrazi met with Vladimir Putin in Moscow in early March 2001. The two sides were to work on the Caspian Sea delimitation issue, but a statement issued at the meeting noted little progress. Among other Caspian issues, Moscow rebuffed Iran's call for the demilitarization of the Caspian Sea. The issued statement, however, appeared to mark agreement between the two sides that the question of the legal status of the Sea must be resolved by the littoral states before trans-Caspian pipelines are built. In keeping with the history of contradictory agreements, however, Russia's position regarding the pipelines appeared to waiver when Kaluzhny traveled to Kazakhstan in mid-March 2001 and endorsed the idea that "economically beneficial" undersea pipelines should be built, seemingly overlooking the previous statement that the Sea's legal status must first be determined.

After its meeting in Moscow, Iran announced that it would not be able to attend the planned Caspian summit later in March, ostensibly because of a scheduling conflict, but it could attend a meeting in mid-April. Kaluzhny then visited Kazakhstan, Turkmenistan, Iran, and Azerbaijan to discuss a 20- to 30-point Russian draft delimitation document that could be signed at the rescheduled summit. According to rumors the draft called for settling the status of the Sea in stages, with the first stage involving dividing the seabed along equidistant lines, and later devising rules for fishing and navigation. After it appeared that Iran had rejected this draft, Putin requested that summit-host Viktor Niyazov again postpone the summit until October 2001. On April 20, 2001, Russian Premier Mikhail Kasyanov voiced optimism that the legal status of the Caspian could be settled by the end of the year.

BIBLIOGRAPHY

Amirahmadi, Hooshang, ed. *The Caspian Region at a Crossroad: Challenges of a New Frontier of Energy and Development.* New York: St. Martin's Press, 1999.

Ascher, William, and Natalia Mirovitskaya. *The Caspian Sea: A Quest for Environmental Security.* Dordrecht: Kluwer Academic Publishers, 2000.

Clagett, Brice M. "Ownership of Seabed and Subsoil Resources in the Caspian Sea under the Rules of International Law," *Caspian Crossroads Magazine,* vol. 1, no. 3, Fall 1995.

Coe, Charles. "Caspian Presidents Plan Meeting on Sea's Status," *Newsbase FSU Oil & Gas Monitor,* week 4, January 30, 2001.

Cutler, Robert M. "Five States (Still) in Search of a Caspian Sea Legal Regime," *Central Asia/Caucasus Anaylst,* April 25, 2001.

———. "Russia Reactivates its Caspian Policy with New Demarcation Approach," *Central Asia/Caucasus Analyst,* June 21, 2000.

Gustafson, Thane, Aleksey Reteyum, and Laurent Ruseckas. *The Caspian Sea: Whose Waters? Whose Oil?* Cambridge, MA: Cambridge Energy Research Associates, 1995.

Horton, Scott. "International Law Ownership of the Caspian Seabed," *CIS Law Notes,* September 1998.

Kochumov, Yagmur. "Issues of International Law and Politics in the Caspian in the Context of the Turkmenistan-Azerbaijan Discussion and Fuel Transport," *Caspian Crossroads,* vol. 4, no. 2, Winter 1999.

Kreil, Erik. *Caspian Sea Legal Issues.* U.S. Department of Energy, Energy Information Administration, Washington, DC, June 2000.

Mamedov, Movsun. "Although There Are Not Yet Any Borders in the Caspian, There Are Border Violators," *Current Digest of the Post-Soviet Press,* vol. 52, no. 31, August 30, 2000, p. 21.

Mehdiyoun, Kamyar, "Ownership of Oil and Gas Resources in the Caspian Sea," *American Journal of International Law,* vol. 94, no. 1, January, 2000, pp. 179–89.

Mizza, Arthur P. "Caspian Sea Oil, Turmoil, and Caviar: Can They Provide a Basis for an Economic Union of the Caspian States?" *Colorado Journal of International Environmental Law & Policy,* vol. 7, 1996, pp. 483–504.

Oude, Elferink A.G. "The Legal Regime of the Caspian Sea: Are the Russian Arguments Valid?" In Brynjulf Risnes, ed., *The Legal Foundations of the New Russia.* Oslo, Norway: The Norwegian Institute of International Affairs, 1998, pp. 25–42.

Oxman, Bernard H. "Caspian Sea or Lake: What Difference Does It Make?" *Caspian Crossroads Magazine,* vol. 1, no. 4, Winter 1996.

Peimani, Hooman. *The Caspian pipeline dilemma: political games and economic losses.* Westport, CT: Praeger, 2001.

Racka, Witt. "A Sea or a Lake? The Caspian's Long Odyssey," *Central Asian Survey,* vol. 19, no. 2 (2000), pp. 192–221.

Uibopuu, Henn-Juri. "The Caspian Sea: A Tangle of Legal Problems," *World Today,* vol. 51 (June 1995), pp. 119–23.

—Jim Nichol

CHINA'S MUSLIM CHALLENGE: CONFLICT IN XINJIANG

In February 1997 the border town of Yining, in China's northwestern region of Xinjiang, witnessed one of the worst outbreaks of ethnic violence since the advent of China's economic reforms in 1978. Although the numbers of killed and wounded remain in dispute, the incident itself was a bloody reminder of long-standing tensions in this predominantly Muslim area on China's sensitive border with the newly independent state of Kazakhstan.

The incident began when crowds of young people held a series of demonstrations in the city streets to protest Chinese policies. Most of the demonstrators were Uighurs, the single largest ethnic group in northwestern China. While Chinese reports described this as an anti-government movement, Uighurs contend that they were protesting detention of Muslim students and Chinese attempts to limit *meshreb*, a traditional gathering to discuss recent events and conduct business. Both sides agree that the outcome was lethal. On February 5, 1997, the local police and military cleared the streets by opening fire. As a result, according to official Chinese sources, nine people were killed, 198 were injured, and some 500 people arrested. Uighur accounts put the numbers much higher. Citing eyewitnesses, overseas Uighur groups reported a total death toll in the hundreds, with many more wounded and nearly one thousand arrested. In the months which followed, the crackdown on what the government labeled "separatist" or "splittist" activities continued with the arrests of Uighur men and women accused of seeking independence for the Xinjiang region.

The city of Yining is just one of many towns and cities to experience outbreaks of violence in the 1990s. Most of these incidents involve the Chinese

THE CONFLICT

The province of Xinjiang, a region historically predominantly Muslim and ethnically, culturally, and linguistically distinct from the Han Chinese, has struggled against what it perceives as the central government's indifference. Faced with a growing Han population that threatens to overwhelm the majority Uighur population, residents of Xinjiang have often protested for increased rights and autonomy, and against the perceived inequities of the government in Beijing. Violent clashes have only served to engender more tension and resentment.

Cultural

- The ethnic Uighur inhabitants of Xinjiang province in northeastern China advocate autonomy, which the Chinese government in Beijing is reluctant to give.

- The Uighur are a group culturally and linguistically distinct from the Han Chinese.

Political

- The northwest region of China, which the Uighurs inhabit, has and still is a hotly contested area, for both its natural resources and its geographical location.

- China has sent millions of Han Chinese to live in the area since the 1950s. The Uighurs see this as the government's attempt to suppress their autonomy.

military and police forces on one side, and local minorities on the other. Yining, a picturesque town in the fertile Ili River valley some 3,000 miles (4,800 kilometers) from the Chinese capital of Beijing, is a good example of the complex mix of ethnic groups living in the Xinjiang region. Yining's population of 290,000 includes Uighurs, Kazakhs, Mongols, and Hui (Chinese Muslims), as well as Han Chinese, who are among the newest arrivals. Although historically the non-Chinese groups lived in relative harmony, policies of the Chinese government have served to increase existing tensions, primarily between the Chinese and the Muslim residents of the Ili Valley.

Like other incidents over the years in Xinjiang, the February 5, 1997, incident in Yining had its roots in a long-standing pattern of interaction between local Muslims and Han Chinese. From the Muslim population's viewpoint, there are many issues that divide them from the Chinese who dominate the region's political and military system. Religious freedom has been an issue since the Chinese Communist Party's (CCP) assumption of power in 1949, but over the years new issues have contributed to rising tensions. Language and cultural policy, limits on family size, exploitation of local resources for export to central China, testing of nuclear weapons within the region's borders (in a sparsely inhabited area around Lop Nor), and central government plans for economic development are among the issues that most concern Uighurs and other Muslims.

The greatest factor in increasing confrontations between Muslims and Chinese, however, has been the in-migration of millions of Han Chinese into the area since the 1950s. As more Chinese move into Xinjiang, the degree of Chinese control over local development and local culture has appeared increasingly threatening to local people, who feel that the central government is more concerned for the Chinese majority than for minority people whose standard of living has remained below that of the ordinary Chinese citizen.

In 2000 a new issue was added to those mentioned above. Local attention focused on the government's ambitious new plans for developing all of China's northwestern provinces and autonomous regions. In the view of some of Xinjiang's minorities, these new plans are only another way for the government to exploit the oil and other natural resources of what they consider their homeland for the benefit of the rest of China rather than for the benefit of the local people. Most of the budget is, in fact, earmarked for specific projects such as an oil

and natural gas pipeline, which will move Xinjiang's massive and valuable reserves to the eastern coastal cities of China to fuel the rapid economic expansion underway there. As outlined thus far, the new development plans do not address the deep poverty of the southern Xinjiang cities nor the inadequate educational or medical facilities throughout the region. Therefore, the "northwest development" plans have done little to dissuade some groups from their belief that the central government only cares about the Chinese and is unconcerned about the welfare or the future of the non-Chinese peoples of Xinjiang.

The rhetoric which has accompanied the new plans also has deepened the resentments of Muslims who were already disturbed by what they see as the arrogance of the Chinese officials sent to administer Xinjiang. Government reports often note how "backward" the area is, both in its culture and economic development. Such arrogance and cultural superiority is deeply resented, as is the case whenever such attitudes prevail among ruling elites.

From the Chinese government's viewpoint—a view largely shared by the millions of Han Chinese settlers who have flocked to the region in growing numbers since 1978—Xinjiang is an integral part of China. According to the Chinese constitution, the People's Republic of China (PRC) is indivisible: no part may secede. In the government's view, the great, unexploited natural wealth of regions like Xinjiang are rightfully the property of all the people of China and should, therefore, be used for the benefit of all, not just for the citizens in that particular region.

The official view also emphasizes the strategic position of the region as China's western "backdoor." During China's last dynasty, control of Xinjiang was considered important to protect China from possible encroachment from Russia. In the twentieth century the region had a common border with the Soviet Union, and when a dispute broke out between the leaders of the Soviet Union and China, the border was an extremely sensitive one. Since the 1991 dissolution of the Soviet Union, strategic Xinjiang suddenly shared its borders with the newly independent Muslim states of the former Soviet states. This dramatic change required immediate action, and China's government moved quickly to open talks with all of its "new" neighbors. For their part, new states such as Kazakhstan quickly agreed to maintain good relations with their East Asian neighbor. Once trade agreements were in place, China requested that these new states agree to limit the activities of any

MAP OF CHINA, WITH THE XINJIANG UIGHUR AUTONOMOUS REGION DELINEATED. *(The Gale Group.)*

anti-Chinese groups that might seek to organize just outside China's borders. This, too, was accepted as part of doing business with China. Nonetheless, during the 1990s several Uighur groups were permitted to organize in Almaty, Kazakhstan, across the border from Yining, despite Chinese pressure.

Finally, when it comes to dealing with any minority area within its own borders, the central government in China believes that any sign of weakness in dealing with minority complaints or demands could set an unwelcome precedent elsewhere. For example, if the Chinese government should relent in Tibet and allow greater religious and cultural freedom, then the Muslim minorities might demand similar freedoms and greater tolerance of religious practice for themselves as well. Therefore, the government approach is to require

minority areas to conform with central government policies, some of which are deeply resented.

The probability of another incident like that at Yining in 1997 is, therefore, high. If the current economic plans go forward and little effort is made to include members of the local minority groups in the implementation and benefits of those plans, the resentments of the past half-century will be greatly reinforced. For much of Xinjiang's history Chinese policies have been marked by a general disregard for the views or wishes of the local population. The challenge of convincing Xinjiang's people that the current government is different from governments of the past is considerable, but without such efforts, the tensions long-present in Xinjiang will continue to threaten the region's stability as its troubled history clearly shows.

HISTORICAL BACKGROUND

Before turning to the reasons behind the events in Yining and elsewhere in Xinjiang, it is important to understand that China is home to many different ethnic minority groups, not only to the Chinese people themselves. Referred to in China as "national minorities," there are 55 officially recognized minorities whose cultures and languages differ from that of the Chinese majority, who are often referred to as Han Chinese in border areas like Xinjiang. Of all of the national minorities, the Tibetan people are perhaps the best known in the United States, largely because of the international recognition accorded the Tibetan religious leader, the Dalai Lama. While the Tibetan people have a strong advocate in their self-exiled religious leader, other minority groups do not have internationally recognized figures as advocates outside of China. Among these are the Uighurs, a Turkic Muslim group whose population in Xinjiang in 1998 totaled over 9 million. Because of the Uighurs' numerical dominance, the Chinese government renamed the area the Xinjiang-Uighur Autonomous Region in 1954. The second more populous national minority is the Kazakh nationality. The region's 1.2 million Kazakhs share the Muslim faith of the Uighurs and also speak a Turkic language, rather than Chinese. Most of China's Kazakhs are related to the 8 million Kazakhs who live across the border in Kazakhstan, formerly a part of the Soviet Union. Xinjiang is also home to half a million Mongols, as well as other less numerous national minorities.

Although all of the region's minorities have experienced the impact of Chinese policies over the years, conflicts between Muslims and the Han Chinese have proved the most difficult to resolve. For China the fall of the Soviet Union in 1991 added new problems. The newly independent states of Muslim Central Asia, once part of the Soviet Union, became free, and, as a result, Islam could be openly practiced. Concern that these new states will encourage China's Muslims to demand their own independent homelands remains a challenge for the Chinese government.

The Roots of Conflict

The situation in Xinjiang has its roots in the region's tumultuous past. China's northwest has been a "land of passage" through which many armies have passed over the centuries. The ancient Turks, whose original homeland was most likely in what is now Mongolia, once dominated the area, primarily seeking to control the lucrative trade routes, now collectively known as the "Silk Road,"

which traversed northern China and then crossed Xinjiang's arid deserts and high mountain ranges.

Turkish power in the far northwest gave way to the Mongols of Chingis Khan (Genghis Khan) in the thirteenth century. At that time, local Uighur kings ruled portions of what is now Xinjiang; in 1209 the Uighurs at present-day Turpan (in eastern Xinjiang) pledged allegiance to the Mongol Khan, or leader, and Uighur men joined the Mongol army heading west into Central Asia. Many of the townspeople were Buddhist, but by the time that Mongol power waned in the fourteenth century Islam had spread across the region from Kashgar in the far west to oasis towns on the fringes of the Gobi Desert in eastern Xinjiang. The dominant religion thus became Islam, but the impact of the earlier Turkic culture also remained, both in some cultural practices and in the language of the local peoples, the majority of whom still speak Turkic languages.

Local Turkic Muslim rulers held sway until China's last dynasty, the Qing (1644–1912), which conquered Xinjiang in a series of bloody battles in the eighteenth and nineteenth centuries. In 1884, for the first time in history, the area was incorporated as a province of China. The name "Xinjiang" means New Territory, and is a reference to the Qing's military conquest and incorporation of the lands into its empire. The local population at that time was under 3 million. While some of the wealthier "begs," or landlords, supported the Qing by serving as tax collectors and judges, others periodically rebelled against their Manchu, or Qing, overlords. By the time the dynasty fell in 1912 only a small number of Han Chinese had settled in Xinjiang. Most were the families of officials sent to administer this remote outpost; others were prisoners sent to serve out their sentences in exile far from the centers of power. Some chose to leave in 1912 when the new Republic of China was founded. Those that remained lived in the region's cities and small towns, usually serving in the new government or provincial army, or working as businessmen involved in domestic and international trade.

Xinjiang in the First Half of the Twentieth Century

The revolution that ended the Qing dynasty did not end Chinese rule in the Muslim northwest. Although in 1911–12 a small group of Muslims attempted to found a Muslim government in Xinjiang, this effort was quickly crushed by local Chinese military units, which transferred their allegiance from the old Qing-appointed government to

CHRONOLOGY

1884 Xinjiang is incorporated as a province of China.

1911–12 A small group of Muslims attempt to establish a Muslim government in Xinjiang.

1912 Han Chinese begin to settle in Xinjiang.

1933 The East Turkestan Republic (ETR) is declared, but is quickly squashed by General Sheng Shicai, who establishes a clear power base in Xinjiang.

1944 The East Turkestan Republic is again declared by minority leaders in Xinjiang.

1945 The Uighur population explodes, accounting for 75 percent of the region's people.

1949 The Chinese Communist Party, led by Mao Zedong, assumes power and declares the People's Republic of China.

August 1949 Top ETR leaders are invited to attend a meeting in Beijing with Chairman Mao and fly to Beijing. En route, however, the plane crashes and all on board die.

1954 The Chinese government renames the Xinjiang area the Xinjiang-Uighur Autonomous Region (XUAR).

1957–58 Xinjiang is ordered to participate in the One Hundred Flowers and the Great Leap Forward campaigns, along with the rest of China. These programs fail miserably and cause severe famine in rural areas.

1960s The Chinese government encourages the in-migration of Han Chinese settlers into XUAR.

1962 Government soldiers fire on protestors in Xinjiang, who were demonstrating against the government's refusal to allow Muslims to exit the coun-try and escape famine. This becomes known as the Ya-Ti incident.

1966–69 During the Cultural Revolution in Xinjiang an unknown number of Muslim sacred objects, such as mosques, icons and literature, are destroyed by Red Guards. Muslim clerics and others in the region face interrogations and beatings by the Red Guards. Wang Enmao, governor of Xinjiang, pleads with the central government to end the Cultural Revolution in Xinjiang.

1980s Student demonstrations calling for political reform, more autonomy, and minority rights erupt in Xinjiang.

1986 The one-child policy is enforced on the Uighur minority in Xinjiang.

1990 Violence erupts at Baren, near the southern city of Kashgar, in Xinjiang. The incident begins over the building site of a mosque. Official government figures place the number of dead at 22, but Uighurs assert that more were killed.

February 5, 1997 Ethnic violence breaks out in the border town of Yining.

April–July 1997 Separatist activists are executed in Xinjiang.

January 1999 The central government executes activists supporting Xinjiang's independence. An angry demonstration ensues, with about 300 Uighurs arrested.

2000 The local population remains suspicious of Chinese intentions, while Uighurs overseas organize to bring more attention to the plight of people back home.

the new republican administration. The provincial capital, known locally as Urümqi, continued to be known official by the old Qing name "Dihua," which can be translated as "guided by China."

During the period of the republic (1912–49) the Xinjiang region was ruled by a succession of military commanders, commonly referred to as warlords. The first of these, Yang Cengxin, maintained relative stability, despite the limited number of troops available to him. He relied on local leaders and tolerated local prerogatives, which gained him a certain degree of compliance from the Muslim population. Further, he sought to keep the region free of "dangerous" outside influences, particularly communism and nationalism. Nonetheless, both of these new ideas began to take root, particularly after the Russian Revolution and the founding of the Soviet Union in 1917. The new Soviet government took control of all of Central Asia and thus became China's new western neighbor. Governor Yang sought to limit Soviet influence and to some extent was successful, but the Soviet Union was soon to play a role in Xinjiang's history.

Governor Yang's assassination by one of his own Chinese officials in 1928 inaugurated a period of turmoil. His successor was unable to maintain stability and in 1931 rebellion led to bloody fighting between government forces, which were mainly Han Chinese, and local Muslim militia. When a group of Russian mercenary troops also rebelled against the governor in 1933, the governor fled the region. Out of the chaos that followed, a new Chinese strongman emerged. With the support of Soviet troops and military equipment General Sheng Shicai, who was affiliated with the Nationalist government in Nanjing, vigorously defended Dihua (Urümqi) and drove off Muslim troops. Building on this victory he then turned his attention to another threat to Chinese power that had also emerged during this time. This was a Muslim group in southern Xinjiang that had declared its independence of China and founded the East Turkestan Republic. Although this Muslim republic was led by notable local leaders, internal divisions hampered their efforts to gain control of the region's scattered oases. General Sheng, making good use of Soviet support, was able to crush the republic and drive its top leaders into exile. By 1935 Sheng had restored order and become the new power in Xinjiang.

Initially General Sheng appeared to support political reforms that would, finally, give the local Muslim majority a voice in local government. He announced plans for a provincial government that would guarantee positions for each of what he termed the fourteen races of Xinjiang. He fostered cultural activities based on ethnic identity, and as part of these efforts encouraged the majority of the population to use the name "Uighur" rather than simply "Muslim" or Turki, both of which were commonly used before the 1940s to identify the region's single largest Muslim group.

He also opened the region's borders to trade with the Soviet Union and signed a number of agreements, without central government sanction, that allowed the Soviet Union to explore for oil, uranium and gold. When Japan invaded China in 1937, beginning World War II (1939–45) in Asia, Sheng allowed Soviet troops to be stationed in Xinjiang at Hami, the largest town in eastern Xinjiang. He also invited members of the Chinese Communist Party to Dihua, where they taught in local schools and also served in his government. It seemed that under Sheng, the region was becoming tied to the Soviet Union, but given the threat from Japan, there was little the central government was able to do to prevent this unwelcome development.

Despite the region's relative isolation and periodical upheavals, Xinjiang began to change in significant ways during the 1920s and 1930s. The first automobiles arrived, as did electricity, the telegraph, and radio service. Airline service linked the region to the Soviet Union and Germany to the west, and to China's coastal cities to the east. Some towns had model schools, and internal trade flourished.

Along with these outward signs of change the region also underwent a national awakening, with the Uighur people coalescing into a distinct and self-conscious nationality. Altogether, the Uighurs accounted for 75 percent of the region's population, which totaled approximately 4 million in 1945. Although the oasis towns and cities where the majority of Uighurs lived were scattered over long distances, trade networks linked the towns and brought news quickly from one town to another. The short-lived East Turkestan Republic had also ignited a sense of self-determination, fostering Uighur nationalism and a sense of solidarity with the region's other Muslim peoples.

This growing sense of nationalism increased after 1940, when General Sheng shifted toward more oppressive policies. His tax levies increased, as did requisitions of goods and horses for his army. Sheng's attempt to disarm the Kazakhs, who relied on their guns for hunting and protection, led to violent confrontations between Kazakh and Chinese troops. Fearful of possible rebellion in urban areas, he also arrested suspected opponents of his government, as well as foreign missionaries, detaining many hapless individuals in his merciless prison system. Opposition to Sheng spread quickly as conditions worsened.

In 1942 Sheng reconsidered his alliance with the Soviet Union and decided to turn to the Chinese Nationalist government for support. To show his sincerity he detained the members of the CCP he had originally invited into Xinjiang. Some were expelled from the region and sent to the communist base at Yenan. At the time, China's Nationalists, led by Chiang Kai-shek (Jiang Jieshi), and Communists, led by Mao Zedong (Mao Tse-tung), were engaged in battle for control over the country. The Nationalists had control over the central government. A few of the more high-ranking CCP individuals were executed by Sheng, including communist leader Mao Zedong's brother, Mao Zemin.

Increasingly anxious to leave the region where he had so many enemies, Sheng in 1944 accepted a position in Chiang Kai-shek's government and flew to the dubious safety of China's wartime capitol, Chongqing, in Sichuan province. The Chinese government appointed a successor, Governor Wu, but before Wu could reach Xinjiang, rebellion erupted once again.

This time the rebel forces were based in Yining, in the Ili River valley, the future site of the 1997 incident. A second East Turkestan Republic (ETR) was founded there in November 1944. The leadership was a coalition of Muslims whose ethnicity reflected the mixture of groups in the Ili area. An Uzbek, Ali Han Ture, was named as Chairman, and the new governing council members included Uighurs, Kazakhs, and Kirghiz. The new government also included some "White" Russians, men who had opposed the "Red" Bolshevik revolution in Russia and had fled to Xinjiang in the 1920s.

The second East Turkestan Republic was somewhat more successful than the first. From their base at Yining the new leaders successfully expanded the area under their control to three districts of westernmost Xinjiang. With China still fighting Japan, the central government could do little. Even with the defeat of Japan and its surrender in August 1945, Chinese troops were needed elsewhere. Therefore, in an attempt to prevent the loss of further districts to the Ili Valley-based government, Chinese officials agreed to talks on the future of Xinjiang with leaders of the ETR. In January 1946 the two sides reached a compromise that led to the formation of a coalition government in Dihua; East Turkestan officials and Chinese appointees began to govern Xinjiang. For the local population this was an opportunity for a more equitable form of power sharing and for insuring religious and political freedoms.

Despite the agreement and the hope with which the settlement was greeted in Xinjiang, neither side trusted the other and the coalition soon fell apart. The men from the East Turkestan movement withdrew to Yining, where they continued to govern the three districts, independent of the government in Dihua. The central government's response was to move government troops into Xinjiang. The Nationalist government was thus firmly established as the new power everywhere except in the three districts.

The new Nationalist troops, all of whom were Han Chinese, did little to enhance relations between Han and Muslim. The military requisitioned food, paying in inflated and nearly valueless Na-tionalist currency or simply demanding supplies outright. Corruption, already an established part of the Chinese military, heightened Han-Muslim friction. By 1947 some 100,000 armed men from central China were stationed throughout the region.

In 1948–49 a final battle between the Nationalists, under the leadership of Chiang Kai-shek, and the Chinese Communist Party under Mao Zedong, ended in a decisive defeat for the Nationalists. The Nationalist leaders quickly evacuated to Taiwan; as many troops as could be transported from ports along the southern coast and Hong Kong joined them there. The CCP now controlled eastern China. By the autumn of 1949 communist troops were marching west into Xinjiang, one of the last areas to be brought under CCP control. The Nationalist troops there were stranded; they dared not flee into the Soviet Union, and the roads to the south, across the Himalayas, were already closed for the winter. The Nationalist leaders in Xinjiang therefore surrendered and declared allegiance to the new power in China, the CCP.

The Xinjiang Region after 1949

For the region's Muslim population the new authorities represented only a change in political party, not a change in the ethnicity of the ruling elite, which, once more, were Han Chinese. Initial promises of full equality were proved meaningless when the top leaders appointed for the transition were Han Chinese. Burhan Shahidi, a local Muslim serving as governor for the Nationalist government since 1948, was re-appointed. A political survivor, Burhan was once more moving with the winds of change, and inside Xinjiang he was widely viewed as a mere figurehead.

The first years of CCP rule gave control over the region to the Chinese military, which secured each major city and took the surrender of the Nationalist troops. Many of the latter were not allowed to go home to their native provinces in China, but, rather, were assigned to build roads and open wasteland, often back breaking manual labor with minimal supplies and pay. Leaving these men in Xinjiang provided local authorities with a workforce and, perhaps more importantly for the new government, boosted the number of Han Chinese living in this strategically important area.

In the Ili valley, where supporters of the East Turkestan Republic continued to administer the three districts, the principal concern was their collective fate in the new change-over to communist control. In August 1949 the top ETR leaders were

A UIGHUR BOY IN XINJIANG WALKS PAST A WALL WITH A SLOGAN IN CHINESE THAT READS, "PEOPLE OF DIFFERENT NATIONALITIES HOLDING HANDS TOGETHER." MANY ETHNIC UIGHURS SEEK AUTONOMY FROM THE CHINESE GOVERNMENT. *(AP/Wide World Photos. Reproduced by permission.)*

invited to attend a meeting in Beijing with Chairman Mao and, with Soviet assistance, the men arranged to fly via Soviet territory to the national capital. The plane, however, reportedly crashed somewhere in Mongolia, and all on board died. A second delegation was quickly put together. This second group announced that the East Turkestan forces would be joined with the People's Liberation Army (PLA) and that the three districts would be peacefully reunited with the rest of the province. The Soviet role in these arrangements remains unclear, but because the Soviet and Chinese leaders officially declared themselves allies, the independence movement based in the Ili area could no longer count on Soviet support. They had little option but to agree to the unification in the fall of 1949.

With the issue of the East Turkestan movement settled, in the spring of 1950 the Chinese military began mopping up operations. These military actions, called "bandit suppression" campaigns, sought to eliminate any armed opposition to the CCP. Among those intent on resisting the CCP

were small groups of Kazakhs, but the PLA's superior numbers and equipment resulted in most of them being defeated or driven out of Xinjiang altogether. By 1953 the PLA had secured control and the region entered a new phase of its history.

Some local leaders chose to give the new government an opportunity to implement promised changes, including a voice in local government for all minorities and eventual autonomy within the Chinese state. In addition to Burhan, young Uighurs and other minority group representatives adopted a wait-and-see attitude. Of particular interest to them was the PRC plan to establish a system of autonomous regions in China's minority areas. One of these was formed prior to the CCP victory: in 1947 the Inner Mongolian Autonomous Region (IMAR) was established as a model for future minority areas. Led by Ulanfu, a Mongolian communist cadre (official), this government was to be composed primarily of Mongols who would determine policy and oversee cultural and economic development in Inner Mongolia.

Thus, despite the violent bandit suppression campaigns of the first three years of CCP administration in Xinjiang, when the new government passed the Program for Enforcement of Nationality Regional Autonomy in August 1952, it appeared that the new leaders intended to keep their promise. The new regulations included a provision that the governments of such autonomous regions be formed principally of personnel of national minorities and an "appropriate number" of personnel of other national minorities and Han Chinese. Further, the regulations called for the use of the minority group's language, the right to administer the area's finances, the right to enact laws and regulations as long as they did not conflict with the Chinese constitution and were approved by the higher levels of government, and the right to adopt measures for the development of culture and education.

New laws also used the term "national minority" (*shaoshu minzu*) to refer to those groups which had official recognition from the government. In the 1950s many ethnic groups sought this special status, but ultimately the government only recognized 55 groups as "nationalities." Those recognized ranged in population from a few thousand to more than five million.

Early Years in the Autonomous Region

In 1954 Xinjiang's name and status were changed. In recognition of the Uighur majority the new name was the Xinjiang-Uighur Autonomous Region (XUAR). The capital city's former name of Urümqi was restored. Lower level autonomous governments were also established, with prefecture, district, and county level units set up for the Kazakh, Hui, Mongol, Kirghiz, Tajik, and Xibo nationalities. These lower level governments also had rights and responsibilities and were to be governed by representatives of all nationalities resident in the area. To some extent this political activity offset the continued arrival of Chinese troops and officials, so that despite complaints from some quarters, the atmosphere was mixed with hope as well as concern over what the future held.

While the rest of China experienced land reform and the early stages of socialist re-organization of the economy, minority areas like Xinjiang moved more slowly. Conditions in such areas were viewed as more backward than other areas of China and thus reforms would only be gradually introduced. Nonetheless, in 1957 both the "One Hundred Flowers" campaign and the "Anti-Rightists" campaign began in Xinjiang, just as they did throughout China. During the period of the Hundred Flowers, in May and early June 1957, individuals were encouraged to offer criticism of the CCP and its policies. Reluctant to speak up at first, with the CCP's encouragement criticisms began to surface. In minority areas much of the sharpest criticism focused on chauvinism of the Chinese officials sent to administer these areas. For their part, Chinese in the minority areas singled out "local nationalism" as the main problem, pointing out that minority groups that wanted their own communist party or limitations on the number of Han Chinese moving into their region were guilty of being too focused on their own group and not enough on the country as a whole.

Unfortunately for those bold enough to speak up, the Hundred Flowers was abruptly ended later in June 1957. In a stinging rebuke to its critics, the CCP initiated a widespread movement that required re-education through physical labor for those who had voiced criticism of the CCP's record. In Xinjiang, as elsewhere in China, the would-be critics, some of whom were long-term supporters of the CCP, disappeared into labor camps. At the labor camps they were to undergo re-education, as well as spend long hours "laboring with the masses" in order to understand the importance of the revolution for the common people. Uighurs and other minority individuals, as well as Chinese accused of being "Rightists," spent periods ranging from months to years laboring in harsh conditions. The message was clear—critics of the Party had no future within the organization and risked everything should they speak out.

Xinjiang was also ordered to participate in the Great Leap Forward, the disastrous economic movement initiated by Mao in 1958. Some in the Party hierarchy did not believe that moving faster toward socialism would help China's stagnating economy, but Mao's personal stature meant that any idea he personally espoused was immediately embraced. The year 1958 saw all of rural China organized into communes, huge and unwieldy organizations subdivided into brigades and teams of workers. All land was worked in common, with a set quota of the production going to the central government and the rest divided among the commune members. In an effort to show revolutionary enthusiasm many commune leaders far over estimated the ability of their communes to produce crops. At the end of the summer, communes sent off enormous quantities to the government in an effort to meet their quotas, leaving so little behind that during the winter of 1958–59 extreme shortages became obvious. Unable to redistribute or pro-

ANCIENT ANCESTORS

Recently, the world was startled to learn of the existence of 4,000-year-old Caucasian mummies discovered in the arid deserts of China's Xinjiang-Uighur Autonomous Region. Incredibly well preserved, the men and women were tall, over six feet (180 centimeters), and wore long woven wool robes with high leather boots. Their skin had been painted with spiral designs, and their hair, ranging in color from reddish-brown to ash blond, was worn in long braids. A Uighur scholar, Dolkun Kamberi, was among the first to recognize their significance when he first unearthed the mysterious bodies in the 1980s. In 1994, *Discover* magazine carried a special article on the mummies in its April issue. A video, "Riddle of the Desert Mummies" produced by the Discovery channel in 1999, also focused on this amazing find. Study of the mummies and their clothing by anthropologists and archaeologists suggests that they were among the earliest inhabitants of Xinjiang. Today's Uighur population, which is Indo-European in appearance, may have its origin in these remarkable ancient people.

cess the surpluses it had collected, the government warehoused large amounts of food crops, which simply rotted as the crisis in the rural areas increased.

The disaster was compounded by the government's order that each commune be self-sufficient in making iron and steel. Untrained peasants built their own primitive blast furnaces, which consumed every available fuel, denuding wooded areas throughout the country. Not surprisingly, the resulting metal was mostly unusable.

In the summer of 1959 the CCP was acutely aware of the extent of the disaster. At a meeting in July of that year, however, the Party chose to continue the communes. Mao, the architect of what was now clearly a mistaken policy, stepped down as President of China, but retained his position as Chairman of the CCP. In the months that followed, Liu Shaoqi took over as president and attempted to revive the economy through small modifications of the Great Leap policies. It was three years, however, before the country began to recover. During that time more than 25 million people died from causes directly attributable to the Great Leap Forward. Because of government control of the Chinese media and limitations on peo-

ple's travel during this time, most Chinese were unaware of the extent of the disaster.

In Xinjiang the rapid transformation of nomadic herders and oasis farmers into commune members also took its toll. Animal herders resented the process, and after 1958 the animal population dropped significantly. Sheep constituted the primary source of meat in Muslim Xinjiang, but nomadic people also relied heavily on animals for dairy products. The decline in the number of animals therefore greatly reduced their usual diet. As elsewhere in China, the policies of the Great Leap led to food shortages, and rationing was introduced in an effort to share what was available more equitably. In 1960 conditions in the towns and cities deteriorated, and local residents stood in line each day for what little food was available.

Mismanagement and inefficiency were problems all over China, but in Xinjiang the dire conditions took on other dimensions as local people blamed the Chinese in command of Xinjiang's economy. Dissatisfaction deepened as the impact of the Great Leap intensified.

By 1962 food shortages led Muslim residents of the Ili River area, the former base of the East Turkestan Republic, to take drastic measures. In that year, many crossed the border into the Soviet Union, seeking relief from the famine conditions. This exodus led to what is now referred to as the Yi-Ta Incident. On May 25, 1962, a large crowd of people gathered in the center of Yining to protest the government's attempts to stop them from leaving. Because so many families had already fled, the government announced that anyone wishing to leave had only three days in which to sell their house and belongings. After those three days no one would be allowed to cross the border. Angered by what was an impossible requirement in districts where so many of the people wished to leave, the people staged a massive protest in Yining.

The angry protestors appeared so threatening to the authorities that soldiers brought in to contain the crowd suddenly opened fire. There is no verifiable number of those killed or wounded during this incident, although local residents insist that hundreds were shot. The area was closed to the outside and a crackdown began, with arrests and prison sentences meted out to participants. The numbers of Han Chinese troops and border militia in the Yining area increased. Among those arrested following the incident was the prominent Uighur writer Zunun Kadir. Along with others, he was arrested and sentenced to a work camp, where he remained for 17 years. Predictably, tensions remained high in the Ili area for many months afterwards.

In the 1960s the CCP decided to increase the movement of Chinese settlers into all of its border regions, but especially into Xinjiang, where the Yi-Ta incident was a reminder of just how small a minority the Chinese were in the XUAR. The CCP had already formed the basis for an increase in Chinese settlers by expanding the activities of a para-military organization, the Production-Construction Corps (PCC). The majority of the PCC members originally came from the demobilized Nationalist army, stranded in Xinjiang at the end of the civil war in 1949. To this group were added more former soldiers, as well as ordinary workers who volunteered to serve in the border regions. Some of these volunteers hoped to prove themselves to the Party by agreeing to work in harsh and "backward" conditions. Some were young people who came to Xinjiang as part of the "Down to the Countryside" Movement of the 1960s, when zealous city youth who had few prospects of a job in the overcrowded and under-industrialized cities were persuaded to serve their country by going west. By 1962 the PCC operated 182 state farms and cultivated over one-third of the region's arable land. It also ran stock-breeding ranches and large enterprises such as the Karamai oil fields.

From the beginning, the PCC was resented by the local population, which saw it as the primary vehicle for introducing growing numbers of Han Chinese into Xinjiang. When the railroad line was finally extended into the region, this made it easier for migrants to make the long journey from central China to the northwest, but as the numbers of Chinese grew, so did the resentment and the suspicion among many minorities that the government intended to dilute the region's Muslim culture with waves of new Chinese residents.

The official population figures for Xinjiang in the period from the 1940s through the 1970s are not fully reliable, but even these, which are widely believed to be underestimates, show the rapidly growing Chinese presence. In 1965 official reports put their numbers at 1,396,000, an enormous increase from 220,000 in 1949. Many of the newcomers became employees of the PCC, enabling it to expand its holdings of arable land and its contribution to the Xinjiang economy.

Xinjiang and the Cultural Revolution

By the time Xinjiang and the rest of China had begun to recover from the deprivations of the Great Leap Forward, Chairman Mao was already planning his next major political campaign. The Great Proletarian Cultural Revolution began in the summer of 1966. Mao called upon the young people, the "revolutionary successor" of China's 1949 revolution, to smash remnants of China's past, which, he said, continued to hold the country back and prevented its rapid progress on the road to socialism.

In unleashing China's young people Mao began a chaotic and violent chapter in modern Chinese history. From 1966 until his death in 1976 he orchestrated mass violence intended to purge the CCP of any who might oppose his vision for China's future. In the process he also sought to temper China's youth in the blood of revolution. He was successful beyond his own expectations as China was submerged in a sea of confusing and contradictory messages from Beijing and an ocean of zealous, angry, and misguided young people who followed their leader, Mao, in devastating attacks on Party members, teachers, intellectuals, and any who still clung to "old" thoughts or ideas.

"Old" ideas included all religious belief. As religion was still followed by most of China's national minority groups, young Chinese converged on minority areas with the intent of destroying all

Nationalities of the Xinjiang-Uighur Autonomous Region

Nationality	1953*	1982*	1990**
Uighur	3,640,000	5,949,000	7,194,000
Han	300,000	5,286,000	5,695,000
Kazak	594,000	903,000	1,106,000
Hui	200,000	681,500	570,000
Kirghiz	70,000	112,900	139,700
Mongol	59,000	117,400	137,700
Other	64,100	139,800	198,100

Source: *Linda Benson and Ingvar Svanberg. *The Kazaks of China.* Uppsala, Sweden: Studia Multiethnica Upsaliensia, 1988.
** FBIS Daily Report, December 28, 1990.

MANY NATIONALITIES MAKE UP THE POPULATION OF XINJIANG PROVINCE. THE UIGHURS HAVE THE HIGHEST NUMBERS, WHILE THE HAN—TRANSPLANTED FROM EASTERN CHINA—HAVE GROWN QUICKLY IN SIZE. *(The Gale Group.)*

vestiges of these "superstitious" beliefs. In Xinjiang young Chinese Red Guards, aged 12 through their late teens, arrived from central China and targeted mosques as centers of "old" ways of thinking. Between 1966 and 1969 an untold number of mosques, Muslim books, and sacred places were damaged or destroyed by zealous young Red Guards. Muslim clerics sustained humiliating treatment and beatings, appalling and angering Muslims who were forced to watch. Public observation of religious holidays ended, and even wearing traditional clothing invited attack by Red Guards. The misery and suffering of this period remains a bitter memory for many of Xinjiang's Muslim residents, adding to a long list of abuses suffered by Xinjiang's population at the hands of Chinese officials. Although much of the fighting that erupted during this chaotic period involved Chinese fighting other Chinese, the assault on Islam was an unforgivable offense in the eyes of many Muslims, and anger and frustration over Chinese policies deepened.

Top local officials showed far more concern over the impact of the Red Guards than authorities in Beijing. The XUAR's Chinese chairman, Wang Enmao, made a number of personal visits to Beijing in order to point out the strategic importance of the region and the dangers of allowing the Cultural Revolution to proceed. Because of the Sino-Soviet split in 1958, which effectively ended the alliance between China and the Soviet Union, and due to the increased number of Soviet troops along Xinjiang's western border, Wang asserted that the Cultural Revolution could have extremely serious ramifications. Any disruption to China's nuclear testing, conducted in Xinjiang, could also hurt China's ability to defend itself. Mao nonetheless refused to end the campaign in Xinjiang, although the nuclear site was made off limits.

International events finally brought a halt to Mao's last great political campaign in Xinjiang. In the summer of 1969 a brief shooting war broke out on the Xinjiang border between Soviet and Chinese soldiers. Wang Enmao made another plea to the central government to end the Cultural Revolution before the situation on the border escalated, and this time he succeeded. In announcing the end of the Cultural Revolution in Xinjiang, Mao pronounced the Cultural Revolution a great victory for all of China's people. With the political campaigning officially over, Chinese and minority residents alike could now assess the damage and begin the process of rebuilding the region's economy and salvaging what they could of Chinese-minority relations.

Although the region began to recover economically from the worst excesses of the Cultural Revolution, unease and distrust remained. The destruction of mosques and Muslim schools, and the public burning of copies of the *Quran*, the sacred book of Islam, left indelible memories. The thousands of Muslims who had been humiliated, beaten, and forced to work at hard physical labor by young Red Guards and the Chinese military could not easily set aside such experiences. It would take radical changes to repair the damage.

With Mao's death in 1976 the opportunity for such change arrived in the person of Mr. Deng Xiaoping, who, in 1978, became China's new "paramount" leader. Under his guidance, China entered the "reform era" which brought an end to extreme Maoist policies. While some aspects of life improved dramatically in minority areas as a result, in other ways the burden of past events continued to divide Muslim and Chinese.

China in the Reform Era (1978 to the present)

The major reforms undertaken in China after 1978 transformed the Chinese economy. One of the first significant changes was the elimination of the old commune system. As part of the reforms, farmers leased land and planted crops, which could then be sold for profit on the new free markets that emerged at the same time. Initially, farmers had to sell part of their crop at fixed prices to the government, but as the reforms deepened, that requirement was removed.

In Xinjiang the reforms meant that farmers on the region's oases could once again raise their own crops and market them. It also meant that herding families, whose animals had been taken into communal herds in the late 1950s, now received animals that became the basis of family-owned herds. The government, however, collected a fee for the use of all grasslands, and an animal husbandry tax was imposed on all herders. Nonetheless, the frustration and economic hardship associated with the old economic system was at last relieved, and both farming Uighurs and herding Kazakhs returned to a lifestyle closer to the one that they once knew.

Other aspects of the old policies, however, changed little. The Production Construction Corps' massive state farms and ranches continued to operate as government enterprises, and overall the PCC increased its role in the local economy. In the 1990s these state-run enterprises produced 24 percent of the region's agricultural output, 40 percent of the textile production, and controlled 30

CHINESE ECONOMIC DEVELOPMENT PLANS DO NOT ADDRESS THE CRUMBLING INFRASTRUCTURE OF XINJIANG'S CITIES, RAISING CONCERNS THAT THE CENTRAL GOVERNMENT IS UNCONCERNED WITH THE WELFARE OF MOST OF THE PEOPLE IN THE PROVINCE. *(Archive Photos. Reproduced by permission.)*

percent of all arable and irrigated land. The PCC employed 2.4 million people, the majority of them Han Chinese. The para-military organization thus had enormous clout in the region and dominated the economy in the northern half of the Xinijang.

Closely related to the presence of the PCC was the ongoing issue of the growing number of Chinese living in Xinjiang. In the 1980s Han Chinese made up 40 percent of the region's total population. Uighurs, who comprised 75 percent of the population in 1949, were reduced to 42 percent. As the numbers of military personnel are not usually included in population figures, the total number of Chinese probably exceeded that of the Uighurs by the mid-1990s.

The growing Chinese population and the economic power of the PCC together became a target of criticism leveled at the government in the 1980s. The Chinese authorities repeatedly defended the PCC and its role in Xinjiang, while at the same time declaring the necessity of welcoming Han Chinese into the area to help with modernization. Official support of the PCC was interpreted as evidence of Chinese plans to inundate the region with Chinese and thereby undermine the dominance of Turkic culture and religion.

This impression was heightened in the late 1980s when it was announced that, in response to the requests of the people of Xinjiang, China's new family planning policy now applied to national minorities as well as Chinese. Originally, the 1980 "one-child policy" did not apply to minorities on the grounds that their overall populations were so small. Further, most lived in under-populated border areas, where space for large families was not an issue. However, when the government announced in 1986 that minority areas were expected to limit their family size as well, many Muslims believed this was an attempt to limit their numbers while allowing more Chinese to move into the area. Even though the new regulations usually allowed minority families to have two children in urban areas and as many as three in the countryside, the new policy was added to the existing list of grievances against the Chinese government.

In the relatively more open atmosphere of the 1980s and 1990s, across China there were student demonstrations calling for everything from greater democracy and economic freedom to a crackdown on the growing problem of corruption. In minority areas, too, the first public protests appeared, but the focus was somewhat different. In addition to calls for more political reform, minority students added a call for more autonomy for the minority areas.

In Xinjiang the local government sought to forestall criticism with a number of changes. Mosques reopened and new ones were built. Some religious instruction was allowed, and Muslims once more gained permission to go on "hajj," the pilgrimage to Mecca. Minorities were admitted to universities with somewhat lower scores than their Han Chinese counterparts, although most then had to spend their first year studying Chinese and taking remedial classes in any areas where they were deemed deficient. The Arabic script was restored in 1980 after years of government efforts to impose other scripts. Increased ownership of private companies by Uighur and other minority entrepreneurs allowed some families to become wealthy.

As the standard of living rose, however, the number of public protests increased, rather than diminished. Usually led by university students, some of the demonstrations in the 1980s became sharply critical in tone. The memory of the East Turkestan Republic was again revived, and some demonstrators carried the flag of the former Yining-based government, angering the local authorities, who declared such acts counter-revolutionary. Anyone convicted of being a counter-revolutionary faced the death penalty. Undaunted, student demonstrations erupted in Urümqi and other towns across the region in the late 1980s.

As demonstrations became more frequent, clashes between Muslim and Chinese authorities also grew more violent. One of the first widely reported major incidents came in 1990, at Baren, near the southern city of Kashgar, a strongly Uighur area with only a small Chinese population. According to Chinese reports the incident began over the building site of a mosque, although the exact details remain a matter of debate. In the fighting that erupted, official government figures gave a total of 22 dead; in contrast, the Uighurs claimed many more Muslims died when the military intervened. In what became usual practice in the 1990s the area was closed to foreigners and travelers until the authorities felt that they had fully restored order.

But incidents continued. After Baren, attacks on Chinese officials and on Uighurs, as well as other minorities who worked for the government, increased. Bus bombings in Urümqi and an explosion at a hotel in Kashgar made international headlines in the mid-1990s. Although most foreign travelers to the region did not witness such scattered instances of violence, local papers carried stories that reflected increasing anger and increased access to weapons, some of which entered the region via nearby Pakistan and Afghanistan, the latter country embroiled in a civil war.

Because of the way some incidents have been reported in the Chinese press, it is difficult to know the extent of support for independence among Xinjiang's Muslim population. In the 1990s some individuals were clearly committed to that goal and gave their lives to the cause. But while many Uighurs were angry over aspects of Chinese administration and limits on cultural expression, others appeared to accept Chinese rule and, like many ordinary people elsewhere in China, hoped that China would continue its more open policies. Small numbers of Uighurs, Kazakhs, and other minorities still took positions in local, regional, and national governments, although the regard in which many of these individuals were held at home in Xinjiang was not (and still is not) high. It appears that opinions about Chinese rule covered the full spectrum, from support to total rejection. Since the Yining incident in 1997, however, a new hardline approach in Xinjiang threatens to erode whatever support the CCP has garnered.

RECENT HISTORY AND THE FUTURE

Although plans for economic expansion in Xinjiang announced in 2000 appear to show central government concern over the future of the region, the local population remains suspicious of Chinese intentions. The region's past history won few strong supporters among the Muslim population, and Chinese rule has often seemed tenuous. In recent years the increased number of Chinese military and police in the region and the continuation of a police crackdown begun in 1997 have heightened tensions. In this atmosphere, concerns are growing over the future stability of Xinjiang.

One clear sign that the Chinese authorities are taking an unyielding stance in dealing with minorities can be seen in the arrests and imprisonment of Muslims since the Yining incident of 1997. Uighurs in particular complain that any Uighur who rises to prominence immediately become a target of the Chinese. One recent example is that of a wealthy Uighur businesswoman, Rabiya Kadeer, whose varied business enterprises brought her great financial success. In an effort to help other women she set up an organization intended to assist Muslim women to follow her example. An elected member of the Chinese People's Political Consultative Conference (CPPCC), in 1995 she was also a delegate to the United Nations' Fourth World Conference on Women, held in Beijing. In 1997 Rabiya Kadeer came under surveillance by the authorities, and in 1998 she was told that she could not stand for re-election to the CPPCC. The following year she was accused of revealing state secrets and was detained. Her trial ended as expected, in conviction on all charges, and she received an 8-year prison sentence. Her husband, a resident in the United States since 1996, drew U.S. media attention to his wife's case through repeated requests to the U.S. government for its intervention on her behalf, but these efforts have been unsuccessful.

Such arrests and detentions anger many local people, who see them as evidence of increasing Chinese oppression. Even stronger emotions are generated by the public execution of men and women accused of separatist activities. These executions are intended as a warning, but in fact they become highly charged, emotional occasions that are often followed by further disturbances. Such was the case after the April 1997 execution of Uighurs accused of participating in the Yining incident, which had occurred just three months earlier. Further executions came in July 1997, and again in January 1999. The latter was followed by an angry demonstration in Urümqi during which some 300 Uighurs were reportedly arrested by the police. In yet another incident linked to the past, in February 2001 a group of young Uighurs reportedly killed a Uighur judge who had supported the execution of 26 Uighurs blamed for the Baren incident of 1990. In an old and well-documented cycle, acts of violence on both sides have led to a repetitive pattern that becomes increasingly difficult to stop. In the process, the gulf between Chinese and Muslims grows ever wider.

Although neighboring Muslim states thus far have shown little interest in supporting Xinjiang's Muslims, this situation could change. Reports are surfacing of Uighurs training in Afghanistan, Pakistan, and Chechnya. With the borders of Xinjiang increasingly open to trade, the movement of men and arms passing from Central Asia to China has increased, adding to the threat of regional instability. The huge oil reserves of Kazakhstan and its neighbors, and the massive international investments that are being made to tap and transport their oil and natural gas to the West, mean that the international community certainly has an interest in preventing disturbances in this important part of the world.

Internationally the Uighurs have begun to organize outside of China. Several Uighur organizations now are based in Europe and the United States. Using web sites and e-mail, they keep close watch on events in their homeland and have become active in contacting politicians and U.S. congressmen, as well as human rights organizations, to draw international attention to the circumstances of Uighurs in Xinjiang. Their new voice, often allied to that of the Tibetan cause, has brought them new recognition. Although their numbers are still small, many are well-educated men and women who understand the importance of organizing and allying with other groups to pressure the Chinese government. Their existence is one more reason why the central government of China will need to pay closer attention to its handling of minority matters.

In sum, Chinese policy is relying on economic improvements combined with a hardline approach to any activity labeled separatist as its answer to stability in Xinjiang. As events in the recent past have already shown, however, a higher standard of living does not mean that long-standing issues between different ethnic groups are automatically resolved. Further, the harsh penalties meted out to people who are viewed by some as national heroes create modern martyrs, particularly in regions where people distrust the news reported by their local media. Ultimately, however, Xinjiang's ethnic problems may only be lessened when the CCP itself accepts that it must be accountable to the people it governs. Until then, they will have to contend with the spreading anger and disaffection they have helped create in contemporary Xinjiang.

BIBLIOGRAPHY

Barber, Elizabeth Wayland. *The Mummies of Urumchi*. New York: W.W. Norton & Company, 1999.

Benson, Linda. *The Ili Rebellion: Muslim Challenge to Chinese Authority in Xinjiang*. Armonk, New York: M.E. Sharpe, Inc., 1990.

Benson, Linda and Ingvar Svanberg. *China's Last Nomads.* Armonk, New York: M.E. Sharpe, Inc., 1998.

Fletcher, Joseph. "Ch'ing Inner Asia c. 1800," in John King Fairbank and K.C. Liu, eds., *The Cambridge History of China*, vol. 10, part I. New York: Cambridge University Press, 1980.

Foreign Broadcast Information Service (FBIS). Translations of Chinese radio and television programs by the USA Department of State. Various reports from the 1980s and 1990.

Gansu Province Nationalities Research Institute, ed. *Yisilan Jiao zai Zhongguo (The Muslim Religion in China).* Ningxia, Gansu: Ningxia People's Press, 1982.

Geng, Shimin. "On the Fusion of Nationalities in the Tarim Basin and the Formation of the Modern Uighur Nationality, *Central Asian Survey*, 3:4 (1984), 1–14.

Hsu, Immanuel C.Y. *The Ili Crisis: A Study of Sino-Russian Diplomacy 1871–1881.* London: Oxford Clarendon Press, 1965.

Ili-Kazakh Autonomous Prefecture Survey Compilation Committee. *Yili-Hasake Zizhizhou Gaikuang* (A Survey of the Ili-Kazakh Autonomous Prefecture). Urümqi: Xinjiang People's Press, 1985.

Jarring, Gunnar. *Return to Kashgar.* Translated by Eva Claeson. Durham, NC: Duke University Press, 1986.

Lattimore, Owen. *Pivot of Asia.* Boston, MA: Little, Brown & Co., 1950.

———. *The Desert Road to Turkestan.* Boston, MA: Little, Brown & Co., 1929.

———. *High Tartary.* Boston, MA: Little, Brown & Co., 1930.

Li, Sheng. *Xinjiang dui Su (E) Maoyishi 1600–1990* (Xinjiang Trade with the Soviet Union [Russia] from 1600–1990). Urümqi: Xinjiang People's Press, 1993.

Light, Nathan. *Qazaqs in the People's Republic of China: The Local Processes of History. Occasional Paper No. 22.* Bloomington, IN: MacArthur Scholars Series, 1994.

MacKerras, Colin. *China's Minority Cultures.* New York: St. Martin's Press, 1995.

McMillen, Donald H. *Chinese Communist Power and Policy in Sinkiang 1949–1977.* Boulder, CO: Westview Press, 1979.

Millward, James. *Beyond the Pass: Commerce, Ethnicity and the Qing Empire in Xinjiang 1759–1864.* Stanford, CA: Stanford University Press, 1998.

Seymour, James D., and Richard Anderson. *New Ghosts, Old Ghosts: Prisons and Labor Reform Camps in China.* Armonk, NY: M.E. Sharpe, Inc., 1998.

Xinjiang Academy of Social Sciences Research Committee. *Xinjiang jianshi* (A Concise History of Xinjiang), 3 vols. Urümqi: Xinjiang People's Press, 1990.

Xinjiang-Uyghur Autonomous Region Gazetteer Editorial Committee. *Xinjiang Nianjian 1995 (Xinjiang Yearbook 1995).* Urümqi: Xinjiang People's Press, 1995.

—Linda Benson

Unrest and Assassination in Congo-Kinshasa

Laurent Kabila, the president of the Democratic Republic of the Congo (DROC), was assassinated on January 16, 2001. The assassination took place in Kabila's office in Kinshasa, Congo's capital. The assassin was a trusted bodyguard, Rashidi Kasereka, a man Kabila had himself recruited in the early days of his bid for power. Kasereka approached Kabila in his office, where the president was conferring with an adviser, and gestured to him, indicating that Kasereka had something to say to the president privately. As Kabila leaned forward, Kasereka drew his pistol and shot him once in the head and at least twice in the belly.

As Kasereka tried to flee he was gunned down and killed by other guards, ensuring that a vital question may remain forever unanswered. Was Kasereka part of a larger plot, or was he simply acting out of the anger many of Congo's civil servants and soldiers felt at their low wages, poor living conditions, and the government's refusal to pay them for several months at a time? The answer to this question may never be known.

Kabila was buried in a lavish ceremony in a mausoleum facing the Palace of the Nation. His son, Joseph Kabila, at 29 years old, became the world's youngest head of state. The younger Kabila was appointed to office in secret, even before his father's death was announced. For a country awash with violence, both at its borders and internally with the assassination of Laurent Kabila, it was important to have a new leader in place as quickly as possible.

The assassination of the elder Kabila and his son's ascent to power were but the latest events in Congo's long history of violent political upheaval. They also raised new questions about the outcome

The Conflict

The Democratic Republic of the Congo, or Congo-Kinshasa, is the third largest country in Africa. Its immense mineral wealth and plentiful natural resources have made it the prize of kings and dictators. President Laurent Kabila, who came to power in a coup, was assassinated in January 2001. His son succeeded him while the Congolese people and the world waited to see if Joseph Kabila would follow in his father's footsteps or forge a new future for a ravaged country.

Political

- Laurent Kabila's death prompted the sudden ascension of his 29-year-old son Joseph into leadership, making the younger Kabila one of the youngest leaders of a nation.

- With at least three separate rebel groups and six neighboring countries fighting in the current conflict, in Congo, the war has been called the African World War. Joseph Kabila's handling of the situation could shift the balance in the region towards peace.

- The younger Kabila must contend with a restive public, intrusive foreign interests, and international scrutiny as he solidifies his authority and takes control of the country.

CHRONOLOGY

1960 The Democratic Republic of the Congo (DROC) wins independence from Belgium.

1965 Mobutu Sese Seko becomes president and serves as a dictator for 30 years.

1971 Mobuto renames the DROC "the Republic of Zaire."

mid-1990s Zaire's Katanga region establishes itself as an autonomous entity, with its own currency and trade agreements. This is easily accomplished due to the poor infrastructure of the country.

1994 More than one million Tutsis fleeing genocide in Rwanda pour into eastern Zaire.

1996 Zaire's government tries to exile ethnic Tutsis from the country. Tutsi revolutionaries form militias, including the Armed Forces for the Liberation of Congo-Zaire, headed by Laurent Kabila.

1997 Mobuto is forced by the rebels to flee the country. Kabila takes over and renames the country the Democratic Republic of the Congo.

1998 Kabila betrays the Tutsis who brought him to power, attempting to exile them from the country just as Mobuto did. Tutsi revolutionaries remobilize, and war begins again.

1999 Kabila and the Tutsis sign a cease-fire agreement.

2001 Laurent Kabila is assassinated, and his son, Joseph Kabila, assumes the presidency.

of the war that had been raging in Congo for years. Often known as Africa's First World War, the fighting claimed the lives of 1.7 million people and left the government of the Democratic Republic of the Congo in control of only half of the country at the time of the assassination.

Congo's great size, central location, and immense mineral wealth ties the fate of Africa to it inextricably. With Kabila's assassination and an uncertain future the country's internal affairs have repercussions far beyond its borders.

HISTORICAL BACKGROUND

The third largest country in Africa, the Democratic Republic of the Congo is about one-third the size of the United States, and about as wide as western Europe. Since the capital of Congo is Kinshasa, the Democratic Republic of the Congo is sometimes referred to as Congo-Kinshasa to avoid confusion with its neighbor, the Republic of Congo (sometimes referred to as Congo-Brazzaville). More than two hundred ethnic groups speaking four language dialects make their home in the Democratic Republic of the Congo.

Lush with savanna and forest, rich with gold, diamonds, and other mineral wealth, the DROC has been the prize of kings, revolutionaries, foreign governments, and greedy dictators at least since King Leopold II of Belgium claimed the country as his own in 1885. In that year, at the Berlin Conference of 1884–85, the European powers recognized King Leopold II of Belgium as the ruler of central Africa, including what was then known as the Congo Free State.

By many accounts Belgium's rule was among the most brutal of Europe's African colonies. Ten million Congolese are thought to have been killed by Belgian colonists, many of whom are said to have punished their Congolese slaves by hacking off their hands. The Belgians also forced the relocation of large numbers of people, laying the groundwork for ethnic strife in later years. Hutus and Tutsis native to the region currently known as Rwanda were moved into Congo to farm. The Belgians also made miners out of the ethnic Luba, native to south-central Congo, moving them into the southeast.

The Post Colonial Era

Congo gained independence from Belgium on June 30, 1960, with Patrice Lumumba serving as prime minister, and Joseph Kasavubu as president. It was at this time that the country first took on the name of the Democratic Republic of the Congo.

The choice of leadership, however, did not sit well with Belgium, or with the United States, which at the time was in the midst of the Cold War with the Soviet Union. Anxious to have a leader in Congo who would fall firmly on the side of the United States rather than be sympathetic to the Soviet Union, the U.S. Central Intelligence Agency (CIA) and Belgium supported a coup against Lumumba. The coup, staged by Congo's army just five days after independence, was led by Joseph Mobutu, later known as Mobutu Sese Seko, who ousted Lumumba and assumed power. For a short time Mobutu ceded power back to President Kasavubu. In 1965, however, he staged another coup. This time declaring himself president. In

MAP OF THE DEMOCRATIC REPUBLIC OF THE CONGO. *(Maryland Cartographics. Reproduced by permission.)*

1970 he was elected without opposition and centralized power firmly into his own hands.

Mobuto ruled Congo for 35 years. His longevity is attributed both to strong support from western Europe and the United States, and to his systematic theft not only of public funds, but also of World Bank and International Monetary Fund loans earmarked for the development of the country. Mobutu personally appropriated millions of dollars from state funds, transferring the money to personal bank accounts in Europe. He also shored up his presidency with generous bribes to important state officials. While Mobutu grew richer by some US$5 billion, the people of his country grew poorer, and the country's infrastructure steadily deteriorated. The United States looked the other way at Mobutu's improprieties, willing to continue its support for him in an attempt to gain dominance over the Soviet Union.

Despite U.S. support Mobutu's rule did not go unchallenged. In spite of his best efforts to foster Congolese nationalism based on loyalty to the state rather than to areas of the country, regional conflicts remained a constant. Mobutu renamed the country the Republic of Zaire in 1971, waging a campaign of "Africanization." Mobuto decreed that all colonial or Christian names, public and private, would be changed to Zairean names. He renamed himself Mobutu Sese Seko Kuku Ngbendu wa za Bana, meaning "the all powerful

JOSEPH KABILA

1972– Little is known about Joseph Kabila outside his close circle of associates. He was appointed to succeed his father as president of the Democratic Republic of the Congo after his father was assassinated in January 2001. Born in 1972, Joseph Kabila was raised in neighboring Tanzania. He arrived in Congo's capital, Kinshasa, when his father was swept into power in 1997.

Joseph Kabila received military training in both Tanzania and Uganda. At the time of his father's death he was receiving further training in China. In the military Kabila, age 29, bore the rank of major general and was in charge of the army. Little was known of Kabila prior to his father's death. Rumored to be more fluent in English than in Congo's official language of French, the younger Kabila made few public appearances in the country after his father's death. Since assuming office, however, he has made a number of appearances internationally, meeting with world leaders and diplomats to express his vision of Congo's future.

Kabila's apparent willingness to negotiate where his father dictated has earned him warm receptions abroad, and many outside observers see in him some hope for a peaceful settlement to the fighting that has raged without cease in central Africa for years.

warrior who, because of his endurance and inflexible will to win, will go from conquest to conquest leaving fire in his wake."

Mobutu's position became tenuous after the collapse of the Soviet Union in 1991, after which the United States withdrew support for his government. Domestic protests lead Mobutu to agree to the principle of a multi-party system with elections. It was not until two years later, however, that the Sovereign National Conference was held, with the election of Archbishop Laurent Monsengwo as its chairman and Etienne Tshisekedi as prime minister. By the end of 1992 Mobutu had created a rival government with its own prime minister. Although elections were repeatedly scheduled over the next two years, they never took place. Factors contributing to Mobutu's eventual downfall included the scarcity of internal investment, and the lack of usable roads led directly to his inability to control large sections of territory. By the mid 1990s the Katanga region had become autonomous—issuing its own currency, and negotiating formal trade agreements with neighboring countries—and Mobutu could do little to stop it.

In April 1994 a plane carrying the presidents of Rwanda and Burundi was shot down and both leaders were killed, precipitating an explosion of violence in central Africa. In the aftermath of their deaths an extremist group of Rwanda's ethnic majority, the Hutus, known as the *Interahamwe*, "those who attack together," instigated a program of systematic genocide against the minority Tutsi population in Rwanda. Over a 100-day period, 800,000 ethnic Tutsis were violently murdered, often with machetes and spears. Soon afterwards, a group of Tutsi revolutionaries called the Rwandan Patriotic Army (RPA) retaliated from bases in Uganda, defeating the Interahamwe in short order and gaining control of the country. Nearly one million Rwandans, many of whom had been involved in the genocide or simply feared mass reprisals, fled west into eastern Congo, where they were sheltered in refugee camps and were provided with weapons by Mobutu's government.

Rwanda's new Tutsi-led government, with the help of the government of Uganda and of ethnic Tutsi militia groups in Congo, attacked the refugee camps in 1996. Their intention was to secure their respective borders with Congo, but the attack went so well that the combined armies were able to keep moving west towards the capital. The Tutsis and their allies soon controlled large parts of eastern Congo, and a man named Laurent Kabila rose to prominence as their leader.

Mobutu, who was in Europe undergoing treatment for prostate cancer, rushed home to a country at war. Just seven months after the attack began, Kabila's army wrested control of the country from Mobutu and forced him to flee. The long-reigning dictator was ousted and the country's new leader, Laurent Kabila, marched unopposed into the capital on May 20, 1997.

Laurent Kabila Takes Control

Kabila declared himself president of the country and changed its name back to the Democratic Republic of the Congo. To appease his supporters Kabila placed Tutsis from both Congo and Rwanda in high government posts. Many outside of Africa were hopeful that Kabila would bring some measure of civility to his embattled country. Then-U.S. Secretary of State Madeleine Albright met Kabila in 1997, and indicated that she was hopeful that Kabila would steady the DROC's government and bring an end to the long cycle of violence that had plagued the region.

Kabila, however, proved to be just as dictatorial as his predecessor. Far from making good on his promise to hold elections soon after his "temporary" government gained power, he in fact set about jailing or killing opposition leaders. Within his first year in power, whatever popular support Kabila had enjoyed as the usurper of Mobutu had eroded. Under his leadership foreign investment in the country dropped. In fact, money was often raised by jailing foreign executives and demanding money for their release. The Dutch beer company Heineken, for example, paid US$1 million to secure the release of two of its executives in Kinshasa. Actions like these ensured that foreign investment practically dried up.

Kabila betrayed his allies, the Tutsis—who had helped bring him to power—by removing them from positions of power in his government and ordering them to leave the country in July 1998. In a matter of days the Tutsis sparked a counterrevolution in eastern Congo. The rebels, backed by the governments of Rwanda, Uganda, and Burundi, and calling themselves the Congolese Rally for Democracy (RCD), subsequently split into three quarrelling factions.

Kabila brought new allies to the fight on his side. The governments of Angola, Zimbabwe, Namibia, Sudan, and Chad all sent troops to support him. The violence in central Africa became a confusion of fighting factions and concerned parties. The war reached an impasse with the three rebel groups, backed by Rwanda and Uganda, controlling the eastern half of the country, and Kabila's government and his allies controlling western Congo, including the capital.

A ceasefire agreement, called the Lusaka Accord, was signed by all government and rebel groups in 1999. Under the terms of the agreement there was to be no more violence against civilians, and humanitarian aid was to be delivered via specially established aid corridors. Monitoring of the agreement was to be overseen by a Joint Military Commission, which was also to oversee the disarmament of various groups. Also as part of the agreement, a United Nations peacekeeping force was to be sent into the region at some to-be-determined date.

Despite the agreement, fighting continued, and although the United Nations recommended that a mission of 500 military observes and 3,400 soldiers be sent to Congo, the UN Security Council was reluctant to send a peacekeeping force without assurances that a ceasefire would hold. By August 2000, after violations on all sides, the ceasefire had

YOUNG WOMEN CRY AS THEY HOLD A PORTRAIT OF SLAIN LEADER LAURENT KABILA AT HIS FUNERAL. KABILA WAS ASSASSINATED BY ONE OF HIS OWN GUARDS. *(CORBIS Corporation (Bellevue). Reproduced by permission.)*

fallen completely apart, with the government of Congo officially suspending the agreement. It was in this stalemate of violence and opposition that Laurent Kabila was assassinated, throwing into question the balance of power for the country and for the region.

RECENT HISTORY AND THE FUTURE

The economy of Congo had all but disintegrated under Laurent Kabila and his predecessor, Mobutu Sese Seko. As 2001 opened in Kinshasa, families grew cabbages in the shadow of the central bank, and others lived in the shattered remains of office buildings, hanging their washing out of broken windows and roasting their meals over open fires in former boardrooms. Four to five million people make their home in Kinshasa. Of these, only about 20 percent have jobs, most of which pay less than the equivalent of US$10 a month.

Most of the streets in Kinshasa remained unpaved. The sewage system and other essential utilities were falling apart from neglect. Although gasoline was supposed to be sold at an official rate, gas stations were often empty, and black market street peddlers took up the slack by selling it in cans for two or three times the official rate. Due to the long term fighting and lack of stable infrastructure in the country shortages abounded and the black market thrived. A strong leader was needed to fill

CASUALTIES OF WAR

As foreign armies and rebel groups began to pull back from fighting in the Democratic Republic of the Congo (DROC), aid agencies were able to take a closer look at the humanitarian effects of the conflict. The New York-based International Rescue Committee (IRC) found that between 1999 and 2001 there were 1.1 million people displaced from their homes; inflation was at a rate of 333 percent; and infectious diseases such as cholera and meningitis, as well as health ailments, including malnutrition, were rampant. While refugees and the deterioration of health in the country were not unexpected effects from the war, the actual numbers were much higher than expected. Indeed, some researchers questioned the accuracy of the IRC's findings. The British medical aid group Merlin, however, documented deaths in Maniema province to be two and one half times higher than births, a number that does lend support to the IRC's survey results. Additionally, the IRC's claim of approximately 3 million deaths over the 32-month war have been confirmed and replicated by independent researchers and follow-up studies. Three million deaths over a 32-month period equals more than 77,000 deaths per month.

A proportionally small number of victims—a few hundred thousand—can actually be attributed to the battles waged by the Congolese army, rebel groups, and foreign troops fighting on both sides of the conflict. In fact, family members and witnesses to these violent killings reported that they were committed at a similar frequency by both government and rebel forces. The violence is indiscriminate; women and children accounted for 47 percent of the violent deaths reported in the eastern half of the country. Despite this, the vast majority of deaths in the DROC are not the result of battles wages, but are caused by starvation, disease, and deprivation.

IRC estimates show that 40 percent of Congo's wartime deaths could have been avoided by access to basic health care. The health care system, already in a precarious situation prior to the war, collapsed under the stress of the fighting. This breakdown allowed treatable illnesses such as malaria, diarrhea, and respiratory infections to run unchecked. A projected 75 percent of children born during the war may never reach their second birthday. The soaring number of deaths, combined with the country's decimated infrastructure and its precarious political situation, create a tenuous environment in which Joseph Kabila can maneuver for peace. If the war in Congo does continue to subside, it is hoped that infrastructure can be rebuilt, health can be restored, and the people of the Democratic Republic of the Congo can begin to rebuild their lives. The path back to peace and prosperity, however, will be a long one, and the social face of Congo will undoubtedly be forever changed by the scars of war.

the void, end the violence, and make this resource-rich country prosperous.

The automatic selection of Joseph Kabila as his father's successor did not sit well with many of the ordinary citizens of the DROC, who wanted a say in the leadership of their country. The international community watched the developments in Congo carefully. Would Joseph Kabila, a young man untested in the waters of government, continue in his father's footsteps or change course? Would he lead the country further into violence or back toward the promise of peace?

Joseph Kabila: Congo's New Hope?

Little was known about Joseph Kabila when he assumed power. He was born and educated in Tanzania, where he grew up speaking Swahili and English. He is not fluent in French, his country's official language, or in any of Congo's native languages, and officials have kept his appearances on national television to a minimum. He is said to have no experience in politics. Joseph Kabila was serving as a major general of the army when his father was assassinated and he was called upon to take up the presidency.

The younger Kabila's first act upon assuming office was an effort to appease any disgruntled soldiers and civil servants who might have sympathized with his father's assassin. He authorized the payment of several months of back pay to soldiers. It was a first step outside his father's shadow. Laurent Kabila's leadership had regularly neglected to pay soldiers. The younger Kabila's effort clearly indicated that he was not his father.

In the first three months of Joseph Kabila' leadership he began working to end the diplomatic stonewalling practiced by his father, visiting numerous Western capitals and inviting other African

JOSEPH KABILA BECAME ONE OF THE YOUNGEST LEADERS IN THE WORLD WHEN HE ASSUMED POWER OF CONGO-KINSHASA AFTER HIS FATHER'S DEATH. *(AP/Wide World Photos. Reproduced by permission.)*

leaders to Kinshasa for talks. Joseph Kabila visited the United States in February 2001, soon after he became president, at the invitation of U.S. President George W. Bush. There, he met with U.S. Secretary of State Colin Powell and the president of Rwanda, Paul Kagame. He also addressed U.S. mining executives, affirming his commitment to the economic development and success of his country and determining to make the DROC more appealing to foreign investors.

The removal of the elder Kabila from power seems to have invigorated the peace process, with most of the warring factions retreating from their formerly intractable positions, and the United Nations finally agreed to deploy peacekeeping

forces in significant numbers to help maintain the peace. Joseph Kabila invited back the mediator appointed by the Organization of African Unity, Ketumile Masire, who was so stymied by the elder Kabila in his efforts to further the peace process that he closed his office in Kinshasa and left the country. With Joseph Kabila's support, Masire again set to work organizing talks between the government of Congo, rebel groups, and political opponents.

In an attempt to put his own stamp on the government and to distance his administration from that of his father's the younger Kabila dismissed his father's cabinet. The dismissed members were allowed to stay in their jobs until a new government was formed, at a future date not yet determined. Formation of a new government, according to Kabila, would have to wait until all foreign powers involved in the war had withdrawn.

Congo's future, and therefore Africa's, may well depend on how committed, or even able, the new president is to enact changes within his government. As D. Jean-Baptiste Sondji, fired for being critical of the elder Kabila's regime while he served as his minister of health, told the *New York Times*: "So far things have improved under the son. But everyone is worried. If the new cabinet is a flop, I don't think he'll have a second chance."

BIBLIOGRAPHY

Berkeley, Bill. *The Graves Are Not Yet Full: Race, Tribe, and Power in the Heart of Africa.* Basic Books, 2001.

"Congo Erupts, Again," *The Economist*, August 15, 1998.

"Congo Without Kabila; Congo After Kabila," *The Economist*, January 20, 2001.

"Death of a Dictator," *Newsweek*, January 29, 2001.

"Democratic Republic of the Congo: The Regional Picture," BBC News. Available online at http://news.bbc.co.uk/hi/English/static/map/congo/democratic_republic_congo.htm (cited July 20, 2001).

International Rescue Committee. "D.R. Congo," May 2001. Available online at http://www.intrescom.org/greatlakes/drcongo/cfm (cited June 29, 2001).

"In the Heart of Darkness; Congo's Unnoticed War," *The Economist*, December 9, 2000.

Jane's Information Group. "Central Africa Risk Pointers: Democratic Republic of the Congo (Zaire)." Available online at http://www.janes.com/regional_news/africa_middle_east/sentinel/central_africa/democratic_republic_of_congo.shtml (cited July 20, 2001).

Onishi, Norimitsu. "Death in Congo," *New York Times*, March 5, 2001.

———. "Pressure Rises on Outsiders in Congo War," *New York Times*, April 17, 2001.

———. "Who Runs Congo? The People, New Leader Says," *New York Times*, April 15, 2001.

Smith, Stephen. "Beyond the Sentries of Hell," *New Statesman*, January 29, 2001.

U.S. Department of State. "Congo, Democratic Republic of," *Background Notes.* Available online at http://www.state.gov/www/background_notes/congo_0001_bgn.html (cited June 4, 2001).

Vick, Karl. "An Apocalypse in Congo," *The Washington Post National Weekly Edition*, May 7–13, 2001, p. 16–17

Wrong, Michela. *In the Footsteps of Mr. Kurtz: Living on the Brink of Disaster in Mobutu's Congo.* New York: HarperCollins, 2001.

—Michael P. Belfiore

THE DIAMOND CARTEL: MONOPOLIZING AN INDUSTRY

In 1999 *Advertising Age* magazine published a special issue with a list of the top advertising slogans of the twentieth century. The winner was "A Diamond Is Forever," a slogan that has been printed in magazine ads and broadcast worldwide for several decades. Coined in 1947, the slogan was first used in the United States, the world's largest market for diamond jewelry. Gradually, the famous slogan made it's way into the rest of the world—and that these words do magic is strongly supported by statistical facts. While the diamond engagement ring was almost unknown to Japanese brides up until the 1960s, two-thirds of them received one from their fiancé in 1996. Between 1980 and the mid-1990s the value of diamond jewelry sold around the globe has more than doubled. After a temporary downturn caused by the severe economic crises in Japan and Southeast Asia and a drop in demand from Europe, global demand for diamond jewelry has enjoyed a robust two-digit growth once again since 1999.

For thousands of years diamonds have been a symbol of everlasting love. "Diamonds are a girl's best friend," sang Marilyn Monroe and Jane Russell in the movie *Gentlemen Prefer Blondes*. What can be better for a woman than receiving an engagement ring from a man as a sign of his love and commitment? But why are diamonds so valuable? What makes people spend one month's salary or more on a diamond ring for their prospective fiancé? And where does the diamond on the ring actually come from? This has been one of the world's best kept secrets by one of the world's most secretive industries.

Diamonds change hands, and borders, several times before they hit the retail stores. To enhance their natural qualities and give them the significant

THE CONFLICT

For about 112 years the South African diamond conglomerate De Beers, which is controlled by the Oppenheimer family, has dominated the world's diamond industry. Between 70 and almost 100 percent of the worldwide diamond production at any given time has been funneled into the company's cartel, the Central Selling Organization. Diamond prices are kept artificially stable by releasing only the number of stones the market can bear at the established high price level.

Economic

- An uncontrolled diamond market would be intensely volatile at times. Adjusting their output to the demand helps diamond producers avoid critical situations and realize higher profit margins.

- While prices of other commodities fluctuated heavily during the last 100 years, price levels for rough and polished diamonds have remained relatively stable, at a high level compared to production costs.

- Diamonds are not a necessity. In most consumers' perception, diamonds are a rare commodity, which can give them a high value. De Beers generic advertising campaign has helped sustain the high-value appeal in diamonds over the last decades.

Political

- The diamond industry is a truly global industry. Diamond producers are concentrated in Africa, Russia, Australia and Canada, while the world's three biggest markets are the United States, Japan and Europe. These countries do not allow cartels, but their anti-trust laws cannot be enforced in other countries. De Beers conducts its business through a complex network of subsidiaries, so their business partners might not always be aware that they are dealing with a cartel.

- The governments of many diamond producing countries, especially in Africa, depend highly on diamond revenues. They have an interest in keeping price levels high.

CHRONOLOGY

1871 Johannes Nicholas and Diederik Arnoldus de Beer sell their farm, rich with diamond mines, in South Africa.

1888 De Beers Consolidated Mines Limited is established.

1890 The London Diamond Syndicate is formed.

1917 Ernest Oppenheimer founds Anglo American PLC.

1929 Ernest Oppenheimer becomes the chairman of De Beers.

1930 Diamond Corporation Limited is founded.

1939 All De Beers mining operations are closed down after World War II begins in Europe.

1958 Rich diamond deposits are discovered in Siberia.

1994 De Beers and the government of Namibia establish a diamond mining joint venture, Namdeb Diamond Corporation.

1996 Australia's Argyle mine terminates its contract with De Beers to sell its production on the open market.

1998 "Conflict diamonds" get media exposure, drawing public attention to diamonds sold illegally by Angola's UNITA rebels to fund civil war.

August 2000 De Beers' is approved for a hostile takeover of the Canadian diamond producer Winspear.

August 19, 2000 Harry Oppenheimer dies in Johannesburg at age 92, and is succeeded by his son Nicolas.

Summer 2000 De Beers launched a new program called "Supplier of Choice," designed to encourage diamond producers to voluntarily use De Beers' diamond center to process its stones. This policy marked a change in De Beers' traditional practice of controlling the supply side of diamonds, which had become an increasingly expensive route.

February 1, 2001 De Beers announces a planned takeover of Anglo American.

shape of a sparkler, they are polished and cut, most likely in one of the world's major manufacturing centers such as Israel, Belgium, India, and the United States. There are two ways for diamond manufacturers to purchase their raw material, called rough diamonds. The first is to become a member of one of the world's diamond bourses (exchanges), most of which operate out of Ant-

werp, Belgium; Ramat Gan near Tel Aviv, Israel; New York City; and Moscow, Russia. The second way for manufacturers to purchase raw material is to go to London every five weeks, receive a brown plastic box, and pay a fixed price for whatever rough diamonds are in the box, with no questions asked. Where do these boxes come from and who would choose to do business under such conditions?

For over a century the South African diamond conglomerate De Beers, which is controlled by the Oppenheimer family, has dominated the world's US$13 billion diamond industry. Between 70 and almost 100 percent of the worldwide diamond production at any given time has been funneled into the company's cartel, the Central Selling Organization (CSO). The main purpose of this organization is to keep diamond prices stable—and high—through the total regulation of the supply chain for rough diamonds. To better understand this mechanism it is helpful to look at the history of the diamond trade.

HISTORICAL BACKGROUND

The Early Days of the Diamond Industry

The modern global diamond industry started taking shape about 100 years ago. Humans, however, have been digging for diamonds for many centuries. Although scientists suggest that the first diamonds were probably found in India some 3,000 years ago, the earliest preserved written material—a work by an Indian scholar for Hindu jewelers about how to profit from the diamond boom—dates back to the third or fourth century BCE. Diamonds had become a sought after commodity in Turkey and the Near East and trade was spreading to China and Greece. The Indian emperors kept the best stones for themselves and the rest made their way to Europe's kings and other noblemen.

Golconda, an Indian fortress city near Hyderabad, became the world's first diamond center. It was here that the basic principles of today's diamond industry were established. The people involved in the trade understood that the high value of diamonds rested on their rarity—and helped keep them rare by limiting production. They also understood that promoting the myths about the stone's "magical qualities" helped keep demand high.

The Dutch East India Company became the first Western industry leader to control the diamond trade. The rough diamonds were brought to London, where the company sold them to a selected group of mainly Jewish dealers. Most of the diamonds were then processed in the Lowlands of southern Scotland and then sold to other dealers or jewelers. The company reached profits exceeding 100 percent, and the government profited through heavy taxation. Having yielded an estimated two and one half tons, or 12 million carats of diamonds, the Indian diamond fields dried up in the late seventeenth century.

By the early 1700s the world's emperors were starving for diamonds and a new source opened up in Brazil's gold fields. After diamonds were discovered near Tejuco, a town 250 miles (400 kilometers) away from the Atlantic Ocean, the area soon became overcrowded by fortune-seekers. It was later renamed Diamantina. The new stones from Brazil, which was then a Portuguese colony, were at first seen as low quality or as fakes since no one had ever heard of diamonds from somewhere else but India. Clever businesspeople bypassed this obstacle by shipping the stones from Brazil to Europe via India, claiming them as "Indian goods," or by letting the stones be cut and polished "Indian style." When the growing supply for diamonds threatened to break down established price levels, the Portuguese government limited production by pushing out diamond rushers and taking control of the diamond fields. The fields became unprofitable at the end of the 1860s.

In 1866 the 15-year-old son of a poor farmer found a shiny stone near the Orange River in Hopetown, in South Africa's Northern Cape Province. It turned out to be a 21.25 carat diamond, and several others were found in the same region. Three years later, in spring 1869, a native African found a rough diamond of more than 83 carats, which later became known as the Star of Africa. Word about the diamond spread fast and initiated another great diamond rush to South Africa. Within a few months about 10,000 people were digging for diamonds along the Orange and Vaal rivers.

Another few months had passed when diamonds were found in two different places on a South African farm owned by the de Beer brothers in early 1871. The Dutch settlers sold their farm and the diamond diggers moved from the riverbanks to the new site. Almost overnight a new town popped up between the two "dry diggings" at the farm. At first called New Rush, the town soon grew into the Cape Province's second largest city, with 50,000 inhabitants, and was renamed Kimberley after British Colonial Secretary John W. Kimberley.

A JEWELER EXAMINES A 42.25 CARAT DIAMOND. DIAMONDS OF THIS SIZE ARE VERY RARE AND VERY EXPENSIVE. *(The Gamma Liaison Network. Reproduced by permission.)*

A New Diamond Monopoly is Formed

One of the diamond diggers at Kimberley was Cecil John Rhodes, the son of an English clergyman. By 1872, at age 19, Cecil Rhodes had achieved financial independence from his claim's profits. Equipped with a natural sense for business opportunities, Rhodes set up a partnership with one of his neighbors, fellow countryman Charles Dunell Rudd. In 1872 they invested in an ice-making machine and started selling ice to their fellow diggers as a side business. With their profits they acquired more claims in the De Beers mine, one of the two mines at the former de Beer farm.

In April 1880 Rhodes and his partner, together with two other large claim-holders, established the De Beers Mining Company, and within five years gained control over the De Beers mine. In the same year, Kimberley Central Mining Company was formed at the Kimberley mine with far better yields. Led by Barney Barnato, son of a Jewish shopkeeper in London's East End, the company was the biggest claim-holder in the Kimberley mine. There was no doubt that Barnato was in the stronger financial position. After several years, as the rivalry between them hurt the profits of both companies, Barnato finally agreed to a merger of his company with Rhodes-controlled De Beers.

The merger of Barnato's mining company and De Beers Mining Company resulted in the formation of De Beers Consolidated Mines Limited in March 1888. While Barnato remained the largest shareholder of the new company, Rhodes, now in his mid-thirties, took over as chairman. The new entity controlled the two biggest producers, De Beers and Kimberley, and acquired control over more mines in South Africa. Aside from a few remaining individual diamond diggers, De Beers was without competition—a diamond monopoly had been established.

The De Beers monopoly was further strengthened when Rhodes then convinced ten of the most important merchants in London's diamond district to buy a portion of De Beers' total output. In return, the merchants agreed to feed Rhodes crucial information about the diamond market so he was able to adjust his production. In February 1890 the London Diamond Syndicate was formed as the vehicle to carry out that plan.

In 1897 Rhodes lost his business partner Barnato, who had become a close friend, when, suffering from alcoholism and derangement, he jumped from a ship coming back to Capetown from London. He was aged 44. Struggling with health problems stemming from his childhood, Rhodes died five years later at age 49 in 1902.

De Beers Cartel is Spelled O-p-p-e-n-h-e-i-m-e-r

The year 1902 was a turning point for the diamond industry. In that year a gigantic diamond mine—the Premier mine—was discovered in the northern part of South Africa. The 3,106-carat Cullinan, weighing over one pound, was found there, and in 1908 diamond production at Premier outgrew De Beers. Soon after, other new deposits were found outside the De Beers mining realm, in German South West Africa and in the Belgian Congo.

The new competition was a serious threat for De Beers. Since Rhodes' death in 1902 the company had lacked a strong leader. During that same year, however, a young man from Britain named Ernest Oppenheimer came to Kimberley to oversee the office of a diamond-trading firm. The German-born son of a Jewish cigar merchant had learned all about diamonds at the firm's London office. He

moved in with his cousin Fredrich Hirschhorn, a major figure in the diamond industry who also had a seat at De Beers' board of directors. Ernest Oppenheimer accompanied his cousin to some De Beers' board meetings and became acquainted with Barney Barnato's nephew and spokesman for the Barnato Brothers Co., Solly Joel, as well as with other leading heads of the industry.

After World War I, Oppenheimer founded Anglo American Corporation of South Africa, which became an important player in the gold mining industry, and soon after in the diamond industry. Oppenheimer had acquired a controlling interest for Anglo American in the newly formed Consolidated Diamond Mines, Ltd. (CDM), which De Beers had unsuccessfully attempted to acquire. Anglo's position in the diamond industry became stronger when the company, together with Barnato, was given control over the diamonds of the Belgian mining company Forminière, which had mining sites in Angola and the Belgian Congo. Whenever there was an opportunity, Oppenheimer also acquired De Beers shares.

De Beers managed to buy the Premier mine in 1921 and greatly profited from the economically swinging 1920s. In the meantime new diamond sites had been discovered in 1925–26 at South African Lichtenburg and Namaqualand, near the Atlantic coast and the additional output of the new independent diggers flooded the diamond market. In 1924 Oppenheimer's Anglo American Corporation became a member of the London Diamond Syndicate, but was soon asked to leave because of its aggressive business tactics. A year later Oppenheimer formed the new Diamond Syndicate, which applied for and won the exclusive right to trade and market all of De Beers' rough diamond production, a right formerly held by the London syndicate. Eventually the old syndicate was dissolved into the new one, contributing to its profits. In 1926 Oppenheimer was elected to De Beers board of directors where he promoted the idea of consolidating all major diamond producers under De Beers. During the next four years Oppenheimer and Solly Joel acquired controlling interest in sites at Lichtenburg and Namaqualand with the best prospects and Oppenheimer managed to buy the huge rough diamond collection of pioneer prospector Dr. Hans Merensky. From this strengthened position he was able to convince De Beers' board of directors to make him the new chairman in the same year. Oppenheimer held the top positions at both De Beers and Anglo American, a role that the Oppenheimer family still holds today.

CONFLICT DIAMONDS

An estimated 3.7 percent of the world's total diamond production in 1999 came from three African countries that were involved in violent conflict. These US$225 million in diamond revenues are allegedly used by violent political groups to buy weapons and to finance their activities.

Angola contributes about 7 percent to the world's rough output of diamonds. Its stones are of a high quality and value. They are mined in the Cunago valley, in the country's northern province Lunda Norte. The Angolan government controls diamond mining through its company Endiama, but issues concessions to other mining companies to run the mining operations.

Angola has been involved in violent conflict for several decades. Since the country gained political independence in 1975, political groups have struggled for power. In 1993 one of the larger groups, UNITA, had 70 percent of the country under its control, including the diamond fields. During the 1990s Angolan diamonds generated between US$200 million and US$700 million annually. An untold amount of this money was diverted to fund UNITA and continue the war. Between 1992 and 1995 alone, about 300,000 people were killed in Angola's civil war, many of them by land mines.

The Democratic Republic of Congo is among the world's largest diamond producers, mining 5.8 percent of the total rough output value. Kisangani, Congo's third largest city in the northeastern part of the country, is an important alluvial mining center. It is also the campaign headquarters for Ernest Wamba dia Wamba, who represents the Democracy-Liberation Movement (RCD-ML).

Civil war has been raging in Congo since the mid-1990s when Mobutu Sese Seko was running the country. Laurent Kabila seized power in 1997, but he was unable to bring peace to the warring factions of tribal militias and rebel armies. In fact, Kabila fed the flames of rivalry by eliminating many fractious members from his government. In 2001, Kabila was assassinated by one of his bodyguards. An estimated 8.8 percent of the Congo's rough are "conflict diamonds."

Sierra Leone's diamond fields are spread out over about 7,700 square miles (20,020 square kilometers) in the southeast, around the town of Kenema. Only one percent of this area contains diamonds, including Kono, Tongo, and the Sewa Valley. By the end of the 1980s about half of Sierra Leone's output came from underground mines in the Yengema kimberlite pipes. Sierra Leone's gemstones are of exceptionally high quality. Almost all of these diamonds are octahedral and their weight most commonly ranges between 0.3 and 5 carats.

In 1992 a group called the Revolutionary United Front (RUF) ended the corrupt dictatorship of Joseph Momoh, which had lasted for 30 years. Led by 27-year-old army captain Valentine Strasser, the RUF successfully took control of the country and tamed inflation. However, often unidentifiable groups of "rebels" have imposed their violent rule upon the countryside. Disguised as politically motivated and equipped with automatic weapons, these rebels often seem to be driven by material, more than ideological, motives.

Convinced that the diamond industry could only be stabilized if the number of diamonds released to the market were controlled and adjusted to the demand, Oppenheimer actively pursued the path Cecil Rhodes had laid out in the industry's early days. Heading both the De Beers mines and the Diamond Trade Syndicate, he was finally in the position to do so. There were two elements to his plan. The first one was to control the production end. Oppenheimer was the driving force behind the formation of the Diamond Corporation Limited (DCL) in 1930, a cooperative that included the major non-De Beers producers, De Beers and its subsidiaries, and the Anglo American and its affiliates. Oppenheimer became its chairman and DCL replaced the old syndicate's function and took over the contracts and diamond stockpiles.

The second element in Oppenheimer's strategy to control the world's diamond supply was to sell it through only one channel, which enabled him to control the amount of diamonds available on the market and to dictate wholesale prices to a certain extent. This was carried out through the establishment of the Central Selling Organization (CSO), which marketed the total output of all DCL producers. The CSO released diamonds in times of high demand and stockpiled them when demand was low, thereby keeping price levels high. Through a system of contracts with the major diamond producers the CSO channeled their production to a selected group of diamond traders and manufacturers and sold them a certain amount of rough diamonds for a fixed price.

One Channel Marketing

Up until World War II, De Beers directors hadn't given much thought to advertising their gems. Furthermore, many of them believed that advertising could even harm their business by negatively influencing their image. But when the company ceased diamond production because of the war, they gave it a second thought. De Beers' first attempt—a diamond jewelry collection designed by Madame Chanel—did not bring the desired results. In the late 1930s Sir Ernest Oppenheimer's son Harry convinced his father to let him travel to the United States, the world's single biggest market for diamond jewelry, to explore ideas in regards to diamond advertising.

After running the idea by several people in the U.S. advertising industry, Harry Oppenheimer found a partner in New York-based agency NW Ayer. The results of the consumer survey conducted by the agency surprised everybody. Despite the diamond's undeniably luxury appeal, American consumers bought them as *the* symbol of love. Based on these findings NW Ayer ran the first advertising campaign for diamonds in 1939. Suddenly catching millions of eyes, the symbol of the very rich soon started diffusing into America's middle class. In 1947 a young copywriter at NW Ayer invented a new slogan for the diamond campaign. First used in 1948, "A Diamond Is Forever" made its way into many parts of the world and greatly contributed to the rising consumer demand for diamond jewelry, especially engagement rings.

New Players Enter the Diamond Market

The emergence of new West African Producers in the 1920s began a new era of challenge for De Beers. In the 1940s new mines that produced high-quality gemstones were discovered in Sierra Leone. One of these mines produced the Star of Sierra Leone, weighing 969 carats. In addition, in 1940 Canadian geologist Dr. John Williamson found immense deposits at the Mwadui Mine. Sir Ernest Oppenheimer died in 1957, and his son Harry became De Beers chairman. He was unsuccessful in his efforts to convince Williamson to comply with the De Beers vision for the industry, but after Williamson's death, De Beers acquired a 50 percent share in Williamson's diamond holdings.

CECIL JOHN RHODES HELPED FOUND THE DEBEERS CONSOLIDATED DIAMOND MINES IN 1888. *(Archive Photos, Inc. Reproduced by permission.)*

The days when De Beers had dominated diamond production were finally over when several new developments changed the diamond market forever. The first development was an immense increase in individual diamond digging in West Africa beginning in the 1950s, where rich alluvial deposits turned out to be easy to mine without huge capital investments. Consequently, many African diggers flocked to the new sites after African countries gained sovereignty and their new governments allowed individual diamond mining. This development was encouraged by dynamically rising diamond prices and the increasing demand for industrial diamonds.

In the 1930s, when machine engineering got into gears, diamonds were discovered as an optimal tool to modify other materials, such as tungsten and silicon carbide. The low-quality stones that couldn't be used as gemstones for jewelry finally found their market, which greatly expanded with technological progress over the coming decades. Additionally, diamond producers looked for new ways to utilize diamonds in industry and came up with quite a number of products, such as diamond drills, polishing powders, engraving tools, glass cutters, and radiation counters. However about 80 percent of all industrial diamonds today are produced synthetically.

The 1970s saw an average annual production of natural diamonds at about 40 million carats. About 30 percent of this yield was in gemstones. By the early 1980s Africa accounted for roughly 70 percent of the world's natural diamond production by weight. De Beers put out about a quarter of the world diamond production in the early 1970s. But when demand started growing in the second half of the decade, De Beers' expanded production was at about half of the world's total, or 21.3 million carats.

Growing Political, Economic and Social Pressure in the 1990s

During the 1980s and 1990s there were major changes under way in De Beers' mining grounds. In Angola, one of De Beers' traditional mining grounds, in the mid-1980s the Angolan government canceled De Beers' contract to manage Angola's diamond mines and left the CSO.

A few years later, in August 1992, rumors grew about a wave of diamonds swamping the market that was bypassing the CSO. In that year Angola's UNITA rebels, fighting against the government, won control over the diamond-rich Cuango valley. The civil war in Angola later came to a temporary halt, but the uncontrolled diamond mining activities brought about an unexpected inflow of rough diamonds, worth hundreds of millions of dollars, into the world's cutting centers. De Beers was left to acquire them on the open market at great cost. The pressure faded when UNITA agreed to return the Cuango valley to the government in early 1998. However, De Beers seemed to have bad luck in the race to win Angola's diamond concessions. The Angolan Cuango valley was divided between three companies for prospecting, Angola's state-owned diamond company Endiama, Brazilian firm Odebrecht, and Australian Ashton Mining. Other African governments also attempted to gain more influence over their domestic diamond industries, which were run by De Beers, the revenues of which their budgets highly depended.

The collapse of the Soviet Union in 1991 changed the diamond world dramatically. The succeeding, cash-starved Russian government became an increasingly unreliable partner for De Beers. The company tried to bind the Russians to sell through the CSO, but Moscow's power over more remote parts of the country was fading and a growing percentage of Russian production was sold independently. New competitors also appeared in Australia and Canada. By 1985 Australia had become the world's largest diamond producer by volume. Around that time, diamond producer Argyle Diamonds, which mines in the Australian Kimberley Plateau region, took a bold step when the company decided to change consumers' perception of colored diamonds. Argyle's mines yielded a considerable amount of pink, yellow, and brown gems. In 1990 Argyle launched a successful marketing campaign in the United States that created a high-fashion market for its colored stones under the brand name Champagne Diamonds. By 1994 Argyle's U.S. sales of champagne and cognac colored diamonds reached US$165 million. The third threat for De Beers monopoly in the 1990s arose from the opposite side of the globe where abundant diamond fields were discovered in Ekati, Diavik, and Windspear in the Northwest Territories of Canada.

Despite the ongoing changes in the diamond industry the decade between 1985 and 1995 became one of the most successful ones for the industry. In those ten years alone, worldwide sales of diamond jewelry more than doubled from $24.9 billion to $56.1 billion. Part of that growth came from the new "tiger economies" in Asia and the Pacific Rim, partly due to De Beers' massive consumer advertising, finding an ever growing audience of people moving into middle class status. Japan, which hadn't even existed as a market for diamonds in the first half of the twentieth century, became the world's second largest diamond market by 1995, absorbing one third of all diamond jewelry.

The growing diamond streams originating from outside the cartel, however, became a huge challenge for the system. Trying to absorb the additional supplies to prevent a breakdown of established price levels, the CSO's stockpiles kept growing between 1992 and 1998, passing the $1 billion mark. De Beers cut back on its mining activities and imposed production quotas on other producers in the network. After a record sales year for the CSO in 1997, the Asian financial crisis crushed the market De Beers had so carefully built. By 1998 Japan's world market share had fallen to under 20 percent, compared with 33 percent before the crisis broke.

Besides the growing economic pressures, De Beers was watched suspiciously by U.S. and European antitrust regulators. The most serious threat for De Beers, as well as for the diamond industry, arose not from legal institutions but from the media. When the U.S. media took notice of "conflict diamonds" after the United Nations had published several reports and the U.S. Congress had held several hearings on the issue, De Beers' practices

DIAMONDS THROUGH THE PIPELINE—FROM THE GROUND TO THE CONSUMER

Seventy percent of diamonds mined each year go through De Beers' Diamond Trading Company. De Beers attempts to match diamond supply to demand. Along with other producers, it determines the volume of rough diamonds to be released onto the market, controlling supply and maintaining stable prices. In 1999 rough production was valued at US$8.4 billion. Among the largest producers of rough diamonds were Botswana, Russia, and South Africa.

ROUGH PRODUCTION OF DIAMONDS, 1999

in billions

Angola	$0.6
Australia	0.4
Botswana	1.8
Namibia	0.4
Russia	1.6
South Africa	0.8
Other	0.8
From stockpiles	1.6

Source: Nicholas Stein. "The De Beers Story: A New Cut on an Old Monopoly." *Fortune.* February 19, 2001.

(The Gale Group.)

As these diamonds go through the process of cutting and polishing to arrive at the finished state of earrings, necklaces, and other jewelry items marketed to the public, their value increases. Once the $8.4 billion in rough diamonds were cut and polished, their value rose by about 40 percent, to a collective value of $11.8 billion. Retailers bought the polished stones wholesale for a total of $13.1 billion in 1999. The United States was the largest site of wholesale diamond purchases in that year, with retailers buying $6.3 billion worth of the stones.

WHOLESALE DIAMONDS, 1999

in billions

Asia-Arabia	$0.6
Asis-Pacific	0.4
Europe	1.8
Japan	0.4
United States	1.6

Source: Nicholas Stein. "The De Beers Story: A New Cut on an Old Monopoly." *Fortune.* February 19, 2001.

(The Gale Group.)

The cut and polished diamonds were then set into jewelry and made available to consumers by retailers. In 1999 these finished diamonds were sold to the public for a total sale of $56 billion. Accounting for 44 percent—$24.6 billion—of worldwide diamond jewelry sales for that year, the United States is the largest diamond market. Japan and Europe accounted for 19 and 14 percent respectively and are the next largest markets for diamond consumption.

came under increasing scrutiny and criticism. Profits from conflict diamonds have been used to fund destabilizing and destructive conflicts in Africa. Protests by organizations such as Physicians for Human Rights and Amnesty International further fueled the media's harsh criticism of De Beers for purchasing a considerable amount of conflict diamonds to preserve the cartel's high price levels.

On November 1st, 1999, Ohio Congressman Tony Hall presented the Consumer Access to Responsible Accounting of Trade Act, also known as the CARAT Act. The proposed bill required a certification of the country of origin for diamonds used in jewelry sold in the United States. De Beers promised to take measures to stop the diffusion of conflict diamonds into its marketing channel. In May 2000 representatives and critics of the diamond industry met with government officials in Kimberley, South Africa, to discuss possible solutions. The result was Rough Controls, a concept that required diamond mining countries to export their rough in tamper-proof containers, including documentation of the contents' place of origin. Rough importing countries were required to reject stones without proper documentation. Two months later the World Diamond Council (WDC) was formed with the promise to eliminate conflict diamonds from the market. In December 2000, however, WDC abandoned Congressman Hall's bill and presented its own—the Conflict Diamond Act of 2000—which was less strict. The diamond industry, including mining countries and jewelers, began several lobbying campaigns to support the WDC bill.

The Global Diamond Pipeline

In 1999 global sales of diamond jewelry grew by 11 percent, totaling about $56 billion. The United States alone accounted for $24.6 billion, or 44 percent, of the total. Most of the diamonds contained in jewelry that is made in the United States come from three countries, which are also the world's major centers for cutting, polishing, and selling polished diamonds. Almost half of the polished diamonds imported into the United States come from Israel. Another quarter of all United States diamond imports come from India, while one-fifth is imported from Belgium. Most of the stones travel directly from customs to New York City's diamond district. The United States is also an important manufacturing center for the diamond industry. The domestic market absorbs about two-thirds of all polished imports while one-third is exported again after getting the right cut.

On a global scale, the United States is only a small diamond manufacturer as are South Africa and Israel. The world's biggest diamond manufacturer by volume and value is India where cheap labor makes it possible to polish large amounts of small stones such as industrial diamonds. Almost half of all diamonds by value are polished and cut in India. The world's second largest diamond polishing and cutting center is Israel, which contributes about a quarter of the total value. And where did these manufacturers purchase their rough diamonds?

Much like 110 years ago, when ten times a year the world's 125 most important diamond traders and manufacturers traveled from the diamond districts in New York, Antwerp, and Tel Aviv to De Beers London headquarters to pick up the brown plastic boxes with rough diamonds worth several million U.S. dollars. The content was derived from De Beers' own network of mines in South Africa, Botswana, Namibia and Tanzania, as well as from Canada's Ekati mine and from Russia. The combined percentage of diamonds channeled into the CSO was about 69 percent of the world's total output in 1999. After arriving at De Beers in London, the rough diamonds are separated into 14,000 categories. After that, 500 sorters allocate them into the famous "boxes." After the "sightholders" paid the pre-set price for the content of their box, they take them back to their factories where they are cut and polished.

In 1999 producers and affiliates of De Beers contributed about 44 percent to the world's total rough production of $6.8 billion, approximately equaling the share of all African countries. In terms of countries of origin, Botswana was the world's number one diamond miner, with Russia closely behind. These two countries together accounted for 40 percent of the world's diamond output. However, the production of all diamond mining countries accounted for roughly four-fifths of the total. The other 19 percent, worth $1.6 billion, were released from stockpiles. Industry experts estimate the stockpiles of rough diamonds at De Beers London headquarters, Europe's "most secure" building, at up to $5 billion.

RECENT HISTORY AND THE FUTURE

De Beers' New Strategy

On August 19, 2000, Harry Oppenheimer, the second Oppenheimer to rule over De Beers, died at the age of 91. This was not only the end of an era for De Beers, but for the world's diamond industry as well. The empire that ruled the diamond industry for over a century started sketching out new rules to secure its market position. The company was led by Harry's son, Nicolas, who took over as chairman in 1998. Together with new managing director Gary Ralfe and the consulting firm Bain & Co., they came up with a strategy called "Supplier of Choice" in the summer of 2000. This strategy abandoned the idea of controlling the supply side, which had become increasingly difficult and expensive.

At the core of "Supplier of Choice" was the idea that, unlike in past times, diamond suppliers would voluntarily sell their production to De Beers for the value added through marketing and branding. To set their strategy into practice, De Beers decided to change its approach to advertising. For more than 50 years, the company had financed its global advertising campaign that, in the 1990s amounted to around $300 million per year, or about 4 percent of sales. This was not much if compared with the 20 percent that other luxury goods manufacturers invest in marketing, but every diamond producer benefited from the investment, including the fringe producers outside the cartel. On January 16, 2001, De Beers announced the

MUCH OF THE SUPPLY FROM MINES LIKE THE CATOCA DIAMOND MINE IS ROUTED THROUGH THE CENTRAL SELLING ORGANIZATION, WHICH TO A LARGE EXTENT CONTROLS THE AMOUNT OF DIAMONDS AVAILABLE ON THE MARKET. *(AP/Wide World Photos. Reproduced by permission.)*

formation of a new company to develop a retail strategy for the company's own diamond brand.

To gain control over some of the new diamond producing competitors, De Beers announced two hostile takeover bids in July 2000. The takeover of the Canadian producer Winspear was approved a month later, while the second attempt—to acquire Australian Aston Mining—failed. While old tactics still worked sometimes, the mighty giant's most recent step took the industry completely by surprise. On February 1, 2001, De Beers announced that there were negotiations with Anglo American PLC, the other Oppenheimer family firm that had become one of the world's most important mining conglomerates, about a possible takeover. Up to that point, De Beers held 37 percent of Anglo American, while Anglo American had a 33 percent interest in De Beers. Both companies remained heavily influenced by the Oppenheimer family, which holds a large number of each company's shares.

The Future of the Diamond Industry

The last 50 years have seen an enormous expansion of activities to explore and exploit new diamond fields. Rough diamond production is expected to grow by 8 percent until 2008 with the value of the output increasing by almost 120 per-

cent. One of the industry's future trends might be that middlemen in form of diamond dealers might sooner or later become obsolete if diamond producers, manufacturers, and retailers work closer together or form strategic alliances. The major advantage for the diamond producer would be that he could put the dealer's margin in his own pocket by selling directly to affiliated manufacturers. The manufacturer would cut purchasing cost and could get a part of the dealer's margin. Another effect would be the shortening of the diamond pipeline from two and a half years to 24 months or even shorter and therefore the reduction of working stock.

In a competitive diamond market, producers will have to win over a loyal client base in order to stay in business. De Beers is already on its way to creating its own diamond brand and marketing strategy, following the example of Australian producer Argyle. Producers will move up the value chain to recreate the total control of the cartel at least within their sphere of influence. Strategic alliances between diamond producers, manufacturers, and retailers seem likely and competitive advantages will increasingly depend on whole supply chains. On the production level, the differences of cost-profit ratios between producers will play a much more important role. Production cost for

$1.00 of diamond value range from $0.07 at the Jwaneng mine in Botswana, to $0.46 at the Russian Udachnye mine, up to $0.56 at the Argyle mine in Australia. To make up for these differences, producers might branch into diamond cutting and polishing, diamond jewelry manufacturing, and, with the help of the Internet, diamond marketing.

The governments of many producer countries such as Russia, Botswana, Namibia and South Africa depend heavily on revenues generated by the diamond industry. One plausible trend seems to be that diamond processing and jewelry manufacturing will move closer to the diamond's country of origin caused by government interference. An example is South Africa where the government required goods worth $400 million from the CSO in 1999. A project for a local diamond cutting industry was being developed in north-west Canada. Other possible scenarios include government subsidies to encourage diamond exports or pressures for producers to sell their rough diamonds below market prices to domestic processing plants.

Consumer demand is expected to grow due to the expected increase in advertising activity to introduce new diamond brands. It seems possible that two different price levels will develop which can go in opposite directions. In 1999 larger stones accounted for roughly one third of total production while they represented 85 percent of the total value. On the other hand, about two thirds of the rough diamonds in carat will translate only into 15 percent of the total value. The majority of the smaller stones which are worth much less come from Australian and Russian mines. Diamond jewelry sections of retails stores might take the shape much like today's perfume and cosmetics departments where diamonds will be present.

Chaim Even-Zohar, an industry insider, painted a possible picture at the World Diamond Conference in Toronto in 2000 of the "post-cartel era" in the diamond industry. It seems, however, that the giant De Beers still has some powers it could use to get back to the old ways. As a high-margin producer and owner of mines that yield high-quality gemstones, the company could use it's position to drive smaller players out of the market over time. Using its enormous cash reserves and backed up by mining giant Anglo American, De Beers seems well positioned for a quick merger at the right time. Because of the industry's global scope, the political environment will always be a major uncertainty. Other possible scenarios include the invention of new technologies that make it possible to synthesize larger diamonds, NGO cam-

paigns against environmental pollution caused by diamond mining companies, or the exhaustion of De Beers African diamond mines. However, taking into account the growing media coverage of the industry's long-kept secrets, the main factor of influence that will determine the industry's future will be if consumers keep their faith that "Diamonds are forever."

BIBLIOGRAPHY

"Angolan Diamonds: De Beers's Worst Friend," *The Economist*, August 22, 1998.

Callahan, Maximillian S. *Insider Secrets to Diamond Dealing: How Real Money is Made*. Boulder, CO: Paladin Press, 1996.

"Diamond Cartel Enlists UN in Effort to Quash Competition," National Center for Policy Analysis. Available online at http://www.ncpa.org/pi/internat/pd080300b.html (cited June 22, 2001).

Epstein, Edward Jay. *The Rise and Fall of Diamonds: The Shattering of a Brilliant Illusion*. New York: Simon and Schuster, 1982.

Even-Zohar, Chaim. "1999 Diamond Retail Jewelry Market Grew by 11 Percent," Diamond Industry Consultants Tacy Ltd., March 20, 2000. Available online at http://www.diamondconsult.com/TACY-Articles/mar190013.htm. (cited April 16, 2001).

———. "Conflict Diamonds, Illicit Diamonds, Rough Distribution Channels and Lack of Transparency," Diamond Industry Consultants Tacy Ltd., January 15, 2001. Available online at http://www.diamondconsult.com/TACY-Articles/Jan15017.htm. (cited April 5, 2001).

———. "Global Overview of the Diamond Industry Pipeline," Diamond Industry Consultants TACY LTD. Available online at http://www.diamondconsult.com/TACY-Articles/jun21001.htm. (cited April 16, 2001).

"The Gems of War," *Newsweek International*, July 10, 2000.

"Glass with Attitude," *The Economist*, December 20, 1997.

Greenhalgh, Peter. *West African Diamonds 1919–1983: An Economic History*. Manchester, Great Britain: Manchester University Press, 1985.

Hunter, Jennifer. "Business: Behind All the Glitter," *Maclean's*, December 29, 1997, p. 89.

Jackson, James O. "Business: Diamonds, Is Their Luster Fading?" *Time International*, March 4, 1996, p. 44.

Kanfer, Stefan. *The Last Empire: De Beers, Diamonds, and the World*. New York: Farrar Straus Giroux, 1993.

Koskoff, David E. *The Diamond World*. New York: Harper and Row, 1981.

Lenzen, Godehard. *The History of Diamond Production and the Diamond Trade*. New York: Praeger Publishers, 1970.

"Lust for Diamonds Kills Thousands in African Wars," CNN, January 12, 2000. Available online at http://

www.cnn.com/2000/WORLD/africa/01/12/ africa.diamonds/index.html. (cited May 10, 2001).

Ransdell, Eric. "War for the Sake of War," *U.S. News and World Report,* July 17, 1995.

Ratnesar Romesh, and Peter Hawthorne. "Time Select/ Global Business: A Gem of a New Strategy," *Time,* September 25, 2000.

Silberstein, Ken. "Diamonds of Death," *The Nation,* April 23, 2001.

Smith/Perth, Roff. "Marketing: In a Few Weeks' Time, as the Leaves Turn to Gold around the Shores," *Time International,* August 29, 1994.

Stein, Nicholas. "The De Beers Story: A New Cut on an Old Monopoly," *Fortune,* February 19, 2001.

"Washed Out of Africa," *The Economist,* June 3, 2000.

—Evelyn Hauser

ECONOMIC SANCTIONS: A VALUABLE WEAPON?

Afghanistan under the Taliban, Angola, Burma (Myanmar), Burundi, Cuba, Ethiopia, Eritrea, Iran, Iraq, India, Liberia, Libya, North Korea, Pakistan, Sierra Leone, South Africa, Sudan, and Yugoslavia are just a few of the countries that have been subjected to economic sanctions over the past few decades. At times carried out with group support (multilateral)—as in the cases of South Africa and the Taliban—or initiated by one country with little international backing (unilateral)—as in the case of Cuba by the United States—sanctions are a diplomatic tool used in lieu of force to indicate displeasure in a country's behavior and to encourage change. Sanctions can be initiated for a number of reasons, including discouraging armed conflict, hindering drug trafficking, and preventing weapons proliferation. They may be applied to the target country via arms embargoes, a withdrawal of diplomatic relations, reducing or cutting off foreign aid, limiting or ending trade, or various other means.

While the aim of sanctions is to apply pressure on a country's leadership to bring about a desired result, the problem exists that such pressures could, and often do, backfire. If sanctions limit the number of supplies coming into a country, that country's government can better control the distribution of goods. The general population of a country targeted by sanctions is rarely untouched by the measures. As scarcity of supplies increases and conditions in a country worsen, the people are likely to consider those who are applying the sanctions as the source of their problems, rather than see their government as responsible. This is the situation that has developed in Iraq. Subjected to sanctions at the end of the Persian Gulf War (1991), the conditions of the Iraqi people have worsened over more than a decade. As a

THE CONFLICT

Economic sanctions are a tool in international relations used in order to attempt to force one country to comply with another's wishes. The United States is by far the largest implementer of economic sanctions in the world. While some see sanctions as a low-cost method for accomplishing foreign policy goals, the toll in human suffering is often extreme, due to shortages in food, medicine, and other basic supplies. It is also argued that sanctions damage international relations and exact a high price on the sender in terms of lost jobs and trade opportunities.

Political

- Economic sanctions are sometimes imposed to achieve goals, such as democratization, or to condemn practices, such as human rights abuses and terrorism.

Economic

- Sanctions are ostensibly an economic issue, although ramifications are often humanitarian as well. The idea is to punish countries for reprehensible behavior by restricting trade with them, thus forcing them to change their policy, but economic sanctions may often have a greater effect on a country's general population than on its leaders.

result public opinion has turned more negative towards the United States, the main proponent of the sanctions, than it has against Iraq's authoritarian leader Saddam Hussein.

As in the instance of Iraq, sanctions often have a negative impact on a population of the targeted country, though this is not their intent, while the true purpose of the restrictions just as often is left unfulfilled. After more than 40 years of sanctions against the island nation of Cuba, the United States has failed to achieve its goal of ousting Fidel Castro and his communist regime from power in that country. Meanwhile, the Cuban people experience shortages in supplies and look for assistance from other sources while the United States denies itself what could be a lucrative trading relationship with its southern neighbor. In Iraq, more than 10 years of sanctions has seen the erosion of the population's health. The Iraqi health care system has experienced a breakdown, as available medicine stocks are not nearly enough to cover the people in need. According to a 1997 Multiple Indicator Cluster Survey carried out by the Iraqi government and UNICEF, 32 percent of children under age five were malnourished, indicating a jump of 72 percent since the time of the Gulf War in 1991.

When sanctions are not well defined, fail to receive broad support, and possess no clear goal, their use inflicts hardship and suffering on people. When applied with a consensus of agreement, with a clearly defined purpose and course of action, sanctions can achieve their goal. One case in point is South Africa. After South Africa implemented the stratified racial system called apartheid in the 1950s, under which it was ruled by a white minority while its predominantly black population lived in oppression and poverty, many countries, including the European Community and the United States, used sanctions to discourage the policy's continuation. Over the course of more than 10 years, the sanctions remained in place. South Africa revoked the legal framework surrounding apartheid in 1991, and gradual forms were instituted until free all-race elections were held in 1994. In this instance, sanctions were a success. In instances where such a high level of international support is absent, however, sanctions can be far less effective, and the people suffer. Given their increasingly frequent use on the world stage, how valuable a weapon are economic sanctions?

HISTORICAL BACKGROUND

Economic sanctions are a way of attempting to force one country (the target) to comply with the wishes of another country or organization (the sender). According to the Heritage Foundation's "User's Guide to Economic Sanctions" (O'Quinn, June 1997), these measures can include:

> limiting exports to the target country; limiting imports from the target country; restricting investments in the target country; prohibiting private financial transactions between a sender country's citizens and the target country's citizens or government; and restricting the ability of a sender country's government programs . . . to assist trade and investment with the target country.

There are a number of reasons why a country or organization may choose to enact economic sanctions. According to the Heritage Foundation these can be divided into three main categories: "national security objectives; other foreign policy objectives; and international trade and investment dispute resolution."

National security is the issue when one country invades another. To express its disapproval, a sender country (or organization such as the UN) may impose sanctions. This was the case when the United Nations agreed to sanctions in response to Iraq's invasion of Kuwait in 1990, as well as when the former Yugoslavia sent troops into breakaway republics. Stopping weapons proliferation also falls under the category of national security. Agreements such as the Wassenaar Arrangement, the Missile Technology Control Regime, and the Australia Group attempt to restrict the export of military technology and equipment. The aforementioned agreements are all multilateral sanctions in which the United States participates. The United States also occasionally imposes controls on the export of military technology to countries that, while not direct threats, may be perceived as potential aggressors.

Evidence linking a nation's government to terrorist activity is another reason for imposing sanctions. It is on this basis that the United States forbids all investment in Iran and has severe restrictions on trade with that country. The United States also limits trade with Cuba, Iran, Iraq, Libya, North Korea, Sudan, and Syria under the same justification.

Sanctions can also be imposed for a variety of foreign policy objectives, including encouraging democratization in the target nation. For example, the military government of Burma (also known as Myanmar) denied that it had been defeated in a May 1990 election, and it kept opposition leader Aung San Suu Kyi under house arrest for six years. On May 20, 1997, in response to the government's continued refusal to follow democratic practices, then-U.S. President Bill Clinton (1993–2001) an-

CHRONOLOGY

1960 U.S. President Dwight Eisenhower severs economic relations with Cuba and imposes trade restrictions.

1980 The United States enforces a grain embargo and oil pipeline sanctions against the Soviet Union; both are declared failures and called off the following year.

1986 The United States and the European Community impose sanctions against South Africa in protest of apartheid.

August 6, 1990 After Iraq invades Kuwait, the United Nations (UN) imposes sanctions against Iraq.

January 16, 1990 to February 28, 1991 The Persian Gulf War occurs. U.S. and NATO forces take action to eject Iraqi leader Saddam Hussein from Kuwait after Hussein refuses to evacuate.

1992 The UN imposes sanctions against Libya, demanding the extradition of bombing suspects in the 1988 Pan Am flight 103 attack.

August 8, 1993 Most sanctions against South Africa are lifted in response to ongoing reforms in that country.

1995 An oil-for-food program is enacted by the UN in an effort to alleviate the suffering of the Iraqi people due to continued sanctions against their country.

March 1996 The Helms-Burton Act is passed by the U.S. Congress, allowing the United States to punish other countries who do business with Cuba in violation of the U.S. unilateral sanctions against that country.

May 30, 1996 The United States imposes trade restrictions against China in concern over environmental ramifications of the Three Gorges Dam project.

August 5, 1996 The U.S. Congress passes the Iran/Libya Act, which punishes non-U.S. companies that invest more than $40 million in petroleum resources in those countries.

November 27, 1996 The UN General Assembly calls for the repeal of extraterritorial laws and sanctions against companies of third states who violate unilateral sanctions.

March 1997 U.S. President Bill Clinton eases travel restrictions to Cuba.

1999 The UN lifts sanctions against Libya when its leader, Muammar Qaddafi, agrees to release the Pan Am bombing suspects for trial.

October 19, 2000 Speakers in the UN General Assembly condemn the use of unilateral economic sanctions.

November 9, 2000 The UN General Assembly calls for the United States to end its long-standing embargo against Cuba. This is the ninth such request from the Assembly in nine years.

November 15, 2000 UN Secretary General Kofi Annan speaks to the International Rescue Committee about the humanitarian impact of economic sanctions.

December 19, 2000 The United Nations Security Council imposes new sanctions against the Taliban in Afghanistan.

April 2001 The UN considers sanctions against Uganda, Burundi, and Rwanda for their looting of natural resources from their mutual neighbor, the Democratic Republic of Congo.

May 2001 Sanctions are issued by the UN against Liberia.

nounced that the United States would not engage in any new investments in the country. Going a step further, some U.S. states such as Massachusetts initiated sanctions of their own against Burma to further restrict relations with that country. These sanctions, however, were overturned by the U.S. Supreme Court.

Human rights violations pose another foreign policy objective that may prompt the use of sanctions. Ironically, it can be argued that sanctions themselves have caused large-scale violations of human rights. Especially in countries such as Iraq and Cuba, sanctions have caused extreme suffering and have denied many people such basic necessities as food, safe water, and emergency medical treatment. Other motivations for the application of sanctions include drug trafficking—applied by the United States against Colombia in 1996—and environmental protection—initiated by the United States against China for its Three Gorges Dam project in 1996, which threatens a wide expanse of land and requires the relocation of millions.

A MAN HOLDS A PRO-CUBAN SIGN AT A RARE BASEBALL GAME BETWEEN THE CUBAN ALL STARS AND THE BALTIMORE ORIOLES. THE UNITED STATES HAS MADE FEW EFFORTS TO EASE RESTRICTIONS OF ITS SANCTIONS AGAINST CUBA, DESPITE INTERNATIONAL DISAPPROVAL. *(The Gamma Liaison Network. Reproduced by permission.)*

When it comes to international trade and investment dispute resolution, economic sanctions are usually limited. Their use depends upon the degree of the infraction committed by the target country. Such disputes are more commonly resolved through mediation by the World Trade Organization (WTO), coalitions such as the European Union (EU), accords such as the North American Free Trade Agreement (NAFTA), or other bilateral agreements.

Unilateral vs. Multilateral Sanctions

Unilateral sanctions involve a single country restricting its business with another country, whereas multilateral sanctions involve several countries agreeing to cut off financial interaction with the target country. Many multilateral sanctions are imposed through actions of the United Nations Security Council. The United States is virtually the only country in the world that imposes unilateral sanctions, certainly the only one that does so with any regularity.

During the Cold War, between 1945 and 1989, the United States primarily imposed sanctions against communist countries to prevent them from developing and gaining access to weapons technology. Sanctions were also employed as a response to military aggression or the threat of such aggression. Such sanctions during the 1980s proved largely ineffective and, in fact, were at times even counterproductive. The grain embargo and pipeline sanctions against the Soviet Union are prime examples. In 1980, when the Soviet Union invaded Afghanistan, the United States condemned the action by refusing to sell grain to the Soviet Union. In response, countries such as Brazil and Argentina dramatically increased their production in order to fill the void in the market. In 1981 then-U.S. President Ronald Reagan (1981–89) revoked the embargo, declaring that it was not achieving its goals. The pipeline sanctions, attempting to cut off the Soviet oil supply, were equally unsuccessful and were also aborted.

In the mid-1990s, during the Clinton administration, economic sanctions reemerged as a popular weapon in the U.S. arsenal in battles ranging from terrorism to drug trafficking. According to a 1997 study by the National Association of Manufacturers, between 1993 and 1996, the United States imposed new economic sanctions on more than 30 countries. Many of these sanctions were unilateral, meaning they did not have broad international support. The organization estimates that sanctions denied American companies 2.3 billion potential customers—42 percent of the world's population—constituting $790 billion in export markets, or 19 percent of the world's total market.

Unilateral sanctions are increasingly ineffective in a more globalized economy. When the United States, for example, decides it will not trade with a country, there are many more nations ready to step in and take its place. Even in the case of the multilateral UN sanctions against Iraq, illegal trade across the border with Turkey, Syria, Jordan, and Iran poses a threat to the ability of the sanctions to isolate the target country and achieve their purpose. Due to a lack of compliance by many other countries, the effectiveness of sanctions suffers.

The United States has instituted several acts in the 1990s in an effort to combat this problem. The Helms-Burton Act and the Iran/Libya Sanctions Act threaten punitive action against companies from countries that do not restrict business in Cuba, Iran, and Libya. These acts, however, run the risk of angering third-country corporations, who in turn can retaliate against U.S. companies by refusing to do business with them. In the instance of unilateral sanctions, such laws by the United States are seen as an attempt to coerce international compliance with U.S. goals. Many countries have responded to U.S. actions like the Helms-Burton Act by passing so-called "blocking statutes." These laws, already enacted by Canada and the European Union, compel these countries not to follow the U.S. legislation such as the Helms-Burton Act or the Iran/Libya Sanctions Act. They place the same restrictions on U.S. subsidiary companies located in Canada or EU nations, thus putting these corporations in the awkward position of being bound to two conflicting sets of requirements.

The Iran/Libya Act, passed on August 5, 1996, threatened punitive action against any U.S. or foreign company that invested over $40 million in either Iran or Libya, especially in the hydrocarbon sector. The Cuban Liberty and Democratic Solidarity Act, commonly known as the Helms-Burton Act, was signed in March 1996. The expressed intention of the act was to encourage Cuba's democratization. As it targeted primarily European and Canadian investors in Cuba, however, the act raised questions as to the scope of U.S. jurisdiction and to what extent one country can enforce its policies beyond its national borders. For example, does the United States have the right to tell a Canadian airline that it cannot service Cuba? Canada does not think so. The law goes so far as to state that products consisting of more than 20 percent of U.S.-made components can not be sold to Cuba by any company and those with between 10 to 20 percent require a license to be sold. The fact that the United States felt the need to pass the Libya/Iran Act and the Helms-Burton Act is an indication of the flaws inherent in unilateral sanctions. Without the cooperation of other nations, sanctions have limited potential to injure the economy of the target country. Indeed, unilateral sanctions can at times violate international law. On October 19, 2000, several speakers in the UN General Assembly condemned unilateral sanctions on this basis and on the basis that they were an infringement on the principles of State equality and presented barriers to free movement and international commerce.

Pros of Economic Sanctions

When one country engages in action that others feel is reprehensible, the disapproving nations often assume a moral obligation to react. While war is the most extreme and unequivocal expression of such disapproval, for many reasons it is usually not the most appropriate. War is costly for everyone involved, both financially and in terms

of human repercussions. Economic sanctions are often seen as a more humane method of getting one country to comply with the wishes of another without resorting to violence. In theory the repercussions are primarily at the upper level, and the primary injuries are sustained by the government and large corporations rather than by the people of the targeted country.

Another argument for sanctions, in the case of Iraq for example, is that it allows the sender to direct where that country's income is going. According to Patrick Clawson of the Washington Institute for Near East Policy (Gwen Ifill, interview, May 3, 2000), "if the sanctions weren't in place, the situation would be worse in Iraq because Saddam [Hussein] would spend money on arms and on arms industry. . . . And if there weren't UN controls which force [Hussein] to spend money on humanitarian goods, I think he would be using that money for nefarious purposes instead."

When combined with other factors, sanctions can be a powerful incentive in encouraging governments to change their policies. One case in point is South Africa. The European Community (currently known as the European Union) imposed sanctions against South Africa in the mid-1980s due to its policy of apartheid. Also at this time, in 1986, the U.S. Congress imposed strict trade limitations with South Africa, overriding President Ronald Reagan's veto. The South African economy, which had grown rapidly from the end of World War II (1939–45) through the 1970s, suffered under the sanctions, which resulted in a lack of investment capital. Diplomatic pressure from outside and civil unrest and violence within the country, led to the election in 1989 of the reformist presidential candidate F.W. de Klerk. Changes in South Africa's apartheid policy were enacted gradually. In 1989 de Klerk did away with the Separate Amenities Act. The following year he repealed a ban on 33 opposition groups that had spoken out against apartheid, including the African National Congress (ANC). Also in 1990 ANC leader Nelson Mandela was freed after 27 years in prison. In January 1991 black students were allowed for the first time to enter all-white public schools. That year saw the repeal of other apartheid laws as well, and on July 10, 1991, U.S. President George Bush (1989–93) lifted most U.S. sanctions against South Africa. On October 8, 1993, the UN rescinded most of the remaining sanctions against the country.

Sanctions tend to be most successful when they are multilateral and have a clear, specific, and

SANCTIONS AND THE UNITED NATIONS

Article 41, Chapter VII, of the United Nations Charter allows the organization's Security Council to "apply measures not involving the use of armed force in order to maintain or restore international peace and security." In other words, the Security Council is authorized to impose sanctions on countries. In the organization's history it has called upon its Member States to take such action 15 times, including against the countries of Afghanistan, Angola, Ethiopia and Eritrea, Federal Republic of Yugoslavia/Kosovo, Haiti, Iraq, Liberia, Libya, Rwanda, Sierra Leone, Somalia, South Africa, Southern Rhodesia, Sudan, and the former Yugoslavia.

Though the United Nations may issue multilateral sanctions against a country, the action does not mean that all Member States are in agreement. In December 2000 Pakistan criticized plans to tighten economic sanctions against the Taliban in Afghanistan. The sanctions were targeted specifically at the Taliban and exempted opponent groups in the north. Pakistan asserted that sanctions should be applied to Afghanistan as a whole rather than piecemeal to different opposition groups in the country. Additionally, for the ninth time in as many years the UN General Assembly called for the United States to end its unilateral sanctions against Cuba. The sanctions, in place since 1960, restrict economic, commercial, and financial transactions between the two countries.

In an attempt to expand the effectiveness of its sanctions against Cuba, the U.S. Congress in March 1996 enacted the Helms-Burton Act, which sought to punish third countries and companies who did business with Cuba, in violation of U.S. sanctions. In other words, the United States wanted to punish countries that did not comply with its unilateral sanctions against Cuba,

even though those countries were not party to supporting the sanctions in the first place. In August 1996 the United States followed-up on the Helms-Burton Act with the Iran/Libya Act, which, in an attempt to make sanctions more effective against those countries, punished non-American owned companies for investing more than US$40 million in petroleum resources in Libya or Iran. These measures generated anger in many nations, which saw the U.S. laws as an effort to control their practices. On November 27, 1996, the UN General Assembly called for a repeal of unilateral extraterritorial laws and sanctions such as the Helms-Burton and Iran/Libya Acts. It encouraged Member States not to comply with such laws because they ran contrary to the UN Charter, impeded the liberalization of world trade, and hurt the economies of developing nations. Despite the Assembly's appeal, the Helms-Burton and Iran/Libya Acts remain in place in the United States, though foreign compliance with the U.S. laws may vary.

While the United Nations can issue sanctions and reprove countries for acting outside of its Charter, as in the case of the United States with the Helms-Burton and Iran/Libya Acts, it can not enforce such measures. The success or failure of sanctions issued by the United Nations is dependent on the cooperation of its Member States. Additionally, the United Nations has no control over the laws passed by its members. The U.S. measures, while against the UN Charter, are valid in the United States. Their continuation or their repeal depends on the U.S. Congress, which is not obliged to bow to the requests of the United Nations if it does not so choose. It is actions like these, and the difficulty of obtaining true multilateral agreement, that make effective sanctions difficult to achieve.

limited aim. The sanctions against South Africa had a specific goal—the end of apartheid—and were successful in meeting that goal. In contrast, sanctions against the Middle Eastern country of Iraq have met with much less success, though restrictions have been in place for more than 10 years. Patrick Clawson of the Washington Institute for Near East Policy contends that one of the reasons why the Iraq sanctions have lasted so long and with such debatable efficacy is because there is no consensus in the international community that Hussein needs to be removed from office, which was the goal of the United States at the time the

sanctions were put into place. With the international community split on the purpose of the sanctions, their effect and the extent to which they are upheld suffers.

Cons of Economic Sanctions

In the United States economic sanctions are often seen as a low-cost way of compelling other countries to conform to international law or will on an issue, or even to the U.S. leadership's view of how things should be, such as in the case of Cuba, which has been subjected to decades of sanctions from the United States due to the Cuban government's adherence to communism. As one of the most powerful nations, the United States can wield heavy influence on smaller nations and their policies. The negative impact of economic sanctions are not as immediately evident as those of war, but they can be just as devastating and long lasting, for both the target and the sender.

Despite claims to the contrary on the part of senders, the population at large of a target country often suffers greatly under sanctions. Trade barriers mean that goods essential for survival— food, medical supplies—can not reach the country. While the elite can almost always find access to these goods, it is the poor who are hit hardest. Sanctions often make it difficult or impossible for even humanitarian aid to reach the people of a target country. For this reason, numerous humanitarian groups have expressed their opposition to sanctions in many cases. The supply shortages also create a flourishing black market, in which those with money can still obtain the desired products. This situation encourages illegal activity and exaggerates the gap between the wealthiest and poorest in the target country.

Sanctions exact a price from the sender as well as from the target. When imposing sanctions a nation must be willing to sacrifice its market in that country, which can at times mean considerable loss of revenue and jobs at home. This impact is often felt immediately, but there are also long-term implications. When a country gets a reputation for imposing economic sanctions liberally, as the United States has in the past decade, it makes other nations reluctant to do business with that country. If a nation feels that there is a real prospect of being cut off, it will be less willing to make an investment in developing economic relations with that supplier and will instead seek out what it perceives as more stable options. For these reasons the National Association of Manufacturers, an American business organization, opposes sanctions. According to a 1995 study conducted by the group, sanctions have lost the United States US$6 billion annually in export sales, and put 120,000 American jobs at risk.

Another disadvantage of economic sanctions is their increasing ineffectiveness in a global economy. Even in the case of multilateral sanctions, during which several nations band together to isolate the target country, there are often other suppliers ready to step in. In this sense the sender can end up not only hurting its own economic prospects, but also giving business to those countries with a conflicting agenda who choose not to comply with the sanctions.

Sanctions without Success

In addition to putting the sanctioned country's general population at risk, sanctions also run the possibility of accomplishing the opposite of their intended goal. One case in point is Libya. In 1982 the Reagan administration declared the Libyan government under Muammar Qaddafi to be associated with terrorist activities and imposed an embargo on oil from Libya, forbade the sale of technical equipment to the country, and banned American travel there. In 1985 Reagan extended the sanctions when Libya was implicated in terrorist attacks at airports in Rome and Vienna. The U.S. president issued a declaration stating that Libya was endangering the national security and foreign policy of the United States. He cut off all political and economic relations and mandated that any Americans in Libya leave the country. Animosity between the two countries escalated. The U.S. Navy held maneuvers in the Gulf of Sidra, which Libya considered its territory. The two countries had a run-in in these waters, after which Reagan ordered a bombing of Libyan missile sites, declaring that it was Qaddafi's intention to target U.S. diplomats worldwide.

In April 1986, after a suspected Libyan terrorist bombing in West Berlin, the United States attacked Qaddafi's compound, Libya's naval academy, and air bases in Tripoli and Banghazi. Fifteen people were killed, including Qaddafi's infant daughter, and 60 were wounded. It can be argued that in this case, economic sanctions did not avert violence, but rather were one step in escalating tensions that eventually led to events in which a number of people died. Neither the sanctions nor the military maneuvers in the country weakened Qaddafi's government; in fact, they appeared to cement his support base both within his country and in other Arab nations and confirmed perceptions of the United States as an imperialist aggressor.

In both Cuba and Iraq as well, sanctions appear to be in many respects self-defeating. While the goals of the sanctions have been to remove Fidel Castro and Saddam Hussein, respectively, from power, it can be argued that the sanctions have instead cemented their leadership. In order to remove a ruler from power in a democratic fashion, which is the goal of the sanctions against these countries, public support is necessary. The intention is that the people of the target country will turn against the leader, at least in part to have the sanctions overturned. Rather, it is more often the case that the leader uses the sanctions to turn public sentiment against the sender. Shortages give the leader greater control over the population in the form of rationing, and provides a scapegoat for any of the government's own faults. This is evidenced in Cuba, where government propaganda continues to portray Castro as a righteous David battling the imperialist American Goliath.

Regarding Iraq, it may seem that Saddam Hussein in fact supports the sanctions against his country. In a March 2001 summit meeting of Arab nations in Amman, Jordan, a resolution calling for the repeal of the sanctions was opposed by only one country—Iraq. Iraq's issues with the resolution were minor. The agreement would have compelled the country to respect Kuwait's sovereignty, which it has already done; the Iraqi delegates claim that this point implies that Iraq is not trustworthy, and they refused the resolution.

Another risk of economic sanctions is that they can provoke the target country into an escalating contest with the sender. Iraq, for example, rather than backing down when sanctions were in place, issued further threats against Kuwait. "If sanctions aren't lifted," the Iraqi foreign minister threatened, "no Kuwaitis should sleep well at night."

Controversy over Iraq

The United States and other Western nations have long had a precarious relationship with Iraq, depending on the country for oil, yet often disapproving of Iraqi politics. One major bone of contention has been Iraqi antagonism toward the state of Israel. Another has been its treatment of the Kurds within Iraq, and the genocide perpetrated against them by the Iraqi government. Yet despite condemnation of these policies, it is also the case that U.S. money and support cemented Saddam Hussein's hold on power in the first place.

Iraq has long played an important role in the international economy because of its oil production. In 1931 the country signed an agreement with the Iraq Petroleum Company, an international conglomerate composed of several Dutch, English, French, and U.S. oil companies. The agreement gave these companies the exclusive right to develop the oil fields in the Mosul area of the country in exchange for annual royalties paid to the Iraqi government. These payments increased under new agreements in 1950 and 1951. In 1952 they again increased, giving Iraq 50 percent of the profits. Between 1972 and 1975 Iraq nationalized all oil companies operating in the country. In 1973, when an international oil shortage caused prices to rise sharply, Iraq's revenue also rose accordingly.

Between the 1950s and 1990 oil revenues brought significant increases in the standard of living for the majority of the Iraqi population, including advances in agricultural production and health care. The infant mortality rate fell from 120 per 1000 live births in 1960, to 45 per 1000 in the late 1980s. After sanctions were enacted against Iraq the rates skyrocketed to more than 100 by 1998.

Iraq's monarchy was overthrown in a 1958 revolution. Several leaders rose and fell in quick succession amid political turmoil. When Hasan al-Bakr resigned in 1979, Saddam Hussein took his place as president and chairman of the Revolutionary Command Council. That same year, an Islamic revolution arose in neighboring Iran. The Iranian dictator, the Ayatollah Khomeini, called for the overthrow of the Iraqi government. War broke out between the two countries on September 16, 1980, when Iraq invaded. The United States supported Hussein's forces throughout the indecisive eight-year war. The countries arrived at an inconclusive peace agreement on August 20, 1988.

Throughout the 1980s the United States and Britain kept Hussein's regime supplied with electronics, chemicals, and other goods, and provided an ample market for Iraqi exports. When the war ended Hussein attacked the Kurds, a minority in his own country who had sided with Iran during the fighting. The Iraqi army used chemical weapons and nerve gas against the Kurds, many of whom were forced to flee to Turkey and Iran. The United States and Britain not only continued their supplies to Iraq. The war against the Kurds entailed the destruction of agricultural areas, and the United States offered more subsidized food to Iraq, declaring that it would allow the country to better handle human rights issues.

When Hussein invaded neighboring Kuwait on August 2, 1990, however, with the intention of obtaining the oil reserves there, the United States and other Western powers withdrew their support and cut off all aid to Iraq. The United Nations Security Council called for Iraq's withdrawal from the council on August 3, and on August 6 it imposed an international trade ban against the country. The United States and its NATO allies sent troops to Saudi Arabia in an operation called Desert Shield, to prevent a possible attack on that country and present a unified front against further Iraqi aggression.

Iraq failed to comply with a November 29 Security Council ultimatum to evacuate Kuwait by January 15, 1991, and on January 16 and 17, the United States led massive air attacks on Baghdad,

FINGER-POINTING OVER WHO IS RESPONSIBLE FOR THE IRAQI PEOPLE'S SUFFERING UNDER ECONOMIC SANCTIONS HAS INCREASED AS INTERNATIONAL SUPPORT FOR THE SANCTIONS HAS WANED. *(Danziger. Reproduced by permission.)*

the Iraqi capital. Operation Desert Storm (the air attacks) and Operation Desert Sabre (the land offensive) lasted until February 28, 1991, by which point the Iraqi resistance had entirely crumbled. U.S. President George Bush declared a ceasefire. Kuwait regained its briefly interrupted independence, and a UN commission was sent to supervise while Iraq destroyed its medium-range missiles and chemical and nuclear weapons research facilities. The sanctions remained in place as inspectors suspected non-compliance regarding Iraq's weapons destruction efforts, a required component of the ceasefire agreement.

In April 1995 the sanctions were eased slightly with the introduction of the oil-for-food program. This gave Iraq permission to export $2 billion in oil every six months; of this revenue, $1.3 billion was to be spent on food and medicine, $600,000 would go into a compensation fund to pay for war damages, and $80,000 would go to pay UN expenses. While the oil-for-food program may have averted a truly disastrous famine it has been inadequate in alleviating the day-to-day situation in Iraq. The UN estimated that Iraq needs $2.1 billion in food

and medicine every six months just to keep the already poor conditions from sinking lower. Revenue from the oil-for-food program is also unevenly distributed; much more of it goes to the northern region of the country than to the south; the north also receives significantly greater aid from international donors, even though the region comprises only 9 percent of the country's land area and 13 percent of the population. It does, however, contain 48 percent of Iraq's arable land. The north has historically been better off than the south, and this imbalance is perpetuated and compounded by the distribution of funds from the oil-for-food program.

Bureaucratic red tape has also prevented the oil-for-food program from being as successful as it could be. Whole shipments of humanitarian goods are often held up if the list includes one or two items to which someone on the UN sanctions committee objects. For example, pencils have been forbidden as part of aid packages. The reasoning is that the carbon in them could be used to coat airplanes to make them invisible to radar. As a result, millions of Iraqi children go without even

THE HUMANITARIAN COST

The UN representative of Burundi reported in October 1996 that since economic sanctions had been applied to his country, food production had fallen by 30 percent and industrial growth decreased 10 percent. The people were at risk of famine and an economic crisis was spreading to Burundi's neighbors. The Director-General of the World Health Organization (WHO), Dr. Hiroshi Nakajima, stated about Iraq in 1997 that, after six years, "The consequences of [the sanctions] are causing a near breakdown of the health care system, which is reeling under the pressure of being deprived of medicine, other basic supplies and spare parts." ("Iraqi Health System Close to Collapse," February 27, 1997) In February 1997 Iraq received only 30 percent of the medical supplies it needed to meet the needs of its people. The circumstances experienced by Burundi and Iraq are not unique. UN Secretary General Kofi Annan noted in an address to the International Rescue Committee on November 15, 2000, that "Too often, innocent civilians have become victims not only of the abuses of their own government, but also of the measures taken against it by the international community."

When sanctions are applied to a country it is often the people who suffer. As they are most often applied, sanctions limit the goods and services going in and out of a country. The country or organization issuing the sanctions, as the source responsible for the limited supplies, often becomes the recipient of backlash. Instead of putting pressure on a government to change its behavior, sanctions may actually create more popular support for the government, which can step into the role of provider for the now limited resources. The leadership can also use the sanctions to raise nationalist feelings against those who would interfere with the country's sovereignty by trying to impose their will on the country through coercive means.

In the case of Iraq, more than 10 years after sanctions were applied, malnourished children are a common sight, their condition evident by their distended bellies. Twenty-five to 30 percent of children between the ages of one and six are chronically malnourished. The United Nations estimated in 1997, that over one million Iraqi children did not have enough to eat. Malnutrition was not a problem in the country before 1991, when Iraq was pushed back from its takeover of neighboring Kuwait during the Persian Gulf War. Since the war and the economic embargo that followed, meager rations and high prices have meant that the average family spends 80 percent of its income on food.

Health is not the only area of life in Iraq affected by the sanctions. Education, infrastructure, and other elements of society have deteriorated significantly since sanctions were imposed in 1990. A 1997 Multiple Indicator Cluster Survey completed by the Iraqi government and UNICEF found that 96 percent of people in urban areas had access to a water supply. Only half the people in rural areas had this access. Additionally, people in rural areas had an immunization rate 10 to 15 percent below those in urban areas. Primary school enrollment for children between the ages of six and eleven years was reported at 73 percent, meaning that over a quarter of Iraqi children are missing out on an education. Virtually every aspect of public life has been touched by sanctions.

To offset the humanitarian impacts in Iraq, the United Nations implemented the oil for food program. Established in 1997, the oil for food program allows Iraq to trade an agreed upon level of oil for necessary supplies such as food. Under this program the first shipment of oil left Iraq in December 1996, and the first food shipments arrived in March 1997. As of 2001 a committee of the UN Security Council has approved contracts valuing US$18.5 billion. More than $13 billion in supplies and equipment have been delivered to Iraq since the program began. These measures, while helpful in alleviating some of the strain placed on Iraqi society due to the sanctions, can not be arranged for every nation that is subject to sanctions. In addition, such programs do not alleviate the cause of hardship, thus, the problem persists until that cause—the sanctions—is removed.

There will always be a cost in imposing sanctions on a country. No action meant to coerce change can bring about that change without a measure of harm. That is, after all, the intent—to make a situation so undesirable for the target country, whether through diplomatic ostracism, trade restrictions, or other means, that it will adjust its behavior accordingly in order to improve its circumstances. Often, however, economic sanctions harm those who are innocent of the infractions for which their country is being punished, while the political elite remains relatively unscathed and may even benefit from the sanctions. Special programs, such as the oil for food program for Iraq, and specific, realistic goals can help lessen the humanitarian costs that befall the people of a country under sanction. The welfare of the general population should be the responsibility not only of the target country, but of the sanctioning body as well.

the most basic in food, health, and educational materials.

As conditions in Iraq continue to deteriorate and worldwide oil production fluctuates, effecting supply to many nations, France and several other countries have begun to call for an end to the sanctions against Iraq. Pointing to the sanctions' lack of clear direction and their obvious negative impact on the general population, nations who once supported the economic sanctions are now divided over the matter.

The Case of Cuba

Like Iraq, Cuba has also been the subject of sanctions with a questionable purpose. Cuba has a long history of economic dependence on other countries. Under the dominion of Spain, the island's commerce was restricted largely to produce goods primarily for sale to the colonial power. In the nineteenth century, however, Spain opened Cuba's markets and U.S. investors came in large numbers, buying land and sugar refineries, as well as putting money into the transportation, tobacco, and banking industries. The United States began to eclipse Spain as the dominating force in the Cuban economy; a 1902 agreement guaranteed that a certain amount of sugar annually would be sold to the United States. While this system proved beneficial for Cuba's economy in some respects, providing a sense of stability and a guaranteed income, it also perpetuated a system in which the Cuban workforce remained underpaid and capital was consistently drained from the island.

It was partially in response to this economic inequality that Cuban dictator Fulgencio Batista's government was toppled in 1959. The revolution that put Fidel Castro in control promised to address the issue of this imbalance both within Cuba and in relation to the United States. This made the United States uneasy, particularly because the Cold War was in full swing, and the United States greatly feared what it perceived as the incursion of communism into the Western Hemisphere, only 90 miles from U.S. soil. U.S. President Dwight Eisenhower (1953–61) severed diplomatic relations with Cuba in 1960, and passed a partial trade embargo prohibiting the import of Cuban products.

By isolating the country economically the United States believed that Castro would eventually be forced to modify his policies or would be replaced. Instead, Castro, with a groundswell of popular support, undertook a program of increased nationalization. Among the businesses brought un-

der government control were $8 billion in U.S. assets. Rather than capitulate with U.S. demands on how Cuba should govern itself, the island nation appealed to the Soviet Union for support. The Soviet Union, grateful for both the ideological and economic alliance, offered its assistance.

With the Soviet Union/Cuba alliance, Cold War tensions were heightened. The United States, already sensitive to having a communist nation so close to its shores, was further alarmed at Cuba's closer ties with the Soviet Union and with the incoming Soviet assistance. In a plan engineered by the U.S. Central Intelligence Agency (CIA) the United States prepared to invade Cuba and assassinate Castro, believing that this action would eliminate the communist threat. The infamous Bay of Pigs invasion in April 1961 resulted in a terrifyingly close brush with nuclear destruction, but it had no effect on Castro's hold on power. The invasion, largely launched by CIA-trained Cuban expatriates, did not receive full U.S. support, and it failed in its endeavor. Little more than a year later, the Cold War reached its height with a standoff over Soviet missiles in Cuba. In October 1962 the Cuban missile crisis was resolved when the Soviet missiles were removed from Cuba and the United States agreed not to invade the island.

While Soviet missiles were no longer supplied to the island, Soviet support to Cuba continued. The Cuban economy managed to do well despite sanctions imposed by the United States in 1960. In many ways the economic relationship that Cuba had with the United States before communism was replicated in its relationship with the Soviet Union in the early years of Castro's regime. Cuba exported sugar and several other raw materials to the Soviet bloc in exchange for technology and manufactured goods.

When communism collapsed in Eastern Europe in the late 1980s, Cuba's $3 to $4 billion a year in aid dried up; the country also lost the market for over 80 percent of its exports. The country's gross domestic product fell 35 percent between 1983 and 1993, with the steepest decline between 1990 and 1993. In the early 1990s, to make up for this sudden loss, Cuba increasingly opened its economy to foreign investors and at the same time instituted strict rationing of basic necessities for the majority of the population.

In 1991 the Cuban government eliminated all references to Marxism from the constitution. In 1993 Castro allowed the use of the U.S. dollar in monetary transactions. At the same time, the United States began to allow Cuban Americans to send more money back to relatives in Cuba. Together these policies have brought significant sums of the currency into circulation in Cuba. In 1994 the Cuban economy began to recover from its losses of the previous decade, and in 1995, the government made explicit its goal to bring in more foreign currency. Foreign investment has grown steadily in the sectors of biomedical products and tourism.

The explicit goal of the United States in permitting more dollars to be transferred to Cuba was to encourage capitalism within the country in the hopes that it would translate into internal political opposition. While no such opposition materialized as of 2001, there has been a noticeable shift toward capitalist policies within Castro's government, although often in such a way that the primary beneficiaries are not the Cuban people, but investors from other countries.

Despite Castro's continued insistence on his adherence to socialist principles, Cuba is taking an increasingly active role in global capitalism. The government prides itself on the freedom of operation it allows foreign corporations, which is one indication of a country moving away from a socialist system. Money from Spain, the Netherlands, and other European countries has built luxury hotels, bars, restaurants, and other facilities to service tourists. The income from the tourist industry is currently $1 billion a year.

Yet at the same time, capitalist activity among the Cuban population itself is actively discouraged; the government restricts the entrepreneurial activity of its citizens to a limited scope. This means that the majority of the money generated by the tourist boom goes to either foreign investors or to the Cuban government. Those who are prospering have relatives abroad who send money back, or are benefiting from the illegal activity that tourism has spawned, including prostitution and other crimes. Meanwhile, unemployment remains at 25 percent.

Despite the continued persistence of U.S. sanctions, Cuba endures. The U.S. hope that the Cuban people will overthrow their leader has not been realized. The unilateral sanctions have been ignored by many countries and, in fact, serve as good propaganda for Castro's anti-American speeches. While the sanctions remain in place the United States loses out on what could be lucrative trade with Cuba and risks angering allies who do wish to trade with Cuba, but who risk doing so at the displeasure of Cuba's much larger and influential neighbor to the north.

RECENT HISTORY AND THE FUTURE

Toward the end of the Clinton administration in the United States it appeared that the sanctions against Iraq, which have faced increasing opposition in the UN, were nearing their end. The sanctions have come up against resistance from Russia, Spain, and France; Great Britain and the United States remain the sole hard-line supporters of the sanctions. Colin Powell, the U.S. Secretary of State under the George W. Bush administration (2000–), however, is in favor of revamped "smart" sanctions, which would be intended to ease the situation of ordinary Iraqis, but have a harder effect on Hussein's government.

The new plan would loosen restrictions on trade and would allow commercial flights to and from Iraq to resume. At the same time, Iraq's income from oil exports would continue to be directed through the UN, and increased control would be exerted to cut off sources of income outside the purview of the UN, such as oil smuggling. The intention of these measures is to bring more money into the country in the hopes of alleviating poverty, food shortages, and medical crisis, while at the same time limiting the control Hussein has over the Iraqi economy. Under the sanctions repression has increased and the Iraqi economy has become more centralized. Travel, freedom of speech, and the dissemination of information remain restricted, and anyone wanting to conduct trade abroad must petition the government in Baghdad for permission.

Despite opposition and the prospect of revised policies, many still see sanctions as the only possible recourse. In an interview by Ray Suarez for *PBS Online NewsHour* (April 25, 2001), U.S. Representative Tony Hall asserted that sanctions can and should be "sharpened," though he noted that humanitarian assistance is needed. "We've got to have . . . a better sanctions committee," he told Suarez. "We've got to . . . allow emergency equipment and emergency goods for humanitarian purposes to go in immediately. We need serums for cholera and diseases. We need more international workers. . . . as far as the sanctions on weapons of mass destruction, those in my opinion should not be lifted."

At the same time, the George W. Bush administration has vowed to take a more active role in attempting to remove Saddam Hussein from power. The Bush administration has indicated its intent to provide financial and material backing to the opposition in Iraq, with the intention of building a strong enough base to bring down Hussein's

FIDEL CASTRO LEADS PROTESTORS DURING A DEMONSTRATION IN HAVANA, CUBA, PROTESTING NEARLY FOUR DECADES OF U.S. EMBARGOES AGAINST THE COUNTRY. *(AP/Wide World Photos. Reproduced by permission.)*

government. The country's opposition groups, however, have historically suffered from a lack of organization and effectiveness. Political and religious divisiveness and the lack of strong leadership are a perennial problem. The possibility of a strong and broadly supported opposition movement arising in Iraq under the existing conditions is slim, even with U.S. support.

While opposition against continued sanctions in Iraq has grown, so, too, has opposition to the U.S. policy. On November 9, 1999, the UN General Assembly issued a declaration supporting the end of the embargo on Cuba. While this was the ninth time the UN had voiced disapproval of the embargo, this vote was the most strongly in favor of abandoning the sanctions. Only two countries, Israel and the United States, dissented; eight countries abstained from voting.

While reluctant to abandon its sanctions against Cuba the United States has made moves to ease the restrictions. In March 1997, after an appeal from Pope John Paul II, President Bill Clinton relaxed some travel and shipping restrictions to the island, restored direct humanitarian charter flights, and allowed Cuban Americans to send remittances of up to $1,200 a year back to relatives in Cuba. Additionally, in October 2000 the United States passed a law that allowed U.S. farmers to sell food to Cuba. It was a small concession, however, as the policy stipulated that Cuba must use U.S. dollars to purchase the food, and forbade American banks from helping to finance any transactions. The Cuban government scorned the policy as insignificant and stated that it would not buy goods from the United States.

It remains to be seen whether continuing trends toward free trade, both globally and specifically within the Americas, will have an affect on the sanctions against Cuba. In an April 2001 summit meeting in Quebec, Canada, President George W. Bush reaffirmed his commitment to free trade among the nations of the Americas. Cuba was not invited to attend the summit, which included representatives from 33 countries. The Bush administration stated that, despite the recent loosening of restrictions, the embargo against Cuba would remain firmly in place. It is estimated that the sanctions are costing the United States an estimated $1 billion in potential sales annually.

There are bills in the U.S. Congress that would amend the embargo to allow food and medicine to be sent to Cuba, as well as ease travel restrictions. These bills have a strong support base, and, while not momentous, if passed, they would certainly be a step toward normalized relations with Cuba, and would allow Cubans access to some much-needed goods.

A Valuable Weapon?

The human cost of sanctions continues to be documented, in Cuba, Iraq, and other nations. But there also exists a human benefit, as exemplified by South Africa. After free elections were held for the first time in 1994, the country began to heal the wounds of apartheid through the establishment of the Truth and Reconciliation Commission. It has since held another round of free elections and experienced a peaceful transfer of power from Nelson Mandela to Thabo Mbeki. Much remains to be done in South Africa to redress wounds gouged out of decades of social, economic, educational, and political division, but the first steps have been taken. Restrictions have been lifted and international assistance is once again flowing into South Africa. Had the international community not expressed its disapproval of apartheid and applied sanctions to discourage the policy's continuation, South Africans might still be living without many of the freedoms available to them today.

An alternative to the type of sanctions most commonly employed, such as those used on South Africa, which tend to target imports of supplies that are often needed by the target country's population, is the use of what is being called "smart sanctions." Smart sanctions aim to be more focused and more effective, with a lower humanitarian cost. They seek to punish those who have control over the target country's actions—the government and political elites—rather than the general public. To do this, smart sanctions will target the financial assets of a country and its leadership and establish mandatory measures early on to maintain a clear focus for the sanctions. By focusing on financial measures smart sanctions have a better chance of reaching the people in charge rather than inflicting humanitarian costs to the general population through the prohibition of much needed supplies through trade. Exemptions to some smart sanction measures could be made if they are considered to incur humanitarian costs.

In instances where sanctions might not be appropriate, where the costs to the population exceed the achievements of the restrictions, there are alternatives to consider. It is possible for a sender country to impose non-economic sanctions. Rather than impacting the target country's economy, these sanctions attempt to undercut the nation's legitimacy, prestige, or international reputation. These measures could include refusing to hold ministerial and summit meetings with the target country; restricting diplomatic relations with the country; denying the country admission to international organizations; denying foreign aid; pressuring other countries to deny the target nation foreign aid; and a variety of other actions. This type of sanction is primarily symbolic; but while there is less at stake for the target country, there is also little chance of non-economic sanctions harming the sender, and few if any humanitarian concerns.

Another option that may lessen the risk of humanitarian costs is the practice of conditional engagement. Conditional engagement combines the narrow use of sanctions with political and economic exchanges with a country. These interactions are made conditional on the basis of specific behavioral changes on behalf of the target country. For instance, conditional engagement could be used by the United States to encourage India and Pakistan to resolve their nuclear standoff, which at times has led to high tension in the region. Through offering incentives to these countries and tying their behavior to them, the United States could perhaps achieve its goal of maintaining a nuclear détente, without resorting to the full use of economic sanctions.

The effectiveness of economic sanctions as a tool of persuasion may or may not work. Much depends on the scope of the sanctions, their purpose, and the level of support behind them. What is clear is that economic sanctions alone are not the only non-violent means available to try to influence countries into compliance with international laws, agreements, and will. As a weapon of diplomacy and engagement, it is a tool that must be exercised carefully. UN Secretary General Kofi Annan stated in an address to the International Rescue Committee (November 15, 2000) that "Sanctions must and will remain an important instrument for compelling compliance with the will of the international community.... The challenge is to achieve consensus about the precise and specific aims of the sanctions, and then provide the necessary means and will for them to succeed."

BIBLIOGRAPHY

Annan, Kofi. Speech to the International Rescue Committee. United Nations, Press release SG/SM/7625, November 15, 2000.

Arnove, Anthony, ed. *Iraq Under Siege: The Deadly Impact of Sanctions and War.* Cambridge, MA: South End Press, 2000.

Center for Strategic and International Studies. *Altering U.S. Sanctions Policy.* Washington, DC: CSIS, February 1999.

Chacon, Richard. "Havana is polishing its old city," *The Boston Globe*, April 25, 2001.

Collins, Joseph J. and Gabrielle D. Bowdoin. *Beyond Unilateral Economic Sanctions.* Washington, DC: CSIS, March 1999.

Cortright, David and George A. Lopez. "Creating Incentives," an excerpt from *Sanctions and Contending Views of Justice: The Problematic Case of Iraq.* Available online at http://www.webcom.com/scripts/articles/stories/default.cfm?id=10589&category_id=39 (cited June 1, 2001).

Cortright, David and George A. Lopez, eds. *The Sanctions Decade: Assessing UN Strategies in the 1990s.* Lynne Rienner Publishers, 2000.

Drezner, Daniel W. *The Sanctions Paradox: Economic Statecraft and International Relations.* Cambridge, MA: Cambridge University Press, 1999.

Expert Seminar on Targeting UN Financial Sanctions, March 17–19, 1998. Available online at http://www.smartsanctions.ch/interlaken1.htm (cited June 29, 2001).

Flynn, Stephen E. "Beyond Border Control," *Foreign Affairs*, November/December 2000.

Haass, Richard N. "Economic Sanctions: Too Much of a Bad Thing," The Brookings Institute, Policy brief #34, June 1998.

Haass, Richard N., and Meghan L. O'Sullivan, eds. *Honey and Vinegar: Incentives, Sanctions, and Foreign Policy.* Washington, DC: Brookings Institution, 2000.

Hufbauer, Gary Clyde. *Economic Sanctions Reconsidered*, third ed. Institute for International Economics, 2001.

Hufbauer, Gary Clyde, et al. *U.S. Economic Sanctions: Their Impact on Trade, Jobs, and Wages.* Institute for International Economics, 1997.

Hyland, Julie. "TV Doctor Exposes Devastating Toll of Sanctions Against Iraq," World Socialist Web Site, March 11, 2000. Available online at http://wsws.org/articles/2000/mar2000/iraq-m11.shtml (cited June 1, 2001).

Ifill, Gwen. "Sanctioning Iraq," interview with Hans von Sponeck and Patrick Clawson. *PBS Online NewsHour*, May 3, 2000. Available online at http://www.pbs.org/newshour/bb/middle_east/jan-june00/iraq_5-3.html (cited June 1, 2001).

"Iraqi Health System Close to Collapse Says WHO Director-General," World Health Organization, Press Release WHO/16, February 27, 1997. Available online at http://www.who.int/archives/inf-pr-1997/en/pr97-16.html (cited June 27, 2001).

Leogrande, William M. "U.S. Policy is Consistent—but Wrong," *Los Angeles Times*, April 22, 2001.

Lindsay, James M. "The New Apathy," *Foreign Affairs*, September/October 2000.

MacLeod, Scott. "Saddam in a Box," *Time*, April 9, 2001.

"Nearly One Million Children Malnourished in Iraq, Says UNICEF," UNICEF Information Newsline, November 26, 1997. Available online at http://www.unicef.org/newsline/97pr60.htm (cited June 27, 2001).

O'Quinn, Robert P. "A User's Guide to Economic Sanctions," The Heritage Foundation, *Backgrounder*, no. 1126, June 25, 1997.

Paul, James A. "Sixteen Policy Recommendations on Sanctions," Global Policy Forum, presented in Bonn, Germany, March 31, 1998. Available online at http://www.globalpolicy.org/security/sanction/jpreccs.htm (cited June 1, 2001).

Persaud, Avinash. "The Knowledge Gap," *Foreign Affairs*, March/April 2001.

Ramsay, William C. Testimony before the U.S. Senate Banking Committee on the Iran and Libya Sanctions Act, October 30, 1997. Available online at http://www.state.gov/www/issues/economic/971030_ramsay_sanctions.html (cited June 1, 2001).

Roy, Joaquin, and John M. Kirk. *Cuba, the United States, and the Helms-Burton Doctrine: International Reactions.* University Press of Florida, 2000.

Said, Edward. "Apocalypse Now." Available online at http://www.salam.org/iraq/apocalypse.html (cited May 21, 2001).

Schweid, Barry. "Powell Offers Rare Praise of Castro," Associated Press, April 27, 2001.

Snow, Anita. "Castro Criticizes Latin Nations," Associated Press, April 26, 2001.

"South Africa's Apartheid Era and the Transition to Multiracial Democracy," *Facts on File World News.* Available online at http://www.facts.com/cs/o94317.htm (cited June 1, 2001).

"Speakers Condemn Unilateral Economic Sanctions in General Assembly," United Nations, press release GA/9791, October 19, 2000.

Suarez, Ray. "Iraqi Sanctions," interview with Representative Tony Hall." *PBS Online NewsHour*, April 25, 2001. Available online at http://www.pbs.org/newshour/bb/middle_east/jan-june00/iraq_4-25.html (cited June 1, 2001).

United Nations Office of the Iraq Programme. "Oil for Food," United Nations. Available online at http://www.un.org/Depts/oip/ (cited June 27, 2001).

———. "Weekly Update, 16–22 June 2001," United Nations, June 26, 2001. Available online at http://www.un.org/Depts/oip/latest/wu26Jun01.html (cited June 27, 2001).

United Nations Office of the Spokesman for the Secretary-General. "Use of Sanctions under Chapter VII of the UN Charter," May 2001. Available online at http://www.un.org/News/ossg/sanction.htm (cited June 1, 2001).

Weiss, Thomas G., David Cortright, George A. Lopez, and Larry Minear, eds. *Political Gain and Civilian Pain.* Lanham, MD: Rowman and Littlefield Publishing, 1997.

Whitaker, Brian. "Saddam Supports Sanctions," *Guardian Unlimited* April 16, 2001.

—*Eleanor Stanford*

CURRENCY EXCHANGE: ECUADOR ADOPTS THE U.S. DOLLAR

Faced with the worst economic crisis in modern Ecuadorian history, President Jamil Mahuad appeared on television screens throughout the nation on January 9, 2000. In a stunning move, he announced in a twenty-minute speech that he would fight to reform Ecuador's economy with a series of abrupt changes. Foremost among these changes in Mahuad's plan, Ecuador's currency, the *sucre*—which had been plummeting in value along with the nation's economy—would be scrapped in favor of using the U.S. dollar as the standard currency. Mahuad also insisted that many of Ecuador's state-owned enterprises, which were extremely inefficient and tremendously overstaffed, would be sold off to private investors. Finally, Mahuad announced that his cabinet of advisors had resigned and that he planned to appoint ministers who would support his economic plan.

In light of the crises that had enveloped the country in the past year, Mahuad's announcement was born of desperation. After piling up billions of dollars in foreign debt to finance infrastructure schemes and subsidize the domestic economy, Ecuador defaulted on its bonds from foreign lenders in 1999. The annual inflation rate ran to almost 61 percent, and the nation's gross domestic product (GDP), the measure of goods and services produced, fell by about seven percent. Contributing to the loss, continuing low prices for oil—the most important source of Ecuador's foreign trade exports—meant that state-owned energy firms brought in less revenue to help pay off the debt and fill the government's coffers. As a result of these broader trends, about one in four Ecuadorians earned less than a dollar a day. In addition, with the failure of 16 banks in 1999, about 70 percent of the nation's deposits were temporarily frozen, hurting

THE CONFLICT

In January 2000, responding to a series of economic crises, Ecuadorian President Jamil Mahuad announced plans to replace the nation's currency, the *sucre*, with U.S. dollars and to privatize many state-owned enterprises. Within weeks, indigenous groups protesting his economic policies as unfair to the nation's poor forced Mahuad from office. His successor, Gustavo Noboa, however, announced that he would implement the dollarization and privatization policies, which were substantially carried out within the year.

Economic
- Ecuador's government came to rely too heavily on income from oil exports to subsidize domestic spending. When oil prices slumped in the 1980s, successive governments ran up huge budget deficits instead of drastically reducing spending. Calls for austerity in government spending were met with protests that sometimes turned violent.

- The country's foreign debt, at $13.7 billion, is too large for the country's economy to sustain, and Ecuador defaulted to international bond holders in 1999.

- In order to pay off its foreign debt, successive Ecuadorian governments printed up relatively large amounts of sucres, which spurred huge increases in domestic inflation.

Political and Social
- Without stable political leadership, including the democratic transfer of power between successive governments, economic reforms stipulated by the IMF will be harder to implement and the international business community will avoid investing in the country.

- Leaders of Indian groups within Ecuador argue that austerity measures, such as the switch to dollarization, will hurt the poorest segments of society.

- The continued interference by the military in Ecuadorian politics demonstrates the fragile character of democracy in the nation. Largely independent of the executive or legislative branches of the government, the military also controls vast economic resources within Ecuador for its own use. As long as military forces are not accountable to Ecuador's elected officials, international investors will be wary of the nation's stability.

the middle-class as well. Not all of the crises could be attributed to human failure, however. The disastrous effects of *El Niño* also wreaked havoc with the environment in 1998, leading to huge agricultural losses and a subsequent downturn in the vital sector of Ecuador's export market.

Mahuad's bold maneuver, ostensibly designed to reform Ecuador's economy in dramatic fashion, was also a bid to shore up his own sagging popularity among the Ecuadorian public while appeasing the country's ruling elite, comprised of business leaders and military officials. After a number of military coups, Mahuad was the country's fourth president in as many years, a pattern that characterized Ecuador's tumultuous political scene. Seventeen months after being elected to office, Mahuad sensed that his days as president were numbered unless he could announce decisive action to turn the economy around and thereby stabilize the country's fragile democracy. Indeed, in the first days after his action, Mahuad's strategy seemed to be working. The military high command announced that it would support Mahuad, and business leaders were generally pleased with his actions. Most Ecuadorians agreed, and approval ratings for the president's plan reached about 59 percent.

Less than two weeks after his announcement, however, Mahuad was ousted from office and replaced by the man he beat in the last presidential election, vice president Gustavo Noboa, who became Ecuador's fifth president in four years. Mahuad's overthrow began with a massive protest against his reforms by poor Indian farmers from Ecuador's highlands, who had in recent years begun to demonstrate their political power. With the assistance of some nationalist army officers under Colonel Lucio Gutierrez, thousands of the protesters stormed into Ecuador's Congress in its capital, Quito, on January 21, 2000. Subsequently, Gutierrez and the Indians' leader, Antonio Vargas, announced plans to form a more populist government to replace Mahuad's reformist government. In the meantime, head of the armed forces General Carlos Mendoza declared that Mahuad had been forced from office and that he, Mendoza, was now leading the junta, or provisional government. Mendoza quickly stepped aside, however, after the United States suggested that another government ushered in by military junta would not be recognized by the international community. Vice President Noboa assumed the nation's highest office, and Mendoza had Gutierrez arrested. For his part, former president Mahuad publicly declared his support for the new president and urged him to carry on with the reforms.

ECUADORIAN PRESIDENT GUSTAVO NOBOA CONTINUES TO PUSH THROUGH ECONOMIC REFORMS, DESPITE PUBLIC CONCERNS OVER THE IMPACT OF THE REFORMS ON THE POOR AND INDIAN GROUPS. *(AP/Wide World Photos. Reproduced by permission.)*

HISTORICAL BACKGROUND

Pre-Columbian and Colonial Ecuador

The nation of Ecuador, located on the western coast of South America, was part of the indigenous Indian kingdom of Quito from about the year 1000. Sometime in the 1400s, it was subsumed into the larger Inca Empire of Peru before being conquered by the Spanish in 1532. As a Spanish colony, Spanish settlers controlled large areas of land and enslaved the aboriginal people to labor on the estates. The Spanish built a few administrative centers in the country, most notably at Quito, located in the highlands away from the coast. Even from the colonial period, tensions between coastal and highland dwellers existed because of the different, and sometimes conflicting, regional interests. Broadly speaking, residents of Quito were more conservative and allied with the country's military elite, while those living in the coastal city of Guayaquil, a more dynamic city for trade and commerce, provided much of the country's liberal leadership. Without free elections or universal suffrage, however, most Ecuadorians were shut out of the political system. The concerns of native Indians were almost completely ignored in the process, as were the fortunes of Ecuador's small African population.

As part of the move for independence from colonial rule, Ecuador joined with Colombia and Venezuela to form *Gran Colombia* under the leadership of Simón Bolívar and Antonio José de Sucre, who defeated the Spanish in the Battle of Pichincha in 1822. *Gran Colombia* proved to be a transitional step into individual sovereignty for the countries and the coalition ended in 1830. Ecuador's early years were unsettled; civil war broke out between conservative and liberal political elements; a border war with Colombia erupted in 1832; and regional tensions between Guayaquil and Quito threatened national unity. Throughout the nineteenth century, with the lack of strong federal leadership and lagging economic development, most of the country settled into local rule, with little interaction with the capital or other parts of the country. Much of this would change at the end of the century, however, as booming cocoa exports brought capital improvements to Ecuador's export sector.

Benefiting from its position as Ecuador's primary port, Guayaquil's political importance almost eclipsed the nation's capital during this period. The Revolution of 1895 ousted the conservatives from power and an almost uninterrupted period of liberal rule began. While the liberals lived up to their promises of limiting the power of the Roman Catholic Church in Ecuador, few other promises were kept and the government continued to be thoroughly corrupt and inefficient. A series of military juntas rocked the country in the 1920s and 1930s, as the country continued down an irregular path of limited economic development, political instability, and social inequality. Ecuadorian Indians played almost no role in the nation's political system and were dominated economically and socially by Ecuadorians who claimed European descent.

In addition to domestic social tensions Ecuador faced continuing border disputes with Peru over Amazonian territories that it claimed on its western border. In 1941 outright warfare broke out between the nations. The following year, under great pressure from the United States and the western Allies, Ecuador signed the Rio Protocol and eventually ceded most of the disputed territory to Peru. The agreement remained a source of bitterness for Ecuadorians for years to come, with the 1990s witnessing renewed hostilities with Peru over the region.

Modern Ecuador

The most significant changes in Ecuador in the first half of the twentieth century were ushered in by the establishment of a banana plantation by the United Fruit Company (UFC) in 1933. UFC had operations in several Central and South American countries by that time, and had gained a reputation for running the governments of these countries like "banana republics," that is, carefully monitoring and protecting its interests. For example, UFC not only owned about a million acres of land in Latin America, but the docks and communications networks of the primary banana-producing nation, Guatemala, as well. After World War II (1939–45), Ecuador gained a competitive edge over Central American countries for lower labor and production costs, and UFC raised exports accordingly. Between 1947 and 1955, export earnings for Ecuador increased eight-fold, and by 1960 the country was producing 30 percent of the world's banana exports. In addition to increased export revenues Ecuador also gained some infrastructure development related to banana production and export. After the mid-1950s, however, with banana production leveling off, Ecuador's leaders also supported further industrialization to diversify the country's economy. Using import-substitution policies similar to other Latin American countries, Ecuador raised tariffs on consumer goods and granted tax incentives to encourage the production of goods by domestic enterprises. While consumers sometimes paid higher prices for inefficiently produced domestic goods, the manufacturing sector of Ecuador's economy increased during the 1960s from 15.5 percent of the GDP to 17 percent. Notwithstanding this gain, Ecuador's economy remained tied to agricultural exports during this period.

The growth brought on by the "banana boom" held out hopes for the political realm as well. After 1948, three successive presidents were elected to office and served out their full terms, a novelty in Ecuadorian politics. But the ouster of the president in 1961, followed by an outright military junta in 1963, brought such stability to an end. The modernization of the economy continued, but without an accompanying series of political reforms. While Ecuador was increasingly tied to the international economy and took advantage of its growing ties to the world through improved communication and transportation networks, the country was by no means on a solid path to democracy. The government, intermittently under the direct control of the military, resorted to harsh repression to staunch opposition movements throughout the 1960s. Despite these measures, strikes and demonstrations continued to rock the country.

The discovery of oil reserves in the *Oriente* region of Ecuador in the 1960s heralded another period of economic growth. By 1972 oil was beginning to flow through pipelines owned by the Texaco-Gulf Corporation, and the government's share of the revenue promised to be huge. Once again, in 1972, a military junta overthrew the president, who had himself disbanded Congress in order to rule as a dictator not long before. This time, the military claimed that the government would mismanage the incoming revenues from oil exports and defended its actions by promising to manage the revenue in a manner to benefit the entire country. Despite this promise, military leaders funneled some of the oil revenue into their own pockets and invested the oil money in enterprises that would generate income for the military, not for the government. To stem opposition from international investors in the oil industry, the military also nationalized oil production, taking away the investment of Texaco-Gulf in the name of the Ecuadorian state. Now oil production and export would be a state-run enterprise. Now oil production and export would be a state-run enterprise. While output remained small in comparison to Middle East nations, Ecuador joined the Organization of Petroleum Exporting Countries (OPEC) in 1973. Despite the diversion to politically connected projects and corruption, oil revenue accounted for a large part of Ecuador's domestic budget from the early 1970s onward. By 1985 oil revenues accounted for 60 percent of the domestic budget.

The oil boom of the 1970s promised to transform Ecuador in many fundamental ways. Economic growth, as measured by per capita growth, was spectacular, reaching 11 percent in 1972 and 21.6 percent in 1973. Under the Industrial Development Plan, instituted by the military junta, manufacturing output increased by fourfold during the decade. By 1983 a majority of the population was urbanized, and literacy rates, life expectancy, and health care substantially improved for Ecuador's citizens. Yet there were troubling signs even during this golden age of the Ecuadorian economy. Despite the massive increases in export revenues, successive governments borrowed heavily to subsidize domestic consumption and infrastructure developments. The foreign debt, which stood at a half-billion dollars in 1975, grew to US$6 billion by 1982. Foreign loans were easily obtained against the promise of future oil revenues, a situation that changed dramatically when interest rates spiked in the late 1970s and oil prices plummeted in the early

1980s. The Ecuadorian economy, which had been growing at a pace of about three percent annually, was in sudden decline after 1981. Between 1982 and 1988, per capita GDP declined by 17 percent, and the ratio of debt relief payments to export earnings reached 33.4 percent by 1984. To make matters worse, general strikes in 1986 and 1987 and a major earthquake in the latter year caused additional economic losses. Rising expectations among the Ecuadorian public only seemed to make the situation more desperate. After a decade of economic growth and social improvements, many Ecuadorians had a hard time accepting the country's difficult straits.

Years of Crisis

Given the continuing political instability in Ecuador, attempts at reform were fitful and ineffective throughout the 1980s, as the country lurched from crisis to crisis. Gradually, however, the nation's leaders became committed to market reforms to deal with the economic crises. The most serious efforts were instigated under President Osvaldo Hurtado Larrea in 1983 to cut back on government spending, limit government subsidies for many consumer items, and devalue the sucre in accordance with guidelines of the International Monetary Fund (IMF), which was enlisted to help end Ecuador's economic problems. Hurtado's efforts, however, brought about strikes and protests that turned violent. His successor, Leon Feres Cordero, also attempted to introduce free-market reforms and likewise met with strong resistance. The failure of these reforms led Ecuador to default on its foreign debt payments in 1987. A major earthquake that interrupted oil deliveries through the Trans-Andean pipeline for two months was a contributing factor to the latest crisis.

Reform-minded leaders faced massive opposition from both ends of the political spectrum. The political elite had benefited enormously from decades of corruption and its connections to the heavily state-managed economy. By 1990 Ecuador was a country of about 150,000 civil service employees—in contrast to manufacturing employment of about 60,000—and the power of these bureaucrats as a political bloc was considerable. Well connected Ecuadorians also took advantage of lax oversight of government contracts and bank loans to line their own pockets, and large landowners continually blocked attempts at land reform that would benefit Indian farmers. For their part, the growing political consciousness of Indians was often directed at protesting against government subsidy cuts and other market reforms. On the other hand, the largest

CHRONOLOGY

1890s–1920s Exports of cocoa spur economic development along the coast.

1925 An economic downturn brings along a military takeover of government.

1948–1960 Ecuador enters into a period of relative political stability, with three presidents democratically elected.

1963 A military coup occurs, renewing political instability.

1972 Oil exports begin to flow from Ecuador's *Oriente* region. After a period of civilian rule, the military takes over again in order to control oil revenues and nationalize foreign oil holdings.

1973 The per capita growth rate in Ecuador reaches 21.6 percent.

1970s An era of massive government spending ensues. Despite increases in oil revenues, foreign debt balloons from a half billion dollars in 1975 to over $6 billion in 1982.

1978 A new constitution restores civilian government.

1980s High interest rates on foreign debt and depressed oil prices usher in economic and political instability.

1983 Austerity measures and the devaluation of currency requested by the IMF for debt service are met with violent protests and strikes.

March 1987 A massive earthquake, which interrupts oil deliveries through the Trans-Andean pipeline for two months, contributes to economic instability.

August 1998 Jamil Mahuad, mayor of Quito, wins the presidency over Gustavo Noboa, who becomes vice president.

1999 Ecuador is struck by the worst economic crisis in its modern history. GDP falls by 7 percent for the year, and the sucre loses 65 percent of its value against the dollar. Ecuador defaults on its foreign debt.

2000 Eighty percent of Ecuadorians live under the poverty line, up from 39 percent just five years earlier.

January 9, 2000 President Mahuad announces plans to dollarize Ecuador's currency and privatize many state-owned enterprises.

January 22, 2000 As a result of protests by indigenous political groups, Mahuad is overthrown and Gustavo Noboa takes over. With the backing of business groups, Noboa pledges to carry through on Mahuad's announcement of dollarization and privatization.

March–September 2000 The initial stage of dollarization stabilizes the economy. Interest rates and inflation drop, GDP begins to grow, and the IMF grants new financing and refinances outstanding foreign debt.

March 9, 2001 Deadline to exchange sucres for dollars are extended for 90 additional days.

Indian group, the Ecuadorian Confederation of Indigenous Nationalities (CONAIE), spoke out forcefully after its founding in 1986 for an end to officially sponsored corruption. CONAIE also argued for a pluralistic identity for Ecuador, one that acknowledged the distinct culture and history of indigenous people, along with a greater voice in political decisions.

The 1990s witnessed further deterioration of economic and social conditions in Ecuador. As oil prices remained low, export income failed to prop up Ecuador's budget as it had in the 1970s. With foreign debt service taking up a larger share of state revenue, government enterprises such as telephone service, health care, and electricity distribution fell into disrepair. For the hundreds of thousands of Ecuadorians living in squatter settlements outside of Quito and Guayaquil, living conditions were even worse, with substandard housing that lacked clean water or other necessities. The country also faced an increase in drug production associated with Colombian drug cartels, which established cocaine processing facilities in Ecuador because of the country's lax supervision and corrupt police and judiciary. Among the few bright notes, flowers and shrimp were added to Ecuador's list of major legitimate export products, and the country became the world's largest exporter of roses.

Politically, a series of governments continued to urge economic reforms, but could not muster sufficient consensus among rival political groups to unite the country behind any one set of proposals.

The most dramatic political upheaval occurred with the election of Abdalá Bucaram to the presidency in 1996. Although he campaigned on populist economic issues, including opposition to privatization and reform of the pension system, Bucaram pushed through austerity measures while in office. After Bucaram ordered prices for electricity doubled and even greater increases for natural gas and public transportation, another series of protests forced the president to declare a state of emergency. Citing Bucaram's unusual public behavior, including singing with a rock band and other outrageous appearances, Congress removed him from office on the grounds of mental incapacity. The deposed president fled to Panama, where he was subsequently charged in exile with stealing an estimated $26 million from the Ecuadorian treasury during his six months in office. Bucaram remained a force in Ecuadorian politics, however, as the candidate he endorsed in the next presidential election, Alvaro Noboa, placed second in a field of several candidates.

The incoming administration presided over the most disastrous year that the Ecuadorian economy had seen. Flooding from unusual *El Niño* weather patterns devastated the country's production and export of flowers, bananas, and other agricultural items. Prices for oil in the global market remained depressed. With oil income accounting for 50 percent of public sector revenue and 36 percent of export earnings, Ecuador's budget remained in crisis. Essentially bankrupt, Ecuador defaulted on its foreign bonds in 1999, and the banking system faced total collapse. A series of mismanaged loans to politically connected investors and a lack of regulatory supervision forced 16 banks to be taken over by the government, locking up 70 percent of deposits in the country. During the year, the value of the sucre plummeted from around 7,000 to 29,000 to the U.S. dollar, inflation reached 60.7 percent, and the GDP declined by 7.3 percent. So desperate were conditions that about one to three million of Ecuador's twelve million people by now worked abroad, with about a quarter million living in New York City and an additional 180,000 in southern California.

Dollarization, Privatization, and the Political Economy of Plurinationalism

With the country once again sliding into public protests and political infighting, President Mahuad declared a state of emergency and announced plans for a crash course in economic reform. For the moment, he fixed the value of the sucre at 25,000 to the U.S. dollar; after a brief period, Mahuad hoped to complete the "dollarization" of the economy, adopting the U.S. dollar as the exchange currency for Ecuador. In doing so, Mahuad would link Ecuador's wildly fluctuating economy with the more stable monetary policies of the U.S. Treasury. No longer would Ecuador's government be able to issue unlimited amounts of sucres to pay off loans or salaries, which would help reduce inflation by limiting the country's money supply. In addition, interest rates would now be set by the U.S. Treasury, which would help reform Ecuador's banking system.

While scrapping the nation's currency was a blow to its nationalist pretensions, the switch to U.S. dollars was not as dramatic as it might appear. For years, many Ecuadorians had preferred to keep their assets in dollars, aware that deposits made in sucres might become worthless as a result of hyperinflation. About 60 percent of all bank deposits were made in dollars, and the remittances sent into Ecuador from abroad, estimated at $1.3 billion, largely came in dollar denominations. Globally, about 90 percent of export commodities were priced in dollars, and 29 other countries already used the dollar as their official currency. In Latin America, Panama had used the dollar since its independence in 1903, and Argentina had adopted a currency board—certifying that its currency was fully backed by dollars—in 1991. Argentina's attempt to stem hyperinflation by linking its *peso* to the dollar was successful, and its economy stabilized after its introduction. Even communist Cuba stipulated that dollars be used by visiting tourists.

Because the use of dollars was familiar to many Ecuadorians, especially among the urban middle classes, reaction to the dollarization plan was positive. Most Ecuadorians hoped that the adoption of a more stable currency would have a host of beneficial effects on the economy, as it would increase confidence in the financial system. International observers, however, were skeptical of dollarization's impact without fundamental reforms of other segments of Ecuador's economy. First, the banking system remained corrupt, with bad loans continuing to drain resources away from legitimate investments. In fact, the switch to dollarization complicated matters even further by threatening to make it easier to funnel drug money in dollars through Ecuadorian banks. Second, dollarization would not in itself abate the budgetary problems that plagued Ecuador since the 1970s. Without easing subsidies and reducing the amount spent on servicing foreign debt, the government's finances would remain in disarray. Third, the lack of political consensus meant that implementing dollarization might introduce even more chaos into Ecuador's political arena. Without a comprehensive set of economic reforms to accompany dollarization, the impact of its stabilizing effects would be lost.

More controversial was Mahuad's announcement that he would push for the privatization of state-owned enterprises. Widely acknowledged to be inefficient, overstaffed, and unresponsive to market and consumer demands, the government's ownership of the nation's telecommunications and electricity networks, along with its extensive holdings among the country's oil production facilities, would be opened up to foreign investment. The decision to open up state firms to majority-foreign ownership sparked immediate criticism from Ecuador's labor unions, which viewed privatization as a step in firing many workers and decreasing the power of the unions in politics. CONAIE leaders as well criticized privatization and other changes in Ecuador's labor laws as designed to hurt the working classes, who would have less job security if the proposed reforms were implemented.

While Mahuad's popularity bounced from a low of less than ten percent approval before the declaration to over 59 percent approval for the reforms, public demonstrations led by CONAIE's Antonio Vargas brought thousands of Indian farmers to the streets of Quito shortly after the president's announcement. Seeking an opportunity to oust Mahuad, nationalist military leader Lucio Gutierrez joined with Vargas to declare a military junta against Mahuad. On January 21, 2001, after several countries condemned the move, the head of the armed forces, General Carlos Mendoza, announced that the junta would step aside so that Vice President Gustavo Noboa could assume office. The business community rallied around Noboa, who was one of Ecuador's top banana exporters, and the new president quickly assured the country that the promised dollarization of the economy would continue. Mahuad moved to the United States, where he had previously studied at Harvard University, and subsequently faced an indictment for his action to freeze Ecuadorian bank assets in 1999.

Noboa gained approval for the dollarization plan, which was passed by Congress on February 29, 2000. The first official day of the dollar's use as Ecuador's currency was set for September 12, 2000, although sucres would still be accepted as currency after that date. Because dollars were already widely used, an informal dollarization had already taken

MONETARY EXCHANGE RATES

number of Ecuadorian sucres equal to one U.S. dollar

Date	Sucres
1970s (fixed exchange rate)	25
12/83	54
07/84	67
01/85	109
06/87	206
12/87	280
06/88	550
12/88	500
12/89	648
1999	18,500
03/01	25,100

Source: Michael Handlesman. *Culture and Customs of Ecuador.* Westport, CT: Greenwood Press, 2000. Dennis M. Hanratty, ed. *Ecuador: A Country Study,* 3rd ed. Washington, DC: Library of Congress, 1991. Oanda.com web site. Available online at http://www.oanda.com/convert/classic (March 18, 2001).

ECUADOR'S EXCHANGE RATE WITH THE UNITED STATES HAS INCREASED MARKEDLY SINCE THE 1970S, FROM A LOW OF 25 SUCRES TO ONE U.S. DOLLAR TO A HIGH OF 25,100. *(The Gale Group.)*

place; the government also commenced an educational series to encourage the public to exchange sucres for dollars to ease the transition. For day-to-day transactions, however, the use of dollars presented some problems. Many Ecuadorians were confused by using both sucres and dollars during the transitional period, a matter not helped by the fact that ATM users might get currency in either denomination when they withdrew money. Many retailers and vendors rounded prices in sucres up in order to convert their prices into dollar-based values, a situation that caused some inflationary pressures in the economy and seemed to justify CONAIE's criticism of dollarization as discriminating against the poor. Indeed, in a country where two-thirds of the people earned less than $30 a month, it was difficult to conduct transactions in any bills larger than five-dollar denominations. Many Ecuadorians also lamented the demise of the sucre out of nationalist sentiments, viewing the adoption of the U.S. dollar as yet another example of the nation's decline.

THE IMF, ECUADOR, AND GLOBALIZATION

Organized in 1944 by the Allied powers in the concluding days of World War II, the International Monetary Fund was designed to promote economic cooperation by stabilizing exchange rates and providing short-term loans to member nations. The IMF has expanded its services and now helps to create development and recovery plans for nations in addition to its international financial services.

The IMF has had a troubled relationship in its role as advisor to Ecuador in the past two decades. Its calls for raising taxes, cutting government subsidies on consumer items, and reforming the banking system have met with political resistance by Ecuador's leaders, who generally have not been willing to follow through on measures that were sure to prove unpopular with the public. The IMF has also pointedly criticized Ecuador's political instability as contributing to its economic problems.

In the midst of its economic crisis, Ecuadorian officials suspended negotiations with IMF representatives in October 1998. Talks resumed during the following year, although President Mahuad's weakening domestic support meant that further economic reforms could not be implemented in line with IMF guidelines. During the dollarization process, however, Ecuador and the IMF worked together to ensure a stable transition; as a result of this collaboration, a twelve-month IMF standby credit of $304 million was granted in April 2000 to help complete economic stabilization and recovery in Ecuador.

CONAIE has led domestic opposition to the IMF's role in Ecuador's economy. Along with other working class and indigenous groups, CONAIE has argued that the IMF has worsened the economic suffering of Ecuador's poorest citizens. With important decisions over Ecuador's future now made in conjunction with international agencies, some Ecuadorians also deem the IMF, with its calls for economic austerity and reform, an unwelcome interference on the country's political life.

Despite the criticism, dollarization was substantially completed by the September starting date. The government estimated that about 98 percent of the $400 million worth of sucres had been exchanged, and it was working to convert sucre deposits frozen in the previous year's banking fiasco into dollars for withdrawal. President Noboa had also started discussions with the IMF that resulted in offers to inject additional funds into Ecuador's economy to ease the monetary crunch during the transition, as the country had only about $100 million left after exchanging sucres for dollars. Working with IMF advisors, Noboa and finance minister Jorge Guzman renegotiated payments to resume Ecuador's debt obligations and saved the country about $300 million in the process. Further aid from the IMF was pending as the agency awaited passage of several additional economic reforms by Ecuador's Congress. In March, the IMF announced that it would grant Ecuador about $2 billion over three years to help Ecuador through the initial transition period.

Finance Minister Guzman's resignation in May 2000, in protest over stronger reform measures which the president was reported to have opposed, dimmed hopes that Ecuador's privatization process would stick to IMF's demands. Although Congress had approved money for an additional trans-Andean pipeline to increase oil production, decreasing energy subsidies, which cost the government an estimated $360 million annually, was a political bombshell. There was also continued opposition to dollarization itself from CONAIE, which pointed to the record-high monthly inflation rate of 14.3 percent in January 2000—just as the dollarization plan was announced—as evidence that wages would be eroded through the scheme. While inflation declined to 1.4 percent by August 2000, CONAIE nevertheless ordered a series of strikes to coincide with the official dollarization date in September. In the meantime, the government was granted a respite from the worst of its economic crisis by rising oil prices, which brought in higher revenues to ease the ongoing budget crunch.

RECENT HISTORY AND THE FUTURE

The immediate effects of dollarization were judged a success by most observers, who noted that the growth rate for Ecuador's GDP, helped along by higher oil prices to 2.3 percent for 2000, beat all expectations for the economy, which had shrunk by over seven percent the previous year. The days of near hyperinflation had also passed; although the inflation rate remained Latin America's highest, at 91 percent for 2000, estimates for 2001 predicted that inflation would slow down to between 20 and 30 percent. Signifying the economy's new stability, about $600 million in currency flowed into Ecuador's banks in the first nine months after dollarization was announced. In addition, a second trans-Andean pipeline, whose construction was urged by the IMF, promised to add about 60 percent to Ecuador's oil exporting capacity. With its anticipated completion in 2003, the pipeline may also create about 50,000 jobs through subsidiary businesses.

Yet serious obstacles remain in Ecuador's path to economic recovery. Foremost among the challenges, political consensus has yet to build behind free market reforms in Ecuador, jeopardizing continued IMF support after the transition. Labor unions have been among the strongest opponents to privatization measures, and they have been joined by political elites who fear that their privileges as the country's bureaucratic class may be ending. Wealthy Ecuadorians have also opposed reforms in the country's tax system and succeeded—against IMF prescriptions—in passing legislation in March 2001 reducing their taxes from 25 to 15 percent. Congress also rejected IMF demands to raise the value-added tax on consumer items to 15 percent. Without these additional taxes to finance Ecuador's budget, the country will remain mired in foreign debt and budgetary deficits.

Thus, while President Noboa was successful in quickly implementing dollarization, most other reforms have stalled. Significantly, privatization of state-owned enterprises has progressed only fitfully. While the President announced plans to sell off 51 percent of state ownership in electrical production and telecommunications in February 2000, Congress has yet to approve such measures. Without foreign investment to improve these networks in terms of efficiency and service, Ecuador's infrastructure will fall into further disrepair. In 2001 President Noboa renewed calls to sell off a majority ownership in the state's electrical firm and restated his commitment to seeing the sale through to completion.

The ascendency of indigenous interest groups, most notably CONAIE, also creates uncertainty for Ecuador's political stability. While CONAIE has succeeded in achieving a more equitable distribution of government projects to benefit rural areas inhabited by Indian groups—its relationship with Ecuador's authorities has been marked by confrontation instead of consensus. Dominated by ruling elites for generations, Ecuador's political system will have to adapt to manage conflicting interest groups, a challenge that has traditionally led to the rapid overthrow of administrations since Ecuador's independence. In serving as a watchdog over government corruption, however, CONAIE will play a vital role in making Ecuador's government more responsive to the needs of its constituents.

The military in Ecuador, traditionally the strongest of all interest groups in the country, has maintained its authority over the government. While it has refrained from establishing another military junta in recent years, it nonetheless has continued to force presidents out of office for pursuing agendas not to its liking. Indeed, it confirmed President Mahuad's ouster in 2000, and has indicated its willingness to force President Noboa out of office if demonstrations against him become too disruptive. In sum, its support, or lack thereof, remains a force to be reckoned with in any policy determination by Ecuador's elected officials. As long as the military remains largely unaccountable to the public or to elected officials, a significant threat to Ecuador's fragile democratic institutions exists. The country has had five different presidents since 1996, making coordinated policy implementation extremely difficult. Not since the 1950s has Ecuador enjoyed a decade of democratic transition by elected presidents.

Ecuador also faces external forces that could disrupt its economic and political transition. Although its border with Peru is now largely peaceful as a result of their settlement of the dispute in 1998, the area bordering Columbia is within close proximity to numerous cocaine-processing labs. With the United States pouring $1.3 billion into Colombia for anti-drug operations, international leaders are worried that the drug cartels may move their operations into Ecuador. In 1999 the United States and Ecuador signed a ten-year lease to allow American military aircraft to conduct surveillance operations from an Ecuadorian air base. Indeed, Ecuador has a history of being a shipment point for contraband goods, in part because it failed to require visas for entry and exit by foreigners until 1998. The country is also the center of global immigrant smuggling operations, which is not banned by Ecuadorian law. Many Asian and Arab immigrants use Ecuador as a stop on their route to entering the United States illegally. Between March and July of 1999 the U.S. Coast Guard, which patrols the international waters off Ecuador's coast in search of drug shipments, stopped nine ships loaded with illegal immigrants headed for the United States. Illegal immigration to the United States by Ecuadorians alone may be between 1,500 to 2,000 each month, according to U.S. estimates.

The Dollar Trend

With the recovery of Ecuador's economy through dollarization and privatization, the international community hopes that the outflow of Ecuadorians to the United States and Europe will be

A WOMAN RECEIVES A U.S. FIVE DOLLAR BILL IN CHANGE FOR A PURCHASE AT A MARKET IN ECUADOR. THE DOLLARIZATION OF ECUADOR'S CURRENCY IS A CONTROVERSIAL MOVE TO STABILIZE AND BOLSTER THE ECONOMY. *(AP/Wide World Photos. Reproduced by permission.)*

reversed. Indeed, Ecuador may be in the forefront of globalizing its economy ahead of some of its Latin American neighbors. In January 2000 the Central American nation of El Salvador joined Ecuador and Panama in adopting the U.S. dollar as its currency along with its national currency, the *colon*. Although its economy had avoided the dire situation faced in Ecuador, El Salvador hopes that the currency conversion will lower interest rates, stabilize its currency, and attract foreign investment. Guatemala also passed legislation in 2001 to allow business contracts and bank deposits to be made in dollars, a first step in implementing dollarization. Other Latin American countries have followed a similar trend. Argentina already uses a currency board to certify that each of its *pesos* is backed in full by U.S. currency. About seventy percent of bank deposits in Nicaragua are already in dollars, and an estimated fifty percent of business loans in Costa Rica are made in foreign currencies, usually dollars.

With the growing list of Latin American countries informally or officially pursuing dollarization, North and South America may soon be using the *de facto* common currency of the U.S. dollar. Like the European Union's *euro*, such a currency may help to reduce trade barriers and make it easier to do business across national bound-

aries without the difficulties in figuring out fluctuating exchange rates. Such an arrangement for the Americas will be strengthened if a central authority, such as Europe's European Union agencies, exists to set official prime interest and exchange rates. With a meeting held for leaders from North and South America in April 2001 to discuss the formation of a free trade area for the region by 2005, the creation of a common market for the Western Hemisphere is already in the works.

Long-term reforms and structural changes, however, will not necessarily take place in the wake of Ecuador's dollarization. While its leaders have pledged to carry through reforms in cooperation with IMF guidelines, the results of this commitment have yet to be realized. Controversies over privatization may again threaten to depose President Noboa, who is vulnerable from both the political right, which opposes cutbacks to the bureaucracy, tax increases, and land reform, and the political left, which has attacked dollarization and privatization as programs that harm poor and working-class Ecuadorians. Despite recent advances, convincing the 70 percent of Ecuadorians living below the poverty line to support the transition to a market-oriented economy remains a primary challenge to future administrations.

BIBLIOGRAPHY

Anderson, Joan B. *Economic Policy Alternatives for the Latin American Crisis*. New York: Taylor and Francis, 1990.

AP Worldstream. "Ecuador President Pegs Currency to U.S. Dollar, Cabinet Resigns," January 9, 2000.

Buckman, Robert T. *Latin America 1998*. Harpers Ferry: Stryker-Post Publications, 1998.

Barro, Robert J. "The Dollar Club: Why Countries Are so Keen to Join," *Business Week*, December 11, 2000.

Chacon, Richard. "With its Economy Hurting, Ecuador Warily Switched to the Dollar," *Boston Globe*, June 1, 2000.

Cisternas, Carlos. "Ecuador," in Shirley Christian, ed., *Investing and Selling in Latin America*. Shawnee Mission: Morning Light Publishing Company, 1995.

Conaghan, Catherine. *Restructuring Domination: Industrialists and the State in Ecuador*. Pittsburgh: University of Pittsburgh Press, 1988.

Darling, Juanita. "Adoption of Dollar Irks Salvadorans," *Los Angeles Times*, January 6, 2001.

"Divided about the Dollar," *The Economist*, January 6, 2001.

Dodds, Paisley. "Ecuador's President Says He'll Push through Reforms despite Opposition," *AP Worldstream*, September 6, 2000.

"Dollar Politics," *The Economist*, March 18, 2000.

"Dollars and Dolours," *The Economist*, February 19, 2000.

Drake, Paul W., ed. *Money Doctors, Foreign Debts, and Economic Reforms in Latin America from the 1890s to the Present*. Wilmington: Scholarly Resources, Inc., 1994.

"Ecuador on the Brink," *The Economist*, January 15, 2000.

"Ecuador's Post-Coup Reckoning," *The Economist*, January 29, 2000.

Ecuador: Public Sector Reforms for Growth in the Era of Declining Oil Output. Washington, DC: The World Bank, 1991.

Handelsman, Michael. *Culture and Customs of Ecuador*. Westport: Greenwood Press, 2000.

Hanratty, Dennis M., ed. *Ecuador: A Country Study*. Washington, DC: Federal Research Division, Library of Congress, 1991.

Hemlock, Doreen. "Some Latin Nations Adopt U.S. Dollar, But It's Not an Easy Fix," *(South Florida) Sun-Sentinel*, March 13, 2001.

Hodgson, Martin. "Disgust and Confusion in Dollars and Sucres," *Christian Science Monitor*, August 30, 2000.

"The Indians and the Dollar," *The Economist*, March 4, 2000.

Lanier, Alfredo S. "Developing Nations Closely Watching Ecuador's Dollarization," *Chicago Tribune*, September 15, 2000.

Mountford, Peter, and Margalit Edelman. "Ecuador's Dollarized Eecovery," *Christian Science Monitor*, June 20, 2000.

Solano, Gonzalo. "Ecuador's Switch to Dollar Shows Positive Results a Year after its Launch," *AP Worldstream*, January 9, 2001.

Radcliffe, Sarah, and Sallie Westwood. *Remaking the Nation: Place, Identity, and Politics in Latin America*. London: Routledge, 1996.

Rotella, Sebastian. "As Crises Converge on Ecuador, an Exodus," *Los Angeles Times*, July 13, 2000.

Tamayo, Juan O. "U.S. Dollar, Oil Prices bring Measure of Stability to Ecuador's Finances," *Miami Herald*, November 9, 2000.

Tyson, Laura D'Andrea. "The Message in Letting Ecuador Default," *Business Week*, October 25, 1999.

U.S. Department of State. *Background Notes: Ecuador*. Washington, DC: U.S. Department of State, April 2001.

U.S. Department of State. *FY 2001 Country Commercial Guide: Ecuador*. Washington, DC: U.S. Department of State, July 2000.

—Timothy G. Borden

OPENING EUROPE'S SECRET COLD WAR FILES

THE CONFLICT

Backed by the Soviet Union, the governments of eastern Europe were taken over by national Communist Parties after World War II. Chief among the repressive instruments used by totalitarian governments in Eastern Europe was the secret police force. These state agencies cultivated informants from among the populace, in addition to using techniques such as wiretapping, eavesdropping, and infiltrating suspected dissident groups. With the downfall of communist governments after 1989 in eastern Europe and the transition to democratic rule, conflicts arose over the disposition of secret police files as well as the question of retribution against the network of secret police bureaucrats and informants.

Political

- There have been vigorous debates over how widely the information contained in secret police files should be disseminated.

- Those who argue for the widest possible dissemination of the files maintain that only with full disclosure can the countries come to terms with the past.

- Others argue that access to the files may lead to blackmail against those who played even minor or unwilling roles in past state actions.

Historical

- Although some of the countries of eastern Europe had established fragile democracies during the inter-war period, none of them had experienced a sustained democratic political system before 1989. Without a tradition of democratic governance and in light of the harsh repression of the communist era, trust in state institutions has been very low throughout the region.

Social

- The opening of police files has raised questions of accountability for individuals that took part in the state-sanctioned repression of the communist era.

- The process of establishing past collaboration with the secret police forces has also raised the issue of due process for the accused informants.

When the Berlin Wall fell on November 9, 1989, it capped a decade of unrest and calls for reform in eastern Europe. It also symbolized the irreversible downfall of communist governments throughout the region. The momentum generated by the founding of the Solidarity trade union in Poland in 1980, the distribution of *samizdat* dissent literature in Czechoslovakia, and widespread dissatisfaction with declining living standards in every socialist country had finally ended more than 40 years of communist rule. Prior to the Wall's destruction Solidarity's Lech Walesa was already in office as the first non-communist president of Poland, and by the end of the year Communist Party leaders had ceded power in Czechoslovakia, East Germany, and Hungary. Democratic reforms were promised in Bulgaria, Romania, and Yugoslavia, and the Baltic Republics of Estonia, Latvia, and Lithuania stated their demands to declare independence from the Soviet Union. Everywhere in eastern Europe, it seemed, communism was giving way to democracy.

The transition to democracy, as symbolized by the tearing down of the Berlin Wall, brought about fundamental political and social changes for eastern Europeans. Chief among these changes was the inevitable reckoning with the region's history under its various communist regimes. Freed from the repression of the state, individuals now had to account for how responsible they were for maintaining the state's power for so long. Given the extensive police files kept in each country, the question had considerable relevancy to every citizen. Some of the considerations were practical in nature. If the files were opened, who should see them, and who would guarantee their safe maintenance? Other concerns were more ethical in nature. Could the files themselves be trusted for accuracy and honesty? And how widely should the information in the files be disseminated? Certainly, the victims of official repression should read their files, but who else should learn of their contents? Finally, the existence of the files pointed to broader, more philosophical questions. How culpable was each citizen who stayed silent in the face of injustice? And what about those who informed on their fellow citizens, whether out of idealism or petty gain—was retribution in order? These conflicts represented nothing less than a coming to terms with the totalitarian past in Eastern Europe—a confrontation of memory, morality, and national identity conducted on a massive scale by the individuals and nations that had lived through it. As writer Tina Rosenberg commented in her work *The Haunted Land: Facing Europe's Ghosts after Communism* (1995), "This is more than a debate over the past. The struggle to define the past is one of the most important ways eastern Europeans compete for control of the present."

HISTORICAL BACKGROUND

Country by country, Soviet-backed Communist Parties came to power throughout eastern Europe in the wake of World War II (1939–45). The path to power varied somewhat given the region. In Czechoslovakia, for instance, a popularly elected communist minority governed as part of a coalition before seizing power outright, whereas in Poland the communists ruled only after a brutal civil war to eliminate their rivals. By 1949, by whatever path, the process of Communist Party domination was complete. The 1955 ratification of the Warsaw Treaty Organization, commonly known as the Warsaw Pact, by Albania, Bulgaria, Czechoslovakia, East Germany, Hungary, Poland, and Romania was a mere formality, for by then each country was fully enmeshed with the foreign and domestic policies of the pact's sponsor, the Soviet Union. The once independent Baltic Republics—Estonia, Latvia, and Lithuania—were even more tightly bound to the Soviets, as they were annexed and declared republics of the Soviet Union. In the entire region only Yugoslavia, under the communist leadership of Josip Broz Tito, declared itself nonaligned with the Soviet Union in 1948. Although Yugoslavia's bold move threatened to bring a Soviet invasion of the country, aid from the West and Tito's own skillful maneuvering prevented war from breaking out.

Whether by civil war, electoral corruption, or genuine popular support, the consolidation of com-munist power in Eastern Europe by the end of the 1940s ushered in an age of totalitarian rule in the region that lasted until the 1990s. The primary goal of totalitarian authority under the communists was to make the state pervasive in both the public and private spheres in each country. Going beyond mere authoritarian rule, totalitarianism attempted to redefine its human subjects by asserting state control over family life, education, religion, and other facets of private life until no aspect of every-day existence was left untouched by the state. Thus, the communists' first priority in the aftermath of World War II was to eliminate any autonomous spheres that might challenge their power, most notably any rival political parties or critics in the press or clergy.

To eliminate the opposition and to control civil society, the totalitarian governments of postwar eastern Europe took their lessons from their Soviet trainers in a deliberate campaign to consolidate their power. Scholar Hannah Arendt remarked in *The Origins of Totalitarianism* (1973) that mass propaganda was vital in winning popular support for the transition away from burgeoning democracies and into totalitarian rule. The organization of state propaganda followed the same pattern in each country, with messages repeated again and again in ritualistic fashion to indoctrinate the masses and convince them of the regimes' legitimacy. In addition, communist state propaganda reminded citizens of the threats by Western powers to destroy their way of life. In this dichotomy Soviet communism was the savior of Eastern European peoples, bringing them peace, stability, and economic progress, while Western capitalism threatened to bring disruption, poverty, and exploitation. Not that the propaganda did not have real meaning behind it. As Markus Wolf, head of the East German Foreign Intelligence Service reminded readers in his memoir *Man Without a Face* (1997),

> Now that the Cold War is history, it is easy to conclude that the Soviet Union was a mangy, ill-coordinated creature, inferior in many regards to its arch rival, the United States, and doomed to failure from its inception. But during the four decades that the superpower conflict dominated world affairs, it did not seem that way at all. On the contrary, the West's fears that Moscow would fulfill Nikita Khrushchev's promise to catch up and overtake the capitalist countries was the motor that drove espionage and propaganda with a historically unprecedented intensity.

On an individual level this propaganda also attempted to get individuals to identify their interests solely with the interests of the state. Control-

THIS MAP ILLUSTRATES THE EASTERN AND WESTERN BLOC NATIONS OF EUROPE DURING THE COLD WAR. *(The Gale Group.)*

ling and manipulating information was a key step in the process of sublimating individuals to the state. Once the independent press was eliminated, for example, most people were forced to rely on state-sponsored news services for information; as a result, the state appeared to be not only omnipresent but omniscient as well. Carrying the process a step further, communist regimes attempted to erase the judicious sense in individuals by arbitrarily choosing their victims. The enemies of the state were no longer those who had committed crimes, but rather those who were viewed *categorically* as being potential enemies. Further destroying the individuality of its subjects, the totalitarian state also demanded that its very victims take part in their own terrorization, for example, by forced confessions that often implicated others in alleged criminal activities.

East Germany's Ministry for State Security: Spying in the Name of the People

Anti-capitalist propaganda was not the only device used to control civil society. Despite vigor-

ous propaganda efforts real repression was also needed to keep people in line. Indeed, an elaborate system of bureaucracies was created in each country, including secret police agencies, to enlist the force of the state against its suspected enemies. The Ministry for State Security in the German Democratic Republic (GDR), also known as East Germany, developed the most comprehensive secret police bureaucracy. The Ministry and its secret police agents became known colloquially as the Stasi, a term that gained infamy. From its founding in February 1950, the Stasi grew to employ more than 90,000 East Germans as Ministry staff members. A fraction of these workers, about 5,000 Ministry employees, devoted themselves to foreign espionage, while the others spied on their own countrymen.

To carry out the bulk of its fieldwork the Stasi used almost twice as many unofficial collaborators as it had Ministry employees. Of its 170,000 informers as many as 110,000 routinely reported to their Ministry handlers on their families, friends, and colleagues. In Timothy Garton Ash's memoir

The File: A Personal History (1997), which recounts his experiences after reading his own secret police file, Ash noted that the number of people directly involved in Stasi affairs amounted to one out of every 50 East Germans, a figure that earned the country the distinction of being the most heavily infiltrated, in terms of domestic espionage, in history. About six million of East Germany's 16 million citizens—fully half of all adults—had Stasi files compiled on their activities.

In terms of its effectiveness the Stasi succeeded in preventing public dissent from appearing in East Germany until the late 1980s, when widespread popular unrest eventually led to the downfall of the communist government there. Indeed, East Germany became a model of compliance within the Warsaw Pact during the Cold War. After an outburst of demonstrations in June 1953, no major political protests occurred for more than 30 years, a testament to the ruthless effectiveness of Stasi repression. Lutz Niethammer observed in his study of memory and totalitarianism in East Germany, *Where Were You on 17 June* (1992), "Throughout a period longer than in any other of the industrialized, avowedly socialist countries, the GDR was able to dampen and contain social conflict, although at the cost of a spectacular degree of self-isolation within its own nation in the wake of the wall's construction."

Reality as Propaganda: Romania's Securitate

While East Germany's Stasi relied on an elaborate network of informers to implicate large numbers of people in state-sponsored repression and thereby dampen dissent, the secret police agencies of other countries resorted to more brutal tactics. Among the most terrifying of these domestic espionage agencies was Romania's *Securitate*, under Communist Party leader Nicolae Ceausescu. The number of Securitate officers was much smaller than that of the Stasi, but its blatant repression made Romania the most totalitarian of the Eastern European states. Ceausescu's attempts to create a cult of personality around his own achievements—as well as those of his scientist wife, Elena—also fostered a national paranoia that, as in East Germany, made every citizen complicit in the regime's actions. Petru Popescu, an author who suffered his first Securitate interrogation at the age of 13 and later defected from Romania as an adult, remembered in *The Return: A Family Revisits Their Eastern European Roots* (1997),

Reality became propaganda, and vice versa. Ceausescu was openly addressed as conductor,

leader. . . . He was 'the best beloved son of the people.' The identities of ordinary Romanians no longer melted in the We of Communism victorious, but into the He of the leader. Ceausescu had a thirst for personal worship to which the Romanians responded with a thirst for self-abolishment, with a desperate, addictive dependency on the fateful leader.

As Romania's economy worsened throughout the 1970s, however, Securitate repression intensified, and not even the force of Ceausescu's personality could keep Romanians from noticing bare store shelves, electrical outages, and food shortages.

Under Ceausescu, Romanians took it for granted that all telephone lines were tapped, that all conversations were recorded, and that any contact with foreigners was duly documented by the Securitate. In many instances these assumptions were correct, as state control over private life in Romania exceeded that in any other communist-ruled country. The most infamous example of state control concerned the enforcement of Romania's pronatalist policies, which were enacted in the 1960s to increase the birth rate and thereby demonstrate the strength and vitality of the nation. Abortion and contraception were outlawed, and to ensure compliance with these mandates, state officials often conducted compulsory and unannounced pregnancy exams on Romanian women in their workplace or if the women sought routine medical attention for some other reason. In the end the effect was the same as in East Germany. Open dissent was not tolerated in Romania, and the period leading up to Ceausescu's 1989 overthrow was marked by strict compliance with the regime's edicts, at least on the surface.

Between the Stasi and the Securitate

Secret police efforts in the other Warsaw Pact countries ranged between the two extremes of the well-equipped Stasi and intensely ruthless Securitate. Most countries could not afford to keep so many staff members and informers on the payroll, a policy that only East Germany, as the region's most economically developed country, could pursue. Nor were most Communist Party leaders in Eastern Europe so careless in the face of popular opinion as was Ceausescu. Indeed, most other countries followed a strategy that combined economic incentives to forestall any uprisings while secretly infiltrating dissent organizations and discrediting them through the traditional means of state propaganda. In Czechoslovakia, for example, the government offered guarantees of a higher standard of living than in many other Eastern Bloc countries, a fact that helped stifle dissent after the Prague Spring of 1968, a period of reform in the Czechoslovakian

CHRONOLOGY

1980 The Polish trade union Solidarity is formed.

1989 Partially free elections in Poland result in a Solidarity-led coalition government, ending decades of Communist Party rule in Poland.

1989 Soviet President Mikhail Gorbachev announces the right to self-determination for countries in the Soviet Bloc and pledges noninterference by the Soviet Union.

November 9, 1989 The Berlin Wall is opened between East and West Berlin, symbolically marking an end to the Cold War.

December 1989 Czechoslovakia's "Velvet Revolution," puts a non-communist government in charge of the nation.

December 25, 1989 After violent demonstrations shake the country, Romania's President-for-Life Nicolae Ceausescu and his wife are executed.

Late 1989–91 The Baltic Republics—Estonia, Latvia, and Lithuania—undertake the process of securing independence from the Soviet Union.

1991 Joachim Gauck is appointed to oversee the opening of the former East Germany's Stasi files, under an office that is known as the "Gauck Authority."

March 1991 The Warsaw Pact is dissolved; the Soviet Union agrees to withdraw troops from Czechoslovakia, East Germany, and Hungary.

August 18–21, 1991 A failed coup against Soviet President Gorbachev hastens the break up of the Soviet Union.

October 1991 The Czech lustration law is enacted, to be in effect until December 31, 2000.

September 1997 Secret police files in Hungary's Office of History in the Interior Ministry are partially opened.

1999 The Institute of National Remembrance is created to oversee the opening of Polish secret police files, but arguments over appointing a chair for the commission delays its work.

October 1999 The Romanian parliament enacts the *Ticu Dumitrescu* law to open up Securitate files. Wrangling over the law's implementation delays the opening of the files.

January 15, 2001 Securitate files are opened to the Romanian public.

January 2001 The first documents from Poland's secret police files are opened to victims of its repression.

April 2001 A list of 30 current officeholders who worked for the Securitate is released by the Romanian government.

May 2001 Tensions between Hungary and Bulgaria increase, with Hungary's call for Bulgaria to sever its espionage ties with Russia.

Communist Party that ended with a Soviet-backed invasion and a return to conformity. The government also continued to retain an array of informants among religious organizations, writers' groups, and political activists, ensuring that no single group ever got too far away from state control.

Poland followed a similar strategy through most of the 1970s. Consumer items filled store shelves and food prices were increasingly subsidized until it was actually cheaper for farmers to use bread instead of grain as feed for their animals. From a deficit of US$2.5 billion in 1973, Poland's foreign debt ballooned to over ten times that amount, or $27 billion, in 1980. Yet the public was not entirely quiescent in the face of these material incentives. Major strikes and protests broke out in Poznań in

1956, in Gdańsk in 1970, and across the country in 1976. Crucially, the government failed to infiltrate the Roman Catholic Church, which remained largely independent of state control and served to validate many opposition demands. Remembering the non-aggression pact between the communist Soviet Union and Nazi Germany in 1939 that led to the invasion of their country and the onset of World War II, Poles also remained antagonistic toward their Russian and East German neighbors, which in turn diminished their commitment to the ideal of socialist unity.

As the governments of Eastern European countries responded with superficial reforms, limited economic incentives, and varying degrees of repression through the 1980s, they remained tied to

Soviet authority in the Cold War between the communist East and capitalist West. Although most of the countries had taken steps away from direct totalitarian rule, however, their reform efforts were too superficial, too insincere, and far too late to forestall demands for outright democratic reform among the populace. Encouraged by the example of Solidarity's peaceful transition into power in Poland and by the opening of the Berlin Wall in 1989, almost every communist power in the region had fallen by the end of the year. Those socialist regimes that remained, as in Albania, Bulgaria, and Romania, quickly shuffled their administrations and promised substantive reforms. In Yugoslavia, the country descended into secession, civil war, and ethnic cleansing under Slobodan Milosevic, delaying any real transition to democracy for another decade.

The Gauck Authority: Coming to Terms with the Past

One of the most important post-socialist reforms concerned the curtailment of the extensive domestic espionage operations that had existed since the 1940s. Just as East Germany had conducted the most comprehensive espionage operations during the Cold War, the united Germany quickly announced after unification that it would open Stasi files to victims of its repression, a massive undertaking in itself. Although Stasi staff members had destroyed many sensitive documents in the days before the Berlin Wall came down, most of its files were intact. In fact, the linear shelf space of the Ministry's paper files amounted to about 111 miles, or 117 kilometers, of documents. Once the government distributed applications for citizens to review their files, some 1.7 million inquiries poured into the Federal Authority for the Records of the State Security Service of the former German Democratic Republic, the agency in charge of maintaining and disseminating the files. More commonly, the agency was known as the Gauck Authority after its director, Joachim Gauck, a former clergyman and East German dissident. Soon, Germans talked of being "Gaucked" to let everyone know they reviewed their Stasi files, or had been cleared of collaboration with the Stasi.

The reunified Germany took a deliberate approach to preserve the Stasi files and open them up to the public. There was general agreement that the victims of Stasi repression deserved to learn the truth about those who had informed on them. In addition, the preservation of the files would serve as a reminder—and, therefore, a warning—to future generations of the misdeeds committed by the

totalitarian state. Further, the relative openness of the Gauck Authority would prevent criticisms that many Germans had come to level at their government and its Western allies in the de-Nazification process after World War II. Although the Nuremberg Trials (1945–46) had publicized Nazi atrocities among the Party's leaders, very few public officials were removed from office in western Germany in the wake of the war. So eager were the Allies to keep West Germany from falling into the Eastern Bloc that they did not push for a full accounting of Nazi crimes among the general public. Essentially, West Germany was prevented from fully coming to terms with its Nazi past, an issue that resonated with the so-called "Generation of '68," the sons and daughters of those who lived through the war. This generation was determined that no nullification of the Stasi's activities, no matter how convenient, would take place.

Although the aims behind its mandate were broad the Gauck Authority performed its functions with a clear set of guidelines in handling the sensitive information under its agency. Some files, particularly those containing information still considered vital to national security, continued to be held in secret by the German government. Otherwise, individuals could petition to view their files, which were opened to them only after all the names of innocent third parties mentioned in the transcripts were deleted. Journalists could also gain access to the archives for research purposes. Of the 400,000 people to see their Stasi files through the end of 1997, most found the process difficult, yet liberating. In some cases, families were torn apart as individuals learned that close relatives such as parents, siblings, or even spouses had turned informant. Aside from the personal confrontations that former Stasi informants sometimes encountered, they also faced possible employment obstacles in the new, united Germany, as public-sector employers could petition the Gauck Authority for information on potential employees and deny them employment if evidence of collaboration turned up.

Lustration Laws in Eastern Europe

Barring former informants from certain jobs was also one of the theories behind the lustration law passed in Czechoslovakia in 1991. With the goal of "lustrating" post-socialist public life—a term used to denote both the illumination and purging of past misdeeds—the law barred collaborators with the *Statni Bezpecnost* (the Czechoslovakian secret police, also known by its initials StB) from a range of offices, including the state's judiciary and central bank, along with some high level

THE INTELLIGENCE AGENCIES OF MANY EAST EUROPEAN COUNTRIES MAINTAINED FILES ON THEIR CITIZENS UNTIL THE END OF THE COLD WAR. THE FILES WERE GRADUALLY MADE AVAILABLE TO THE PUBLIC, THOUGH NOT WITHOUT CONTROVERSY. *(CORBIS CORPORATION (Bellevue). Reproduced by permission.)*

civil service, armed forces, intelligence, and academic positions. While the law was not widely utilized in Slovakia after the mutual breakup of Czechoslovakia in 1992–93, it led to more than 300,000 lustration screenings in the Czech Republic from 1991 through 1997. The entire process was intended to be completed before the end of 2000, when the lustration law would lapse. After that date, no more hearings would occur, and anyone not subject to its prohibitions would be presumed fully innocent of any past collaboration.

From the start the lustration process engendered controversy. Initially, files were grouped into ambiguous categories that included a "candidate" label for individuals who had merely been approached by the StB to become informers, even if they had turned down the offer. Although an estimated two-thirds of all "candidates" did indeed walk away from the StB, the appellation now threatened their professional lives by merely appearing in its files. In addition, in the less than five percent of cases that turned up concrete evidence of collaboration, the lustration committee's findings were usually reversed by outside agencies. A majority of the cases appealed to the independent lustration commission were in fact overturned, a situation that soon led to the entire category of "candidates" being made exempt from the lustration process. Further, cases appealed to the Prague Municipal Court were routinely reversed on the grounds that the microfiched information the lustration committee used in its hearings was inadmissible as evidence in court. Because of this technicality, 80 percent of the lustration cases brought into the court were nullified.

In the first years of lustration very few past StB informers were ousted from their current positions; one estimate put the figure at just 19 removals at the end of 1991, while four years later it was estimated that no more than 100 Czech citizens had been barred from a position as a result of the investigations. Further, most of those who were found to be guilty of past collaboration were rarely fired outright; instead, they were almost always demoted or reclassified to a position that was not one of the jobs subject to lustration. In the end, despite a few well-publicized cases of past StB involvement by some public officials, lustration became a routine bureaucratic process in the Czech Republic. While some observers praised the law for preventing retribution against collaborators and helping Czechs slowly come to terms with their country's communist past, others questioned whether it had gone far enough. Because most of the lustration procedures took place out of public view, an open debate on the accountability and culpability of the StB in Czech affairs did not take place with the same intensity as in the united Germany.

Other countries approached lustration aware of the controversies that accompanied the process in the Czech Republic and the former East Germany. Bulgaria used lustration only for certain high-level academic positions, while the Hungarian lustration law, passed in 1997, was limited to a small group of public officials. In addition, the Hungarian lustration commission was allowed to publicize its findings only after giving the individual in question the chance to resign his or her position and avoid public exposure. Before opening up any files to the public the Hungarian agency responsible for maintaining the files, the Office of History in the Interior Ministry, also blacked out any names in the files; this provision ensured a higher degree of anonymity for anyone named in the files, although it was often still possible for readers to guess the identities of those who had informed on them.

In Poland the debate over lustration took years to settle, with legislation taking effect only in 1998. Part of this delay resulted from the country's unique transition away from communism, which took place as part of a negotiated settlement between the Solidarity Party and the ruling Communist Party. Although Solidarity won an overwhelming victory in the first partially-free elections that took place in 1989, it ruled only as part of a coalition with the communists, who were guaranteed a certain number of seats in the Polish parliament, the *Sejm*, under the terms of the roundtable agreement. As a result of this arrangement there was no rush to expose the files of the Polish secret service, partly over the direct political confrontation that this would entail, and partly because the communists were still powerful in the government, albeit as minority members of the governing coalition. When politicians did intervene to publicize information from the files, as anti-communist Interior Minister Antoni Macierewicz did in 1992, the results were disastrous: Macierewicz was forced to resign from office after being accused of using the secret files to smear his political opponents.

As the Macierewicz case demonstrated, the potential for mudslinging would remain until the files were opened, at least until the lustration of public officials occurred. Proceeding cautiously, the Sejm passed a law that formally began the lustration process in 1998. A full opening of all the security files to the public would wait until a special commission was appointed. In the meantime, elected and some appointed public officials were required to sign a declaration that stated whether or not they had consciously collaborated with the Polish secret service during the period of communist rule. A special Vetting Court would then investigate each individual to verify the statement. Unfortunately, merely appearing at the Court sometimes gave the impression of guilt, a situation not helped by the Court's controversial role in the presidential election of 2000.

During the election, charges surfaced that the two best-known candidates, sitting President (and former Communist Party member) Aleksander Kwasniewski, and Solidarity Party leader (and former President) Lech Walesa, had files that showed them to have collaborated with the secret police. For Kwasniewski, the charges were plausible, as he then led the successor party to the Communists, the Alliance of the Democratic Left. Yet the charges directly countered Kwasniewski's claims that he had never served as an informer. For Walesa, the accusation produced incredulity; as Solidarity's leader, he was the leading dissenter of the anti-communist movement, a place that earned him the Nobel Prize in 1983. In the end the Vetting Court cleared both men. The documents produced against Kwasniewski were probably fraudulent, and an investigation revealed that the secret service had for many years deliberately produced false documents to implicate Walesa. In addition to the dubious documents, former secret service agents testified that Kwasniewski had only met with them in an official capacity and never to inform on anyone. In the election itself the scandal appeared to have had little impact, aside from giving the whole campaign a negative tone. Kwasniewski maintained his lead in the polls, and won a convincing majority in the multi-candidate field, returning to office for a second term as president.

RECENT HISTORY AND THE FUTURE

As the controversy surrounding the 2000 presidential election showed, Poland's initial experience with lustration was marked by confusion and contention, and many questioned whether the experience was worth it. Nevertheless, plans moved forward to open the files to those who had been spied on by the Polish secret police. The Institute of National Remembrance was entrusted with the duty to release all state files dating back to 1939, when the country was invaded by Germany, through 1989, when the coalition government ended communist rule. Unfortunately, the Institute went without a director for several months after its establishment in 1999. Not only did it suffer from a lack of support from President Kwasniewski, who had opposed its creation, but the Sejm was also unable to reach the necessary consensus over who should lead the agency. As a result the Institute failed to meet its first target date of March 2000 for opening its files. Eventually, in June 2000, Leon Kieres was appointed director, and the following January the Institute began processing applications from Poles who had police dossiers. In a symbolic act, Foreign Minister Wladyslaw Bartoszewski, who had been imprisoned by both Nazi and communist authorities, was the first to receive an application from the Institute. More than ten years after Czech lustration had begun—and after its term had expired—Poland's secret police files were being released to their subjects.

As in Poland, a complicated political situation delayed the opening of Romania's police files. For years rumors had circulated about the Securitate's power in Romania, even after Ceausescu was over-

thrown. The secret police force had expropriated enough funds during the communist era to set up its own businesses and trade agencies, and it continued to use these funds to support favored political candidates in the emerging democratic system in Romania after 1990. Ion Iliescu, the first elected president of Romania in the post-Ceausescu era, was himself rumored to have Securitate ties. His long-standing association with the communist regime included a number of high-ranking posts, which led many Romanians to assume that he had significant Securitate dealings as well. Ironically, it was one of Iliescu's chief political rivals, ultra-nationalist Corneliu Vadim Tudor, who benefited directly from the Securitate's continuing influence in Romanian political life in the 1990s. Employing a number of former Securitate staff members as functionaries of his Greater Romania Party, Tudor added to his image as a nationalist with anti-Hungarian rhetoric, contributing to the excesses of the extreme right wing in Romanian politics. In the presidential elections of 2000 Tudor placed second in the voting behind Iliescu, whom most Western observers had endorsed as the lesser of two evils.

After protracted wrangling by the parliament and Iliescu, who was reelected as president in 2000 after losing the office to Emil Constantinescu in 1995, the process of opening Securitate files began in earnest in January 2001. Under the law, named after prominent dissident Ticu Dumitrescu, an independent committee of 11 members would open up the files, which were placed under the administration of the National Council for the Study of the Securitate Archives. Since 1999 the agency had vetted the backgrounds of a select group of public officials and duly announced the results to the public in the hope of eliminating the use of the files for political blackmail. As of 2001, however, anyone who was subject to Securitate spying could petition to see his or her file, although no retributive actions against informers were mandated by the law.

With an estimated 700,000 informers and 125 million files, the process of opening up the Securitate files promised to be a drawn-out affair with a fair number of disquieting revelations along the way. In March 2001, after newspapers began reporting the Securitate's past infiltration of religious institutions in Romania, Romanian Orthodox Priest Eugen Jurca disclosed that he had been a Securitate informer. Jurca had signed an agreement with the Securitate in 1980 and was required to report to the agency on all religious texts that came into Romania. Urging other clerics to follow his example, Jurca cited his confession as a necessary step in national reconciliation between those who

MARKUS WOLF: SPYMASTER

1923– The life and career of Markus Wolf have spanned the most tumultuous movements in recent world history. Born in Hechingen in southwestern Germany in 1923, his childhood was a prosperous, if unconventional one. His father, Friedrich Wolf, was a doctor, naturalist, and committed Marxist; he was also Jewish, which made the family an immediate target once the Nazi Party solidified its grip on power in 1933. Friedrich Wolf was able to secure asylum in the Soviet Union and the family arrived in Moscow in March 1934. Markus Wolf would not return to Germany until the end of World War II (1939–45).

Sharing his father's commitment to communism, Wolf was given a series of important positions in the Soviet-controlled area of Germany after the war. His first major assignment as manager of the sector's Berlin radio station gave him training in propaganda and communication technology, important skills for his appointment as the chief of foreign intelligence in the Ministry of State Security in the newly formed German Democratic Republic in 1952. Second only to Erich Mielke in the spy bureaucracy of East Germany, Wolf held the position for the next 34 years.

Acknowledged to be the best espionage agency in the Soviet bloc, Wolf's office successfully placed agents throughout state offices in West Germany. In 1973 the arrest of East German agent Günter Guillaume, a top aide to West German Chancellor Willy Brandt, shocked the international community and forced Brandt to resign from office. In addition to monitoring events in West Germany, Wolf's agency also sponsored international terrorist groups, most notably the Palestine Liberation Organization (PLO). After German reunification Wolf fled to Moscow, where he was disappointed with his former mentors' lukewarm reception. Eventually, Wolf returned to Germany and made numerous television appearances in defense of his past work.

FORMER EAST GERMAN SPY CHIEF MARKUS WOLF LEAVES A COURTROOM IN DUESSELDORF, GERMANY, AFTER RECEIVING A TWO-YEAR SUSPENDED SENTENCE FOR FOUR COLD WAR-ERA KIDNAPPINGS. *(AP/World Wide Photos. Reproduced by permission.)*

Although he acknowledged that some excessive measures were used by his ministry, Wolf insisted that his actions in support of East German and Soviet espionage were undertaken simply to prevent a return to the fascism of the Nazi era. Nevertheless, Wolf was convicted of treason against West Germany in 1993, a finding that was later overturned on appeal. In 1997 Wolf was convicted of kidnapping in three different cases that dated back to the 1950s; he negotiated a suspended sentence and did not serve any jail time. In contrast to his years as a mysterious figure during the Cold War, Wolf remains a frequent presence on television programs exploring East Germany's past, and his memoir, *Man Without a Face* was published in 1997.

had worked, however unwillingly, with the Securitate, and those who were its victims. In the months after the Jurca exposé, lists of elected officials who were Securitate informers also shook up the political landscape. Ristea Priboi, who had been appointed by Iliescu to oversee intelligence services in Romania, quickly resigned after his association with the Securitate was brought to light. In May 2001 another intelligence minister, Radu Timofte,

was falsely accused of Securitate collaboration based on forged documents that allegedly showed a connection between Timofte and the Soviet secret police, the KGB. Timofte was cleared of the charges, but the episode revealed the dangers of taking Securitate documents at face value.

In Germany, where the first and most aggressive attempts at opening up secret police files took place, scandals were still unfolding a decade later. Investigations into illegal fundraising activities by the Christian Democratic Party, once the most powerful party in Germany under Chancellor Helmut Kohl, revealed that Kohl was a one-time target of Stasi spying and that Stasi tapes revealed Kohl's familiarity with his party's illegal activities. As investigators pressed to open up the Stasi files to learn more, Kohl, by now retired from public life, asserted that his right to privacy was under attack. The Gauck Authority agreed with the investigators, however, and despite misgivings that Stasi information was not necessarily credible, the investigation moved forward. Many residents of the former East Germany were pleased by the outcome, as they had viewed Kohl's demand to keep his Stasi files closed as patently unfair; after all, East Germans were fully accountable for their Stasi pasts, and there was no reason to exempt one-time West Germans from the same standard, albeit under different circumstances.

Overall, then, the opening up of secret police files in eastern Europe produced some surprising outcomes that could not have been predicted when their communist regimes collapsed after 1989. Yet the results were ambiguous in terms of whether the lustration process helped citizens come to terms with the past or, indeed, whether it strengthened democracy in the region. A 1999 poll showed that more Czechs, Hungarians, and Poles believed that the fall of communism was worthwhile than not, and that an overwhelming number believed that it was more possible to state their thoughts publicly after communism's demise. Yet equally large numbers of those who responded claimed that material living standards had gone down, that security in employment was a thing of the past, and that crime was rampant. Most eastern Europeans still viewed official institutions with suspicion. A 1995 poll of Romanians ranked the country's judiciary, parliament, and government in general with substandard approval ratings. Only the Orthodox Church and the army received approval from a majority of respondents. Given these figures, it is clear that the lustration process was not a curative in itself, but merely one step in the transition to real democracy and the support of the burgeoning civil societies in eastern Europe.

BIBLIOGRAPHY

Arendt, Hannah. *The Origins of Totalitarianism.* reprint, New York: Harcourt Brace Jovanovich, 1973.

Ash, Timothy Garton. *The File: A Personal History.* New York: Random House, 1997.

———. *History of the Present: Essays, Sketches, and Dispatches from Europe in the 1990s.* New York: Random House, 1999.

Behr, Edward. *Kiss the Hand You Cannot Bite: The Rise and Fall of the Ceausescus.* New York: Villard Books, 1991.

Brand, Madeleine. "Analysis: Struggle in Poland to Determine How to Deal with the Truths of Its Communist Past," National Public Radio, *Morning Edition,* August 16, 2000.

Crampton, R.J. *A Concise History of Bulgaria.* Cambridge, MA: Cambridge University Press, 1997.

Gallagher, Tom, with Allan H. Meltzer. "Ceausescu's Legacy," *National Interest,* Summer 1999.

Gallagher, Tom. *Romania After Ceausescu.* Edinburgh: Edinburgh University Press, 1995.

"Germany: Open the Files!" *The Economist,* April 8, 2000, p. 54.

Goldfarb, Jeffrey, C. *Beyond Glasnost: The Post-Totalitarian Mind.* Chicago, IL: University of Chicago Press, 1992.

Hansen, Liane. "Profile: Former German Chancellor, Helmut Kohl, Objects to Release of Stasi Files Compiled While He Was in Office," National Public Radio, *Weekend Sunday Edition,* January 7, 2001.

"Hungary's Prime Minister Urges Bulgaria to Reform Intelligence Services," AP Worldstream, May 18, 2001.

Jordan, Michael R. "Spy Files of Communists Still Put Hungary on Edge," *Christian Science Monitor,* November 13, 1997.

Kriseova, Eda. *Vaclav Havel: The Authorized Biography.* New York: St. Martin's Press, 1993.

Lovatt, Catherine. "Securitate Shuffle," *Central Europe Review,* vol. 2, no. 15 (April 17, 2000). Available online at http://www.ce-review.org/00/15/lovatt15.html (cited July 10, 2001).

Mutler, Alison. "Opening of Secret Files Show Eavesdropping Was Prevalent," AP Worldstream, March 29, 2001.

———. "President Enacts Law Allowing Romanians Access to Some Securitate Files," AP Worldstream, December 12, 1999.

"New List of Politicians Who Collaborated with Communist Secret Police," AP Worldstream, April 24, 2001.

Niethammer, Lutz. "Where Were *You* on 17 June?," in *Memory and Totalitarianism,* Luisa Passerini, ed. New York: Oxford University Press, 1992.

"Panel Names New Candidate to Head Institute Overseeing Communist-Era Files," AP Worldstream, April 3, 2000.

Pasek, Beata. "Polish Minister Gets First Application to See Communist-Era Police Dile," AP Worldstream, January 31, 2001.

Pond, Elizabeth. "Romania: Better Late Than Never," *Washington Quarterly,* Spring 2001.

Popescu, Petru. *The Return: A Family Revisits Their Eastern European Roots.* New York: Grove Press, 1997.

"Prominent Dissident Calls for Securitate Files to Be Opened," AP Worldstream, February 20, 2001.

Ramet, Sabrina. *Nihil Obstat: Religion, Politics, and Social Change in East-Central Europe and Russia.* Durham: Duke University Press, 1998.

Rohozinska, Joanna. "Struggling with the Past: Poland's Controversial Lustration Trials," *Central Europe Review.* Available online at http://www.ce-review.org (cited May 30, 2001).

"Romania: Spy Chief," AP Worldstream, May 7, 2001.

Rosenberg, Tina. *The Haunted Land: Facing Europe's Ghosts After Communism.* New York: Random House, 1995.

Rothschild, Joseph. *Return to Diversity: A Political History of East Central Europe Since World War II.* Second Edition, New York: Oxford University Press, 1993.

Rubin, Trudy. "Central Europeans Still Falter at Coming to Grips with History," *Philadelphia Inquirer,* July 31, 1998.

Schopflin, George. *Politics in Eastern Europe 1945–1992.* Oxford: Blackwell Publishers, 1993.

Weir, Fred. "In Russia, Privacy is a Commodity," *Christian Science Monitor,* July 19, 2000.

Wolf, Markus, with Anne McElvoy. *Man Without a Face: The Memoirs of a Spymaster.* London: Jonathan Cape, 1997.

—Timothy G. Borden

FEMALE CIRCUMCISION: CULTURE OR CRUELTY?

THE CONFLICT

Female circumcision has been practiced for more than two thousand years in various parts of the world. Since the mid-twentieth century, however, its continued practice, chiefly in Africa, has led to conflict that has increasingly drawn in the United Nations, numerous countries, human rights and feminist organizations, and individuals on both sides of the issue.

Political

- In colonized African nations such as Kenya, government-imposed bans on female circumcision led to public revolt.

Health

- The United Nations has taken a continually more active role in trying to halt female circumcision, largely on health grounds.

Cultural

- Proponents of female circumcision support it as a ritual that helps to carry on cultural heritage.

- Western opponents of female circumcision rely on a body of "international human rights" to override the practices of people in individual nations who see it as a cultural practice.

- Activism against female circumcision in Africa has become more grounded in indigenous organizations.

- An ongoing conflict exists between Western and indigenous organizations on how best to eliminate the practice.

Religious

- In many Islamic nations, especially in Africa, female circumcision is considered a religious necessity.

In 1997 a young Ghanian woman arriving in New York was stopped at the airport by immigration officials. Her passport, which identified her as Adelaide Abankwah, had been altered, and the officials prepared to deport her. The woman claimed asylum and, at her hearing several months later in a U.S. courtroom, she told a terrifying story. Abankwah testified that she was the daughter of a Ghanian tribal queen; after her mother died, she said, she was going to be forced to undergo female circumcision against her will. Abankwah gained support from many feminist groups and from notables such as Julia Roberts and Hillary Rodham Clinton. After two years in detention she was finally granted asylum. In late 2000, however, it was revealed that "Adelaide Abankwah" actually was a Ghanian hotel worker, Regina Norman Danson, and that she had adopted the identity of the real Adelaide Abankwah, whose passport was allegedly stolen. Danson insisted that she really would have been forcibly circumcised if returned home, even though she was not the woman she claimed to be. Although this case provoked a scandal, it nevertheless brought a great deal of media attention to the issue of female circumcision.

Female circumcision has been performed in various parts of the world for at least 2,500 years. It was reported as early as the fifth century BCE by the Egyptian historian Herodotus. Like male circumcision, it is a ritual that might have arisen as a symbolic substitute for human sacrifice. Today, it is performed in at least 28 African countries, as well as some Asian and Middle Eastern countries. Many but not all of these nations practice the Islamic religion, but not all Islamic nations endorse female circumcision. With the recent increase in immigration from countries where it is a tradition, the practice has also spread to North America and Europe. The World Health Organization (WHO), an agency of the United Nations (UN), estimates that between 100 and 132 million girls and women worldwide have undergone circumcision.

Unlike male circumcision, female circumcision is not usually performed on infants and is not necessarily a minor removal of skin. Instead, it is a rite of passage performed into the teenaged years or later. It can involve complete removal of genital organs and stitching up of a girl's labia so that she cannot engage in intercourse until marriage. The stitching is then removed at marriage, but often is replaced after childbirth. Most female circumcisions are done by village women who use makeshift tools, without anesthesia or sanitary precautions. Female circumcision involves many serious or even fatal health risks, and often is performed on girls too young to consent or performed involuntarily on older girls. While the practice was known to Western travelers and researchers at an earlier time, it only began to be publicized and protested against in the West during the 1970s. As a result, WHO and many human rights groups such as Equality Now have renamed the practice "female genital mutilation" (FGM) and have been trying to eliminate it. Supporters are equally adamant that the practice is a private religious and cultural matter, and that westerners who oppose it are trying to impose their own cultural standards on other societies.

HISTORICAL BACKGROUND

Ancient Origins of Female Circumcision

Probably the earliest historical reference to female circumcision was made by the Egyptian historian Herodotus in the fifth century BCE. Mention of the practice also appeared on Greek papyruses during the second century BCE. In ancient Rome slave girls were subjected to infibulation—the most extreme form of circumcision, in which the labia are stitched together—to keep them from becoming pregnant and thus unable to work. Reasons given for female circumcision have varied and include: meeting a religious requirement, promoting cultural heritage, reducing sexual desire, preventing promiscuity, guaranteeing fidelity within marriage, enhancing fertility, and maintaining women's health.

Circumcision is a requirement for male Muslim children, and many of the countries in which female circumcision has become a tradition practice the Islamic religion. However, in some devoutly Islamic countries, such as Saudi Arabia,

CHRONOLOGY

circa 400 BCE First written mention of female circumcision, by Egyptian historian Herodotus.

1925 Europeans begin limiting the practice of female circumcision in African colonies.

1952 The United Nations Commission on Human Rights discusses the issue of female circumcision for the first time.

1956 A ban on female circumcisions in Meru, Kenya, leads to protests in which groups of girls circumcise each other.

1959 The Egyptian government bans female circumcision in its Ministry of Health hospitals and clinics.

1979 WHO sponsors its first Seminar on Harmful Traditional Practices Affecting the Health of Women and Children and votes to recommend an end to all types of female circumcision.

1980 A clash occurs between indigenous and Western activists at the UN Mid-Decade Conference on Women and the NGO Forum.

1981 The UN adopts the Convention on the Elimination of All Forms of Discrimination Against Women (Women's Convention).

1984 A group of African human rights organizations forms the Inter-African Committee on Traditional Practices Affecting the Health of Women and Children (IAC).

1990 The UN Committee on the Elimination of Violence Against Women (CEDAW) recommends international action against female circumcision.

1993 The UN Declaration on the Elimination of Violence Against Women includes female circumcision and genital mutilation within the definition of "violence against women."

1996 The United States enacts Federal Prohibition of Female Genital Mutilation Act.

1996 WHO releases the first large-scale study of the prevalence of female circumcision.

1997 An Egyptian court rejects religious groups' challenge to the Ministry of Health ban on female circumcisions.

LEADERS OF NOW LOOK ON AS REP. CAROLYN MALONEY TALKS TO THE MEDIA ABOUT THE ASYLUM CASE OF ADELAIDE ABANKWAH. THE CASE BROUGHT A GREAT DEAL OF ATTENTION TO THE ISSUE OF FEMALE CIRCUMCISION. *(AP/Wide World Photos. Reproduced by permission.)*

female circumcision is not practiced. The Islamic holy text, the Koran, does not mention female circumcision. Islamic supporters of female circumcision rely on a conversation that Mohammed was said to have had with Um Habibah, a woman circumciser of female slaves. He reportedly told the woman that, "If you cut, do not overdo it, because it brings more radiance to the face and is more pleasant for the husband." Female circumcision also is not limited to Islamic countries or even to followers of Islam. It is a tradition among some Christian sects, such as Egypt's Copts and the Ethiopian Christian Church, and has been practiced in some Asian countries and Indonesia, as well as among

indigenous tribes of South America. Traditionally, female circumcision has been performed by older women in a village, whose profession is honored for carrying on a cultural ritual.

Rebellion Against Female Circumcision Ban in Kenya

Around 1900, European administrators and Christian missionaries in colonized African countries began to denounce the practice of female circumcision, which they considered barbaric. Laws and church rules were created to prohibit the practice. Some native peoples, however, strongly resisted what they saw as one more instance of foreigners taking over and destroying their cultures. For instance, in the early 1900s colonial administrators in Kenya, who selected members of local councils, decided to try to end female circumcision. Around 1925 these councils began to prohibit female circumcision done without a girl's consent and to limit the types of procedures that could be used.

In one Kenyan district, Meru, these restrictions imposed by foreigners resulted in a long-lasting political and cultural conflict. Protestant missionaries working in the area enlisted the help of humanitarian and feminist groups in London to try to stop the practice, and Kenyan converts to Christianity had to take a vow to renounce the ritual. This approach backfired. Within a short time after the Methodist Church of Meru adopted such a vow in 1930, its membership dropped from seventy to six. The people of Meru ignored the restrictions, since they viewed female circumcision as a vital step toward marriage and childbirth, and they began to protest publicly. Men and women in the villages performed a dance and song called *Muthrigu*, in which they angrily criticized the missionaries and the colonial government for trying to destroy their customs and seize their land.

In the 1930s Kenyan local councils controlled by Europeans enacted further restrictions on female circumcision, most of them limiting the severity of the procedure. Methodist missionaries and government administrators in some areas, realizing that the local residents would not abandon the practice, oversaw circumcisions and trained circumcisers, and some doctors even became involved in performing them. Presbyterian missionaries took a strict stand; girls who had been circumcised would be expelled from their schools. In Meru, girls were not circumcised until after puberty; if they became pregnant before circumcision, they obtained abortions. To stop these abortions, which they considered both a health hazard and a risk to population growth, the colonial administrators in Meru called in government police to round up masses of prepubescent girls and had them all circumcised.

From 1952 to 1957 an uprising against the British colonial government, known as the Mau Mau Rebellion, raged in Kenya, fueled by many years of resentment against Britain's appropriation of Kenyan land. The rebellion sought Kenya's freedom from its colonial status and was supported by many young Kenyans, men and women alike. In 1956 the *Njuri Ncheke*, the district council in Meru, unanimously passed a total ban on female circumcisions, ostensibly because of the complications they caused during childbirth. At the same meeting, it passed a

WARIS DIRIE

1967– Waris Dirie, born into a Somalian nomadic family with twelve children, traveled far to become a supermodel. At the age of thirteen her father sold her to a much older man in exchange for a few camels. Before the marriage she fled across the desert and eventually made her way to London. There she was discovered by a photographer while working at a fast food restaurant and rose to international fame as a model. Behind this success story, however, was a harrowing tale that she finally made public in her 1998 autobiography, *Desert Flower*.

At the age of five, Dirie was circumcised by a woman using a dull razor, and then her vagina was sewn shut with thorns. She endured constant pain into adulthood and finally had surgery in England to reopen her vagina. In 1997 Dirie became a special United Nations ambassador, speaking out against female circumcision. Rather than debate the practice on cultural grounds, Dirie focuses on the health problems of women who have undergone this procedure. In addition to her own physical agony, one of Dirie's sisters died of an infection after being circumcised. She says, "I think God gave me a voice to speak for other little girls."

tax on coffee; both of these measures were probably a gesture of thanks toward the colonial government for creating an independent Meru land district. The only female member of the council, Martha Kanini, was college educated and had not been circumcised. Although she was present at the council meeting, she was excluded from the discussion and voting. In a 1995 interview quoted in Shell-Duncan and Hernlund's *Female Circumcision in Africa* (2000), she recalled, "I was there alone and . . . the District Commissioner told me not to speak. . . . He wanted men to discuss it. Because I am concerned, I should keep quiet. . . to hear what men say."

As soon as news of the ban on female circumcisions spread, women of the district began to defy it. Traditionally, circumcisions had been times of village celebration, in which feasts and dances honored the groups of girls who were being circumcised. Older women who performed the circumcisions were secluded with the girls for months afterward, observing the healing and teaching the girls about how women should behave. During the next three years following the ban, however, Kenyan adolescent girls bought razor blades and secretly went into the wilderness to circumcise each other, without the help of older women. They became known as *Ngaitana,* which translates as "I will circumcise myself." This was a dangerous act of rebellion since the colonial government was already routinely torturing Mau Mau rebels and burning rebel villages. Although several thousand people were arrested or fined for defying the ban, by 1959 the government realized that it was ineffective and the ban was rescinded.

Female Circumcision in Great Britain and the United States, 1850s–1960s

During the mid-1800s many respected British physicians believed that diseases of women could be cured by surgically removing or cauterizing the clitoris. These physicians included Isaac Baker Brown, who became president of the Medical Society of London. The "diseases" being treated were believed by Victorian society to be potentially fatal ailments among women: masturbation, nymphomania, hysteria, melancholia, and lesbianism. This theory soon became less popular in Great Britain, perhaps because the society of the time was reluctant to discuss sexual matters. By the late nineteenth century, however, it already had spread to the United States, and female circumcision became an accepted medical procedure as a means to stop masturbation and the insanity that it would supposedly cause.

By the 1950s female circumcision as a way to control behavior was not as common in the United States. Instead, it became employed as a cosmetic medical procedure in situations where a girl's clitoris was considered abnormally large. The prestigious *Journal of Surgery* still endorsed complete removal of the clitoris in 1966.

Increased Anti-circumcision Activity Begins in 1960s

During the 1960s and 1970s educational efforts began in some African countries, including Nigeria, Somalia, and Sudan, in the hope that teaching the public about the health damage caused by female circumcision would help stop the practice. Most of these efforts were led by indigenous women's groups, as well as doctors who had observed the results of circumcision and began to write about them in medical journals. It was, however, largely a chance encounter that triggered modern interest in female circumcision in the United States.

While traveling in Africa during the 1970s American journalist Fran Hosken overheard a discussion about female circumcision. After learning more she became horrified and began to write about it. She published research about her discoveries in *The Hosken Report,* set up an organization to fight female circumcision—Women's International Network (WIN)—and testified before hearings held by congressional committees and international agencies. Soon Western-based human rights and feminist groups, including Amnesty International and more recently created groups such as RAINBO and Equality Now were investigating the issue. Individual activists such as noted African American author Alice Walker publicized the harm they thought was done through female circumcision. These western activists and organizations largely focused on circumcisions performed in Africa.

At the same time, African women were becoming more active in efforts to stop female circumcision. In 1980 four African women traveled to Copenhagen, Denmark, to address the United Nations Mid-Decade Conference on Women and the NGO Forum. Unfortunately, the approaches of these women and the Western feminists who addressed the conference were completely at odds. According to Rahman and Toubia in *Female Genital Mutilation: A Guide to Laws and Policies Worldwide* (2000), the African women thought that some of the Western women who spoke were "condescending and confrontational." Rahman and Toubia note that this event is pointed to by those who want to "fuel the fire of cultural conflict," as "the great schism between Western feminists and African cultural conservationists."

Out of this conference, a network of African-based activists emerged. In 1984 a group of African women organized a conference in Senegal. There African human rights organizations formed the Inter-African Committee on Traditional Practices Affecting the Health of Women and Children (IAC). By the late 1990s the IAC had affiliates in 26 African countries, working to educate both the public and African governments about female circumcision. Several well-known women of African origin, including model Waris Dirie [See sidebar], also stepped forward to announce that they had been circumcised and worked to help end the practice.

The Role of the United Nations

The United Nations Commission on Human Rights discussed the issue of female circumcision for the first time in 1952. Until the 1970s, however, the UN did not pay substantial attention to the issues facing the world's women, including female circumcision. Problems such as domestic violence often were considered internal national issues, not

EDUCATIONAL EFFORTS SUCH AS THIS POSTER HELP TO INFORM THE PUBLIC IN AFRICA ABOUT THE DANGERS OF FEMALE CIRCUMCISION. *(CORBIS CORPORATION (Bellevue). Reproduced by permission.)*

human rights abuses that the UN should require its individual member countries to address. Many early UN instruments adopted by member nations could have been applied to women's issues, including female circumcision, but were not. Chief among these were the UN Charter itself, which states that one of the purposes of the organization is to promote "respect for human rights and for fundamental freedoms for all without distinction as to race, sex, language, or religion;" and the 1948 Universal Declaration of Human Rights. A rising international human rights movement and a simultaneous growth of feminist legal scholarship, however, made it impossible for the UN to remain so silent on women's issues.

In 1979 the World Health Organization (WHO), a United Nations agency, voted to recommend an end to all types of female circumcision at its first Seminar on Harmful Traditional Practices Affecting the Health of Women and Children. This seminar was held in Sudan, where female circumcision was almost universal and where national government efforts to regulate the practice during colonial times had failed. Since 1979 WHO has become one of the most active players in the effort to stop female circumcision.

In 1981 the UN adopted the Convention on the Elimination of All Forms of Discrimination Against Women (Women's Convention). This instrument was followed by the recommendation of international action against female circumcision by the UN Committee on the 1990 Elimination of Violence Against Women (CEDAW); and the inclusion, in 1993, in the UN Declaration on the Elimination of Violence Against Women, of female circumcision and genital mutilation within the definition of "violence against women." These instruments, along with the worldwide attention directed to many women's issues after the World Conference on Women held in 1995, led to a much more active role for the UN on the issue of female circumcision. Waris Dirie was appointed as a special United Nations ambassador to speak out on the issue.

WHO now officially refers to female circumcision as "female genital mutilation" (FGM), the term used by most Western human rights and feminist groups. Its "Female Genital Mutilation Information Pack" and *Female Genital Mutilation: An Overview,* for example, both define FGM as "all procedures which involve partial or total removal of the external female genitalia or other injury to the

FAUZIYA KASINGA

1977– In 1996 the U.S. Board of Immigration Appeals made legal history, when for the first time it granted political asylum to a woman who was threatened with involuntary circumcision in her native country. Fauziya Kasinga, a teenager born in the African nation of Togo, had not been circumcised as a child because her wealthy father opposed the practice. After his death, however, Fausinga's aunt arranged a marriage and circumcision was inevitable.

Using a false British passport, Kasinga escaped from Togo and tried to enter the United States in late 1994. She was detained and then imprisoned for over a year while her case was pending before the U.S. Immigration and Naturalization Service. During that time, she claimed, she often was shackled and denied health care. Finally, after her situation was publicized, Kasinga was released to the custody of a relative until her case could be heard. An immigration judge rejected her plea for asylum, saying that her story "lacked credibility," but after the Immigration Board heard Kasinga's appeal, it decided that the fear of undergoing female circumcision constituted persecution and that she was entitled to asylum. This 1996 ruling became binding on all United States immigration judges.

female genital organs whether for cultural or any other non-therapeutic reasons." In these publications, WHO classifies such procedures into four types:

- Type I: Excision [removal] of the prepuce with or without excision of part or all of the clitoris.

- Type II: Excision of the prepuce and clitoris together with partial or total excision of the labia minora.

- Type III: Excision of part or all of the external genitalia and stitching/narrowing of the vaginal opening (infibulation).

- Type IV: Unclassified; includes pricking, piercing or incision of clitoris and/or labia; stretching of clitoris and/or labia; cauterization by burning of clitoris and surrounding tissues; scraping (angurya cuts) of the vaginal orifice or cutting (gishiri cuts) of the vagina; introduction of corrosive substances into the vagina to cause bleeding or herbs into the vagina with the aim of tightening or narrowing the vagina; and any other procedure which falls under the definition of FGM given above.

In 1996 WHO released a study it had conducted on the estimated prevalence of FGM in Africa. According to WHO, Types I and II are now the most common types, constituting up to 80 percent of all procedures. Type III, infibulation, accounts for approximately 15 percent of all procedures. It is the most extreme and, according to WHO, can be responsible for many severe health problems. In its "Female Genital Mutilation Information Pack," WHO gives a graphic description of the infibulation procedure and its possible complications. According to the organization, however, all types of female circumcision can result in serious health complications or death, especially if they are conducted without sanitary precautions. The immediate and long-term complications that WHO describes include: shock, hemorrhaging, recurring infections, urine retention, incontinence, infertility, HIV transmission, painful intercourse, menstruation difficulties, problems during pregnancy and childbirth, and long-term psychological trauma.

Based on its 1996 study WHO estimated that between 100 and 132 million girls and women worldwide have undergone FGM, and that another one to two million are at risk every year. It believes that most of these people live in the African countries covered by its study, but that the practice also takes place in some Middle East and Asian countries. Because of increased immigration from countries where female circumcision is practiced, WHO believes FGM is becoming more common in Australia, Canada, Europe, New Zealand, and the United States as well.

The WHO study showed that the percentage of girls and women who have been circumcised varies widely from country to country in Africa, even among countries where the same religion is practiced. In Uganda and the Democratic Republic of the Congo, for example, the estimated rate of female circumcision is only about five percent; but in Djibouti and Somalia it approaches 100 percent. In some countries girls and women of all religions are circumcised; for Côte d'Ivoire the estimate is 80 percent of the Muslim population, 15 percent of Protestants, and 17 percent of Catholics. Fifty percent of Ethiopian girls and women are circumcised; the practice exists among Muslims, Coptic Christians, and Jews alike. The types of circumcision also vary; in Egypt 80 percent of girls and women are circumcised, mostly via the less extreme types (Types I and II). But in Sudan, with an estimated rate of almost 90 percent, the most extreme type of circumcision (Type III, infibulation) is the most common.

Cultural Clash in Egypt

WHO estimates that 97 percent of Egyptian women have been circumcised, most via the simplest ("Type I") procedure. Efforts to change the practice of female circumcision in Egypt have been concentrated on the health damage it causes. In 1959 the Egyptian government banned female circumcision in its Ministry of Health hospitals and clinics, hoping to send a message to the public. In 1994 during the United Nations International Conference on Population and Development, which was being held in Cairo, the CNN television network broadcast a segment in which a young girl was circumcised in a village, using the traditional method rather than in a hospital. Public outcry in the West was enormous; at the same time, many Egyptians felt they had been publicly humiliated by the broadcast. The Grand Sheikh of Al Azhar Gad el-Haq, a prominent Egyptian religious leader, reacted by decreeing that it was the duty of all Egyptian women to be circumcised.

To prevent a surge in circumcisions performed under unsanitary conditions, Egypt's Ministry of Health lifted its 1959 ban and issued a new policy once again allowing female circumcisions to be performed in government hospitals. In the mid-1990s, however, under pressure from WHO and human rights groups, the Ministry of Health issued a decree outlawing female circumcisions in its hospitals unless a senior gynecologist prescribed them. Although religious groups challenged this decree, it was upheld by an Egyptian court in 1997. Some Western activists expressed outrage that the government's approval of the "medicalization" of female circumcision would allow continuation of the practice.

Egypt's parliament, as of 2001, had not passed any law prohibiting female circumcision, and the Ministry's decree was largely unenforced. Instead, Egyptian health officials and feminist groups, aided by UN funding, began a public education campaign against the practice. Much of this effort has been headed by native activists, such as Joann Salib, a Coptic Christian nun who heads a Christian-Islam group opposed to female circumcision.

Female Circumcision in Modern North America

Female circumcision has been performed in modern times in the United States and Canada, although there are no reliable statistics on how many women have undergone this procedure. There are two situations in which female circumcision has occurred: among immigrant groups from countries where female circumcision is a custom;

Estimated Prevalence of FGM in Select African Nations

As a percentage of female population

Country	Estimated Prevalence, %
Burkina Faso	72
Central African Republic	43
Côte d'Ivoire	43
Egypt	97
Eritrea	95
Guinea	99
Kenya	38
Mali	94
Niger	5
Nigeria	25
Somalia	96
Sudan	89
Tanzania	12
Togo	23

Source: World Health Organization, May 2001. Data for all estimates, except Somalia and Togo, obtained from National Demographic and Healthy Surveys, Marco International Inc., Calverton, MD. Data for Somalia taken from: *Fertility and Family Planning in Urban Somalia*, 1983. Ministry of Health. Mogadishu and Westinghouse, 1983. Data for Togo taken from a national survey carried out by the Unité de Recherche Démographique (URD) in 1996. (The reference of the unpublished report is Agounke E, Janssens M, Vignikin K, *Prévalence et facteurs socio-économiques de l'excision au Togo, rapport provisoire*, Lomé, June 1996. Results are given in Locoh T. 1998. "Pratiques, opinions et attitudes en matière d'excision en Afrique." Population 6: 1227-1240.)

FEMALE CIRCUMCISION, ALSO REFERRED TO AS FEMALE GENITAL MUTILATION (FGM), IS PRACTICED WITH VARYING DEGREES OF FREQUENCY ACROSS AFRICA. *(The Gale Group.)*

ALICE WALKER

_1944–_ American writer Alice Walker is best known for her novel _The Color Purple,_ which won the Pulitzer Prize for 1983 and was made into a successful film. In 1992 her novel _Possessing the Secret of Joy_ dealt graphically with the subject of female circumcision, and instantly brought Walker critical praise as well as controversy.

The following year Walker became more involved in publicizing the practice of female circumcision. With Indian director Pratibha Parmar, she co-produced and narrated an equally graphic film documentary on ritual female circumcision in Africa, _Warrior Marks._ Walker also wrote a book by the same name, which tells how the two women filmed the documentary and also contains Walker's personal reflections and poetry.

and among girls and women on whom circumcision is performed for medical or psychological reasons.

During the late 1990s the federal Centers for Disease Control and Prevention (CDC) attempted to determine how many women and girls in the United States either had undergone circumcision or were at risk of having it performed on them. Using figures compiled by WHO of the prevalence of circumcision in African countries and United States census figures for immigrant populations, the CDC estimated that in 1990 there were 168,000 girls and women in this group.

No large-scale study has taken place in Canada, but there have been studies of smaller groups. For instance, in Somalia, female circumcision that involves stitching up a girl's labia ("infibulation") is almost universal. A study of 60 Somalian immigrants in Canada, all of them new mothers who had been circumcised by infibulation during childhood, was discussed in _Chatelaine_ (November 2000). Not only did half of these women want to be restitched after childbirth, but most also wanted their own daughters to undergo the same drastic circumcision procedure.

Because of concern over female circumcision among immigrant groups, both the United States and Canada have outlawed the practice. In the United States, the Federal Prohibition of Female Genital Mutilation Act of 1996 (Public Law 104-140, 110 Stat. 1327) makes it illegal to perform circumcision in the United States on girls under the age of eighteen. Canada's law, passed in 1997, goes one step further; it outlaws female circumcision within the country and also makes it illegal to have a child sent abroad to have it performed. In both cases the laws were passed after highly publicized cases caused a public outcry from feminists and human rights activists and the medical community raised concerns over the serious and possibly fatal health problems caused by female circumcision. Enforcement of these laws, however, is difficult. In Canada there had been no prosecutions as of 2000, and there is such secrecy among the immigrant population that no proof is available on how many circumcisions are taking place.

During the 1960s and 1970s there was an upsurge in female circumcision in the United States, a strange byproduct of the "Sexual Revolution." Some physicians and popular magazines encouraged surgery, in which skin covering the clitoris was removed, claiming that this would make a woman more sexually responsive. Insurance companies put an end to most of these procedures by saying that they were ineffective and refusing to pay for them.

According to researcher Martha Coventry, writing in _Ms._ (October-November 2000), at least 2,000 children in the United States have cosmetic genital surgery every year. Most of these patients are girls whose clitorises are considered abnormally large and are reduced in size. While some of these children might be intersexed (born with genitals that make their gender unclear), Coventry noted how much pressure exists to have cosmetic genital surgery to meet societal standards of "normal." Genital surgery within the United States, occurring both during the nineteenth and twentieth centuries, has not attracted the level of public attention given to female circumcision that takes place in other countries.

RECENT HISTORY AND THE FUTURE

The Future of Female Circumcision

Several African countries now have laws prohibiting female circumcision, including Burkina Faso, Egypt, Ghana, Guinea, and Senegal. A great incentive toward enacting these laws has been the United States' annual country report on human rights, prepared by the State Department. This report lists the countries that allow female circumcision, and it can result in a reduction in foreign aid to those countries. Few countries, however, enforce their laws against female circumcision, since they

A WOMAN WEEPS AFTER A MANDATORY CIRCUMCISION IN KENYA IN 1995. *(The Gamma Liaison Network. Reproduced by permission.)*

would result in the arrests of possibly millions of people. Many indigenous groups fear the type of backlash that resulted when Kenya and Egypt imposed bans on female circumcision. Instead, they prefer to try to educate the public about the health risks of female circumcision and to convince people to adopt alternative rituals. Their hope is that these substitute rites of passage will eventually replace female circumcision as a way of carrying on cultural heritage and religious tradition.

Laws limiting or banning female circumcision also have been enacted in several countries with sizable numbers of immigrants from countries where female circumcision is practiced. These include Australia, Norway, Sweden, and the United Kingdom, as well as the United States and Canada. In addition to the federal law in the United States, eight individual states passed their own laws prohibiting female circumcision during the 1990s. According to WHO, these states were California, Delaware, Louisiana, Minnesota, North Dakota, Rhode Island, Tennessee, and Wisconsin.

WHO took a strong stance in the twenty-first century that female circumcision should be eliminated, and that this action should originate largely within nations employing the practice. As the

agency states in its 1998 publication *Female Genital Mutilation: An Overview,*

> Many have reached the conclusion that, recognizing the imbalance of power between men and women that underlies the practice, the most effective strategies for dealing with female genital mutilation include helping women to empower themselves within their own culture and community. Essentially this means that the struggle to stop the practice as a health risk and a violation of women's rights must be led by women from the communities where it occurs.

WHO sees the role of international aid groups and human rights organizations as contributing technical and financial resources and maintaining a united stand against the practice, but not as the grassroots leadership of the movement.

The modern effort to halt female circumcision that has originated within African countries has focused attention on education about its health risks. Local campaigns have attempted to recruit community leaders, including religious authorities, into these educational activities. People in countries where female circumcision is practiced are also having increased contact with countries where it is not practiced (via the media, the Internet, and foreign travel). This contact, along with the existing outreach network for AIDS prevention, could have a major effect on female circumcision.

Although there is great international pressure to end female circumcision, particularly its most extreme forms, many Arab and African women still support the continuation of the practice. A 1996 Hastings Center report, "Judging the Other," noted that there are many other important problems facing these women, such as domestic violence, and that there is resentment that Westerners consider the circumcision ritual barbaric and label it "mutilation." There is a growing acknowledgement, however, even among advocates of female circumcision, that the more severe forms are dangerous to women's health and should be modified. In *Taking Sides: Clashing Views on Controversial Issues in Human Sexuality* (1998), multicultural professor P. Masila Mutisya criticizes Western activists for "dictating and imposing their morality on non-westerners without offering any viable alternative or accommodation." Mutisya suggests an alternative to traditional female circumcision: a symbolic nicking of the clitoris, performed by a physician and preceded by educating the girl about the meaning of the practice and the role of women in society.

In several African countries, the rate of circumcision has gradually declined since the 1980s. In Sudan, where infibulation is the predominant

VIEWPOINTS

The subject of female circumcision brings up a wide range of questions and opinions. In the countries where female circumcision is widely practiced, those trying to eliminate the practice are faced with deeply entrenched beliefs and traditions. It is an obstacle that has proven difficult to overcome.

Fran P. Hosken, in her speech "Female Genital Mutilation: Strategies for Eradication," presented at the First International Symposium on Circumcision on March 1–2, 1980, explained that "Over the centuries and due to their isolation, women have come to believe that the mutilation of their genitals are 'necessary.' Indeed, many women think that they are done all over the world. Thus, they are accepted as 'natural.'" It is this acceptance that human rights and health organizations are trying to combat and have mounted international and local campaigns to inform women of their choices.

Culture or Cruelty? On April 12, 1994, the Director-General to the World Health Organization's Global Commission on Women's Health, addressing the cultural claims of female circumcision, stated, "Our purpose should not be to criticize and condemn. Nor can we remain passive, in the name of some bland version of multiculturalism. . . . [W]hat we must aim for is to convince people, including women, that they can give up a specific practice *without* giving up meaningful aspects of their own culture" (quoted in the World Health Organization's "Female Genital Mutilation Information Pack").

Culture. Richard A. Shweder asserts the importance of understanding the cultures in which female circumcision is practiced. In "What About 'Female Genital Mutilation'? and Why Understanding Culture Matters in the First Place" (*Daedalus*, Fall 2000), Shweder encouraged insight into the cultures and societies that support the custom. "[I]nstead of assuming that our own perceptions of beauty and disfigurement are universal and must be transcendental we might want to consider the possibility that there is a real and astonishing cultural divide around the world in moral, emotional, and aesthetic reactions to female genital surgeries."

Cruelty. While cultural beliefs and practices should not be discounted, women's health and safety also should not be ignored. In a call to arms against female circumcision, Tilman Hasche, an attorney for Lydia Oluloro—who sought asylum in the United States to prevent the circumcision of her daughters in Nigeria—said, "If I told the average American we were sending young boys back to Africa to have their penises cut off, I think they'd agree that the claims for asylum are clear." (Brownless and Seter. "In the Name of Ritual," *U.S. News and World Report*, February 7, 1994).

While it may not be clear if female circumcision is a cultural tradition or a practice in cruelty, it is clear that the issue will continue to receive international attention and that efforts to inform women of the health risks will carry on. With more information, women may at least have the chance to choose.

procedure, the number of circumcised women between 15 and 49 dropped ten percent during the 1980s. And in Kenya—where earlier attempts to end circumcision had resulted in the *Ngaitana* rebellion—a 1991 survey showed that only 78 percent of adolescent females had been circumcised, as opposed to virtually 100 percent of women over fifty. An alternative to circumcision, *Ntanira Na Mugambo* ("circumcision through words") has been devised cooperatively by the Kenyan organization Maendeleo Ya Wanawake and the international organization Program for Appropriate Technology. Similar to the Jewish ritual of Bat Mitzvah for adolescent girls, the Kenyan ritual involves education and celebration at a coming of age day, but does not include any genital alteration. During its first two years, 300 young women went through this alternative ritual. In other countries female circumcision might possibly end more quietly. One of the most prominent circumcisers in Guinea, who had been the target of protests by Western human rights groups, confessed that she had never actually "cut" any girls. As quoted by *Lancet*, Younkara Diallo Fatimata said, "I'd just pinch their clitorises to make them scream and tightly bandage them up so that they walked as if they were in pain."

BIBLIOGRAPHY

Branigin, William, and Douglas Farah. "Asylum Seeker Impostor, INS Says," *Washington Post*, December 20, 2000.

Brownlee, Shannon, and Jennifer Seter. "In the Name of Ritual," *U.S. News and World Report*, February 7, 1994.

Burstyn, Linda. "Female Circumcision Comes to America," *Atlantic Monthly,* October 1995.

Chelala, Cesar. "An Alternative Way to Stop Female Genital Mutilation," *The Lancet,* July 11, 1998.

Coventry, Martha. "Making the Cut," *Ms.,* October-November 2000.

Dirie, Waris. *Desert Flower.* New York: William Morrow, 1998.

"Egypt's Battle Against Female Circumcision," *Christian Science Monitor,* February 27, 2001.

"Eradication of Female Genital Mutilation (FGM) in Kenya," *UN Chronicle,* Fall 1999.

"Female Genital Mutilation: Is It Crime or Culture?" *The Economist,* February 13, 1999.

Fennell, Tom. "Finding New Grounds for Refuge," *Maclean's,* August 8, 1994.

Francoeur, Robert T., and William J. Taverner. *Taking Sides: Clashing Views on Controversial Issues in Human Sexuality.* 6th ed. Guilford, CT: Dushkin/McGraw Hill, 1998.

"Ghanaian Woman Wins Asylum," *Washington Post,* August 18, 1999.

Gollaher, David L. *Circumcision: A History of the World's Most Controversial Surgery.* New York: Basic Books, 2000.

Hosken, Fran P. "Female Genital Mutilation: Strategies for Eradication," March 1–2, 1989. Available online at http://www.nocirc.org/symposia/first/hosken.html (cited June 1, 2001).

Jones, Wanda K., et al. "Female Genital Mutilation/Female Circumcision: Who is at Risk in the U.S.?" *Public Health Reports,* September-October 1997.

Kiragu, Karungari. "Female Genital Mutilation: A Reproductive Health Concern," *Population Reports,* October 1995.

Lane, Sandra D., and Robert A. Rubinstine. "Judging the Other: Responding to Traditional Female Genital Surgeries," *Hastings Center Report,* May-June 1996.

Leyden, Liz. "Adelaide Abankwah Fled Ghana to Avoid a Tribal Ritual," *Washington Post,* July 21, 1999.

Lightfoot-Klein, Hanny. *Prisoners of Ritual: An Odyssey into Female Genital Circumcision in Africa.* New York: Harrington Park Press, 1989.

Morris, Rita. "The Culture of Female Circumcision," *Advances in Nursing Science,* December 1, 1996.

Price, Joyce, and Brian Blomquist. "Immigration Judges to Decide if Tribal Ritual Merits Asylum," *Insight on the News,* June 3, 1996.

Rahman, Anika, and Nahid Toubia, eds. *Female Genital Mutilation: A Guide to Laws and Policies Worldwide.* London, New York: Zed Books, 2000.

Scott, Sarah. "The Deepest Cut of All," *Chatelaine,* November 2000.

Shell-Duncan, Bettina, and Ylva Hernlund, eds. *Female "Circumcision" in Africa: Culture, Controversy, and Change.* Boulder, CO.: Lynne Rienner Publishers, 2000.

Shweder, Richard A. "What About 'Female Genital Mutilation'? and Why Understanding Culture Matters in the First Place," *Daedalus,* Fall 2000.

Walker, Alice. *Possessing the Secret of Joy.* New York: Pocket Books, 1992.

Walker, Alice, and Pratibha Parmar. *Warrior Marks: Female Genital Mutilation and the Sexual Blinding of Women.* New York: Harcourt, Brace, 1993.

World Health Organization. "Female Genital Mutilation Information Pack." Available online at http://www.who.int/frh-whd/FGM/infopack/English/fgm_infopack.htm (cited March 15, 2001)

World Health Organization. *Female Genital Mutilation: An Overview.* Available online at http://www.who.int/dsa/cat98/fgmbook.htm (cited March 15, 2001).

—Gerry Azzata

OVERTHROWING DEMOCRACY: FIJI'S COUP

THE CONFLICT

The nation of Fiji faced political unrest even before its declaration as an independent republic in 1970. Early British control of the island as a Crown Colony, as well as tensions between ethnic Fijians and the Indian population recruited in the 1870s to work in the agricultural industry, lie at the heart of the nation's struggle to maintain democracy.

Political

- Fiji has suffered through years of political unrest, with three major coups taking place since 1987.

Ethnic

- Inter-ethnic conflict between ethnic Fijians and the country's Indian population is partially to blame for Fiji's political instability.

On May 19, 2000, gunmen invaded Fiji's parliament, taking Prime Minister Mahendra Chaudhry and other cabinet members hostage. The gunmen's leader, George Speight, proclaimed himself head of a "civilian Taukei government," or native Fijian government. Fiji's president declared a state of emergency, and the country entered into a tense negotiating period with Speight that lasted for 56 days, until the hostages were released. This was not the first time the Taukei movement that motivated Speight's coup gained widespread attention. Fourteen years earlier another coup overthrew the Fijian government in the name of Taukei, the seeds of which were sewn in Fiji's unique society and history.

Speight's gunmen followed in the footsteps of the May 14, 1987, coup, in which armed soldiers wearing hoods entered the Fijian parliament. Led by Lieutenant Colonel Sitiveni Rabuka, they ushered members of a coalition elected the previous month, outside. There these parliamentarians were put into waiting trucks to be transported to military barracks. Rabuka then announced his coup to Fiji's governor-general, who, after consulting with the country's judiciary, declared a state of emergency and assumed executive authority. Fiji had achieved the unwelcome distinction of becoming the first Pacific Island nation to suffer a military coup. The nation would suffer two additional coups in the ensuing years, culminating in the standoff between the Fijian government and George Speight in 2000.

Rabuka's intent was to firmly establish the dominance of ethnic Fijians over Fiji's sizable population of Indians—descendants of indentured laborers brought to the islands to work in the sugar industry. He set in motion 14 years of political unrest in one of the larger and more prosperous countries in the Pacific. Since troops first marched these legally elected parliamentarians out of Government House, Fiji has gone through a second Rabuka-led coup, the promulgation of two different constitutions, and in May 2000 a third coup led by someone widely described in the media as a "failed businessman." He and his followers were in turn imprisoned by military forces who then had to survive threats of mutiny within their own ranks. As of May 2001, Fiji was ruled by an interim government that possessed dubious constitutional authority, while social order depended very much on military might.

From an outsider's viewpoint there might have seemed little reason to expect such turmoil in an oceanic region named after the Latin word for "peaceful." Composed of more than 300 islands, one-third of them inhabited, Fiji seemed to fit the image of a South Pacific paradise and was becoming an increasingly popular tourist destination. The country enjoyed high average life expectancy and adult literacy rates. The economy, based primarily on sugar production, was ranked by the World Bank as lower-middle-income, better off than many impoverished, "underdeveloped," countries elsewhere. Ratu Sir Kamisese Mara, who had served as prime minister since the country achieved independence in 1970, was regarded as a major figure in regional politics.

Yet behind this idyllic image lay an early history of indigenous warfare among Fijian chiefs, followed by almost a century of colonialism that set the stage for modern inter-ethnic conflict that has yet to be resolved.

HISTORICAL BACKGROUND

More than 3,000 years ago, intrepid voyagers sailed in outrigger canoes from a Southeast Asian homeland through the western Pacific Ocean to settle islands in the east. Archaeological finds suggest that the ancestors of the Fijians arrived in the archipelago about 1,100 years before the beginning of the Christian era. The neighboring island groups of Samoa and Tonga were settled at about the same time as Fiji, and there continued to be frequent interaction among these three populations throughout the succeeding centuries. Though a number of European explorers sighted the Fijian islands, beginning with the Dutch captain Abel Tasman in 1643, they seldom landed or had much direct contact with Fijians until the end of the 1700s. Fijians came to have a reputation for violence; early travelers in the Pacific often referred to Fiji as "The Cannibal Isles." This reputation had a factual basis in frequent

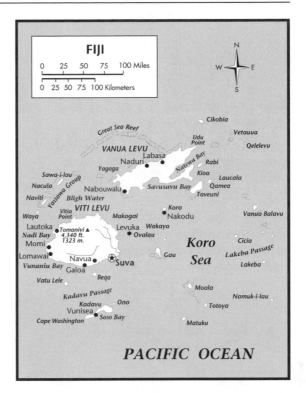

MAP OF FIJI. *(Maryland Cartographics. Reproduced by permission.)*

wars fought over the control of land and succession to chiefly rank. Competition for leadership never ceased. Though rank was based on kinship, it had to be maintained and increased by force. Chiefdoms expanded, contracted, or completely disappeared. Yet none of these chiefs ever commanded more than a portion of the islands.

Enter the Outsiders

Intense relations between Fijians and the outside world began when Europeans learned that sandalwood could be obtained in Fiji. As a result Fiji was thoroughly involved in trading relationships with outsiders by the mid-1800s. The islet of Bau, off the southeast coast of the main island of Viti Levu, came to occupy a key position in these relationships. Trade for firearms added a new dimension to the ongoing political conflicts among chiefs, and Bauan chiefs were well placed to exploit contacts with the outside world.

Another kind of outside influence came from Wesleyan (Methodist) missionaries, who arrived in 1835 from England by way of Australia and Tonga. Missionaries developed a system of writing, heretofore lacking, for the Fijian language. The question of conversion to the new faith also became entangled with Fijian politics. Tongans had earlier accepted Christianity and many served as Wesleyan missionaries to Fiji. Tongan chiefs had long inter-

CHRONOLOGY

1801 Attracted by sandalwood forests, Europeans begin trading with Fijians.

1872 Chief Cakobau of Bau establishes the kingdom of Fiji.

1875 Faced with continuing social unrest, Cakobau cedes the kingdom to Great Britain as a Crown Colony.

1879 Planters begin importing laborers from India under an indenture system.

1882 The Colonial Sugar Refining Company begins operations.

1919 The indentured labor system ends, after more than 60,000 Indians have come to Fiji.

1970 Fiji becomes an independent nation and a member of the British Commonwealth. Ratu Sir Kamisese Mara of the Alliance Party becomes the new country's first prime minister under a parliamentary system of government.

1977 The National Federation Party, representing Indo-Fijian interests, wins a majority of seats in parliament but is unable to form a government. The governor-general appoints Mara to create an interim cabinet.

1987 A coalition headed by the Fiji Labor Party upsets Alliance to win a parliamentary majority. At the first sitting of the new government, Lieutenant-Colonel Sitiveni Rabuka leads a coup to restore ethnic Fijian dominance in the country.

1990 A new constitution is developed, giving ethnic Fijians a clear advantage in government.

1995 Faced with domestic unrest and international criticism, Fiji's government creates a committee to review the 1990 constitution.

1997 The new constitution is unanimously approved by parliament.

1999 In the first general election under the new constitution, Mahendry Chaudhry leads the Fiji Labor Party to an absolute parliamentary majority, becoming Fiji's first Indo-Fijian prime minister.

May 2000 Gunmen led by part-Fijian George Speight invade parliament, taking Chaudhry and others hostage. They are released after 56 days and Speight is later imprisoned by the military. An interim government is formed and creates a new constitutional review committee.

married with residents of Fiji, and the Tongan Chief Ma'afu settled in Fiji in 1852. By then Chief Cakobau of Bau had taken advantage of his location to amass both traditional and imported wealth. Even within his base on Bau and adjoining Viti Levu island, Cakobau could not rest easily, as traditional rivalries over succession to chiefly titles continued unabated.

In the mid-1800s other nations began to contend for economic and political power in the Pacific. Fijians were not immune to these struggles. Increasing numbers of settlers from Britain, Australia, the United States, and elsewhere, wanted land in the archipelago. Some were drawn to Fiji by the possibility of developing cotton plantations in response to the demand created by the U.S. Civil War (1861–65). Settlers' activities fomented continual unrest. Several Americans claimed that Cakobau, whom they saw as the chief of all the islands, owed them substantial debts and were threatening to bring in U.S. warships to collect.

In 1870–71 approximately 1,500 new settlers arrived, tripling the "white" population. The outsiders usually brought with them the ideas of racial superiority then prevalent in their home countries. Few, if any, could accept traditional Fiji political patterns of competing chiefdoms, but instead demanded what they thought of as stable government. Despite sentiment that such a government should be controlled by foreigners, in 1871 a monarchy was set up with Cakobau as king of all Fiji.

Though Cakobau had considerable prestige throughout the islands, he lacked the coercive power to control all the factions that competed in his kingdom. These included planters, traders, and missionaries—often backed up by the warships of their governments—and, as always, rival Fijian chiefs. Violence between Fijians and settlers, as well as among the "whites" themselves, was all too common. In the early days of the kingdom, Cakobau had to deal with warfare in the interior of Viti Levu, when mountain dwellers resisted plantation development.

The Tongan chief and Fiji resident Ma'afu shared with many of the settlers the belief that cession to a European nation was the best solution to Fiji's problems. The question of annexation had already been raised in the British House of Commons. J.B. Thurston was both a confidante of Cakobau and the current British consul. In January 1873 he cabled the British government to clarify the situation. Two commissioners were appointed by London to make an assessment. Although a group of 18 chiefs expressed their opposition to cession, an agreement was finally reached that turned over the government—but not the land or the Fijian people—to Great Britain.

Cakobau signed the deed of cession in September 1874 and the document that transformed Fiji into a British Crown Colony was formally promulgated on October 10, 1874. The first months of Fiji's new status were marked by tragedy as a measles epidemic swept through the islands in 1875. Lacking natural immunity to the disease, perhaps one-fifth of the population died, including many chiefs.

The Crown Colony

Sir Arthur Gordon was Fiji's first governor appointed by the British Colonial Office, which retained final authority over all major decisions taken in the colony. Three years later, the position was combined with that of the Western Pacific High Commissioner, with jurisdiction over British subjects in much of the region. Gordon collaborated with J.B. Thurston, who eventually succeeded him, in shaping colonial policy. An important feature was the preservation of Fijian lands in the hands of Fijians, in contrast to what had happened in other Pacific realms such as Hawai'i and New Zealand. European notions of land tenure never really matched what can be known of Fijian culture before foreign influence. Just as Fijians traditionally had never had a single ruler, there was regional variation in customary land tenure. Populations were mobile and the gardens that provided people's subsistence shifted accordingly. Nor did chiefly rank correlate neatly with the size of a chief's landholdings; more important was a chief's ability to mobilize labor or warriors. Nevertheless, establishing a stable government approximating British ideals required codified laws which had the effect of reducing the flexible characteristics of tradition. The Native Land Ordinance of 1880 made Fijian land inalienable and, though the law was modified in later years, Fijians today firmly hold to the belief that they alone should control their land.

Following the principle of "indirect rule," a system of provinces and districts was created. Each province was governed by a paramount chief, and in 1875 they formed a Great Council of Chiefs to advise the governor. Lower-ranking chiefs were in charge of districts and, as governance developed, they also filled magistrate and other administrative positions. Succession to chieftainship continued to be contentious. Instead of the violent clashes of pre-colonial times, there was a tendency for first-born sons to inherit automatically from their fathers. Fijians were taxed but payment was commonly made in produce, usually copra, the dried meat of coconut. Before World War I (1914–18), politics involved three major elements: colonial administration, Fijians represented by chiefs, and a growing commercial sector run by European settlers.

Sugar

Policy as set by Gordon and Thurston, his successor until 1897, was guided by a vision of Fijians as small-scale agricultural producers. Thurston, however, also pursued a goal of larger capital investment. To this end, the colonial government invited an Australian firm, Colonial Sugar Refining Company (CSR), to establish plantations and mills in Fiji. Beginning in 1882 CSR's operations became the basis of the colony's economy with far-reaching consequences for modern politics.

Sugar production is an extremely labor-intensive operation involving back-breaking work in the tropical sun. Fijians, firmly possessed of the land they needed for their own subsistence, could not be expected to join the work force required. Though workers from other Pacific islands had been recruited for plantation labor before the Colony was established, this recruitment had come under attack as being nothing short of kidnapping. CSR had to look elsewhere for the labor it needed.

In 1879 planters had begun to recruit laborers from India under an indenture system. This system meant that workers were brought to Fiji under a contract that legally required them to work five years for their employers. At the end of the indenture period, workers could return to India at their own expense or, if they contracted for a second five-year term, employers would provide return fare at term's end.

When the indenture system ended in 1919 more than 60,000 Indian men and women had come to Fiji. Though some 24,000 returned to India after varying periods of residence, others settled in Fiji permanently. These laborers had been recruited from different areas and language groups. Their Fiji-born descendants formed a distinctive community. Very few intermarried with ethnic Fijians, and their adopted name "Indo-Fijians" emphasized long-term residence rather than any "racial" mixture. Even before the indenture system ended, Indians took advantage at the end of their contracts to become small-scale traders or free laborers. In rural areas, some began to lease land, often from Fijian landlords.

By 1900 CSR was enjoying increased profitability and moving toward monopoly status, obtaining land and mills formerly owned by others.

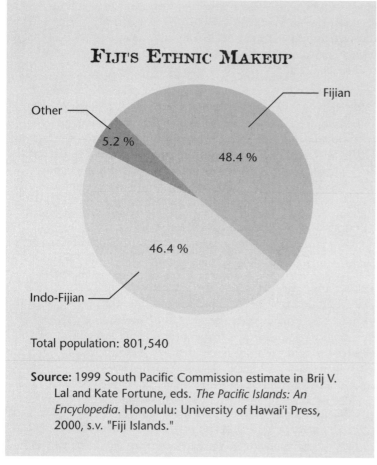

FIJI'S ETHNIC MAKEUP

Other
5.2 %

Fijian
48.4 %

Indo-Fijian
46.4 %

Total population: 801,540

Source: 1999 South Pacific Commission estimate in Brij V. Lal and Kate Fortune, eds. *The Pacific Islands: An Encyclopedia.* Honolulu: University of Hawai'i Press, 2000, s.v. "Fiji Islands."

FIJI HAS A LARGELY HOMOGENOUS POPULATION. THE TWO MAIN GROUPS ARE THE NATIVE FIJIANS AND THE INDO-FIJIANS, MANY OF WHOM ARE DESCENDENTS OF INDENTURED SERVANTS. DIFFERENCES BETWEEN THE TWO GROUPS HAVE RESULTED IN POLITICAL UPHEAVAL. *(The Gale Group.)*

Changing conditions caused the company to reorganize its operation to deal with more independent growers. By the 1930s cane production was about equally divided between that grown on land leased from the Company and that leased from Fijians. The Indo-Fijian community continually pressured for long-term leases, since they were the primary growers. In 1940 leasing from Fijians was put in the hands of a Native Land Trust Board, which was mandated to ensure sufficient land for Fijian needs.

These changes did not alter CSR's dominance of the colony's economy. Gold had been discovered in the early 1930s, but sugar remained the mainstay. There were social consequences as the European business community continued to resist anything that might serve Indo-Fijian interest. Ethnic Fijians as represented by the Great Council of Chiefs generally concurred, though their own membership in the Legislative Council that advised

the governor was limited. Not until 1937 did the Colonial Office reorganize the council to include representation by the three major ethnic groups.

War and Its Aftermath

World War II (1939–45) marked a watershed in the history of all Pacific Islands. Although no battles were fought in Fiji, there were inevitable social repercussions. Some 8,000 Allied troops were stationed in Nadi, heretofore a little town devoted to sugar production. The sudden influx of so many "whites" was unsettling to Fijian and Indo-Fijian alike.

Ethnic Fijians participated enthusiastically in the war effort, and chiefs led successful recruiting drives. Indo-Fijians responded rather differently. They could not help but be aware of Gandhi's "Quit India" campaign and the collaboration of some Indians with the Japanese to get rid of the British. In addition, both government and CSR urged their community to devote itself to agricultural work. Mounting grievances against the company, however, led to a major strike by sugar farmers in 1943. Though CSR could be said to have won the ensuing settlement, many issues remained unresolved.

During wartime, administration of Fijian affairs was reorganized. The Fijian Affairs Board was created in 1944, effectively becoming the executive and administrative arm of the Great Council of Chiefs, which was itself expanded and reorganized. This administration assumed uniformity across villages, overlooking regional variation as well as the different interests of urban and rural Fijians. The Board's increased regulation of their lives produced an even greater sense that Fijians were a special people, set apart from others. This division was heightened by wartime population changes—for the first time there were more Indo-Fijians than ethnic Fijians in the colony. Both Fijians and "whites" became more outspoken in denouncing a perceived threat to their interests, and repatriation of the entire Indo-Fijian community to India was openly discussed in the 1950s.

During the same decade, organized labor became a significant force. Several strikes took place in various industries, and one in the oil industry led to a riot in Suva. This event was noteworthy because it appeared to target the European business community, suggesting a developing solidarity along class, rather than ethnic, lines. The next major industrial clash took place in the sugar industry and initially it appeared that both Indo-Fijian and Fijian cane growers might join forces against

CSR. However, unity among the different growers' associations could not be maintained, while the Great Council of Chiefs offered to aid the government against the strikers.

Even more significant changes were on the horizon. Decolonization of Africa and Asia was proceeding rapidly, and the growing block of newly independent countries in the United Nations increased pressure on European powers to rid themselves of their overseas possessions. In November 1960 Fiji's governor announced his intention to modify the existing constitution. Ratu Kamisese Mara, a high-ranking chief from Lau with an Oxford education, had emerged as the leader of Fijians. Mara expressed his people's concern over the speed with which political change was progressing but a new constitution was produced in 1966.

Fiji was pointed on the road to a Westminister, or parliamentary, system of government. A method for legislative representation had to be developed as a compromise among ethnic groups. The result was an electoral system that maintained ethnic divisions, gave a slight numerical advantage to Fijians over Indo-Fijians, and produced a significant over-representation of Europeans. Two seats were to be filled by nominees of the Great Council of Chiefs.

Political parties contested the 1966 elections. A lawyer who had been a leader in sugar strikes headed the National Federation Party (NFP). His party soon became the voice of Indo-Fijian interests, demanding a common roll, rather than representation by ethnic group, and condemning European dominance. Mara headed the Alliance Party, which grew out of an earlier association that had consistently demanded Fijian paramountcy in any future government. By 1965 Alliance also included some members of the Indo-Fijian, Chinese and European communities. This party won a clear majority in 1966. When Mara became chief minister in 1967, NFP forced a by-election that increased its majority in the nine seats reserved for Indo-Fijians. This in turn created a backlash among Fijians and there was rioting in some areas.

New leadership of NFP was more willing to compromise; the party no longer demanded a common roll. In turn, the Alliance Party accepted the principle of full independence from Britain. Details of the transition were worked out in 1969. Parliament would consist of an appointed Senate and a fully elected House of Representatives. In the latter, a complicated system of voting was established, with some seats reserved for ethnic groups and others to be contested regardless of ethnicity. The Great Council of Chiefs was empowered to review all legislation affecting Fijians, and to appoint 8 of

Mahendra Pal Chaudhry

1942– In 1999 Mahendra Chaudhry was elected Fiji's prime minister, the first of Indian ancestry to hold that office, but was deposed a year later in a coup led by gunmen claiming to speak for ethnic Fijian interests. He is presently struggling to restore the 1997 constitution, which paved the way for his electoral victory. Chaudhry began an active career in labor politics when he became general secretary of the Fiji Public Service Association in 1975. He served as national secretary of the umbrella Fiji Trades Union Congress 1988–92. With the late Dr. Timoci Bavadra, an ethnic Fijian civil servant, Chaudhry established the National Farmers Union to represent sugar cane growers, most of whom are Indo-Fijian. He was thus well-placed to join Dr. Bavadra in founding the Fiji Labor Party (FLP).

Elected to parliament in 1987, Chaudhry briefly served as Minister of Finance and Economic Planning until the Bavadra government was deposed by the first military coup led by Sitiveni Rabuka. Taking over the FLP after Bavadra's death, he led the party to the electoral victory that surprised most observers by its magnitude. His confrontational style and the circumstance that sugar land leases were due to expire 2000–01 added to Fijian resentment of his ethnicity. Though he claims that lawsuits now in progress will return him to power, many observers feel that ethnic Fijians will never again permit any suggestion of Indo-Fijian political control.

the 22 members of the Senate. The result was that, at any time, half or more of the Senate were Fijians. This scheme, complicated enough to outside observers, assumed that voters would always follow their ethnic membership and that other divisions—rural vs. urban, economic classes, one geographic area vs. another, commoners vs. chiefs—would remain irrelevant, despite continuing socioeconomic change. It was with this system that Fiji began its independence on October 10, 1970, with Ratu Mara as Fiji's first prime minister.

Independence Politics

In fact, demographic change was on its way. By the 1980s Fijians had begun to outnumber Indians, and there was continued migration to urban areas. It was in towns that the notion of a "multiracial" society had some reality as people mingled in schools, voluntary associations and sporting activities. Intermarriage between Fijians and Indians was still rare, however.

Fiji held its first post-independence general election in 1972. By this time, Ratu Mara was at the height of his renown. He had been knighted in Great Britain in 1969, and in the same year succeeded to a title that made him paramount over the entire Lau region in Fiji. He led international forums and seemed to dominate politics throughout the Pacific, where larger island groups had yet to achieve independence.

For 17 years Ratu Mara's Alliance Party and the NFP were the primary rivals to rule Fiji. Alliance was able to command enough support from Indo-Fijian and other ethnic groups to prevail until 1977, when the NFP won a narrow majority of seats. Plagued by intra-party squabbles, the NFP could not form a government under Westminister rules. The governor-general, acting within constitutional right, appointed Ratu Mara prime minister to form a minority government. After this government fell to a no-confidence vote, a new general election took place. Alliance leaders worked hard to get back Fijian voters, while the NFP was divided by leadership struggles. Mara's party scored a clear majority. The 1982 election, however, was more closely contested than all of those earlier. The NFP's new leader managed to form a coalition with a Fijian party which expressed the resentment of westerners who felt ill-used by successive Mara administrations. Campaign and post-election rhetoric was filled with all manner of accusations. The final result carried Alliance to a close victory. Ethnic voting patterns continued, and Alliance embarked upon an effort to strengthen the chiefly system at local levels.

In 1985 Fiji's national politics changed forever with the formation of the Fiji Labor Party (FLP). The FLP boasted of its genuine multi-ethnic nature. Its membership drew heavily on younger, less conservative Fijians and Indo-Fijians. With close ties to labor unions, the FLP described itself as "democratic socialist" in orientation. Its inaugural president was a Fijian from the west, Dr. Timoci Bavadra, a retired community health specialist. He was also president of the powerful Fiji Public Servants' Association, whose secretary, Mahendra Chaudhry (or Chaudhary), was a prime mover in the FLP's founding.

As the 1987 general election approached, the FLP decided to form a coalition with the NFP, despite some misgivings on both sides. This meant that for the first time leaders of both major parties, Bavadra and Mara, would be ethnic Fijians. Those in Bavadra's group were willing to ask whether the old structures of Fijian society remained adequate for modern, more urban living. They also questioned whether the west had received fair treatment from Alliance. The presence of the NFP in the Coalition, however, could raise Fijian fears about what had always been the "Indian party."

Suffering a low Fijian voter turnout, Mara's Alliance Party lost the election. The coalition's strength was notable among urban Fijians and the general electors. In the aftermath of this surprising outcome, people wondered whether the coalition could actually form a government. Timoci Bavadra was sworn in as Fiji's second prime minister on April 13, 1987. His chosen cabinet consisted of seven Fijians and seven Indo-Fijians.

The Coups of 1987

Parliament was in its third day of sitting when the drama that is now called "the first coup" unfolded, but Fijian anti-coalition sentiment arose as soon as the election results were announced. Though the Fijian community was and is divided along regional, social class, and other lines, it has never been difficult to gather large groups against a perceived threat of Indo-Fijian control. The Taukei (roughly, "ethnic Fijian") Movement articulated and organized this sentiment, beginning with a protest march in Suva. "Taukei" remains a label and a rallying cry that advances a policy of "Fiji for the Fijians." It does not constitute a formal political party. Despite the actual and threatened unrest that followed the election, the coalition did not crumble until Sitiveni Rabuka made his move and initiated a coup on May 14, 1987.

The governor-general represents the British monarch, who is officially head of state in Fiji. Ratu Sir Penaia Ganilau held the office in 1987. He was also Rabuka's paramount chief. When Rabuka told the governor-general what he had done, a series of confusing events ensued in which Ganilau vacillated over the constitutional issues. After the Great Council of Chiefs came out in favor of the coup, Ganilau created a complex plan to return the country to parliamentary government. This involved a review of the 1970 constitution. Rabuka's followers released the coalition parliamentarians, and Bavadra indicated willingness to participate in the review process, though expressing doubt that change was necessary. What emerged was an agreement for a bipartisan caretaker government in which the two major parties would attempt to resolve the constitutional crisis.

This new agreement did not meet the demands of Rabuka and the increasingly militant Taukei. Fearful lest a caretaker government reduce

PROTESTORS CONDEMN THE ACTIONS OF GEORGE SPEIGHT ON MAY 24, 2000. AT THE TIME, DEPOSED PRIME MINISTER MAHENDRA CHAUDHRY WAS BEING HELD HOSTAGE BY THE COUP LEADER. *(CORBIS CORPORATION (Bellevue). Reproduced by permission.)*

the power of the military, Rabuka led a second and more tightly controlled coup on September 25, 1987. A curfew was imposed, communications with the outside world were restricted, and some 200 individuals who were perceived as unfriendly to the Taukei Movement were detained. Rabuka declared Fiji a republic, with himself as head of an interim government. On October 1, 1987, the 1970 constitution was formally revoked.

The New Regime

International reaction was mixed. Pacific Island nations like Tonga were generally supportive, but the British Commonwealth of Nations allowed Fiji's membership to lapse. Australia and New Zealand were critical of a series of decrees that limited civil freedoms. The economy suffered as cash and professional members of the Indo-Fijian community poured out of the country. Tourism

SITIVENI LIGAMAMADA RABUKA

1948– Since bursting upon the Pacific Island political scene in 1987 as the leader of the region's first military coup, then-Lieutenant Colonel Rabuka has undergone a number of career and personality transformations. The style of his takeover made "Rambo" an easy pun on his name. He quickly rose through officers' rank to become Major-General and commander of the Fiji Military Forces in 1988. But after making statements about his lack of interests in politics, in 1991 he joined the Soqosoqo Vakavulevu ni Takei (SVT) political party. Though the SVT was backed by the Great Council of Chiefs, the commoner Rabuka was elected party head over two chiefly opponents. During the same year, he belied his "Rambo" tag by helping Ratu Mara, the interim prime minister, settle a sugar farmers' dispute.

The 1992 election was the first held under a new constitution and Rabuka led the SVT to win 30 parliamentary seats. However, he was only able to achieve the post of prime minister by joining forces with the Fiji Labor Party, whose government he had overthrown. When his budget was not approved, constitutional procedures required a new general election and in 1994, the SVT won two additional seats. Rabuka was returned as prime minister in a renegotiated coalition. His mercurial temperament and the continuing factionalism of Fijian politics made his tenure a turbulent one.

Rabuka had frequently demonstrated humility and willingness to listen to others. When SVT was resoundingly defeated in the 1999 election, he accepted blame personally and resigned as party head. In that year, as ethnic conflict threatened political stability in the Solomon Islands, Rabuka took on the role of Commonwealth special envoy to broker negotiations between the contestants. Whether as "Rambo" or conciliator, his own political future is as much up in the air as that of his country. He has disavowed any connection with the most recent coup.

dropped by 26 percent from the previous year's level. Even the chiefs were uneasy about the new power of the military and the commoner Rabuka. On December 3, 1987, Rabuka, recently promoted to Brigadier General, dissolved his military cabinet and turned over power to a newly appointed president, Ratu Ganilau.

Ratu Ganilau in turn called upon Ratu Mara to serve as prime minister in a new government. Consisting of Mara and 21 appointed ministers, this

government ruled Fiji from December 1987 until 1992. In 1990 a new constitution was formally developed that was clearly designed to strengthen the political dominance of Fijians, who were to have a large majority of seats in the House. All voting was to be on a purely ethnic basis; Fijians and Indo-Fijians could only vote for representatives of their own group. Electoral boundaries were redrawn so that only five of the Fijian electorates were in urban areas. This reduced the voting strength of urban Fijians who had supported the FLP in 1987.

The constitution provoked considerable debate and a number of new political parties were formed, including the Soqosoqo ni Vakualewa ni Taukei (SVT), claiming to speak for Fijian interests. In 1992 this Rabuka-led party won a majority of the Fijian seats but could only form a government in coalition with other parties. Rabuka was chosen prime minister. Rabuka was not able to control the domestic dissatisfaction and international criticism that his coups had generated. Economic problems like the downturn in tourism continued to beset the nation. In 1995 a Constitutional Review Commission was established in an effort to deal with these issues. This commission spent almost two years at its task, and its recommendations were unanimously adopted in parliament in July 1997.

The new constitution created a system that would avoid purely ethnic politics and at the same time take account of Fijian concerns. It specified that the president, who is head of state, must always be a native Fijian, and gave increased recognition to the Great Council of Chiefs. Not only would the council nominate and participate in electing the president, but would take particular responsibility for all matters dealing with native Fijians. Parliament was to consist of two houses. The Lower, where all legislation originates, would have 71 members. Forty-six seats were communal: 23 for Fijians, 19 for Indians, 3 for general electors, and 1 for Rotuma Island. The remaining were to be "open" seats, contested on a common roll basis without reference to ethnicity, either for the voters or candidates.

The president would appoint as prime minister the member of parliament who commanded majority support of the Lower House. Further, the constitution provided for mandatory power sharing in cabinet. Any party with more than 8 seats in the House was entitled to join cabinet in proportion to the number of seats it held. The Upper House was to consist of 32 appointed members: 14 nominated by the Great Council, 9 by the prime minister, 8 by the leader of the opposition, and 1 by the Council of Rotuma. Parliament was to serve for a maximum of four years after a general election, though it could be dissolved by the president acting on the advice of the prime minister.

Armed with this new constitution, Fiji looked forward to the 1997 election for a way out of the troubles of the preceding decade. New political parties organized for the contest, and new alliances were formed. Timoci Bavadra died in 1989, and leadership of the Fiji Labor Party was taken up by Mahendra Chaudhry. Rabuka's SVT party surprised many by forming a coalition with the NFP to contest the election. This development undermined the Fijian vs. Indian opposition of the past, as did the coalition of the FLP with two smaller Fijian parties. The latter called itself "The People's Coalition." Another new element was the use of the preferential ballot, in which voters must indicate not only their first choice but their order of preference for as many candidates are in the running.

Fiji Labor Party scored what amounted to a landslide victory. FLP candidates won 37 seats; Rabuka's SVT took only 8; and the once powerful NFP won no seats at all. Mahendra Chaudhry became Fiji's first prime minister descended from Indian indentured laborers. He maintained his "People's Coalition." He chose 11 Fijians and only 6 Indians in his first cabinet; his two deputy prime ministers were Fijians, one a titled woman.

Almost immediately, Fijians began expressing their outrage at the idea of an Indo-Fijian prime minister. Chaudhry's personal style, often described as "abrasive," aggravated the situation. A more practical problem was that of sugar leases, most of which were held by Indo-Fijian farmers on Fijian land and were scheduled to expire in 2000–2001. In the context of Chaudhry's victory, any effort by farmers to obtain long-term leases was likely to be interpreted by Fijians as another part of an Indian take-over, yet the sugar industry needed this kind of stability to continue as the mainstay of the country's economy. Despite a new constitution that attempted to deal fairly with Fijians' concerns and Chaudhry's efforts to reach out to their community, a century of suspicion would not disappear.

Chaudhry Ousted by Speight

On May 19, 2000, twelve years and five days after Sitiveni Rabuka's coup, another group of gunmen invaded parliament. They took prime minister Chaudhry and other members hostage. Their leader, part-Fijian George Speight, pro-

FIJI COUP LEADER GEORGE SPEIGHT, RIGHT, AND OTHER FIJIAN OFFICIALS AGREE TO RELEASE DEPOSED PRIME MINISTER CHAUDHRY AND 26 OTHER MEMBERS OF PARLIAMENT, WHOM SPEIGHT WAS HOLDING CAPTIVE. *(CORBIS CORPORATION (Bellevue). Reproduced by permission.)*

claimed himself head of a "civilian Taukei government." Ratu Mara, now president, declared a state of emergency, in which he was supported by the police and the army.

Ten days later the armed forces persuaded Mara to step aside so that they could restore order. Under Commodore Frank Bainimarama, the military declared martial law and abolished the 1997 constitution. Speight attempted to arrange the appointment of a prime minister of his choice, but, with military support, an interim cabinet was instead appointed. Laisenia Qarase, a commoner from Lau, took over as acting prime minister. On July 13, 2000, Chaudhry and the last of the hostages were released. Though negotiations leading up to their freedom had promised Speight and his close associates amnesty, two weeks later they were arrested and eventually charged with treason.

Speight portrayed himself as a Fijian nationalist defending against an Indo-Fijian takeover, but things were not so clear-cut. He had lost out on a lucrative timber deal when Chaudhry's administration awarded the concession to another firm. Part of his maneuver to create a new government appeared to favor western and northern chiefs who had chafed under the rule of Mara and the easterners. The extent to which Speight was backed by business interests that cut across ethnic lines is still under scrutiny.

RECENT HISTORY AND THE FUTURE

Once a success story of Pacific Island decolonization, Fiji remains in political limbo. In July

GEORGE SPEIGHT

1956– Though George Speight claimed to be taking over on behalf of ethnic Fijians when he took the Indo-Fijian prime minister and other parliamentarians hostage in May 2000, his persona and motives remain open to question. Of mixed Fijian ancestry, his background fits uneasily with Fijian tradition. Until recently, Speight was carving out a business career. He earned a management and finance degree at Andrews University, a Seventh-Day Adventist institution in the United States. First employed in Australian financial offices, he returned to Fiji in 1996 amid rumors of bank fraud.

When an older friend, also of mixed ancestry, became Finance Minister in Fiji, Speight was appointed to oversee government-owned timber reserves. While holding this office, he formed an association with an American company seeking to harvest the forests, but when the Chaudhry government took over in 1999, Speight lost his position.

Speight's coup raises further questions about his backers. Besides the overthrow of a government that had dashed his financial hopes, he is reported to have sought the downfall of President Sir Ratu Kamisese Mara and associates in favor of northern and western chiefs who had long resented the domination of easterners. His one success to date was forcing Mara into apparent retirement. However, Speight is presently in prison awaiting trial for treason, the punishment for which is death.

2000 an interim government was appointed with the approval of the Great council of Chiefs and of the military. Headed by a Fijian banker, Laisenia Qarase, as interim prime minister, this government was committed to write a new constitution, which is likely to give greater power to Fijians at the expense of Indo-Fijians. This process is scheduled for 2001, with an election in 2002, but these achievements do not seem likely. Qarase is cast as a moderate compared to those Fijians who have continued sporadic acts of violence against Indians in rural areas, but he is committed to continuing Fijian control and improving the economic position of ethnic Fijians.

Fiji's economy appears to be recovering slightly, but sanctions imposed by Australia, the fears of potential tourists, and the likely continued exodus of educated and professional Indo-Fijians are bound to create problems. More worrisome is that the precedent of Fiji's coups seems contagious—Papua New Guinea has suffered through years of secessionist war in its Bougainville province, while two years of ethnic clashes in the Solomon Islands culminated in the forced resignation of the nation's prime minister. As the new millennium begins, the islands no longer seem so "pacific," or idyllic.

BIBLIOGRAPHY

"Fiji's Prime Minister Rallies Nation as Troops Search for Mutineers," CNN.com, November 3, 2000. Available online at http://www.cnn.com/2000/ASIANOW/australasia/11/03/fiji.gunfire/index.html. (cited July 12, 2001).

"Fiji Treason Case Starts," CNN.com, May 28, 2001. Available online at http://www.cnn.com/2001/WORLD/asiapcf/southeast/05/28/fiji.speight/index.html (cited July 12, 2001).

"Fiji Treason Hearing Postponed," BBC News, June 11, 2001.

Kelly, John D. *A Politics of Virtue: Hinduism, Sexuality, and Countercolonial Discourse in Fiji.* Chicago, IL: University of Chicago Press: December 1991.

Lal, Brij V. *Another Way: The Politics of Constitutional Reform in Post-Coup Fiji.* Canberra, Australia: National Centre for Development Studies, 1998.

———. *Broken Waves: A History of the Fiji Islands in the Twentieth Century.* Honolulu, Hawai'i: University of Hawai'i Press, 1992.

Lal, Brij V., and Kate Fortune, eds. *The Pacific Islands: An Encyclopedia.* Honolulu, Hawai'i: University of Hawai'i Press, 2000.

Lawson, Stephanie. *Tradition Versus Democracy in the South Pacific: Fiji, Tonga and Western Somoa* (Cambridge Asia-Pacific Studies). London: Cambridge University Press, April 1996.

Ravuvu, Asesela. *The Façade of Democracy: Fijian Struggles for Political Control, 1830–1987.* Reader Publishing House, 1999.

Scarr, Deryck. *Politics of Illusion: The Military Coups in Fiji.* Kensington, Australia: New South Wales University Press, 1988.

———. *A Short History of Fiji.* La'ie, Hawai'i: The Institute for Polynesian Studies, 1984.

Sutherland, William. *Beyond the Politics of Race: An Alternative History of Fiji to 1992.* Canberra, Australia: Australian National University, 1992.

—Eugene Ogan

HAITI'S ROCKY ROAD TO DEMOCRACY

On November 26, 2000, Haitian voters elected Jean-Bertrand Aristide as president for a second time in that country's history. These elections, boycotted by a large group of opposition parties, were characterized by numerous incidences of violence. The November elections constituted yet another page in the turbulent post-Duvalier experiment with democracy in Haiti. In the aftermath of the elections, some members in the U.S. Congress condemned the Haitian government and accused Aristide of plotting to impose a dictatorship on the Haitian people. Nevertheless, election observers in Haiti felt that the results reflected the will of the people. Aristide's re-election offers a new opportunity for Haiti to pull itself out of the rubble, resulting from centuries of social and political turmoil.

While Haiti is considered to be the poorest country in the western hemisphere, it possesses one of the most complex and compelling histories in the Americas. Certainly, no other country in the world, within the last 300 years, has had the type of historical episodes as Haiti. Therefore, to explain political and social developments in the Haiti of today it is imperative to have a comprehension outline of certain important events which led to the evolution of this nation state.

HISTORICAL BACKGROUND

European Conquest and Slavery

In 1492 Christopher Columbus landed on a small Caribbean island which the Spanish would later called Hispaniola. The indigenous Arawak people, however, referred to the country as "Hayti," which means mountainous land. The Spanish enslaved the Arawak people who produced many products for export to the European market. The

THE CONFLICT

When Family Lavalas, a political party led by Jean-Bertrand Aristide, was awarded most of the seats in the Senate by the Provisional Electoral Council, the Group de Convergence, a coalition of opposition parties in Haiti, called for the nullification of the results of the May 21, 2000, legislative elections. Unable to reach a compromise with Family Lavalas, the opposition coalition boycotted the presidential elections. When Aristide won the presidential elections in November the Haitian government was reprimanded by the Clinton administration in the United States and the Group de Convergence threatened to set up an alternative government.

Economic

- Haiti is a desperately poor country which needs international financial assistance in order to develop.

- To access financial assistance the Haitian government needs to be seen as a legitimate body, especially by the U.S. government.

Political

- Disagreement between the coalition of opposition parties and Family Lavalas has resulted in political violence and a standoff between the main political parties in the country.

- The U.S. State Department, Canada, and the European Union, have accused the Haitian government, which oversaw the 2000 legislative and presidential elections, of undemocratic practices.

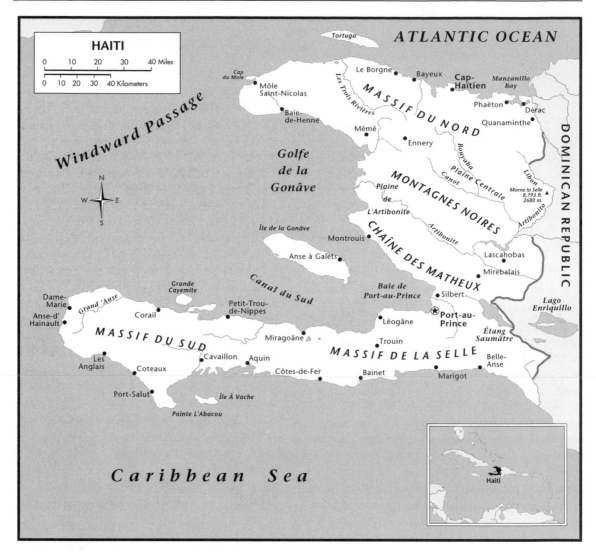

MAP OF HAITI. *(Maryland Cartographics. Reproduced by permission.)*

harsh treatment, coupled with diseases that were brought to the country by the Spanish, resulted in the virtual extinction of the Arawaks. Later, African slaves were imported from West Africa to supplement the labor shortage. Because Hispaniola was economically and strategically important, since it was claimed by the Spanish in the fifteenth century, it was sought after by major European powers.

The Spanish settlement of Hispaniola, however, was restricted to the eastern end of the island, leaving the western portion unimpeded. In 1664 French pirates established Port-de-Paix in the northwest of the country, and the French West India Company took possession. The French took control of the western portion of the island by the Treaty of Rijswijk of 1697. The French renamed it Saint-Dominique. The eastern portion remained in

the hands of Spain. During the eighteenth century the population of Saint-Dominique increased dramatically as the French imported African slaves to work on plantations. Saint-Dominique became France's most important trading partner, exporting sugar, coffee, cocoa, indigo and cotton—all produced by slave labor. By the second half of the eighteenth century Haiti was one of the wealthiest countries in the world.

The Haitian Revolution

By the 1770s Saint Dominique had a population of over 500,000, 90 percent of whom were slaves. The remainder were both whites and free blacks. In 1791 the slaves rose in rebellion against their slave masters. The rebellion was led by the son of an educated slave, Toussaint Louverture, who in 1794 abolished slavery in that country.

Toussaint Louverture was an educated slave who wrote and spoke French, and in 1777 he became legally free. When a slave revolt broke out in the north in 1791, Louverture joined the revolt with an army he had trained in the tactics of guerilla warfare. When Spain and France went to war in 1793 his involvement proved decisive in helping the Spaniards to win the eastern two-thirds of Hispaniola. He was hailed as a brilliant tactician, possessing extraordinary military ability in his campaign against the French. Louverture's military campaign won him respect and admiration from his black followers, in addition to the whites and mulattoes in the country. He set about improving the economy and even allowed some white planters to return to run plantations. Although he used military discipline to get the former slaves to return to work, black Haitians were free and shared in the wealth of the plantations.

In 1801 Louverture took control of the Spanish section of Hispaniola, abolishing slavery there, and also treating the white and mulatto population with great kindness. Determined to get rid of Louverture, the French invaded the country in 1802. Many of Loverture's supporters defected and he was sent into retirement on a plantation. In 1803 Louverture was tricked into going to France, where he eventually died.

In 1804 the entire island was declared an independent nation and renamed Haiti, its original Arawak name. The economy of Haiti had been destroyed because of the wars with France. France had failed to recapture the country. In 1804 General Dessalines declared himself Emperor, but he was killed in 1806 while trying to stop a mulatto revolt. Later, civil war broke out in the island with Henry Christophe (Dessalines' successor) in the north and Alexander Petion in the south. Spanish rule was restored to the eastern end of Haiti in 1809, when the British assisted the Spaniards in the war.

Following the death of Christophe in 1820 Jean-Pierre Boyer who was the leader of the mulatto-led south, became president of Haiti. He invaded Santo Domingo, the eastern side of the island, which had declared its independence from Spain, in 1822 and abolished slavery there. In 1844, however, the Haitians were expelled from Santo Domingo during a popular uprising.

During this time the country was under siege by a number of European powers that tried, unsuccessfully, to capture it. Haiti suffered the most comprehensive trade and military embargo in modern history. In return for almost 100 million francs

CHRONOLOGY

1492 Christopher Columbus sights the island and names it *La Isla Española*, and the Spanish colonize the island.

1790 The Haitian revolution begins. Led by Toussaint Louverture, the rebels eventually take control of the entire island of Hispaniola and abolish slavery.

1804 The entire island is declared independent and is renamed Haiti.

1915 The U.S Marines occupy Haiti under the Monroe Doctrine and remain until 1934.

1934 Pressured by the U.S government Haiti adopts a new constitution that makes it legal for foreigners to own land.

1935 A plebiscite amends the constitution so that future presidents will have to be elected by popular vote.

1957 François Duvalier is elected president.

1964 Duvalier names himself president for life.

1971 François Duvalier dies and his son Jean-Claude Duvalier becomes president.

1986 Jean-Claude Duvalier flees Haiti after widespread social protests against his regime. A six-person military junta runs the country until presidential elections are held in January 1988. Two coups result in the installation of two governments.

1990 The first free and fair elections in Haiti's history are held.

1991 Jean-Bertrand Aristide takes office as president, but is later overthrown by General Raoul Cedras. Aristide is forced to flee; the United States and the Organization of American States impose a trade embargo against Haiti.

1994 The United States invades Haiti and Aristide is restored to office as president.

1996 Réne Préval takes over from Aristide, after winning the elections by a landslide. This is the first smooth and democratic transfer of power to occur in Haiti's history.

1999 Préval suspends the legislature and promises to call elections.

1999 Jean-Bertrand Aristide is elected president of Haiti for the second time. He assumes power in February 2001.

THE NOVEMBER 2000 PRESIDENTIAL ELECTIONS WERE MARKED BY NUMEROUS ACTS OF VIOLENCE AND WERE BOYCOTTED BY SEVERAL GROUPS. *(AP/Wide World Photos. Reproduced by permission.)*

per year for the next 62 years, France recognized Haiti's independence in 1825. Britain recognized it in 1833, and the United States in 1862.

Since the overthrow of Boyer in 1843, Haiti saw a succession of at least twenty rulers, most of whom were assassinated or overthrown. Since the 1890s the United States has attempted to play a more important commercial and military role in Haiti. By 1905 United States business interests had secured a foothold in the country.

The American Occupation

In 1915 U.S. Marines began their occupation of Haiti, with the intent to restore peace and expand the U.S. sphere of influence. The Monroe Doctrine, which proclaimed U.S. protection over the western hemisphere, and humanitarian concerns were used to justify this intervention. With the military occupation of Haiti came improved infrastructure such as roads, hospitals, schools and a sewage system. This was usually accomplished, however, with the use of forced Haitian labor.

The Americans also incurred the wrath of Haitians who saw the U.S. presence as an assault on Haitian sovereignty. In addition, many poor Haitians were of the view that the Americans were less interested in their welfare and more concerned with using them for political ends. In fact, it was during the American occupation of Haiti that Haitians of a lighter complexion (the mulattoes) tended to have far greater power in the country. American anti-black racism was introduced into the way they dealt with Haitians on a daily basis. The American occupation of Haiti resulted in changes to the laws, which ultimately benefited American commercial and political interests. For example, in the Marine-supervised election of 1918, the constitution was changed to allow foreigners to own land in Haiti.

In 1934 the United States withdrew from Haiti, nine years after it had originally agreed to stay. This withdrawal came following the election of nationalists to the national assembly in 1930. Even after its withdrawal, however, the United States retained indirect fiscal control over Haiti up until 1947.

The Rise and Fall of the Duvaliers

Throughout the period 1930 to 1957 there was a great deal of political instability and social unrest in Haiti, as well as conflict between Haiti and the Dominican Republic. In 1937 a conflict between Haiti and the Dominican Republic led to the massacring of thousands of Haitians on the Haitian-Dominican Republic border. The Dominican Republic, with its largely mulatto population, looked down upon the Haitians, who were largely black. Haitian labor, however, played a critical role in keeping the Dominican economy afloat.

In 1946 there were violent demonstrations against the Hatian regime of Elie Lescot, who succeeded Stenio Vincent in 1941. Lescot was deposed by the military and a succession of two other coups saw two more regimes take power, only to be overthrown later by the military.

This unstable situation paved the way for the entry of François "Papa Doc" Duvalier. In 1935 under the presidency of Vincent, the Haitian constitution was amended to allow for future presidents to be elected by a popular vote. In 1957 Duvalier, running on a platform of black nationalism and political reform, was elected president. A medical doctor, "Papa Doc" used the religious symbols of voodoo to mobilize popular support.

Duvalier's presidency was characterized by the use of the brutal military police, called the *Tontons Macoutes*, who were used to eliminate opposition to his leadership. The Macoutes were responsible for the death and disappearance of many Haitian civilians and political activists. In addition, it was during this time that a large number of Haitians went into exile or sought refuge in other countries, especially the United States. In 1964 Duvalier named himself president for life. Isolated by a number of countries for terrorizing the population, Duvalier presided over a country with an economy in shambles. Before his death in 1971 he appointed his 19-year-old son, Jean-Claude "Baby Doc" Duvalier, to the post of president.

Although Jean-Claude's regime did engage in some political and economic reforms, which revived the economy and reduced repression, there was no significant departure from his father's policies. The Tontons Macoutes were still terrorizing people and the oppressive social and economic conditions forced many Haitians to flee their country in search of better living conditions.

In 1985 popular demonstrations against the Duvalier government broke out across the country.

Haitians had had enough of the terrible social, economic and political conditions. Unable to repress the demonstrators, Jean-Claude Duvalier fled Haiti, leaving the country in the charge of General Henri Namphy and a five-member council made up of military persons and civilians.

From Namphy to Aristide

During the Namphy regime elections were held in January 1988 and were won by Leslie Manigat. Those elections were considered to be fraudulent, however, and later that same year Namphy overthrew Manigat. Following this, General Prosper Avril, who held the post of president until 1990 when he was forced to resign, overthrew Namphy in September 1988.

In 1990 Jean-Bertrand Aristide was elected president of Haiti. Aristide's election—considered the freest and fairest in Haiti's history—signaled a change in Haiti's turbulent history, or so it seemed. Aristide, a left leaning Catholic priest, won in a landslide victory in an election in which 67 percent of the electorate voted for him. Eight months after taking office in February 1991, however, Brigadier General Raoul Cedras overthrew Aristide. Apparently, there were many in the Haitian military and among the Haitian elite who felt that Aristide was making too many radical statements about the bad treatment of the poor people in the country and the role of the military in that process. For the next three years the military junta that ousted Aristide was responsible for the death of more than three thousand Haitians.

After being ousted from office, Aristide went into exile in Venezuela and the United States. Following the coup the United States imposed a trade embargo against Haiti. It was not very effective, however, because Haitians traded and smuggled goods across the Haitian-Dominican Republic border. The U.S government, the United Nations (UN), and the Organization of American States (OAS) all tried to negotiate a settlement to the impasse. In 1993 an agreement was reached with General Cedras for Aristide to return to power. This agreement was later breached by General Cedras.

The world looked on as once again, Haiti began to slip back into a state of anarchy. Thousands of Haitians left Haiti in rickety boats bound for the United States. The large number of boat people who went to the United States and the many who died trying to get there or who were returned to Haiti resulted in an outcry from many Americans, particularly African Americans and Haitian

JEAN-BERTRAND ARISTIDE

1953– Jean-Bertrand Aristide was born to a working class family in the coastal town of Port-Salut, Haiti. He and his family moved to the capital city of Port-au-Prince, where he attended elementary and high school run by the Salesian Fathers of Haiti. In 1974 he graduated from the College of Notre Dame in Cap-Haitian, and subsequently completed studies at the Salesian seminary in La Vega, Dominican Republic. He returned to Haiti and did postgraduate studies in philosophy at the Grand Seminaire Notre Dame, and postgraduate studies in psychology at the State University of Haiti. In 1979 he traveled to Rome and Israel where he pursued biblical theology for the next two years.

In 1983 Aristide returned home, was ordained, and appointed curate of a poor parish church close to Port-au-Prince. He was subsequently moved to St. Jean Bosco which is close to the one of Haiti's largest and most notorious slums. As a priest Aristide became active among the poor and acquired a reputation as a left-leaning theologian who followed some of the tenets of liberation theology. Although fluent in Portuguese, Spanish, Italian, Hebrew, English, and French, Aristide communicated with his parishioners in the vernacular, Creole. He was a fierce critic of the 'Baby Doc' Duvalier regime and became a national figure because of his broadcasts on Catholic radio. When he met René Préval in the 1980s together they helped to organize opposition to the Duvalier regime. Through the organization, "Honor and Respect for the Constitution," Aristide was being groomed to become a future leader of Haiti. As a result of his involvement in politics, he was expelled from the Salesian order.

Following the fall of Duvalier and a short-lived civilian government, successive military regimes took control of Haiti. During this time Aristide was harassed and many of his supporters targeted and murdered. Aristide himself survived numerous attempts on his life. Although arsonists burned down his church, Aristide continued his work among the poor, including La Fanmi Selavi, a home founded for street children in 1986.

In 1990 Aristide contested Haiti's first free and fair elections. He won in a landslide with 67 percent of the popular vote. This victory was not without costs, as

JEAN-BERTRAND ARISTIDE. *(AP/Wide World Photos. Reproduced by permission.)*

many people were killed during the campaign, including four children at his La Fanmi Selavi home.

In 1991 he assumed the post of President of Haiti, but was soon overthrown by the military, who felt that some of his ideas about Haitian development were too radical. For the next three years Aristide was exiled in Venezuela and the United States. While in exile he traveled to many countries seeking support for his return to Haiti. It was during this period that the Haitian military introduced repressive measures, reminiscent of the François Duvalier era. The military routinely imprisoned or murdered supporters of Aristide and the pro-democracy movement.

In 1991, with the assistance of the Clinton administration in the United States, Aristide was re-installed as president of Haiti. He served his country until 1996, when his former prime minister and long-time friend, René Préval, was elected president. As a leader of the reformed political party, Lavalas Family, and with the support of his new wife, Aristide contested and won the 2000 election. In early 2001 Aristide assumed the post of president of Haiti for a second time.

Americans. Many of them argued that American immigration policy towards Haitians was racist. The Congressional Black Caucus called on the Clinton administration to do more to resolve the Haitian crisis. Under siege by the boat people and seemingly unable to find a peaceful solution to the problem, the Clinton administration, with the support of the United Nations, the OAS, and Aristide, invaded Haiti in September 1994 in an attempt to restore power to Aristide. While the Marines began to converge on Haiti, former U.S. president Jimmy Carter was sent to Haiti to persuade General Cedras to leave the country. After almost two days of intense discussion, Cedras agreed to leave Haiti and ordered his troops not to resist the American occupation. On September 19, about 20,000 U.S. soldiers, under the banner of "Uphold Democracy," began their occupation of Haiti. On October 19, President Aristide was restored to office. The American soldiers remained in Haiti until March 1995, however, when a United Nations peacekeeping force replaced them.

From Aristide to Préval

Jean-Bertrand Aristide returned to a country which was in even greater disarray than when he had taken over as president in 1991. Ravaged by internal conflict and an economic embargo, this Catholic priest who had limited experience as a politician had the task of uniting a country in seemingly permanent chaos. Although he maintained a high level of popular support, Aristide and supporters of his Lavalas party were often criticized by public commentators and members of the Haitian National Assembly for creating further political divisions within the country.

In regards to the management of the economy, many observers of Haitian politics felt that Aristide's populist policies did little to help the economy. For instance, Aristide refused to privatize industries as advised by the U.S. government, which was providing much needed aid to his government. To be fair to Aristide, however, it was virtually impossible for any leader to solve Haiti's extreme social and economic crisis in just a few short years. Furthermore, much of the financial assistance that the U.S government and the international community had promised Haiti was not received by the country. In addition, while the United States, France, and Canada provided assistance with training a new police force, following the demobilization of the army and the police of the pre-Aristide era, the assistance was not enough to fulfill the demands of maintaining a new and democratic Haitian state.

In 1995 when national elections where due, Aristide contemplated running for another term. The Haitian constitution, however, forbids a person from holding the office of president for two consecutive terms. The decision by Aristide to run for a second term was in part based on his view that he had not served his five-year term, since he was out of office for almost three years. In the end Aristide bowed out of the race and his long-time friend and former prime minister, René Garcia Préval, won the presidency in December 1995.

Préval's Difficult Tenure

In 1996 when Préval was sworn into office Aristide left the priesthood and decided to retire to his mansion in the suburbs of Port-au-Prince with his new Haitian-American wife. He vowed to continue his work with the poor in the slums of the Port-au-Prince. The Lavalas Party had thrown its support behind Préval. Préval's inauguration was the first time in Haiti's history that there was a peaceful transfer of power from one democratically elected president to another.

Préval's honeymoon was short-lived, for even though he secured 88 percent of the popular vote in the elections, only 28 percent of the eligible electorate actually voted. Furthermore, one of the conditions for economic assistance from the Clinton administration was that the Haitian government would have to institute austerity measures, which included privatization of states enterprises and a cut in social spending and subsidies. In an already impoverished country these policies led to public disaffection with the Préval government. This, combined with a split in the Lavalas Party in the legislature, weakened the Préval presidency. The right-wing section of the Lavalas party eventually composed itself into a new political party, the Struggling People's Organization (OPL), headed by Gerald Pierre-Charles. Aristide, in the meanwhile, reorganized his party under the name Family Lavalas.

Further erosion of Préval's popular support occurred when Aristide distanced himself from the austerity measures adopted by Préval. For five years Préval led a government that was virtually deadlocked. After the resignation of Rosny Smarth as prime minister in June 1997, Préval was unable to win confirmation from the legislature, of another candidate for that post. Unable to gain the confidence of the legislature, Préval dissolved it in January 1999. The next afternoon motorcycle gunmen shot his sister and killed her driver. International observers saw these events as a return to political chaos in the country, but Préval held firmly to

THE HAITIAN POLICE STOOD GUARD AGAINST ELECTION-RELATED VIOLENCE AND VOTER INTIMIDATION IN 2000.
(AP/Wide World Photos. Reproduced by permission.)

power, determined to overcome the 17-month stalemate that virtually paralyzed the government.

The dissolution of the legislature meant that Préval would have to call elections. On February 2, 1999, in an address to the nation, he promised to set up an electoral commission and establish an election timetable. The postponement of the elections and a struggle between Aristide's supporters and opponents threatened to plunge Haiti into yet another political crisis. During this period Préval was locked in a battle with the leader of the OPL, Gerald Pierre-Charles, over what was perceived to be the subversion of democracy in Haiti. Pierre Charles was opposed to both Préval's leadership of

the country and a possible return of Aristide to office. Local and international opposition to Préval grew when he postponed the legislative elections.

It should be noted that Haiti's government is made up of three branches: the judiciary; the executive branch—which comprises the president and the prime minister, who is appointed by the president—and the legislative branch, which is a bicameral National Assembly comprised of the Senate and the Chamber of Deputies. Elections for all of these branches of government were pending and Préval's opponents were beginning to argue that these postponements signaled a return to "Duvalierist" policies.

In March 1999 Préval appointed, by decree, a new Prime Minister along with the Provisional Electoral Council (CEP), which began the task of preparing the country for legislative elections.

RECENT HISTORY AND THE FUTURE

The Return of Aristide

On May 21, 2000, Haitians voted for candidates running for parliamentary and local government seats. When the votes were counted Aristide's party won control of the majority of the seats in that chamber. Family Lavalas won 16 of the 17 Senate seats and 28 of the 83 seats in the Chamber of Deputies in the first round. In the run up to these elections, however, opponents and supporters of Aristide clashed, and by the end of the elections at least 15 people were killed, most of them supporters of the opposition party. In addition members of the opposition accused the government of rigging the elections in favor of Aristide and creating an environment of intimidation. Of importance though was the fact that 60 percent of the eligible voters turned out for the elections—a significant increase from the 1997 parliamentary elections figure when only six percent of voters cast their vote.

In the aftermath of these elections the leader of the U.S. observer team in Haiti, Congressman John Conyers, gave support to the final results. The OAS and several of the Haitian opposition parties, however, opposed the elections. For weeks opposition members demonstrated throughout Haiti, calling on members of the CEP to resign. The OAS mission leader, Orlando Marville, and the CEP engaged in a stand-off in which the CEP was accused of using a flawed methodology and CEP leader president, Leon Manus, accused Marville of interference in Haitian internal affairs. Other international observer bodies felt that the OAS criticisms were valid. On June 20 the CEP, in defiance of criticism from some international observers made an official publication of the May 21 elections.

When Haiti's parliament convened on August 28, 2000, with Lavalas Senator Yvonne Neptune as president of the Senate, the U.S. State Department questioned the legitimacy of the body. On September 6 the Clinton administration warned that the United States would impose sanctions on Haiti unless steps were taken to implement meaningful democratic reforms to the electoral system, especially in anticipation of the partial senatorial and presidential elections scheduled for November of

that year. Both Canada and the European Union (EU) also threatened to impose sanctions due to perceived electoral irregularities.

In an effort to force the hands of the CEP and the Préval government, the opposition parties organized themselves into a coalition under the name "Group de Convergence," and threatened to boycott both the partial senatorial and the presidential elections in November. In an effort to diffuse the impasse, negotiations were held between the opposition groups and Family Lavalas. During these meetings Aristide's party made a large number of concessions, including a decision to have a commission investigate the methodology used to determine the May elections. The Group de Convergence, however, demanded that the entire May elections be declared null and void, as it was rigged to allow Aristide to win. While the OAS had suggested that there were problems with the methodology used by the CEP to arrive at the winners of the elections, none of the observers supported the view that the elections were rigged to allow a victory for Aristide's Family Lavalas. The U.S. State Department also stopped short of demanding that the entire results of the May poll be thrown out. Aristide and his party, by all accounts, appeared to be the most popular candidates among the Haitian electorate.

Unable to settle the impasse the opposition parties decided to boycott the November elections. In addition, the United States withdrew financial aid for the elections and decided against sending an observer team to Haiti. Other international bodies, including the OAS, followed suit by not sending observers to the November poll. Observers from the Caribbean Community (CARICOM) and the Quixote Center and Global Exchange did send observers. The number of observers who refused to monitor the elections indicated early on that the results would be questioned.

Although Aristide had no serious rivals for the presidential contest he conducted a spirited campaign. He traveled around the country holding meetings, marches, and other activities to mobilize his supporters. The Haitian electorate seemed electrified by the campaign. Unfortunately, the elections were once again marred by violence. In early November, gunmen in a car murdered seven people. On November 10 bombs exploded at the CEP headquarters. The U.S. State Department quickly responded by issuing a travel advisory for Haiti. International observers who saw no evidence of anti-American or anti-foreigner rhetoric or attacks during the campaign, however, criticized the advi-

THE DUVALIER DYNASTY

The name Duvalier has a special resonance in Haiti because it is often linked to two of the most ruthless dictators the country has seen in the twentieth century. François "Papa Doc" Duvalier was born in 1907 in Port-au-Prince. He graduated from the University of Haiti School of Medicine, where he served as a physician for nine years.

As a young man Duvalier became interested in the works of mystical scholar Lorimer Denis and became a member of the group of Haitian writers, "Le Groupe des Groits." This group promoted black nationalism and voodoo as main aspects of Haitian culture. Duvalier would later use both voodoo and black nationalism as political mobilization tools.

Throughout his professional career Duvalier held a number of important positions. He was director general of the National Health Service in 1946, and directed the anti-yaws program two years later. He held a number of political positions under the presidency of Dumarsais Estime, including minister of public health and labor and under-minister of labor. When Estime was overthrown by a military junta of Paul Magloire, Duvalier organized opposition to Magaloire. Following the resignation of Magloire in 1956, Duvalier ran for the office of president, under a populist program which emphasized Haitian nationalism. In 1957 Duvalier was elected to the presidency.

In the aftermath of his victory Duvalier set about consolidating his power by reducing the size of the army and setting up his personal security force, known as the "Tontons Macoutes." Duvalier used this militia to murder and terrorize his opponents. He manipulated the legislative elections of 1961 to have his term extended to 1967.

In 1964 he declared himself president for life. By manipulating voodoo symbols Duvalier portrayed himself as a prophet who had the right to rule Haiti. During his term in office he was ruthless in dealing with people whom he believed threatened his power-base. He spared no one. His personal chief aide, Clement Barbot, the man who helped Duvalier form the Tontons Macoutes, was murdered after attempting an insurrection.

So rife was the abuse and corruption within the Duvalier government that the U.S. government reduced aid to Haiti, and a number of countries, including the Vatican, isolated the regime. For fourteen years Duvalier ruled Haiti, achieving a remarkable degree of political stability in a country historically characterized by political chaos. When he died on April 21, 1971, he passed on the reins of to his 19-year-old son, Jean-Claude Duvalier.

A young and inexperienced politician, Jean-Claude "Baby Doc" Duvalier became the youngest president in the world when his father died. Unlike his father, Jean-Claude did not complete university, but spent a short time as a law student at the University of Haiti. While in office his regime was forced by the United States to reduce repression and corruption in government. He made some changes, including appointing a new cabinet, releasing political prisoners, and instituting minor judicial reforms. His regime continued the dictatorial practices of his father, however, squashing political opposition and murdering some opponents. In 1980 he married Michele Bennett, who became an influential person in his government. Michele was ruthless in dealing with opposition and used the money of the Haitian people to support her lavish lifestyle.

In 1986, when the Haitian people decided that they had had enough of the Duvalier dynasty, social unrest engulfed the country. With the help of the United States the Duvaliers fled the country. After their departure, a six-member council was appointed to oversee the affairs of the country.

sory, which claimed that Americans in Haiti might be targeted.

In the week prior to the elections at least ten bombs exploded in different parts of the capital city and the airport. The bombs resulted in the deaths of at least two persons and injuries to many others. The Haitian police arrested several people suspected of being responsible for the bombings, which appeared to be aimed at preventing Haitians from voting in the elections. However, this effort was not successful. On November 26 the presidential and partial senatorial elections were held with a remarkable degree of efficiency. An estimated 60 percent of eligible voters cast their ballots and in the end Aristide was elected president of Haiti for the second time. Aristide got more than 90 percent of the votes. According to reports from a coalition of international observers (the Quixote Center and Global Exchange), the elections were generally free and fair.

In the aftermath of the elections, the opposition parties condemned the elections and threatened to set up a parallel government. Various Republicans in the U.S. Congress criticized Aristide and accused him of setting up a dictatorship. Of importance though, is the fact that most of the opposition in the U.S. Congress to Aristide had historical precedence. Republicans in Congress were opposed to Aristide even after he won Haiti's first free and fair elections in 1990. Many Republicans in the U.S. Senate, in particular Sen. Jesse Helms, repeatedly complained that Aristide's politics were too liberal.

In an effort to diffuse the tensions between the U.S. government and the Aristide administration, a meeting was held between special White House Envoy Anthony Lake and President-elect Aristide. At the meeting Aristide was told to implement eight reforms if Haiti was to improve its relationship with the United States. Elements of these reforms had to do with the inclusion of opposition members in his new administration, the establishment of a new electoral council, the implementation of human rights and negotiating bodies, runoffs for ten Senate seats which were awarded to Lavalas, and the implementation of an economic reform program with the World Bank.

Haiti's Future

When Aristide took over the presidency from Préval, the Haitian economy was still in deep crisis. During Préval's tenure, the Haitian dollar had been devalued to the U.S. dollar, unemployment had risen above 70 percent, and inflation was on the rise. In addition, social services had been reduced and many Haitians had lost faith in the ability of the government to turn the country around. Despite this situation Haiti had managed a third generally peaceful transfer of power from one president to the next. Préval had also implemented a number of painful but necessary economic reforms in the country.

Whether or not Haiti will be able to rise from the political and economic decay in which it finds itself will largely depend on the skillfulness of

Aristide as a leader as well as the resolve of the Haitian people to find a way out of what appears to be perpetual social chaos. Aristide's job is made harder by the fact that Haiti is now considered one of the most important trans-shipment points for drugs from Colombia to the United States. Many Haitians have long turned to drug trafficking as a means of earning an income. On the other hand, as a new member of CARICOM, a group of Caribbean countries that has recently formed a trading bloc and engages in different forms of functional cooperation, Haiti has additional allies in its struggle for democracy and development. Nonetheless, the involvement of the international community in helping to strengthen the economy and civic institutions in Haiti should go a long way toward ensuring its prosperity.

BIBLIOGRAPHY

Arthur, Charles. *Haiti in Focus: A Guide to the People, Politics, and Cultures.* Northampton, MA: Interlink Publishing Group, 2001.

Central Intelligence Agency. *The World Factbook 2001,* s.v. "Haiti." Available online at http://www.ciagov/cia/publications/factbook/geos/ha.html (cited July 12, 2001).

Gibbons, Elizabeth D. *Sanctions in Haiti.* Washington, DC: Center for Strategic and International Studies, 1999.

"History of Haiti," *Encyclopaedia Britannica.* Available online at http://www.britannica.com/eb/article?eu = 127859 (cited May 30, 2001).

James, C.L.R. *The Black Jacobins: Toussaint L'Ouverture and the San Domingo Revolution.* New York: Vintage Books, 1989.

Miles, Melinda, and Maoira Feeney. "Elections 2000: Participatory Democracy in Haiti," Report prepared by the Quixote Center and Global Exchange, February 2000.

Norton, Michael. "Aristide Wins Haitian Senate," The Associated Press, May 30, 2000.

Reding, Andrew. "Exorcising Haiti's Ghosts," *World Policy Journal,* vol. 13, no. 1, Spring 1996.

Wilentz, Amy. *The Rainy Season: Haiti Since Duvalier.* New York: Touchstone Books, 1990.

Wucker, Michele. *Why the Cocks Fight: Dominicans, Haitians, and the Struggle for Hispaniola.* New York: Hill and Wang, 1999.

—Ian Boxill

Hong Kong: Walking the Tightrope between Capitalism and Communism

The Conflict

The resumption of Chinese rule over Hong Kong in 1997 meant that the world's leading communist nation would absorb one of the world's leading capitalist economies. International observers questioned whether the "one country, two systems" approach would work for the integration of Hong Kong into the People's Republic of China.

Economic

- Although China has undergone some policy changes since the 1970s that have taken its economy further into market-based responses, it is still guided by state control and central planning. In contrast, the economy of Hong Kong has been one of the most market-based in world history, with the private sector taking the leading role in economic growth and planning.

- Hong Kong's greatest value to China is its dynamic capitalist economy. Hong Kong is the major point of transfer for Chinese goods bound to the West, and the entrepreneurial expertise of Hong Kong's business community has further aided China's ties to the capitalist world. Because Hong Kong's economy exists in direct contrast to communism's stated goals a fundamental conflict exists between its capitalist accomplishments and China's communist platform.

Political

- Despite the establishment of Special Economic Zones to experiment with "capitalism with Chinese characteristics," China remains a bastion of communism and levies restrictions on its people's freedoms of speech, expression, and civil liberties. Hong Kong, meanwhile, is a prime example of capitalism, with a society accustomed to many of the freedoms Beijing so commonly restricts.

- Under the agreement reached under the transition negotiations with Britain, China promised to allow Hong Kong's elected officials a great degree of autonomy in governing the region. In contrast, as the only recognized party in China, the Communists have a monopoly on the ballot box and do not allow truly free elections to occur. Because of Hong Kong's ambiguous status within China, it is unclear how much discretion Communist officials will allow for Hong Kong's elected officials.

As midnight on June 30, 1997, approached, the world witnessed one of the most remarkable transitions of power in the modern era. Henceforth, one of the last colonial outposts of the British Commonwealth, Hong Kong, would be known as the Hong Kong Special Administrative Region (HKSAR) of the People's Republic of China. In the hours before the transition government officials hastily removed the emblems of colonial rule from buildings, signposts, and uniforms, while Chinese troops quietly moved over the border to replace their British and Hong Kong predecessors at the region's military bases. After a departing address from Governor Christopher Patten, given in a driving rainstorm, the ceremony moved indoors to a convention center. While Chinese President Jiang Zemin and British Crown Prince Charles awaited the official transfer of power, "God Save the Queen" played for the last time as the colony's anthem, and the British flag was lowered. Just after midnight the yellow stars and red background of China's flag reigned supreme, joined by a new flag for HKSAR.

The overnight changes for the colony involved more than just a different flag or a new name. Effective immediately, protests against Chinese actions in Tibet or protests in favor of recognizing Taiwanese independence were outlawed in HKSAR. Other civil liberty restrictions limited the right of free association and public protest. Although democratic elections were promised, a body of lawmakers appointed by the Chinese took over in the interim. Some protests against the impending communist Chinese takeover roused the city in the days just before the transition, but most residents accepted the changes with a passive ambivalence. After all, why would China undertake political actions that could threaten Hong Kong's dynamic economy and its position as a center of world trade? To repeat the parable invoked by most observers, killing the goose that laid the golden egg made no sense, especially given the emphasis on economic development that characterized Chinese leadership since the death of Mao Zedong in 1976.

Hong Kong's business community had, for the most part, decided to make the best of the transition. Despite the Cold War tensions between China and the West, Hong Kong maintained extensive ties with both spheres, welcoming Western technology to develop its financial sector while moving most of its manufacturing sites to mainland China to take advantage of vastly cheaper labor costs. As long as China lived up to its commitment to keep HKSAR's economy free from government interference and maintain the rule of law, business could go on as usual. Hoping for the best yet planning for the worst, many of the region's wealthier citizens hedged their bets. Emigration from Hong Kong tripled in the years after the 1984 announcement of the transition, with most residents hoping to establish a claim on citizenship in another British Commonwealth country such as Canada or Australia, or in the United States, as a sort of insurance against possible threats of intimidation by the new regime. In 1992 alone, a full one percent of the region's residents left Hong Kong, a figure that had increased sharply after the violent political repression against Chinese dissidents at Tiananmen Square in Beijing in June 1989.

The majority of the population, lacking the resources to emigrate, even if temporarily, resigned themselves to Chinese rule. Politics had always taken a back seat to the pragmatism of making money in Hong Kong, and most residents hoped that the transition would entail only a momentary interruption in their daily activities and the continued prosperity of the colony. Despite the worldwide attention focused on the events of June 30, 1997, both public protests and open celebrations over the transition were rare. With the official schedule disrupted by almost constant rain showers, most of the citizens enjoyed the long weekend by staying indoors and watching the events on television or, in typical Hong Kong fashion, going shopping.

HISTORICAL BACKGROUND

The integration of one of the world's most dynamic capitalist economies into the world's leading communist nation is one of the most recent chapters in the unique history of Hong Kong. Col-

CHRONOLOGY

1841 The Treaty of Nanking concludes First Opium War between China and Great Britain. Under the treaty, China cedes Hong Kong to the British.

1843 Hong Kong becomes a Crown possession of Great Britain.

1860 China cedes Kowloon Peninsula to Great Britain.

1898 The New Territories, the third portion of Hong Kong, is leased to Great Britain by China for 99 years.

December 1941–45 Japanese forces occupy Hong Kong during World War II.

1949 The People's Republic of China is declared by communists leader Mao Zedong.

Late 1970s With 15-year leases coming up for renewal in the New Territories, discussions between Britain and China begin over Hong Kong's status after 1997.

1984 The Sino-British Joint Declaration is issued, setting forth basic principles for Hong Kong's status after 1997.

1990 The Basic Law for Hong Kong Special Administrative Region of the People's Republic of China is passed by Chinese legislature. Basic Law guarantees Hong Kong's autonomy for a period of 50 years after the handover.

June 30, 1997 The Final day of British rule in Hong Kong arrives. At midnight, control of Hong Kong reverts to China.

Late 1997 Southeast Asia experiences the Asian financial crisis, which threatens the economies of several countries in the region.

1998 Hong Kong is hit by a recession brought on by the Asian financial crisis.

1999 Economic growth returns to Hong Kong. Chief Executive Tung Chee-hwa's popularity plummets as he faces public criticism for several scandals involving cronyism.

November 2000 Executive Secretary Anson Chan speaks at a Heritage Foundation Conference, stressing the need for Hong Kong to be ruled by Hong Kong people and not by officials in Beijing.

January 2001 Anson Chan resigns her post as Executive Secretary of HKSAR.

DIGNITARIES AND OTHER GUESTS WITNESS THE HONG KONG HANDOVER CEREMONY AND WATCH AS THE CHINESE FLAG IS RAISED. *(AP/Wide World Photos. Reproduced by permission.)*

onized by Great Britain as an outpost of the international drug trade in the 1840s, Hong Kong's history also represented the humiliation suffered by China as its own empire dissolved from internal corruption and warfare. Located on the Kowloon Peninsula and part of a strategic group of islands in the Pearl River estuary on China's southeastern coast, the region had for centuries been a favorite of pirates taking advantage of the many natural harbors to prey on the area's trade. Portuguese traders entered the region in 1514 and established a base on the southern part of the Pearl River delta in Macao, which remained a Portuguese territory until it was transferred back to China in December 1999. British interests eclipsed Portuguese trade in the 1700s, however, after the British public took to drinking a new beverage, tea, in vast quantities. The tea trade made fortunes for many Cantonese traders, as the Chinese usually insisted that the British pay for the export in silver bullion. To get around the trade imbalance the British East India Company found a product that was in growing demand in the Chinese market—opium. Produced in British-controlled India and readily sold through Chinese merchants the opium trade became a major source of revenue for the British East India Company. So successful were British efforts at selling the drug that Chinese imperial officials, alarmed at the revenue lost to drug sales, banned the drug and destroyed shipments of it in 1839.

Ignoring the ban, British traders continued the opium shipments and called for military reprisals against the Chinese.

Unequal Treaties

The resulting First Opium War of 1839–41 was a resounding defeat for imperial China. Not only did the country have to open new trading posts to foreign powers and pay an indemnity for any opium it destroyed, it also ceded Hong Kong Island to Britain in perpetuity under the Treaty of Nanking, an agreement that lived on in Chinese memory as an "unequal treaty." Declared a Crown possession in 1843, the new British colony expanded along the Kowloon Peninsula after the Second Opium War of 1856–58, which resulted in further Chinese losses and another "unequal treaty." After yet another disastrous war in 1894–95, this time against Japan, China acquiesced to another British demand for more land. Under the agreement signed in 1898, the British leased an area known as the New Territories, further up the Kowloon Peninsula, for a period of ninety-nine years. The growth of the British colony of Hong Kong represented a national humiliation for the crumbling Chinese empire.

From a population of about 7,000 in 1842, Hong Kong grew to include about 300,000 residents by 1900. As a trade center and manufacturing base the colony attracted immigrants from China seeking their fortunes as well as refugees from the country's instability, as the empire declined into frequent political rebellions. The Japanese invasion of Manchuria in 1931 along China's northern region, followed by a series of military attacks southward, caused an estimated one half million Chinese to flee to Hong Kong in the 1930s. They found only temporary refuge in the colony, however; with the onset of World War II (1939–45) the Japanese occupied Hong Kong from the end of 1941 until their eventual defeat in 1945. During the occupation many residents fled for their lives, leaving about 600,000 residents in Hong Kong by war's end.

The colony's population rebounded to about 1.8 million people shortly after World War II. Yet any expectations for a return to stability were dashed by the ongoing civil war in China, which reached its conclusion after decades of fighting. While Chinese Nationalist and Communist forces had temporarily united in order to fight the Japanese invasion in the 1930s, they resumed their struggle once the occupiers has been vanquished. By 1949 the Communists, led by Mao Zedong, were victorious, and the People's Republic of China was proclaimed in October. As Nationalist forces fled to the newly established Republic of China on the island of Taiwan, an estimated 775,000 Chinese crossed over into Hong Kong. The refugees increased Hong Kong's population to more than two million by 1951, instigating a desperate housing crisis in the overcrowded colony. In 1953 the colonial government finally stepped up its efforts to build public housing and ease the worst of the housing situation.

The Economic Miracle

While the explosive growth of the colony's population put a strain on its resources, the immense influx of refugees to Hong Kong also represented an enormous benefit to the colony. Given the nationalization of enterprises by the Communist Chinese, it was not surprising that the entrepreneurial class fled to Hong Kong and set to rebuilding their businesses. With the comparative advantage of cheap wage rates, manufacturing exports from the colony soared. In 1950 just 10 percent of Hong Kong's exports came from the manufacturing sector, a rate that skyrocketed to 70 percent just ten years later. In short order, manufacturing firms made Hong Kong a center of textile, plastics, and eventually electronics production.

As Hong Kong's traditional position as a trade and financial center continued, the political insta-

CHRISTOPHER PATTEN

1944– Oxford-educated Christopher Patten began a career in diplomacy in the 1960s. After leading Prime Minister John Major's successful 1992 campaign but losing his own seat as a Conservative Party representative in the House of Commons, Patten was appointed Governor of the Colony of Hong Kong in 1992. As the last British Governor of the Colony, Patten oversaw the transition of power to the People's Republic of China, which took place at midnight on June 30, 1997. Patten spoke forcefully in favor of continuing Hong Kong's free-market economy and was critical of potential Communist Party interference in Hong Kong's affairs.

bility in Southeast Asia persistently affected its fortunes. The Korean conflict that commenced in June 1950 disrupted trade throughout the region, and China's international isolation and anti-capitalist posturing, along with its attempts at economic self-sufficiency, diminished Hong Kong's role as a distribution point between China and the rest of Asia, not to mention the West. Despite these tensions China remained an important trading partner with Hong Kong. Although the colony shipped an overwhelming majority of its manufactured items elsewhere, China was a vital source of Hong Kong's food supply, almost all of which had to be imported. Once the open hostilities of the Korean conflict ceased and China's isolationist tendencies abated, reopening avenues for trade, Hong Kong businessmen made the colony the world's leading newly industrialized nation of the postwar era.

In contrast to Hong Kong's dynamic capitalist success after the mid-1950s, Communist China lurched from one economic mishap to another. Determined to raise collectivized agricultural production and develop the industrial sector simultaneously, China's Great Leap Forward (1958–61), begun in 1958, depended on centralized planning that set high goals for production while often misallocating vital resources. Many projects were inaugurated in the name of national pride instead of actual need or viability, and the results were disastrous—an estimated 16 to 27 million Chinese died of starvation during the Great Leap Forward, a testament of the inefficiency of the command economy under Mao Zedong. The years of the Cultural Revolution (1966–69), inaugurated by Mao in 1966, were little better. Attempting to equalize resources between rural and urban areas and root out supposedly pro-Western influences, the system of higher education essentially ceased functioning until the 1970s. Export products generally remained limited to raw materials, and the economy remained stunningly inefficient in both the agricultural and industrial sectors. The contrast between China and neighboring Hong Kong could not have been more stark.

It was only with the death of Mao Zedong in 1976 that Chinese leaders undertook market-oriented economic reforms. After a brief power struggle Deng Xiaoping emerged as China's new leader, and it quickly became apparent that the country's policies of self-sufficiency, central planning, and state ownership would be modified or abandoned. In 1978 China joined the International Monetary Fund (IMF) and the World Bank. The following year four Special Economic Zones (SEZs) were established to attract foreign investment in manufacturing enterprises. Almost immediately Hong Kong investors rushed to take advantage of the cheap labor supply; indeed, the percentage of the colony's manufacturing workforce plunged from 46.5 percent in 1980, to a mere 12.6 percent in 1997, as more firms relocated to China.

In just a decade after Mao Zedong's death the Chinese economy underwent some fundamental reforms. Peasants now had strong incentives to sell their crops on the market and retain the profits; hundreds of thousands of Chinese migrated to the Special Economic Zones to work in one of the new manufacturing facilities financed and managed by foreigners; and Chinese firms themselves gained more experience working in a market environment. The economy as measured by the gross domestic product (GDP) grew by an annual average of 9.2 percent in the decade after 1979. While this expansion did not match the 11.9 percent annual growth rate of Hong Kong between 1976 to 1981, it nevertheless represented a dramatic turnaround for the previously sluggish and insulated Chinese economy.

The success of the economic reforms encouraged Chinese leaders to continue the country's integration into the global economy. Specifically, China looked for closer ties with Hong Kong, which had supplied the crucial investments and expertise to fuel China's economic boom in the post-Mao period. Border restrictions were eased to allow easier passage of shipments and travelers, and trade between China and Hong Kong grew by an average rate of 24 percent a year after 1978. In the first official visit to China by a Hong Kong Governor since 1949, Governor Murray MacLehose trav-

eled to Beijing in March 1979 to meet with Deng Xiaoping, in order to foster the normalization of relations between Hong Kong and China. As it turned out, MacLehose's visit marked the beginning of the end of British rule in Hong Kong.

Negotiating the Handover: "One Country, Two Systems"

Although the People's Republic of China took steps to reintegrate itself into the international economic and diplomatic order in the 1970s, it by no means had forgotten the foreign interventions of its imperial past. The loss of Hong Kong under the "unequal treaties" of the nineteenth century remained a source of contention for the Chinese leadership. In order to redeem the nation's honor the only acceptable fate for Hong Kong would be re-absorption into China. For the Chinese, any other outcome was unthinkable. In contrast, an overwhelming number of Hong Kong residents favored the status quo. Few residents could see the sense in changing the colony's status, particularly if it would cause uncertainty in the business sector. Even immigrants to the colony from China, most of whom maintained ties with their homeland once relations became normalized, were not convinced of the wisdom of ending British rule.

Because the 99-year lease on the New Territories of Hong Kong was due to expire in 1997, the dilemma of Hong Kong's future came to the forefront of Sino-British relations in the late 1970s. Almost all of the land in the New Territories was actually held by the Hong Kong government, which in turn leased the land for periods of fifteen years, with typically automatic renewals for lease holders. With the 1997 expiration of Britain's hold on the land, however, Hong Kong's officials feared that they could no longer issue land rights to investors with any guarantee of their rights to retain the use of the land past that date. Urged to at least find some clarification of the lease issue for the colony, Governor MacLehose brought up the matter with Deng Xiaoping, who responded by calling for an official series of meetings on the topic. It soon became apparent that China was intent on gaining control over the New Territories upon the expiration of Britain's lease; furthermore, Chinese officials restated their belief that the "unequal treaties" that ceded much of Hong Kong to the British were invalid. In short, China expected to regain all of Hong Kong. Not only was the redemption of China's imperial humiliation at stake, the country also hoped to set a precedent for its demands to acquire Taiwan, where the Nationalists had set up the Republic of China in 1949.

PROTESTORS DEMONSTRATED AFTER THE CHINESE LEGISLATURE OVERTURNED THE RULING OF A HONG KONG COURT ON IMMIGRATION. THIS ACTION MAY HAVE FAR REACHING IMPLICATIONS FOR THE CONTINUED INDEPENDENCE OF HONG KONG'S JUDICIARY. *(AP/Wide World Photos. Reproduced by permission.)*

Although Britain insisted that the treaties of 1841 and 1860 were legitimate, it nonetheless conceded that China's takeover of Hong Kong was inevitable. Talks over the transition began in earnest in 1982, and the resulting Sino-British Joint Declaration in 1984 spelled out the future of the Hong Kong Special Administrative Region of the People's Republic of China, as the colony would be known after June 30, 1997. The subsequent Basic Law of the HKSAR, ratified by the Chinese legislature in 1990, codified the region's status and authorized several provisions that guaranteed the region's autonomy from China. Together, these documents promised to allow Hong Kong to retain its own common law, system of capitalism, and private property rights. English would be kept as one of the HKSAR's official languages. China also promised not to change HKSAR's market economy for a period of 50 years after the takeover. In sum, China promised a "one country, two systems" approach to integrating HKSAR into the People's Republic of China.

While the agreements formally put HKSAR under the direct control of China, British officials insisted that the provisions for its autonomy would guarantee continued economic success. It was not clear, however, just how these provisions would be enforced. The violent repression of Tiananmen Square pro-democracy protesters in June 1989,

shortly before China ratified the Basic Law agreement, seemed to indicate that Chinese officials could not be trusted to maintain their guarantees of HKSAR's autonomy.

The arrival of Christopher Patten as the Governor of Hong Kong in July 1992 further intensified the rhetoric between Chinese and British officials. Patten was appointed governor knowing that he would be Britain's last colonial representative there, and he was determined to usher in a more democratic form of government for the colony in the hope that such changes, once instituted, would survive the transition to HKSAR under China. Under Patten's plan more representatives of Hong Kong's legislature would be directly elected by the voters, and the government would undertake more social programs than it had in the past. In response, China threatened that it would rescind the reforms after the takeover and added that any contracts signed without the approval of Chinese officials in Beijing would be invalid after the takeover. Although China had agreed in the 1984 Joint Declaration to honor any outstanding contracts the announcement in November 1992, sent a shock wave through the colony. The Hang Seng index on Hong Kong's stock market, a measure of its leading stocks, immediately lost almost a quarter of its value as investors became nervous over the colony's long-term prospects. After reassurances to the

TUNG CHEE-HWA

1937– Son of a wealthy Shanghai shipping magnate, Tung Chee-hwa grew up in Hong Kong after World War II and completed his college education in Great Britain. Based in Hong Kong after 1969, Tung enjoyed a lengthy international career in his family's shipping business. In 1996 he was elected Chief Executive of the Hong Kong Special Administrative Region of the People's Republic of China, the first election held for the post. Although Tung was generally praised for leading a smooth transition from British to Chinese rule, his resistance to democratic reform was criticized by those who viewed him as too deferential to Chinese communist officials.

business community from China, however, the stock market rebounded and continued its rapid growth for the year.

Despite the tensions between Patten and the Chinese, the transition moved along through a joint planning committee, which discussed issues ranging from the design for Hong Kong's new flag to the need to translate the colony's common laws into Chinese. Meanwhile, less obvious, but more fundamental changes were taking place. After a sluggish period in 1982–83, GDP rebounded to an annual growth rate of 8.1 percent from 1984–88, with investment and trade between China and Hong Kong fueling the growth. In the decade after 1979 Hong Kong's foreign investment represented about 58 percent of the total direct foreign investment in China, outstripping the combined investment from the United States and Japan by more than three times in the same period. About five million Chinese workers were employed by Hong Kong firms in China, a majority of them living in the Guangdong province bordering Hong Kong. In the most common pattern of investment, Hong Kong manufacturing firms relocated their assembly operations in China, arranging for raw materials or semi-finished components to be imported into the country for final assembly, and then re-exporting the item back through Hong Kong to international markets. Through this arrangement China provided cheap manual labor, and Hong Kong provided the financing, marketing, and managerial capabilities.

The division of labor with China also fostered the development of a postindustrial economy for Hong Kong. By the year of the takeover only 12.6 percent of its workers were employed in the manufacturing sector, while service-sector employees, including those in the vital import and export sector, grew to include 43.8 percent of all workers, a stunning rise from just 22.8 percent in 1980. Similarly, those engaged in transport or communications activities included 7.8 percent of all workers in 1997, up from 3.8 percent in 1980; the gain in those providing business and financial services grew from 6.4 percent to 17.9 percent. In less than two decades the colony had made the switch to a service-sector economy with a basis in the technological, financial, and managerial professions. Hong Kong's economy enjoyed almost continuous growth during the 1980–97 period.

Despite the successful economic integration between the two entities, doubts lingered in the final days of British rule about the potential for Hong Kong's political integration into China. Most of all, pro-democracy critics voiced concerns that China had no intention of respecting Hong Kong's autonomy and rule of law and might soon rescind HKSAR's Basic Law after the takeover. Chief among these critics was the colony's last governor, who made a number of speeches during the last months of British rule designed to increase international scrutiny of China's handling of Hong Kong after his departure. "The rule of law implies respect for the individual," Patten reminded the Chinese in one speech to the American Chamber of Commerce in Hong Kong shortly before the takeover, "And the rule of law implies willingness of government to hold itself accountable, and that is fundamental to the respect, the credibility, and the authority which government needs if it is to serve the community." Indeed, whether China would allow Hong Kong to continue its capitalist ways with a minimum of government intrusion into the personal freedoms of its residents was a chief question in the days of transition.

The Asian Financial Crisis

Once the official events marking the transition had ended most of Hong Kong's residents hoped that political events would again take a secondary role to the region's economic accomplishments. Ironically, the rest of 1997 would indeed be dominated by economic news, but not the kind of news that put Hong Kong's residents at ease. In fact, 1997 would mark the first real economic downturn in the region's modern history. Even more ironic was that the economic problems had little to do with the transition to Chinese rule, as most investors had once feared.

At the beginning of the year, an International Monetary Fund (IMF) review of Hong Kong's economy predicted that it would survive the transition without significant interruption; in its May 1997 report the IMF even forecast that Hong Kong's GDP was expected to grow more than 5 percent for the year. The collapse of the Thai currency the day after Hong Kong's official handover, however, put all such predictions in doubt. The countries hardest hit by the Asian financial crisis, as the recession came to be known, included Thailand, Malaysia, Korea, and Indonesia, although Singapore, China, Vietnam, and Taiwan were also affected. Each of the first group of countries held overvalued currencies that quickly collapsed at the threat of interest rate hikes by Japan, Canada, and the United States, which suggested a withdrawal of investment from the Asian countries. Once the financial stampede out of Asia began it triggered a rapid collapse of local stock markets and banks, which in many cases had extended risky loans. Adding to the problem, massive government subsidies and cartel arrangements in some of the countries had allowed many local industries to follow inefficient practices that contributed to the economic slump once it began. Finally, the crisis exposed widespread corruption among many business and government officials in the region, making it harder to attract foreign investment to revive the national economies in recession.

Hong Kong's economy was better situated than most Asian economies to weather the crisis. Its banks had been far more conservative with their loans, so widespread financial collapse was only a remote possibility. Additionally, with a market-oriented economy that could respond rapidly to global economic changes, Hong Kong's business leaders also remained confident of their competitive edge over their Asian neighbors. Yet serious structural problems remained that eventually brought on Hong Kong's first economic downturn in its modern history. Chief among these problems was the overvaluation of HKSAR's real estate market. In the period between the Sino-British Joint Declaration and the handover, property values had far outpaced other economic indicators at a rate of 19 percent average growth per year, versus 11.8 percent for per capita GDP growth and 13.5 percent for the overall GDP itself. As a result, bank loans and the stock market became dominated by real estate investments as capital sought the best possible returns. Adding to the speculation, many observers noted a massive capital inflow from China into Hong Kong's real estate and stock markets in the months prior to the handover. With this

ANSON CHAN

1940– Appointed the first ethnic-Chinese Chief Secretary of Hong Kong in 1993 by Christopher Patten, Anson Chan was referred to as the "conscience of Hong Kong" for her insistence on rule of law and freedom of the press after the 1997 transition to Chinese rule. Chan had served in numerous government posts in Hong Kong from the early 1960s and became the Director of Social Welfare in 1984. Her appointment as Chief Secretary gave her the second-ranking position in Hong Kong government. Because of her demands for political reform after the transition of power in 1997, Communist officials viewed her as too democratic and western-oriented. Chan resigned from office early in 2001.

investment pattern in place, rents in Hong Kong soared and consumers had less to spend on other goods or services. The imbalance in the economy also generated worsening income inequality in the colony, as poorer residents failed to profit from the real estate boom.

Once the Asian financial crisis spread, Hong Kong's stock market indices plummeted as much as 50 percent from August to October 1997. In response, the Chief Executive of HKSAR, Tung Chee-hwa, announced a comprehensive set of initiatives to abate the crisis and limit the potential effects on the Hong Kong economy. Chief among the programs was a government plan to build 55,000 housing units each year in order to alleviate the bubble in the real estate market. Tung also promised to undertake more social programs, especially for the elderly, which he hoped would narrow income inequality among HKSAR's residents. At the same time, however, Tung also ordered the government to undertake some stock market purchases to avert a total collapse of the exchange, which spurred charges of a government bailout for well connected investors. In the end, however, while Tung's actions represented a departure from Hong Kong's traditional "hands-off" mode of governing, they were not enough to stem the tide of recession, which caused HKSAR's economy to shrink by 2.7 percent in the first quarter of 1998, and by 5.2 percent the following quarter.

The economic contraction in 1998 confirmed the generally pessimistic mood of Hong Kong's 6.8 million residents. Unemployment reached a historic high of 6.3 percent in 1999. Real estate prices remained exorbitant by most standards, and the stock market's wild swings continued to create uncertainty for investors.

Economic conditions regained some stability in Asia throughout 1999, as the IMF helped several countries restructure their finances and undertake reforms to prevent a repeat of the crisis. Although Hong Kong did not need to negotiate with the IMF for a relief package, it nonetheless benefited from the agency's activities, which helped put the region's economies back on track and revived Hong Kong's trade sector. Indeed, with one of the soundest economies before the crisis, Hong Kong was the first to rebound in 1999; its GDP growth led all others in the region in the first quarter at 14.3 percent, continuing the trend with a 10.8 percent rise the following quarter. It seemed that Hong Kong had recovered from its first major post-transition challenge.

RECENT HISTORY AND THE FUTURE

Despite the lifting of Hong Kong's economic gloom, Chief Executive Tung's popularity plummeted, as he became a symbol of long-standing popular dissatisfaction. Elected in 1996 to serve as Hong Kong's highest elected official after the transition, Tung came to office with China's endorsement for his experience in business and in dealing with Hong Kong-Chinese matters. Tung's ties to Beijing's leaders and Hong Kong's business establishment quickly turned into a liability with his critics in the months after the transition. Martin Lee Chu-ming, head of the Democratic Party, led the political opposition to Tung and voiced his concerns that the Chief Executive disregarded the HKSAR Legislative Council in his policy making, preferring to make decisions out of public view and in consultation with Beijing. More troubling, Tung refused to discuss further democratic reforms of HKSAR's legislature, which were scheduled to allow direct elections for all of its representatives as early as 2008. Finally, Lee pointed to several scandals that demonstrated Tung's cronyism. In one instance, the government awarded a noncompetitive bid worth US$1.7 billion to the son of one of Tung's friends; in another, Tung refused to let prosecution charges proceed against a longtime associate. One of Tung's assistants was also accused of trying to interfere with the publication of a public opinion poll that showed Tung's approval rating at dismal levels.

Tung's position on the Falun Gong movement also deepened fears over his commitment to Hong

TUNG CHEE-HWA WAS APPOINTED BY THE LEADERSHIP IN BEIJING TO SERVE AS THE FIRST CHINESE HEAD OF HONG KONG SINCE THE LAND WAS GIVEN TO BRITAIN UNDER THE TREATY OF NANKING. *(AP/Wide World Photos. Reproduced by permission.)*

Kong's autonomy. Exiled from the People's Republic of China, Falun Gong leader Li Hongzhi retained a following in his homeland estimated in the millions. Although Falun Gong, a mediation and exercise program, did not claim any explicit political meaning, communist officials who labeled it a dangerous cult viewed it as a threat. After 10,000 Falun Gong practitioners made a silent protest for religious freedom outside of the Party's headquarters in Beijing in 1999, Chinese officials banned its practice. Tung endorsed their decision and indicated that he would not support Falun Gong protests in Hong Kong, where the practice was still ostensibly legal. When Falun Gong supporters organized a demonstration in Hong Kong's city hall, Tung expressed his utmost disapproval. Tung also refused to disclose whether he would ban Falun Gong from Hong Kong in accordance with Beijing's wishes, which caused additional uncertainty over his commitment to democracy and free speech in HKSAR.

Upholding the Rule of Law

Perhaps the leading critic of Tung's deference to Beijing was Chief Secretary Anson Chan, who served as HKSAR's top-ranking civil servant, a position second only to the Chief Executive. During her years as Hong Kong's second-ranking official, Chan had often taken exception to Tung's attitude toward Beijing. After Chinese officials cautioned Hong Kong businesses to stop trading with Taiwan, Chan openly rebuked the directive as a violation of HKSAR's Basic Law. The Executive Secretary was also critical of the scandals that plagued Tung's administration and fought vigorously to keep Hong Kong's civil servants at arm's length from political issues, offering the belief that transparency in government dealings was necessary to win the public trust and ensure social stability. Chan also supported the Falun Gong's right to free speech in HKSAR. For these measures, Chan earned the nickname "the conscience of Hong Kong," a tribute to her integrity as a civil servant and her willingness to speak out when Beijing interfered in Hong Kong's rights. As Chan addressed a November 2000 Heritage Foundation Conference, "It is crucial to our autonomy that we settle our arguments here in Hong Kong. Hong Kong people running Hong Kong means just that: Hong Kong people running Hong Kong here in Hong Kong." The implied directive to Beijing to stay far removed from HKSAR's governance could not have been more clear.

In January 2001, however, Anson Chan abruptly resigned as Executive Secretary. Although she publicly stated that her departure related only to her desire to spend more time with her family, most observers believed that her conscience would no longer allow her to serve in an administration that she no longer felt served Hong Kong's best interests. Far from solving Tung's problems, Chan's exit heightened scrutiny of his actions; because the HKSAR's government seemed shaken by mismanagement, support of Tung diminished even further. Chinese leaders expressed their support of Tung by flying in a group of influential Hong Kong businessmen for a pro-Tung rally, but their actions seemed counterproductive in terms of his popularity with the public.

China's pledge to refrain from interfering in Hong Kong's political system, then, had been only partially fulfilled since the transition, and it demonstrated the difficulties in making the "one country, two systems" approach a reality. While overt control over Hong Kong's affairs had not been demonstrated, the hesitancy of Chinese leaders to articulate a long-range, transparent policy toward Hong Kong raised concerns about its political stability, a major factor in whether it could continue its economic growth. Given the lack of credible and concrete information from Beijing regarding Hong Kong's future, HKSAR officials, particularly Tung Chee-

THE BASIC LAW OF THE HONG KONG SPECIAL ADMINISTRATIVE REGION OF THE PEOPLE'S REPUBLIC OF CHINA (SELECTED ARTICLES FROM CHAPTER 1: GENERAL PRINCIPLES)

Article 1 The Hong Kong Special Administrative Region is an inalienable part of the People's Republic of China.

Article 2 The National People's Congress authorizes the Hong Kong Special Administrative Region to exercise a high degree of autonomy and enjoy executive, legislative, and independent judicial power, including that of final adjudication, in accordance with the provisions of this Law.

Article 4 The Hong Kong Special Administrative Region shall safeguard the rights and freedoms of the residents of the Hong Kong Special Administrative Region and of other persons in the Region in accordance with law.

Article 5 The socialist system and policies shall not be practiced in the Hong Kong Special Administrative Region, and the previous capitalist system and way of life shall remain unchanged for 50 years.

Article 6 The Hong Kong Special Administrative Region shall protect the right of private ownership of property in accordance with law.

Article 8 The laws previously in force in Hong Kong, that is, the common law, rules of equity, ordinances, subordinate legislation and customary law shall be maintained, except for any that contravene this Law, and subject to any amendment by the legislature of the Hong Kong Special Administrative Region.

hwa, were increasingly accused of trying to second-guess their own initiatives in the hope of currying favor with China. The calls for further democratic reforms on the part of Democratic Party leader Martin Lee Chu-ming and the departure of Anson Chan from the government also increased tensions for Tung's administration.

By most measures, Hong Kong remained throughout the handover and its aftermath the most market-oriented economy in the world. Although this market orientation led to over-speculation in the stock market and real estate sector in the mid-1990s, Hong Kong's economy responded quickly once the financial crisis became apparent, with the government taking on greater responsibility for overseeing HKSAR's financial health. Despite the dissatisfaction with the Tung administration and suspicion over Chinese motives, HKSAR also continued to enjoy a greater number of political freedoms than the People's Republic and retained a vastly higher standard of living than across the Chinese border or among its regional rivals, though the extent of these freedoms has been tested under the new administration. Considering the traditional entrepreneurial spirit of its citizens, it seemed likely that Hong Kong would press to take full advantage of its unique history and opportunities to serve the financial and trading sectors as the most international city in Asia.

BIBLIOGRAPHY

Bereuter, Douglas. "Pragmatic Presence: U.S. Policy and Hong Kong's Transition," *Harvard International Review*, Summer 1997.

Chan, Anson. "Economic Freedom in Hong Kong," Heritage Foundation Conference Address, November 1, 2000.

Cheung, Clare. "Standard & Poors Upgrades Hong Kong Rating," *Hong Kong Standard*, December 8, 1999.

"China's Man Pushes Out Hong Kong's Woman," *The Economist*, January 20, 2001.

Ching, Frank. "A Hong Kong Perspective on the Hong Kong Transition," *China Business Review*, March/April 1997, p. 50.

Clifford, Mark L. "Is Hong Kong a Free Market?" *Business Week*, September 21, 1998.

Clifford, Mark L. and Rose Brady. "Hong Kong: Another Body Blow to the Rule of Law?" *Business Week*, January 29, 2001.

"Clouds over Hong Kong," *The Economist*, August 14, 1999.

Dodsworth, John, and Dubravko Mihaljek, eds. *Hong Kong, China: Growth, Structural Change, and Economic Stability During the Transition*. Washington, DC: International Monetary Fund, 1997.

Dorgan, Michael. "Falun Gong in Hong Kong Tests China's 'One Country, Two Systems' Vow," *Knight Ridder Washington Bureau*, February 8, 2001.

Dunphy, Stephen H. "Reporting from Hong Kong," *Seattle Times*, April 2, 2000.

"Hong Kong Countdown," *World Trade*, May 1997.

"Hong Kong's Pessimism about Chinese Rule Hits New High," AP Worldstream, April 19, 2001.

"Hong Kong's Troubled Voice," *The Economist*, October 23, 1999.

Hudson, Christopher, ed. *The China Handbook: Prospects onto the Twenty-first Century*. Chicago, IL: Glenlake Publishing Company, 2000.

"IMF Expects Growth to Stay Weak in First Half of 1999," *The Hong Kong Standard*, November 11, 1998.

Liebhold, David, Susan Jakes, and Wendy Kan. "Wrong Touch," *Time South Pacific*, July 10, 2000.

Lui, Tai-Lok. "Hong Kong Society: Anxiety in the Post-1997 Days," *Journal of Contemporary China*, March 1999.

Marshall, Tyler. "Hong Kong Economy Stabilizing as Growth in GDP Slows to 10.8 Percent," *Los Angeles Times*, August 26, 2000.

"Meddling in Hong Kong," *The Economist*, September 30, 2000.

Patten, Christopher. *East and West: China, Power, and the Future of Asia*. New York: Times Books, 1998.

———. "Hong Kong," *Presidents and Prime Ministers*, May/June 1997.

Rifkind, Malcom. "Hong Kong's Future," *Presidents and Prime Ministers*, March/April 1997.

Roberts, J.A.G. *A Concise History of China*. Cambridge, MA: Harvard University Press, 1999.

Segal, Gerald. *The Fate of Hong Kong: The Coming of 1997 and What Lies Beyond*. New York: St. Martin's Press, 1993.

Shipp, Steve. *Hong Kong, China: A Political History of the British Crown Colony's Transfer to Chinese Rule*. Jefferson, NC: McFarland and Company, Publishers, 1995.

Spaeth, Anthony, and Sandra Burton. "Hong Kong Jitters," *Time Australia*, April 22, 1996.

Switow, Michael. "Hong Kong Still Hung Up on Problems," *Christian Science Monitor*, July 13, 1998.

Tran, Van Hoa, and Charles Harvie, eds. *The Causes and Impact of the Asian Financial Crisis*. New York: St. Martin's Press, 2000.

Tsang, Donald. "Hong Kong's Clear Skies," *The Economist*, August 28, 1999.

Tsang, Shu-Ki. "The Hong Kong Economy: Opportunities Out of the Crisis?" *Journal of Contemporary China*, March 1999.

Tse, Raymond Y.C. "China's Real Estate Market and the Asian Financial Crisis," *Emerging Market Quarterly*, Winter 2000.

"Tung-Tied Hong Kong," *The Economist*, April 22, 2000.

Welsh, Frank. *A Borrowed Place: The History of Hong Kong*. New York: Kodansha International, 1993.

Xu, Xiaobing, and George D. Wilson. "The Hong Kong Special Administrative Region as a Model of Regional External Autonomy," *Case Western Reserve Journal of International Law*, Winter 2000.

Zhang, Wei-Wei. *Transforming China: Economic Reform and its Political Implications*. New York: St. Martin's Press, 2000.

—*Timothy G. Borden*

INDONESIA: GRAPPLING WITH UNREST IN IRIAN JAYA AND ACEH

On December 2, 2000, Indonesian police shot and killed seven people in the town of Merauke in the province of Irian Jaya. Police claimed the victims had initiated a riot when told to take down the "Morning Star" flag, a symbol of their independence. The following day, over two hundred heavily armed troops descended on a cultural center in the provincial capital of Jayapura, arresting sixty-one members of the militia, known as *Satagas Papua*, or the Papua Taskforce. The group had been using the building as its headquarters for the previous six months. Among those arrested and jailed were the leaders of the region's separatist political body, the Papuan Presidium Council. These actions were in response to celebrations on December 1 marking the thirty-ninth anniversary of the declaration of independence of the Indonesian province. The declaration—which has failed to achieve its goal—was celebrated throughout the region by the flying of the banned "Morning Star" flag.

Guerrilla fighting continued after the police shooting, and on December 15, Indonesian Army Corporal Sahrudin and several soldiers decapitated a flagpole bearing the Morning Star. Fifty guerrilla warriors of the Dani tribe surrounded the men, who began firing their automatic weapons on the group of rebels, who were armed only with bows and arrows. A nine-hour battle ensued, resulting in the death of Sahrudin and four Dani.

At the other end of the Indonesian archipelago, in the province of Aceh, on the northern tip of the island of Sumatra, similar violent outbreaks between Indonesian police and rebels have occurred. Negotiations between the government and rebels there have not been successful in quelling fighting. On February 10, 2001, while peace talks

THE CONFLICT

The Indonesian regions of Aceh and Irian Jaya have flared with violence as ethnic populations reject the authority of the Jakarta government and call for independence. The government has responded harshly and clashes have escalated to include common citizens and humanitarian aid workers. With Indonesia's president implicated in several scandals, the growing unrest in Indonesia's provinces contributes to a leadership already on shaky ground.

Economic

- Aceh is a primarily Muslim area that is rich in resources, especially oil, which brings in a large revenue for the Indonesian government.

- As in Aceh, fighting in Irian Jaya has escalated since Suharto's fall from power. The government, wanting to retain the resource rich land, has offered Irian Jaya increased autonomy, a proposal the region turned down. However, Indonesia is at this point unwilling to enter into independence negotiations.

Ethnic

- Irian Jaya (also known as West Papua) shares an island with Papua New Guinea, but has been part of Indonesia since 1969. The region is culturally distinct from the rest of Indonesia, sharing more with Melanesian peoples from Papua New Guinea and Australia.

Political

- Aceh, a territory at the northern tip of Sumatra, has been agitating for independence from Indonesia since the 1970s.

- Between 1990 and 1998, the Indonesian government declared Aceh an area of designated military operations and killed, raped, and tortured thousands of citizens suspected of working for independence.

- The independence movement in Irian Jaya dates to the early days of annexation, which was achieved through a vote engineered by the Indonesian government.

were underway, four citizens of the village of Kruef Lintang, in the Peureulak district of East Aceh, were killed by federal troops. The soldiers entered a coffeehouse where the men were sitting, shot them and arrested several others. The village chief claimed that the men, all prawn farmers, were not affiliated with the independence movement. The East Aceh police chief, however, said that the men were rebels who had ambushed troops on a routine patrol of the town. The chief claimed that the men fired first and died in the ensuing gunfight. A report from the local hospital, however, found torture marks on the men's bodies.

The fighting in Aceh continued to flare into mid-2001, in spite of a ceasefire drawn up in Geneva in June 2000. While the accord seemed to stem violence for a period of time, and the agreement was renewed in September, its conditions are vague, and it is in effect more of a mutual understanding than an officially binding agreement, as it makes explicit no punishment for violating the terms. The ongoing negotiations broke down in February 2001, and since then violence has been escalating in the area.

The rebels have gained ground, fueled by popular outrage at Indonesian military excesses, as well as by the guerrilla terrorists' own tactics, which have silenced internal opposition. A day-long occupation of the town of Idi Rayeuk in February was seen as a landmark in the movement's growing momentum. Although the government took back the town after 24 hours, the event was indicative of a situation that may soon come to a head.

HISTORICAL BACKGROUND

A Brief Portrait of Indonesia

The archipelago of Indonesia consists of 13,670 islands, of which over 7,000 are uninhabited. It stretches 3,200 miles (5,100 kilometers) from one end to the other, covering a total of 735,310 square miles (1,904,444 square kilometers). On the western end of Indonesia, Irian Jaya shares an island with Papua New Guinea, while the large island of Borneo is shared with two Malaysian states and the Kingdom of Brunei. The island of Timor is divided into East and West; the eastern half gained its independence in 1999, while the western portion remains part of Indonesia. The other main islands are Java (where the capital, Jakarta, is located); Sumatra (where Aceh is located); Bali; Sulawesi; and the Moluccas. Indonesia is the largest country in Southeast Asia in terms of area, and the fourth most populous nation in the

world—a July 2000 estimate placed the population at 224,784,210.

Indonesia's economy is based primarily on agriculture. Rice is the main crop, and much of what is produced is consumed within the country itself. Nevertheless, Indonesia is not self-sustaining and is forced to import basic foodstuffs. The largest cash crops are coconut, rubber, and tea. Tin, other minerals, and timber are also exported, as is petroleum. (It is the largest exporter of petroleum in Asia.) Manufacturing accounts for 21 percent of the Gross Domestic Product (GDP). Many of the country's industries in this sector have received international criticism for their horrendous working conditions and use of child labor, a condition indicative of Indonesia's depressed financial situation. The government attempted unsuccessfully to nationalize industry in the 1960s. It is currently in the process of re-privatizing, in hopes that this will help revitalize the suffering economy.

Religious and Ethnic Diversity

Ironically, for a country founded on principles of religious tolerance, Indonesia is being torn apart by conflicts stemming largely from religious differences. As a center of maritime trade, the islands were influenced by a variety of outside cultures and traditions, including Hindus from India, Buddhists from East Asia, Muslims from Malaysia, and Christians from Holland and Portugal. Each of these religions still has followers in Indonesia. Hindus, who comprise two percent of the population, live primarily on Bali. Eight percent of Indonesians are Christian, and one percent are Buddhist. The majority of the country (88 percent) is nominally Muslim. However, most of these people practice a form of the religion that combines elements of Hinduism and Buddhism, as well as the indigenous animism.

The principles on which Indonesia was founded were laid out in a speech by Achmed Sukarno in 1945, and are known as *pancasila*. This Sanskrit word encompasses the ideals of humanism, national unity, democracy, social justice, and belief in one god. While *pancasila* upholds freedom of religion for all, some Muslims saw this institutionalized value system as an underhanded attempt to impose the culture and religion of those in power on them.

In 1984 President Suharto proposed a law making *pancasila* the official philosophy of the nation. Muslims opposed what they saw as a further attempt to marginalize their belief system. There were violent protests in Jakarta, including fires and

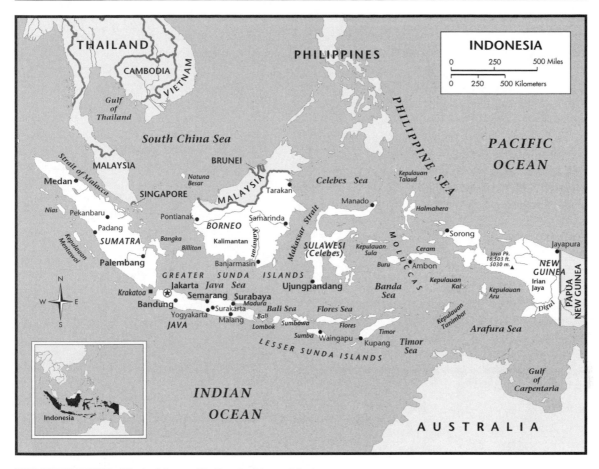

MAP OF INDONESIA. *(Maryland Cartographics. Reproduced by permission.)*

bombings, but nevertheless, the law was passed the following year.

There is a vocal contingent of more devout Muslims on the island of Java. Soon after independence, the group known as *Darul Islam* (House of Islam) held demonstrations in Jakarta, protesting what it saw as the marginalization of Islam in the government. These insurgencies were supported by Muslims from Aceh, the country's largest stronghold of the Islamic faith. Indonesian Muslims feel a connection to Islamic nations in the Middle East, and the Acehnese have received support from Libya in particular. Javanese have tried to cast the Acehnese as Muslim fundamentalists, while the Acehnese counter that it is rather the case that the religion practiced in Java is so diluted and commingled with other traditions that it cannot properly be called Islam.

Indonesia also has a small but significant population of Christians. Five percent of the population is Protestant, and three percent is Roman Catholic. The island of East Timor, originally col-onized by the Portuguese, is primarily Roman Catholic. There are also Christian populations on the Moluccas, who have recently come into conflict with the Muslims there. Some of the ethnic groups on Irian Jaya are also Christian, which serves as yet another marker of their difference from the Javanese. Others practice indigenous religions which, unlike in Java, have remained largely uninfluenced by Hindu and Muslim influences.

Chinese settlers have been a presence in Indonesia for hundreds of years. Most settled in trading posts in northern Java, where they lived primarily in insular communities and often came to dominate the commerce of the area. They were merchants and moneylenders, professions Indonesians typically scorned. This contributed to discrimination against the Chinese; they were prohibited from working in the government and in many other professions. This long-standing animosity toward the Chinese flared during the economic crisis in 1998. Chinese communities in Jakarta were attacked; many Chinese were killed or forced to flee the country.

CHRONOLOGY

August 17, 1945 Sukarno declares Indonesia's independence. War ensues between Indonesia and its colonizer, Holland.

1949 The war for independence from Holland ends; Indonesia wins its sovereignty; Sukarno becomes president.

1959 Aceh is given "special territory" status.

1961 Irian Jaya (West Papua) declares its independence from the Dutch.

1963 The Dutch cede Irian Jaya to the United Nations.

1965 Indonesia experiences a coup attempt, put down by army General Suharto.

1968 Suharto officially becomes president of Indonesia.

1969 Irian Jaya is incorporated into Indonesia by a vote engineered by President Suharto.

1976 Aceh Merkdeka (Free Aceh) is founded.

1990–98 Aceh is declared an area of military operations, and countless atrocities are perpetrated on the citizens of the area in the name of putting down insurgencies.

1997 Economic crisis strikes all of Southeast Asia, including Indonesia.

May 21, 1998 President Suharto resigns and is replaced by his vice president, B.J. Habibe.

1999 Abdurrahman Wahid defeats Habibe in the country's first democratic presidential election.

February 1, 2001 President Wahid faces charges of financial misdoing and threats of impeachment.

April 30, 2001 Parliament officially censures Wahid.

May 2001 Corruption charges against Wahid are dropped, but parliament votes to impeach Wahid for incompetence.

July 2–23, 2001 Wahid calls for a state of emergency to preempt impeachment proceedings, but security forces do not support him. Wahid is impeached and removed from office. Megawati Sukarnoputri is sworn in as president.

July 2001 Twenty civilians are killed in the regions of Aceh and Irian Jaya.

Early History and Colonization

Most of the Indonesian islands were settled by people from Asia known as the Proto-Malays. The exception is Irian Jaya, whose people trace their ancestry back to Melanasian roots, similar to the natives of Australia, New Zealand, and Papua New Guinea. Chinese and Indian traders first arrived in the islands in the fifth century CE; Arab traders landed on the northern island of Sumatra two centuries later. In the ninth century two kingdoms arose in Central Java: the Sailendra and the Mataram. In 1294 much of present-day Indonesia and Malaysia were united for the first time under the reign of the Majapahit kingdom.

Indonesia's primary importance in international trade was in spice. Muslim traders from the Middle East and Malay long dominated commerce in the area, but the Portuguese took the city of Malacca, in nearby Malaysia, in 1511, in an attempt to gain entry into the profitable enterprise. England and Holland soon followed.

The Dutch arrived in 1602, and by 1619 ruled most of present-day Indonesia, then known as the Dutch East Indies, from the capital of Jakarta, which they renamed Batavia. By the end of the nineteenth century Holland had incorporated all of what would later become Indonesia under its colonial regime. The Dutch introduced coffee and other crops to the islands and reaped large financial benefits from the agricultural production. While exploiting the colony for financial gain, the Dutch did contribute to the development of agriculture, health, education, and transportation in the islands, and it was these aspects of colonization that partially made possible the idea of a free, united Indonesia.

The independence movement developed under the leadership of Indonesians educated in the West. The Indonesian Nationalist Party (PNI) was established in 1927. Achmed Sukarno was one of the founding members and was arrested twice for his activities. Along with fellow nationalists, including Mohammad Hatta, Sukarno fought not only to repel the Dutch but also to unify factions within the country, which were divided along religious, political, and regional lines.

During World War II (1939–45) the Japanese occupied Indonesia, replacing the Dutch. Sukarno offered Indonesian support for the Japanese in exchange for being allowed to promulgate his nationalist ideas. In 1945, when the Japanese surrendered, Sukarno issued a declaration of independence. The Dutch were not prepared to give up their colony,

INDONESIAN SOLDIERS MARCH NEAR A MOSQUE IN ONE OF THE COUNTRY'S RESTIVE REGIONS IN DECEMBER 2000. SOLDIERS AND REBELS HAVE CLASHED WITH INCREASING FREQUENCY, AND CIVILIANS HAVE NOT BEEN EXEMPT FROM THE VIOLENCE. *(AP/Wide World Photos. Reproduced by permission.)*

however, and a four-year war ensued. Indonesia finally won its independence in 1949.

Sukarno and Suharto

From 1949 until 1957, the fledgling democracy went through seven different administrations. The motto of the new country was *Bhinneka Tunggallka*, "Unity in Diversity." This goal was partially achieved through the spread of a national language, Bahasa Indonesia, and through intermarriage and internal migration among islands, which the government encouraged. However, the 300 different ethnic groups, with over 300 different languages, spread throughout thousands of islands, did not naturally coalesce into one unified nation. Tensions between Java and the outer islands were high due to cultural and religious differences, as well as resentment on the part of the outer islands that the

government was controlled primarily by Javanese, who did not necessarily have in mind the interests of other regions of the country.

In 1957 Sukarno overthrew the parliament and instituted martial law. In an attempt to instill order and unity in the country, President Sukarno put in place an authoritarian system he called "Guided Democracy." Despite his socialist policies, the gulf between the rich and the poor widened, and civil unrest ensued; uprisings occurred in Sumatra and Sulewesi, and a coup attempt in 1965 threatened Sukarno's presidency. The coup was put down, but Sukarno's hold on office was tenuous at best.

General Suharto, who was responsible for defeating the coup attempt, began to assume more power. After moving up the government ranks he officially became president in 1968, replacing

ECONOMIC CRISIS AND ITS RAMIFICATIONS

Indonesia's size and its largely untapped resources—both natural and human—have made the country an attractive market for foreign investors. The United States has labeled it a Big Emerging Market (BE), and since 1967, U.S. companies have invested over $12 billion in the economy, primarily in such industries as energy, aerospace, construction and mining, and financial services. Indonesia is the world's largest supplier of plywood, as well as a significant source of such goods as clothing, machinery, petroleum, coffee, and natural rubber. Japan and South Korea are also major trading partners.

When an economic crisis struck Asia in 1997 Indonesia's growing economy bore the brunt of the impact. The value of the rupiah fell drastically, factories closed down, and investors lost confidence in the economy and left. In November 1997 the International Monetary Fund (IMF) offered a support package, consisting of technical aid, food, and medical supplies, under conditions of wide-sweeping reforms in the monetary, banking, and corporate systems of the country.

The economic downturn compounded the growing dissatisfaction with Suharto's government. As the president faced charges of corruption, student protests erupted in the streets of Jakarta, demanding reform of the authoritarian regime. Economic instability fed political instability, and as the situation in East Timor escalated, secessionist stirrings intensified in other regions of the country as well, including Aceh and Irian Jaya.

Economic Crisis, Suharto's Fall, and the Reign of Habibe

In 1997 all of Southeast Asia was hit by economic recession. Indonesia's currency, the rupiah, was devalued. In the face of the inflation and mounting debt, many foreign investors lost confidence and pulled out of the country. The International Monetary Fund offered to help bail Indonesia out, under the condition that the country institute certain humanitarian and economic reforms.

However, rising unemployment and poverty caused growing dissatisfaction among the populace. Political instability was compounded by the fact that President Suharto was facing charges of corruption. In March 1998, in an effort to cement his increasingly shaky hold on power, Suharto extended his term by five years. Protests, riots and ethnic violence erupted in the cities of Jakarta and Medan. Hundreds of people were killed; ethnic Chinese, who had controlled a large portion of the economy, were a primary target. The economic situation continued to worsen. Inflation rose as high as 70 percent, and most remaining foreign investors left the country. On May 21, 1998, President Suharto resigned, and was replaced by his vice-president, Bacharuddin Jusuf Habibe.

Habibe took office in October 1999. From the beginning, Habibe's public support was qualified at best. Despite his professed openness to East Timorese independence, it was too late to allay the violence that had been brewing. The situation escalated, and when East Timor voted for independence in 1999, police and army troops were sent in to put down rebellions and student protests.

During his early days in office, Habibe approached the issue of independence in both Irian Jaya and Aceh with a conciliatory stance. He allowed the "Morning Star" flag to be flown, and permitted the use of the term "West Papua," which separatists prefer to "Irian Jaya." However, Habibe soon caved in to pressure from other political parties, who feared that concessions to these independence movements would encourage further secessionist activity in other areas of the country.

In fact, these fears were realized as the situation in East Timor continued to worsen. Indignation mounted as more and more atrocities perpetrated by the Indonesian government in the area were revealed. The movement had the backing of the Portuguese government (the island's former colonizer), and various other Western nations and international organizations. Eventually Australia and the United Nations (UN) got involved; the UN

Sukarno. Suharto paid lip service to a government reform and economic restructuring, but his administration engaged in the same corruption and cronyism that had plagued Sukarno's presidency. Under Suharto the military took an increasingly powerful role; army officers retained control of the oil, mining, and forestry industries, and members of the military comprised half of Suharto's cabinet. Suharto and his political party, Golkar, maintained tight control of the government, ensuring the president's reelection in five consecutive elections.

During Suharto's rule, Indonesia expanded to include two new territories: Irian Jaya in 1969 and East Timor in 1976. Particularly in East Timor, annexation was a violent process, involving the massacre of thousands in the Timorese city of Dilli.

sent a small number of troops to the island, and Australia dispatched considerably more. Many Indonesians who felt it was purely a domestic dispute resented the outside interference. By the time East Timor was finally granted independence, the new country was virtually destroyed. The incident had taken its toll on Indonesia as well. The head of the army, General Wiranto, was removed, and Habibe was replaced by Abdurrahman Wahid—the first democratically elected president in the country's history. The rupiah, Indonesia's currency, was ailing; relations with Australia were tense; and unity, both within the parliament and in various regions of the country, was increasingly fragile.

History of Irian Jaya

The province of Irian Jaya is located on the western portion of the island that also contains the independent nation of Papua New Guinea. Culturally, the Irian Jayans are closer to Papua New Guineans and other Melanasian people than they are to Indonesians. They prefer to refer to themselves as "Papuans" and to their region as "West Papua;" in this essay, these terms are used interchangeably with "Irian Jaya" and "Irian Jayans." There is a marked distinction in the region between outsiders who have settled there and the indigenous people, who, outside of a few coastal towns, live almost entirely as they have for centuries. There are a large number of so-called transmigrants, brought from other islands by the Indonesian government; of a total population of 2.5 million, over one-fourth are transmigrants. The majority of the top government positions on the island are held by nonnatives. These are mostly Javanese bureaucrats, who comprise a relatively small percentage of the population and live in the capital of Jayapura.

Irian Jaya is the largest and least explored area of Indonesia. It comprises 22 percent of the country's total land area. However, it is also one of the most sparsely populated zones, containing only two million people, or one percent of the country's population. Anthropologists estimate that this number includes at least 250 different ethnic groups; the most prominent of these are the Asmat and the Dani. The Dani in particular, who live in the highlands in the island's interior, have retained their ancient cultural practices into contemporary times. They wear little clothing, and many still live in traditional basic conditions similar to those of their early ancestors.

The island of Papua, which contains both Irian Jaya and Papua New Guinea, is thought to have been connected to the continent of Australia during the last Ice Age. It is estimated that it was once home to as many as one thousand different tribes and languages.

Irian Jaya declared its independence from the Dutch in 1961. Two years later, the colonizers finally ceded the territory, at the time called West Irian, to the United Nations. Indonesia officially incorporated the region in 1969. The government had promised a referendum, but fearing that they would vote for independence, President Sukarno decided instead to conduct a vote of specially selected delegates. Not surprisingly, the council of 1,025 voted in favor of annexation. Many Irian Jayans were bitter about what they saw as, in effect, the replacing of one colonial regime with another, and were outraged at the undemocratic process by which it was done. The area's separatist movement dates back to these early days as a province of Indonesia.

As early as the 1950s the Indonesian government began a campaign to redistribute its population, resettling landless peasants from the more crowded islands of Bali, Java, and Madura to other less populous ones, including Irian Jaya. This effort was renewed in 1986. The government offered settlers houses, farming equipment, and supplies to relocate; thanks to these financial incentives, the numbers have risen to a total of six million settlers receiving assistance, and as many as another six million without.

While the resettlement movement is ostensibly an effort to improve the conditions of poor Indonesians on other islands, it is also in part intended to spread the cultural influence from these islands in order to create a more unified Indonesia. Instead, the migration has caused a good deal of ethnic tension between settlers and locals. The government has exploited these tensions as a way to make villains out of independence fighters in the region and portray them as dangerous and anti-Indonesian. The settlers, most often poor farmers unable to make a living in their home states, have in many cases become the victims of violent attacks by Papuan, or Irian Jayan, separatists.

Irian Jayans resent the infringement upon their land and culture, which they have managed to preserve virtually unchanged into modernity. Actions taken by the Indonesian government in the region, when not outright oppressive, are seen by Papuans as patronizing, offensive, or irrelevant. For example, in the 1980s, the Indonesian government attempted to convince the Dani people to adopt more Western modes of dress. The surface motive was to protect the Dani from the cold weather to which the region is sometimes prone; the Dani, however,

A SUPPORTER OF THE FREE ACEH MOVEMENT HOLDS UP ACEH'S FLAG. MANY FEEL THE GROUP WILL SETTLE FOR NOTHING LESS THAN INDEPENDENCE FROM INDONESIA. *(The Gamma Liaison Network. Reproduced by permission.)*

who had retained their traditional minimal body covering for centuries, saw it as an obvious attempt to force outside culture on them, and the effort was a failure.

More than 80 percent of West Papua is covered by rainforest, which is home to a wide variety of flora and fauna, including birds of paradise, for which the island is famous. The Papuans are concerned about the destruction of this rainforest, as well as other environmental damage that the influx of people has caused.

There are several separatist groups active in Irian Jaya. The most prominent is the Free Papua Organization (OPM). While Irian Jaya is home to an estimated 250 different ethnic groups, one of the largest and most active in the independence struggle are the Dani, who live in the central highlands.

The government proposed autonomy for Irian Jaya as an alternative to independence. At a June

2000 congress held in the city of Jayapura, tribal leaders rejected the proposition, instead electing a 31-member group called the Papua Presidium to enter into separation negotiations with the government. The government refused to negotiate and renewed its crackdown on the independence movement.

The region's flag has also been a focal point for disagreement. On October 6, 2000, Indonesian troops attempted to take down a flag in the town of Wamena. They killed six Papuans, and local soldiers retaliated by killing 24 Indonesian settlers in the area. After negotiations between the government and the Papua Presidium, an accord was reached on November 9, allowing the flag to be displayed in five specified locations.

History of Aceh

Aceh is located on the northernmost tip of the island of Sumatra. It is a resource-rich area, supplying a large percentage of Indonesia's natural wealth, including much of its oil. When these resources leave Aceh, it is often to the financial benefit of Javanese rather than locals. Similarly, while growing industry in the region has produced jobs, much of the work has been taken by immigrants from other islands.

Of all areas of Indonesia, Aceh has the longest history of contact with the outside world. There are records of it in documents of Chinese exploration dating back to the early sixth century. When Marco Polo landed there in 1292, he noted six active trading posts in the area. Muslim traders first came to the area in the seventh and eighth centuries, and their religion took hold; in 804, the first Islamic kingdom, called Perlak, was established. Aceh became an area of Portuguese influence in the sixteenth century. Islamic culture, however, continued to exert the strongest cultural influence. In the sixteenth and seventeenth centuries, the area developed an active literary scene, and works springing from it were read throughout the Islamic world.

The British and Dutch fought over the area in the early nineteenth century, and in 1824, the Treaty of London declared it the property of Holland. However, the people of Aceh rebelled, and fought a war that lasted from 1873 until 1942. It was the longest war ever fought by the Dutch. They lost a total of 10,000 soldiers, while Acehnese casualties were more than ten times that. Most Dutch troops withdrew after 1942, and a 1949 treaty transferred the region from Holland to Indonesia.

In 1958 Sukarno's government suppressed an armed uprising in Sumatra. This uprising had the backing of the U.S. Central Intelligence Agency (CIA), which feared the communist tendencies of Sukarno's regime. In response, Sukarno appealed to the Soviets for help, and it was Soviet aid that allowed Indonesia to win Irian Jaya from the Dutch.

In response to separatist sentiment, Aceh was given "Special Region" status in 1959. This gave it greater autonomy in regard to religious and political freedom, while still keeping the region under the rule of the central government. In actuality, however, the region was never allowed to exercise many of these rights.

The Acehnese independence movement began in the early 1970s. The *Gerakan Aceh Merdeka* (GAM), or Free Aceh Movement, was founded in 1976. It is known by the Indonesian government as the Aceh Security Disturbance Movement. It gained momentum in the late 1980s when troops

who had been trained in Libya and provided with arms by the Libyan government returned to their country. In 1996 the Indonesian government claimed that it had effectively eliminated GAM. However, the underground movement only continued to grow.

Between May 1990 and August 1998, the region was designated an area of military operations (*daerah operasi militer*, or DOM). Giving the area this status allowed the government to run counter-insurgency operations, which prompted killing of the Acehnese with impunity; thousands of civilians were arrested, held without trial, and tortured. Bodies were mutilated and left by roadsides; many women whose husbands and sons were associated with the rebels were raped.

Popular support for the movement reached a critical mass only after the fall of Suharto's dictatorship in 1998. The new government's failure to address the atrocities committed under Suharto's regime has resulted in increased public anger. GAM has gained in strength as many of its numbers have returned from exile or hiding. The movement has also been inspired by the recent success of East Timor in that region's battle for independence from Indonesia.

Unfortunately, as GAM has grown in influence and power, it has developed a criminal element that imposes a system of illegal taxation on businesses and individual households. GAM leaders deny the existence of this illegal activity, claiming that all donations to its cause are voluntary. In many areas, GAM has replaced the role of the federal government; GAM leaders issue marriage licenses, for instance, and resolve local disputes.

When Suharto's government fell, many of these atrocities were revealed, and the Acehnese hoped that the new administration would attempt to address the wrongs that had been perpetrated there. However, Habibe ignored Acehnese demands for justice, which further fueled anger and the desire for self-rule in the region.

Continued violence in March 2001 forced the Indonesian branch of the U.S. oil company Exxon Mobil to close its gas fields in the region. Since then, skirmishes have broken out at the fields, when rebels attacked police who were guarding the area. On several occasions, gunfire has been exchanged.

Among much of the populace, the police and the rebels inspire equal degrees of fear. One woman whose husband was killed by the military in the late 1980s stated, "Before, at least you knew the military is behind the killings. Now the killers are always

TARGETING AID WORKERS IN ACEH

Violence in Aceh has in many cases spread to include civilians. Both the Indonesian police and GAM rebels are guilty of numerous human rights abuses. Humanitarian aid workers have become targets as well. In a well publicized case Nazaruddin, a 22-year-old from the village of Simpang Kramat who worked as a volunteer for a nongovernmental organization, found himself a victim of the unrest. He works for the Rehabilitation Action for Torture Victims in Aceh (RATA), which provides counseling and rehabilitation services to victims of torture and abuse in Aceh. On December 6, 2000, Nazaruddin, along with three other RATA workers, was kidnapped and tortured by men they suspected to be cuaks (government informers) and TNI (Indonesian police). Nazaruddin gave his testimony to Human Rights Watch, available online at http://www.hrw.org/press/2000/12/acehtest.htm (cited July 18, 2001).

I am a 22-year-old field worker for the nongovernmental organization [NGO] Rehabilitation Action for Torture Victims in Aceh (RATA). We provide counseling and rehabilitation services to victims of torture and abuse in Aceh. Before working for RATA, I worked for the Indonesian Red Cross and helped collect the bodies of victims of the conflict....

The cuaks [government informants] kept their guns pointed at us, and started questioning us.... We explained that we were not political, but humanitarian workers. Ampon said we were lying....

We responded that we had an official letter [surat tugas] which allowed us to work freely in Aceh. The men wanted to see it, so I took it out of my wallet and gave it to them....

Then the cuak ordered us to take off our shoes, and told us to get out of the car. It was about 1 p.m. and we were still in Lapang village. They started threatening us, and began to beat us. When we fell down from the beating, the cuak would order us to get up again, and fire their rifles near our feet, not hitting us but getting close. I was hit hard on the side of my head, near the right temple, with a rifle butt. Bachtiar and I were dripping blood. Those doing the beatings were not only the four cuaks, some of the others also gathered around and took turns beating us. One of the other armed men ... was filming the entire beating and the abuse with a large shoulder-supported camera.

.... Ampon came to us and said, "Now you are going to confess and say what's what if you want to live. We will give you 15 minutes." One of us said, "What can we confess, we are just volunteers?" "Then it's clear you want to die," Ampon replied....

We were marched for about a meter, and when we got closer to the house I just ran. I later heard two shots as I took off, and believe that Bachtiar and Rusli were killed then. The men opened fire on me as I was running and emptied a full magazine trying to hit me.

I ran for about 15 minutes without stopping through tall grass. When the sun set, I was still in the forest. I went up a small hill and saw a house with a light in the distance. I went to the house and called out, but the family inside was scared. I was dressed only in my underwear. Eventually, they took me in and gave me food. I asked to be taken to the next village and they helped me, and finally I managed to make it home.

unknown." The police have a reputation for targeting humanitarian workers, but GAM also has a record of human rights violations and victimizing civilians; it has been known to torture and kill those suspected of being informers or collaborators. In fact, those in most danger are nonviolent advocates of independence, as they are targets of both GAM and the Indonesian troops. Immigrants from other islands have also become GAM targets. More than six thousand people have died fighting in the area in the past decade, and over two hundred have been killed in the renewed violence in the first three months of 2001.

The rebels' military chief is Abdullah Syafii. Teungku Hasan di Tiro, another prominent leader in the Acehnese independence movement, was exiled to Sweden in 1980, where he continues to work for the cause.

RECENT HISTORY AND THE FUTURE

Abdurrahman Wahid's hold on the presidency was somewhat tenuous in mid-2001. He was accused of two accounts of graft and on February 1, 2001, the parliament issued a censure of his involvement in these scandals. Wahid set a deadline of July 20, 2001 for a compromise agreement for legislators not to pursue impeachment proceedings, which were scheduled for August 1. Short of a compromise that met Wahid's terms, the president planned on declaring a state of emergency in an attempt to hold onto power.

These events came to pass in late July 2001. Wahid declared a state of emergency in an attempt to suspend parliament's impeachment hearings against him. Security forces called upon to support Wahid, however, ignored his orders. The parliament voted to dismiss Wahid from the presidency and, minutes later, Vice President Megawati Sukarnoputri was sworn in as the next president of Indonesia.

Student protests in Jakarta have expressed dissatisfaction with Wahid and their preference for Megawati Sukarnoputri. The daughter of former president Sukarno, Megawati is staunchly opposed to independence for either Irian Jaya or Aceh, where 20 civilians were killed in July 2001. Among Megawati's first tasks must be an attempt to settle the continuing unrest in these regions.

Humanitarian groups such as Amnesty International have expressed concern that the political turmoil in Jakarta will divert attention from the independence movements in places such as Aceh and Irian Jaya, and that human rights offenses with be ignored in the confusion. A spokesperson for Amnesty International worries, "While all eyes are turned towards Jakarta, the Indonesian security forces are intensifying their repressive approach in Aceh, and peaceful political activists in Papua [Irian Jaya] are being silenced behind prison bars." (Amnesty International News Service, March 13, 2001.)

According to Indonesian minister Sisilo Bambang Yudhoyono the country is currently facing three major crises. The first is the scandals involving the now former-president Wahid, and resulting dissent among top-level politicians. Another is the financial situation; this is the fourth consecutive year of economic crisis in Indonesia. Finally, political instability and insecurity in regions such as Aceh and Irian Jaya threaten to continue the break up of the country begun by the secession of East Timor.

There have been stirrings of unrest in other regions of Indonesia as well, including Riau and East Kalimantan (both areas rich in natural resources), in North Sulawesi, and in Makassar (historically an important trading center). Additionally, in February 2001 native Dayaks on the island of Borneo launched a series of attacks on settlers from Madura. Approximately 500 Madurese were killed in one month, and army troops were sent in to stabilize the situation. Unresolved land disputes, and resentment on the part of the Dayaks that the settlers were taking jobs from them, led to the conflict. The Dayaks have vowed to continue the attacks as long as Madurese continue to inhabit the island.

Future Prospects for Irian Jaya and Aceh

As the central government in Indonesia becomes more wracked with problems and dissention, it is likely that it will become increasingly difficult for the country to maintain control over outlying areas. As more far-flung regions begin making demands for increased autonomy, the unity of the country as a whole is taxed, and a large-scale fragmentation appears to be a possibility.

While Indonesia's military power is superior to that of rebels in either Irian Jaya or Aceh, the guerrilla fighters generally have more personally invested in their struggle than do the Indonesian soldiers. They are willing to put themselves on the line in situations where they are outnumbered or overpowered and are ready to accept high losses.

On March 20, 2001, a helicopter carrying two senior government ministers to Aceh was fired upon, causing Wahid to cancel a planned visit to the region. The area has been largely cut off from humanitarian aid since January as well, due to security concerns. The prospect of increased violence and antipathy towards the central government appeared to be intensifying.

The Wahid government hoped to appease Acehnese secessionists with terms of increased autonomy similar to those proposed in Irian Jaya. While the Indonesian government has agreed to new laws granting the area more autonomy it is not making concessions to demands for independence. There are fears among many in the region that compromise will result in a splintering of the GAM, which could cause extremists in the movement to feel even more alienated and resort to further violence, not just against Indonesians from Java and other islands, but also against more moderate Acehnese.

In Irian Jaya the proposed terms of autonomy resulted in no such internal division. Instead the response was a more determined and unified effort at obtaining full independence. In Aceh, unlike in Irian Jaya, Acehnese themselves have become targets of the guerrilla movement. While Papuan separatists have attacked civilians, these victims have been primarily settlers from other islands. In Aceh, internal dissention appears to be more of a threat to the independence movement, as GAM has targeted Acehnese whom it suspects, often with minimal evidence, of not fully supporting the cause.

Compared to East Timor, Aceh's rebels are significantly better armed and trained, thanks to their support from Malaysia, Thailand, and Libya. East Timor had the backing of the Catholic

ABDURRAHMAN WAHID (LEFT), SITTING NEXT TO THEN-VICE PRESIDENT MEGAWATI SUKARNOPUTRI, WAS OVERCOME BY SCANDAL AND REMOVED FROM OFFICE. HE WAS REPLACED BY MEGAWATI. *(AP/Wide World Photos. Reproduced by permission.)*

Church and many other Western organizations, as well as expatriate communities in Portugal and Australia. Aceh, as a Muslim region, has garnered some sympathy from other Muslim nations, and has an expatriate support network in Malaysia. How the new government of Megawati Sukarnoputri will handle the separatist goals remains to be seen.

If East Timor is any indication, Indonesia will not relinquish the territories until it becomes a war of attrition for the country, and the government faces enough opposition from outside nations. Unlike East Timor, both Aceh and Irian Jaya are extremely rich in natural resources—one reason why Indonesia is reluctant to let either of them go. Aceh in particular, with its oil reserves, is a main source of income for the country, and since the oil fields closed in March 2001, the government has been forced to seek out alternative supplies of liquefied natural gas. It has attempted to reassure buyers in Japan and South Korea that supplies will not be affected, but investor confidence, already low, has continued to fall as a result. Irian Jaya has large reserves of tin and copper. Both regions, however, despite their resources, remain two of the poorest and least developed regions of the country.

It is uncertain what an independent Aceh or West Papua would look like. It would not be an easy task for either region to build a new country out of the ashes of war. The economy and local administration in both Irian Jaya and Aceh are currently dominated by Javanese. The majority of the natives are not as well educated as these outsiders, and it remains to be seen how locals would replace the outside powers in these upper level positions.

Initiatives supported at the Papuan People's Congress in June 2000 make clear that an independent West Papua would not offer much change in the status quo. While Papuan leaders have insisted that investors would be forced to respect the environment and the culture of the region, there are no stipulations as to what such respect would entail, and it is evident that retaining the support of the investors is the primary concern. Thus, it remains doubtful that current conditions—sweatshops, low wages, and environmental damage—would change under an independent government.

Forced to compete in a global economy, it is likely that an independent West Papua or Aceh would become dependent upon loans and foreign investment; politically, such a situation could effectively put either state in the pocket of one of the major global powers.

The current situation in East Timor bears out such fears. Independence there has not meant democratic rights for the populace, or an improvement in the standard of living. Jobs continue to be scarce and workers underpaid; housing is in many cases substandard; and the government has not been able to provide its citizens with basic health care and other social services.

Despite these foreboding signs, public sentiment in Irian Jaya continues to support independence. In Aceh, the increasing intolerance by GAM members has begun to instill doubts in some Acehnese as to whether independence would indeed be an improvement. Granted assurance of anonymity, citizens in Aceh have expressed these concerns to journalists. As one woman says, "Our leaders have no education, only brawn. If we are given independence, we still won't be free."

BIBLIOGRAPHY

Ali, Muklis. "Gunfire Hits Indonesian Minister's Copter in Aceh," Reuters, March 20, 2001.

———. "Indonesia Hunts for LNG after Arun Woes," Reuters, March 11, 2001.

Anh, Lily. "Irian Jaya's Valleys of Death," *The Japan Times Online*, February 22, 2001. Available online at http:// www.japantimes.co.jp (cited April 5, 2001).

"Disintegration Dreaded," *The Economist*, December 7, 2000.

Djalal, Dini. "A Bloody Truce," *Far Eastern Economic Review*, October 5, 2000.

Fisher, Frederick. *Indonesia*. Milwaukee: Gareth Stevens Publishing, 2000.

Hill, Hal. *The Indonesian Economy*. New York: Cambridge University Press, 2000.

"Indonesia: Political Crisis Deepens in Jakarta while Repression Continues in Aceh and Papua," Amnesty International, March 13, 2001. Available online at http:// web.amnesty.org/802568F7005C4453/0/ 78A0140C4201DE7380256A0F006D939E!Open (cited April 5, 2001.)

Kell, Tim. *The Roots of Acehnese Rebellion, 1989–1992*. Ithaca, NY: Cornell Modern Indonesia Project, Southeast Asia Program, Cornell University, 1995.

Manning, Chris and Van Diermen, Peter, editors. *Indonesia in Transition: Social Aspects of Reformasi and Crisis*. London: Zed Books, 2000.

Murphy, Dan. "In Rebel Aceh, Neutral Isn't Safe," *Christian Science Monitor*, January 24, 2001.

Napier, Catherine. "Analysis: Indonesia's Fragile Archipelago," BBC News, September 13, 2000.

"A Political History of Aceh," September 9, 1999. Available online at http://www.refugees.org/news/crisis/ indonesia/indonesia.htm (cited April 5, 2001).

"A Reign of Terror: Human Rights Violations in Aceh 1998–2000 executive summary," TAPOL, the Indonesia Human Rights Campaign. Available online at http://www.gn.apc.org/tapol/ (cited April 5, 2001).

Schwarz, Adam. *Nation in Waiting: Indonesia's Search for Stability*. Boulder, CO: Westview, 2000.

"Street Protests Continue in Jakarta," BBC News, March 14, 2001.

"Wahid Outlines States of Emergency Plans," CNN News, July 12, 2001. Available online at http://www.cnn .com/2001/WORLD/asiapcf/southeast/07/12/wahid .impeach/index.html (cited July 12, 2001.)

"Why Indonesia is Exploding," Human Rights Watch, August 27, 1999. Available online at http://www.hrw.org/ campaigns/indonesia/aceh0827.htm (cited April 5, 2001).

—Eleanor Stanford

ISRAEL'S ASSASSINATION OF THE OPPOSITION

THE CONFLICT

After stalled peace negotiations, violence flared anew in Israel and the occupied territories of the West Bank and Gaza in late 2000. As tensions continued to escalate, Israel acknowledged exercising a policy of assassination against those it deemed to be Palestinian terrorists or organizers of terrorist acts. International attention was drawn to the matter as Palestinians, human rights groups, and foreign governments decried the policy. Israel, under the new leadership of hardliner Ariel Sharon, refused to back down.

Political

- Despite United Nations Security Council Resolutions 242 and 338, which call for Israel's withdrawal from the occupied territories of the West Bank and Gaza, Israel maintains a presence in the region.

- Palestinians insist upon autonomy in the West Bank, East Jerusalem, and Gaza and demand just settlement for Palestinian refugees.

- Peace negotiations have proven difficult, with hardliners in both Israel and the Palestinian Authority speaking out against compromise.

- After violence returned to the region in waves at the end of 2000, Israel admitted in January 2001 to a policy of assassination toward those it deemed a security threat.

- Palestinians, human rights groups, and foreign governments have spoken out against the policy and demanded it be stopped, but the Israeli government, led by Ariel Sharon, stands behind its policy, creating an even more difficult environment for peace.

Following the deaths of seven Palestinian protestors on September 29, 2000, shot dead by Israeli forces at holy sites in East Jerusalem, a second massive Palestinian *intifada* (uprising) began later that day. For months following, newspaper headlines daily announced further escalations of violence, primarily in the occupied territories of the West Bank and Gaza: trucks bombed; activists and civilians killed, including women and infants; peace negotiations stalled. Images of rock-throwing Palestinian youths beset by Israeli security forces, endless checkpoints, house demolitions, and street shootings continued to dominate news accounts of the region. By the end of December, the continuing violence had taken its toll on the local economy, as tourists stayed away in droves from Jerusalem and Bethlehem. Restaurants and hotels stood empty at what normally would have been the busiest time of year, putting thousands of Palestinians and Israelis out of work. The Christian Christmas hymn "Silent Night" took on a particularly haunting dimension for the small number of visitors to Bethlehem in December 2000. Shrouded in a silence that spoke volumes about the effects of the on-going conflict between Arabs and Jews, Bethlehem remained under curfew—streets empty and shops closed. No public religious celebrations took place in the most holy of Christian cities at the most holy of times.

As the violence grew on both sides, reports of planned assassinations by Israelis of Palestinian political figures became prominent. The assassination policy was not openly acknowledged until the death of Dr. Thabet Thabet, a Palestinian dentist and a senior official in the Palestinian Ministry of Health, in January 2001. The policy immediately sparked controversy. Although Israel has long held an unspoken policy of assassinating anti-Israeli terrorists, the policy admitted to after the death of Thabet Thabet was one that went beyond targeting those involved in terrorism to targeting those who directed others in the carrying out of those acts. Abdul Jawad Saleh of the Palestinian Legislative Council condemned the policy as a violation of human rights under the Geneva Convention. Ephraim Sneh, Israeli deputy minister of defense under former prime minister Ehud Barak, defended the policy as an effective and "just" means of preventing terrorist attacks. These two very different positions underscore the long-standing unrest that has become a part of everyday life in Israel and in the West Bank and Gaza, also referred to as the Occupied Territories. International opinion on Israel's policy of assassination varies. Human rights groups such as Amnesty International, along with Israeli peace activists, have publicly attacked Israel's policy as a violation of human rights and demanded the practice be stopped. The United States, long an interested player in maintaining peace in the region, took a noncommittal stance. Israel's policy of assassination has remained a touchy subject in an already volatile region.

HISTORICAL BACKGROUND

Tensions between Palestinian Arabs and Israeli Jews stretch back decades, even centuries. In its most simple form, the conflict between Arab and Jew in the Middle East boils down to one thing: the land. Arabs and Jews alike simultaneously claim primary allegiance and exclusive right to the land west of Jordan. Formerly known as Palestine, and now known as Israel, the West Bank, and the Gaza Strip—often referred to as the occupied territories—this land has been home to generations of Palestinians who have grown olive trees and herded sheep on its dry, rocky soil, dependent on the land for their very survival. It is also home to Jews, the oft-persecuted people of the earth who fulfilled their dream of a land of their own when Israel became a state in 1948. Dispersed from Palestine in the first century by the Roman conquest, Jews throughout the world cherished for centuries the dream of a return to their Holy Land.

Palestinian Arabs and Israeli Jews tell two very different stories, both based in their own cultural, social, and religious claims to the land. Neither side has indicated an understanding of the other's point of view, even though their goals—to live and raise families safely in their ancestral homelands—are similar. The very land that unites these two groups has also created a deep and seemingly permanent chasm between them that turns neighbors into ene-

CHRONOLOGY

1948 The State of Israel proclaims its independence, and the first Arab-Israeli war ensues.

1987 The first Palestinian *intifada* begins in the West Bank and Gaza.

1993 The Oslo Peace Accords are signed between Israeli Prime Minister Yitzhak Rabin and PLO Chairman Yassir Arafat.

July 2000 A peace summit at Camp David encounters a stumbling block over claims to the city of Jerusalem and ends with little progress having been made.

September 27, 2000 Ariel Sharon visits the Temple Mount/Harem-al-Sharif and violent protests result, setting off a new wave of unrest in the region.

November 9, 2000 Hussein Abyat is killed in an Israeli helicopter attack that targeted his truck.

December 31, 2000 Thabet Thabet, founder of the Palestinian Committee for Understanding and Reconciliation, is assassinated outside of his home by Israeli soldiers.

January 2001 Israel admits to an official policy of assassination.

February 2001 Ehud Barak loses his bid for reelection and Ariel Sharon becomes Israel's new prime minister.

July 30, 2001 Six Palestinians are killed from a bomb. Palestinians claim it was an Israeli assassination. Israel, which has declared responsibility for previous assassinations, denied the charge.

mies and children into soldiers, destroying individual lives, whole families, and entire communities. Attempts at peace talks alternatively progress, then break down, leaving both sides in a state of chaos.

Roots of the Current Conflict

Although Jews throughout the centuries kept alive the dream of a return to Zion, or the Holy Land, it was not until the nineteenth century that an organized political Zionism emerged. Although conditions for Jews began to improve in western Europe, Jews in eastern Europe continued to experience persecution. To escape, many immigrated to the United States. Others turned to a new, political Zionism, as much national in character as it was religious.

ISRAELI PROTESTORS ARGUE AGAINST THEIR COUNTRY'S ACKNOWLEDGED POLICY OF ASSASSINATION TOWARD PALESTINIAN ACTIVISTS. *(CORBIS CORPORATION (Bellevue). Reproduced by permission.)*

In 1896 Theodor Herzl's *The Jewish State* appeared, arguing for a separate Jewish state. Enthusiasm for nationalist Zionism, fueled by this book, resulted in the first Zionist Congress, which met in Basel, Switzerland in 1897. From that Congress came the Basel Declaration, which officially stated its goal to establish a legally recognized Jewish state in Palestine. The World Zionist Organization was founded to work toward this goal.

Convinced that supporting the Zionist cause for a Jewish national state in Palestine would have a positive impact on British imperial interests in the Middle East, including providing the British a strategic position next to the Suez Canal, the British cabinet approved the Balfour Declaration on November 8, 1917. In a letter to Lord Rothschild, a prominent British Zionist, the British foreign secretary Arthur Balfour announced the support of the British government for the Zionist goal of a na-

tional Jewish state in Palestine. At the same time, the declaration vowed to protect "the civil and religious rights of non-Jewish communities in Palestine." Thus did British policymakers effectively offer primacy of the land to both Arabs and Jews in Palestine, setting the stage for the dilemma that continues to plague the region. Although the British appointed a civilian high commissioner to the region who attempted to set up a representative government, Arabs never accepted the Balfour Declaration. Arab and Jewish communities grew further and further apart, developing parallel but separate spheres of economic, social, and religious infrastructures.

Regional Turmoil

From these beginnings Jewish Zionist organizations were better organized, better funded, and better recognized than Arab organizations in Pales-

HOME DEMOLITIONS AND SETTLEMENT EXPANSION

Jeff Halper, coordinator of the Israeli Committee Against House Demolitions, has written that house demolition orders, along with land expropriation, massive settlement expansion, and the building of new roads for settlers, are all part of Israel's "Master Plan" of Annexation. Housing demolitions and settlement expansions have been cast as responses to Palestinian terrorism in the same way that political assassinations have become official Israeli policy, and Halper charges that the goal of Ariel Sharon's government is to force Palestinians to submit to Israeli dictates.

Prime Minister Sharon has commented that he sees no reason to evacuate any settlements and, upon taking office, announced that settlement expansion would, in fact, continue. With each new settlement Israel creates what it calls "facts on the ground," which it can use to argue Israeli ownership. The Sharon government has announced plans for seven hundred new homes in the West Bank, with intentions for an additional five thousand on land yet to be marketed. Even the United States, long a staunch supporter of Israel, has denounced these plans as provocative and inflammatory. Daniel Williams of the *Washington Post* reported in "A Recharged Tug of War for Land" (April 16, 2001) that "human rights groups have taken an unbending position that the settlements are illegal under the Geneva and 1907 Hague conventions."

Human Rights Watch issued a report in April 2001 stating that Israeli policy of continued settlement expansion is objectionable on the basis of international humanitarian law in that it transfers civilians from Israel into the occupied territory and creates permanent changes in the occupied territory that do not benefit the occupied population. Israel rejects these legal statutes, arguing that they do not apply to West Bank and Gaza settlements, which Israel does not view as foreign land. Israel's policy of settlement expansion, therefore, continues. Palestinians in the West Bank and Gaza continue to face an influx of Israeli settlers on land that Palestinians believe to be theirs. This creates increased tension in the region on both sides, as the Palestinians resent the Israeli settlers, and the Israelis are determined to reclaim land that is part of their historical heritage. Palestinian have seen their homes destroyed as they have been pushed off of what has long been their family's land by Israeli settlers moving in and building new homes in an area that is part of *their* historical heritage. Just who is the rightful owner in this scenario?

Interpretations over systems of land ownership have failed to settle questions of control. Israel has designated approximately half of the West Bank as "state lands," authorizing Israel itself to retain control over the land. Palestinians have resisted land confiscation by presenting land documents and witnesses to military courts, but to date Israel's policies of home demolition and settlement have prevailed.

tine. Jewish access to British authority was also greater, although Zionism was plagued by divisiveness within itself. During the 1930s Arabs failed to gain support for legal recognition of their rightful inhabitance of Palestine. The key issues creating tension at this time were Jewish immigration and land acquisition, issues that have continued to be at the heart of the conflict.

In response to the turmoil in the region and to Britain's own concerns for its vital interests, the British government issued a new policy in a White Paper (an official statement) published on May 17, 1939. For the first time, Britain declared unequivocally that it was not part of British policy that Palestine should become a Jewish state, as this would be "contrary to [British] obligations to the Arabs under the Mandate." Within five years Jewish immigration to the area would cease completely unless Palestinian Arabs agreed that it could continue. Land transfers would be restricted to particular areas. Within ten years the British Mandate would end, and Palestine would be granted independence.

At a time when Jews in Europe were struggling to flee Hitler's Germany, Britain's announcement threw the Zionist community into a tailspin. As World War II (1939–45) broke out and news of the Jewish Holocaust became known, popular support among western nations for a Jewish state in Palestine grew. This was especially prominent in the United States, where American Jews pressed for open immigration to Palestine and for the formation of a Jewish state. Meanwhile, among Palestinian Arabs, fear of a Jewish-dominated Palestine continued to stir angst. Between 1945 and 1947 political and social conditions in Palestine worsened to the point that the British foreign secretary, Ernest Bevin, requested intervention from the United Nations.

Establishment of the State of Israel

On November 27, 1947, based on recommendations from a special committee, the United Nations General Assembly approved an independent Palestine divided into separate Jewish and Arab states. Because of the deep religious significance of Jerusalem to Muslims, Jews, and Christians, Jerusalem was designated as an internationalized district.

Upon the departure of the last British high commissioner from Palestine on May 14, 1948, Israel was proclaimed an independent state, and its borders were open to Jewish people everywhere. As Jewish settlers poured into Israel to begin new lives in the long-sought-after independent state of Israel, Palestinian Arab communities were displaced. With leadership dispersed throughout the Middle East, Palestinian Arabs lacked the cohesiveness of the well-organized Jewish settlers. Conflict between the two groups continued to erupt as Israel celebrated its birth.

As Israel became an independent state in 1948, the world balance of power was changing. The Cold War developed, with the United States and Russia now center stage. The more than 700,000 Arabs living within the borders of the newly defined state of Israel became refugees as entire communities abandoned ancestral lands in response to Israeli threats on their lives. Many suffered forced evacuations and entered a permanent exodus. Tents originally set up to provide temporary housing for the refugees eventually gave way to permanent camps of concrete block, maintaining their inhabitants in a kind of cultural limbo.

War and the Intifada

Palestinian resistance groups mobilized throughout the Arab world during the late 1950s and the early 1960s. In response to this increase in Arab solidarity, which threatened the new Jewish state's very existence, Israel entered into massive air strikes against Egypt, Syria, and Jordan on June 5, 1967. By June 11, just six days later, Israel had destroyed the air forces of those countries and taken control of the West Bank, the Golan Heights, Gaza, Sinai, and East Jerusalem. Within a few short days, the contours of Israeli-controlled territory changed dramatically, creating once again a massive Palestinian Arab refugee crisis. Thousands of Palestinians, suddenly finding themselves on Israeli-controlled land, fled. At the same time, Israel's residents now included an Arab population of 1.5 million.

Although Israel won the war, it did not achieve peace. Assured in its position of power, Israel was unwilling to make concessions, and the Arab nations it defeated in the Six-Day War were just as reluctant to negotiate from a position of weakness. The United Nations (UN) intervened in hopes of providing a framework for peace in the region. After months of debate the UN Security Council passed Resolution 242 (UNSCR 242), which called for Israel's withdrawal from territories occupied in 1967 and for a "just settlement of the refugee problem." It further affirmed the "right to live in peace within secure and recognized boundaries free from threats or acts of force" for all living in the region. Resolution 242, among the most frequently cited documents relating to the Palestinian-Israeli conflict, was later reaffirmed by UNSCR 338 after the 1973 Arab-Israeli War. Despite these international resolutions, however, Israel continued to expand its settlements into Palestinian-controlled areas, and tensions remained high between both Israelis and Palestinians.

On December 9, 1987, four Palestinians were killed and several others injured after an accident in Gaza involving an Israeli military vehicle. The incident drew thousands of Palestinian protestors, some of whom were killed by Israeli army personnel. A full-scale *intifada*, or uprising, broke out, rapidly gaining support from all levels of Palestinian society. Among the goals set up by the leaders of the uprising were two key demands on Israel: (1) to recognize an independent Palestinian state under the leadership of the Palestinian Liberation Organization (PLO), and (2) to stop annexing Palestinian land to build settlements. The leaders also called for an end to all taxes levied exclusively against Palestinians.

Leaders of the uprising called for massive general strikes and demonstrations, forced shop closings, and refusal to pay taxes. Stone throwing was the common form of aggression against Israelis, though violence later escalated to include incidents of stabbings and shootings. Israel retaliated with the use of military force against the mass demonstrators. Entire Palestinian communities were punished collectively through a policy of home demolitions. The Israelis cut off electricity to entire villages and closed schools and universities. Olive trees and gardens were uprooted to prevent Palestinians from achieving economic self-sufficiency. Despite the hardships imposed, or perhaps because of them, Palestinian resolve only deepened.

AN ISRAELI BORDER POLICEMAN AND A PALESTINIAN CITIZEN CONFRONT EACH OTHER AT THE GATES OF THE AL-AQSA MOSQUE IN EAST JERUSALEM'S OLD CITY. DESPITE YEARS OF NEGOTIATIONS FOR PEACE, TENSIONS REMAIN HIGH. *(AP/Wide World Photos. Reproduced by permission.)*

Continued violence in Israel and the occupied territories prompted the Madrid Conference on the Israeli-Palestinian conflict, sponsored jointly by the United States and Russia. On October 30, 1991, representatives from Israel, Palestine, and neighboring Arab countries gathered to discuss peace. Although the conference did not result in concrete proposals for a peaceful settlement, it did lay the groundwork for ongoing negotiations. As talks progressed it became clear to many that Israel's expanded settlement program in the occupied territories was the major block to any potential breakthroughs in the peace process.

Olso Peace Accords, 1993

In late summer 1993, at a follow-up discussion in Washington, DC, which stemmed from the Madrid Conference, Israeli and PLO officials disclosed secret agreements authorizing Palestinian autonomy in the West Bank and Gaza. Organized and hosted in secret by the Norwegian government, the historic face-to-face talks brought the Nobel Peace Prize to Israeli prime minister Yitzhak Rabin, Israeli foreign minister Shimon Perez, and PLO chairman Yassir Arafat.

The fruit of their secret meetings resulted in two unprecedented agreements. The first was a document of "mutual recognition." In it the Palestinians recognized Israel's right to exist in peace and security, and Israel recognized the PLO as the rightful representative of the Palestinian people.

The second agreement was the Declaration of Principles on Palestinian Self Rule, which outlined a timetable and procedures for granting Palestinian autonomy in the occupied territories. Israel agreed to end settlement expansion and to consider negotiations regarding the future of East Jerusalem, the site of the most holy of places in both the Muslim and Jewish religions, known to Palestinians as Harem al-Sharif, and to Jews as Temple Mount.

Although the agreements raised the hopes of many for peace in the region, in the end nothing changed. Palestinian perception at home was that Arafat had sold out by accepting less than complete autonomy of the West Bank. Many Israelis, on the other hand, accused Rabin of dismantling Israel. Both sides remained deeply suspicious of each other. Palestinians remained convinced that the unrecognized imbalance of power between themselves as an occupied people and Israel as the occupying power prevented a successful conclusion to the peace negotiations.

Tensions Escalate despite the Peace Accord

In an attempt to revive peace negotiations, in July 2000 U.S. President Bill Clinton (1993–2001) invited Palestinian leader Yassir Arafat and Israeli prime minister Ehud Barak to Camp David for intensive talks. Once again Israel refused to concede to demands for the repatriation of Palestinian refugees, and Palestinians refused to compromise claims in East Jerusalem. Neither side was able to meet the deadline for an agreement. On September 27, 2000, an Israeli soldier was killed in Palestinian-ruled Gaza. The next day Israeli Foreign Minister Ariel Sharon's visit to Temple Mount/Harem-al-Sharif brought forth protests from Palestinians. Sharon was a well-known and controversial hardliner in Israel's Likud Party. He objected to many of the concessions made by Prime Minister Barak during the peace process and was particularly against any compromises regarding the city of Jerusalem. Sharon's visit to a holy site held in high importance to both Jews and Muslims caused tensions to escalate sharply as Palestinians reacted in outrage. Dozens were wounded in clashes between Israeli security forces and Palestinian protesters.

On September 29 Israeli soldiers shot and killed seven Palestinian protesters in Jerusalem, beginning the second *intifada*. In a marked increase in the use of violent methods, those on both sides of the conflict have ruthlessly attacked the other in a seemingly endless cycle of retaliations. While Palestinians escalated their use of firearms, the Israeli military increased its use of heavy military equipment, including tanks, missiles, and helicopters.

THE ECONOMIC TOLL

The economies of Israel and the areas of the West Bank and Gaza, under the nominal control of the Palestinian Authority, have spiraled downward since the second *intifada* began in September 2000, bringing still further hardship to people on both sides of the conflict. Tourism in particular, one of Israel's most important industries, declined sharply in the last quarter of 2000, showing a 43.2 percent decline in tourist arrivals. The Christian holiday of Christmas is usually a heightened season for tourists in Israel, but in December 2000, many hotels were all but empty as tourists stayed away for fear of being caught in the crossfire of the violence running through the region. Israel's housing and construction industries also suffered with the renewal of fighting, with a 64 percent decline in housing completions and a 12 percent decline in housing starts in the last quarter of 2000. Unemployment rose by .4 percent to 8.9 percent, while the number of new immigrants dropped 22 percent for the same period. The Tel Aviv Stock Exchange dropped from 480 in October 2000, to 378 in March. The economic repercussions of continued violence were felt across Israeli society.

The effects of the violence were also felt in Palestinian areas. Already at a disadvantage due to years of little to no economic development and a stagnant economy, the West Bank and Gaza experienced vast declines in the period from October 2000 to March 2001. This was contributed to partly by increased security measures on the part of Israel, which often closed the border between Israel and the occupied territories, making it difficult for goods and supplies to get across. Construction was down 78.7 percent, while agriculture was down 73.8 percent. Trade declined by 59 percent, while unemployment soared to 33 percent during the same period. Forced closings of Palestinian shops and companies since the 1993 Oslo peace accords showed an increase of lost working days, up 79.7 percent in 2000, from 6.1 percent in 1993.

For both Israel and the Palestinian Authority, long engaged in violent battle, the experiment with peace and return to violence clearly illustrated one thing economically: Peace pays.

Between October 1, 2000, and April 7, 2001, violence in Israel and the West Bank claimed the lives of more than 450 people, 375 of them Palestinians. As Matt Rees of *Time* reported in an article entitled "The Work of Assassins" (January 15, 2001), "From both sides of the *intifadeh*, high-tech hit squads and low-tech vigilantes wield street jus-

tice." Throughout the course of the conflict, however, it was not until January 2001 that the word "assassination" was used to describe Israel's official policy toward Palestinian political figures.

Israel's Policy of Assassination

Dr. Thabet Thabet, a Palestinian dentist killed by Israeli assassins on New Year's Eve 2000, was well known to those on both sides of the Arab-Israeli conflict. Active in peace work in Jerusalem and a founder of the Palestinian Committee for Understanding and Reconciliation with the Israeli People, Thabet was nonetheless viewed by Israelis as a dangerous terrorist who was instrumental in plotting attacks against Israelis in the West Bank. A senior official in the Palestinian Ministry of Health, Thabet was also a local leader in Yassir Arafat's Fatah political faction in Tulkarem on the West Bank. As he was leaving his home on December 31, he was gunned down in his car by Israeli soldiers using a long-range precision machine gun known as a Shayetet 1.3. His home had been under intense surveillance for three nights prior to his death.

Thabet was neither the first to be assassinated by the Israelis using sophisticated, high-technology weaponry, nor the last. His death became particularly significant because it marked the first time the Israeli government acknowledged publicly its policy of assassination. Seldom admitting to specific killings, Israel admitted that Thabet's death was in direct retaliation for the death earlier the same day of Israeli activist Benjamin Kahane.

On January 8, 2001, a week following Thabet's assassination, the *Washington Post* ran a front page headline announcing "Israelis Confirm Assassinations Used as Policy." In the article, writer Keith B. Richburg wrote that key Palestinians were routinely targeted. Although Israeli peace activists reported that eight or nine similar assassinations had taken place up to that time, Palestinian and other sources reported between twenty and thirty assassinations. Some victims were killed using air-to-surface rockets launched from Israeli helicopters; others fell victim to the Barrett M82 semiautomatic sniper rifle. Fitted with a scope that has the capacity to allow the shooter to identify a human target at five hundred meters (about 547 yards), the rifle can easily fire on a target at 1,500 meters (1,640 yards).

Some weeks earlier, on December 22, 2000, Deborah Sontag reported in the *New York Times* article, "Israel Acknowledges Hunting Down Arab Militants," that senior Israeli officials had admitted

SIHAM THABET, WIDOW OF THABET THABET, SITS UNDER PORTRAITS OF HER DECEASED HUSBAND. HIS DEATH MARKED THE FIRST TIME THE ISRAELI GOVERNMENT PUBLICLY ACKNOWLEDGED ITS POLICY OF ASSASSINATION. *(AP/Wide World Photos. Reproduced by permission.)*

to hunting down individual Palestinian militants and killing them in retaliation for attacks on Israelis. At that point, however, Israeli army officials denied that political figures had been targeted. Observers voiced concern over the inevitable escalation that would occur, warning that an endless cycle of retaliations would begin.

Israeli military strategists have placed a priority on developing and maintaining a high-technology, cutting-edge surveillance system. A network of antennas set up throughout the West Bank enables Israel's domestic security service, Shin Bet, to pinpoint within mere yards the location of a cell phone user. Matt Rees of *Time* magazine reported in "The Work of Assassins" (January 15, 2001) that "drones," flying as high as a mile above ground,

have the capacity to zoom in on targets and beam live video back to Shin Bet's offices in a Tel Aviv suburb. "The drone can follow a target as he travels, building a thick intelligence dossier on his movements or relaying to snipers on the ground that their mark is approaching." With the names of about one hundred people whom the Israelis have identified as terrorists against Israel, Shin Bet works closely with highly skilled Israeli marksmen when the army decides to take action against someone.

The first designated assassination has been traced to the death of Hussein Abyat. A Palestinian nationalist and commander of the Tanzim paramilitary group heavily involved in violent action against Israelis, Abyat was killed on November

9, 2000, when an Israeli helicopter aimed rockets at his pickup truck in Beit Sahur in the West Bank. Using a powerful machine gun stolen from the Israeli army, Abyat had become a recognized figure in the West Bank since the beginning of the second *intifada* in September. He was killed in retaliation for his attacks on Israeli military personnel, but the assault also killed two female bystanders. Israeli military personnel referred to the assault against Abyat as a "surgical strike."

Deaths under the Palestinian Authority

Although Israel has publicly acknowledged the sanctioned use of assassination, not all assassinations are carried out by the state of Israel. Yussef Abu Sway, a Palestinian Muslim active with the radical Islamic Jihad, was killed on the street in front of his parents' home while on his way to visit them to break the Muslim fast of Ramadan. Assassinated by an Israeli special unit because of his anti-Israeli political activities, Abu Sway's assassins were led to him by a Palestinian collaborator. Five days later members of the Rapid Deployment Force of the Palestinian Authority dragged Adnan Shahine into the street and killed him with a pistol while his mother watched in horror. Suspected of collaborating with the Israelis, Shahine was targeted as the Palestinian responsible for leading the Israeli forces to Abu Sway, though it is not certain that Shahine actually played a role in Sway's death.

Unlike Israel, the Palestinian Authority does not have an official, organized policy of assassination towards those it deems as a threat to its security. The PA is far less organized than Israel, especially as Palestinian communities are increasingly cut off from one another by on-going Israeli settlements. Palestinian suicide bombers, however, are a significant threat to Israelis, though these bombers are not under the direct control of the Palestinian Authority.

RECENT HISTORY AND THE FUTURE

Around the same time that Israel publicly announced its policy of assassination, Prime Minister Ehud Barak declared his intention to resign from office, hoping to be reelected in a vote of confidence. In February 2001 Barak lost in his bid for reelection to Ariel Sharon, the right-wing Likud politician whose visit to the Temple Mount/Harem-al-Sharif had sparked violence in September 2000. Sharon volubly announced his commitment to increasing security for Israel, which he defined as eliminating Palestinian resistance. In the atmosphere of increased tension and violence that had engulfed the region for the past several months, promises of increased security appealed to many Israeli voters. Sharon, a former solider who fought in the 1948–49 Arab-Israeli war, has voiced continued support for settlement expansions in the West Bank and Gaza and open approval of Israel's assassination policy.

The controversial nature of Israel's policy of assassination has provoked much criticism. Many have called for its immediate end, citing international law. In October 2000 the United Nations Security Council adopted a resolution condemning Israel's excessive use of force against Palestinians. A statement from the American-Arab Anti-Discrimination Committee (ADC) called for the U.S. government to use all its influence to end Israel's use of assassination, citing the fourth Geneva Convention, which obligates Israel as an occupying power to protect Palestinians living within occupied territories. In an announcement made on January 5, 2001 ("Israel's Assassination of Palestinians Must End"), the ADC characterized Israel's practice of assassination as "an overt policy of 'liquidation' designed to suppress protests. . . ." Perhaps most telling are comments of members of the Israeli Knesset, or Cabinet, showing a split among Israeli policy makers. Some members have demanded an immediate end to the policy, terming it unacceptable and illegal.

Israel has managed to retain control in the region through its command of a superior military and with the benefit of being an established state, with all of the organization, funding, and support that goes with that official status. The Palestinians in the West Bank and Gaza have spent years living in economically depressed areas with few options available in terms of education and employment. Residents under Israel and the Palestinian Authority would benefit from peace, but both sides are unwilling or unable to set differences aside and make the compromises that would put an end to the fighting. Instead, the circle of violence continues, with Israel openly admitting to a policy of assassination, and the Palestinian Authority determined to fight back.

BIBLIOGRAPHY

Arab-American Anti-Discrimination Committee. "Israel's Assassination of Palestinians Must End," January 5, 2001. Available online at http://www.adc.org/press/2001/05january2001v002.htm (cited June 21, 2001).

Ashrawi, Hanan. *This Side of Peace.* New York: Touchstone, Simon and Shuster, 1995.

Cleveland, William L. *A History of the Modern Middle East.* Boulder, CO: Westview Press, 1994.

Halper, Jeff. "Despair: Israel's Ultimate Weapon," Information brief no. 72, March 28, 2001. Center for Policy Analysis on Palestine. Available online at http://www.palestinecenter.org (cited June 21, 2001).

Justice and Peace Commission. Jerusalem (Catholic Church). "Violence in Palestine: Origins of a Conflict and Struggle for the Self Determination of a People," December 6, 2000. Information paper available from Justice and Peace Commission, P.O. Box 20459, 91204 Jerusalem.

Kifner, John. "Resistance Grows to Mideast Plan in Opposing Camps," *New York Times,* December 31, 2000, sec. A1, p.6.

Kuttab, Daoud. "The Two Intifadas: Differing Shades of Resistance." Available online at http://www.palestinecenter.org/news/20010208.html (cited June 21, 2001).

Laqueur, Walter and Barry Rubin, eds. *The Israel-Arab Reader: A Documentary History of the Middle East Conflict.* New York: Penguin, 1984.

Mendelsohn, Everett. *A Compassionate Peace: A Future for Israel, Palestine, and the Middle East.* New York: The Noonday Press, Farrar, Straus, and Giroux, 1989.

Rees, Matt. "The Work of Assassins," *Time,* January 15, 2001.

Richburg, Keith B. "Israelis Confirm Assassinations Used as Policy," *Washington Post,* January 8, 2001.

Shipler, David K. *Arab and Jew: Wounded Spirits in a Promised Land.* New York: Times Books, Random House, 1986.

Smith, Dita. "Intifada Fallout," *Washington Post,* April 7, 2001, sec. A13.

Sontag, Deborah. "Israel Acknowledges Hunting Down Arab Militants," *New York Times,* December 22, 2000, International Page.

Wallach, John and Janet. *Still Small Voices. Forward by Teddy Kollek, Mayor of Jerusalem.* New York: A Citadel Press Book, 1990.

Waskow, Rabbi Arthur. "Back from the Brink?—or Beyond It? The Joint Survival of Conjoined Twin Nations." Available online at http://www.shalomctr.org/html/peace13.html (cited June 21, 2001).

Waskow, Rabbi Arthur. "Sharing Our Grief, Burying Our Fears," Available online at http://www.shalomctr.org/html/peace25.html (cited June 21, 2001).

Williams, Daniel. "A Recharged Tug of War for Land," *Washington Post,* April 16, 2001, sec. A11.

—Lolly Ockerstrom

ELECTING CHANGE IN MEXICO

THE CONFLICT

The Institutional Revolutionary Party (PRI) dominated the political life of Mexico for 71 years. Although the 2000 elections were hotly contested, the opposition parties succeeded in breaking the PRI's political dominance. Under the PRI's leadership, Mexico has had mixed fortunes, at times achieving high levels of economic development and social progress since 1929, but also experiencing serious economic downturns and social problems during the past two decades. The people of Mexico have thus chosen to place the fate of the country into the hands of the National Action Party (PAN), at least until the next election in 2006.

Political

- Mexicans are frustrated with the political corruption and the undemocratic practices of the past PRI governments. They expect the new president, Vicente Fox of the National Action Party (PAN), to make sweeping changes to the political life of the country.

- The Zapatista rebels have demanded better treatment for the indigenous people of the country. Unless a settlement is reached with them, the country may suffer continued political instability.

Economic

- The Mexican economy is currently stable, but for the past two decades it has lumbered from crisis to crisis.

- The new Fox administration wants to strengthen free trade between the United States and Mexico.

Social

- Mexico suffers from many social problems including crime, corruption, and drug trafficking. Additionally, there are many poor people who feel that the economic reforms of the 1980s and 1990s have not helped them.

On July 2, 2000 Mexico witnessed one of the most significant changes to its political landscape in 71 years—the election of Vicente Fox, of the National Action Party (PAN) to the post of president. Fox won the election over the Institutional Revolutionary Party (PRI) candidate Francisco Labastida. The PRI has dominated national politics in Mexico since 1929. The Fox victory offered hope to alter a long and often controversial period in Mexico's social and political history. The PRI has been blamed for many of the problems currently faced by the Mexican society: political corruption, poverty, drug trafficking, crime, and the Chiapas rebellion. When Fox, an unorthodox, brash, and outspoken critic of successive PRI administrations, assumed the presidency, he promised to tackle and resolve these problems.

HISTORICAL BACKGROUND

The origin of the modern Mexican state can be traced back to the Spanish conquest of the country in 1521. Under the leadership of Fernando Cortez, the Spanish defeated the Aztec empire, which was ruled by Cuauhtemoc, and maintained control of this colony until 1821, when independence was achieved. Mexican independence, however, did not lead to the immediate improvement in the lives of the people. For many years following the proclamation of independence, Mexico was characterized by a situation in which power was concentrated in the hands of a few elites, thereby resulting in sharp divisions between the elite and the mass of poor—mainly peasant—people. This situation was, in part, the result of the policies of President Porfirio Díaz, a man who refused to give up power and ruled Mexico between 1884 and 1911.

Francisco I. Madero opposed the presidency of Díaz, arguing that his governing was not consistent with advancing democracy and prosperity in Mexico. Madero created a political party, which campaigned across the country against Díaz's re-election. As a result of his opposition to Díaz, Madero was imprisoned by Díaz. Madero, however, was able to flee to the United States, where he continued to organize opposition to Díaz. In 1910 Madero initiated the Mexican Revolution (1911–20) by issuing the "Plan of San Luis," a manifesto which declared the election of Díaz as fraudulent. In 1911, as a result of the armed rebellion aimed at removing him from office, Díaz fled Mexico. His departure ushered in democratic changes to the Mexican political system. The period from 1911–24 was marked by a high degree of political instability and conflict. It was only after 1924, with the election of Plutarco Elías Calles, that some semblance of political stability began to emerge in the country. It was also during this period that a new political party emerged in Mexico. This party would change the face of Mexican politics for the next 71 years.

The PRI and Mexican Development

The PRI is Mexico's oldest political party and was the world's longest ruling party until it lost power in July 2000. It was formed in 1929 under the name of the National Revolutionary Party (PRN), after the Mexican Revolution. Within the first ten years of its inauguration the PRI developed a reputation for being a left-wing party that challenged the hegemony of the church and spoke on behalf of the poor. This was due primarily to the work of Lázaro Cárdenas who became president of Mexico in 1934.

It should be noted that Cárdenas was the successor to presidents Emilio Portes Gil, Pascal Ortiz Rubio, and Aberlardo Rodríguez—all three of whom served between 1928–34. While these three men were presidents in name, however, the country was actually being run by their predecessor, Plutarco Elías Calles, the man who founded the PRN and who eventually supported Cárdenas for president in 1934. Calles' influence resulted in conflict, and later complete separation, between the state and the Catholic Church. After leaving office Calles became increasingly corrupt and was even considered by some to be moving in the direction of fascism. Calles, originally Cárdenas' ally, was banished from Mexico by Cárdenas because he was becoming a political threat.

In 1938 the party, under the leadership of Mexico's most revered and radical political leader,

CHRONOLOGY

1521 Fernando Cortez defeats the Aztecs and Mexico becomes a colony of Spain.

1821 Mexico achieves its independence from Spain.

1911 The Mexican Revolution begins and lasts for the next nine years.

1924 Gen. Plutarco Elías Calles becomes president of Mexico.

1929 The National Revolutionary Party (PRN) is founded.

1934 Lazaro Cárdenas becomes President of Mexico.

1938 Cárdenas nationalizes the oil industry and institutes radical populist reforms.

1939 The National Action Party (PAN) is formed.

1946 The Party of the Mexican Revolution changes its name to the Institutional Revolutionary Party (PRI). The PAN wins its first congressional seats.

1988 Carlos Salinas de Gortari is elected Mexico's president. The elections are considered fraudulent. Cuauhtemoc Cárdenas forms the Party of the Democratic Revolution (PRD). The PRI makes a decisive shift to the right ideologically, embracing neo-liberal social and economic policies.

1989 PAN wins it first governorship in the state of Guanajuato.

1994 The commencement of the North American Free Trade Association (NAFTA) occurs. The Chiapas rebellion begins. Luis Donaldo Colosio, PRI presidential candidate, is assassinated.

1994 Ernesto Zedillo Ponce de Leon is elected president of Mexico. For the next six years he institutes sweeping political reforms, but continues the neo-liberal policies of Salinas.

2000 The election of Vicente Fox of the PAN ends the 71-year-old domination of the PRI in Mexican politics.

2001 The Mexican government reopens negotiations with the Zapatistas.

Lázaro Cárdenas, changed its name to the Party of the Mexican Revolution. Part of the reason for Cárdenas' popularity in Mexico had to do with his strong nationalist ideology and policies aimed at improving the lot of the poor and landless. In 1938

Cárdenas nationalized the country's oil industry. In addition, he carried out an extensive land reform program in which land from large haciendas was distributed to many poor Mexican people. Although the nationalization of the oil industry resulted in serious negative economic repercussions for Mexico, Mexicans hailed Cárdenas as a hero. As a result of the perceived honesty and sincerity of Cárdenas, the party became associated with honest political leadership. This changed, however, when Cárdenas left office in 1940.

In 1940 Manuel Avila Camacho became president of Mexico, moving the party's policies more to the right of those of his predecessor, Cárdenas. In 1946 the party changed its name to the Institutional Revolutionary Party (PRI), signaling a change in its populist policies, at least for the next 12 years. The main reason for this was that Camacho and his two successors, Miguel Alemán Valdes and Aldolfo Ruiz Cortines, were much more business oriented and less populist than Cárdenas. Cortines, in particular, was a fiscal conservative who sought to correct perceived extravagant spending habits of his predecessors. He attempted to create an efficient, stable government with its economic house in order.

Since 1946 the PRI has sought to enlarge its political base by embracing different segments of the Mexican society, including the Mexican elite and the business sector. This has caused many critics to see it as an amorphous political organization, which has lost its revolutionary zeal and is simply concerned with maintaining power. Between 1958 and 2000 the PRI went through many ups and downs. In 1958 when López Mateos took over the presidency he re-introduced many populist policies that were similar to those of Cárdenas. Although he was quick to reprimand those who broke the law, including trade union leaders and many leftist organizations, Mateos considered his presidency a movement to the left of his predecessors. Mateos' populist programs included an extensive land reform program, in which he parceled out land to peasants, and the nationalization of American and Canadian owned electric companies. He also instituted an extensive literacy program. Between 1958 and 1964 Mexico gained international respect for its nonaligned foreign policy. Additionally, it was during this time that a portion of Mexican land, the Chamizal, which had been annexed to Texas, was returned to Mexico. Despite Mateos' triumphs and the resurgence in the fortunes of the PRI, turbulent times were ahead.

Mateos' successor, Gustavo Díaz Ordaz, brought improved economic fortunes to Mexico. In addition, Mexico continued the non-aligned foreign polices of Mateos. In Mexico, however, as in other parts of the world, the 1960s brought with it strong radical youth and student movements clamoring for social reform. Although the details are unclear, in 1968, a week before the commencement of the Olympic games in Mexico City, uniformed soldiers and other military and paramilitary squads opened fire on a mass meeting of students at Tlatelolco. These students were primarily from the National Autonomous University (UNAM), Mexico's largest and most radical university. In the aftermath of the attack, the official figures put the death toll at about 43; unofficially the figure was over 500. This incident put a stain on the PRI for the remainder of the twentieth century. Despite its revolutionary name and populist policies, the PRI became identified with the powerful in society, as well as with repression and murder. The PRI no longer seemed to be the party of Cárdenas.

The Economic Crisis

To overcome the political fallout from the student massacre, the next president, Luis Echeverría Alvarez, tried to distance his administration from that of Ordaz. Echeverría increased subsidies to universities—in particular the UNAM—released students who were arrested under Ordaz's administration, and ordered price controls on luxury goods and commodities. Ordaz's policies reflected many of the populist tendencies of the early PRI and recaptured some of its support within the society. However, it was the economic crisis of the post-1970s era which signaled the beginning of the end for PRI.

When Echeverría left office in 1976, Mexico had accumulated a large external debt. However, because of the oil crises of the mid- to late-1970s, Mexico was able to earn more money on the world market for its oil. The huge oil revenues were both a blessing and a curse for Mexico as Echeverría's successor, José López Portillo, engaged in imprudent financial management, and his government became associated with corruption. For most of his presidency, Portillo started extravagant projects, engaged in huge social spending, and nationalized Mexican banks. After the oil glut of 1982, however, Mexico was forced to devalue its peso. This situation plunged the country into social and economic turmoil. At the end of his presidency, the Mexican economy was in decline, and Mexico had again become associated with widespread corruption.

In 1982 Mexico elected the first of its next three PRI ivy-league-educated presidents, the ambitious Miguel de la Madrid Hurtado. Miguel de la Madrid came to power with a promise to restore the economy and put an end to government corruption. In an attempt to reduce corruption, he sent some top officials to jail and also removed others from their positions. Economically, he instituted a number of reforms to Mexico's petroleum sector. In general, however, he failed miserably in both areas. To be sure, the economic and political problems of de la Madrid were made worse with the Mexico city earthquake of 1985, which killed more than 4,000 and caused millions of dollars in damage. In fact, when he ended his presidency in 1988, the peso had experienced yet another devaluation (from 950 to 2,300 to the U.S. dollar), inflation was on the increase, and the external debt was extremely high. Accusations of political corruption, along with authoritarianism and economic mismanagement, led Mexicans to have even less confidence in their government.

The PRI's Shift to the Right

This situation worsened when Carlos Salinas de Gortari became Mexico's next president. He began his presidency on a bad note—many people felt that he came to power through a fraudulent election. In addition, he came to office at time when the PRI was at the lowest point in its popularity. One of the worst blows occurred when Cuauhtemoc Cárdenas, the son of Lazaro Cárdenas, abandoned the party and ran for the presidency under his new party, the Party for Democratic Revolution (PRD). Cárdenas had accused the PRI of being corrupt and dictatorial. Many observers believed that Cárdenas actually won the 1988 elections, but that they were stolen from him by the PRI, eventually leading to the installation of Salinas as president. In response to the widespread criticisms of electoral fraud, the country got its first National Action Party (PAN) governor in the state of Guanajuato. This decision to install a PAN candidate was based on the fact that there had been widespread corruption in the state elections, in addition to the evidence, which pointed to a PAN victory. With the economy in decline, social problems abundant, and the PRI being described as a party of corrupt political elites, Salinas' presidency would lead to yet another change in the polices of the PRI—a decisive shift to the right.

Salinas came to power when left-wing politics were on the decline globally, and neo-liberal ideas had started to achieve prominence. The Eastern socialist bloc was on the retreat, and free market capitalism was triumphing. Consistent with those changes, Salinas privatized Mexican banks and attacked the powerful trade unions, thereby reducing their influence in the bargaining process. He also reversed two policies which represented the cornerstones of the PRI political platform—support for the agricultural cooperatives and an anti-clerical stance.

The cooperatives, which were the result of successive land reform policies of the PRI, were aimed at providing land for the poor rural people. The reversal of the PRI's support for this *ejido* ("common land") system encouraged wealthy Mexicans to obtain control of much of the peasant land, thereby returning parts of Mexico to a situation similar to the pre-Cárdenas era, when there was a mass of landless poor. Salinas also moved closer to the Catholic Church—allowing it to own property and re-open religious schools—and re-established relations with the Vatican.

Salinas also decentralized education by passing the Education Reform Act, which transferred control of public education from the federal government to the states. The act also raised the number of years of obligatory schooling from six to nine.

Salinas, however, is perhaps best remembered for his support of the North American Free Trade Association (NAFTA). There were many in his party, and throughout Mexico, who stoutly resisted NAFTA because it was seen as a form of American imperialism that would ultimately lead to the destruction of Mexican businesses. Salinas countered by calling his critics the "new reactionaries."

It may be argued that many of Salinas' policies were necessary for the revival of the Mexican economy and society. Certainly, he did have great success in reducing inflation and restoring some level of confidence to the Mexican economy. For this and other reforms he gained popularity, both for himself and his party. In fact, he had succeeded in turning around his image from one of a corrupt PRI official to that of a strong economic manager who had a vision for the country. But even this perception was short-lived. On January 1, 1994, the day NAFTA took effect, an uprising in Chiapas occurred. Under the leadership of Subcomandante Marcos, the indigenous people of Chiapas challenged the hegemony of neo-liberal ideology, which had resulted in the further marginalization of indigenous people, particularly themselves.

It is important to note that despite the economic progress made by Mexico, there was, and

MEXICAN PRESIDENT ERNESTO ZEDILLO CASTS HIS VOTE DURING THE COUNTRY'S 2000 ELECTIONS. MOST ANALYSTS AGREED THAT WITHOUT ZEDILLO'S ELECTORAL REFORMS, PAN CANDIDATE VICENTE FOX WOULD NEVER HAVE WON THE ELECTION. *(CORBIS CORPORATION (Bellevue). Reproduced by permission.)*

continues to be, a simmering ethnic problem in the country. Indigenous groups have, for centuries, been locked out of many aspects of Mexican social life. In many states, like Quintana Roo and Chiapas, many people live on the periphery of the Mexican mainstream. On the other hand, Mexicans are extremely proud of the important contributions that indigenous people have made to present-day Mexican society. The economic crisis of the 1980s and Salinas' reform measures conspired to further exclude many indigenous groups from Mexican society. Salinas also learned some hard political lessons when many members of the same Catholic clergy that he had stoutly defended gave their support to the Zapatista rebels. As followers of tenets of liberation theology they were opposed to many of Salinas' neo-liberalist policies.

The Chiapas crisis was only the tip of the iceberg in terms of what was about to happen to Mexico. In 1994 Luis Donaldo Colosio, Mexico's presidential candidate for the PRI, was assassi-

nated. The incident shocked the entire country, more so when it was rumored that his death may have been linked to his opposition to Salinas' policies. Other political killings followed, which eventually discredited Salinas. In addition, the violent crime rate in Mexico City was on the increase, and drug trafficking, apparently involving high-ranking members of the PRI, had become widespread. Many people blamed NAFTA and the policies of Salinas for this situation. By the end of 1994, when the Yale-trained economist Ernesto Zedillo became Mexico's next president, the country was in social and economic crisis. Crime and corruption had now become rife, the economy was unstable, the Chiapas rebels were attracting international attention, and the presence of drug lords became part of Mexico's everyday life.

Zedillo's presidency brought about important changes to Mexican politics and society. The young technocratic-styled president went on another "moral crusade," not dissimilar from that of de la

LAZARO CÁRDENAS

1895–1970 Lazaro Cárdenas is Mexico's most revered political leader. In large part this reverence is due to his radical populist policies and his favorable treatment of the poor and promotion of education while he was president from 1934 to 1940. Additionally, he developed a reputation for being an honest politician. This perception obviously finds resonance in a country in which there is a long history of political corruption.

Born in 1895 in Jiquilpan, Michoacan, to a lower-middle-class family, he was forced to support his large family following the death of his father. Cárdenas distinguished himself as a military officer, although he was known to be against militarism. In 1920 Cárdenas became a general in the Alvaro Obregon administration. Cárdenas had fought on the side of Obregon in the battle against Pancho Villa in the forces of Gen. Plutarco Elías Calles, Obregon's successor as President. As a top military official, Cárdenas became known as a person who could not be corrupted.

In 1928 Cárdenas became the governor of the state of Michoacan. With a strong populist agenda he set about developing the state's infrastructure, organizing peasants, farmers, students, and other interest groups into movements for social and economic development. In 1934 this young 39-year-old idealist became presi-dent of Mexico. Guided by radical nationalist ideals, he set about nationalizing the oil industry in 1938, expropriating the assets of seventeen foreign companies in Mexico. While he was hailed as a hero in Mexico, many countries, the United States and Britain in particular, decided to boycott Mexican petroleum. This led to difficult times for Mexico, as it immediately lost its export markets. Following World War II (1939–45), however, the demand for oil increased and Mexico arrived at a financial settlement with the countries from which it had expropriated the industry. Although Mexican petroleum was exported to these countries again, Mexico was saddled with a huge debt.

Cárdenas' honesty and seriousness of purpose was reflected in numerous acts of generosity and service to his country. For instance, he used part of his house as a free clinic for the indigenous people in the region. Cárdenas was not simply a politician who depended on nice-sounding rhetoric to gain popularity. This man of action instituted many radical reforms to the Mexican society including, among others, extensive land reform, the formation of people's cooperatives to improve their economic bargaining power in the market place, and the promotion of rationalist/secular education through the construction of schools which were not beholden to the powerful Catholic Church.

Madrid, to clean up Mexican politics. He gained respect for tackling corruption in the justice system and for arresting the brother of former president Salinas, who was accused of killing a high-ranking political figure. Zedillo also abandoned some of the paternalistic governing practices of his predecessors and committed his government to openness and democratic principles. His government was more receptive to input from opposition members than any other in the past. He instituted significant political reforms, some of which were opposed by hardliners in his party. For instance, he abandoned the *dedazo*, or "fingering of the candidate'—the tradition of the president to name his party's presidential nominee. Instead, for the first time the presidential candidate was elected through an open primary.

A concern with reducing the disparity between the rich and the poor, fighting poverty, and improving the infrastructure of the county also char-acterized Zedillo's term. He also entered negotiations with the Zapatistas, at one time preferring to negotiate rather than push home a military advantage after the military had captured rebel headquarters in 1995. This concession almost led to a military coup in the country.

In respect to the economy, after devaluation in late 1994, Zedillo was able to stabilize the economy, later achieving upwards of six percent growth in 1997. Due to these positive changes, Zedillo's popularity was high within the Mexican society and he managed to restore some level of respectability to the office of the presidency and his party. When he left office his popularity among Mexicans was at its highest.

Despite Zedillo's enormous efforts and accomplishments, many things remained unchanged in the society. Political corruption remained rife, and members of the Zedillo administration were implicated in a number of scandals. In fact, so serious was the perception of corruption in the country that all of the candidates in the 2000 elections ran on a platform of eradicating corruption. Additionally, despite Zedillo's efforts, he was unable to resolve the Zapatista rebellion. Between 1994 and 2000, the Zapatista movement captured the imagination of many Mexicans, especially the student movement, who saw Subcomandante Marcos as a true Mexican hero. The government's problems with students at Mexico's largest university, the UNAM, resulted in the students closing the university for many months.

As a sign of what was likely to come later for the PRI, Zedillo's political reforms contributed to the crushing defeat of his party in the congressional elections. For the first time the PRI had lost control of Congress, and the left wing Cárdenas of the PRD was elected mayor of Mexico City. Ironically, this situation occurred when, for the first time, Zedillo opened up the seat for election, instead of following the tradition of the president appointing the mayor.

Zedillo was hailed for instituting many reforms to the political system and restoring some semblance of stability to the Mexican economy. But by now the Mexican electorate was looking for a change in governance. The PRI had departed considerably from its revolutionary past to one that advocated neo-liberal policies and seemed to represent the interests of the wealthy and political elites. It had become tarnished by political corruption, drug trafficking, and electoral fraud. Many in Mexican society appeared to have grown PRI-fatigued.

RECENT HISTORY AND FUTURE

In 1999 the PAN and the PDR began negotiations aimed at forming an alliance in order to defeat the PRI in the 2000 elections. The negotiations deteriorated, and eventually there were three main contenders in the presidential race: Vicente Fox of the PAN, Francisco Labastida of the PRI, and Cuauhtemoc Cárdenas of the PDR. The election campaign was a bitterly fought one as both Fox and Cárdenas accused the PRI of corruption and mismanagement of the economy. Labastida distanced himself from the accusations of corruption in the PRI and promised to institute changes aimed at combating corruption, advancing democracy, and stimulating economic growth. He focused on developing education, fighting poverty and crime. He also tried to distance himself from both the tradi-

tional populist wing of the party and the free-market advocates of the right. While the polls placed Labastida and Fox in a dead heat, after the July 2, 2000 elections Fox was victorious, securing more than 45 percent of the votes.

Fox came to office with a program of economic, political, and social reform. He promised to deal with corruption and reduce the gap between the rich and the poor. Presenting himself as a hardworking, hands-on, no-nonsense man of the people, he promised to institute reforms to the government, making it more transparent and democratic. He promised to deal with the alienation of the indigenous people in the country from the mainstream of Mexican society. In one interview he promised to solve the Chiapas problem "in fifteen minutes." He said that he would build health clinics, making them available to more people. He promised fiscal discipline and annual growth rates of seven percent annually. Fox's campaign was based on projecting an image of a president who was willing to change the practices of the PRI and make radical changes to the moral decay which he said had come to characterize the tenure of the PRI.

In the area of foreign policy Fox was in favor of closer links with the United States and was critical of the U.S. government's certification program. The program recommends which countries are to be denied aid if they are not considered to be actively combating the drug trafficking problem. Fox argued that the United States was partially to blame for the drug trafficking problem since that country had the consumers. Fox also suggested that there should be open borders between the United States and Mexico, which would allow for the free movement of Mexican workers. He is in favor of extending the NAFTA arrangement in order to facilitate an open border within five to ten years.

Although ideologically Fox's party may be described as being on the right, Fox himself appears to be a more moderate politician. He is perhaps best described as a pragmatist and possibly even a nationalist. He once said that he was opposed to PRI's brand of "capitalism" which produced poverty, exclusion, and lack of development. Instead he advocated a Third Way, or a "Fox Way," similar to that of Britain's Tony Blair. On the other hand, he also argued that there was a need to "bring the economy in line with the market." Fox can therefore be considered a free-market supporter, but also somewhat of a populist.

Since taking up office on December 1, 2000, Fox has begun to make an impact internationally

VICENTE FOX

1942– Born to a Mexican father and a Spanish mother, Vicente Fox made history in July 2000 by becoming the first person to defeat an Institutional Revolutionary Party (PRI) presidential candidate since 1929. A divorcee and father to four adopted children, Fox comes from a wealthy farming family in the state of Guanajuato. Prior to winning the presidency he was a governor and also managed a large farm in his state, where he raised cattle and exported vegetables to many parts of the world.

Standing at a commanding six foot five inches, Fox has had many firsts in his life. For instance, Fox joined Coca-Cola Corporation at the age of 22 years, and within a period of 10 years he became president of the company's Mexican operations, making him the youngest soft drink company president in the history of the company's operations in Mexico. During his tenure Fox established Coca-Cola's dominance in the market over its rival Pepsi-Cola.

Fox also had a meteoric rise through the ranks of his political party, the National Action Party (PAN), which he joined in 1987. During the 1988 elections he rose to national prominence by poking fun at the PRI candidate, Carlos Salinas de Gortari, for alleged electoral corruption. In 1991, when he ran for governor of Guanajuato and failed, he again gained national attention when he pointed to fraudulent electoral practices that seemingly robbed him of a victory. The PRI candidate was eventually removed, but was replaced by another PAN member, instead of Fox. Fox was eventually victorious in 1995, when he was elected governor of his home state.

Although he studied business at Mexico's Iberio-American University and at Harvard University in the United States, Fox is considered poles apart from his more cautious and ostensibly more sophisticated predecessor, Ernesto Zedillo. During the elections Fox por-

VICENTE FOX. *(AP/Wide World Photos. Reproduced by permission.)*

trayed himself a hardworking down-to-earth person who knows what it is to do manual labor. Fox prefers to wear jeans and cowboy boots than business suits. His Spanish is not the polished language of Mexico's educated elite, and he is often described as being blunt and crude. For instance, during the presidential campaign he called his main rival Francisco Labastida a "sissy" and a transvestite.

Although his party is to the right of the PRI, Fox is much more liberal than a large number of members in his party. He is, perhaps, much better described as a pragmatist, rather than as having strong allegiance to any political ideology. This pragmatism has worked for him, as he has already made significant steps towards resolving the conflicts with the Zapatistas of Chiapas.

and domestically. In the area of foreign affairs, Fox has moved Mexico even closer to the United States, especially the Republican Party. Since coming to office Fox has met with U.S. President George W. Bush on a number of occasions, and has been paid a visit by one of Mexico's harshest critics, Senator Jesse Helms. Helms has had high praise for Fox and his administration and has expressed interest in working closer with the government.

Domestically, Fox has moved quickly to appoint a cabinet made up of people with strong human rights records and reputations for rooting out corruption. In terms of management of the economy, Fox has appointed a number of people with experience in the corporate world to several cabinet posts. Alphonzo Zarate, a Mexican political scientist, argues that Mexican politics has moved through four stages, with the Fox presi-

PRI AND PAN: MEXICO'S OLDEST POLITICAL PARTIES

The Institutional Revolutionary Party (PRI) is Mexico's oldest party. Formed in 1929 under the name National Revolutionary Party, it later changed its name to the Party of the National Revolution under its most famous leader, Lazaro Cárdenas. Cárdenas' radical populist policies endeared his party to the Mexican people. In 1946 the party underwent organizational changes and was renamed the PRI.

The PRI has held political office in Mexico from 1929 to 2000, the longest for any political party in the world. The PRI's fortunes began to falter in 1988, when Cuauhtemoc Cárdenas, the son of Lazaro Cárdenas, broke away from the PRI and formed his own party, the Party of the Democratic Revolution (PRD). By now the PRI had come to be associated with widespread political corruption and economic mismanagement. In the mid-term elections of 1997, the PRI lost majority control of the lower house of Congress and of Mexico City.

Even though former president Ernesto Zedillo instituted democratic reforms within the party and also improved its image from being a party of corruption and economic mismanagement, the PRI lost the 2000 general elections to the National Action Party (PAN) candidate, Vicente Fox.

Mexico's second oldest political party, the PAN, was founded in September 1939. The PAN has always been ideologically to the right of the PRI and has traditionally viewed the policies of the PRI as populist tactics aimed at maintaining power, but not necessarily serving the interests of the country. The PAN has had historical links to the conservative Catholic Church. During the 1980s its popularity increased as it called for democratic reforms in the country and protested against the high level of political corruption in Mexican electoral politics.

In 1989, following protests against electoral fraud, the party won its first governorship in the state of Guanajuato. Since its formation the PAN remained Mexico's main opposition party, never being able to capture the imagination of the Mexican people like the PRI has. In 1946 it won its first four congressional seats; however, prior to the victory of Fox, the PAN's highest vote tally was about 26 percent. In the 2000 election the PAN, led by Vicente Fox, beat the PRI candidate, Francisco Labastida, thereby ushering in a new era in Mexican politics.

dency representing the last stage. He argues that Mexico has moved from having a political system dominated by the military, to one dominated by the lawyers, then by technocrats, and now by managers. Fox and his managers have shown a great interest in advancing the NAFTA, and also the Free Trade Area of the Americas (FTAA), due to commence in 2005. Fox is also in support of the Puebla-Panama project, which is an attempt to extend the free trade area through the Americas, with Mexico being a gateway to the rest of Latin America. Some of Fox's critics argue that the fulfillment of the Puebla-Panama project and FTAA is connected to a resolution of the Chiapas crisis. That is, unless the Chiapas crisis is resolved then the project will be jeopardized.

Whether or not this is true, Fox's most important achievement thus far has undoubtedly been his handling of the Chiapas impasse. On his first day in office he took steps to begin peace talks with the Zapatista freedom fighters. He ordered the Mexican military to retreat from Zapatista zones in Chiapas, and then set about to send Congress an Indian rights bill—an act which was rejected by his predecessor Zedillo. Fox also tried to meet all of the Zapatistas' conditions for the resumption of peace talks with the government: withdrawal of troops from the conflict zone, release of Zapatista political prisoners, and congressional adoption of a peace framework, which was approved by the negotiators but shelved by the PRI.

Fox's efforts at forging peace with the Zapatistas have been greatly assisted by the new Chiapas governor, Pablo Salazar, also of the PAN. Salazar has bitterly criticized the policies of the PRI for their handling of the Chiapas rebellion. In his inaugural speech as governor, he committed himself to ending the war and said that the Zapatista war was an authentic expression of a need for democracy and freedom for all in the country.

The president's approach succeeded in bringing the Zaptistas to the bargaining table and permitted them to travel to Mexico City (wearing their masks) to address gatherings at UNAM. Perhaps the most far-reaching measure of all was the Zapatistas' address to the Mexican Congress on March 28, 2001. In this session, the Zapatistas outlined some of their grievances and pledged not to engage in any military offensive in the areas from which the Mexican military has withdrawn. Following the return of the Zapatista delegation to Chiapas, President Fox pledged to work with Congress to pass a bill on Indian rights. The bill was based on the San Andres accords of 1996, which was the outcome of negotiations between the Zedillo administration and the Chiapas guerrillas.

On April 28, 2001, Congress passed an amended bill, which was subsequently rejected by the Zapatistas. The guerrilla leader, Subcomandante Marcos, rejected the bill, charging that changes to the bill would have left indigenous people worse off than before. The bill was amended because some congressmen thought it could lead to the breakup of Mexico. Although disheartened with this setback, Fox and the other leaders hope to unite the Mexican people and deliver what the PRI couldn't—a society free of political corruption, poverty, drug trafficking, crime, and an end to the Chiapas rebellion.

BIBLIOGRAPHY

Batalla, Bonfil Guillermo. *Mexico Profoundo: Una Civilizacion Negada.* Mexico City: Grijalbo, 1989.

"Comandante Esther's Address to the Congress of the Union," March 28, 2001, translated by Irlandesa. Available online at http://www.zmag.org/ZNET.htm (cited July 12, 2001).

Heusinkveld, Paula. *Inside Mexico: Living, Traveling and Doing Business in a Changing Society.* New York: John Wiley and Sons, 1994.

Meyer, Michael C., William L. Sherman, and Susan M. Deeds. *The Course of Mexican History.* London: Oxford University Press, 1998.

Milner, Kate. "Profile: Vicente Fox," BBC News, Available online at http://news.bbc.co.uk/hi/english/world/americas/newssid_813000/813206.stm (cited June 12, 2001).

Mexico Connect. Various articles available online at http://www.mexconnect.com/index.html. (cited June 12, 2001).

"Mexico, U.S. Establish New Spirit of Cooperation," *USA Today,* updated June 19, 2001. Available online at http://www.usatoday.com/news/world/2001-04-18-mexico.htm. (cited July 20, 2001).

"No Legislamos para de Vetar la Ley de Derechos y Cultura Indigena, Solo del Ejecutivo," *La Jornada,* May 1, 2001.

Ruiz, Ramon Eduardo. *Triumphs and Tragedy: A History of the Mexican People.* New York: W.W. Norton and Company, 1993.

Smith, James. "New Chiapas Governor Initiates Process to Release Rebels," *Los Angeles Times,* December 9, 2000.

Womack, John, ed. *Rebellion in Chiapas: An Historical Reader.* New York: The New Press, 1999.

—Ian Boxill

PAKISTAN'S COUP: NEW REGIME OR OLD TRADITION?

THE CONFLICT

Elected heads of state in Pakistan have been overthrown four times by military dictators since Pakistan's founding in 1947. The last elected leader, Nawaz Sharif, was ousted by Pakistan's chief of the armed forces, General Pervez Musharraf, in October 1999. The question remains whether Musharraf will allow a smooth transition back to civilian government or if he will take to the role of dictator.

Political

- Government in Pakistan has been strongly influenced by the military, which, under Nawaz Sharif's administration, demanded an official say in how things were run.

- Though ousted in a military coup and convicted by the courts for corruption, former Prime Minister Nawaz Sharif challenged the validity of the coup in Pakistan's supreme court. The court rejected his appeal, granting legitimacy to General Musharraf's actions as the country's leader.

- Musharraf claims that national elections will be held in 2002, and that he will return power to a civilian government at that time. Uncertainty remains over whether or not this will occur.

On October 12, 1999, General Pervez Musharraf introduced the fourth military coup in Pakistan since the country's inception in 1947. Pakistan's democratically elected leader, Nawaz Sharif, was removed from power in a quick and bloodless military coup. Tensions between Sharif and the military were common during his time in office. When Sharif moved to create more support for himself in the military, those tensions quickly escalated into a struggle for power over who would have ultimate control of Pakistan's leadership.

Prior to the coup Sharif held a majority of support in parliament and had taken several measures to strengthen his position as prime minister, including attempts to curtail the military's influence on how the government was run. A few weeks before Sharif's ousting, senior party members of his Pakistan Muslim League joined in a controversial opposition alliance against the military. When General Pervez Musharraf ousted Sharif from office it was the culmination of a long, tense relationship between Sharif and the military. Musharraf succeeded three previous army generals who had also initiated coups against Pakistan's leadership: Ayub Khan in 1958; Yahya Khan in 1969; and Zia ul Haq in 1997. With the fourth coup in little over 50 years, however, the question arose: Would Musharraf's coup usher in a new regime or would it be the same old tradition of corruption and instability?

HISTORICAL BACKGROUND

Officially known as the Islamic Republic of Pakistan, the country is predominantly a Muslim nation (about 97 percent). The country was in fact founded because of the religious makeup of its

MAP OF PAKISTAN. *(Maryland Cartographics. Reproduced by permission.)*

population. Part of the same British colony as India in the 1800s and into the 1900s, Pakistan was granted independence, along with India, in 1947. Pakistan was actually created in two parts, about 1,000 miles (1,600 kilometers) apart, with a portion of India in between. This division was based on religious differences of the people—West Pakistan and East Pakistan were predominantly Muslim, while India was predominantly Hindu. Religious tensions between the two new nations frequently flared to violence.

Pakistan became a new nation on August 14, 1947, as a member of the British Commonwealth of Nations. Muhammad Ali Jinnah, who had been head of the movement to separate Pakistan from India, became Pakistan's first head of state. With 1,000 miles of Indian territory separating West and East Pakistan, the country's unity was fragile.

Fighting between Hindus and Muslims did not stop with the partition. In a massive movement of people, ten million refugees migrated between the two countries—Muslims who found themselves living in the new India fled to Pakistan, while Hindus and Sikhs who found themselves in Pakistan left for India.

Full war erupted between India and Pakistan in October 1947 over the territory of Kashmir. Since the majority of the population of Kashmir was Muslim, Pakistan claimed it for its own. The Hindu ruler of Kashmir, however, declared the region to be part of India. Pakistan sent in troops. The war raged until 1949, when the United Nations (UN) brokered a peace agreement. Maintaining the peace was more difficult. The dispute over Kashmir continued on a quieter scale until 1965, when fighting again erupted between Paki-

CHRONOLOGY

August 14, 1947 Pakistan and India are granted independence from the British Empire. Pakistan, however, is divided into two parts—East and West Pakistan, with a portion of India dividing the two sides.

October 1947 Pakistan and India go to war over the disputed territory of Kashmir.

1949 A cease-fire is brokered by the United Nations.

October 27, 1958 Army chief Ayub Khan takes control of Pakistan.

1965 Pakistan and India again engage in war over Kashmir. The UN brokers another peace agreement.

March 1969 Army chief Yahya Khan takes control of Pakistan after Ayub Khan resigns.

1971 East Pakistan declares itself the independent nation of Bangladesh. West Pakistan sends in troops to prevent succession, but, supported by India, Bangladesh wins its autonomy and is established as a separate nation. Also in this year, Yahya Khan resigns and Zulfikar Ali Bhutto becomes president of Pakistan.

1973 A new constitution for Pakistan calls for a separate president and prime minister. Bhutto remains president, while Chaudhri Fazal Elahi serves as prime minister.

March 1977 Elections keep Bhutto in power, though allegations of fraud and calls for new elections are made by opposition groups.

July 5, 1977 General Mohammed Zia ul Haq, chief of the armed forces, takes over the country and declares martial law.

April 6, 1979 Bhutto is executed by ul Haq's regime.

August 17, 1988 Ul Haq dies in a plane crash.

November 1988 After national elections are held, Benazir Bhutto becomes prime minister of Pakistan.

August 1990 President Ishaq Kahn removes Benazir Bhutto from office.

October 1993 Benazir Bhutto again becomes prime minister after national elections. Farooq Leghari serves as president.

November 1996 President Leghari removes Benazir Bhutto from office.

February 1997 Bhutto loses her bid for reelection, and Nawaz Sharif becomes prime minister.

October 12, 1999 General Pervez Musharraf, chief of Pakistan's armed forces, removes Sharif from office and takes over the country.

July 2000 Sharif is convicted of corruption, fined, and sentenced to fourteen years in prison.

February 2001 Pakistan's supreme court rejects an appeal challenging Musharraf's takeover and grants him legitimacy as the country's ruler.

stan and India. Again, the UN brokered a fragile peace agreement. Fighting continued to erupt over time, with no clear resolution in sight.

Pakistan's Civil War

Growing resentment among East Pakistanis over West Pakistan's control of their government was exacerbated by the crisis presented by a natural disaster in 1970. In that year a cyclone and a tsunami, a giant tidal wave, killed more than 266,000 people in East Pakistan. When West Pakistan was slow to deliver food and other badly needed supplies it contributed to strained relations between the two parts of the country.

A new National Assembly was elected in 1970, with the responsibility of writing a new constitution. Since East Pakistan made up about 56 percent of Pakistan's population, a majority of the Assembly was from East Pakistan. These members pressed for greater autonomy for East Pakistan. The president of the country, General Yahya Khan, responded by postponing the Assembly's first meeting, and East Pakistanis took to the streets to protest the action. Violence erupted when Yahya Khan sent troops into East Pakistan, which declared itself a separate nation called Bangladesh in December 1971, launching an internal war.

India took sides in what became Pakistan's civil war, allying itself with Bangladesh, and Pakistan again found itself at war with India. By the time Pakistan surrendered, just two weeks after India entered the fray, more than one million people had been killed in the fighting. General Yahya Khan resigned as president less than a week after

PERVEZ MUSHARRAF'S COUP MARKED THE FOURTH TIME AN OVERTHROW MADE HEADLINES ON PAKISTAN'S NEWSPAPERS. *(CORBIS CORPORATION (Bellevue). Reproduced by permission.)*

the war ended. He was replaced by Zulfikar Ali Bhutto, the leader of the Pakistan People's Party.

With Indian troops still occupying Pakistani territory, Bhutto returned his country to constitutional, civilian rule. India withdrew its forces from Pakistan in 1972, but kept them in Kashmir, leaving that region again open to contention.

The 1977 Coup

A new constitution in 1973 established the separate posts of president and prime minister. Zulfikar Ali Bhutto became prime minister, while Chaudhri Fazal Elahi was elected president. Elec-

tions in March 1977 kept Bhutto in power, but charges of corruption resulted in violence between Bhutto's government and political opponents. Many of Bhutto's opponents were Muslim fundamentalists representing the aristocracy and the Islamic clergy. Bhutto, in an attempt to appease these groups, many of whom objected to his "Westernized" style of government, shut down nightclubs and outlawed alcohol.

It was too little too late for the prime minister, however. The army took over the country for the second time in July 1977, with General Mohammed Zia ul Haq as leader. Bhutto was forced from office

NAWAZ SHARIF

1949– Born in 1949, just a year after his country's founding, Sharif grew up in the city of Lahore. His family, prominent and successful business owners, operated an iron foundry. Sharif was educated at the Government College of Lahore, where he received a law degree, and at the Punjab University Law College in Lahore.

Sharif first gained national attention in 1981, when he was named first finance minister and then also chief minister of Punjab Province. By then his family business included the largest private steel mill in the country, a sugar mill, and four textile factories, and employed about 10,000 people. Sharif was primarily supported by urban voters. First elected prime minister in 1990, Sharif was dismissed by President Ishaq Khan in 1993. He was followed in that post by opposition leader Benazir Bhutto. A second chance at leadership came around to Sharif in 1997, when he was again elected to the office of prime minister. This time he had strong support from parliament, as well as from other branches of the government. Where his support was weakest, however, turned out to be his downfall. Relations between Sharif and the military were tense, and when Sharif moved to install a friendly figure in the post of chief of the armed forces, he encountered strong opposition from most senior military officials, as well as the man who currently held that post, General Pervez Musharraf. In a struggle for power between Sharif and Musharraf, Sharif lost. On October 12, 1999, he was placed under house arrest and removed from office in a bloodless coup.

Put on trial by Musharraf's regime for hijacking, kidnapping, and attempted murder, as well as other crimes, Sharif was denied the right to testify at his own trial. He did, however, deny the charges against him, saying that they were fabricated by Musharraf as an excuse to remove him from office and jail him. Sentenced to life in prison for hijacking and terrorism, Sharif was later also convicted on corruption charges. Sharif was eventually allowed to leave the country, fleeing to exile in Saudi Arabia.

and the country entered ten years of military rule, in spite of the general's promise that elections would soon be held. President Elahi stayed on in his post as a figurehead until he finally quit, and ul Haq became president in name as well as in actuality.

Meanwhile, Bhutto was tried by ul Haq's government for the murder of a political enemy and, in 1979, he was executed. Ul Haq had hoped to squelch the former leader's popular following, but

Bhutto instead became a martyr. His death became a rallying point for those who wanted ul Haq removed from leadership and democracy restored. These people included much of the working class, as well as professionals such as attorneys and physicians, who were not afforded the same benefits that ul Haq's supporters, the landed gentry, received. A coalition of such people, many of whom shared little but a hatred of ul Haq, came together in a group called the Movement for the Restoration of Democracy (MRD).

The largest group within this organization was Bhutto's now-outlawed Pakistan People's Party (PPP). After Bhutto's death, his widow, Nusrat Bhutto, became head of the PPP. In failing health and lacking political expertise, however, she passed the torch of leadership on to her daughter, Benazir Bhutto. When ul Haq allowed elections in 1985, Benazir Bhutto put her name on the ballot. Ul Haq, however, did not like the voting results. He suspended the newly elected parliament and the prime minister and affirmed his position as ruler. When ul Haq died in a plane crash in August 1988, Ghulam Ishaq Khan, then acting-head of the senate, appointed Benazir Bhutto head of state.

From Benazir Bhutto to Nawaz Sharif

Elections in November 1988 confirmed the democratic election of Benazir Bhutto as the new prime minister, earning her a place in history as the first woman ever to be elected head of a predominantly Muslim country. Ghulum Ishaq Kahn became president, and he distanced himself from Bhutto by accusing her of corruption. In 1990 Kahn ousted Bhutto from office and scheduled new elections for October. In these elections the Islamic Democratic Alliance, which was made up of several allied political parties, gained more than half of the seats in parliament, and Nawaz Sharif was elected prime minister. Sharif was a member of the Pakistan Muslim League, the main party of the Islamic Democratic Alliance.

The new government did not last long. Bowing to pressure from the military, which held a significant amount of power in the country, Khan and Sharif resigned in July 1993, just three years after taking office. Elections in October 1993 returned the Pakistan People's Party to power with a majority of the parliament seats, and Benazir Bhutto was again elected prime minister. Farooq Leghari took the office of president.

Leghari, in a by now familiar move, dismissed Prime Minister Bhutto from office, accusing her of corruption. Elections were held in February 1997, in

NAWAZ SHARIF IS TAKEN AWAY UNDER ARMED GUARD AFTER GENERAL PERVEZ MUSHARRAF SUCCESSFULLY INITIATES A COUP AGAINST PAKISTAN'S ELECTED LEADER. *(CORBIS CORPORATION (Bellevue). Reproduced by permission.)*

which the Pakistan Muslim League gained most of the seats of parliament, and Sharif returned to his old job of prime minister. He was elected to office on a campaign platform that promised to restore Pakistan's ailing economy. Instead, he appropriated state funds and international aid funds to serve his own ends. Under Sharif, foreign debt soared while foreign investment all but vanished. Massive inflation coupled with record unemployment added to Pakistan's woes.

It was under Sharif's reign that Pakistan, in 1998, became a nuclear power. This was in large part a response to nuclear testing initiated by India earlier. Relations between Pakistan and India were always tense, particularly over the matter of Kashmir, and their cold war nearly erupted into a hot war in May 1999. Pakistani and Indian troops faced off in Kashmir with deadly results when Pakistani troops violated the Kashmiri neutral zone and crossed into territory controlled by India. Full-

out war was averted when Sharif, in response to the urging of foreign countries, including the United States, withdrew Pakistan's army from the disputed area.

During his second stint in office, Prime Minister Nawaz Sharif enjoyed an overwhelming majority of support. Perhaps conscious of how easily his first post as prime minister had been lost, Sharif took advantage of the powers available to him. In fact, he abused his power, making it illegal to disagree with him, dismissing critics from parliament, and sharply reducing the power of the president, the press, the Pakistani courts, and the country's labor unions to disagree with him or his party. Among his actions after becoming head of state were the dismissal of the chief justice of the supreme court and a reversal of the April 1997 amendment to the constitution that made it illegal for the president to fire the prime minister. Sharif's efforts against the press included the freezing of one newspaper company's assets and the seizing of its newsprint. Sharif also had the publisher of another newspaper jailed without charging him with a specific crime and had that newspaper's published editions confiscated and its Web site disabled.

Musharraf Makes His Move

Sharif's tenure as prime minister came to an end in October 1999, when General Pervez Musharraf, head of Pakistan's military forces, forced Sharif from office, suspended the constitution, and established a "transitional" military government, complete with a national security council and a cabinet. Sharif's efforts to solidify his power base were for naught. In the power struggle for control, the military proved to be the winner.

Sharif's actions leading up to the coup indicate that he was well aware of the forces against him. On October 12, 1999, General Musharraf was out of the country on an official visit to Sri Lanka when he learned that Sharif planned to fire him from his post as chief of armed forces and install the head of the Inter-Services Intelligence Agency, General Ziauddin, in his place. He quickly caught a plane back to Pakistan and made plans to mobilize military troops for action.

While Musharraf was flying back to Pakistan, Sharif made the change official. Musharraf was out; Ziauddin was in. Senior military officers, however, refused to accept Ziauddin's appointment. Ziauddin informed Sharif of suspicions that a coup was already underway and suggested that the only way Ziauddin would gain control of the military was if Musharraf's plane was prevented from landing in Karachi. While agreeing to attempt to forestall Musharraf's arrival, Sharif also publicly announced Musharraf's "retirement." This announcement proved to be the impetus the military needed to move against the prime minister.

Military troops soon lined the streets of Islamabad. Soldiers took over the state television station, abruptly cutting off broadcasts. Sharif's guards were disarmed and the prime minister was placed under house arrest. Across Pakistan troops took control of government buildings and forced Sharif supporters to submit to house arrest. All of this occurred while Musharraf was still in the air.

As the plane approached Karachi it was denied permission to land. Musharraf ordered the pilot to ignore air traffic control. The plane continued to circle the city, despite being low on fuel. Troops soon arrived at the airport and surrounded the control tower, and the plane was allowed to land. Musharraf was back in Pakistan, and the coup was

virtually complete. Television broadcasts resumed with the announcement that Nawaz Sharif had been dismissed from office. Musharraf was in control. In a televised speech to the nation Musharraf acknowledged the country's social and political turmoil and announced that he had taken over the country in an attempt to avoid further destabilization.

Musharraf's coup did not bode well for Pakistan's cold war with fellow nuclear power India. Pakistan's stance against India, mainly focusing on disputed land in Kashmir, quickly hardened under Musharraf. Musharraf's foreign minister, Abdus Sattar, was known to be fiercely anti-India; in a speech quoted by Mohammed Ahmedullah in the *Bulletin of the Atomic Scientists* ("Pakistan: After the Coup," January 2000), he called a peace accord signed by the Indian prime minister and Nawaz Sharif "insignificant." India refused to acknowledge Musharraf's government, and Pakistan soon found itself suspended from the 54-nation British Commonwealth.

One of Musharraf's first acts as Pakistan's leader was to pull Pakistani troops away from India's border. Although firm in his stand that "Pakistan is Kashmir and Kashmir is Pakistan," he did open dialogue with India on the issue, according it first priority in talks with India. India, in turn, played down the troop withdrawal, announcing that a more significant move would have been to stop sponsoring attacks by Muslim separatists in Kashmir. Though Kashmir remains an issue between the two countries, Musharraf's initial actions in dealing with the matter did scale back the chance of tensions quickly overflowing into violence.

Former Indian prime minister I. K. Gujral cautioned, however, that dismissing Musharraf's government could be a mistake. He stated that there had been no anti-military demonstrations, reports of military repression, or human rights abuses in Pakistan in the wake of Musharraf's coup, all of which would be signs of Musharraf's unpopularity. For the most part, Pakistanis seemed unconcerned that their country was once again ruled by the military. After the plague of corruption that seemed to infest democratically elected leaderships, Musharraf's promises of reform were welcome to many. Indeed, inflation fell two percent in the first year of Musharraf's government, and the Pakistani currency, the rupee, held its own against foreign currencies.

Though he assured Pakistan and the world that democracy would be restored to the country over time, Musharraf has shown no intention of stepping down any time soon, saying only that elections were planned for 2002 and that his goal was to have reforms in place to ensure that his restructuring could not be reversed. Due to achieving office in a coup, Musharraf's position as Pakistan's leader has no expiration date, but his time as army chief did—October 7, 2001. In March 2001, however, Musharraf admitted that he had no intention of relinquishing his title as army chief. Whether or not his word about holding democratic elections in 2002 is valid remains to be seen.

RECENT HISTORY AND THE FUTURE

Musharraf's two major goals for Pakistan were to boost the economy and to end corruption in government. Indeed, he seemed committed to making the tough economic decisions required to revive Pakistan's economy, enacting unpopular sales and farm taxes. These measures resulted in higher prices for consumers. Foreign bankers and analysts praised Musharraf's efforts to control Pakistan's large debt, half of which is from foreign lending. This was a problem civilian governments typically had a difficult time controlling. Musharraf worked hard to cut government spending and undertook the privatization of many government-owned businesses. The International Monetary Fund responded favorably in November 2000, lending Pakistan more than one-half billion dollars for development.

Despite the unpopular taxes he has levied, Musharraf has won praise at home for his fight against corruption. His administration's National Accountability Bureau prosecuted crooked politicians, business people, and government workers, recovering around US$500 million by early 2001. Former Prime Minister Nawaz Sharif is one who has felt the full force of Musharraf's anti-corruption campaign. Sentenced to 14 years in prison under corruption charges in July 2000, Sharif was also fined 20 million rupees, or US$400,000, and was barred from holding public office for 21 years.

Musharraf has also made it clear that he will tolerate no dissent within Pakistan's government. When six judges of the Supreme Court refused to swear allegiance to him in March 2000, he had them removed from office. Additionally, Pakistan's Islamic fundamentalists also fell under Musharraf's consideration. In June 2000 Musharraf reinstated many of the Islamic laws set forth in the suspended Pakistani constitution.

Public support for Musharraf eroded in 2001. Widespread poverty, crime, and tribal blood feuds, as well as Pakistan's costly and dangerous nuclear

PERVEZ MUSHARRAF

1943– General Pervez Musharraf was the head of Pakistan's armed forces when he deposed elected leader Nawaz Sharif in October 1999. He enjoyed initial popular appeal as leader or Pakistan and promised to hold elections by 2002. Born in 1943 Musharraf started out life with his family in New Delhi, in what became India, until 1947, when the country of Pakistan was created. Musharraf and his family then moved to Karachi, Pakistan.

Musharraf attended the Pakistan Military Academy in 1961, earning his commission in three years before joining an artillery regiment. He became a decorated veteran after the 1965 conflict with India, and he fought again as a company commander in the Pakistani civil war that split East Pakistan from West (Bangladesh).

By 1991 Musharraf was a major general in the armed forces. He quickly moved up in rank to make lieutenant general by 1995. Also in the early 1990s he studied at the Command and Staff College at Quetta, Pakistan's National Defense College, and at the Royal College of Defense Studies in Great Britain. Promoted to the rank of general in 1998 Musharraf was appointed chief of staff of the army by Prime Minister Nawaz Sharif. Shortly thereafter he became head of Pakistan's Joint Chiefs of Staff. Ironically, Sharif appointed Musharraf to the cabinet post in order to replace the former army chief of staff, who had pushed for a joint military-civilian government for Pakistan.

On October 12, 1999, when Musharraf, out of the country on official business, heard that Sharif was planning to replace him, he acted quickly to preempt the prime minister. Musharraf returned to Pakistan immediately. With the support of several senior military officials and the full force of the armed forces behind him, Musharraf had Sharif and several of his supporters arrested. He took control of the country without one shot being fired. With the eye of the world upon him, Musharraf assured Pakistan that civilian rule would be restored. But first, changes needed to be made. Detailing a list of goals, including the revival of the economy and a fight against corruption, Musharraf promised to fulfill his goals and create a stable basis for Pakistani government. Local elections have been successfully carried out under his leadership, with national elections slated for 2002.

competition with India all contributed to his troubles. Fighting in neighboring Afghanistan between the ruling Taliban regime and its adversaries resulted in an influx of refugees, drugs, and arms runners into Pakistan. "Initially, people were very

MUSHARRAF (LEFT) GREETS MEMBERS OF THE PAKISTANI COMMUNITY. MUSHARRAF HAS GAINED SOME SUPPORT FOR HIS REGIME BY BATTLING CORRUPTION AND WORKING TO IMPROVE PAKISTAN'S ECONOMY. *(AP/Wide World Photos. Reproduced by permission.)*

motivated and very spirited, and Musharraf was in a position to exploit that spirit," Khalid Rahman, director of the Institute of Policy Studies in Islamabad, told Gregg Jones of the *Dallas Morning News* on February 26, 2001. "[Now] he has lost that opportunity, and things are becoming difficult for him."

With 70 percent of Pakistan's budget committed to military spending and the servicing of foreign debt, Musharraf does not have a large margin for error. Hundreds of thousands of Pakistani troops remained deployed along the boarder with India as 2001 opened. Pakistan's navy announced plans in February 2001 to deploy nuclear missiles on its fleet of submarines. The country's apparent willingness to enter into a nuclear arms race with India could prove devastatingly costly to its economy, making Musharraf's efforts to revive Pakistan's economy more difficult.

Musharraf allowed elections on a local level in December 2000, but it was not initially clear how much, if any, impact this would have on restoring democracy to the country as a whole. Musharraf also said that he would abide by a Pakistan Supreme Court ruling that required him to hold national elections by the close of 2002. Only time will tell if he will make good on his promise. In February 2001, however, in an appeal by Nawaz Sharif challenging the legality of the coup, the Supreme Court reiterated that Musharraf must hold elections by October 2002. In the same ruling, the court rejected Sharif's appeal, allowing Musharraf to remain in power, but making it difficult for him to claim any mandate past the 2002 date.

Repeating his promise of national elections to come, Musharraf stipulated that neither Nawaz Sharif nor Benazir Bhutto would be allowed to participate in politics, citing convictions of corruption against both former prime ministers. Musharraf's stated plan is to start transitioning government back to civilian control in a gradual process, beginning with local elections, followed by provincial polls, and then finally a national vote. Democracy could yet evolve from the 1999 coup.

BIBLIOGRAPHY

Ahmedullah, Mohammed. "Pakistan: After the Coup," *Bulletin of the Atomic Scientists,* January 2000, p. 14.

"Bhutto Becomes the First Woman Elected to Lead a Muslim Country," in *DISCovering World History.* Farmington Hills, MI: The Gale Group, 1997.

"Bhutto, Zulfikar Ali," in *Columbia Encyclopedia,* sixth edition. New York: Columbia University Press, 2000.

"Chief Executive of Pakistan: General Pervez Musharraf." Available online at http://www.pak.gov.pk/public/chief/ce_profile.htm (cited May 10, 2001).

Cloughley, Brian. *A History of the Pakistan Army: Wars and Insurrections.* London: Oxford University Press, 2000.

"Getting to Know Pakistan's Dictator," *The Economist,* February 19, 2000, p. 41.

"India-Pakistan Wars," in *Columbia Encyclopedia,* fifth edition. New York: Columbia University Press, 1993.

"Interview: Pakistani Gen. Pervez Musharraf," PR Newswire, February 11, 2001, p. 184.

Jones, Gregg. "For Pakistan, a Stable Dream—Peaceful Prosperity Elusive for Besieged Country, Leader," *Dallas Morning News,* February 26, 2001.

"Lust for Power: Pakistan; Army Power in Pakistan," *The Economist,* March 31, 2001, p. 3.

Mian, Zia. "Nuclear Neighbors," *Nucleus: The Magazine of the Union of Concerned Scientists,* vol. 19, no. 1, Spring 1997.

"Nawaz Sharif," in *Encyclopedia of World Biography Supplement,* vol. 19. Farmington Hills, MI: The Gale Group, 1999 and 2000.

"Pakistan Court Rejects Coup Appeal," BBC News, February 7, 2001.

Sardar, Ziaruddin. "A Very Pakistani Coup," *New Statesman,* October 18, 1999, p. 11.

"Sharif Convicted of Corruption," BBC News, July 22, 2001.

Shuja, Sharif M. "The Pakistani Military Coup of 1999: Some Explanations," *Contemporary Review,* April 2000, p. 183.

Women's International Center. "Benazir Bhutto: Prime Minister of Pakistan." Available online at http://www.wic.org/bio/bbhutto.htm (cited May 10, 2001).

Ziring, Lawrence. *Pakistan in the Twentieth Century: A Political History.* London: Oxford University Press, 2000.

—Michael P. Belfiore

WHOSE MARBLES ARE THEY? CONTROVERSY OVER THE PARTHENON MARBLES

In 2000 officials from Athens, Greece, reported plans for a citywide revival, including a state-of-the-art subway system and a brand-new Acropolis Museum. The museum, which had been on the Greek agenda since the 1980s, would replace the small, outmoded, nineteenth-century-built galleries and would stand in view of Greece's greatest national monument, the Parthenon. Plans for the structure included a vast centerpiece gallery to hold the world-renowned Parthenon Marbles, also known as the Elgin Marbles, a group of fifth-century BCE friezes, pediment sculptures, and statues regarded as some of the finest examples of Classical Greek art. There was one glitch. Since 1817 the marbles have resided in the British Museum, and the British have flatly refused to give them back.

The Greeks have been bereft over the loss of the Parthenon Marbles for two centuries, since a British foreign ambassador known as Lord Elgin hatched a plan for their removal in 1801. Greece has been actively seeking their return since the country's independence in 1821, making this quite possibly the longest-lasting nonviolent international dispute in history. The Greek government questions the legality and ethics of the manner in which Britain acquired the marbles, and it calls into debate such issues as the ownership of antiquities and where such antiquities belong.

Bitterness over the marbles is evident in a squabble over the very name used to describe them. While the British Museum refers to them as the Elgin Marbles—museum officials are required to use this name according to an act of Parliament passed upon the marbles' purchase—Greeks, Greek-sympathizers, and an increasing number of historians call them the Parthenon Marbles,

THE CONFLICT

The Greek government seeks the return of its cultural treasures, the Parthenon Marbles, which were removed in the early nineteenth century by foreign ambassador Lord Elgin and installed in the British Museum.

Political

- The British government claims that it obtained the marbles legally, citing Elgin's receipt of a *firman*, or decree, from the Turkish sultan.

- The Greek government questions the legality and ethics of Elgin's removal of the Parthenon Marbles, claiming that Elgin stretched the terms of the *firman* and bribed Turkish officials.

Cultural

- Greece claims the marbles were removed illegally and are an integral part of the Parthenon.

- While British Prime Minister Tony Blair opposes returning the marbles to Greece, a majority of the ministers of Parliament (MPs), as well as a majority of the British public, support the repatriation of the artwork.

CHRONOLOGY

1801 Thomas Bruce, seventh earl of Elgin, hires a team of men to begin removing marbles from the Parthenon in Athens.

1810 Elgin's team completes the removal of the marbles.

1810–16 Elgin stores the marbles in a shed on the property of his London home while negotiating a price for them with the British government.

July 1, 1816 Under an act of Parliament the British government purchases the marbles for £35,000 (about half the sum that Elgin originally sought) and presents them to the British Museum for display.

1817 The British Museum displays the marbles in a temporary exhibition space, moving them to a more permanent gallery in 1831.

1846 Britain transfers the sovereignty of the Ionian Islands to Greece, boosting Anglo-Greek relations.

1940 Courting Greek support during World War II, Britain drafts a plan to return the marbles to Greece after the war. The plan is never enacted.

1950s During the anti-colonial uprising on Cyprus, Britain hints that it will return the marbles to Greece; in return, Greece is expected to cease supporting the Cypriot's terrorist campaign against the British colonial government.

1983 Greek Minister of Culture Melina Mercouri makes an impassioned plea to Britain for the marbles' return. Britain's Labour Party vows that it will return the marbles when it comes back into power.

1986 Greece begins to make plans for a new Acropolis Museum that will include exhibition space for the Parthenon Marbles. Objections to the museum's proposed design delay the project's progress.

1997 The Labour Party returns to power in Britain with the election of Tony Blair as prime minister. The new government reverses its position on the marbles, however, and declares that they will remain in Britain.

2000 Greece announces its goal to open the new Acropolis Museum in 2004, when Athens hosts the Olympic Games. Plans for the museum feature a grand gallery to house the Parthenon Marbles—a gallery that will remain empty if Britain maintains its refusal to return them.

eschewing recognition of the British lord who orchestrated their removal.

Contemporary visitors to Greece cannot help but get a sense of the country's long-standing grief over its missing artwork. In Athens activists hand out leaflets explaining the story of the plundered Parthenon and outlining Greece's demands for the marbles' return. Art exhibits featuring the Parthenon Marbles as a theme appear in the city's newly unveiled subway stations. In July 2000 a British doctor, Chris Stockdale, swam from Delos to Paros (neighbor islands in the Greek Cyclades) to demonstrate British sympathy for the return of the marbles. And famous visitors to Greece, including former U.S. President Bill Clinton and British actor Sean Connery, offer their opinions on the issue. Both Clinton and Connery support the return of the Parthenon Marbles to Greece. Connery, who visited Athens in January 2001, called Greece the "rightful place" to house the marbles. Britain, however, maintains that the best home for the Parthenon Marbles is not in Greece, but in their present location at the British Museum in London. The battle over custody continues to rage.

HISTORICAL BACKGROUND

"A Few Pieces of Stone"

The conflict over the Parthenon Marbles began in 1801, when their removal from the Parthenon was choreographed by Thomas Bruce, the seventh earl of Elgin and the British ambassador to the Ottoman Empire, which in his day included Turkish-ruled Greece. Elgin claimed that when he saw the state of the dilapidated Parthenon, which had suffered damages in wars with the Ottomans and Venetians, he was moved to save as much of it as he could. He also believed that British artists could benefit from a close study of the temple's treasures, which included beautifully crafted metopes (individual sculptures in high relief), friezes (continuous sculptures in low relief), and pediment statues (three-dimensional sculptures placed in the triangular pediments at either end of the temple).

Arranging to remove these artworks, Elgin obtained permission in the form of a *firman*, or decree, from the Turkish sultan. Scholars and legal experts, however, disagree about whether or not Elgin's *firman* gave him license to actually remove and take possession of the artwork. Surviving documents suggest that the sultan gave Elgin permission to draw the sculptures, to cast models of them in plaster or gypsum, and to take "a few pieces of stone." The Greeks and Greek sympathizers believe that Elgin stretched the terms of the *firman* to suit his purposes, translating "a few pieces of stone" into whole panels of friezes and entire metopes. For supporting evidence they point to the fact that Elgin continually bribed Turkish authorities when he encountered obstacles to his plan. The work *Lord Elgin and the Marbles* (1998), by British historian William St. Clair, illustrates that bribery accounted for about a quarter of the total expenses related to the marbles' removal.

Because the marbles were an integral part of the Parthenon, having been carved into the surface of the building after it had been erected, Elgin's men had to dismember the ancient temple in order to extract them. These workmen, led by Elgin's agent, the painter Giovanni Battista Lusieri, used saws, crow bars, and naval pulleys to carry out the marbles' removal, damaging the building and occasionally even destroying works of art in the process.

Elgin's booty from the Parthenon included 56 frieze panels, 15 metopes, and 17 pediment statues. In addition he took a column and a caryatid—an intricately detailed sculpture of a woman that served as a column—from the Erechtheion, another Acropolis structure, as well as many inscriptions and hundreds of vases. The removed sculptures and other works were crated and taken to the shipyard in Piraeus, the port of Athens, where Elgin secured boats for their passage to England. One of these boats, the *Mentor*, sank amid the Greek Islands; the antiquities resting on the floor of the Aegean Sea were eventually retrieved by Elgin's men. The entire job, from the marbles' extraction to their shipment to England, took almost ten years to complete. The last shipload of antiquities departed from Piraeus in 1810, aboard the warship *Hydra*.

The first shipload, containing 65 crates of antiquities, arrived in London in January 1804. Elgin, however, was not there to receive them. While he was traveling through France, war broke out between that country and Britain, and Lord Elgin was detained and imprisoned by an order of Napoleon. He languished in a French prison for two years, returning to Britain in 1806.

Once back in England Elgin attempted to sell the antiquities to the British government, which was not willing to pay the sum he demanded. The treasure-filled crates remained for years in a shed at Elgin's Park Lane house in London, where the marble sculptures fell prey to the country's dampness while Elgin negotiated. But there were other

hindrances to the sale besides the money involved. The acquirement of these artworks, which had been taken from Athens via dubious means, was already controversial. Many members of Parliament objected to the manner in which Elgin had attained them, suggesting that he had abused his powers as an ambassador and that his looting antics had brought disrepute to the nation. Some MPs felt that the marbles should be held only until the city of Athens insisted upon their return.

Eventually, however, the British government agreed to purchase the treasures and to house them in the British Museum. The motion carried by a slim parliamentary majority, with 82 favoring the purchase and 80 opposing it. The act of Parliament, which passed on July 1, 1816, stipulated that the government would pay Elgin £35,000, the equivalent of about US $2.7 million in 2000—only half the amount that he had originally requested—for the entire collection. Deep in debt, Elgin accepted this offer. The act also stated that the collection must remain intact and must bear the name the Elgin Marbles.

In early 1817 the British Museum set about transferring the marbles from Elgin's damp London shed to a temporary exhibition space. It was not until 1961 that the museum relocated the marbles to their current space, the Duveen Gallery, built expressly for them by Sir Joseph Duveen, a wealthy art dealer and patron.

Meanwhile, the marbles came to influence the art and architecture of nineteenth-century Britain. Churches, residences, and other buildings featured the Classical Greek style, which was regarded as the pinnacle of artistry. Poets waxed lyrical about the marbles, including John Keats, whose experience viewing the antiquities moved him to pen the sonnet "On Seeing the Elgin Marbles."

Critics, including the prominent British poet Lord Byron, wrote of the marbles' presence in Britain as shameful and passionately voiced the opinion that the marbles should be returned to their motherland. Byron included a passage to this effect in his poem "Childe Harold." Addressing the Parthenon as if it were a living spirit, Byron wrote,

Dull is the eye that will not weep to see
Thy walls defaced, thy mouldering shrines
    removed
By British hands, which it had best behooved
To guard those relics ne'er to be restored.
Curst be the hour when from their isle they roved,
And once again thy hapless bosom gored,
And snatch'd thy shrinking gods to northern
    climes abhorred!

GREEK FOREIGN MINISTER GEORGE PAPANDREUO, ACCOMPANIED BY HIS FAMILY, VIEWS A SECTION OF A FRIEZE FROM THE PARTHENON MARBLES AT THE BRITISH MUSEUM IN 2000. *(AP/Wide World Photos. Reproduced by permission.)*

A lover of Greek culture and people, Byron died fighting the Ottomans for Greek independence.

A later poet, Roger Casement, an Irish revolutionary who was hanged by the British during World War I (1914–18), wrote quite plainly of his opinion that the marbles should be returned: "Give back the Elgin marbles, let them lie/Unsullied, pure beneath the Attic sky. . . ."

Greece was an occupied country when Elgin took the marbles from the Parthenon, and the subjugated Greek people were unable to press for their antiquities' return with official statements and government action. But following Greek independence in 1821, the country made its feelings known about the missing marbles. Although the British seemed determined to hold on to these treasures, in some instances it seemed that negotiation might be possible. Such was the case in 1864, when the British empire transferred sovereignty of the Ionian Islands to Greece, ushering in a period of strong diplomatic relations between the two countries. Yet despite this, Britain rebuffed an appeal from Greece for the marbles' return at that time.

Later, Britain would use the marbles as a trump card when it wanted something from Greece. In 1940, needing a new ally after the fall of France in World War II (1939–45), Britain went so far as to draw up a plan for the marbles' return come peacetime. After the danger had passed, Britain's Foreign Office put the plan on hold, never to complete it. The British used similar tactics in the 1950s, when they wanted Greece to stop supporting a terrorist campaign against the British colonial government on Cyprus. Again, after the danger had passed in Cyprus, the British stopped suggesting that the marbles' return was a possibility.

A 200-Year-Old Debate

Over the years the basic arguments surrounding the Parthenon Marbles conflict have altered little. The British government has consistently claimed that it obtained the marbles legally, with a valid *firman* from the Turkish sultan. British officials have also supported the theory that Elgin's intention in taking the marbles was of a generous nature, since his goal was apparently to protect them from total destruction by the invading Turks.

Britain has also suggested that the Greeks seemed indifferent to the marbles' removal at the time, having passively witnessed Elgin's handiwork. Although the British acknowledge that contemporary Greeks are far from indifferent to the marbles' removal, they claim that air pollution in Athens would damage the marbles if items were returned to the Acropolis today or in recent history. Included in these latter points is an implication that Greece would not have been able to provide the fine stewardship of the marbles that has been given by the British Museum. Greek responses to this suggestion of British superiority have been particularly vehement.

Perhaps England's most insistent and persuasive defense for keeping the marbles is the theory that giving them back to Greece would set a precedent for the return of other "dubiously acquired" antiquities to their countries of origin and would trigger a lamentable emptying-out of museums around the world. At stake, this theory suggests, are the fine collections that have been acquired at world-renowned institutions like the Metropolitan Museum of Art, in New York City, and the Louvre, in Paris. These museums, like the British Museum, feature extensive Egyptian and Roman as well as Greek art holdings. The British suggest that if a precedent were set with the return of the Parthenon Marbles, then other countries, such as Egypt and Italy, would demand similar restitution.

Many museum curators, art historians, and government officials support this theory—not just Britons. These critics warn that dividing up artworks along national lines would have a regrettably provincial effect on the world's museums. Since most antiquities were acquired via dishonest means—wartime plunder, illegal archaeological digs, etc.—then the return of these antiquities, hundreds of years after their acquirement, would have a devastating effect on the world's museums. Only Egyptians would be able to exhibit the riches of their ancient tombs, and only Italians could display the preserved frescos of Pompeii, leaving other peoples of the world ignorant, perhaps, of these cultural achievements.

The Greeks have responded to all of these arguments from the British and have raised a few new points of their own. First, they have repeatedly declared that Elgin was not the protector that he claimed to be. They point out that he caused irreparable damage to the Parthenon, dismembering it to remove the artworks that had been integral to its structure. Indeed, because the sculptures and friezes were not displayed within the Parthenon but were carved into the sides of the building after it had been constructed, the marbles differ from other works of art in that they were part of a national monument. Greek officials claim that the marbles' return would restore integrity to this monument, even though they can never be reunited with it structurally.

MELINA MERCOURI

1925–1994 Although she first became famous as an actress and singer, Melina Mercouri was always politically active and passionate in her beliefs. This political zeal was a birthright, perhaps, as her grandfather had served as mayor of Athens for several years.

As an actress, the blond, green-eyed Mercouri was perhaps best known for her role as the kind prostitute in Jules Dassin's film *Never on a Sunday* (1960). Mercouri married Dassin, an expatriate American, in 1966 and collaborated with him on nine films.

Outspoken against the military dictatorship that ruled Greece at the time, Mercouri was exiled from her country in 1967. She returned after the fall of that government in 1974 and became increasingly involved in Greece's Socialist Party, winning a Parliament seat in 1977.

In 1981 she assumed the role of minister of culture, making the fight for the Parthenon Marbles' return the centerpiece of her career. She held the position of minister of culture through two socialist governments, totaling eight and a half years (1981–89 and 1993–94).

Mercouri died of lung cancer in 1994, and her State funeral was an occasion of great mourning throughout Greece.

Greece also maintains that it had not been indifferent to the marbles' fate when Elgin removed them. It points out that because the Turks had subjugated them, the Greeks were unable to take action to prevent Elgin's looting. For proof of nineteenth century Greeks' deep feelings for the Parthenon, scholars profess that when Turkish soldiers plundered the temple for lead to make bullets, their Greek adversaries sent some of their own bullets and begged the Turks to leave their monument alone. Many stories chronicle the Greeks' grief upon the marbles' removal, such as the myth that the remaining caryatids could be heard weeping at night for their lost sister. Historians point to quotes from Greeks in mourning for their lost marbles, such as this one (in Latin) appearing as graffiti in Athens in 1813: *Quod non fecerunt Gothi, hoc fecerunt Scoti* ("What the Goths did not do, the Scots did here"). Also often quoted is an alleged remark from an anonymous Greek in 1810: "Lord Elgin may now boast of having ruined Athens."

THOMAS BRUCE (A.K.A. LORD ELGIN)

1766–1841 A career diplomat, the Scottish nobleman Thomas Bruce, the seventh earl of Elgin, was appointed ambassador to the Ottoman Empire, which included Turkish-ruled Greece, in 1799. Desiring to be of service to the arts in Britain, Elgin hatched a plan to remove some of the famed Parthenon Temple sculptures and transport them from Athens to England. He assembled a team of artists and architects to oversee this job.

The dismantling of the Parthenon Marbles began in 1801; Elgin periodically visited the site to monitor his team's progress. While he was traveling through France in 1804, war broke out between France and Britain, and Elgin was imprisoned by an order of Napoleon. He was not released until 1806, although his wife, Mary, had been allowed to leave earlier.

Meanwhile, Elgin fell into debt from expenses related to the removal of the Parthenon Marbles. Discovering that his wife had had an affair while he was imprisoned, Elgin divorced her, incurring yet more debt. When the British government purchased the Parthenon Marbles in 1816 for £35,000—less than half the sum that Elgin had originally requested, but enough to pay his debts—he accepted.

Impoverished, Elgin died in 1841 in France, where he had gone to escape his creditors.

In response to Britain's claim that air pollution in Athens would harm the marbles, Greece concedes that pollution has been a problem in the past, yet it maintains that this is no longer so. Atmospheric pollution in Greece reached an all-time high in the 1960s, and the Parthenon suffered damages during that time from sulphur dioxide exposure. To salvage the antiquities Greece removed several Parthenon sculptures and installed them in the current Acropolis Museum, where pollution would not harm them. Meanwhile, efforts in Greece to reduce emission levels have been successful. The Greek government banned the use of cheap heating oil and low-grade diesel fuel in an effort to improve air quality. By 1998 Greece cited atmospheric reduction in the levels of smoke, nitrousoxide, and especially in sulphur dioxide, which dropped from two hundred micrograms per cubic meter to less than 40. In addition to these improvements, Greece points out that pollution wouldn't harm the marbles anyway, since upon their return they would be installed in the new Acropolis Museum.

Claims of superior British stewardship of the marbles have been under fire as well. In 1998, with the publication of a book by William St. Clair, details emerged about the museum's botched attempt to clean the marbles in the 1930s. Lord Duveen, the art dealer and patron who financed the gallery space that now houses the marbles, had ordered that the marbles be cleaned to remove their honey-colored patina and make them appear more white. The museum employed unskilled workmen to do this delicate work, which was carried out with wire brushes and harsh cleaning agents. Inevitably, the cleaning resulted in irreparable damage to the surface of the marbles. St. Clair claims in his book that the British Museum covered up the incident, preferring to remain seen as the marbles' trusted guardian.

Finally, Greece claims that the marbles' return does not have to set a precedent for the return of other treasures. The Greek government does not necessarily support the "fundamentalist" view that all artworks acquired via dubious means must be returned to their countries of origin. Greek antiquities reside in various museums around the world, but the Greek government is asking only for the repatriation of the Parthenon Marbles, since they are integral to a national monument.

"There Are No Elgin Marbles"

Greece's efforts to reclaim the Parthenon Marbles reached a new level of intensity in the 1980s, when a fiery Greek actress-turned-politician named Melina Mercouri entered the fray. Mercouri was named Greek minister of culture in 1981, and her fight for the return of the Parthenon Marbles became the cornerstone of her career. Soon after she became minister of culture, in an interview with the British Broadcasting Corporation (BBC), the British television network, Mercouri presented her request for the return of the marbles, launching an intense political campaign that she would continue for the rest of her life.

It is Mercouri who first insisted that the antiquities be called the Parthenon Marbles instead of the Elgin Marbles. In a 1986 speech to the Oxford Union, Britain's world-renowned debating society, she stated: "There is a Michael Angelo David. There is a Da Vinci Venus. . . . There are *no* Elgin Marbles!" In her plea for the marbles' return, she went on to appeal for understanding that the marbles were Greece's pride and a symbol of the nation's history and aspirations that should be

MELINA MERCOURI, A FORMER ACTRESS AND GREEK MINISTER OF CULTURE, SPOKE STRONGLY IN FAVOR OF HAVING THE PARTHENON MARBLES RETURNED TO GREECE. *(Corbis Corporation (Bellevue). Reproduced by permission.)*

Melina Mercouri died of cancer in March 1994. On the day of her State funeral, all Greeks, regardless of political affiliations, mourned her death. In an oft-repeated quote she is remembered to have said, "I hope to see the marbles back when I'm still alive. If they come later, I'll be reborn."

The Labour Party finally did come back into power in Britain in 1997, with the election of Tony Blair as prime minister in a landslide victory. All of Greece looked to Britain, remembering Labour's promise to return the marbles. Evangelos Venizelos, then Greek culture minister, wrote a letter to Britain's new government only hours after Blair's election, and he received a prompt and firm reply—the marbles would not be returned.

With Greece's hopes dashed, some placed the blame on Venizelos' hasty tactics. A few influential Athenians had been working quietly with the British Committee for the Restitution of the Parthenon Marbles, a group that had formed in the 1980s to campaign for the marbles' return. Venizelos' letter seemed to undermine these efforts. Most Greeks, however, did not blame their culture minister, but blamed instead Britain's Labour government for reversing its position on the issue.

Does Greece have reason to raise its hopes once again? While statements from Prime Minister Tony Blair seem to suggest that it does not, public opinion polls taken in 1998 and in subsequent years point to a change in public attitudes in Britain. In a 1998 poll a majority of Britons—more than two to one—said they supported returning the marbles to Greece. In a similar poll taken among British MPs, 47 percent favored returning the marbles, while 44 percent opposed their return. In 2000 *The Guardian* suggested that the majority was gaining ground, with 66 percent of MPs now supporting the marbles' return.

The fate of the Parthenon Marbles remains to be decided, and it seems to depend greatly on the personalities and preferences of those in power in Britain in future years. Greece has vowed that as long as the marbles reside in Britain, it will press for the antiquities' return. Whether or not the British government will ever part with the vast collection, which is perhaps the finest artistic gem featured in the British Museum, remains to be seen.

RECENT HISTORY AND THE FUTURE

Plans for Athens to host the Olympic Games in 2004 added a new sense of urgency to Greece's

returned to their homeland. "They are the essence of Greekness," she said.

Although it did not lead to immediate action on the part of the British, Mercouri's passionate campaign had far-reaching influences. More than ever, the dispute over the Parthenon Marbles fell into the international spotlight, and Mercouri's name became synonymous with a particularly Greek fighting spirit. In preparation for the return of the marbles, which she felt certain would happen one day, Mercouri launched plans for the construction of a new Acropolis Museum. It was she who first envisioned reserving a vast empty gallery that would await the marbles return to their homeland.

Although Britain's then-Prime Minister, Margaret Thatcher, paid little attention to Mercouri's campaign, other politicians in Britain were beginning to listen and to sympathize. Neil Kinnock, who led Britain's Labour Party from the early 1980s to the early 1990s, declared that when his party returned to power it would give the marbles back to Greece. Michael Foot, who preceded Kinnock as party leader, had also supported the return of the marbles. Neither Kinnock nor Foot, however, would become prime minister, so their promises were never realized.

ON SEEING THE ELGIN MARBLES

My spirit is too weak—mortality
Weighs heavily on me like unwilling sleep,
And each imagined pinnacle and steep
Of godlike hardship, tells me I must die
Like a sick Eagle looking at the sky.
Yet 'tis a gentle luxury to weep
That I have not the cloudy winds to keep
Fresh for the opening of the morning's eye.
Such dim-conceived glories of the brain
Bring round the heart and undescribable feud;
So do these wonders a most dizzy pain,
That mingles Grecian grandeur with the rude
Wasting of old Time—with a billowy main—
A sun—a show of a magnitude.

John Keats

efforts to regain the Parthenon Marbles. Anticipating that all eyes would be on Athens, with media coverage of the Games from every country, Greece hoped to showcase its cultural treasures, with the Parthenon Marbles being foremost among these.

Motivated by the 2004 goal, Greece's Foreign Minister George Papandreou paid a visit to London in the summer of 2000 to resume negotiations for the marbles' return. His intent was to cast aside former feelings of rancor over the issue and to bring a tone of camaraderie to the debate. "We want to move from controversy to partnership," he told British ministers of Parliament (MPs). The foreign minister also stated that Greece would no longer make an issue of the legal ownership of the marbles and suggested that Greece was open to exploring new ideas, including custody of the marbles by the European Union or the United Nations. The main objective for Greece, Papandreou suggested, was not to win back ownership of the marbles, but simply to restore them to their original site at the Parthenon temple in Athens.

Papandreou went on to propose a deal to the British government. If the British agreed to return the marbles, Greece would present the British Museum with some enticing rewards: a rotating exhibition of Greek art and a full set of state-of-the-art copies of the Parthenon Marbles, paid for by Greece. The British Museum would be the only institution in the world to receive such an offer, and the rotating exhibition and copies would assure that no rooms in the museum would remain empty

upon the marbles' return. Papandreou concurrently suggested that Britain would demonstrate enormous international goodwill if it returned the marbles in time for the 2004 Olympic Games.

Although Britain made no official response to the Greeks' offer for many months, initial replies from London suggested that the offer would be rejected. Alastair Campbell, spokesman for British Prime Minister Tony Blair, told the press that Britain had no intention of returning the marbles, and British Museum Director Robert Anderson held fast to a long-standing objective to retain the Greek treasures, which draw millions of visitors to the museum each year. Anderson pointed out what he considered to be a false suggestion in Papandreou's argument: If the marbles were given back to Greece, they would reside in a museum near the Parthenon, and—for reasons of safety—would not be reintegrated onto the temple itself, as Papandreou had implied.

Prime Minister Blair remained silent on the issue for many months and did not make a public response to the Greek offer until March 2001. His response was clear: The marbles would remain in the British Museum, and the exclusive offers of the Greek government would be rejected. In an interview published in *To Vima*, Athens's daily newspaper, Blair stated that the six million people who visit the British Museum each year are able to enjoy the Parthenon Marbles. As it stands the museum cannot single-handedly decide to return the Parthenon Marbles to Greece; only an act of parliament can make their return possible.

What will happen to the new Acropolis Museum in Greece, with its plans for a grand centerpiece gallery to house the marbles, if the marbles are to stay in Britain? According to Greece's Minister of Culture, Theodoros Pangalos, who spoke of the museum during a visit to New York in 2000, the centerpiece gallery will not be altered. Rather, the magnificent exhibition hall will remain empty until the marbles' return. Should the British never return them, said Pangalos, the space will remain empty forever.

BIBLIOGRAPHY

"Blair Rejects Elgin Marbles' Return," CNN News, March 24, 2001. Available online at http://www.cnn.com/2001/WORLD/europe/03/24/uk.marbles/index.html (cited June 1, 2001).

"Connery Calls for Marbles Return to Greece," CNN News, January 25, 2001. Available online at http://www.cnn.com/2001/WORLD/europe/01/25/greece.connery (cited June 1, 2001).

Gadney, Reg. "Steal Your Own Marbles," *Guardian*, June 7, 2000.

"Greece Pushing for Deal with Britain for Return of the Parthenon Statues," CNN News, June 5, 2000. Available online at http://www.cnn.com/2000/STYLE/arts/06/05/elgin.marbles.reut (cited June 1, 2001).

Hitchens, Christopher. *Imperial Spoils: The Curious Case of the Elgin Marbles*. New York: Hill and Wang, 1987.

Lennon, Troy. "Elgin's Idol Moments," *Daily Telegraph* (Sydney, Australia), December 1, 2000.

Lewis, Jo Ann. "Underground in Athens, a Dig at the British," *Washington Post*, November 12, 2000.

Loftus, Margaret. "They've Lost Their Marbles," *U.S. News and World Report*, June 26, 2000.

The Melina Mercouri Foundation. Available online at http://www.culture.gr/4/41/411/e41101.html (cited June 1, 2001).

Melina Mercouri's Speech to the Oxford Union. Available online at http://ares.math.utk.edu/marbles/speech.htm (cited June 1, 2001).

"The Parthenon Marbles." Available online at http://www.greece.org/parthenon/marbles/index.htm (cited June 1, 2001).

"Playing for All the Marbles: Greece, Britain Battle for Antiquities," *Christian Science Monitor*, June 25, 1998.

Randal, Jonathan C. "Greece Still Going for All the Marbles," *Washington Post*, May 31, 1997.

St. Clair, William. *Lord Elgin and the Marbles*. London: Oxford University Press, 1998.

"Stones to Die For," *The Economist*, March 18, 2000.

"Unplundering Art," *The Economist*, December 20, 1997.

—Wendy Kagan

Fujimori and Montesinos: Power, Politics, and Scandal in Peru

The Conflict

Alberto Fujimori served as president of Peru for ten years, from 1990 to 2000. Vladimiro Montesinos was the shadowy figure behind Fujimori's success. Employing near totalitarian rule under the auspices of a democratic society, Fujimori fell from power in September 2000, when he was implicated in a web of corruption, blackmail, and bribery run by Montesinos, his long-time advisor. With Fujimori fleeing to his ancestral homeland of Japan and Montesinos on the run from authorities, Peru faces the challenge of rebuilding its fragile democracy.

Political

- After first being elected president in 1990, Fujimori successfully battled the problems of hyperinflation and the onslaught of the rebel group *Sendero Luminoso* (Shining Path), which had crippled the nation for the previous decade.

- Fujimori was reelected in 1995 under a new constitution that centralized power in the office of the president and his actions as president became increasingly autocratic.

- Amidst widespread allegations of election fraud, Fujimori ran and won the election for the presidency again in 2000, even though the constitution prohibited a third term.

- After Fujimori fled Peru and stepped down as president, new elections brought Alejandro Toledo to power. Toledo must rebuild the people's trust in government and resolve the scandals left in the wake of Fujimori and Montesinos.

Economic

- Peru continues to be burdened by an international debt of more than $21 billion.

- Although Fujimori was able to slow inflation, prices and unemployment rates skyrocketed. The country has been in a recession since 1997.

For ten years President Alberto Fujimori ruled Peru with an ironclad hold on power. On July 28, 2000, he was inaugurated for an unprecedented third presidential term and, despite protests of election fraud, it appeared as though Fujimori remained firmly in control. During his administration the Peruvian economy, at the edge of total collapse in 1990, had been salvaged and the revolutionary groups *Sendero Luminoso* (Shining Path) and *Movimiento Revolucionario Túpac Amaru* (Túpac Amaru Revolutionary Movement; MRTA) had been brought under control. Having established a stable—albeit not completely healthy—economic and political system, no one could predict that before the end of the year, Fujimori would call for new elections, flee the country, resign from office, be denounced by the Peruvian Congress, and come under a variety of political and criminal charges.

The soap opera-like series of events were set into motion on September 14, 2000, when Lima's only independent television station, Channel N, aired a tape of Vladimiro Montesinos, Fujimori's long-time close adviser and head of the National Intelligence Service (SIN), offering a US$15,000 bribe to Luis Alberto Kouri, an opposition member of Congress, in return for his support of the president. The ensuing events brought near political chaos to Peru as allegations of widespread abuse and corruption within the Fujimori administration began to unfold.

HISTORICAL BACKGROUND

The future for Peru's fragile democracy remains in the balance of the most recent upheaval, but upheaval is not new to the people of Peru. Since the conquest of the great Inca civilization by Francisco Pizzaro in 1533, Peruvians have struggled with serious issues of military intervention, economic development, land reform, political unity, rebel factors, and corruption in places of power.

Spanish Influence

Although humans had most surely inhabited the land for thousands of years before, a reliable telling of Peru's history begins in 1438, with the ascension of Pachacuti to the throne of the Inca Empire. During the last half of the sixteenth century, under the leadership of Pachacuti, and later his son Topa Inca, the Inca civilization grew rapidly. Pachacuti is credited with the development of the city of Cuzco and many of its great structures still stand today. When it reached its maximum size, the Inca Empire encompassed nearly 380,000 square miles (984,195 square kilometers), from the present Colombia-Ecuador border to central Chile, and covered 2,500 square miles, or 6,475 square kilometers, of the west coast of South America.

In 1524 Spaniard Francisco Pizarro explored the area of Peru and became convinced of the vast wealth of the Incas. By 1927 Pizarro had returned to Spain and secured the permission of Charles I to conquer and control the area extending 600 miles (965 kilometers) south from Panama on behalf of the Spanish government. Pizarro established a base at San Miguel on the north coast with a force of 180 soldiers. Taking advantage of the internal strife caused by a civil war within the Inca Empire as Topa Inca's sons Inca Atahuallpa and Huayna Capac struggled for control, Pizarro traveled across the mountains to approach Atahuallpa, who had recently gained power over his brother. With 30,000 troops supporting him, Atahuallpa scoffed at the tiny band of European invaders. Upon meeting with Pizarro and refusing to acknowledge Spanish rule, however, he was taken prisoner. After securing a large ransom from Atahuallpa's officers Pizarro ordered the Inca ruler's execution, for his supposed involvement in the murder of his brother Huayna. In November 1533 Pizarro overtook the capital of Cuzco, and Spanish control effectively began.

The ensuing period of early colonization was fraught with conflict. Pizarro developed the city of Lima to serve as his headquarters and divided the lands among individual conquerors. Native Indians, who were forced into the service of the new landholders, revolted in 1536 under the leadership of Manco Capac. Indian rebellion, coupled with strife among the Spaniards, culminated in the assassination of Pizarro by rival factions in 1541. A series of viceroys appointed by the King of Spain failed to bring order to the chaos. Finally, in 1569, Viceroy Francisco de Toledo managed to organize the region, subduing the native population and controlling the greedy conquerors. Indian leaders were allowed to govern their local communities under traditional customs, but were required to collect a tribute and provide forced labor. Toledo also ordered the execution of Manco Capac's son, Túpac Amaru, fearing his rebellious activities would threaten stability. Under Toledo's administration the vast territory extended to all of South America, save Venezuela and Portuguese Brazil. Agriculture, based on forced Indian labor, was the primary industry; however, discovery of silver and mercury mines in regions that are now Peru and Bolivia became a source of vast wealth, most of which was centralized in Lima.

Beginning in the seventeenth century and continuing into the eighteenth century, Spain experienced a decline in international power and the result was reflected in growing difficulties in colonized South America. Spanish rulers gradually moved viceroy control out of Lima and into other regions, causing Lima to lose much of its prestige and power as the primary export city. In addition, Indian rebellions came with new force in the 1780 when Túpac Amaru II, a highly respected descendant of the last Inca emperor, led a revolt that extended throughout Peru and Ecuador. Although Túpac Amaru II was captured and executed in 1781, the revolt continued for several more years before finally being put down by the Spaniards.

Peruvian Independence

Peru's independence from colonial rule eventually came from forces outside the country. General José de San Martin of Argentina, hoping to take control of the silver mines of Upper Peru (now Bolivia) and rid the area of Spanish control, liberated the Peruvian seaport of Pisco and subsequently entered Lima. As a result, Peru declared independence on July 28, 1821. Unable to overcome the Spanish forces still residing in the interior, San Martin withdrew and left the liberation of the remainder of Peru to Simón Bolívar, who had already decolonized the northern regions of South America. After several important battles during 1824, Peru was permanently loosed from Spanish rule.

The transition from a colonized region into an independent state did not prove easy. After Bolívar withdrew in 1826 caudillos, or military leaders, who gained power and prominence during the struggle for independence, began to vie for power. The

CHRONOLOGY

1990 Political newcomer Alberto Fujimori defeats frontrunner Mario Vargas Llosa to win the presidential election.

1992 Fujimori suspends the constitution, dismisses Congress, and institutes martial law.

1995 Under a newly written constitution that allows for a president to serve two terms, Fujimori easily defeats Javier Pérez de Cúellar to win reelection.

May 28, 2000 Despite protests that his reelection to a third term is unconstitutional, Fujimori wins the presidential election in a runoff with Alejandro Toledo.

July 28, 2000 Amid violent demonstrations and claims of wide-spread election fraud and voter intimidation, Alberto Fujimori is sworn in for an unprecedented third term as Peru's president.

August 21, 2000 Fujimori and Vladimiro Montesinos, head of Peru's intelligence agency, hold a press conference to announce the dismantling of an international arms trafficking operation.

September 14, 2000 Peruvian television station, Channel N, airs a 57-minute video of Montesinos offering a $15,000 bribe to an opposition member of Congress.

September 16, 2000 Fujimori calls a press conference to announce his resignation from office, the dismantling of Peru's intelligence agency, and plans to hold new elections. Montesinos, now a fugitive, goes into hiding.

November 20, 2000 From Tokyo, Japan, Fujimori emails his resignation from the office of the presidency of Peru.

November 22, 2000 Valentin Paniagua is named Peru's acting president.

April 8, 2001 Presidential elections are held, resulting in a run-off between three main candidates.

June 3, 2001 Alejandro Toledo wins the runoff election and is elected to the presidency.

June 2001 Vladimiro Montesinos is arrested in Venezuela, and measures are immediately initiated to extradite him to Peru.

deposits (bird droppings) collected along the coast and offshore islands, which could be sold to other countries as fertilizer. The industry was developed by foreign corporations, but taxes on revenues provided the main source of national income for several decades. Castilla appeased liberals by relieving Indians from the burden of paying tributes and emancipating black slaves. Conversely, he placated conservative landowners by allowing the import of thousands of Chinese to provide a sufficient supply of cheap labor. He also established a state education system. The constitution adopted under his rule lasted into the 1900s.

Characteristic of much of Peru's history, advancements were followed by setbacks. In 1864 Spain failed in an attempt to regain control of Peru, but in the process put a heavy strain on the Peruvian financial resources. In the 1870s military rule was replaced by the success of the Civilian Party, a newly established cooperative of landowners and merchants, in its efforts to place Manuel Pardo as president. Pardo instituted a program of extensive internal development. The major undertaking was a railroad system that eased the isolation of the mountainous Peruvian interior. Beset by corruption on the part of government officials and contractors, however, the project cast Peru deeply into debt. The country's problems were further exacerbated when Peru lost its four-year war with Chile in 1883 and was forced to turn over control of the mineral-rich province of Tarapacá. The expense of the war, combined with the loss of income from the lost nitrate fields, put a further strain on Peru's national budget. In an attempt to stabilize the economy, Peru was forced to make heavy concessions to its foreign creditors. Under the agreement reached, Peru turned over control of the railroads for sixty-six years, allowed for the mining of three tons of guano annually, and to provide thirty-three annual payments of £80,000, or about US$115,000 in contemporary dollars.

By the turn of the twentieth century the Democratic Party had formed as a rival to the Civilian Party, creating a stable political environment based on direct, popular vote. Industrial development increased, most importantly copper mining and the agricultural production of sugar, cotton, and wool. The country, however, continued to depend heavily on foreign loans to finance internal developments. Under a new constitution adopted in 1920, communal Indian lands were protected from seizure and sale, but the failure to enforce the provision left much of the Indian population feeling bitter and disenfranchised from the ruling parties, which consisted almost exclusively of

governance of Peru came under a succession of ambitious military leaders. In 1845 General Ramón Castilla became president; he served until 1851, and again from 1855 to 1862. He instituted an economic program based on the export of guano people of European descent, leaving the door open for the formation of radical factions among the Indian population.

Military Rule

The American Popular Revolutionary Alliance (APRA), whose members became known as *apristas,* was formed by Victor Raúl Haya de la Torre, a then-exiled intellectual living in Mexico City. Created as a workers' union, the APRA wished to unify the Indian population and eliminate foreign imperialism, especially as it regarded U.S. interest in the Peruvian economy, by establishing a planned economy and nationalizing foreign-owned companies. The movement became popular among the poor masses and many intellectuals. In 1930 a military junta removed President Augusto Leguía y Salcedo, a member of the Civilian Party, from his 11-year rule. The following year the military allowed general elections, and Sánchez Cerro defeated APRA candidate Haya de la Torre. The APRA complained that the election results were fraudulent. The dissatisfaction of the APRA led to an organized uprising in the coastal town of Trujillo in July 1932, and the assassination of Sánchez Cerro in 1933 by apristas.

General Oscar Benavides, Sánchez Cerro's successor, moved quickly to reduce the power of the apristas by declaring the APRA party illegal, harassing its leaders, and appeasing the poor by creating social assistance programs. In 1939 presidential elections, the APRA supported the winning candidate, Manuel Prado, and during his administration, the APRA became a legal party again. The years of World War II (1939–45) proved prosperous for Peru—who sided with the Allied nations—due to the increased sales of petroleum, cotton, and minerals. With a stable economy, Peru looked toward improving its political stability as well. In 1945 José Luis Bustamante y Rivero, a lawyer with slightly liberal leanings, was elected president. The APRA won a majority of seats in the House of Representatives and one half the seats in the Senate. When Bustamante failed to follow the wishes of the aprista leadership, however, the APRA withdrew its support. Turning again to violent uprisings, the APRA led an insurrection in Callao, a city near Lima, which resulted in the party being outlawed once again.

In 1948 General Manuel Odría led a nonviolent coup and claimed control of the government. Instituting authoritarian rule, Odría aggressively sought to minimize the power of the APRA. Haya de la Torre found refuge in the Colombian embassy for five years before being forced to leave Peru for a time. Odría's restrictive reign did restore political stability, and the onset of the Korean War (1950–53) in the early 1950s helped fuel the economy, although, once again, much of the influx of money was from foreign-controlled sources. Manuel Prado returned to office, with the support of Odría, in the 1956 presidential election, defeating National Front Party candidate Fernando Belaúnde Terry. Although the economy improved, the plight of the country's landless and jobless poor was unaltered.

Political tensions, based on underlying economic problems, resulted in the stalemate election of 1962. With no candidate receiving the necessary one-third vote the military once again seized control of the government and called for new elections the following year. Belaúnde, now under the party name Popular Action, was awarded the victory in 1963. Over the next five years Belaúnde began a program of agrarian reform that resulted in the redistribution of more than a half million acres of land. He also began community development and irrigation programs, education reforms, and a plan for an improved road system. In 1968, however, the military forced Belaúnde to resign and a military junta, headed by Juan Velasco Alvarado, imprisoned political opponents and suspended the constitution.

Under a program of economic nationalization, the junta seized the holdings of the U.S.-based International Petroleum Company and instituted a policy that required a majority of stock in all Peruvian enterprises be held by Peruvian nationals. Other businesses, such as the fishmeal industry, were nationalized outright. Its strict control over the country, in which all press was censored, nationalized, or shut down, was tempered by such reforms as the recognition of women's rights, the establishment of rural schools, and the granting of autonomy to universities. Despite its efforts, the junta failed to obtain economic security as prices of fishmeal and copper dropped and the loans taken to create internal reforms once again added to the heavy burden of national debt.

In 1975 another military junta took charge, this time under the leadership of General Francisco Morales Bermúdez, but ever-changing policies did little to stabilize the economy. Determined to reinstitute constitutional rule, Morales called for the popular election of a Constituent Assembly, which was then charged with writing a new constitution. The APRA held a majority in the Assembly and Haya de la Torre was elected president. The new constitution went into effect on July 12, 1979, and the elections of 1980 returned Fernando Belaúnde Terry to the presidency. Belaúnde quickly denationalized all remaining state-held enterprises and opened Peru's doors to foreign imports. His free-market policies combined with falling prices of Peru's main exports, the overwhelming national debt, and the devastating effects of El Niño, put the economy on the brink of collapse. In the five-year period between July 1980 and June 1985, the inflation rate rose a staggering 3,240 percent, and the sol, the issue of Peruvian currency, lost so much value that it was replaced by the inti in 1986.

With the country in a state of economic chaos, the APRA was able to secure the election of its presidential candidate for the first time in 1985. The new president, Alan Garcia Pérez, boldly declared that Peru would only commit 10 percent of its export earnings to its foreign debt, totaling almost $14 billion. As a result, the International Monetary Fund announced that Peru would be ineligible for any further foreign loans until a more plausible repayment plan was in place. Unable to jumpstart the economy, Garcia moved to nationalize the banks in 1987, which provoked a nationwide panic. By the end of his term, the country was nearing political and economic upheaval. A series of large-scale general strikes and the increasing guerrilla activities of the Shining Path provoked Garcia's own party to reject him.

"El Chino" Enters Office

It was with this political and economic history of upheaval and into this dire situation that Alberto Fujimori came as the country's political and economic savior. Prior to serving public office Fujimori, the son of Japanese immigrants, worked as a dean at Peru's Agrarian National University in La Molina and later hosted a television talk show, *Getting Together*, which blended agricultural issues with politics. In 1989 he created *Cambio 90*, or Change 90, a political party with the simple theme "honesty, technology, and work." Fujimori adeptly read the political minds of Peruvians, who were resentful of so many years of failed politics. As an outsider, he incited the imagination of the people, convincing them that positive change was possible.

Fujimori obtained his success by appealing to the poor and marginalized. He traveled extensively among the poor, listened to their plight, and assured them of his commitment to improving their conditions. Embracing the nickname "El Chino," even though it means "Chinese" in Spanish, he often donned blue jeans, a brightly colored Andean poncho and a *chullo* (hat) as he rode a tractor around the countryside. Always reminding the resi-

PUBLIC PROTESTS TOOK PLACE AGAINST PRESIDENT ALBERTO FUJIMORI AND HIS CLOSE ADVISOR VLADIMIRO MONTESINOS AFTER A BRIBERY SCANDAL ERUPTED. *(AP/Wide World Photos. Reproduced by permission.)*

dents of shantytowns of his humble beginnings, he told them he would be "*un presidente como tu*" (a president like you). He made a connection with the poor, who had long felt left out of the political process and ignored by the political elite.

Fujimori's main opponent in the 1990 presidential election was award-winning Peruvian novelist Mario Vargas Llosa, a member of the center-right Democratic Front Movement, who was widely considered the frontrunner. Fujimori attacked Vargas Llosa's pledge to "Europeanize" Peru, an idea that made many uncomfortable as it recalled the long years of European colonial rule. Suprisingly, Fujimori, a first generation Peruvian, was able to present himself as the commoner, a candidate of the *informales* (common people), and at the same time successfully cast the long shadow of aristocratic European influence over his native Peruvian opponent. It did not help that Vargas Llosa, in contrast to Fujimori, often appeared stiff and uncomfortable campaigning among the *campesinos* (peasants).

Just three weeks before the election, polls showed Fujimori with as little as five percent of the vote. He gained ground rapidly, however, in what became known as "the Fujimori phenomenon" or the "Fujimori tsunami." The final results of the election gave 32 percent of the vote to Vargas Llosa and 29 percent to Fujimori, with three other candidates splitting 30 percent of the vote. After failing to convince Fujimori to concede, Vargas Llosa scrambled to regain control of the electorate. However, Fujimori, who remained consistently in the middle ground between liberal and conservative factions, was able to paint Vargas Llosa as an uncompromising radical conservative, and the results of the run-off showed the success of Fujimori's tactics. Although Vargas Llosa was able to secure 70 percent of the upper class votes, he only managed to get 20 percent from the shantytown districts and rural areas. The final result gave Fujimori an easy victory, winning 62 percent of the vote to Vargas Llosa's 38 percent.

The Economy

Fujimori entered office and wasted no time in taking drastic measures to curb hyperinflation. Instituting policies that were actually much harsher than those proposed by Vargas Llosa, Fujimori was able to drastically reduce inflation—but not without heavy costs. Price subsidies and social spending were cut and interest rates and taxes were increased. As a result, prices soared at the same time that thousands lost their jobs. Gasoline prices jumped 3,000 percent and food prices rose 500 percent. Within two years the average Peruvian income dropped by one third, and over one half of the population was living in poverty. Surprisingly, despite what became known as "Fujishock," Fujimori's popularity among the poor remained high. It seemed that Peruvians longed for political and economic stability so badly that they were willing to allow the president to take whatever measures necessary. Because he had connected with the masses during the campaign, they now trusted that the decisions made by Fujimori, although harsh, were made in their best interest.

Not only did Fujimori move quickly to regain economic control of the country's flailing economy, he also immediately began working to secure the support of the Peruvian military. In this matter, Fujimori, who never served in the armed forces, turned to Montesinos, a former army captain bounced from the position in the late 1970s for selling state secrets to the U.S. Central Intelligence Agency (CIA). Since that time, Montesinos had served as a lawyer, specializing in defending drug traffickers. He also represented Fujimori prior to the election, helping him clean up some tax problems that had begun to surface in the press. The day after his inauguration, Fujimori replaced the commanding officers of the army and navy. The following year he convinced Congress to grant him the power to promote and retire officers at will, thus doing away with a time-honored system of advancement based on rank. Montesinos, who still had many contacts in the military, was given free reign over military promotions, which he used to place key supporters in important positions and force into retirement any officers who showed opposition to Fujimori's politics.

The Shining Path

Next Fujimori turned to the problem of the rebel groups, the Shining Path and the MRTA. Since its inception in 1970 the Shining Path had claimed over 20,000 mostly civilian lives—including 400 assassinations of public officials, priests, and civic leaders between 1988 and 1992—caused an estimated $15 billion in economic destruction, and created 200,000 internal refugees. The Shining Path has its roots in the isolated south-central Andean region of Ayacucho. Once important as a stop-off point between Lima and Cuzco, Ayacucho had steadily been allowed to deteriorate. By the 1980s more than 50 percent of the area's half-million inhabitants were illiterate, and the per capita income for the peasant communities was below $50 a year.

In 1963 Abimael Guzmán Reynoso came to teach philosophy at Ayacucho's National University of San Cristóbal de Huamanga. In 1966 Guzmán and numerous other facility members and students joined the Lima-based Maoist Peruvian Communist Party-Red Flag (PCP-BR). By 1970, however, the growing Ayacucho communist community left the PCP-BR to form the Peruvian Communist Party-Sendero Luminoso, named after the assertion by José Carlos Mariátegui that "Marxism-Leninism will open the shining path to revolution." In the ensuing years the Shining Path became a dominant force at the university, controlling such important matters as course content and the selection of faculty. University graduates who adhered to Guzmán's Maoist communist vision began to disperse the message throughout the region as they filled teaching positions across the department of Ayacucho.

The Shining Path's strategy turned violent on May 18, 1980, the day that Belaúnde was reelected to the presidency. *Senderista* militants burned ballot boxes in the town of Chuschi, located in the southern part of Ayacucho. Belaúnde took little notice of the action; however, when the Shining Path attacked a police post at Tambo in Ayacucho's La Mar province in October 1981, Belaúnde reacted by placing La Mar, along with four other Ayacucho provinces, under a state of emergency, which suspended several constitutional rights, including the right to public assembly and the necessity of a warrant to issue an arrest or search a house. Belaúnde also sent in the Civil Guard's elite *Sinchi* (meaning "those who can do anything"). The battalion proved to be filled with poorly trained and corrupt officers who reportedly raped, tortured, and killed indiscriminately anyone suspected of being connected to the Shining Path. Furthermore, the Sinchi's efforts provided little protection against the growing force of senderistas.

By 1982 the Shining Path had increased its numbers and expanded guerilla activities. It attempted to shut down local markets to force peasants to remove themselves from capitalist activities. Twice in 1982 it caused blackouts in Lima by dynamiting numerous electrical sources. The Shining Path also began a campaign of assassination, targeting those it deemed to be "enemies of the people," including mayors, government officials, landowners, and business owners, along with peasants who were labeled as traitors to the cause. In March 1982 the senderistas showed their strength and organization in an attack on an Ayacucho prison that resulted in the escape of 247 inmates, many of whom were Shining Path leaders. In September 1982, between 10,000 and 30,000 people attended the funeral of the slain 19-year-old senderista Edith Lago. Clearly the Shining Path had, by fear or admiration, secured the popular support of the region.

As more and more military troops were sent in to put down the uprising, the death toll increased. With the military coming under allegations of widespread human rights abuses, the Shining Path continued to increase its violent activities. Civilians were often caught in the middle. Fearful of both the military and the senderistas, some campesinos took up arms themselves in an attempt to protect themselves from attacks from either side. The situation gained international attention in January 1983 when eight journalists were murdered in the remote village of Uchuraccay. The subsequent investigation led to no conclusions, and every witness to the crime seemingly disappeared.

By the mid-1980s the Shining Path had discovered the lucrative business of the coca trade and struck an attractive arrangement with peasant growers. On one hand, the senderistas protected the peasants from drug traffickers who tried to intimidate them into selling the coca at the cheapest price possible; and on the other hand, they protected the peasants from government officials and police intervention. By levying "taxes" on the narco-traffickers, the Shining Path was able to bring in an estimated $30 million, which allowed the organization to improve its military operations, provide above average salaries for its soldiers—now totaling between 5,000 and 7,000—and expand the area of its control by moving into regions outside of Ayacucho. Throughout the remainder of Belaúnde's administration and into García's term in office, the Shining Path wreaked havoc on the country, and some even began to speculate on the possibility that the senderistas would eventually overtake Lima.

Movimiento Revolucionario Túpac Amaru

As the Shining Path spread northward, another guerrilla organization surfaced. In 1983 the MRTA, led by former aprista Víctor Polay Campos, a friend of Alan García and a victim of Fujimori's forced retirement from the military, began a series of bombings and assassinations in Lima. Unlike the rural beginnings of the Shining Path, the MRTA focused its activities in Lima, targeting foreign companies and banks and often acting in Robin Hood fashion by dispersing stolen food among poor neighborhoods. It maintained a consistent media presence by staging major violent publicity stunts and regularly appearing on radio and television stations it had either seized or blackmailed.

When Fujimori took office, approximately 40 percent of the country was under martial law. The military's battle against the insurgency had proved uncoordinated and ineffectual, and military human rights abuses had earned the fear and condemnation of the peasant communities. Fujimori moved to centralize the power over the military in his hands. In addition to gaining control over military promotions, which could then be exploited for political purposes, at the end of 1991, Fujimori issued a decree that created special military courts to try alleged terrorists. He also issued a decree that members of the military could not be tried for human rights abuses in civilian courts but would always appear before a military court. Since military courts almost never delivered guilty verdicts in cases of human rights violations, Fujimori effectively granted immunity to members of the military in their battle against the Shining Path. As a result, the brutal tactics of the armed forces became a growing counterweight to the indiscriminate violence of the Shining Path.

Other than the capture and imprisonment of Guzmán in 1992, which dealt a serious blow to the

ALBERTO FUJIMORI

1938– Alberto Fujimori served as the president of Peru for ten years (1990–2000) before being driven from office due to a scandal incited by his close advisor Vladimiro Montesinos. Fujimori, the son of Japanese immigrants, was born on 1938, and attended the Agricultural National University in La Molina, where he graduated with honors in 1961. In 1967 he received a Master's degree in mathematics from the American University in Wisconsin.

At the start of his professional career Fujimori served as the dean of the faculty of sciences at the Agrarian National University in La Molina from 1984 to 1989. He also developed a reputation as a political analyst as the host of the television talk show *Getting Together,* which combined agricultural topics with current political issues. Fujimori was married to Susana Higuchi until 1994, four years into his first term as president, when he dismissed her from her duties as first lady for disloyalty. She later earned a seat in Congress as member of an opposition party. They had four children.

Under the party name "Change 90," with the simple slogan, "honesty, technology, and work," Fujimori won the 1990 presidential election. He quickly addressed the economic issue of hyperinflation and, in 1992, suspended the constitution, dismissed Congress, and invoked martial law to stabilize the growing threat from the leftist rebel organization the Shining Path. Easily winning reelection in 1995, during his second term Fujimori came under increasing criticism for his near-dictatorship style of governing. National and international outcry was heard when Fujimori announced that he would run for an unconstitutional third term. Although he won the 2000 presidential election, the growing dissatisfaction of the people, coupled with the explosion of corruption charges instigated by the

ALBERTO FUJIMORI. *(AP/Wide World Photos. Reproduced by permission.)*

actions of intelligence head Vladimiro Montesinos, caused Fujimori to lose his grip on power.

Fearful of pending charges that could vary from corruption to murder, Fujimori fled to Japan, where he sought and received recognition of Japanese citizenship, which would allow him to stay in Japan indefinitely. Speculation has arisen that Fujimori was actually born in Japan, which would have made it illegal for him to serve as Peru's president; Fujimori denies the charge. He is currently working on a book about his experiences and numerous video documentaries. He maintains his innocence and declares that he had no knowledge of Montesinos' wrongdoings.

Shining Path, Fujimori's decision to foster the development of *rondas*, or civilian military patrols, was the most important step in releasing the countryside from the terrorism of the senderistas. Rondas were first established in local communities to combat rustlers and thieves. Later they were forced into service by the military to patrol against the senderistas. By the early 1990s, however, the peasants had grown increasingly tired of the harsh, arbitrary rule of the Shining Path, and Fujimori

wisely took advantage of the turn in sentiment. By replacing often racially biased *costeños* (residents of the coast) with Quechua-speaking military officers who were natives of the interior regions, Fujimori was able to rebuild rapport with the campesinos. The army distributed over 10,000 guns to the rondas, often in a ceremony attended by Fujimori himself. Thereafter, these community-based civil watch groups proved to be effective in reducing the effectiveness of the Shining Path.

"Self Coup"

On April 5, 1992, Fujimori shocked the Peruvian population by declaring a "self coup." After twelve years of democratic government Fujimori dismissed Congress, suspended the constitution, and ordered the arrest of several opposition leaders, including an unsuccessful attempt to arrest Alan García, who had returned to favor in the Democratic Front Party. Declaring that Congress was serving as an obstacle to progress, Fujimori claimed that his action was the first step to creating a true democracy. Although widely denounced by the international community, Fujimori received the approval of the majority of the Peruvian population. When the United States withdrew economic aid and support, however, Fujimori agreed to call for the election of a constituent assembly to rewrite the constitution. After appeasing the international community, Fujimori dismantled the judiciary structure, which was filled with García appointees, and filled the court benches with his own selections.

Just as the Shining Path was moving toward a plan to overtake Lima, Guzmán was unexpectedly captured. Although Fujimori quickly assumed credit for the arrest, the process had begun several years earlier during García's administration. The national intelligence police, known as DINCOTE, trailed a suspected senderista who had just been released from jail. The senderista led DINCOTE agents to Guzmán's safe house. After an elaborate stakeout, agents descended on the house and arrested Guzmán without incident. The DINCOTE arrested two more Shining Path leaders and discovered the master computer files for the Shining Path organization, which in turn led to the detainment of over one thousand suspected senderistas over the following weeks. Although the violence did not completely cease, the arrests dealt the Shining Path a crippling blow and gave Fujimori a boost in popularity before the 1995 elections. Fujimori maintained his grip on power in part due to the dismantling of the Shining Path and the sharp decline in inflation, and in part due to the lack of any viable, organized opposition. No other possible leader stepped to the front to challenge Fujimori.

When the constitution was rewritten in 1993, the new document centralized power in the hands of the president. One significant change permitted a president to serve two terms, which allowed Fujimori to run for reelection in 1995. The close vote on the adoption of the new constitution (52 percent in favor; 48 percent against) showed Fujimori's popularity slipping among the poor, who continued to suffer under his program of stabilization without the institution of economic safety nets previously promised by Fujimori. With less than two years before the next election, Fujimori quickly moved to regain the support of the public by substantially increasing social spending.

In February 1995 a long-standing border dispute with Ecuador was resolved when both countries signed a truce. The easing of tensions along the border, coupled with an improving economy, was enough to give Fujimori an easy victory over former United Nations secretary general Javier Pérez de Cúellar in the April 1995 presidential election. Fujimori continued to stir controversy. In a move to secure the support of the military, in June 1995, he granted full amnesty to those previously found guilty of human rights abuses. Also, his prime minister, Dante Cordova, resigned in protest over Fujimori's rapid implementation of free-market reforms.

Fujimori faced another serious guerrilla attack when the MRTA besieged the Japanese embassy in Lima in December 1997. Fourteen MRTA rebels took hostage approximately 500 diplomats, politicians, and business leaders and demanded the release of 500 prisoners, including leader Victor Polay, and also called for the reversal of Fujimori's free-market policies. The drama continued for months as negotiations, in which Fujimori refused to compromise, dragged on. Several groups of hostages were released, and by April 1998, 72 people remained captive. Fujimori ended the situation four months after it started by ordering a military assault on the embassy. All but one of the hostages were rescued, and all of the rebels were killed. The one hostage not rescued in the assault was killed. Hailed at the time for his decisive action, Fujimori may now face charges of human rights abuse if evidence substantiates the reports that he ordered the secret execution of the rebels during the raid. Media reports have surfaced that two female rebels attempted to surrender but were nonetheless gunned down. Another report, coming from a former hostage, testified that he saw three rebels alive and tied up in the garden after the raid. In March 2001 several MRTA bodies were exhumed so that forensic science could be used to determine whether the rebels died within the context of the battle or were later executed at short range.

Reelection Controversy

In 1999 Fujimori came under extensive criticism at home and abroad when he announced his decision to seek an unconstitutional third term. Fujimori's proponents argued that he had only served one term under the new constitution and was therefore eligible to run for reelection; however, according to a constitutional tribunal, Fujimori was legally prohibited from running in the 2000 election. True to form, Fujimori ignored the tribunal's decision, dismissed the three justices that opposed him, and launched his campaign, which was fraught with accusations of corruption. Reportedly, Vladimiro Montesinos was instrumental in launching a smear campaign of Fujimori's opponents and orchestrating a campaign of dirty tricks, including intimidating the media, paying people to toss eggs at opponents' rallies, and outright ballot fraud. The election held on April 9 failed to give Fujimori an outright majority and a runoff was scheduled for May 28 between Fujimori and his leading opponent Alejandro Toledo. Toledo, however, boycotted the runoff and encouraged Peruvians to do the same. An observer mission from the Organization of American States withdrew prior to the runoff, claiming that conditions for a fair electoral process did not exist.

With public sentiment turning against Fujimori, Alejandro Toledo was successful in staging popular demonstrations, including weekly washings of the Peruvian flags. In the two days leading up to Fujimori's swearing in ceremony on July 28, 2000, Toledo led one of the largest public demonstrations in Peru's history, called the "Marcha de los Cuatro Suyos." As Fujimori was sworn in, violence erupted that resulted in the death of six people and the destruction of numerous government offices. Even before the release of the damaging videos, it appeared that Fujimori had begun to lose the confidence of many of the people who had first placed him in office ten years earlier. The ensuing arms trafficking scandal followed quickly by the bribery scandal took Fujimori from the pinnacle of power to self-instituted exile within four months.

In retrospect many analysts point to the emerging arms trafficking scandal, which led to political tensions with the United States, as the beginning of Fujimori's downfall. Ironically, Montesinos, the man who had helped Fujimori maintain his control of the government for ten years, was largely to blame for Fujimori's fall from power. In March 1999 Peruvians showing military identification reached an agreement with the Jordanian government to purchase ten thousand AK-47 assault rifles, which were then transported across the Atlantic by a Russian-flown airplane. The rifles, however, never arrived in Peru. Instead, they were parachuted over Colombia into the hands of members of the guerrilla group, the Revolutionary Armed Forces of Colombia. By the end of 1999 the

PRESIDENTAL ELECTION RESULTS, 2000

2000 Primary	No. of Votes	%
Alberto Fujimori	5,528,394	50%
Alejandro Toledo	4,460,812	40
7 Other Candidates	1,095,311	10

2000 Secondary	No. of Votes	%
Alberto Fujimori	6,041,685	74%
Alejandro Toledo	2,086,215	25
Null/Blank	3,672,410	0

Source: Oficína Naciónal de Procesos Electorales. Available online at http://200.4.197.67/histo_elec/resant/elecgen/20001_nac.html, and at http://200.4.197.67/histo_elec/resant/elecgen/20002_nac.html.

PERU'S 2000 PRESIDENTIAL ELECTION SPARKED CONTROVERSY WHEN ALBERTO FUJIMORI RAN FOR AN UNPRECEDENTED THIRD TERM IN OFFICE, WHILE MAIN OPPONENT ALEJANDRO TOLEDO LEVELED CHARGES OF FRAUD. TOLEDO WON THE PRESIDENCY IN NEW ELECTIONS HELD IN 2001. *(The Gale Group.)*

United States, an ally of the Colombian government, had discovered that Peru was the source of the rebels' new weapon supply.

Montesinos, known as "The Doctor" for his ability to fix any situation, assured Fujimori that the illegitimate deal had been done by a renegade group of former military officers, using forged documents and identification. Montesinos claimed he had broken up the arms ring and arrested the guilty parties. On August 21, 2000, Fujimori, accompanied by Montesinos who was seldom seen in public, gave a news conference claiming they had made a spectacular bust and had ended the illegal operation. Unknown to Fujimori was the fact that Montesinos had been linked to the scandal and the news was about to break, a latter revelation that caused Fujimori great embarrassment. Some political analysts speculate that the release of the video was timed by the U.S. Central Intelligence Agency's (CIA) decision to divert attention away from the arms scandal, because the CIA and the SIN had been working partners in the war on drug trafficking. The CIA, like Fujimori, quickly came to consider Montesinos a liability and wanted to cut

VLADIMIRO MONTESINOS

1945– Born in Arequipa, Peru, in 1945, Vladimiro Lenin Montesinos Torres served in the army. He rose to the rank of captain before being dismissed from service in the late 1970s for supposedly supplying state secrets to the U.S. Central Intelligence Agency (at a time when Peru was receiving support from the Soviet Union). After his discharge from the army, Montesinos served as a lawyer, specializing in defending drug traffickers. He first represented Fujimori prior to the 1990 election when he called in numerous favors with members of the judiciary to help resolve some of Fujimori's tax problems that had begun surfacing in the press.

As Fujimori's power increased, so did Montesinos' powers expand. Hardly ever seen in public, he acted as Fujimori's closest advisor. He headed the National Intelligence Service and was given free reign to make military appointments. Suspected of corruption for many years, Montesinos quickly went from one of the country's most powerful men to a fugitive when evidence of his illegal activities found its way into the media in September 2000. He was wanted for such crimes as bribery, drug trafficking, and human rights abuses. In June 2001 Montesinos was captured in Venezuela and Peru immediately implemented extradition measures so that he could face justice in Peru.

him loose. When Fujimori learned that Montesinos had tricked him into participating in the bogus news conference, the relationship was permanently fractured between the two, and the beginning of the political end for both of them.

The Video Scandal

The damaging bribery video first came into the hands of congressman Luis Iberico, who received the tape from an unidentified source, assumed to be a member of the military with access to Montesinos' fortress-like SIN headquarters. Iberico, a former television journalist, was previously employed by then-exiled Baruch Ivcher, an Israeli-born owner of a television station that had been previously shut down for airing critical remarks about Fujimori. Iberico had the tape in his possession for two weeks before airing it on September 14, the same day Montesinos likely discovered Iberico had possession of the video. When he began receiving threatening phone calls, Iberico, who believed his life was in imminent danger, decided to air the tape immediately and called a press conference for that evening.

As the 57-minute video played on Channel N, Fujimori was called from a meeting with Algerian dignitaries and hurried to a room with a television. Reports of Fujimori's response varied. Supporters noted that Fujimori was deeply saddened, worried about his own legacy, and that feelings of moral obligation to the Peruvian people determined his decision to commit political suicide at his press conference on September 16, 2000. Other accounts report that Fujimori was furious with Montesinos and fired him immediately. Still other reports describe a daylong exchange of telephone calls between Fujimori and Montesinos that ended with Montesinos issuing a violent threat. Whatever the actual circumstances, clearly the long relationship between Montesinos and Fujimori, which had been seriously strained by the arms scandal, had become completely severed.

On September 16, 2000, just two days after the release of the video to the public, Fujimori addressed the nation in a carefully worded recorded statement saying that he would hold new elections as soon as possible, in which he would exclude himself as a candidate, and that he would disband the SIN, thus signifying a break with Montesinos. "I don't want to become a disturbing factor, much less an obstacle to the strengthening of the democratic systems," he said in his statement. The nation was stunned. Fujimori had long ignored his critics and was not known for being overly concerned with maintaining the purity of democratic systems. Therefore, his seemingly sudden decision left many guessing at the motives for his actions.

For more than a decade Fujimori had held off his opponents and secured substantial power in all areas of government, including the military, the legislature, and the judiciary branch. A great part of the credit for Fujimori's political success is attributed to the behind-the-scenes efforts of Montesinos, a shadowy figure seldom seen in public, who had long been suspected of corruptive practices. After the release of the bribery video, it was soon discovered that Montesinos had over 2,600 other videotapes, secretly recorded in his office, depicting transactions of bribery involving many of the country's prominent leaders. Although no evidence existed that Fujimori had direct knowledge or involvement in Montesinos' activities, the sensational scandal opened the door to a slew of questions regarding Fujimori's connections to his powerful adviser's activities.

At first, Fujimori attempted to backpedal, announcing just three days later, on September 19,

POLITICIANS AND OTHER OFFICIALS WERE IMPLICATED IN BRIBERY WHEN SECRET RECORDINGS, KNOWN AS "VLADIVIDEOS," CAME TO LIGHT. THE RECORDINGS WERE MADE BY VLADIMIRO MONTESINOS, WHO QUICKLY FLED WHEN THEY WERE REVEALED. *(The Gamma Liaison Network. Reproduced by permission.)*

2000, that he would not leave office until July 28, 2001, after elections were held in March or April. In differing occasions, he intimated that he might run for the presidency again in 2006 or perhaps seek a seat in the Congress. His postponement of the new elections and the delay of his own removal from office infuriated his opponents, who quickly called for his resignation and the establishment of a transitional government. As scandalous news continued to flood the press, Fujimori could not regain his grip on power. Montesinos had gone on the run, leaving the country for Panama for a time before allegedly returning in secret to Peru three weeks later, having been denied immunity in Panama. He became the country's most wanted fugitive.

Fujimori Leaves Office

In mid-November Fujimori's chances at political recovery received a deadly blow when Martha Hildebrandt, the Speaker of Congress and one of the president's most ardent supporters, was routed from office. For the first time in eight years the opposition held control of Congress. Just hours before the censure vote on Hildebrandt, Fujimori left the country, supposedly to attend an Asian summit in Brunei on November 16. He only landed in Brunei for a few hours, however, before going on to Japan. At first offering numerous reasons for his stopover—such as wanting to visit his parents, he had a cold, and he was negotiating a loan for Peru—it was soon apparent that Fujimori had no intentions of returning to Peru. In an email sent from Tokyo, Japan, on November 19, Fujimori an-

TERRORIST CASE BROUGHT TO NEW LIGHT IN "VLADIVIDEO"

New Yorker Lori Berenson, a former Massachusetts Institute of Technology student, was sentenced to life imprisonment in 1996 by a Peruvian military court on the charge of treason for her involvement in a thwarted plan to overthrow Congress undertaken by the Túpac Amaru Revolutionary Movement, or MRTA. The United States has pressured Peru to reconsider the case, but until a "Vladivideo," a secret tape made by Vladimiro Montesinos, was revealed, Peru denied any misconduct or denial of due process in the case.

Prior to the Vladivideo's release, on August 28, 2000, Peru's supreme military court overturned the initial ruling and the sentence of life imprisonment for Berenson and ordered a new trial due to pressure from the United States. Because Berenson was not a leader in the rebel group—a prerequisite for a charge of terrorism—the charges against Berenson were lowered to terrorist collaboration and her case was remanded to a civil court. Of the evidence considered against her favor was the request for her release from prison by MRTA rebels who had stormed the Japanese embassy in Lima in 1996.

Berenson has consistently denied any involvement in the plot to overtake Congress and maintains that she did not know that her former housemates were members of the MRTA. Defenders have accused former President Alberto Fujimori of using the case to prove that he is tough on terrorism. New evidence of the political manipulation of the case was revealed in one of the infamous "Vladivideos." The video, secretly recorded by intelligence director Vladimiro Montesinos, shows Montesinos and former Foreign Minister Eduardo Ferrero discussing how to handle the case to appease the United States but without acknowledging that the military court denied her due process.

A new trial began in March 2001, with testimony continuing into April. Berenson's supporters in the United States declared that retrying Berenson constituted as double jeopardy (being tried for the same crime twice) and demanded her immediate release. On June 20, 2001, despite any questions that may have arisen with the discovery of the Vladivideo, the civil court convicted Berenson of terrorist collaboration and sentenced her to 20 years in prison. She was convicted on the basis of several anti-terrorist laws that were enacted during former President Fujimori's reign. Despite his corrupt administration and questions of a fair trial, Berenson's conviction stands. In a meeting with U.S. President George W. Bush (2001–) prior to Berenson's sentence, Peruvian president-elect Alejandro Toledo said that he would consider the case after it was finished in the courts.

nounced his resignation. The opposition-controlled Congress wasted no time in rejecting Fujimori's resignation, instead voting him morally unfit to serve and publicly announcing his removal from office.

After Fujimori's departure for Japan the chaotic situation in Peru continued. Allegations of wrongdoing, fraud, and embezzlement continued to surface against Montesinos and Fujimori. For his part, Montesinos had long been suspected of human rights violations and abuses, including intimidation, torture, murder, disappearances, and bribery. The discovery that he maintained secret bank accounts in Switzerland and the Cayman Islands totaling more than $50 million became further evidence of his corruption. Fujimori, who instigated an illegal raid on Montesinos' offices before departing, is believed to have illegally removed up to 50 videotapes, supposedly with incriminating evidence. A sad commentary of corruption unfolded before the Peruvian people as the remaining videotapes, known as the "Vladivideos," showed media executives, politicians, television stars, judges, army generals, and representatives from local and foreign countries accepting bribes, conspiring to rig elections, and plotting against opponents. Over three dozen public officials have been arrested or charged with corruption.

RECENT HISTORY AND THE FUTURE

On November 22, 2000, just two days after Fujimori sent his resignation from Tokyo, Valentin Paniagua was named the country's acting president, a position he held until the newly elected president took the oath of office in July 2001. He selected Fujimori's 1995 opponent Perez de Cuellar as his prime minister. A member of the Belaúnde's Popular Action Party, Paniagua had just been elected as Speaker of Congress on November 16 as the replacement for the ousted Hildebrandt. Highly respected, Paniagua, who was not allowed to run in the election, made efforts to clean house of Fujimori and Montesinos supporters. General Walter Ledesma, a critic of Fujimori who was forced into early retirement, was named as defense secretary. Ledesma quickly set about dismantling the power structure of the armed forces built by Montesinos.

Montesinos, under suspicion for a wide range of crimes, was the country's most wanted fugitive until his capture in Venezuela in June 2001. Prior to his arrest, many suspected many that friends in the military were protecting Montesinos within the country. Other reports surfaced suggesting that he had fled Peru and may have undergone plastic surgery to alter his identity. In reality, Montesinos had fled the country, but without undergoing plastic surgery. Measures were immediately undertaken to extradite Montesinos to Peru for prosecution. Fujimori, who is now recognized as a citizen of Japan by Japanese officials, continued his stay in Tokyo as of July 2001. Peruvian officials are proceeding with an investigation into his administration, and Congress is still considering the possibility of issuing charges of abandonment of duty and moral laxity against him. However, much more serious charges may stem from the discovery of 120 presidential decrees signed by Fujimori that allocated more than $1 billion in government purchases between 1992–2000, which is the best evidence so far that Fujimori knew of, and was involved in, Montesinos' illegitimate activities. There are also allegations that Fujimori has at least one secret bank account filled with public funds.

In an interview with *Time*'s Tokyo bureau chief Tim Larimer on March 15, 2000, Fujimori placed the blame squarely on Montesinos and his opponents in Congress. "I wonder if those people [in Congress] who want to charge me, they are really willing to find out where this money comes from. What types of crimes Montesinos committed. Why don't they concentrate on this problem? The problem here is that they are focusing on the former president, but that they are leaving alone the other problem. The infiltration of Montesinos may have reached in the Congress, in the judiciary, in the prosecutor, in the armed forces, and in the police." Although he does not rule out someday returning to Peru, Fujimori has no plans to return to face charges lodged against him. He is in the midst of writing a book on his experiences in Peruvian politics and, ironically, is completing a series of video documentaries based on videos in his office of meetings and conversations that he openly taped during his tenure as president.

Despite many efforts, the political stability of Peru remains in question. Numerous political parties vie for power, but do not have the backing or organization to secure the commitment of large sectors of the population, which led to eight candidates being placed on the ballot for April 8, 2001 presidential election. The three main contenders to take control of the country were Alejandro Toledo, Fujimori's opponent in 2000, former president Alan García, who recently returned to the country after charges of corruption against his former administration were dropped, and conservative Lourdes Flores. Both Toledo and García received enough votes on April 8 to force a runoff. On June 3, 2001, Alejandro Toledo won the runoff election and became the first new president of Peru since Fujimori was first elected in 1990. In a victory speech on election night, Toledo promised voters a clean break away from the corruption and scandal that discredited Fujimori's administration, "I swear, brothers and sisters, I will never let you down."

BIBLIOGRAPHY

Conaghan, Catherine M. "The Irrelevant Right: Alberto Fujimori and the New Politics of Pragmatic Peru," in Kevin J. Middlebrook, editor, *Conservative Parties, the Right, and Democracy in Latin America*. Baltimore, MD: The Johns Hopkins University Press, 2000, p. 225–284.

Graham, Carol. *Peru's APRA: Parties, Politics, and the Elusive Quest for Democracy*. Boulder, CO: Lynne Rienner Publishers, 1992.

Klarén, Peter Flindell. *Peru: Society and Nationhood in the Andes*. New York: Oxford University Press, 2000.

Larimer, Tim. "Fujimori Plans a 'Tell-All' Movie," *Time*, March 15, 2001.

Mauceri, Philip. *State Under Siege: Development and Policy Making in Peru*. Boulder, CO: Westview Press, 1996.

Miller, Jon, interview by Bob Edwards. "Profile: Peruvian President Alberto Fujimori," *Morning Edition*, National Public Radio, April 5, 2000.

Rudolph, James D. *Peru: The Evolution of a Crisis*. Politics in Latin America: A Hoover Institute Series. Westport, CT: Praeger, 1992.

—Kari Bethel

ROOTING OUT CORRUPTION IN THE PHILIPPINES: IMPEACHMENT OF A PRESIDENT

THE CONFLICT

The Philippines first made international headlines for government corruption in the 1970s during the administration of President Ferdinand Marcos. While no president since has equaled his flagrant disregard for the nation's laws, cronyism, nepotism, and financial misdoings are problems that continue to plague the Philippines. Rampant corruption culminated in the impeachment of President Joseph Estrada in 2001.

Political

- Since gaining independence the Philippines has often been beset with corruption by its leadership. In October 2000 accusations arose against President Joseph Estrada, alleging bribery, graft, and plunder. Impeachment proceedings began against him, the first democratic measures taken in the Philippines to remove a leader from office.

- Despite the charges against Estrada, he maintained a wide base of popular support among the poor. Demonstrations both in support of and against him took place in the streets, sometimes leading to violence.

- Senate prosecutors in charge of the impeachment proceedings resigned in protest after they were prevented from investigating potentially damaging financial documents.

- On April 25, 2001, Estrada was arrested and detained on charges of economic plunder, a crime punishable by death. He continued to maintain a level of popular support.

Philippine President Joseph Estrada took office on June 30, 1998, and left office less than three years later in January 2001. Scandal and corruption dogged his short term in office. In early October 2000 Luis Singson, a longtime friend of Estrada's, testified at a Senate hearing that the president had asked him to coordinate a nationwide collection of payoffs from an illegal numbers game called jueteng. Along with the US$8.6 million in payoffs from illegal gambling, Estrada received $2.8 million skimmed from provincial tobacco taxes. Based on these accusations of wrongdoing, Congress began an impeachment process against the president.

In addition to graft Estrada was charged with bribery, perjury, and possession of unexplained wealth. On November 13, 2000, Joseph "Erap" Estrada became the first Philippine president to be subjected to the impeachment process. The House of Representatives sent four impeachment charges to the Senate, where a trial began on December 7, 2000. As the impeachment trial proceeded, witness after witness came forward with allegations that Estrada had taken payoffs from illegal numbers games, signed a false name to withdraw millions of dollars from a secret personal account, and had given money and homes to his mistresses. In his 31 months in office he allegedly acquired a total of $82 million through illegal means.

Estrada's corruption outraged much of the public. Not since former president Ferdinand Marcos had corruption reached such levels in the Philippines. Estrada, who captured the public's fancy as a popular movie star in Robin Hood roles, campaigned as a supporter of the poor and lower classes, where his support base was strongest. Despite his high living as president he continued to receive support from this segment of the public once the scandal broke. For a country often buffeted by strong-arm leadership and vice, Estrada's blatant misuse of power was another occasion in a long string of similar events, and this time it was not going to be tolerated.

HISTORICAL BACKGROUND

From Colony to Independent Nation

The Philippines was a Spanish colony for over three hundred years. Shortly before the end of the nineteenth century, in 1898, the United States defeated Spain in the Spanish-American War and occupied the Philippine islands. In 1899 Emilio Aguinaldo launched a war of resistance against the U.S. presence. Aguinaldo was captured in 1901 and swore allegiance to the United States. Further resistance gradually died out through 1902. During this time the islands' infrastructure, sanitation, and health care improved, and the education system also benefited, with schooling made more widely accessible to the general population.

Under U.S. occupation, the Philippines instituted a system of government after the American model, with a president serving as national leader and supported by a Congress consisting of a Senate and a House of Representatives. In 1907 the first legislative assembly was established in the Philippines and remained largely under local control. National elections were held to fill seats in the assembly, with two delegates being sent to the U.S. House of Representatives to represent Philippine interests. A civil service was also initiated. Though it first began firmly under U.S. control, power was gradually shifted to Filipinos, who had complete control of the civil service by the end of World War I (1914–18).

It was during this same time that the U.S. government sold the landholdings of the Church to already wealthy Filipinos, consolidating their power and exaggerating the gap between the upper and lower classes. Despite the professed American goal of democratization this new political model was, in practice, overlaid on a deeply entrenched system with a clearly defined economic and political elite. This divided structure continued to define Filipino politics well after the United States left the Philippines. Despite the patina of Americanization, the new Philippine government functioned similarly to the old colonial one in many ways. Nepotism, cronyism, corruption, and economic inequality continued to flourish. Over the years since its independence in 1946, the Philippines experienced coups to oust corrupt leaders, but the demo-

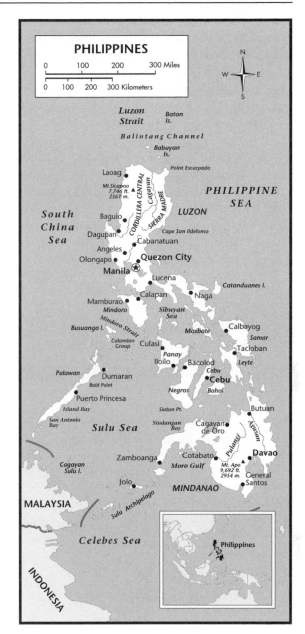

MAP OF THE PHILIPPINES. *(Maryland Cartographics. Reproduced by permission.)*

cratic process of impeachment—a process modeled after and recently used in the United States—was only employed for the first time against Joseph Estrada in 2000.

In 1935 the Philippines became a self-governing commonwealth. This step was intended to help the islands make a 10-year transition to an independent nation. Manuel Quezon was elected to serve as president at this time. Before the 10-year period could be completed, however, World War II (1939–45) began and the Philippines fell to Japanese control in 1942. Two years later, U.S. General

Douglas MacArthur launched the battle to regain the islands. In the process of fighting, much of the islands' organization and infrastructure was destroyed. By the time the United States and the Philippines defeated the Japanese in 1945 with the Battle of Leyte Gulf, the islands were in a high state of disorder.

While the Philippines began the slow process of recovery from war, the United States granted the islands independence on July 4, 1946. The new country, assisted by the United States, struggled to rebuild. In one of its earliest acts as the independent Republic of the Philippines, the country elected its first president, Manuel A. Roxas y Acuñe. Communist guerrillas, called Hukbalahaps, threatened the stability of the new republic from 1945 to 1953. Their demands were met by land reforms and military action until the movement was finally repressed under President Ramon Magsaysay.

The Reign of Marcos

Ferdinand Marcos came to power in 1965 and began what would become one of the most corrupt administrations in Philippine history. He was re-elected to office several times, until finally being forced out in 1986. In response to what he claimed was rampant rebellion and unrest Marcos declared martial law on the Philippines in 1972. He proceeded to rule by decree and exhibited little respect for human rights. His regime was beset with accusations of fraud, ballot-rigging, and widespread corruption. Both Marcos and his wife Imelda were infamous for their excessive, gaudy lifestyle, supported by illegal means.

Under martial law, Marcos employed increasingly dictatorial means by which to govern the country. Human rights were routinely violated, and democratic institutions were repressed. In 1981 Marcos declared an end to martial law, but the government retained wide powers of arrest. The political scene, however, was allowed some amount of freedom due to reforms initiated earlier in 1978. These reforms helped Marcos achieve a third successful election as president in 1981. Under his continued reign the Philippine economy stagnated while the economies of its neighbors grew.

Popular support for Marcos faded over time. One organized group that contributed to his eventual downfall was the Bagong Anyansang Makabayan Party (Bayan). Formed in the mid-1960s the Bayan today is composed of more than one thousand grassroots social and political organizations whose members total over one million. The group became a clandestine organization when Marcos instituted martial law, but was nonetheless instrumental in land reform and other causes. It was one of the main forces behind ousting President Marcos after the 1986 election and continued to remain active. In the late 1990s, for instance, the Bayan denounced the increasing power of oil companies in the Philippines. It also expressed concern during Joseph Estrada's presidency that the government was restricting free speech.

In 1983 protests erupted when opposition leader Benigno Aquino, who had returned to the Philippines after three years in exile, was killed. Many believed that Marcos was responsible for Aquino's assassination. Popular dissatisfaction with Marcos' administration increased. In a 1986 election a coalition of opposition parties supported Aquino's widow Corazon as their presidential candidate. Vote tallies awarded the seat to Marcos, but a wave of popular opposition, called People's Power, rose in support of Aquino. Via this peaceful uprising Marcos was forced from office and out of the country. After an offer from U.S. President Ronald Reagan, Marcos and his wife settled in an expensive villa in Honolulu, Hawaii, where he died in 1989. The Marcos couple's excesses while he was in office earned them a spot in the *Guiness Book of World Records* under the category of "Biggest Robbery." The amount they stole from the Philippine people—through various means including bribe taking, overpricing goods, diverting money from government-controlled businesses, and the levying of taxes that were never subjected to audit—is estimated at between $5 to $10 billion.

The Aftermath

Corazon Aquino, the first female president of the Philippines, gained office on a wave of popular support. Once in power she had to deal with communist insurgents and economic mismanagement, compliments of the Marcos years. Her term in office steered the country back toward a more democratic system. She also initiated an effort to retrieve money stolen from the Philippine people by Ferdinand and Imelda Marcos. Shortly after the Marcos' left the country, Aquino established the Presidential Commission on Good Government (PCGG), which would investigate allegations of misdoing and begin the long process of trying to retrieve the stolen funds.

While the government alleged corruption against Marcos and his wife, the couple denied the charges. Assets contained in the Marcos' Swiss bank accounts were frozen by Swiss authorities in 1986. At the same time, the Philippine government filed a Racketeer Influenced and Corrupt Organizations (RICO) case against the couple in the United States. The RICO case sought to recover $1.55 billion the Philippine government believed had been illegally taken from its treasury by the Marcos.' In a settlement in 1991 assets from the estate of Ferdinand Marcos, as well as money from personal accounts, were transferred to the Philippine government.

Imelda Marcos was allowed to return to the Philippines after her husband's death in 1989. She became an elected member of Congress and consistently denied the charges of corruption levied against her and her late husband. Her protestations of innocence, however, could not stop the PCGG from investigating. Its operations have continued into 2001. The amount recovered by the PCGG represents only a small portion of what the Philippine government believes was taken. Under Corazon Aquino's instruction, the quest for recovery of these funds began its long journey.

When elections were again held in 1992, six years after Aquino's election, she was voted out of office and Fidel Ramos stepped in. Ramos, Aquino's former defense minister, promised to make economic growth a priority, to tackle the problems of corruption, and to raise the general standard of living. Under his administration the Communist Party was legalized and talks began with various rebel groups throughout the country in an attempt at reconciliation. Ramos was able to broker peace agreements in both 1995 and 1996 with separate rebel groups. While insurgency remained across the country, his efforts marked successful attempts at reconciliation versus repression.

The Philippine economy—which was neglected during the Marcos years—was hit by the same financial crisis that struck all of Southeast Asia in 1997. Ramos' promises of economic growth were dashed and the country had difficulty recovering from this new bout of economic malaise. When Ramos' vice president, Joseph Estrada, was elected to the presidency with promises of economic reform and support for the poor, hopes grew. After Estrada's corruption scandal broke, however, confidence in the economy quickly waned.

In his short time as president, Estrada experienced a large level of popularity. He used his movie star past as a Robin Hood character to buoy his support among the poor and lower classes. A flamboyant figure, many of Estrada's excesses while in office were obvious to those close to him. When serious allegations of bribery, perjury, and gambling were officially lodged, however, it was time for this

CHRONOLOGY

1902 The United States gains control of the islands after winning the Spanish American War.

1942–44 The Japanese occupy the Philippines.

1946 The Philippines become an independent nation.

1965 Ferdinand Marcos becomes president.

1973 Marcos institutes martial law.

1986 Marcos is overthrown in popular protests stemming from his oppression and corruption; Corazon Aquino assumes the presidency.

1986 The Presidential Commission on Good Government is established.

1992 Aquino's government is beset by economic and political woes; Fidel Ramos replaces her.

1998 Joseph Estrada, a former movie star, campaigns on a populist platform and wins the presidential elections.

October 2000 Charges are brought against President Estrada concerning financial misdoing.

13 November 2000 Estrada is impeached by the House of Representatives, which leads to a trial in the Senate.

20 January 2001 Gloria Arroyo is sworn in as president.

April 25, 2001 Estrada is arrested for economic plunder and faces a possible death sentence if found guilty.

Robin Hood to pay the piper. Despite the allegations, support for Estrada remained strong amid the lower classes. This support encouraged Estrada to fight his removal from office. He was ultimately unsuccessful and his ousting—via democratic means—continued to solidify the process of political stabilization that began after Ferdinand Marcos was removed from power in 1986.

Filipino Values

To some extent the Filipino legacy of corruption and exploitation by government officials can be traced back to the colonial system imposed by the Spanish. Cronyism and bribery flourished and were not habits easily broken once independence was achieved. In addition, elements inherent in Filipino culture exaggerated corrupt tendencies.

The fact that corruption has been so prevalent in the Philippines stems in part from a value system

ANTI-ESTRADA PROTESTORS CALL FOR THE PRESIDENT'S OUSTING AFTER ALLEGATIONS OF CORRUPTION SURFACED. *(CORBIS CORPORATION (Bellevue). Reproduced by permission.)*

that, while it certainly does not condone the practice, in many regards sets the stage to make it possible. Attitudes endorsing the protection and advancement of family members above others, a high value placed on rank and social status, and a strong group mentality are part of a long-standing cultural ethos that combine to create a climate in which corruption can and has flourished.

The Filipino social structure is defined by clan relationships. There is a strong importance placed on family ties, both through blood and marriage, and these links serve as a mechanism of social control, as an informal system of social security, and as a rung on the job ladder in the workplace. The clan establishes order in the world; one's place is clearly defined in relation to others. Identity is primarily defined by these bonds, as well as by the geographical ties to where the clan originates within the country. This dates back to the precolonial social structure, which centered around the *balangays*, or clans.

Interaction in the Philippines is characterized by what sociologists have called "smooth interpersonal relationships," or SIR. This means that cour-

tesy is of utmost importance, and confrontation is avoided at all costs. It is considered more acceptable to lie or to relate the truth indirectly if it means saving face for either the speaker or the listener. The quality known as *hiya* reflects this sensitivity to others' feelings. Indirect communication is based largely on the quality called *pakiramdaman*, which has to do with intuiting another's intentions. Smooth interpersonal relations also entail a spirit of extreme generosity.

Exchange is often made explicit in relationships by what is known as *utang na loob*, or debt of gratitude. This means that favors must be repaid, and is both an individual and a collective responsibility. *Utang na loob* has had a wide-ranging impact in Filipino government and politics. This value, for example, led the Philippines to feel indebted to the United States after the latter "freed" it from Japanese occupation and granted the Philippines independence. The concept of reciprocity also feeds the system of tit-for-tat, in which politicians trade favors for votes. While this could be seen as a positive, in the sense that government officials are obliged to fulfill their duties toward those who put them in office, in practice, it has often translated

JOSEPH ESTRADA

1937– The former Philippine president was born Joseph Ejercito in 1937, in a suburb of Manila. One of nine children, Estrada had a middle-class upbringing. He was the only one of his siblings not to earn a college degree. Estrada's acting aspirations led him to leave school early. He changed his name because of his father's shame of being associated with the movie business.

Commonly known by the nickname "Erap," Estrada got his big break in the film industry in 1957, and later rose to fame by starring in dozens of B-movies, in which he often played a Robin Hood role. His image as a rogue with the interests of the poor in mind, however loosely based in reality, helped him immeasurably in his campaign for the presidency.

Estrada's political career began in 1967 when he ran for mayor of the city of San Juan. The election results were contested, but ten months after the vote Estrada was finally declared the winner and installed in office. His next venture for political office came in 1987. He ran a successful bid for a seat in the Philippine Senate. As a senator Estrada served on committees for the environment and social reform. He was a strong supporter of the Filipino language and opposed the presence of U.S. military bases in the country. In January 1991 the Philippine Free Press named him Outstanding Senator.

In June 1992 Estrada advanced to the position of vice president of the country. He served under President Fidel Ramos. In January 1999, when Ramos' time in

JOSEPH ESTRADA. *(Gale Research (Detroit).)*

office was up, Estrada was elected to the presidency. He ran on a platform popular with the economically poor populace. Less than two years into his term, however, accusations of corruption emerged and an impeachment trial began against Estrada. The scandal resulted in Estrada's removal from office. In April 2001 he was arrested on charges of economic plunder. If found guilty, Joseph Estrada could face the penalty of death.

---

into vote-buying and a system in which wealthy campaign donors are exempt from paying taxes.

Pakikisama is another defining characteristic of social interactions. It entails submitting one's individual goals or ideas to the collective will. *Pakikisama* has had both positive and negative ramifications in the political mindset of the country. Ideally, it compels leaders to submit themselves to the will of the people whom they are serving. In fact, it has also led to excessive compromise and a stagnant bureaucracy.

These values—strong family ties, *hiya*, and *utang na loob*—combined in the Philippines to create an environment that inadvertently supported corruption. Leaders such as Ferdinand Marcos and Joseph Estrada took advantage of these cultural

traits and of the trust of the Philippine people to benefit themselves. As a relatively young democracy, the Philippines rose to the occasion of Marcos' excesses and pushed him from office. With more years and experience behind it, the country was able to fully utilize its democratic structure to eject Estrada.

Estrada's Corruption Saga

On June 30, 1998, Joseph Ejercito Estrada was elected president. He ran on a populist platform of help for the poor and more power for the largely ignored populace. Unfortunately, he openly bought the votes of many poor people by simply handing out cash in low-income areas. A charismatic former movie star, Estrada proved more interested in his own financial well being than in that of his country.

IMPEACHMENT PROCEEDINGS AGAINST JOSEPH ESTRADA BEGIN WITH THE SWEARING-IN CEREMONY. *(AP/Wide World Photos. Reproduced by permission.)*

Once in office Estrada drained the national treasury and allowed the national debt to mount. As of 2001 there were an estimated 50 billion pesos owed in back taxes by the richest business people in the country, many of whom were Estrada's personal friends and political allies. Estrada's mismanagement, on top of Marcos' embezzlement and the country's slow recovery from the Asian financial crisis, was a further blow to the country's economy.

Less than two years into his six-year presidential term Estrada found himself facing charges of bribery, perjury, and other allegations related to his unaccountable wealth and high living. An impeachment trial began in December 2000, while the public came out both in support of and against President Estrada. The beleaguered president refused to back down, claiming that he was wrongly accused. The president and his supporters managed to interrupt the impeachment process by preventing prosecutors from gaining access to potentially damaging financial records. Trial prosecutors, outraged after the Senate voted 11–10 not to open the documents, resigned.

With the resignation of trial prosecutors the impeachment trial was adjourned indefinitely. Hundreds of thousands of Filipinos took to the streets, demanding that Estrada step down. This was largely a middle-class revolt. Estrada, who had

won the elections by the largest margin in the country's history, retained a fairly strong support base among the poor. It became clear, however, that Estrada was losing his grip on power when the military and the police withdrew their support and shifted allegiance to Gloria Macapagal Arroyo, Estrada's vice president. Most of his cabinet resigned and sided with the protestors. The leader of the Catholic Church in the country—an organization with considerable political clout—called for Estrada to resign. Former Philippine president Corazon Aquino also spoke out against Estrada, calling his actions an outrage and an affront to the country's honor.

A panel of opposition negotiators gave Estrada a deadline to resign. Estrada, in a last ditch effort to prove that he still had a coalition and the support of the people, called for snap elections in May 2001 that he promised not to contest. His announcement was met with immediate dismissal from Vice President Arroyo and her supporters, who, according to the constitution, was first in line to succeed Estrada should he be removed from office

Finally, minutes before a second deadline, Estrada left the presidential palace on January 20, 2001. Although he did not actually resign, Estrada agreed with the decision of the supreme court, which resolved that "the people had spoken" and could not be ignored. The supreme court declared the presidency vacant and appointed Gloria Arroyo the fourteenth president of the Republic of the Philippines.

RECENT HISTORY AND THE FUTURE

Although able to escape a Senate trial Estrada was unable to avoid arrest on charges of economic plunder, a crime punishable by death. The fact that Estrada was arrested on April 25, 2001, is indicative of a shrinking tolerance among the majority of the populace for corruption and of a growing desire to hold leaders accountable for their actions. While punishing the former president for his crimes would go against historical precedent and perhaps challenge some deeply engrained cultural attitudes, there are several indications that many Filipinos are simply fed up with a system that has proved ineffective and has allowed leaders to take advantage of them for years.

Despite being forced from office Estrada was not without supporters. Many of the poor still saw him as the hero from the movies, a Robin Hood. Thousands of supporters were outside Estrada's residence on May 1, 2001, as the police moved in to apprehend the ex-president. A week later thousands of demonstrators attempted to storm the presidential palace. The riots that ensued were the worst seen in 15 years. Four people were killed and hundreds were injured, leading President Gloria Arroyo to declare a "state of rebellion." The declaration allowed the police and the military detain suspects without warrants. As a result, approximately 50 mostly poor supporters of the former leader were jailed. Although the detainees were released a week later Arroyo continued to pursue opposition leaders she said were responsible for masterminding the palace attack in an attempt to seize power. Arroyo came under fire from Philippine lawyers, who condemned the pursuit and arrest of Estrada supporters, prompting Arroyo to lift the "state of rebellion" declaration.

Moving Forward

Congressional elections were scheduled for May 14, 2001. The elections were widely seen as a proxy war between Estrada and Arroyo. Arroyo pushed for all 13 candidates from the People Power Coalition (PPC) to sweep the elections, and said that it was necessary for all of them to win in order for the government to accomplish its goals. The PPC has succeeded in unifying several different parties and coalitions under a common platform of

GLORIA MACAPAGAL ARROYO

1947– Gloria Macapagal Arroyo comes from a family prominent in Philippine politics. Her father, the late Diosdado Macapagal, served as president of the country. Unlike many Filipino politicians, the Macapagals were known for their integrity and unostentatious lifestyle. Gloria Macapagal Arroyo graduated first in her high school class at Assumption Convent. She went on to Georgetown University in Washington, D.C., and graduated *magna cum laude* from Assumption College. Returning to the Philippines, she earned a Master's degree in economics from the Ateneo de Manila University and a Ph.D. in the subject from the University of the Philippines.

Arroyo was appointed Undersecretary of Trade and Industry in 1986, during Corazon Aquino's administration. In the course of her tenure, she wrote 55 laws concerning social and economic reform. She was recognized several times as Outstanding Senator, and was elected vice-president of the country in the same course of elections that put Estrada in office. Estrada appointed her Secretary of Social Welfare and Development. She resigned from the Cabinet on October 12, 2000, in protest of the Estrada financial scandals, but retained her position as vice-president.

Upon Estrada's impeachment and removal from office, Gloria Arroyo became the second woman to serve as president of the Philippines.

"new politics." This includes increased funding for housing, education, and health care, the elimination of graft, and a crackdown on illegal drugs. They also focus on improvement of the Manila metropolitan area, addressing such issues as garbage disposal, traffic, and floods.

The Catholic Bishops Conference of the Philippines has come out in support of the current administration's candidates. However, Cardinal Vidal, a high-ranking figure in the church (and the personal spiritual advisor to Estrada) has expressed his concern at the church taking sides in politics and has made known his own personal neutrality in the elections.

The government took precautions to ensure that the elections were peaceful and the process was democratic. Comelec, the committee that oversaw the elections, attempted to eliminate the possibility of violence by confiscating weapons and establishing safe polling places. In areas on the Philippine island of Mindanao, where the threat of violence seemed high, the committee used military troops as poll supervisors rather than teachers. Despite these efforts, violence could not be completely eradicated. Since January 2, 2001, more than 80 incidents of election-related violence occurred throughout the country. On election day, the military deployed about 45,000 troops to assist the police in keeping the voting peaceful. The democratic process, tested under Estrada's corrupt administration and ousting, continued to turn its wheels, and the people came out to have their say. Despite formidable obstacles, many Filipinos remain cautiously optimistic about living in a truly democratic society.

BIBLIOGRAPHY

Austin, W. Timothy. *Banana Justice: Field Notes on Philippine Crime and Custom.* Westport, CT: Praeger, 1999.

"Arroyo's Gov't Rates Higher than Erap's," ABS-CBN News, March 29, 2001. Available online at http://www.abs-cbnnews.com/abs/newsflash.nsf/Brundown/20010330017 (cited May 31, 2001).

Burton, Sandra. "People Power Redux," *Time,* January 29, 2001.

Cannell, Fenella. *Power and Intimacy in the Christian Philippines.* New York: Cambridge University Press, 1999.

Cavendish, Marshall. *Philippines.* New York: Times Books International, 1991.

Concepcion, John Anthony, et al. "Poll Fraud Afoot—Biazon," *Manila Times,* March 8, 2001.

Contreras, Volt, et al. "Estrada: Ramos Out to 'Demonize' Me," *Philippine Daily Inquirer,* April 2, 2001.

Doronila, Amanda. "People's Coup: Bloodless, Constitutional, Democratic," *Philippine Daily Inquirer,* January 22, 2001.

"Five Banks Surrender Records of Joseph Estrada," *Times of India,* February 17, 2001. Available online at http://www.timesofindia.com/170201/17aspc14.htm (cited April 18, 2001).

Gedman, Eva-Lotta E. *Philippine Politics and Society in the Twentieth Century.* New York: Routledge, 2000.

Gloria Arroyo Official Website. Available online at http://www.kgma.org.

"Government Probes Alleged Attempt to Launder Marcos Money," *Manila Times,* March 14, 2001.

"Philippines: Estrada Charged with Corruption," BBC News, April 4, 2001.

Roque, Pat. "Communist Rebels Free Last Hostage," Associated Press, April 6, 2001.

Smith, Desmond. *Democracy and the Philippine Media, 1983–1993.* Lewiston, NY: Edwin Mellen Press, 2000.

Steinberg, David Joel. *The Philippines: A Singular and Plural Place.* Boulder, CO: Westview Press, 2000.

Sullivan, Margaret. *Philippines: Pacific Crossroads.* New York: Dillon Press, 1993.

Teves, Oliver. "Unable to Recover Marcos' Wealth, Philippines Moves to Negotiate Smaller Settlement," *The News-Times,* October 29, 1997.

Vigilar, Rufi. "Philippine Coup Suspect's Surrender Aborted," CNN News, May 9, 2001. Available online at http://www.cnn.com/2001/WORLD/asiapcf/southeast/05/09/philippines.surrender.aborted/index.html (cited May 31, 2001).

—Eleanor Stanford

FREE TO SPEAK? ESTABLISHING A FREE PRESS IN RUSSIA

In the most dramatic instance of Russian government moves deemed troubling to freedom of the press, Russia's state-owned Gazprom natural gas firm on April 3, 2001, seized formal control of independent nationwide television network, NTV, from shareholder and media magnate Vladimir Gusinsky. He witnessed the takeover from Spain, where he was fighting a simultaneous Russian government request for extradition on embezzlement charges. On April 19, 2001, Spain's High Court rejected the extradition request, deeming the alleged offenses not crimes in Spain. Free to leave Spain, Gusinsky flew to Israel on April 25, 2001. Russian prosecutors filed a new arrest warrant with Interpol on April 22, this time alleging that Gusinsky was involved in money laundering, and voiced their intentions to eventually see Gusinsky face charges in a Russian courtroom. The loss of independence by Gusinsky's NTV appears more serious than other moves by the government of President Vladimir Putin against independent newspapers and magazines because NTV has a nationwide reach, and most Russians now get their news from television rather than from print media.

Commenting on the Russian government moves against Gusinsky, Elaine Monaghan of Reuters reported that the U.S. State Department stated on April 18, 2001, that Gusinsky's Media-Most media holdings had faced "extraordinary pressures from law enforcement and other elements of the Russian government," which "lead reasonable observers . . . to the conclusion that the campaign against Media-Most is politically motivated." The State Department also indicated that it was "extremely troubled" by the takeover of Gusinsky's NTV independent national television network as a sign that freedom of speech is under assault by the

THE CONFLICT

Freedom of speech and of the press became more widely practiced in Russia after the collapse of the Soviet Union. The Russian media began to actively report on the government and to question its actions. When President Vladimir Putin succeeded Boris Yeltsin into office, he implemented restrictions on the media that greatly reduced their freedoms. Putin also began to reinstate government controls over the media and to prosecute media companies and owners who did not comply.

Political

- A free media raises questions that the Russian government under Vladimir Putin clearly does not want to answer. Putin's attempts to restrict the media's freedoms is an effort to control the information available to the public.

- The Soviet Union had a common practice of censorship and controlled media. Russia has had very few years of experience with a free press. Putin's efforts to re-establish government control are a return to a tradition much more established than the relatively new rights of free speech.

Legal

- Russia seized control of the nationwide independent television station NTV, while owner Vladimir Gusinsky fought from Spain to overcome a Russian government request for his extradition on charges of embezzlement, which he claims are false.

- The Russian government has cracked down on granting reporters access to the war-torn region of Chechnya. Rumors persist that the Russian army was responsibly for reporter Andrey Babitsky's initial capture. When Babitsky was released by Chechen rebels in the neighboring province of Dagestan, Russian officials prosecuted him for not having proper travel documents.

Russian government. German Foreign Minister Joschka Fischer and other Western governments also voiced misgivings about the takeover of NTV and other negative democratization trends in Russia. Responding to the U.S. State Department's remarks, the Russian Foreign Ministry rejected the suggestion of political involvement in the Media-Most events, stating that they were, according to Transitions Online in "Russia: Gusinky Free, Independent Media Not" (April 18–23, 2001), "purely commercial and financial" affairs and did "not have anything to do with freedom of speech" in Russia.

Compared to the revelatory aspects of former Soviet President Mikhail Gorbachev's media *glasnost* (openness) policy, and the free media-building period of Russian President Boris Yeltsin's rule, President Vladimir Putin has appeared less disposed to support freedom of the press. Major negative incidents have included the Putin government's clampdown on press coverage of the Chechnya conflict; the military treatment of war reporter Andrey Babitsky; the harassment of media magnate Vladimir Gusinsky and the seizure of control over NTV; the reaction of the Putin government to press reports of the sinking of the submarine Kursk; and Putin's promulgation of a restrictive Information Security Doctrine. The pressure on the press exerted by the Putin government has only been weakly challenged by the courts. Although the Russian constitution upholds freedoms of the press and speech, courts have seldom justified their decisions on the basis of these principles. Existing laws dealing with the press provide piecemeal protection and are contradictory, so that courts sometimes rule to uphold press freedoms and at other times rule against the press even in cases that appear similar.

The Russian government owns about 150 of the 550 television stations in Russia and about one-fifth of the 12,000 registered newspapers and periodicals, but among these are the major national television broadcasters and print media. Many private media are too dependent on government subsidies or financiers. There is a high concentration of private media ownership, and these owners often have used their media holdings for their own commercial purposes, harming the integrity of the press. Nonetheless, the private media has functioned somewhat independently of the government, breaking a state monopoly on information. To the extent that private media are suppressed, the opportunity for the emergence of a freer press is constrained.

Among the owners of major media are state-controlled energy companies Gazprom, Lukoil, and United Energy Systems, the Russian Central Bank, and the state-controlled Sberbank. Oligarchs Vladimir Potanin and Roman Abramovich are major media owners. The holdings of oligarchs Boris Berezovsky and Vladimir Gusinsky, who are out of favor with Putin, are dwindling. Two major foreign media groups include the Independent Media Group and Storyfirst Communications. Berezovsky retains control of TV-6, a small Moscow television station, and Gusinsky retains TNT, a cable company that reaches about one-half of the population, mainly with entertainment programming. After NTV was taken over by Gazprom, many of NTV's employees quit or were fired and went to work at TV-6 or TNT.

Putin's viewpoint that information should be shaped by and serve state interests was set forth in an Information Security Doctrine he promulgated in September 2000. In discussing the Doctrine, Putin's media advisor, Gleb Pavlovsky, in September 2000, stated that freedom of the press in Russia had become a means for the degradation and destruction of society, blaming oligarchs Gusinsky and Berezovsky, among others. He endorsed government efforts against them but also warned that foreign media with non-Russian agendas might try to purchase their media holdings. In an address to editors of mass media in January 2001, Putin stated that the Russian state needed a unified viewpoint from the media, and would continue to ban "illegitimate and extremist ideas." Most recently, in his state of the federation address to the legislature on April 3, 2001, Putin devoted most attention to bolstering free enterprise and some attention to pension, health, and other social issues. He did not, however, mention human rights as a priority concern for the year, and dismissed the conflict in Chechnya as posing no human rights issues.

HISTORICAL BACKGROUND

The main negative trends in press freedom in Russia are exemplified by censorship of the Chechnya conflict—including the government's treatment of reporter Andrey Babitsky—the harassment of Gusinsky's Media-Most independent media firm, and the promulgation of a repressive Information Security Doctrine by the government. While the negative trends began in the latter years of the Yeltsin era, they appeared to receive state sanction by the Putin regime.

Russian media became more vulnerable to manipulation with the consolidation of ownership

CHRONOLOGY

January 15, 2000 Andrey Babitsky is reported missing in Chechnya.

February 25, 2000 Babitsky is freed in Dagestan by his captors.

April 26–27, 2000 Newspapers *Novaya Gazeta* and *Kommarsant* are warned that publishing an interview with Chechen President Aslan Maskhadov, branded a terrorist by Moscow, violates anti-terrorism laws.

May 11, 2000 Tax police raid Media-Most offices, destroying computers and communications equipment.

June 13, 2000 Vladimir Gusinsky, head of Media-Most, is detained by Russian police.

June 16, 2000 Gusinsky is released from detention, but is charged with embezzlement.

July 6, 2000 Babitsky is charged with using false documents in Dagestan.

July 11, 2000 Police raid Media-Most offices.

July 19, 2000 Police seize Gusinsky's property.

July 27, 2000 The prosecutor drops the embezzlement case against Gusinsky, who flees to Spain.

October 6, 2000 Babitsky is found guilty of using false documents and is fined.

November 13, 2000 The Russian Prosecutor General issues a warrant for Gusinsky's arrest on embezzlement charges.

November 21, 2000 A military panel of the Supreme Court dismisses a lower court acquittal in the espionage and treason trial of Grigory Pasko and sends the case back for re-trial.

December 5, 2000 Prosecutors and police raid ORT offices.

January 25, 2001 Court bailiffs raid NTV to freeze its assets.

February 7, 2001 Prosecutors and FSB officers raid Media-Most offices.

April 3, 2001 Gazprom seizes control of NTV at a meeting of its board, removing Gusinsky from control of the television station.

April 19, 2001 The Spanish High Court rejects a Russian request for Gusinsky's extradition on embezzlement charges. Gusinky then flees to Israel.

April 22, 2001 Russian prosecutors file a new arrest warrant with Interpol, alleging that Gusinsky was involved in money laundering.

over major media by a few magnates, or "oligarchs," and finance, banking, and energy firms in the mid-1990s. This consolidation did not appear at first to adversely affect press freedoms, as exemplified by the brave and forthright coverage by some media of the first Russian conflict in its breakaway Chechnya region in 1993–96. A dark side emerged, however, with major media manipulation by the oligarchs in support of Yeltsin's re-election in June-July 1996. Increasingly, it appeared that independent and forthright voices in the media were being stilled by media owners seeking to use their control to advance their own agendas. In addition, media investigations into crime and corruption became more difficult, as criminals and corrupt officials gained increasing power and moved with impunity to kill and harass reporters. Both the 1996 presidential race and the December 1999 State Duma election were typified by media bias and government manipulation of state-owned media, according to the Organization for Security and Cooperation in Eu-

rope and other observers. In the case of the Duma races, government-owned media strongly backed the newly created pro-Putin Unity Party and heavily criticized the opposition Communist Party and others.

Reporting on Chechnya

Events surrounding Putin's election as president in March 2000, witnessed ominous trends in press freedom. The Yeltsin-Putin administration launched a new attack on Chechnya in September 1999. Polls showed that this renewal of conflict was widely supported by the Russian populace, weary of increased theft and lawlessness in the region. Particularly sensational were reports of the kidnapping of hundreds of Russians, including by Chechen criminals who would conduct raiding parties into areas bordering Chechnya to seize hostages. These hostages would be held for ransom or even pressed into "slave labor." This situation, along with a Chechen incursion into Russia's neighboring

THE RUSSIAN MEDIA HAS FACED INCREASING RESTRICTIONS ON ITS FREE SPEECH UNDER PRESIDENT VLADIMIR PUTIN. *(CORBIS CORPORATION (Bellevue). Reproduced by permission.)*

Dagestan region in July-August 1999, ostensibly to establish wider Islamic fundamentalist rule, triggered a renewal of conflict. The Russian military response received added Russian popular support following a series of bombings of apartment buildings in Moscow and elsewhere that raised popular panic, blamed by the Russian authorities on Chechen criminals.

The initial huge support by most Russians for renewed military and police intervention in Chechnya permitted the unpopular Yeltsin to successfully designate his prime minister, Vladimir Putin, as his successor in December 1999. The general apathy that at first greeted the designation of the relatively unknown Putin was soon replaced by popular enthusiasm engendered in part through a pro-Putin media campaign launched by allied oligarchs. Circumstances also enhanced popular support for Putin, particularly the apartment bombings, which

created widespread panic and caused many Russians to welcome Putin's apparent resoluteness. At the same time, Putin and the military-police forces in Chechnya imposed a harsh censorship on reporting from Chechnya to prevent adverse news from harming Putin's electoral chances.

The military has attempted to control media reports from Chechnya through a highly restrictive press accreditation procedure. Under the procedure only pro-Putin reporters have been approved for visits. They are only shown designated sites under armed escort, and their dispatches are screened and censored if necessary. Also, censorship over media accounts of the conflict are imposed throughout Russia by the seven Russian military districts and by regional police offices. The government has used anti-terrorism laws to argue that media cannot legally publish interviews with Chechen leaders.

VLADIMIR PUTIN

1952– Vladimir Putin, an ethnic Russian, was born in 1952 in Leningrad (now St. Petersburg). In 1975 he graduated with a law degree from Leningrad State University. Instead of entering the law field, Putin landed a job with the Foreign Intelligence Administration of the KGB, the Soviet Union's secret police. It was here that he learned to speak German and English in preparation for an international assignment—living undercover as the director of the Soviet-German House of Friendship, a social and cultural club in East Germany.

In 1990 Putin returned to Leningrad and took a job as aide to deputy rector of his alma mater. However, this was reportedly a cover for his continuing intelligence work. Putin resigned from the KGB in 1991 in order to get involved in politics. He became the external affairs aide to St. Petersburg's (the former Leningrad) mayor, and in 1994 became deputy mayor.

In 1997 Putin was asked to join the administration of President Boris Yeltsin and served as deputy head of the Kremlin property office. He left the Kremlin in 1998 to head the Federal Security Service (FSB), the successor to the KGB. In March of 1999 Putin became head of the Security Council, a body that advises the president on matters pertaining to foreign policy, national security, and military and law enforcement.

He served as Acting Premier, then Premier of Russian government from August-December, 1999. On New Year's Eve in 1999 Yeltsin unexpectedly stepped

VLADIMIR PUTIN. *(AP/Wide World Photos. Reproduced by permission.)*

down as president and named Putin as acting president. In accordance with the Russian constitution the election was moved up to March 26, 2000. Putin won the election, garnering 52.6 percent of the vote. He was sworn in as Russia's second president, its first in a free transfer of power in the nation's 1,100-year history, on May 7, 2000.

Reporters have been killed or attacked in Chechnya by both Russian and Chechen forces. Among the most prominent cases involving Russian forces, in January 2000, Andrey Babitsky, a Moscow-based reporter for Radio Liberty, was reported by the Russian military to be missing in Chechnya. The military claimed that he had not abided by accreditation procedures. It was soon revealed, however, that after apprehending him and holding him in the infamous Chernokozovo filtration camp, the military allegedly handed him over to Chechen guerrillas in exchange for two Russian military hostages. In late January Babitsky was released by these guerrillas in neighboring Dagestan, but was then charged by the Russian government with not having proper travel documents at the time when he was freed by the guerrillas. He was found guilty under these charges in October 2000,

but an international outcry helped prevent him from being jailed.

Another reporter who endeavored to provide unbiased coverage of the Chechnya conflict was Anna Politkovskaya, who visited the region several times after September 1999. She was finally detained by Russian troops in February 2001, accused of traveling to areas of Chechnya without permission. Following an outcry by fellow reporters and others, she was released and expelled back to Moscow. She later wrote that she had seen pits at the Khatuni filtration camp where Chechens were allegedly held, often for ransom by Russian soldiers. A commission led by Vladimir Kalamanov, Putin's human rights emissary in Chechnya visited Khatuni in March and reported seeing no such pits. Military prosecutors pronounced Politkovskaya a liar and proposed that she be sued for slander. Supporting the government's denials, ORT television news announcer Mikhail Leontyev, who in May 2001 became a leader of the pro-Putin ultra-nationalist Eurasia movement, called Politkovskaya's report "absurd," saying that he knew Khatuni well and that there were no filtration camps or pits there.

More Media Restraints

Russia's battle with the press gained increasing attention in Chechnya and soon came under even further scrutiny. The widespread popular criticism of the Putin government's treatment of the sinking of the submarine Kursk in August 2000 caused the government to harshly accuse the media of manufacturing and fueling the outcry. Putin's apparently shocked reaction to criticism that he appeared cavalier in the immediate aftermath of the sinking may have contributed to decisions to move more resolutely against perceived anti-government reporting. The sinking of the Kursk witnessed the use of friendly and government-controlled media by the Putin government to deflect criticism. State television RTR was given special access to Putin, and the state-controlled newspaper *Rossiyskaya Gazeta* on August 23–24 condemned attacks against Putin by some "politicians and journalists," singling out Gusinsky's media as seeking to "undermine presidential power" and cause the "dismemberment of Russia." Putin, on August 22, criticized attempts to exaggerate the situation politically for the benefit and interests of certain groups. Slyly questioning the patriotism and motives of Berezovsky, who had collected $1 million to help the families of the Kursk sailors, Putin asserted that those who had collected $1 million for the families had "for a long time contributed to the collapse of the Army, Navy, and state," and that "it would be better for them to sell their villas on the Mediterranean coast."

The U.S. State Department's Human Rights Report for 2000 underscored growing U.S. concerns about the status of freedom of the press in Russia during the first few months of Putin's rule. Responding to the Human Rights Report, Russian Information Minister Lesin, in late February 2001, asserted that there was more freedom of speech in Russia than in the United States, because media in the United States are owned by about fifty wealthy individuals, while Russian media are more widely owned.

Among moves harmful to press freedom the pro-Putin Unity Party and the Liberal Democratic Party sponsored legislative amendments to the 1990 media law that were denounced by the

AFTER REPORTER ANDREY BABITSKY WAS RELEASED BY CHECHEN REBELS IN NEARBY DAGESTAN, HE WAS CHARGED BY THE RUSSIAN GOVERNMENT WITH NOT HAVING THE PROPER TRAVEL DOCUMENTS. AN INTERNATIONAL OUTCRY PREVENTED HIS IMPRISONMENT. *(AP/Wide World Photos. Reproduced by permission.)*

Yabloko Party deputies as threatening freedom of the press. The proposed amendments called for recentralizing the issuing of media licenses, stripping freelancers or stringers of their status as journalists, and allowing prosecutions of media that "deliberately spread false information." Some of the proposals introduced by Unity deputies, such as not permitting reporters to protect their sources, appeared too extreme and were not supported by the Unity faction leadership in the Duma. Other amendments under consideration by Duma committees reportedly included restrictions on foreign information on the Internet.

The State Duma on April 26, 2001, moved to further constrain freedom of the press by overwhelmingly approving a draft bill banning foreign ownership or control of Russian media. The pro-Putin Unity Party, which sponsored the bill, stated that its passage was necessary to safeguard press freedom and national security. The timing of the bill appeared linked to interest by U.S. media magnate Ted Turner in possibly purchasing a share of NTV to maintain its independence from the Russian government. The bill also specifically stated that persons with dual citizenship could not own controlling shares of media firms, appearing to be a clear attack on Vladimir Gusinsky, who holds dual Russian and Israeli citizenship. The bill is part of the implementation of the Information Security Doctrine issued by Putin.

The Information Security Doctrine

The Information Security Doctrine was approved by decree in September 2000 as a policy guide, including the drafting of state-sponsored legislation. The doctrine justifies the strict management of mass media and the construction of new state-owned communications networks for the executive branch of the civilian leadership and for the military and security agencies. As part of this process the Russian government is re-centralizing its control over dozens of regional radio and television affiliates that had fallen somewhat under the sway of the governors and republic presidents.

According to one view the Information Security Doctrine was a response by the Putin government to its decreasing ability to get its message across to the population and to control information flows. State-sponsored news programs were garnering less and less audience share compared to commercial media, creating dissatisfaction among Soviet-thinking bureaucrats. A major rationale was to protect against what some Third World socialists term "information imperialism" by the West. As argued in the doctrine, the West is both trying to impose its views on Russians and to block Russia from making its views known in the "world information space." It warns that foreign influences are trying to take over and control Russia's media. In response it calls for laws regulating foreign media and for more influence by the government over the content of Russia's media, including the ability to block the dissemination of "unlawful information and psychological influences." According to the doctrine, by early 2001, the government is to re-consolidate its effective censorship over the mass media. The doctrine calls for "advisory groups" of trusted journalists to be set up as a top-down means of control. It also calls for stricter standards for the registration of media, which may result in opposition media being stripped of their registration, and for the strict application of laws against the divulgence of military and national security secrets. By 2003 a system of media and communications for military troops is to be operational where they are deployed and based, to be completed by 2005. A major role in military information dissemination is to be played by the Rosinformcentr (Russian Information Center), created in late 1999 to manage news about the Chechnya conflict. According to some reports Russian officials have also proposed that Ros-

informcentr and its head, Sergey Yastrzhembsky, be given added responsibilities for controlling civilian media.

The Information Security Doctrine called for providing "counter-propaganda" to foreign media to counter what it termed "disinformation" on Russia's policies. In a foreign policy address in late January 2001, Putin called for a "struggle for influence over public moods abroad" to "explain Russia's positions." In line with this call Information Minister Mikhail Lesin on February 27, 2001, held a press conference to announce that Russia would begin a "social advertising" campaign in the United States and later in Europe to counter negative Western media accounts of Russia. He also criticized Russian media that he alleged contributed to negative Western media evaluations, singling out Media-Most official Igor Malashenko, who had provided information on freedom of the press in Russia for the U.S. State Department's annual human rights report. Russian critics of the doctrine's call for counter-propaganda have argued that Russia's international image will only change in a positive direction when it seriously pursues democratic and free market reforms.

The Federal Agency for Governmental Communications and Information (FAPSI) not only has responsibility for encryption and security over Russian government communications, but under the doctrine it will also ensure the general security of Russia's "information space." One of its main roles will be to prevent the dissemination of "misinformation." It has moved to carry out surveillance of e-mail and websites on the Internet, along with the Russian Federal Security Service (FSB).

The 2001 Russian state budget reportedly had secret sections dealing with funding for media "rebuilding," including modern communications networks such as microwave and satellite. According to a report in the Russian newspaper Kommersant, it also included funding for the "information struggle." This has reportedly included use of the budgeted funds to gain control over major Russian news sources on the Internet.

Media-Most

The 1998 Russian financial crisis harmed already economically fragile media companies, since advertising revenues and subscriptions plummeted. In the case of Media-Most the crisis led owner Vladimir Gusinsky to seek further loans, contributing to the company's greater financial dependency on state-controlled energy company Gazprom's

AN ASSESSMENT OF FREE SPEECH AND FREE PRESS IN RUSSIA

The U.S. State Department appraised the status of freedom of speech and of the press in Russia. Its observations were noted in *Country Reports on Human Rights Practices, 2000* (February 2001). As this excerpts notes, the Russian government has reached a strong arm across media venues to restrict the free flow of uncensored information.

The [Russian] Constitution provides for freedom of speech and of the press, and numerous national and regional media reflect a multitude of opinions; however, government pressure on the media persisted and in some respects increased significantly, resulting in numerous infringements of these rights. The Government exerted pressure on journalists, particularly those who reported on corruption or criticized officials, by: selectively denying them access to information (including, for example, statistics theoretically available to the public) and filming opportunities; demanding the right to approve certain stories prior to publication; prohibiting the tape recording of public trials and hearings; withholding financial support from government media operations that exercised independent editorial judgment; attempting to influence the appointment of senior editors at regional and local newspapers and broadcast media organizations; removing reporters from their jobs; and bringing libel suits against journalists. Faced with continuing financial difficulties and increased pressure from the Government, many media organizations saw their autonomy erode during the year.... Government intimidation and censorship, both direct and indirect, remained a significant problem during the year.... The Government has also brought considerable pressure to bear on the largest media conglomerates. The most notable example of this phenomenon was the high-profile conflict between the Kremlin and Media-Most (owned by Vladimir Gusinskiy).... The Kremlin has also reportedly sought to strengthen its control over the country's most widely watched television network, ORT.... The press and media NGO's reported a number of killings of journalists, presumed to be related to the journalistic work of the victims, and dozens of other bodily assaults on journalists.

goodwill. Unfortunately, Media-Most was not favored by the Putin government.

Although Gusinsky used his Media-Most holdings to support Yeltsin in the 1996 presidential race, Gusinsky later had a falling-out with Yeltsin. Media-Most media tended to be more critical of government policies and actions in recent years than others. The main holding of Media-Most was its National Television (NTV) station, the only independent, nationwide television station in Russia. Media-Most's support for one of Putin's opponents in the presidential race—the liberal Yabloko Party head Grigory Yavlinsky—was the most immediate source of ire by the Putin regime.

Growing government harassment of Media-Most was highlighted in May 2000, when armed tax police raided the headquarters and television stations NTV and Memonet. The Prosecutor's Office announced that the raid was part of an investigation into financial improprieties by Media-Most's guard service. These raids were followed by dozens of raids on Media-Most offices and the homes of employees. Gusinsky was arrested on June 13, 2000, and charged with embezzlement during the privatization of a television station in St. Petersburg. He was held for three days in jail but was released following an international outcry, and, three weeks later, he left Russia for Spain. Indicating that his departure was negotiated, the prosecutor dropped the embezzlement charges.

Gusinsky, under pressure in July 2000, had acquiesced to the transfer of his share of Media-Most holdings to creditor Gazprom, in return for debt forgiveness and the government's agreement to drop all proposed or possible criminal charges. Gusinsky later denounced the agreement as having been signed under duress and therefore void. The Putin administration claimed it was not a participant in this deal, but Information Minister Lesin later admitted involvement in what some critics termed an attempt to blackmail Gusinsky. Gusinsky, while in Spain, negotiated with Gazprom to protect his investment in Media-Most, but in December 2000, he was detained by Spanish authorities on an Interpol warrant on fraud charges newly brought by the Russian Prosecutor's Office. The prosecutor charged that Gusinsky had received loans from Gazprom by pledging shares of companies that were insolvent. During this turmoil the Putin government claimed it was not politically persecuting Gusinsky, and Gazprom claimed that it was merely pursuing its financial interests.

After a board meeting on April 3, 2001, where Gazprom seized control of NTV and named the president of Gazprom and five other Gazprom officials to the nine-person board, many employees at NTV refused to accept the new management and barricaded the NTV building. Several public rallies took place in Moscow in support of the independence of NTV. Police forcibly occupied the building in a pre-dawn raid on April 14, 2001. Gazprom designated Boris Jordan, a U.S. citizen active in Russian business, as chairman of the NTV board. Jordan argued that the takeover of NTV by Gazprom was strictly motivated by NTV's insolvency and Gazprom's efforts to protect its shares. Moving against other Gusinsky assets, Gazprom bid its shares in alliance with co-owner and manager Dmitriy Biryukov to seize control of the Sem Dnei ("Seven Days") publishing company from Gusinsky. Biryukov then cancelled publication of the liberal newspaper Segodnya and fired the editorial staff of the magazine *Itogi*. Ted Turner, the American head of large U.S. media holdings, in February indicated interest in buying a share of NTV to maintain its independence from Russian state control, but he pulled out of talks in April when it became clear that the government, through Gazprom, intended to retain majority control. Also, many of the top personnel at NTV quit, reducing its value.

Gazprom has maintained that it has no political plans for its new media holdings and may even seek to sell some of its holdings, according to some reports. Some critics, however, claim that the activities of other media it controls do not give room for optimism. They point to the Gazprom-owned newspaper *Trud*, which has few readers, operates at a deficit, and does not address sensitive political issues, as an example.

Other Media Harassment

Oligarch Boris Berezovsky's Logovaz press syndicate was instrumental during the December 1999 Duma races and Putin's presidential election in pushing Putin's agenda and attacking Putin's opponents. Berezovsky also owned 49 percent of ORT, Russian Public Television, with the remaining 51 percent controlled by the government. He too, however, soon faced government harassment. According to Berezovsky, the harassment was linked to critical coverage by ORT of Putin's response to the sinking of the Kursk submarine in August 2000. Immediately after these critical reports, Berezovsky alleged in a letter he released in September 2000 that the presidential administration had demanded that he relinquish his shares in ORT, seeking to completely silence ORT like it was using Gazprom and the prosecutor's efforts to silence NTV. In December 2000 police from several agencies conducted a massive raid on Berezovsky's offices at ORT, claiming ORT had smuggled foreign films into Russia. In January 2001 Berezovsky sold his ORT shares to oligarch Roman Abramovich, whom Berezovsky termed a "middleman" for the government. In February 2001, the government moved to name the remaining members of the board of directors. However, Information Minister Lesin subsequently claimed that Abramovich no longer held the shares and that they had been sold to private buyers.

The Russian Federal Security Service (FSB) and Interior Ministry police have been implicated in several attacks on journalists. In January 2000, in a case reminiscent of Soviet-era practices against dissidents, Moscow police arrested investigative reporter Alexander Khinshtein, accused him of mental illness, and tried to take him to a psychiatric clinic. Among other cases the Putin administration reportedly has been putting pressure on the English-language newspaper *Moscow Times*, which is critical of the Putin regime, to soften its reporting. In late 2000 the *Moscow Times* was forced out of its offices to make way for a new Putin government-created English language newspaper.

Greater government oversight over the content of telephone, cellular, and Internet communications was provided by a Russian Communications Ministry directive issued in July 2000 that called for all state and private operators to facilitate monitoring by the FSB. Communications firms were then required to work with the FSB in designing and installing surveillance equipment and even in training FSB personnel in its use. Although the proposed monitoring was criticized by the public in 1998, during the more restrictive Putin era there were already fewer media outlets willing to air negative commentary, according to observers. In the Internet realm Putin's media advisor, Gleb Pavlovsky, wants the government to restructure its state-owned or controlled media as an hierarchy initially led by the internet site he set up, strana.ru. In October 2000 Pavlovsky took over the news portal vesti.ru, stating that henceforth it would report patriotic and right wing views. A few months later in January 2001 the government news agency NOVOSTI set up a news portal called rian.ru, to promulgate government information, including from state-owned television and radio stations. According to some reports the government also planned to set up an internet provider.

RECENT HISTORY AND THE FUTURE

Polls indicate that the public appears divided on the issue of press freedom. A poll conducted by the well-regarded All-Russia Public Opinion Center in January 2001 found that 42 percent of those polled thought the media have enough freedom, while 18 percent thought the media were too free. On the other hand, 33 percent thought that media did not yet have enough freedom. Another poll showed that public support for the independence of NTV was not overwhelming. According to one poll taken by Center on April 7–8, after the NTV takeover, only 21 percent of respondents decried the Gazprom move to seize management control of NTV. These respondents, however, have been vocal despite their apparent minority status. Yabloko announced at a rally on April 28, 2001, that it had gathered signatures from 863,000 people supporting the continued independence of NTV and freedom of speech. Even the Russian legislature's Audit Chamber in early 2001 questioned the government's harassment of Media-Most. It issued a report on the finances of the state-controlled RTR television station and its parent company, concluding that they were suffering major financial losses. The auditors noted that Information Minister Lesin, the former financial manager at the parent company, retained financial interests there, and questioned why the government was selectively pursuing only Gusinsky and Media-Most for financial improprieties and debts.

A policy forum convened by the International Research and Exchanges Board in December 2000 recommended that the United States and European states take several measures to encourage press freedom in Russia. It called for the development of media centers throughout Russia where journalists could receive training and advice from visiting foreign journalists, and technical assistance for Russian newspaper editors to help them better manage advertising and finances. The forum advocated that government agencies develop their own public relations capabilities rather than pressuring commercial media to act as their mouthpieces. It also called for U.S. and European governments to offer more assistance to the Russian legislature to help it write laws upholding the freedom of information and broadcast licensing.

The Struggle for a Free Press Continues

Despite the pressure on freedom of the press during the Putin era, some free expression remains, as evident in media criticism of Putin's treatment of the Kursk disaster and some continued brave criticism of the Chechnya conflict and government corruption. The Russian government might find it difficult to control information flows where both reporters and the public have become used to certain freedoms. In particular, the government might find it difficult to control the Internet and a less docile judicial system, and might have to tolerate independent voices.

Observers will be monitoring the re-trial of environmental journalist Grigory Pasko, scheduled for early 2001 but delayed into the summer. He was arrested by the FSB and imprisoned in November 1997, charged with handing over allegedly secret documents on radiation waste spills by the Pacific Ocean Fleet to Japanese reporters. The military court of the Pacific Fleet in Vladivostok acquitted him of espionage and treason charges in July 1999, but convicted him on a lesser offense of abuse of office, sentenced him to three years' imprisonment, and then freed him for time served. Pasko appealed this reduced sentence, calling for complete exoneration. A military panel of Russia's Supreme Court vacated the acquittal in November 2000 and remanded the case for re-trial in Vladivostok. The re-trial decision was viewed by Pasko's supporters as political harassment. Pasko's defense in the first trial had been supported by the Glasnost' Defense Fund, the Open Society Institute, and several Russian newspapers, who have called for support for his re-trial. Pasko's future, like that of Russia's media, remains uncertain.

BIBLIOGRAPHY

Blank, Stephen, and Theodore Karasik. "'Reforms that Hark Back to Stalinist Times: Putin is Centralizing Control Over the Media and Tax Revenue to Snuff Out Dissent," *Los Angeles Times*, July 20, 2000, p. B11.

Commission on Security and Cooperation in Europe, U.S. Congress. *Report on the Russian Presidential Elections, March 26, 2000*. Washington, DC: U.S. Congress, October 2000.

Demchenko, Irina. "Russia's Gusinsky Receives New Blow to Media Empire," Reuters, April 17, 2001.

"Factbox—Who Owns What in the Russian Media?" Reuters, April 17, 2001.

Feller, Henry. "Russian Military Reform: Mass Media Control and Information Security," *Jane's Intelligence Review*, January 2001, p. 12–13.

Glasser, Susan B., and Peter Baker. "Russian Network Seized in Raid: 11-Day Standoff Ends; Many Journalists Quit," *The Washington Post*, April 15, 2001, p. A1.

International Press Institute. *2000 World Press Freedom Review*. Available online at http://www.freemedia.at/wpfr/russia.htm (cited June 1, 2001).

Lipman, Masha. "Putin's KGB Way," *The Washington Post*, April 17, 2001, p. A17.

McHugh, David. "Russia: NTV—What's Left," Associated Press, April 17, 2001.

Monaghan, Elaine. "U.S. Says Very Troubled by Moves on Russian Media," Reuters, April 18, 2001.

Paldi, Boaz. "Gusinsky Keeps Low Profile," Reuters, April 25, 2001.

Renaud, Chris. "Russian Roulette: Putin Shoots the Messenger," *Wall Street Journal*, February 23, 2001.

"Russia: Gusinsky Free, Independent Media Not," *Transitions Online*, April 18–23, 2001. Available online at http://www.tol.cz/look/TOLnew (cited June 1, 2001).

"Russia: One Fine Day," *Transitions Online*, April 24–30, 2001. Available online at http://www.tol.cz/look/TOLnew (cited June 1, 2001).

Schoenberg, Cheryl and Courtney Dunn. "The Media in Russia: New Roles, New Rules," International Research and Exchanges Board, 2001.

Shishkin, Dmitry. "Brief Legal Evaluation of Circumstances Attending to Andrey Babitsky's Detention," Glasnost Defense Foundation. Available online at http://www.gdf.ru/english/babitski-eng.html (cited June 1, 2001).

Simonov, Alexsey. "Knock from Below," *Index on Censorship*. Available online at http://www.indexoncensorship.org/100/sim.html (cited June 1, 2001).

Staar, Richard F. "Toward a Police State?" *Perspective,* vol. 11, no. 3, January-February 2001, p. 1, 7–9.

"VGTRK Budget Figures Don't Lie," *RFE/RL Media Matters,* vol. 1, no. 3, February 23, 2001.

Vidal-Hall, Judith. "Russia: In Chechnya," *Index on Censorship,* March 12, 2001. Available online at http://www.indexoncensorship.org/news/russia1120301.html (accessed June 1, 2001).

Yasmann, Victor. AFSB legalizes monitoring of Internet," *RFE/RL Security Watch,* vol. 1, no. 6, August 28, 2000.

———. "Putin's Image-maker Issues Information Policy Manifesto," *RFE/RL Security Watch,* vol. 1, no. 11, October 2, 2000.

———. "Kremlin Moves to Capture Internet Media," *RFE/RL Security Watch,* vol. 1, no. 13, October 16, 2000.

———. "The Roots of Putin's Attack on Media Freedom," *RFE/RL Security Watch,* vol. 1, no. 3, August 7, 2000.

———. "Russia's New Information Security Doctrine—A Threat to Freedom and Democracy," Radio Free Europe/Radio Liberty, *RFE/RL Security Watch,* vol. 1, no. 9, September 18, 2000.

—Jim Nichol

AFTER SOMALIA'S CIVIL WAR: PUTTING THE PIECES BACK TOGETHER AGAIN

THE CONFLICT

Under the dictatorial leadership of Mahammad Siad Barre, Somalia became embroiled in increasing violence throughout the 1970s and 1980s. As public resistance to his regime escalated, Siad Barre's efforts to maintain control grew increasingly brutal as he encouraged ethnic clans to fight one another. In 1991 he fled the country, and it descended into chaos. International intervention failed to achieve a lasting peace and the country has struggled amidst continued fighting to rebuild its government and infrastructure from the ravages of war and to unite its people under one Somalia.

Political

- After dictator Mahammad Siad Barre fled the country, Somalia was left without an organized, functioning central government. A power vacuum ensued, with opposing clans fighting each other for dominance.

- As the violence waned, a transitional government was established to fill the void, which, despite continued opposition, continues its efforts to resume the services of government.

- Though the majority of fighting has ceased, violent opposition by opposing clans lingers, threatening Somalia's stability.

- The regions of Somaliland and Puntland have established governments independent of Somalia. Puntland considers this a temporary arrangement until Somalia becomes more stable, whereas Somaliland maintains that its independence is permanent.

Ethnic

- Somali society, while largely homogenous, is divided along clan lines. Mahammad Siad Barre encouraged clan rivalries and spurred fighting between the clans to offset opposition to his own regime.

- After Siad Barre's departure from the country, clan fighting continued, and international and humanitarian intervention largely failed.

Despite the removal of the brutal dictator Mahammad Siad Barre in Somalia in January 1991, the violence that dominated the country for the previous decade was nowhere near over. The numerous resistance forces that united to oust Siad Barre could not come together in agreement to form a new government. Factions broke off, internal rivalries erupted, and in the civil war that followed, some 50,000 Somalis were killed and 300,000 more died of starvation because international relief supplies could not be delivered amidst the chaotic violence. With no existing government, the economy in virtual collapse, violence out of control, and a drought plaguing the country, Somalia was a land of anarchy and suffering. Despite U.S. and United Nations (UN) intervention and the deployment of peacekeeping troops in the early 1990s, the Somali tragedy went unabated for the remainder of the decade.

Hope was reborn in 2000 when the neighboring country of Djibouti organized the Somali National Peace Conference, which was held on May 2, 2000. More than 2,000 participants traveled to Arta, Djibouti, to attend the conference. A 245-member Transitional National Assembly was selected based on clan representation. After three months of deliberations, on August 26, 2000, the Transitional National Assembly elected Abdiqasim Salad Hassan as the new president of Somalia. The following day Abdiqasim Salad was sworn into office in Arta in an inauguration ceremony attended by heads of state from Eritrea, Ethiopia, Sudan, Yemen, and Djibouti. Representatives from the UN, the European Union, the Arab League, France, Italy, Kuwait, and Libya were also present.

Despite Abdiqasim Salad's election to the presidency, a peaceful and united future for So-

MAP OF SOMALIA. *(Maryland Cartographics. Reproduced by permission.)*

malia was not assured. Somali's traditional clan-based allegiances remain far stronger than any bonds to national unity. Those clans that have felt ostracized from the process have not acknowledged Abdiqasim Salad's right to rule, and they vow to oppose his administration. Not only will Abdiqasim Salad have to contend with clan factions in central and southern Somalia, he will also faces serious challenges to his government from two break-away regions in the north: Somaliland and Puntland. The northwestern region of Somalia declared its independence from the rest of the country in 1991. Now the Republic of Somaliland refuses to acquiesce its autonomy, stating its independence is irrevocable. In 1998 the northeastern

region, known as Puntland, also separated from Somalia to establish its own state. Although the Puntland government considers its independence a transitory state until a satisfactory centralized government can be established, Puntland leaders have refused to participate in the Arta peace talks. After years of war Somalia must struggle to pick up the pieces and put itself back together.

HISTORICAL BACKGROUND

Known as the Land of Punt in ancient times, Somalia was a part of the Ethiopian kingdom of Askum. Somalis began pushing south from the Gulf of Aden coast (now in Yemen) around the ninth or tenth century. It was also around this time that Arabs established the sultanate of Adel and other settlements along the Indian Ocean's coast. When the sultanate of Adel dissolved, the region became dominated by Arabs in the coastal trading communities and Somalis in the pasturelands of the interior. The structure of individual chiefdoms remained intact until the arrival of European imperialism decimated the traditional systems of governance in the nineteenth century.

European Colonization

Although the Portuguese were the first Europeans to explore the region, the British were the first to initiate colonization of Somalia. In 1839 Britain established a refueling station in the Gulf of Aden to service merchant ships. By 1874 Egypt had established control of some of the coastline and several interior villages, but its occupation was short-lived. From 1884 to 1886 the British negotiated friendship treaties with local clans, and in 1887 declared the creation of British Somaliland. By 1905 the governmental administration shifted from Aden to a regional colonial affairs office in British Somaliland. British rule was constantly disrupted from 1899 to 1920 by the "holy war" waged by Sayyid Mahammad Abdille Hasan, known to the British as "Mad Mullah."

Italy established its first colonial foothold in southern Somalia in 1888, when Italian expansionist Vincenzo Filonardi convinced Yuusuf Ali Keenadiid, the Sultan of Hobyo, to agree to Italian "protection." In the same year, rival sultan, Boqor Ismaan Mahamuud of the Majeerteen clan, also agreed to allow Italian presence. By the early twentieth century, Britain agreed to concede the southern Chisimayu region to Italy, which completed the protectorate that became known as Italian Somaliland. Unencumbered by violent conflict, as the British were in the north, the Italians in southern Somalia were able to establish a development plan for the region. Instituting an economic plan, Italian Somaliland launched a series of large-scale development projects, including creating a system of plantations throughout the region. As a result, southern Somalia developed an economic and political infrastructure lacking in British Somaliland.

As a result of the influx of European influence, the largely ethnically homogeneous Somalis were divided into five distinct regions: British Somaliland, Ethiopian Somaliland, French Somaliland, Italian Somaliland, and the far north region known as the Northern Frontier District (NFD), indirectly ruled by Britain through Kenya.

World War II

In 1935, as the conflicts leading to World War II (1939–45) were beginning, Italian troops marched into Ethiopia and removed Ethiopian Emperor Haile Selassie from his throne, thereby effectively also taking control of the Ogaden. In 1940 Italian forces invaded British Somaliland and took charge of the entire region, thus uniting much of the Somali population, except for French Somalia and the NFD, under the Italian flag. The Italians introduced a common currency, set prices, and imposed taxes, which created a monetarized economic system that replaced the traditional system of exchange-in-kind. The shift in control, however, was short-lived. The following year British troops were able to regain British Somaliland and take control of Italian Somaliland and the Ogaden as well, where they established military administrations.

During the 1940s British rule in Somalia proved more effective than in the past. An influx of funding into the northern area resulted in an increase in economic activity. The British also made efforts to improve conditions by expanding the elementary school system, establishing more health and veterinary services, creating better water supplies by digging new wells, and reorganizing the judiciary system by combining elements of British law with traditional or religious customs. The British also invited the Somalis into the administrative process by allowing Somalis to hold lower level offices in civil service and replacing local clan leaders previously appointed by the Italians with clan-elected representatives.

Political Activities

Somali political activity grew as a counterdevelopment to Italian political organizing. Because the British needed experienced civil servants to operate the administration effectively, Italians retained many civil service jobs. Only Italians associated with the military or considered a security threat were exiled or detained. Therefore, a substantial Italian population remained in Italian Somaliland after the British took control of the region. As a result, by 1943 Italians were organizing to promote the return of the area to Italian rule. To counter the political pressure from the Italians, the British encouraged the Somalis to organize politically. The first modern Somali political party was founded in Mogadishu in 1943 as the Somali Youth Club.

With the support of the British administration, the Somali Youth Club expanded quickly, growing to 25,000 members by 1946. The follow-

CHRONOLOGY

July 1960 British Somaliland and Italian Somaliland gain their independence and unite as the sovereign nation of Somalia.

October 1969 Somali President Abdirashid Ali Sharmaarke is assassinated. Days later the military stages a coup and takes control of the government under General Mohammed Siad Barre.

July 1977 Siad Barre declares war on Ethiopia in an effort to reclaim the region known as the Ogaden.

March 1978 Somalia is forced to withdraw its troops and concede defeat after the Soviet Union, formerly Somalia's ally, aligns with Ethiopia.

May 1988 The Somali National Movement (SNM) launches the first major military attack against Siad Barre's increasingly oppressive regime.

December 1990 Armed uprisings break out across Mogadishu as military resistance to Siad Barre's rule intensifies.

January 1991 Siad Barre is forced to flee, and the country falls into chaos as rival factions struggle for control of the country.

May 1991 Somaliland declares its independence.

April 1992 UNOSOM begins its initiative in Somalia, in an attempt to secure the delivery of humanitarian aid to areas affected by severe drought.

December 1992 U.S.-controlled UNITAF takes over command of UN efforts in Somalia.

May 1992 UNITAF returns control to the UN, and UNOSOM II is established.

March 1993 After numerous widely publicized incidences of armed conflict between UN troops and Somalis, the United States removes its military personnel from the country.

March 1994 UNOSOM II officially ends as its remaining UN troops withdraw from Somalia.

1998 Puntland declares its independence in a transition move, pending the establishment of a central Somali government.

May 2000 Somali peace talks are held in neighboring Djibouti. A 245-member transitional parliament is elected based on clan representation.

August 2000 The transitional parliament elects Abdiqasim Salad Hassan as the new Somali president.

March 2001 Faction leaders opposed to the transitional government establish the Somali Reconciliation and Restoration Council.

ing year it was renamed as the Somali Youth League (SYL) and increased its influence by expanding its organization into all regions of Somalia. The SYL's stated goals included the creation of a unified Somalia and the development of a national language. Vehemently opposed to the reestablishment of Italian rule, the SYL also denounced the clannish mentality that so often worked against national unity. To emphasize their commitment to national unity, the 13 founding members, who represented four of the six major clans, refused to reveal their family origins.

After World War II, according to the terms of the Potsdam Conference, Italy was forced to concede its African land interests; therefore, the Allied Council of Foreign Ministers commissioned a four-nation council of Britain, France, the Soviet Union, and the United States to decide Somalia's future. Britain wished to maintain all of Somalia under British rule, a proposal the other commission members found unacceptable. In January 1948 the commission representatives traveled to Somalia to gain a better understanding of the Somalis' wishes. The SYL staged a large demonstration in favor of Somalia's independence. Violence erupted when a counter demonstration supporting Italian rule clashed with the SYL, resulting in the deaths of 24 Somalis and 51 Italians. During its stay the commission representatives heard three proposals from Somali-based groups: the SYL's proposal for an independent, united Somalia after ten years of trusteeship under international authority; a modified request for independence based on a 30-year Italian trusteeship; and a pro-Italian request for the return of Italian rule.

Having heard the proposals, the commission debated over Somalia's fate, each hoping to protect the interest of their individual countries. As deals between the powers were made, the resulting decision created a 10-year transitional period for both

British Somaliland and Italian Somaliland to move toward independence. Britain would remain in Somalia for ten years as the administrator of the trusteeship of British Somaliland. Italian presence would be reintroduced to Italian Somaliland for a 10-year period, after which both trusteeships would become independent. Also, under intense pressure from the United States, the Soviet Union, and Ethiopia's Haile Selassie, whom the British had replaced on the throne after driving out the Italians, Britain returned the Ogaden to Ethiopian rule. Members of the SYL, who saw the possibility of establishing Greater Somalia—incorporating all five divided regions into one united country—destroyed by the decision to return the Ogaden to Ethiopia, protested loudly but to no avail. Somali clan leaders in the Ogaden were assuaged with payment of war reparations, which other Somalis disparagingly referred to as bribes.

The reinstitution of Italian rule in Italian Somaliland was riddled with conflict. Many civil posts were held by members of the SYL, who deeply distrusted Italian presence in the region, and their resentment increased when the Italian transitional administration proceeded to fire some SYL members and arrest others. By the mid-1950s, however, tensions had abated somewhat as the country began to focus on its upcoming independence.

Somalia: Independent and United

Within a four-day period in 1960 Italian Somaliland and British Somaliland were granted independence; the two regions enthusiastically united as the Somali Republic on July 1, 1960. Under an agreement reached by representatives from the north and south, the united country would be governed by a president, a prime minister, and an elected National Assembly of 123 members. Aadan Abdullah Usmaan was appointed by the National Assembly as the first president; a national referendum the following year confirmed his appointment. A member of the SYL, Usmaan named another SYL leader, Abdirashid Ali Shermaarke, as prime minister. In 1964 Usmaan replaced Shermaarke with Abdirizaaq Haaji Husseen. The SYL, which held a strong majority in the National Assembly, split its allegiance between Shermaarke, who favored an aggressive pan-Somalia program, and Husseen, who advocated internal development as the national priority.

In 1967 Shermaarke succeeded Usmaan as president. Despite conflicts within the SYL, the transfer of power occurred peacefully. Shermaarke named Mohammad Ibrahim Egal as prime minister. Egal offered a moderate voice on the issue of Greater Somalia. He hoped to mend relations with neighboring countries to create an environment in which the border conflicts with Ethiopia and Kenya could be resolved peacefully. He succeeded to an extent, and border pressures were eased for a time. In March 1969 municipal and National Assembly elections gave the SYL an incredible advantage over the numerous competing political parties. The National Assembly held 109 of the 123 seats. Discontent began to arise as allegations of ballot fraud, nepotism, and official corruption surfaced. More people increasingly complained that clan-based alliances were becoming more important than political affiliation or national interest. Shermaarke's and Egal's disinterested approaches to those expressing dissatisfaction did little to alleviate rising tensions.

Somalia's fragile democracy soon came to an abrupt end. A bodyguard, reportedly angered by the president's poor treatment of his clan-family, assassinated Shermaarke on October 15, 1969. In the days following the president's death, Egal arranged for the selection of a new president by the National Assembly. Before the process could be complete, however, the military—long dissatisfied with the direction of the country away from establishing Greater Somalia—intervened. A military coup d'état took place on October 21, 1969, when the military, with the cooperation of the police, rounded up government leaders and peacefully took control of the country.

The Rule of Siad Barre

The new military government assumed the name of the Supreme Revolutionary Council (SRC) and appointed Major General Mahammad Siad Barre as president. Major political leaders were detained, the National Assembly was dismissed, and the constitution was revoked. The SRC stated its desire to end corruption, mismanagement, tribalism, and nepotism. It also expounded the firm commitment to Somali unification and renamed the country the Somali Democratic Republic. As the military worked to revamp the government and create an aggressive Marxist-based program of development, Siad Barre continued to increase in prestige and power. On the anniversary of the coup, he announced the Somali Democratic Republic to be a socialist state. Although Marxist ideology is based on class conflict, which did not exist in Somali culture, Siad Barre named tribalism as the "disease" of Somalia that socialism would overcome. Siad Barre's strong commitment to the image of scientific socialism, coupled with the nation's growing dependence on

SOMALIA WAS RAVAGED BY ETHNIC CONFLICT, WHICH BEGAN UNDER THE REIGN OF DICTATOR MAHAMMAD SIAD BARRE. THE COUNTRY NOW FACES THE CHALLENGE OF REBUILDING. *(AP/Wide World Photos. Reproduced by permission.)*

the support of the Soviet Union, led to the popular acceptance of Somalia as a socialist state.

Siad Barre had a grand vision for Somalia. With the assistance of the Soviet Union he undertook numerous large-scale projects. By 1972 a written Somali language had been developed and declared the official national language. With only a five percent literacy rate, Siad Barre established an aggressive urban and rural literacy campaign. He also focused on issues of national development and improvement such as tree planting, construction of schools, hospitals, and health clinics, the development of businesses and roads, and the promotion of women's rights. By 1976 Siad Barre had con-

structed a communist political structure to replace military rule, and in June 1976 the congress of the Somali Revolutionary Socialist Party (SRSP) convened. It replaced the SRC as the governing body on July 1, 1976. Despite the change in organization the country continued to be ruled by military personnel, who now assumed positions within the SRSP, with Siad Barre at the helm.

The Ogaden War (1977–78)

By the end of the 1970s Siad Barre had firmly cemented his power, and his leadership style had moved toward a dictatorial approach. His popularity was waning quickly. Perhaps in an attempt to regain the respect and unity of the people, Siad

Barre, in a bold military move, ordered the invasion of Ethiopian Ogaden in 1977. Widespread drought in Ethiopia the previous two years had weakened the country's defenses, and Haile Selassie's rule was crushed by Ethiopian revolutionary Mengistu Haile Mariam. Taking advantage of the situation, Siad Barre, who had built the Somali army from 5,000 to 37,000 before invading, moved to return the Ogaden to Somalia rule. Unbeknownst to Siad Barre, however, was the Soviet Union's decision to abandon its previous affiliation with Somalia to support Haile Mariam. Thousands of Cuban troops, wielding sophisticated Russian equipment, helped Ethiopia reject Siad Barre's advancing army. Ethiopia was able to regain control of the region, and, as a result, over one million Somali refugees poured across the Ethiopian border into Somalia.

The results of losing the Ogaden War were devastating. Siad Barre, in fear of losing power and no longer supported by the powerful Soviet Union, continued to build army forces until its ranks soared to 120,000. The country was unsettled in the wake of its defeat, and oppositions groups began to emerge. Siad Barre dealt with his detractors quickly and violently, suppressing critics by jail, torture, mass execution, and harassment of certain clans. To protect himself from rebellious factions, he instituted a strategy of "divide and conquer." Whereas clanism had previously been strongly rejected, Siad Barre now used it to his advantage by playing clans against one another. He ordered his troops to attack "hostile" clans and instructed them to arm "loyal" clans. By encouraging clan warfare, Siad Barre instigated one of the most violent and senseless wars in African history.

Clan-Based Society

Clan identity is the most important affiliation in Somali culture. Alliances are made based on the necessity of the situation. Although clan families may unite to overcome a common foe, as soon as the opponent is defeated, the alliance is broken and the clan may then dissolve friendly relations and fight against each other. The relation among clans is therefore very liquid and flexible, making allegiances to national structures almost impossible to sustain. When Siad Barre banned all political parties, making them illegal because, he reasoned that the parties consisted primarily of clan-based affiliations, and he actually strengthened the clannish nature of the society by making it the only political and social outlet for the population. As his power dissolved and he began to pit clan against clan, Siad Barre created an environment where inter- and intra-clan warfare was accentuated.

Although Somalia has one of the most homogeneous ethnic populations in Africa, identity is based almost solely on affiliation with one of the six major clans. Approximately three-quarters of the population belong to one of four pastoral nomadic clan-families that descend from the common tribe of Samaal—the Dir, Daarood, Isaaq, and Hawiye. The Samaal clan families are further delineated into a multitude of subclans. For example, the clan families of Ogaden, Majeerteen, Mareehaan, and Dulbahante all originate from the Daarood clan. Although there is a small population of non-Somali residents, most of the remaining population (approximately 20 percent) belongs to one of the two agricultural clan-families, the Digil and Rahanwayn, who reside primarily in the southern regions of Somalia.

Resistance and Oppression

The Majeerteen clan originates from the Daarood family clan, as did Siad Barre's own Mareehaan clan. Prior to the military coup many important government and military positions were held by Majeerteen. Perhaps resentful of their past influence or fearful of their opposition, Siad Barre singled out the Majeerteen for discrimination as early as 1970s. By the mid-1970s the Majeerteen were effectively alienated from Siad Barre's administration, and in April 1978, an unsuccessful coup d'état was staged by a group of Majeerteen army officers. Seventeen alleged leaders of the coup were executed; several more escaped to Ethiopia, where they established the Somali Salvation Democratic Front (SSDF), led by Yusuf Ahmad, the SSDF became the first military organization to appear with the intent to remove Siad Barre from power. As the SSDF began its military battle in northeast Somalia, Siad Barre unleashed his elite and brutal special military force, the Red Berets, on the Majeerteen clan. The Majeerteen, who had few allies among the other clans, found no support against Siad Barre's forces. By destroying reservoirs around the area inhabited by the Majeerteen, Siad Barre was able to deny water to the clan and its herds. As a result, during a two-month span in 1979, more than 2,000 Majeerteen died of thirst, and the clan lost an estimated 50,000 camels, 10,000 cattle, and 100,000 sheep and goats.

Despite the persecution the SSDF continued its efforts, and by 1988 had extended its control over parts of the western and southern regions. In 1985 the SSDF split, with a new organization forming as the Somali Patriotic Movement (SPM). In 1990 a mass desertion of military officers in the Ogaden region, disenfranchised after the defeat to

Ethiopia in the Ogaden War, aligned themselves with the SPM, giving the organization substantial military power that allowed the SPM to capture and maintain control of several government posts in the south.

The Isaaq clan, which live primarily in the northern region of Somalia, also came under the attack of Siad Barre's forces. In 1981 some 500 Isaaqs living in England organized the Somali National Movement (SNM) with the sole objective of removing Siad Barre from power. In a military campaign launched in 1988 from northwestern Somalia, it managed to gain control of the city of Burao and part of the city of Hargeysa; both cities were almost exclusively inhabited by Isaaqs. Additionally, both were subsequently destroyed by massive bombing attacks ordered by Siad Barre. Hargeysa was completely destroyed and an estimated 50,000 inhabitants were killed. The SNM was forced to withdraw, and more than 300,000 Isaaq sought refuge in Ethiopia. Once again, Siad Barre ordered brutal attacks the Somali people. In the last six months of 1988 reportedly more than 1,000 women and children were murdered by Siad Barre's troops. Although the SNM appealed to other clans to join its efforts the northern region's largest non-Isaaq clan, the Gadaburis, formed its own resistance organization, the Somali Democratic Alliance (SDA).

Siad Barre also systematically repressed the Hawiye clan. The Hawiye occupied a large section of Mogadishu and had held important positions in the government before Siad Barre's regime. Now, disenfranchised with Siad Barre's rule, the Hawiye became Siad Barre's next target for destruction and demoralization. His attempt to crush them proved to be a fatal mistake. Mogadishu had always served as Siad Barre's stronghold, but now he was faced with waging war within the walls of his own fortress. The Hawiye opposition formed the United Somali Congress (USC) in late 1989. It divided in mid-1990 after the death of its charismatic founder. One faction was controlled by businessman Ali Mahdi Muhammad, and the other by General Mohamed Aidid.

By 1989 resistance groups controlled large portions of the north and east. Siad Barre, becoming desperate to maintain his control, ordered wholesale brutality upon the Somali people. Mogadishu became the center of the murderous violence. On July 9, 1989, Salvatore Colombo, the Italian-born Roman Catholic bishop of Somalia and an outspoken critic of Siad Barre, was shot to death in his church in Mogadishu. Although no

MAJOR SOMALI CLANS AND POLITICAL PARTIES

United Somali Congress (USC). Most USC members come from the Hawiye clan of central Somalia, with a heavy concentration of the population of Mogadishu. The USC split into two factions in 1990. One faction is led by Ali Mahdi, and the other is led by Hussein Aidid, son of the USC founder Mohammed Farah Aidid. Aidid's faction is aligned with the Somali National Alliance (SNA). It has since split again with a new USC faction formed by former USC lieutenant Usman Khalil Ali Ato.

Somali Salvation Democratic Front (SSDF). The SSDF was originated by the Majertain sub-clan of the Daarood clan, located in the northeast region of Somalia.

Somali National Front (SNF). The SNF was founded by the Marehan sub-clan of the Daarood in southern Somalia, near the Kenyan border. Former president Siad Barre was a member of this sub-clan.

Somali National Movement (SNM). The SNM was created by the Issaq clan in northwestern Somalia. The SNM was the driving force behind the creation of the independent Republic of Somliland in May 1991.

Somali Patriotic Front (SPF). The SPF is the political arm of the Ogadeni clan, a sub-clan of the Daarood, located partially in the south and partially in the central regions of Somalia. The SPF is divided into two rival factions.

Somali Democratic Movement (SDM). The SDM was founded by the Rahanwein clan, who live primarily in the south and west regions of Somalia. The SDM is also split into two rival factions.

Somali Democratic Association (SDA). The SDA was created by the Dir clan of northwestern Somalia.

gunman was ever identified, his assassination was widely believed to have been ordered by Siad Barre. Just days later, on July 15, 1989, the Red Berets fired on Muslims who were protesting the arrest of their spiritual leaders; 450 were killed and more than 2,000 seriously injured. The following day 47 members of the Isaaq clan were transported to the edge of Mogadishu and executed. The human rights organization Africa Watch estimated that between June 1988 and January 1990, government forces killed as many as 50,000 unarmed civilians, the majority of whom belonged to the Isaaq clan. After the violence of July 1989 the United States, which had provided military equipment and other aid to Siad Barre's government since the end of the Ogaden War, withdrew its support completely from Somalia.

As violence in the form of rape, torture, and genocide continued, the voice of opposition grew stronger. Siad Barre became even more desperate and the situation more dire. On July 6, 1990, an anti-government demonstration at a soccer match erupted into violence. In the ensuing riot, 65 people were killed when Siad Barre's bodyguard panicked and began firing into the crowd. Other military personnel shot into the panicked crowds fleeing the stadium. Later, family members were not allowed to remove the bodies for burial. The following week Siad Barre ordered the execution of 46 prominent citizens who had signed a manifesto calling for elections and improved human rights conditions. Demonstrations outside the trial brought the city to a standstill, forcing Siad Barre to drop the charges. Shaken and quickly losing his footing, Siad Barre retreated to a military bunker near the airport. In January 1991 the USC gained control of Mogadishu, and Siad Barre, hidden in a military tank, fled to Nigeria.

Upon Siad Barre's departure the country fell into chaos as clan militias struggled for control. Siad Barre had effectively played clan against clan so that in his absence the clan relationships once again became the predominate means of affiliation. Now, clans fought rival clans for control of the country. The problem was that Somalia had no internal political structure to replace the one it tore down when Siad Barre was driven from the country. In the absence of any sustainable national government the leaders of the military resistance groups became warlords vying for power and land. In the complex, flexible interplay between clan families, distrust and revenge ruled the day.

The day after Siad Barre's flight from Somalia, the USC, which had gained control of Mogadishu, quickly placed hotelier Ali Mahdi as president. General Mohamed Aidid strongly opposed the appointment. Soon after, full-scale war broke out between the rival factions of the USC. Eventually Mogadishu became divided between Ali Mahdi's USC and Aidid's USC, which formed a coalition with several other opposition groups as the Somali National Alliance (SNA). Just in the capital city alone, an estimated 14,000 people were killed and more than 30,000 wounded as the USC factions fought for control of the city; many of the casualties were women and children caught in the crossfire. Also, the USC had named Ali Mahdi as president

MOHAMMAD IBRAHIM EGAL SERVES AS PRESIDENT OF THE REPUBLIC OF SOMALILAND, A BREAKAWAY REGION OF SOMALIA. UNLIKE PUNTLAND, SOMALILAND INTENDS TO MAINTAIN ITS INDEPENDENCE EVEN AFTER SOMALIA RENEWS A STABLE GOVERNMENT. *(AP/Wide World Photos. Reproduced by permission.)*

without consulting any other clan representatives, leading to other factions to resent the USC's assumption of power. The country, overflowing with a surplus of guns and war paraphernalia left over from Siad Barre's huge arsenal, became a chaotic region of looting, murder, mini-wars, and destruction.

Somaliland

Whereas the southern and central regions of Somalia were divided among rival clans and subclans and their respective warlords, opposition to Siad Barre in the northwestern region had been much more centralized in the efforts of the Isaaq's SNM. As a result, in the aftermath of Siad Barre's fall from power, the region, roughly encompassing former-British Somaliland, held a *shir* (council) on May 18, 1991, and declared its independence.

Although it is still not recognized by any foreign nations, the Republic of Somaliland has its own flag, currency, and police and military forces. The capital was placed in the partially rebuilt city of Hargeysa, which was destroyed in the struggle with Siad Barre's forces. The republic established a legislative assembly with two bodies, one filled with elected representatives and another filled with clan-appointed representatives. Mohammad Ibrahim Egal, former Somalia prime minister under Shermaarke, became president of Somaliland in 1993.

One of the major factors in the decision to break away from the rest of Somalia was that many in Somaliland believed that the fractious chaos in the south would never lead to reunification. Although more stable than the rest of Somalia, Somaliland is not without violence and conflict. Armed opposition to the established government reached a peak in 1994, and sporadic uprisings instigated by clans opposed to SNM's dominance continue to plague the region.

Operation Restore Hope

As the tragedy unfolded in Somalia, a drought beset the central and southern regions of the country. By August 1992 more than 1.5 million—one quarter of the Somali population—were at risk of starvation. A study by the U.S. Centers for Disease Control reported that between August 9, 1992, and November 14, 1992, at least 40 percent of the population of the city of Baidoa had died. Relief organizations estimated that by September 1992, one quarter of all Somali children under the age of five had died. Trying to escape the violence and drought, Somali refugees flooded into neighboring countries. In 1992 an estimated 500,000 Somali refugees had moved across the border into Ethiopia, with another 300,000 in Kenya, 65,000 in Yemen, 15,000 in Djibouti, and approximately 100,000 in Europe.

The problems caused by the drought were exacerbated by rival factions who used food and relief supplies as weapons. Relief supply trucks were stopped and supplies stolen before they could be delivered to the areas in need. At best, relief workers were extorted out of 10 to 20 percent of all incoming aid. They were also often required to pay for armed escorts to "protect" their food deliveries from looting. Due to security risks relief efforts were either grinding to a halt or proving extremely ineffective at providing relief. Whereas some of the distribution trouble was instigated by clan militias, the breakdown in the central government also allowed for the rise of local warlords, who operated essentially as bandits, profiting from foreign aid intended to ease the famine. As news of the happenings in Somalia caught the interest of the media, the public became aware of the plight of the Somali people, and finally, after several years of a hands-off approach by both the United States and the UN, the international community reacted.

SOMALIA'S VOLATILE RELATIONSHIP WITH ETHIOPIA

Tensions between Somalia and Ethiopia peaked in 1977–78, when Somalia invaded Ethiopia in an unsuccessful attempt to gain control of the Somali-inhabited Ogaden region. With each country suspicious of the other's expansionist interests, the relationship has been dominated by distrust and animosity.

Hope for a fresh beginning came in 1991. As Somalia was falling into anarchy, Meles Zenawi, who had lived in Mogadishu as a liberation leader in the 1980s, came to power in Ethiopia. In 1992 he was able to persuade Somali faction leaders to meet for peace talks in Addis Ababa, receiving international commendations for his efforts to restore order in the region. By 1993, however, the talks had broken down, with faction leaders claiming that Ethiopia was aggressively pursuing its own agenda. The short-lived friendly relationship between Ethiopia and Somalia was quickly replaced by long-standing unease and accusations.

After peace talks ended in 1993 Ethiopia began building friendships with specific factions within Somalia. The self-declared independent Republic of Somaliland's president, Mohammad Ibrahim Egal, has traveled to Ethiopia on numerous occasions. Somaliland has a positive history with Ethiopia, who supported the Somaliland-based Somali National Movement's efforts against dictator Mahammad Siad Barre. Landlocked since 1993, when the coastal province of Eritrea declared its independence, Ethiopia is particularly interested in securing the use of the Somaliland port of Berbera.

Connections also exist between Somalia's other self-declared independent region, Puntland. Puntland leader Colonel Abdullahi Yusuf, who served in the Somali army, fled to Ethiopia after staging an unsuccessful coup against Siad Barre. Ethiopia was called upon to persuade Yusuf to participate in the Djibouti peace talks in 2000. Failure to convince Yusuf to attend may have been partially due to Ethiopia's own distrust of the transitional government in Mogadishu.

Ethiopia's presence in southern Somalia is manifested in its continued support of factions that oppose the transitional national government. Despite a trip by Somali President Abdiqassim Salad to Ethiopia in November 2000, relations between the transitional government and Ethiopia have not progressed, as evidence continues to arise that Ethiopia is providing opposition forces with arms and support.

Numerous attempts were made to find a resolution to the conflict. In January 1992 UN Assistant Secretary-General James. O.C. Jonah visited Mogadishu but failed in his efforts to stop the fighting. The following month both sides of the USC met in New York and agreed to a ceasefire, which was signed on March 3, 1992. The fighting resumed shortly thereafter, however, and the delivering of humanitarian aid continued to be problematic. On April 24, UN Resolution 751 established the United Nations Operation in Somalia (UNOSOM) with the intent to secure the delivery of food and aid to drought-plagued areas. In May, Mohammed Sahnoun, a newly appointed UN representative to Somalia, arrived in Mogadishu; in July, 50 military observers also move into the country, and on September 14, the first UN forces, a deployment of 500 Pakistani soldiers, established themselves at the Mogadishu airport, over which they gained control from local warlords on November 10.

Just two months before leaving office, having lost the 1992 election to Bill Clinton, then-U.S. President George Bush (1989–92) ordered the deployment of 28,000 U.S. troops to further the humanitarian and peacekeeping mission in Somalia. On December 12, 1992, 12,000 U.S. military troops landed on the shores of Somalia to begin their assignment, dubbed "Operation Restore Hope." With the arrival of U.S. troops, control of the international peacekeeping operation was placed in the hands of the United States, under UN Resolution 794, which established the Unified Task Force (UNITAF). Most agree that in the first six months of UNITAF, the operation was fairly successful. Despite ongoing isolated conflicts, UNITAF forces maintained sufficient order so that relief supplies could once again be delivered. Given this fact, the United States and the UN began making plans to return control of the operation to the UN. In May 1993 the UNITAF passed command to the UN-led UNOSOM II, which was commanded by Jonathan Howe, a retired U.S. Admiral.

Soon after the establishment of UNOSOM II the situation in Somalia began to deteriorate rapidly. On June 5, 1993, Aidid's forces ambushed a lightly-armed patrol of Pakistani soldiers in Mogadishu, killing 24. The attack was unprovoked and shocking to the UN forces, as it was assumed that because the Pakistanis were Muslims like most the Somali people, their presence would be accepted and welcomed. Having invoked UN Chapter VII, a seldom-used article that allows for military action in UN missions, UNOSOM II began to engage in armed conflict with Somali militias, focusing on Aidid's USC/SNA coalition. Commander Howe placed a bounty on the head of Aidid, but he continually eluded UN forces during a five-month manhunt. On June 12 U.S. aircraft began four days of aerial attacks on SNA-controlled southern Mogadishu. The next day, Pakistani troops fired on demonstrators protesting the air strikes, killing at least twenty people, including women and children.

As tensions grew between UNOSOM II forces and the Somali people, the situation continued to deteriorate. On July 2, 1993, three Italian paratroopers were killed in Mogadishu. Eleven days later, a U.S. military helicopter targeted a meeting of clan leaders, firing into the meetinghouse and killing 54, including highly respected clan elder Sheik Mohammed Iman. Casualties also included women who were serving the elders during the meeting. In the riotous aftermath Somali crowds turned on international journalists who had arrived on the scene to report on the attack; four journalists were beaten to death. In yet another tragic happening, on September 9, crowds violently engaged UN forces, and a U.S. helicopter subsequently fired on the crowd, killing approximately 200 civilians. The deathblow to UNOSOM II came on October 18 when two U.S. Special Forces helicopters were downed in Mogadishu, leading to the death of eighteen U.S. Marines and the capture of a U.S. helicopter pilot and a Nigerian soldier (both were later released). The number of Somalis killed in the mayhem ranges from 300 to 1,000. Video footage of a dead U.S. Marine being dragged through the streets of Mogadishu by the angry crowd was broadcast around the world, turning U.S. public sentiment strongly against further involvement.

Soon thereafter, President Bill Clinton (1993–2000) announced that all U.S. military personnel would be removed from Somalia by the end of March 1994. Germany also announced the removal of its troops from the UN mission. As planned, on March 25, 1994, the last units of U.S. troops left Somalia. One year later, in March 1995, the remaining UNOSOM from other nations withdrew from Somalia under the protection of U.S. Marines, thus ending the UNOSOM II mission. Despite ongoing peace talks during the previous two years, no adequate agreement had been reached. UNOSOM was unable to transfer authority to a legitimate Somali government upon its departure. Somalia was once again on its own.

SOMALI PRESIDENT ABDIQASIM SALAD HASSAN
SPEAKS AT THE UNITED NATIONS. UN INTERVENTION
FAILED TO BRING A HALT TO THE VIOLENCE THAT
TORE THROUGH SOMALIA IN THE 1990S. *(AP/Wide World
Photos. Reproduced by permission.)*

Struggles for Stability

The five years following the end of UNOSOM
II were filled with small pockets of hope, fueled by
a proliferation of external assistance to support reconciliation of the country, countered by continued
disruptions, violence, and a growing number of
factions. In 1994, there were 15 significant factions;
that number grew to 27 by 1997. In August 1996
Aidid was killed in action, and his son Hussein
Aidid, a former U.S. Marine, assumed leadership.
In November the Ethiopian government sponsored
peace talks, but Hussein Aidid boycotted the negotiations. A year later, faction leaders met in Cairo,
but no consensus was reached, leaving Somalia to
continue without a government. Mogadishu still
remained divided along what became known as the
green line, the symbolic line separating north and
south Mogadishu, each controlled by the rival factions of the USC.

The northeastern region of Somalia known as
Puntland declared its independence in 1998 after
failing to see substantial progress in the resolution
of conflict in the south. Colonel Abdullahi Yusuf
Ahmad was selected as president. The region continued to organize its government, but Abdullahi
Yusuf considered the region's autonomy a transitional status as the Somalia leadership in

Mogadishu works out an appropriate governmental
plan. Nonetheless, Abdullahi Yusuf has found
much to criticism about Abdiqasim Salad's government of Somalia and has made a move to extend his
presidency for another year instead of holding elections in mid-2001 as planned. He has warned that
the south's inability to create a viable and fair central government may result in yet another civil war.

Somaliland also continues to maintain its independence, and unlike Puntland, refuses any concessions to its autonomy. For Somaliland, the
dream of Greater Somalia is dead, and the Somaliland government is still pursuing international
recognition as a sovereign state. Despite Egal's
longstanding personal friendship with Abdiqasim
Salad, the Somaliland president does not recognize
the legitimacy of the presidency of Somilia.

RECENT HISTORY AND THE FUTURE

The still shaky Somali transitional government
operates in Mogadishu from a block of hotel rooms
paid for by local businessmen. Although the widespread violence that beset Mogadishu in the mid-
1990s has abated, violent conflicts continue to
occur. The Somali Transitional National Government (TNG) has been the target of numerous attacks. On October 18, 2000, gunmen shot and
killed General Yousuf Talan, the national security
chief and close adviser to President Abdiqasim
Salad. On November 13, Hassan Ahmed Elmi, a
member of the transitional parliament, was also
gunned down. Four days later, gunmen staged an
unsuccessful assassination attempt on Ahmed
Duale Ghele, another member of parliament, killing seven and wounding ten. Four of the dead were
Ahmed Duale's bodyguards, and the other three
were believed to be the attackers.

On January 6, 2001, the Rahanwein Resistance
Army (RRA) attempted to abduct parliament
speaker Abdallah Derrow Issak. Four were killed
and seven wounded in the unrest. Yet another
member of parliament, Abdirahman Duale Ali, has
been held hostage since mid-January. On March
22, 2001, the hotel in which Somali Prime Minister Ali Khalif Galaydh resides was attacked; three
people died in the incident. In a separate incident
seven UN staffers (six international employees and
one Somali employee), along with three members
of the international aid organization Médecins
Sans Frontières, (MSF) who were working to combat cholera in Mogadishu, were taken hostage on
March 27, 2001, after a two-hour gun battle out-

side the MSF offices. Six hostages were released the following day, and two more were let go on March 30. Two UN staffers, both British, continued to be held in Mogadishu as of May 2001.

As sporadic violence continues in the streets of Mogadishu, warlords are finding new resistance from business leaders, who have organized and funded a force to police the streets. Airports have reopened and businesses have begun to operate again. Islamic clerics, gaining authority with the institution of the transitional government, have also begun to organize militias to secure the city for its inhabitants. Those who oppose the new government accuse the TNG of giving power to Islamic fundamentalism; the public, however, has been supportive of the introduction of the severe punishment of the Islamic courts, whose rulings included stoning to death and cutting off of hands and feet for certain crimes.

Faction leaders continue to express staunch opposition to the TNG and have made advancements in attempts to work together. Meeting in Addis Ababa, Ethiopia, in March 2001, Somali faction leaders formed the Somali Reconciliation and Restoration Council (SRRC), with the goal of developing an all-inclusive reconciliation conference and the establishment of a legitimate transitional government. The SRRC consists of five co-chairmen and a first secretary. The chairmanship will rotate among the five co-chairs on a monthly basis, although the first chairman, USC/SNA's Hussein Aidid, received a six-month mandate. Most of the important faction leaders took part in the conference. Notable exceptions included representation from Puntland and Usman Hasan Ali Ato, who broke away from Aidid's USC/SNA to form a new USC faction.

Somalia's future remains far from certain at best. Reasons for hope exist; however, the wounds of the Somali people will not heal quickly. In a closed-door address to the UN Security Council in January 2001, Prime Minister Ali Khalif Galydh told the council that after so many years without a government, "now we are slowly but surely moving from the 'law of the gun' to law and order. . ." He acknowledged that it would take years to heal the wounds of the past and achieve disarmament and security, but "Whatever it takes, however, we are determined . . . to restore hope and normalcy to the nation. We have no choice but to press on until we succeed."

BIBLIOGRAPHY

Adam, Hussein, and Richard Ford. "Removing Barricades in Somalia: Options for Peace and Reconciliation," *Peaceworks*, 24 (October 1998). Available online at http://www.usip.org/pubs/pworks/pwks24/pwks24.html (cited April 19, 2001).

Bowden, Mark. *Black Hawk Down: A Story of Modern War*. New York: Penguin USA, 2000.

Clarke, Walter, and Jeffrey Herbst, eds. *Learning from Somalia*. Boulder, CO: Westview Press, 1997.

Hashim, Alice Bettis. *The Fallen State: Dissonance, Dictatorship and Death in Somalia*. Lanham, MD: University Press of America, 1997.

Lewis, Ioan, and Mayall, James. "Somalia," in *The New Interventionism, 1991–1994: United Nations Experience in Cambodia, Former Yugoslavia, and Somalia*, edited by James Mayall. Cambridge, MA: Cambridge University Press, 1996, pp. 94–126.

Lyons, Terrence, Ahmed I. Samatar. *Somalia: State Collapse, Multilateral Intervention, and Strategies for Political Reconstruction*. Washington, DC: Brookings Institution, 1995.

Mayall, James, ed. *The New Interventionism, 1991–1994: United Nations Experience in Cambodia, Former Yugoslavia, and Somalia*. Cambridge, MA: Cambridge University Press, 1996.

Peterson, Scott. "Somalia: Warlords Triumphant," in *Me Against My Brother: At War in Somalia, Sudan, and Rwanda. A Journalist Reports from the Battlefields of Africa*. New York: Routledge, 2000, pp. 3–172.

Samatar, Ahmed I., ed. *The Somali Challenge: From Catastrophe to Renewal?* Boulder, CO: Lynne Rienner Publishers, 1994.

"*Somalia.*" Library of Congress Federal Research Division, Country Studies. Area Handbook Series. Available online at http://memory.loc.gov/frd/cs/sotoc.htm (cited April 19, 2001).

—Kari Bethel

SOUTH AFRICA'S STRUGGLE WITH AIDS

When scientists and health officials from around the world who study acquired immuno-deficiency syndrome (AIDS) met in Durban, South Africa, in July 2000, it was a momentous occasion. For the first time in the 13 years since its creation, the International AIDS Conference was to be held in a developing nation—which activists hoped would highlight the extreme urgency of the fight against AIDS in Africa, the continent most devastated by the disease. But instead of cooperation and resolve, the meeting brought controversy and division. Several delegates threatened to boycott the conference to protest the AIDS policy of South African President Thabo Mbeki, who rejected Western approaches to diagnosis and treatment and argued that Africans should find their own solutions to the pandemic. Despite grim statistics showing that almost 20 percent of South Africa's adult population is infected with HIV, and that 5,500 people die of AIDS in sub-Saharan Africa each day, Mbeki continued to insist that poverty, not AIDS, was his country's leading cause of death.

Many saw Mbeki's stance as evidence of South Africa's failure to recognize and address the urgent problem of AIDS treatment and prevention. Mbeki's public comments and policies—particularly his opposition to azidothymidine (AZT), a drug effective in preventing a pregnant woman from transmitting the human immunodeficiency virus (HIV) to her fetus, and his statement that HIV does not cause AIDS—created a furor among researchers and health officials. Five thousand scientists, in protest, signed the Durban Declaration, stating that scientific evidence proves unequivocally that HIV causes AIDS.

THE CONFLICT

South Africa has the largest number of people in the world living with HIV/AIDS. Several socioeconomic and political issues have prevented the country from mounting an effective AIDS strategy.

Socioeconomic

- Twenty-two million South Africans live in conditions of abject poverty. They are often undernourished and lack basic health needs, such as decent shelter and running water.

- A high rate of migrant labor facilitates the spread of HIV/AIDS.

- The low status of women, and attitudes that condone multiple sex partners for men, make women particularly vulnerable to HIV infection. Fifty-six percent of South Africans living with HIV/AIDS are women.

- South Africa lacks an effective infrastructure through which to deliver health services to its indigent population and lacks the financial resources to pay for expensive AIDS drugs.

Political

- AIDS emerged as a serious problem in South Africa just as the ANC succeeded in ousting the apartheid government that had deprived blacks of basic rights. Preoccupied with the job of creating a new, democratic government, the ANC did not at first make AIDS a top priority.

- ANC leaders have rejected the AIDS advice of white scientists and health officials. They insist that they must find African solutions to HIV/AIDS, and have resisted authorizing the use of AZT and other AIDS drugs for indigent South Africans.

- The international community has been late in responding to the AIDS crisis in South Africa. Financial assistance from international organizations has been a fraction of the amount specialists say is needed.

- Multinational drug companies did not agree to lower prices for AIDS drugs in South Africa until late in the 1990s. Even then, South Africa insisted that the cost was too high.

Disappointed though many conference attendees were with South African health policies, the Durban conference did focus international attention on the magnitude and complexity of the AIDS problem in Africa. Within less than a year the United Nations (UN) called for concerted efforts to fight the pandemic in Africa; organizations urged Western nations to fund the AIDS war in developing countries; pharmaceutical companies agreed to slash prices of antiretroviralanti-retroviral drugs; and South Africa approved the use of Western drugs for indigent patients. The world's attention had finally been caught—but not in time to stem massive social, political, and economic devastation.

HISTORICAL BACKGROUND

A Mysterious New Killer

AIDS was first identified in 1981 in Los Angeles, California, and in New York City after young and middle-aged adults with no previous serious health problems began to die from infections and malignancies that almost never cause trouble in the general population. By 1983 researchers identified HIV as the cause of this new disease, AIDS. HIV destroys or impairs immune system cells and progressively destroys the body's ability to resist infections and some types of malignancies. AIDS is considered the last stage of HIV infection, and it is fatal.

HIV is transmissible but not contagious. It is contracted mainly through exposure to blood, semen and other genital secretions, and breast milk. It can also be transferred across the placenta during pregnancy, infecting the unborn child. Because the first AIDS cases were found among gay men, it was initially believed that homosexual contact was the primary means of transmission. It is now known, however, that heterosexual intercourse is the major mode of transmission worldwide, accounting for 70 percent of all HIV infections.

The interval between infection with HIV and the appearance of conditions associated with AIDS is, on average, ten years. Affected individuals may remain without symptoms for several years, during which they can unwittingly spread the disease. As HIV weakens the immune system, individuals become susceptible to numerous diseases. Often, these are opportunistic infections—infections caused by organisms that rarely cause harm in healthy individuals, such as cytomegalovirus, *Pneumocystis carinii,* toxoplasmosis, candidiasis, herpes simplex virus, herpes zoster, tuberculosis, and atyp-

THE 2000 AIDS CONFERENCE IN SOUTH AFRICA MARKED THE FIRST TIME THE CONFERENCE WAS HELD IN A DEVELOPING NATION. *(AP/Wide World Photos. Reproduced by permission.)*

ical *Mycobacterium.* Affected individuals also experience an unusually high rate of certain cancers, including Kaposi's sarcoma, tongue and rectal cancers, and non-Hodgkins B cell lymphoma. Death results from the persistent ravages of diseases and malignancies from which the body can no longer defend itself.

Through the 1980s and early 1990s, AIDS cases in the United States increased alarmingly, with no cure and few treatment options. In the early years of the pandemic AIDS patients suffered not only the physical devastation of the disease, but also the shame with which it was associated. Because most known AIDS cases at that time were concentrated in the gay community, as well as among intravenous drug users, the majority culture often stigmatized victims, blaming them for bringing the disease on themselves through "immoral" behavior. Some people went so far as to suggest that AIDS was a punishment from God for engaging in homosexual activities. Yet, as more and more young men died in their prime, activists took up the cause. The gay community rallied to fight misconceptions about the disease and to remove the guilt and shame with which it was often associated. At the same time, AIDS was starting to spread beyond the gay community and intravenous drug users. Demanding funds for AIDS research, activists also promoted educational outreach to warn people of behaviors that increased the risk of contracting HIV: sharing contaminated needles for injecting drugs, and engaging in "unsafe" sex—homosexual or heterosexual intercourse without using a condom. In time, slowed rates of new infections showed that individuals were changing behaviors to minimize their risk of contracting HIV.

Therapy for the first AIDS patients was limited to treatment of the individual infections they contracted and was ineffective in slowing the course of the disease. But in 1987, when annual AIDS deaths in the United States reached 16,000, the first drug known to retard the advance of the disease, AZT, was introduced. By 1996, three-drug combination therapy with antiretroviral drugs became standard treatment in developed countries, precipitating a sharp decline in annual AIDS deaths. Though AIDS remains incurable, these therapies offer the hope of prolonged life and relative health to those patients who receive them.

AIDS in Africa

Though most AIDS research has benefited patients who live in developed countries—which enjoy sophisticated health care systems and a high standard of living—the disease has wrought its most extreme devastation in underdeveloped regions of the world, particularly sub-Saharan Africa. United Nations (UN) epidemiologists estimated in 1991 that, by 1999, some 9 million people in sub-Saharan Africa would be HIV-positive. By 2000 data showed the infection to be 2.5 times that number. Out of a total population of 640 million in the region, the annual death rate from AIDS reached 2.4 million, and the HIV infection rate ranged from 5.06 in Nigeria to 35.8 in Botswana. By contrast, on December 2, 2000, Kevin Toolis of the British newspaper the *The Guardian* reported that Britain, with a population of 59 million, had 31,000 people living with AIDS and a prevalence rate of only 0.11 percent; Germany, with a population of 82 million, had 37,000 AIDS cases and a prevalence rate of 0.10 percent; and the United States, with a population of 276 million, had 850,000 people living with AIDS and a prevalence rate of 0.61 percent.

In South Africa, where more people are infected with HIV than in any other country, 4.2 million people—19.94 percent of the adult population—are HIV-positive, and the rate of new infections is among the highest in the world. According to statistics from the World Health Organization (WHO), some 250,000 South Africans died of AIDS during 1999, and the pandemic has orphaned an estimated 420,000 children. In early 2001 the rate of new infections in South Africa was 1,700 per day.

So huge is the problem of AIDS in developing countries that UN Secretary-General Kofi Annan declared AIDS "a major challenge for human security." In March 2001, U.S. Secretary of State Colin Powell named Africa's AIDS epidemic a national security issue for the United States.

Several factors make AIDS in Africa, as well as in other underdeveloped areas, much more difficult to combat than in developed countries. Poverty, political oppression, migration, and social violence create an environment in which HIV and AIDS can flourish. Lack of education and a reticence to openly discuss sexual matters further exacerbate the problem. At the same time, many areas lack the infrastructure necessary to offer HIV testing or to deliver health services to those most in need. Indeed, the vast majority of HIV-positive individuals in sub-Saharan Africa receive no treatment whatsoever.

South Africa

South Africa is the hardest hit by HIV/AIDS. With 4.2 million HIV-positive adults and children, it has the largest number of people living with HIV/AIDS in the world. Of these, 56 percent are women. In 1999 alone, the country suffered 250,000 adult and child AIDS deaths. And experts point out that this is merely the tip of the iceberg. According to Institute for Security Studies analyst Martin Schonteich, in "Age and AIDS: South Africa's Crime Time Bomb?" (*African Security Review*, 1999), the people now visibly sick and dying in South Africa represent only one percent of those infected in 1990. The dramatic increase in new infections since then will lead to catastrophic death figures within a few years. In 1998 Minister of Health Nkosazana Zuma estimated that HIV would reach its peak in South Africa in 2010, with 6.1 million infected. It is estimated that South African AIDS deaths between 1995 and 2005 will reach 7.4 million. In 1998 alone, more than 100,000 South African children were orphaned because of AIDS; this number could reach one million by 2005.

CHRONOLOGY

1981 The first cases of AIDS are identified in Los Angeles, California.

1987 AZT, the first drug effective in treating AIDS, is introduced; death rate in the United States is 16,000, while death rate in Africa is approximately 150,000.

1990 The first cases of AIDS are identified in South Africa.

1996 Three-drug antiretroviralanti-retroviral combination therapy becomes standard AIDS treatment in developed countries but remains too expensive for African countries; death rate in Western countries slows while death rate in sub-Saharan Africa soars to 1.5 million. Most AIDS patients in South Africa receive no medical treatment.

1997 Then-deputy president Thabo Mbeki and health minister Nkosazana Auma pressure for approval of Virodene, a drug discovered by South African researchers, which they believe can cure AIDS; it is later found to be carcinogenic and ineffective against AIDS.

1998 Five multinational pharmaceutical companies offer to sell AIDS drugs to Africa at substantial discounts.

1999 Mbeki announces that AZT is too toxic to administer to pregnant women.

April 2000 Mbeki suggests that HIV is not the cause of AIDS in Africa. Death rate in developed countries continues to decline dramatically; death rate in sub-Saharan Africa reaches 2.4 million.

May 2000 Five major pharmaceutical companies offer to cut the price of AIDS drugs for Africa by as much as 80 percent.

July 2000 The International AIDS Conference opens in Durban, South Africa. Many threaten a boycott to protest Mbeki's stance against AZT and refusal to acknowledge that HIV causes AIDS. Mbeki opened the conference by stating that extreme poverty, rather than AIDS, was the country's leading killer.

Five thousand scientists around the world sign the Durban Declaration, stating that evidence that HIV causes AIDS is "clear-cut, exhaustive and unambiguous."

August 2000 South Africa rejects an offer of $1 billion in annual loans from the United States to purchase drugs for AIDS treatment.

December 2000 Mbeki's government accepts a $50 million donation of the drug fluconazole from the Pfizer pharmaceutical company and gives conditional approval for nevirapine, a drug that reduces the risk of HIV being transmitted from an infected pregnant woman to her fetus.

February 2001 The Indian drug company Cipla agrees to sell generic versions of AIDS drugs for $350 per patient per year to Doctors Without Borders, and for $600 per year to governments of low-income countries.

February 2001 At the Eighth Annual Retrovirus Conference in Chicago, Illinois, participants draft a comprehensive plan for treating AIDS in Africa that calls on wealthy nations to cover the cost of drugs.

March 5, 2001 Forty-two multinational drug companies sue the South African government, seeking to block the government from enacting a law allowing it to import generic versions of patented drugs.

March 2001 Cipla requests permission to sell generic versions of eight HIV drugs in South Africa. Merck Company agrees to sell two antiretroviralanti-retroviral drugs to poor countries at cost. Bristol-Myers Squibb announces that it will no longer try to block companies from making and selling generic versions of its HIV drugs in Africa. Mbeki announces that his government will not declare AIDS a national emergency in order to obtain generic drugs.

April 2001 Pharmaceutical companies withdraw from their lawsuit; the South African government continues to refuse to make antiretrovirals widely available.

Shockingly, few South Africans receive treatment for HIV infection or AIDS. According to a November 30, 2000 report by Chris McGreal in *The Guardian* ("AIDS: South Africa's New Apartheid"), doctors estimated in 2000 that only 10,000 of the country's 4.2 million HIV-positive individuals can afford expensive antiretroviral therapy, which costs between US$10,000 and $15,000 a year in developed countries. Most of those who get the drugs are gay white men or members of the new black elite. The vast majority of black South Africans suffering from HIV/AIDS receive no treatment because the government has refused to administer AZT and other antiretroviral drugs to those who rely on the public health system, claiming that the drugs' safety and effectiveness were in question and that their cost was prohibitive. This circumstance has led people to call AIDS in South Africa "the new apartheid" and to suggest that failure to provide treatment would be an act of genocide.

The Legacy of Apartheid

Of all the developing countries confronted with AIDS, South Africa should have been well prepared to devise an effective strategy against the disease. The country has an industrialized economy and well-educated elected leaders. But in 1993, when officials began to recognize the scope of the AIDS problem, South Africa was consumed with political issues that deflected attention away from public health. Members of the African National Congress (ANC) were poised to take control away from the apartheid government in the country's first democratic elections.

Under apartheid, the white minority in South Africa had created a racially segregated society that kept people of color, particularly blacks, in inferior positions and denied them basic human rights. This system also created conditions that facilitated the spread of HIV infection. Because blacks were forced to live in separate townships far outside of white areas, where jobs were nonexistent, a pattern of migrant labor emerged. Many had no choice but to travel long distances to find work in urban centers or in the mining industry; denied permission to bring along wives and families, these men often resorted to sex with prostitutes or casual partners for the extended periods that they were away from home. Of the thousands of political dissidents who fled to Zambia, Tanzania, Uganda, and other countries to escape apartheid oppression, some were exposed to HIV in those countries and brought it back with them when they returned to South Africa.

ADULT HIV/AIDS INFECTION RATES

as of December 1999, in percentages

South Africa	19.90%
United States	0.61
Thailand	2.15
Kenya	14.0
India	0.70
Brazil	0.57
Botswana	35.8

Source: UNAIDS. "Epidemiological Fact Sheet on HIV/AIDS and Sexually Transmitted Infections." World Health Organization, 2000. Available online at http://www.unaids.org/hivaidsinfo/statistics/june00/fact_sheets/all_countries. html#s.

SOUTH AFRICA IS ONE OF THE WORST AFFECTED COUNTRIES IN TERMS OF POPULATION INFECTED BY HIV/AIDS. *(The Gale Group.)*

Apartheid policies had also eroded trust in established health services, which were mostly staffed by white physicians. Jon Jeter noted in the July 6, 2000 *Washington Post* article "South Africa's Advances Jeopardized by AIDS," that "After decades of seeing friends and relatives jailed, poisoned, and even sterilized by whites, the ANC shut clinics that could have been useful in treating and counseling patients infected with HIV ... After negotiating an uneasy coexistence with the white minority, the new leaders' initial efforts to address the epidemic were slowed and even sabotaged by white civil servants inherited from the apartheid era." Indeed, fears and suspicions that had burgeoned under apartheid affected the new government's approach to AIDS.

During the elections, apartheid leaders used fear of AIDS, which they associated with the stereotype of the promiscuous and irresponsible black male, to shake public confidence in the ANC. When the ANC proved victorious and Nelson Mandela was elected president, apartheid supporters expressed doubt that his black administration would be competent to govern the country. Amid jubilation and hope for the new regime there also existed defensiveness and division. Faced with the task of building a new, democratic South Africa,

ESTIMATED HIV INFECTION RATE IN SOUTH AFRICA AMONG WOMEN ATTENDING PRENATAL CLINICS

as a percentage of women tested

1990	1
1991	2
1992	3
1993	4
1994	8
1995	10.5
1996	14
1997	16.5
1998	23
1999	22

Source: UNAIDS, Center for the Study of AIDS, University of Pretoria

THE PERCENTAGE OF PREGNANT WOMEN INFECTED BY HIV IN SOUTH AFRICA HAS RISEN STEADILY SINCE 1990. *(The Gale Group.)*

leaders resented the fact that AIDS could deflect resources from such crucial goals as housing and jobs for a country with approximately 22 million people living in "third world" conditions of abject poverty. Some even refused to admit that AIDS was really a problem.

The Status of Women

Attitudes toward women in South Africa also exacerbate the spread of HIV. Though HIV infection in other parts of Africa occurs at the same rate in men and women, in South Africa, 56 percent of infected individuals are women, with the highest infection rates among women aged 20 to 30. Low social status and lack of power make women particularly vulnerable. In an *HIV Insite* report on South Africa (2001), Lisa Garbus cited a 1998 South African Medical Research Council study claiming that 90 percent of men studied believed it was common for men to have multiple sex partners. Two out of three men believed women had no right to refuse sex or insist that their partner use a condom. Indeed, women frequently report being beaten if they object to sex with partners they know are HIV-positive.

Additionally, the belief among some men that having sex with a virgin will cure them of AIDS contributes to sexual abuse of young girls, who contract HIV on average five years earlier than men do. Almost a third of South African teenage girls report being raped as a virgin. In South Africa, Garbus reports, a woman is raped every five minutes, and gang rape is common. When women fear violence from men, they are even less able to say no to sex or to insist on condom use. At the same time, women are the most deprived sector of the population—56.4 percent lack income of any sort. Many are forced to become sex workers to survive, leaving them even more vulnerable to sexual violence and HIV infection.

The high rate of sexually transmitted diseases (STDs) in South Africa—approximately 11 million cases annually—is also a major factor facilitating HIV transmission. Evidence shows that HIV infection is more likely to occur when an individual suffers from certain STDs, particularly gonorrhea and genital herpes.

Denial and Divisiveness

Though the ANC's first AIDS policy was tentative, at least the party had a policy. The apartheid regime's HIV program, was almost non-existent. Nkosazana Zuma, appointed South Africa's first black minister of health by then-President Nelson Mandela, developed an AIDS plan calling for $64 million to devote to education, mass media campaigns, distribution of free condoms, and support programs for HIV-positive individuals. Zuma also urged the creation of a national AIDS commission and suggested that the country's AIDS program be run from the president's office, to ensure it a high level of visibility and respect. But Zuma balked when asked to address other issues contributing to the spread of AIDS, such as the role of migrant labor.

In his first budget, Mandela approved only $15 million for AIDS and assigned the AIDS initiative to the health department. Instead of helping to promote HIV and AIDS awareness, Mandela remained silent. He made no public statement about AIDS until late 1997, when he delivered a speech to the World Health Organization (WHO) in Switzerland. He made no public reference in South Africa to AIDS until 1998, after he had been in office more than three years. Official silence on AIDS, many believed, caused some blacks in rural areas to doubt the actual existence of AIDS and to reject condom campaigns as a ruse to limit black population growth.

THABO MVUYELWA MBEKI

1942– Thabo Mvuyelwa Mbeki succeeded Nelson Mandela as president of South Africa in 1999. The son of teachers and activists, he has devoted his life to the struggle to end apartheid in South Africa and build a new, democratic country. He spent much of his youth in exile, earning a graduate degree in economics in Britain and working for the banned African National Congress (ANC).

Mbeki returned to Africa in 1971, when he was appointed Assistant Secretary to the Revolutionary Council of the ANC in Lusaka, Zambia. Two years later, he was sent to Botswana, where several key ANC leaders were living in exile. During the next decades Mbeki continued to work for the party. In 1989 he led the ANC delegation that participated in secret talks with the apartheid government, which led to the release of ANC political prisoners and finally gave the ANC legal status. In 1993 he was elected ANC chairperson. Mbeki served as executive deputy president of South Africa under its first post-apartheid president, Nelson Mandela.

Mbeki's fervent belief in South Africa's ability to solve its own problems, many say, led to an AIDS policy that was nothing short of disastrous and that undermined his political credibility. But his supporters insist that Mbeki's position was based on his willingness to

THABO MBEKI. *(AP/Wide World Photos. Reproduced by permission.)*

look at all the facts, including dissident views. Late in 2000 Mbeki retreated from his controversial stance on HIV and AIDS and authorized South Africa's public health department to begin using antiretroviral drugs in the fight against AIDS.

Zuma, however, was committed to increasing AIDS awareness. She spent $3 million producing an AIDS awareness play reminiscent of the popular musical *Sarafina*. Despite its good intentions, the play, many felt, communicated a simplistic message about AIDS. Many activists criticized Zuma for spending one-fifth of her annual budget on this project. Their negative perceptions were further cemented when Zuma announced her plan to require HIV-positive individuals to publicly acknowledge their status. Though the health minister intended this as a means of removing the stigma from HIV infection, activists objected that it compromised confidentiality and further stressed AIDS patients. Zuma's staff responded that confidentiality was a Western preoccupation, not an African matter.

African Solutions to African Problems

Tentative as South Africa's first AIDS campaign was, it was distinguished by a strong conviction that black Africans should be skeptical of

white authority and should create their own, uniquely African, solutions to the AIDS pandemic. Nowhere was this attitude more evident than in the government's decision to promote research on Virodene P058. This drug was discovered by three researchers in Pretoria, who claimed the substance could cure AIDS. In 1997 Zuma sought funding and approval for the drug. Though Peter Folb, who directed the approval agency, objected that Virodene research was flawed and further study of it was needed, Zuma and then-deputy president Thabo Mbeki pressured him to approve it. Soon, however, it was revealed that Virodene, which contained an industrial solvent as its active ingredient, was not only ineffective against HIV but was also carcinogenic.

The push for approval of Virodene, officials complained, had been a purely political decision, not one based on scientific expertise. In John Jeter's article "South Africa's Advances Jeopardized by AIDS" (July 6, 2000), he quoted Quarraisha

Karim, first director of South Africa's national AIDS program, as saying, "There was this sense that this drug would be the thing that would offset the perception . . . of Africans as substandard and less than capable. . . . This was driven by this need to show the world: 'Yes, Africans can do this. We can do this. Virodene became our redemption.'"

As late as 1999, when Bristol-Myers proposed to Zuma a new AIDS initiative to fund medical research and education projects, the South African government responded negatively. Zuma's assistant, Nono Simelela, responded that Britsol-Myers should come to Africa to learn how to deal with the virus in the developing world. Simelela further objected to clinical trials in South Africa using drugs that were not affordable to a vast majority of the population.

Money and Drugs

Though many AIDS workers were deeply frustrated with the government's approach, its distrust of Western motives certainly had some basis. By the time AIDS became a crisis in Africa, wealthy nations, where antiretroviral treatments were proving effective, were losing interest in fighting the disease. Though a classified U.S. Central Intelligence Agency (CIA) document, Interagency Intelligence Memorandum 91–10005, predicted the scope of the disaster for Africa when it was first circulated in the late 1980s and warned that the response from developed countries would have at best only a marginal effect, U.S. government response was tepid. The first U.S. budget after release of the document allocated only $124.5 million for overseas AIDS control and remained flat for the next seven years. Small as this amount was, it far exceeded allocations from other countries; the combined AIDS assistance from Europe, Australia, and Japan barely exceeded the U.S. figure.

At the same time, bureaucrats argued about how to distribute the limited funds available. The U.S. Agency for International Development (USAID) balked at paying for AIDS testing overseas, arguing that it was too expensive and that those who tested positive would then want treatment, which would be even more expensive. Duff Gillespie, who supervised AIDS assistance for USAIDS, felt that overpopulation was a much more important problem in Africa than AIDS was, and resisted channeling funds away from the budget for population control. Also at issue was cost-effectiveness. With the number of HIV-positive individuals skyrocketing, many analysts argued that

treatment was financially impossible, and recommended focusing solely on prevention programs.

Indeed, the cost of antiretroviral treatment was staggering. Antiretroviral regimens, which do not cure AIDS, must be administered for the entire life of the HIV-infected individual. And this drug therapy costs between $10,000 and $15,000 per patient each year—a figure far beyond the capacity of South Africa to pay. Though the World Health Organization began as early as 1991 to address the need to make therapies affordable for developing countries, little was actually accomplished until almost a decade later. The major pharmaceutical companies that manufactured AIDS drugs lobbied against plans to offer these drugs at cost, claiming that governments and other sectors were responsible for finding reasonable means of providing the drugs; pharmaceutical companies were concerned primarily with research and development.

One contention against this claim is that drug companies feared that drugs sold to Africa at a steep discount might be re-exported to wealthy countries for a profit. This, in turn, could encourage AIDS patients in developed countries to demand lower prices as well. Also at issue was the protection of intellectual property rights. In 1993 then-U.S. President Bill Clinton, at the urging of pharmaceutical companies, pressed to extend patent laws worldwide. In 1995 the World Trade Organization drew up an agreement on Trade Related Aspects of Intellectual Property Rights (TRIPS), which protected the exclusive marketing rights of patent holders. This meant that the companies that had developed new drugs could control their pricing and marketing. At the same time, TRIPS forbade developing countries from making or purchasing generic (and cheaper) versions of patented drugs.

Yet pressure to make antiretroviral therapies affordable began to mount. In 1998 the executive board of WHO endorsed a Revised Drug Strategy, which stated that public health concerns should have precedence over commercial interests. Soon after, the UN published "Globalization and Access to Drugs," which stated that drug patents conflicted with the human right to equal health care. In response, Glaxo Wellcome (now GlaxoSmithKline), developer of AZT and the two-drug package known as Combivir, announced that it would offer AIDS drugs to developing countries at prices substantially less than in the developed world. Pfizer, which manufactures the anti-fungal treatment Diflucan, needed by 10 percent of AIDS patients, offered to donate the drug to South Af-

DEMONSTRATORS MARCHED AGAINST THE HIGH PRICES OF HIV/AIDS TREATMENT DRUGS DURING THE 2000 AIDS CONFERENCE IN SOUTH AFRICA. MOST PEOPLE IN DEVELOPING NATIONS CAN NOT AFFORD THE EXPENSIVE DRUGS. *(AP/Wide World Photos. Reproduced by permission.)*

rica. Later that year pharmaceutical giants Merck, Hoffman-La Roche, Bristol-Myers Squibb, Glaxo Wellcome, and Boehringer Ingelheim agreed to big discounts on AIDS drugs to developing countries, though they did not specify exact prices. In 2000, the Clinton administration offered $1 billion for the purchase of AIDS drugs. This generous-sounding amount, however, was really a structure of Export-Import bank loans, at commercial interest rates; it was rejected. Though the World Bank, reversing its policy not to underwrite loans for health care, announced a $500 million funding pool to fight AIDS, it still considers antiretroviral drugs to be cost-ineffective. According to the World Bank's concept of "disability-adjusted life year," it is a net loss for a country to spend $1,000 each year to save the life of an individual who earns only $500 a year.

By the time Thabo Mbeki succeeded Nelson Mandela as president of South Africa in June 1999, it was clear that the country was in the midst of a full-blown AIDS crisis. The AIDS strategy that the country had adopted in July 1994 proved ineffective, and in 1997, a review led to a reformulation of national priorities to fight AIDS. In 1998 Mandela created a multi-sectoral ministerial task force on HIV/AIDS, as well as the National AIDS Council. The government also launched a national educational campaign to urge safer sex practices and the use of condoms. But the crucial matter of testing and treatment had yet to be addressed.

Known as an independent and original thinker, Thabo Mbeki quickly distinguished himself for his reluctance to accept Western approaches to AIDS. Though his earlier support for Virodene had resulted in embarrassment, he continued, as president, to insist that solutions to South Africa's AIDS problem should take into account the differences between AIDS in developing countries and AIDS in the West. After studying the opinions of a range of AIDS experts, some of whom questioned the safety of AZT, he determined that the drug was too toxic to administer to pregnant women. Yet AZT is routinely used to prevent maternal transmission of HIV in the United States, Canada, Britain, and most European countries.

The AZT Controversy

Some suggest that part of Mbeki's resistance to AZT and other antiretroviral drugs was their astronomical cost. Since the vast majority of HIV-positive people in South Africa depend on the public health system, the government faced an impossible financial burden if it were to import expensive AIDS drugs. But South African concerns about the safety of AZT are not completely

A Major Challenge for Human Security

Citing the alarming acceleration of the epidemic and its global impact, the United Nations General Assembly decided to convene a special session on HIV/AIDS. In anticipation of the June 2001 fifty-ninth session, UN Secretary-General Kofi Annan presented a report that examined the spread of the epidemic and reviewed its impact. The picture he painted was daunting.

AIDS ... has evolved into a complex social and economic emergency. HIV primarily affects young adults, cutting a broad path through society's most productive layer and destroying a generation of parents, whose death leaves behind orphans, desocialized youth and child-headed households.... In the hardest-hit regions, AIDS is now reversing decades of development. It changes family composition and the way communities operate, affecting food security and destabilizing traditional support systems. By eroding the knowledge base of society and weakening production sectors, it destroys social capital. By inhibiting public and private sector development and cutting across all sectors of society, it weakens national institutions. By eventually impairing economic growth, the epidemic has an impact on investment, trade and national security, leading to still more widespread and extreme poverty. In short, AIDS has become a major challenge for human security.

unfounded. The drug, first developed as a cancer treatment in 1960, can have serious long-term side effects, including loss of muscle, anemia, depression of white blood cells, and bone marrow damage. Other side effects can include nervousness, headaches, dizziness, nausea, stomach pain, confusion, loss of appetite, muscle aches, fever and sweating, sore throat, and abnormal bruising or bleeding. A rare side effect, according to the AIDS Treatment Data Network, is lactic acidosis, caused by damage to liver cells. Dr. Peter Moore, sub-Saharan medical director for GlaxoSmithKline, the maker of AZT, told the *Johannesburg Mail and Guardian* in "Truth and Lies about AZT" (December 1, 1999) that serious side effects such as cancer, anemia, and reduced white blood cell count occurs in about five percent of patients who take the drug for more than six months. When AZT was first approved for AIDS treatment, doses were much higher than are presently recommended; the usual dose has been adjusted to 300–600 mg per day.

The safety of AZT for pregnant women has also been questioned, especially because initial laboratory tests on mice suggested that the drug could cause cancer in the affected fetus. Subsequent re-

search, published in the January 13, 1999, edition of *Journal of the American Medical Association*, (Culnane, "Lack of Long-Term Effects") reported no adverse effects among the group of infants studied. According to the previously cited *Johannesburg Mail & Guardian* report, providing AZT to pregnant women who are HIV-positive could cut the number of South African babies born with HIV—estimated at 600,000 per year—in half.

In February 2001 the U.S. Department of Health and Human Services revised its treatment recommendations regarding antiretroviral drugs. The new guidelines specify that treatment with these drugs should not begin until HIV-positive patients begin to show symptoms of AIDS; earlier, physicians were encouraged to begin aggressive treatment immediately after a patient tested positive for HIV. Also troubling is research released by the University of California at San Diego that indicates that 14 percent of newly diagnosed HIV cases have strains of the virus that are resistant to antiretroviral drugs, suggesting that overuse of these treatments has contributed to the mutation of HIV just as overuse of some antibiotics has been conducive to the development of bacteria that do not respond to known treatments.

The HIV Controversy

Mbeki also questioned theories of how AIDS develops. Two types of HIV are currently recognized. Subtype B is the type spread most often through homosexual contact and intravenous drug use, and occurs more often in the United States, Europe, Australia, Japan, and the Caribbean. Subtype C, found most often in South Africa and India, seems to spread more often through heterosexual contact. Noting these differences, Mbeki stated in a letter to international leaders on April 3, 2000, that he planned to invite to South Africa an international panel of scientists, which included American researchers Peter Duesberg and David Rasnik, as well as British scientists Gordon Stewart and Andrew Herzheimer, to discuss new approaches to AIDS. He also suggested that focusing on HIV might not be the best response for South Africa. "A simple superimposition of Western experience on African reality would be absurd and illogical," he wrote. "I am convinced that our urgent task is to respond to the specific threat that faces us as Africans. We will not eschew this obligation in favour of the comfort of the recitation of a catechism that may very well be a correct response to the specific manifestation of AIDS in the West. We will not, ourselves, condemn our own people to death by giving up the search for specific and targeted responses to the specifically African incidence of HIV-AIDS."

The international AIDS community reacted with horror. Nor were they reassured when, at the Durban conference, Mbeki said in his opening remarks that poverty is a more deadly threat in South Africa than is AIDS. *The Times* diplomatic editor Richard Beeston reported in "Mbeki Controversy Jeopardises Conference Aims," (July 12, 2000), that Justice Edwin Cameron, a white High Court judge in South Africa who is gay and suffers from AIDS, stated at the conference that Mbeki's stance "has created an air of unbelief amongst scientists, confusion among those at risk of HIV and consternation amongst AIDS workers." The controversy stirred by Mbeki's comments overshadow the issue of getting help to the country's AIDS sufferers.

Mbeki insisted that his remarks had been misunderstood. In defense of the president, South Africa's MEC for Health, Dr. M. Sefularo, made the following statement at the AIDS Conference:

> It is unfortunate that President Thabo Mbeki has been misunderstood on the question of HIV and AIDS. The President has never denied either the existence of AIDS nor the causal relationship between HIV and AIDS. He has never said that HIV does not cause AIDS. What we are saying or asking is—'What is it about us in Sub-Saharan Africa, about the HIV virus, about our condition, culture, beliefs, our relationship to the rest of the world and our response to the HIV that has allowed AIDS to so catastrophically destroy individuals, families and communities to a point where it is possible that our economic development, freedom, security and our very existence as a people and a nation may be reduced to nothing?' That is the challenge. We reiterate our view that it is inappropriate to blame everything around this epidemic on the HIV virus. Clearly, the relationship between HIV and other social ills afflicting our society such as poverty and disease, particularly TB and STDs, is complex. We reaffirm our view that a comprehensive response in our country needs to recognise this reality.

In a September 4, 2000 interview with *Time Europe*, Mbeki clarified his position.

> Clearly there is such a thing as acquired immune deficiency. The question you have to ask is, what produces this deficiency? ... A whole variety of things can cause the immune system to collapse. Endemic poverty, the impact of nutrition, contaminated water, all of these things, will result in immune deficiency. If you take the African continent you add to that things like repetitive infections of malaria, ordinary STDs—syphilis, gonorrhea, etc. All of these will result in immune deficiency. ... The problem is that once you say immune deficiency is acquired from that virus your response will be antiretroviral drugs. But if you say the reason we are getting collapsed immune systems is a whole variety

of reasons including the poverty question which is very critical, then you have a more comprehensive response to the health condition of a person.

When asked directly whether he agreed that a direct link exists between HIV and AIDS, Mbeki responded "No, I am saying that you cannot attribute immune deficiency solely and exclusively to a virus."

By September 2000, however, Mbeki had begun to distance himself from the controversy. Senior officials of his ANC party urged him to acknowledge publicly that HIV causes AIDS, and his office admitted that his unpopular stance had cost him credibility. At the same time, pharmaceutical companies, under increasing pressure to make AIDS drugs affordable to developing countries, began negotiating offers. In 1999 Bristol-Myers Squibb announced its Secure the Future initiative, which pledged $100 million over five years to fight AIDS in Africa. But as of December 2000, 77 percent of funds pledged to Secure the Future have gone to U.S. charities and research institutions; only 10 percent of the funds have gone to programs in South Africa. Though five major pharmaceutical companies agreed in March 2001 to offer drastic price cuts on AIDS drugs, only Glaxo has specified a particular price. The companies are still concerned about protecting patent rights. Rather than allow generic AIDS drugs to be sold in Africa, 42 multinational drug companies joined a lawsuit brought by the Pharmaceutical Manufacturers Association of South Africa (PMA) seeking to block the South African government from enacting a 1997 law allowing it to import generic versions of patented drugs. British Prime Minister Tony Blair backed the drug companies, citing the importance of protecting intellectual property laws, but a torrent of international criticism harmed their case. After secret negotiations between the drug companies and the government, brokered with the assistance of UN Secretary-General Kofi Annan, the parties reached a settlement announced on April 19, 2001, which in essence allows South Africa to buy the cheapest available antiretrovirals.

RECENT HISTORY AND THE FUTURE

AIDS threatens to reverse many of the gains South Africa has made in recent years. Most obvious is life expectancy. Laura Garbus reported in "South Africa" (*HIV Insite*, 2001) about a study suggesting that fewer than 50 percent of South Africans now living will reach age 60, compared with an average of 70 percent for developing countries and 90 percent for industrialized countries. She also noted that, without AIDS, life expectancy in South Africa would presently be 65—it is instead 55. The falling life expectancy rate in the country has significant implications for South African society.

The impacts of AIDS will undoubtedly be catastrophic for families and communities. Among adults, HIV and AIDS generally affects young individuals who are likely to be parents and family breadwinners. As HIV-positive adults become increasingly ill, they can no longer work; at the same time, the lack of hospitals and health centers in rural areas means that vast numbers of AIDS patients must be cared for by relatives. This places a disproportionately high burden on women, who are already South Africa's most marginalized group. It also erodes the family structure by exacerbating poverty, and by stigmatizing those affected by AIDS.

By 2005 AIDS is expected to leave approximately 1 million maternal orphans (those whose mothers have died) in South Africa. Care for these children will also fall on family groups; in some cases, orphaned children may become heads of families. With this unprecedented number of AIDS orphans a corresponding increase in crime is likely. Numerous studies in several countries show that crime rates are closely related to age, with teenagers and young adults committing most crimes. In 1996 census data indicated that 34 percent of the country's population was under the age of fifteen, with the largest segments aged five to nine and ten to fourteen; the number of juveniles and young adults as a proportion of the population is expected to peak between 2010 and 2020. By 2010 one out of every four South Africans will be between the ages of 15 and 24. With AIDS expected to bring some 7.4 million deaths in South Africa between 1995 and 2005, and to leave one to two million orphans by 2010, huge numbers of young people left without parental figures and traumatized by the extreme suffering of AIDS will become part of the demographic group most likely to commit crimes.

Economic impacts from AIDS are also expected to be significant. One estimate suggests that the disease will cause South Africa to lose 10.8 percent of its workforce by 2005, and 24.9 percent by 2020. In the article "The Worst Say to Lost Talent: Business and AIDS," *The Economist* (February 10, 2001) reported that a typical South African company will lose 20 percent of its workforce by 2010, and that each HIV-positive workers will cost a

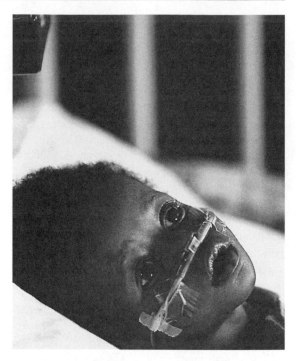

AS OF 1999, 22 PERCENT OF PREGNANT WOMEN ATTENDING PRENATAL CLINICS IN SOUTH AFRICA WERE INFECTED WITH HIV. MANY OF THESE WOMEN PASS THE DISEASE ON TO THEIR CHILDREN. *(AP/Wide World Photos. Reproduced by permission.)*

typical company about twice his or her annual salary. The mining industry, which relies heavily on migrant labor, will be particularly affected. Figures suggest that 10 percent of South African mine workers could succumb to AIDS. The disease cost the industry 114 million rand in 1995, a figure that could rise to 1.5 billion rand in 2010. Indeed, a special United Nations report on AIDS suggests that AIDS "may cut productivity growth by as much as 50 percent in the hardest-hit countries." Because South Africa's population is expected to decline by 23 percent by the year 2015, but per capita income is expected to remain stagnant, demand for South African goods will be affected. At the same time, companies will be hard-pressed to provide benefits such as health and life insurance. They will also face difficulties replacing skilled workers who succumb to AIDS.

Government Response

By the end of 2000, Mbeki's government agreed to accept donated AIDS drugs and to begin treatment of HIV-positive prenatal patients with nevirapine, a drug that reduces the risk that a pregnant woman can transmit HIV to her fetus. But despite further concessions from drug companies early in 2001 about pricing and patents, the government stated that it could not make antiretrovirals more widely available because the infrastructure to deliver them was inadequate and the price—$2 per day in the public sector and $4 per day in the private sector—was still too high.

The government's *HIV/AIDS/STD Strategic Plan for South Africa 2000–2005* lists prevention as its top priority. Its recommendations include making condoms available in all government department buildings; providing condoms at truck stops, mines, brothels, and borders; making clinics and other health facilities "youth friendly;" and training midwives and other reproductive health care providers on HIV/AIDS counseling for pregnant women. A significant part of its prevention strategy is the involvement of "all sectors of government and civil society," including traditional leaders, faith-based organizations, business, entertainment, and the media. The Plan's second priority—the treatment, care, and support of infected individuals—includes measures aimed at ensuring a dependable supply of appropriate medications for treatment of opportunistic infections and other conditions, improving health care infrastructure and training, and poverty-alleviation programs aimed at addressing the root causes of AIDS. The Plan also addresses research, monitoring and surveillance, and questions relating to human rights, including workplace HIV/AIDS policies and the possibility of decriminalizing commercial sex work.

In addition, South Africa has implemented an aggressive educational campaign on HIV/AIDS, aimed primarily at young people aged 12 to 17. The campaign, "Love Life," uses billboards, radio, television, and newspapers to deliver its message about safer sex and condom use. The program hopes to reduce the rate of HIV infection by half within five years. Love Life uses direct language and addresses once-taboo subjects, such as masturbation, foreplay, and gay sex, to encourage open discussion of sexual matters. Love Life also visits sports facilities and schools, and runs the Love Train, a railroad train that travels throughout the country displaying its safer sex message on South Africa's largest billboard.

The government has also established 20 specialized "rape courts" and is developing a rape protocol that may include compulsory HIV testing for all persons arrested in sexual assault cases. South Africa is also revising legislation relating to employment, which may result in classification of HIV/AIDS as a disability, thus protecting infected individuals from discrimination and unwarranted dismissal.

Private Sector Response

Private companies have also implemented policies to deal with AIDS. AngloGold, the country's largest gold mining company, gives its workers and their girlfriends AIDS leaflets printed in various African languages, and also hires specialists to train peer educators among miners and prostitutes. The company also offers voluntary HIV testing and counseling, as well as free treatment of STDs, which, if untreated, can increase the likelihood of HIV infection by 50 percent. South African Breweries (SAB) presents role-playing exercises designed to show workers how fast HIV infection can spread. Like AngloGold, the company also offers testing, counseling, and STD treatment. In February 2000 South Africa's telephone company, Telkom, purchased 5 million condoms to distribute to its workers via restroom vending machines. The company estimates that it will dispense about 100,000 condoms each week.

Health insurance companies, too, are devising measures to cope with the burden of AIDS. Some have established special facilities for HIV/AIDS patients, which allow the companies to cap guaranteed benefits for HIV treatment. As of 2000, average coverage was about $4,000 per person each year. Increased demand for coverage as more infected people become sick, however, is expected to strain the industry, and companies may have to limit health insurance coverage further, as death benefits are expected to rise markedly by 2002.

Anticipating high rates of personnel losses in the coming years, some companies have changed hiring and training practices. Mondi, a company that manufactures paper, trains its employees in a variety of specific jobs so they can easily replace workers who become ill. Other companies may hire as many as three workers for each skilled job to ensure coverage if employees die. In other cases, companies are mechanizing and outsourcing services to subcontractors in order to function with fewer employees.

Further Needs

Despite new commitments to fight AIDS in South Africa, much remains to be done. The UN AIDS office estimates that at least $1 billion is needed to fight HIV/AIDS in Africa. This figure, however, is much lower than other estimates. Jeffrey Sachs, director of Harvard University's Center for International Development, suggested in the *New York Times* article "The Best Possible Investment in Africa" (February 10, 2001) that wealthy countries need to spend between $5 to $10 billion each year for the next decade to combat AIDS in

Africa. The smaller figure, he notes, is the amount that Europeans determined to spend on mad cow disease, which has killed about 80 people while AIDS in Africa has claimed about 17 million lives to date. Sachs observed that prevention and community support measures would cost about $3 billion annually, and treatment would cost between $2 and $7 billion.

In 2000 the United States authorized just under $200 million in development aid to fight AIDS overseas. Its projected budget for 2001 seeks to add about $50 million to this amount. The U.S. contribution represents about half of the AIDS funds from all industrialized countries.

Money and drugs, however, are not enough to stem the tide of AIDS as it washes over South Africa. While governments and pharmaceutical companies argue over various points, the main issue remains that a generation is dying of AIDS in South Africa. The people must be informed and, educated about the risks, precautions, and available treatments, provided with all available information and all available options to give them the best chance at life.

BIBLIOGRAPHY

"AIDS Drugs for Poor Nations," *New York Times,* March 12. 2001.

The AIDS Foundation of South Africa. "AIDS in South Africa," updated November 9, 2000. Available online at http://www.aids.org.za (cited July 18, 2001).

Beeston, Richard. "Mbeki Controversy Jeopardises Conference Aims," *The Times,* July 12, 2000.

Brubaker, Bill. "The Limits of $100 Million," *Washington Post,* December 29, 2000.

Culnane, Mary, et. al. "Lack of Long-Term Effects of In Utero Exposure to Zidovudine Among Uninfected Children Born to HIV-Infected Women," *Journal of the American Medical Association,* January 13, 1999.

Daley, Suzanne. "A President Misapprehends a Killer," *New York Times,* May 14, 2000.

Epidemiological Fact Sheet on HIV/AIDS and Sexually Transmitted Infections: South Africa. World Health Organization, 2000.

The Evidence that HIV Causes AIDS. Bethesda, MD: National Institute of Allergy and Infectious Diseases, 2000.

Garbus, Lisa. "South Africa," *HIV Insite,* Regents of the University of California, 2001. Available online at http://hivinsite.ucsf.edu/InSite.jsp?page = cr-02-01&doc = 2098.410f (cited July 18, 2001).

Garrett, Laurie. *Betrayal of Trust: The Collapse of Global Public Health.* New York: Hyperion, 2000.

———. *The Coming Plague: Newly Emerging Diseases in a World Out of Balance.* New York: Farrar, Straus and Giroux, 1994.

Gellman, Barton. "The Belated Global Response to AIDS in Africa," *Washington Post,* July 5, 2000.

———. "An Unequal Calculus of Life and Death," *Washington Post,* December 27, 2000.

HIV/AIDS/STD Strategic Plan for South Africa 2000. South African Ministry of Health, 2000. Available online at http://www.gov.za/documents/2000/aidsplan2000.pdf (cited July 18, 2001).

Jeter, Jon. "South Africa's Advances Jeopardized by AIDS," *Washington Post,* July 6, 2000.

McGreal, Chris. "AIDS: South Africa's New Apartheid," *The Guardian,* November 30, 2000.

"The Road Ahead: An Interview with South African President Thabo Mbeki," *Time Europe* (web only version), September 4, 2000. Available online at http://www.time.com/time/europe/webonly/africa/2000/09/mbeki.htm (cited July 18, 2001).

Sachs, Jeffrey. "The Best Possible Investment in Africa," *New York Times,* February 10, 2001.

Schonteich, Martin. "Age and AIDS: South Africa's Crime Time Bomb?" *African Security Review,* vol. 8, no. 4 (1999).

Sefularo, M. "Statement by the MEC for Health During the AIDS Conference Report-Back, July 25, 2000." Available online at http://www.gov.za/province/nwest/25jul2000.htm (cited July 18, 2001).

Stolberg, Sheryl Gay. "Africa's AIDS War," *New York Times,* March 10, 2001.

South African Ministry of Health. "HIV/AIDS/STD Strategic Plan for South Africa 2000." Available online at http:www.gov.za.

Swarns, Rachel. "Mbeki Details Quest to Grasp South Africa's AIDS Disaster," *New York Times,* May 7, 2000.

Toolis, Kevin. "While the World Looks Away," *The Guardian,* December 2, 2000.

"Truth and Lies about AZT," *Johannesburg Mail and Guardian,* December 1, 1999.

United Nations General Assembly. *Special Session of the General Assembly on HIV/AIDS.* Fifty-ninth Session. Report of the Secretary-General, 2001.

World Health Organization. *Epidemiological Fact Sheet on HIV/AIDS and Sexually Transmitted Infections: South Africa.* UN World Health Organization, 2000.

"The Worst Say to Lose Talent: Business and AIDS," *The Economist,* February 10, 2001.

—*E.M. Shostak*

RETAINED ASSETS: SWISS BANKS RELEASE PREVIOUSLY HELD FUNDS TO HOLOCAUST SURVIVORS

In a New York courtroom in August 1998, a final chapter in the saga of World War II (1939–45), which had ended more than 50 years before, was written. Before a U.S. district court judge, a consortium of major Swiss banks—under siege by a class-action lawsuit by plaintiffs residing in the United States and joined by several influential international Jewish organizations—agreed to a US$1.25 billion payment in reparation for Holocaust assets looted by Nazi Germany and deposited long ago in Swiss banks. In monetary terms, the amount of the settlement was staggering. In terms of opening up the records of bank accounts in contradiction of traditional Swiss banking secrecy, the agreement was unprecedented. While the settlement was only one step in putting to rest a series of accusations against Swiss profiteering at the expense of Holocaust victims, it marked a fundamental change in the willingness of Swiss banks to come to terms with their actions more than a half-century ago.

Considering that the famed Swiss banking secrecy laws, enacted in 1934, had brought the tiny nation almost unrivaled wealth, the country's hesitation to break with the past was understandable. Not only was the secrecy of banking matters enmeshed with the image of the impenetrable integrity of its bankers, it also went hand-in-hand with the nation's own reputation for impartiality in international affairs. Moreover, the fundamental shift in banking policy meant that the country would now confront the implications of its banking practices as a neutral country in the greatest conflict of the century, World War II. While Switzerland had survived the upheavals of the war intact and unscathed, its reckoning generations later would instigate the biggest foreign policy crisis that the

THE CONFLICT

In the aftermath of the Nazi rise to power in Germany in 1933 and eventual domination of Europe during World War II, thousands of Jewish Europeans opened bank accounts in Switzerland to protect their assets. In addition, the Nazis themselves deposited looted assets from conquered nations and individuals into Swiss banks. After World War II many of these accounts were retained by the banks as heirless assets, while others were liquidated to provide for Swiss property claims in Poland and Hungary. The Swiss also paid a fraction of the Nazi deposits in reparations to the Allied powers, while retaining most of the estimated $400 million in deposits that the Nazis funneled through their country during the course of the conflict. Contemporary efforts to reclaim much of these funds met with the entrenched wall of traditional Swiss banking secrecy.

Historical

- The Allies treated the Swiss with great leniency in the aftermath of World War II in their quest to discover Nazi assets and individual Holocaust victim accounts in Swiss banks. One primary reason for the Allies' reluctance to press the claims was the need to keep Switzerland as a financial center in rebuilding Western Europe after the war. In addition, the Allies feared that the Soviet Union's encroachment into Central Europe would be aided by a destabilized and weakened Switzerland.

Political

- Until recently, Swiss banks were not forthcoming with information on dormant accounts, many of which were opened by European Jews in the 1930s and 1940s, even though some of these accounts could be claimed by their heirs. It was only with immense pressure from international Jewish organizations and the United States government, along with reams of unfavorable publicity for Swiss actions during and after World War II, that the Swiss banks have been willing to conduct an extensive investigation into dormant accounts.

country had witnessed since the outright hostilities of the war had ended.

Finally, the reparations matter caused the international Jewish community to ask its own questions about the effectiveness of asking for indemnity so many years after the events in question. There was by now a cottage industry of lawyers, lobbyists, and advisors at work debating and crafting reparation settlements in Switzerland, the United States, Israel, and elsewhere. While no credible entity argued against paying Holocaust survivors or their descendants their rightful claims, some observers thought that the tactics of some of the more aggressive proponents of reparations, which included singling out Switzerland for boycotts and international censure, went too far. As effective as these tactics may have been in forcing Switzerland to come to terms with its past, they may have inadvertently led to an upsurge in anti-Semitic sentiment among those who resented the confrontational rhetoric and unilateral demands. Other observers also voiced skepticism at the efforts of U.S. politicians to raise awareness of the reparations issue, noting that elected officials may have been more interested in gaining votes than in settling a long-standing moral and ethical dilemma.

HISTORICAL BACKGROUND

The foundation of modern Swiss banking dates to the November 1934 enactment of a set of secrecy laws for its banking sector. Chief among the provisions of the Federal Law Relating to Banks and Savings Banks was the absolute prohibition on all bank employees, officers, auditors, or banking commission members from revealing the identity of any individual holding a bank account in the country, or any details related to such an account. The law also strengthened the regulatory powers of the federal government, through various banking commissions, over Switzerland's banks. Contrary to later opinion, however, the enactment of the Swiss bank secrecy laws had little, if indeed anything, to do with the Nazi Party's rise to power in Germany the year before. In fact, the secrecy laws were a result of a 1932 scandal over tax evasion in France that had strained relations between the two countries over French demands to look at Swiss bank accounts opened to avoid paying taxes in the former country. After some Swiss bankers leaked information to French authorities to aid them with their investigation, the leaders of Swiss banks wanted to guarantee that such an indiscretion would not happen again, at least not without threatening severe repercussions. As enacted, the law provided for

penalties of up to six months in prison and a fine of 20,000 Swiss francs.

While the banking secrecy laws were designed to forestall future scandals and maintain the integrity of Swiss banking procedures, it soon had an unintended benefit. After Nazi Germany promulgated its Nuremberg Laws in September 1935, assets from German Jews began to stream into Swiss banks. The decrees, which stripped German citizenship from Jewish residents and forbade marriage and sexual relations between Jews and Aryans (non-Jewish Caucasians), were just the first step in the total disenfranchisement, marginalization, and eventual brutalization of Jews in Germany and elsewhere under Adolph Hitler. Over the next few years the Nazis stepped up their program against the Jews, taking steps to bar them from certain occupations and seizing their businesses outright and turning them over to Aryans after 1938. As some 60 percent of the half million of Germany's Jews made their living from their own small businesses, the economic decrees delivered a formidable amount of assets into Nazi hands.

Of course, the Nazis were not blind to the possibility of Jewish assets fleeing the country, and they used every means at their disposal to prevent the monetary flow into Swiss banks. In December 1936 the Nazi regime made transferring assets out of Germany a crime punishable by death. In addition to this obvious deterrent, travel restrictions made trips out of the country increasingly difficult, if not impossible, and a series of new laws were enacted to put more assets under Nazi control in the days leading up to World War II. By that time, outright intimidation and physical repression also induced Jews to hand over their remaining assets to the state. Because of the serious risks involved in getting one's assets out of the country, many German Jews used their business colleagues to take assets out of the country on their behalf. In a typical arrangement of this nature, someone wanting to make a deposit in a Swiss bank would hand over cash, securities, precious metals, or jewelry to an intermediary, who would travel to Switzerland and open an account in the first individual's name. Naturally, the transaction depended on the trust between the two parties; however, there is evidence that an informal network of intermediaries developed to ferry Jewish assets out of Nazi Germany and into Swiss banks in the mid to late-1940s.

As Hitler's Germany took over neighboring countries after 1938, however, the network of intermediaries itself was subsumed under Nazi control. Under the Anschluss agreement of March

JEWISH SURVIVORS FROM CONCENTRATION CAMPS LIKE THIS ONE IN DACHAU, GERMANY—IN WHICH THE PRISONERS HAVE JUST BEEN LIBERATED—HAVE DEMANDED REPARATIONS FOR HOLOCAUST ASSETS LOOTED BY NAZI GERMANY AND DEPOSITED INTO SWISS BANKS. *(AP/Wide World Photos. Reproduced by permission.)*

1938, Austria was absorbed into Nazi Germany, as was the Sudetenland region of Czechoslovakia in March 1939. The military aggression against Poland in September 1939, and the subsequent takeover of all of northern and western Europe, save neutral Sweden, Switzerland, Spain, and Portugal, further cut off escape from the Nazi grip. Yet even in the final days before the war, assets flowed into Swiss banks. In the month of August 1939 alone, about 17,000 Swiss bank accounts received transfers of assets by residents of Poland. Once Nazi domination of the continent was underway, the economic conquest of its people became a primary goal of the conquerors, a fact recognized by almost everyone in the region. Alone in Europe, Switzerland represented an oasis of stability and security, a fact demonstrated by the enormous amount of assets deposited there in direct proportion to the rise of the Nazis.

Those who chose to put their assets into Swiss banks had good reason to believe that they had made the best possible choice. To say the least, the political atmosphere in Europe during the late 1930s was tumultuous. Almost every national economy sustained a serious setback in the global economic depression that began after 1929. Although there was some recovery in the latter part of the decade much of this was driven by the Nazis' drive to rearm Germany, matched in part by Benito

Mussolini's military expenditures in Italy, and the subsequent militarization policies pursued by the nascent Axis' rivals, France and Great Britain. Thus, even economic recovery was a mixed blessing for Europe, as it seemed to go hand-in-hand with the nationalist ambitions of Germany and Italy and responses to their aggressive foreign policies. Although Switzerland's government joined in the military preparedness strategies pursued by European countries, it relied more on its natural geographic defenses—surrounded by mountains it was easily accessible only through tunnels that could quickly be shut down—instead of pouring money into its armed forces.

The Swiss also relied on their traditional stance of strict neutrality in international affairs during the anxious years after Hitler's rise to power in 1933. As the founding place and home of the International Red Cross, the headquarters of the International Olympic Committee, and a member of the League of Nations, Switzerland was one of the centers of international relations and prided itself on its contributions to humanitarian causes. The country was also a traditional place of asylum for political refugees and others escaping persecution, although Swiss authorities were always careful to discriminate between those with legitimate claims to asylum and those deemed less desirable, who were usually forced to emigrate elsewhere. The refugee policy was never designed to implement an open door policy for emigrants to Switzerland. In fact the policy reflected another strain of the country's history, a latent xenophobia that caused many Swiss to fear that their country could be overrun by foreigners if too many were allowed to settle there.

Switzerland Deals with Wartime Refugees

In the late 1930s the tenor of Swiss policies towards emigrants swung decidedly against its humanitarian traditions and in favor of keeping refugees from remaining in Switzerland. The change resulted from several factors, including xenophobic and anti-Semitic tendencies among many Swiss residents. Jews had only gained the right to vote, serve in elected office, and move about freely in Switzerland in 1866, and their community remained a small percentage of the country's population. Another one of the main elements in this change was the pressure to curry favor with Nazi Germany, or at least to avoid entangling Switzerland in foreign policy imbroglios with its powerful neighbor. In the most infamous example of Swiss complicity with Nazi anti-Semitic policies, Swiss officials asked Nazi Germany to begin stamping the passports of Jews with the red letter "J" in 1938 to make it easier to identify potential refugees and prevent them from entering the country to seek asylum. Swiss relief organizations also began excluding Jewish children from other countries in holiday programs to Switzerland in the late 1930s out of fear that they might attempt to stay in the country. The fear of mass asylum claims on Switzerland's part, however, was not unfounded. In the summer of 1938, just a few months after the Anschluss, Austrian Jewish children were abruptly ejected from Switzerland along with their parents, who, on the pretext of visiting Switzerland, immediately sought asylum.

For those 7,000 Jews who were allowed to remain in Switzerland as refugees prior to the war, many paid a premium "solidarity" tax for the privilege of staying there, a situation made all the more galling by the employment prohibitions enforced on refugees while in the country. Individual Swiss cantons, or administrative districts, also levied payment on Jewish refugees for permits to remain in the country. In addition, Swiss authorities demanded that international and Swiss Jewish organizations pay for the maintenance of Jewish refugee camps, even as the government paid for settlement centers for other wartime refugees. Even after the onset of World War II on September 1, 1939, Switzerland's immigration polices remained in-

transigent. The government dealt harshly with those who contravened its ban on Jewish refugees. In one case that would become infamous, the police chief of the town of St. Gall, Paul Grüninger, was dismissed from his position after allowing about 3,000 Jewish refugees to cross the border into Switzerland from Austria after the Anschluss. Grüninger also helped to raise funds privately to ensure the refugees sustenance; both acts led him to his prosecution on the grounds of malfeasance, causing him to lose his pension as well. Deemed a social outcast for his actions, Grüninger lived in poverty until his death in 1972. He was honored by his countrymen only posthumously, with an official "rehabilitation" in 1993.

After August 1942 Switzerland had completely shut its borders to those seeking asylum from religious persecution. Considering the government's official stance, efforts to help Jewish refugees went further underground. It is not known how many refugees were turned away from Switzerland's borders or ejected from the country during the war, although 24,000 official asylum rejections were recorded. Thousands of these ejections took place after Swiss officials learned of the Nazi Final Solution, the plan to send thousands of Jews to their deaths in the system of concentration camps in Central and Eastern Europe. It was only in July 1944, however, that Swiss immigration officials changed their policies to allow religious persecution to be grounds for seeking asylum. Overall, during the war about 21,000 Jewish refugees were allowed to remain in Switzerland, along with an additional 30,000 additional civilian refugees.

Wartime Neutrality

Switzerland took such Draconian steps to prevent refugees from flooding its borders in part out of real fears that a Nazi invasion was imminent. What had seemed unimaginable just a few years before—the complete domination of the continent by Hitler's forces—now meant that Switzerland was entirely surrounded by the Axis powers. Although the Swiss prepared plans to block any invasion by destroying the mountain tunnel passes into the country, it was clear that the country's five million people would be no match to German forces if they decided to overrun the country. Even if it offered military resistance, the country still depended on shipments of food and other vital materials through Axis countries to guarantee its survival. Realistically, Switzerland's only hope was to insist on its neutrality and to offer its services as a financial and diplomatic center. Indeed, the country continued to serve as one of the most important international relations theaters in the world, a place where Allied and Axis negotiators and espionage agents could meet on neutral ground.

It was as a financial center, however, that Switzerland not only survived the war, but also prospered. Despite the drastic changes brought about by wartime conditions, Swiss bankers, along with their banking laws, remained above the fray. Bankers continued to insist on secrecy and discretion to maintain the uninterrupted flow of international capital, even when it was apparent that the Nazis were looting the treasuries of defeated countries and stealing from conquered peoples. The amount of plundered assets deposited in Swiss banks during World War II may never be known with certainty; however, estimates by the United States of stolen treasury deposits by the Nazis from conquered countries range up to $579 million, about $5.6 billion in 2001 currency. Of this amount, about $400 million (worth about $3 billion in contemporary dollars) made its way to Swiss banks during the war.

In addition to emptying treasuries of gold deposits throughout Europe, the Nazis also looted the assets of their individual victims. It is nearly impossible to determine with precision the fraction of the $400 million deposited in Swiss banks that came from individual victims. Typically, gold that was stolen from individuals—wedding rings, coins, and the most infamous example, gold crowns and dental fillings—was melted down and recast into gold ingots at Berlin's central Reichsbank. The recast gold was then deposited in Switzerland, which took German gold deposits until the very last weeks of the war. Although Swiss banking officials knew from 1941 that at least part of the Nazi gold deposited in their institutions was looted, they failed to take steps to verify the source of German deposits until 1943. Even then, their efforts were lackluster, and Switzerland remained the favored banking site for Nazi Germany. Through the end of the war, about four-fifths of international capital flow from Germany was routed through Switzerland.

Acknowledging Switzerland's position as the banker to Nazi Germany, the United States responded with a series of measures designed to put pressure on the neutral nation to abandon its stance. In 1940 the United States froze all European assets being held in U.S. banks, with the exception of the unoccupied Allied partner Great Britain. This declaration included, of course, Swiss assets in the United States. In 1944 the United States issued the Declaration on Gold Purchases, which nullified recognition on all gold transfers presumed to be stolen from countries occupied by the Axis powers, a measure clearly aimed at Switzerland's banks. Finally, after intense lobbying by the United States, Switzerland agreed in March 1945, just weeks before the end of World War II, to block Nazi assets and stop purchasing gold from Germany. The neutral nation also agreed to start taking stock of German assets that were deposited in Switzerland, a condition that it soon ignored.

While Switzerland faced the onset of World War II with legitimate security concerns over its possible invasion by Nazi Germany, its strategic location demonstrated by 1943 that it faced no credible threat to its borders. It was safeguarded as the banker for Nazi Germany and the diplomatic courier for the Allied and Axis powers. Indeed, after the German surrender at Stalingrad in February 1943, and particularly after the Allied invasion of Normandy in June 1944, the Swiss knew full well that Nazi power was in decline in Europe, and that Switzerland most certainly would not face military action by the Axis countries. Yet Swiss officials and bankers did not revise their polices regarding refugees, Nazi deposits, and looted assets even as wartime conditions changed. They continued to insist on a strict interpretation of banking secrecy and diplomatic neutrality that precluded them from making the moral judgments that the Allies pressured them to consider. In the course of World War II and its aftermath the Swiss position enriched the country and assured its future as a center of financial transactions; the long-term consequences would not come due for another half century.

The Washington Accord

The negotiations at the end of World War II that resulted in the May 1946 Washington Accord followed the Swiss stance of completely rejecting the moral and ethical arguments that the U.S. and Allied powers invoked. Swiss negotiators refused to acknowledge that much of the German deposits to their banks were looted from national treasuries and individual victims of the Nazi regime, despite evidence from the Allies that showed at least $200 million in monetary gold was stolen. Fortunately for the Swiss, however, the Allies were divided on how far to press the Swiss to make restitution. Some U.S. officials were insistent that the Swiss pay back the greatest possible share of the ill-gotten deposits sitting in their banks, while others favored a quick settlement, even if it meant allowing Swiss banks to keep the stolen gold. In the end, the rising tensions of the incipient Cold War were the de-

CHRONOLOGY

1934 Swiss bank secrecy laws are enacted.

November 1935 The Nuremberg Laws in Nazi Germany strip Jewish residents of their citizenship rights.

September 1, 1939–May 7, 1945 World War II is launched in the European theater.

March 8, 1945 Under pressure from the Allies, Switzerland freezes Nazi German assets in Swiss banks and cuts off trade with Germany, although German deposits to Swiss banks continue through April 1945.

May 26, 1946 The Allied Powers sign the Allied-Swiss Accord, commonly known as the Washington Accord, with Switzerland. The Accord provides for limited reparations by Switzerland to the Allies and certain war refugee agencies for gold and assets known to have been looted by Nazi Germany from Holocaust victims and deposited in Swiss banks.

1995 A growing number of press reports expose Swiss banks' reluctance to identify and distribute Holocaust victim assets.

April 1996 Senator Alphonse D'Amato opens U.S. Senate Banking Committee hearings on Nazi deposits in Swiss banks.

May 1996 Under international pressure, Swiss banks agree to join the Independent Commission of Eminent Persons, also known as the Volcker Commission.

October 1996 Lawsuits are filed by Holocaust survivors and their descendants to reclaim assets in Swiss banks.

December 1996 Outspoken Swiss President Jean-Pascal Delamuraz refers to international efforts to reclaim Holocaust assets as "extortion and blackmail."

January 1997 Security guard Christoph Meili discovers vital documents related to Holocaust assets in the process of being shredded at the Union Bank of Switzerland. Together with Delamuraz's comments, international opinion turns decidedly against the Swiss in the wake of the discovery.

August 1998 Preliminary settlement on Holocaust assets is reached among Swiss banks, U.S. plaintiffs, and international Jewish organizations.

June 1999 Advertisements are placed to publicize Holocaust settlements and solicit applications from potential asset holders.

February 2000 The Volcker Commission dissolves.

July 2000 A U.S. court approves the final settlement among Credit Suisse Bank, Union Bank Switzerland, U.S. class action plaintiffs, and international Jewish organizations.

ciding factor in treating the Swiss with pronounced leniency. With so much of Europe already in ruins and the Soviet Union expanding its sphere of influence throughout Eastern and Central Europe, Switzerland's role as a financial center to rebuilding Europe was vital to U.S. foreign policy in the region. If Switzerland were sidelined during this transitional period, so the argument went, the West would lose ground to the Soviets in the race to secure the rest of Europe. Knowing this, Swiss officials were in no hurry to rush negotiations in Washington and presented a united, and stubborn, front to Allied representatives.

The Washington Accord followed Swiss proposals almost unilaterally. Although $200 million of the $276 million in gold that the Swiss National Bank took into its own accounts in payments from Nazi Germany was estimated to have come from stolen national and individual assets, the Swiss pledged just over $58 million into a Tripartite Gold Commission fund to distribute to countries reclaiming Nazi assets. In return, the Allies agreed to waive all claims against Switzerland to recover stolen assets from its banks. The Swiss also agreed to take inventory of all Nazi deposits and liquidate these holdings on a fifty-fifty split with the Allies; however, legitimate German owners of any liquidated assets would be compensated for their losses by the new German government, not by Switzerland. Switzerland also agreed to take inventory of all heirless assets in its banks and forward these assets to the Allies for refugee relief. For its efforts, Swiss assets in the United States, frozen in 1940, were unblocked; government holdings were released in May 1946, and private assets were released in November of that year.

Overall, the Swiss paid out about $86 million in reparations through 1952. The matter of heirless assets, however, remained largely unexamined until the 1960s. Yet a key agreement with communist Poland in 1949 demonstrated the hard line that the Swiss government took to protect its interests. The Swiss-Polish Agreement signed in June 1949 stipulated that the Polish government would gain control of all heirless Polish assets in Swiss banks—most of which were deposited by Holocaust victims—in exchange for paying off all Swiss property claims from World War II and its aftermath. Swiss authorities did not, however, attach a list of names to the accounts that they determined were subject to the agreement, ensuring that any Polish heirs to the account holders would not be able to claim the assets. Essentially, the Swiss used Holocaust victim assets to pay for their own property losses in Poland, a deal they would also make with communist Hungary in 1950. Further, the diplomatic protocol between these countries kept the deals a secret. Their eventual exposure in 1996 shocked the international community.

As with many unsettled issues of World War II, the matter of dormant accounts in Swiss banks was pushed aside during the years of the Cold War. The United States wanted to reestablish mutually positive relations with Switzerland in the 1950s and did not press further to force Swiss banks to resolve the issue. Further complicating the Cold War atmosphere, many of the individuals who opened Swiss accounts were now, after the war, part of the Soviet Bloc. Even if they could gain access to their accounts, the property would now face claims by the communist states where they resided. Finally, Swiss bankers themselves were anything but receptive to releasing information on the accounts even when they were faced with potentially legitimate claims on the accounts by the heirs of the account holders. Sticking to the letter of Swiss banking secrecy laws, bankers insisted not only on exact identification of the accounts by claimants, but often proof that the holder was now deceased and remitted the account to the heirs. As many of the account holders had perished in the Holocaust, of course, no such specific proof existed. Many of the heirs were affronted that Swiss bankers demanded death certificates and wills to prove their claims, questioning how reasonable it was to expect such documents to have been issued by the concentration camp administrators.

Thus, the claims on Holocaust victim assets by their heirs were another casualty of the Cold War. In addition, the topic remained taboo in political circles because it was often linked with the issue of

THOMAS BORER, HEAD OF THE SWISS TASK FORCE ON ASSETS OF NAZI VICTIMS, TESTIFIES ON CAPITOL HILL ABOUT SWITZERLAND'S INVESTIGATION INTO ITS ROLE AS A FINANCIAL CENTER DURING WORLD WAR II. *(AP/Wide World Photos. Reproduced by permission.)*

Holocaust reparations in general. Although West Germany had paid damages to the state of Israel in the 1950s and established a pension plan for Holocaust survivors that distributes funds to this day, there was serious dissension in Jewish circles over the appropriateness of these payments. Many argued that no amount of money could bring back a single Holocaust victim, and that such payments diminished the true meaning of the horrors of the Holocaust. In light of the debate, the issue of individual claims on looted Nazi assets was secondary to the diplomatic resolution of claims between West Germany and other nations.

A New Leader for the Jewish World Congress

The dramatic revival of the Holocaust assets issue was testament to the direction of the Jewish World Congress under Edgar Bronfman, who assumed its leadership in 1981. Bronfman was already known as the multi-billionaire chairman of the Seagrams Company, a Canadian-based distiller that also held stakes in Universal Studios, Time-Warner, and a host of other companies. The son of Russian Jewish immigrants, Bronfman grew up with a strong Jewish consciousness. His father, who founded Seagrams and helped it grow tremendously as a major supplier of liquor to the United

States during Prohibition, and also was the president of the Canadian Jewish Congress and a major supporter of the establishment of an independent Jewish state of Israel. Bronfman himself stirred up controversy by spearheading the expose of the World War II actions of United Nations Secretary General Kurt Waldheim, which included assisting the Nazis in deporting Greek Jews to the Auschwitz concentration camp. Bronfman also aided Soviet Jews in insisting on their rights to practice their religion in the Soviet Union or be granted exit visas from the country. To be sure, Bronfman did not shy away from a good fight.

Bronfman's efforts in confronting the intransigence of Swiss bankers were aided by the ending of Cold War tensions in Europe. After the fall of the Berlin Wall in 1989 and the subsequent crumbling of communist rule throughout Eastern Europe, new sources came to light that showed the secret dealings of the Swiss government with the Communist regimes. More pressing, thousands of new claimants on dormant Swiss accounts emerged from behind the Iron Curtain with urgent demands spurred by the immediate need to rebuild their lives. Denied from asserting their claims during the communist era, these impoverished Holocaust survivors and their descendents added an emotional appeal that had long been subsumed to diplomatic considerations.

Bronfman's initial meeting with the Swiss Bankers Association (SBA) on September 12, 1995, did not go well. Authorized by the Israeli government to discuss the matter of Holocaust assets with the Swiss through the aegis of the World Jewish Congress, Bronfman approached the meeting with the hope of beginning a series of discussions on opening up a thorough investigation of the dormant accounts and their disposition. In contrast, the SBA representatives viewed the meeting as an opportunity to present a unilateral offer to settle the claims once and for all. Clearly, the Swiss bankers had not changed their tactics since the Washington Accords almost a half century before. This time, however, the Cold War stalemate and any hesitancy on the part of international Jewish organizations to demand a full accounting of the actions of Swiss bankers during and after the war no longer remained. Soon after the meeting, which delivered an affront to Bronfman that drove his subsequent actions, the issue of Holocaust assets in Swiss banks exploded in the media.

While Bronfman's skillful use of the international media helped the cause of the Holocaust survivors and their heirs, the Swiss were equally ineffective on behalf of their own interests. One of the worst public relations fiascoes occurred at the end of 1996, when outgoing Swiss President Jean-Pascal Delamuraz referred to the work of the World Jewish Congress and other international Jewish organizations as "extortion and blackmail" in a Geneva newspaper interview. Delamuraz added that if the Swiss contributed to an interim fund for Holocaust survivors, it would be nothing less than a preliminary admission of wrongdoing before any full investigation had occurred. Finally, Delamuraz voiced concerns that the matter of repatriating Holocaust assets had taken on another, more sinister agenda of trying to destroy Switzerland as an international financial center. Upon the interview's publication, a storm of protest forced Delamuraz to issue an apology to Bronfman, but the damage was done. Many viewed Delamuraz's attitude as proof that Swiss officials had yet to accept the legitimacy of the inquiries into Holocaust assets in their banks. To some observers, Delamuraz's comments also reflected a rise in anti-Semitic rhetoric in Switzerland, where many citizens did indeed resent being scrutinized so carefully by international groups and often directed their frustration specifically at Jewish groups.

Swiss Banking Records Revealed

Just days after Delamuraz's apology, another even more damaging incident cast into doubt Swiss efforts at resolving the Holocaust assets issue in good faith. On January 8, 1997, Christoph Meili, a security guard at the Union Bank of Switzerland, discovered a vast set of documents in the bank's shredding room, waiting to be destroyed. After glancing at the ledgers, receipts, and statements, Meili immediately realized that these documents related to the bank's records from the 1870s through 1965, a period when many accounts were opened by individuals who would later perish in the Holocaust. The records also included documents from other banks that had been absorbed by the Union Bank in the postwar era. In short, Meili discovered an entire archival set of bank records that could be used to verify the identity of at least some Holocaust-era accounts. Once he realized the importance of the documents, Meili was horrified—the bank was deliberately destroying documents that may have directly related to the accounts, in direct contradiction to their own public statements that there was no way of proving the legitimacy of most of the claims. In particular, Meili was shocked to find one ledger that contained information from the 1930s that listed accounts opened by depositors in various German cities, most likely German Jews ferrying their assets out of Nazi Germany.

After taking some of the documents home and discussing it with his wife, Meili turned them over to a local Jewish organization, which in turn contacted the police for further action. When the news became public, it was another bombshell that proved disastrous for Swiss authorities. After denying for decades that any concrete proof existed to facilitate claims on heirless assets, a roomful of documents had emerged at a crucial time in the current investigation. Further, no one seemed to believe the Union Bank's contention that the documents were only inadvertently being destroyed and that it had no knowledge of their contents. Instead, a deliberate plot to erase all evidence of the provenance of the dormant accounts was presumed to be the more likely motive. For his part, Meili was immediately fired from his job and soon was the target of legal threats by the government for violating Switzerland's famed bank secrecy laws. Because of the death threats against him and his family, Meili eventually requested political asylum in the United States, which was granted by Congress in May 1997. Hailed as a hero by international Jewish groups, Meili settled into a new life in California with his wife and children.

U.S. Efforts and the Threat of Sanctions

With the Delamuraz and Meili scandals surrounding the Holocaust assets issue, Swiss authorities gained new incentives to be more forthcoming in the ongoing investigations. These inquiries included the Independent Commission of Eminent Persons, also known as the Volcker Commission, established in May 1996 between various Jewish organizations and the SBA, and the U.S. Senate hearings opened by Alfonse D'Amato, chair of its Banking Committee, in April 1996. While the Volcker Commission would eventually issue a series of reports that largely criticized the past efforts of Swiss banks to resolve claims on dormant accounts, the D'Amato hearings provided ongoing, explosive headlines that condemned Swiss bankers for their evasive actions in dealing with the claims. Yet D'Amato himself often deflected the attention onto his own motives for holding the contentious hearings. With a tough Senate reelection campaign against Democrat Charles Schumer looming in the Fall of 1998, many political pundits argued that D'Amato's aggressive stance with the Swiss bankers was merely a ploy to gain a larger share of New York's Jewish vote in the election. While his efforts kept the Holocaust assets issue in the headlines, however, it failed to serve him politically; despite championing the cause in the Senate, D'Amato was defeated in his reelection bid.

SELECTED LIST OF COMMITTEES STUDYING THE ISSUE OF HOLOCAUST ASSETS

The Independent Commission of Eminent Persons, commonly known as the Volcker Commission after its head, former U.S. Federal Reserve chairman Paul Volcker, was established in May 1996 by the Swiss government in conjunction with several international Jewish organizations. It issued its report on Nazi-era bank accounts in December 1999. The Volcker Commission disbanded the following year.

The Independent Commission of Experts, also known as the Bergier Commission, was formed by the Swiss government in December 1996. It issued two reports: The Bergier Report on Gold Transactions (May 1998) and the Bergier Report on Switzerland and Refugees (December 1999).

The Eizenstat Commission was created by the U.S. government to study the United States' role in returning looted property to its rightful owners or their heirs after World War II. Deputy Secretary of the U.S. Treasury Stuart Eizenstat led the studies, which resulted in two reports in May 1997 and June 1998.

Another major impetus from the United States in bringing Swiss bankers to the bargaining table was the effort by New York City Comptroller, Alan G. Hevesi, who put together a group of about 800 local governments willing to withdraw their investment funds from Swiss banks. In July 1998 Hevesi noted that New York City's retirement fund administrators alone did about $31 million in annual business with Swiss banks that handled their investments. If the coalition carried through on its threats, Swiss banks would lose hundreds of millions of dollars in business, possibly more than $1 billion. Under Hevesi's timeline for sanctions, a gradual withdrawal of business from Swiss banks would occur starting in September 1998, and continue through the following year until the public pension funds had divested themselves of all Swiss holdings. With a schedule of specific sanctions looming, Swiss bankers now redoubled their efforts to come to terms with Jewish groups.

With the ongoing work of the Volcker Commission and the Task Force on Assets of Nazi Victims, created by the Swiss government in October 1996 with Thomas Borer as its chair, the Swiss

A HOLOCAUST VICTIM RECEIVES A CHECK IN COMPENSATION FROM A SWISS BANK. DURING WORLD WAR II MANY HOLOCAUST VICTIMS LOST MONEY DEPOSITED INTO SWISS BANK ACCOUNTS FOR SAFEKEEPING. *(CORBIS CORPORATION (Bellevue). Reproduced by permission.)*

government had hoped to maintain a deliberate pace in its investigation into dormant accounts and negotiations with the World Jewish Congress and other organizations. Under the threat of sanctions, however, these methodical efforts were now secondary to the immediate need to reach a settlement. After years of inactivity two of the major banks involved in the matter, Credit Suisse and United Bank of Switzerland, suddenly agreed to a settlement of $1.25 billion that would absolve them of future claims and commit them to a speedy resolution of all pending claims on dormant accounts. Although the settlement before Judge Edward Korman in the United States District Court for the Eastern District of New York proved controversial to many Swiss, who viewed it as an admission of wrongdoing, others argued that it was a wise business decision, considering it removed future liabilities on other claims that might arise. Still others considered the agreement an act of simple ethics, although in the midst of the announcement this perspective seemed to be the minority view.

The banks admittedly came to the settlement table begrudgingly. Once the court handed down the decision, however, they moved in good faith to resolve the claims. Conversely, the investigations engendered further controversy as the announcement of the number of dormant accounts linked to probable Holocaust victims turned out to be much larger than previously admitted by the banks. Whereas the SBA insisted in February 1995 that only 775 dormant accounts from the Holocaust era existed, the Volcker Commission's final report in December 1999 found 53,388 unclaimed accounts that might be related to Holocaust victims. The great difference between these two figures seemed to justify all of the criticisms that Edgar Bronfman and the World Jewish Congress had been leveling all along.

RECENT HISTORY AND THE FUTURE

Under the guidelines set up by the Volcker Commission in conjunction with the settlements, heirs to the dormant accounts that still had money in them would receive ten times the amount, in order to make up for interest and appreciation. Other accounts that might have been closed under duress by Nazi authorities would be individually reviewed to determine what their value might have been had the individuals retained the accounts. By the end of 2000, some $33.5 million had been paid out in claims, with $6.4 million going to individuals who had direct claims on an account. In a separate group of payments, a fund established by the Swiss in 1997, at the height of the banking controversy, to make payments to currently needy Holocaust survivors, mostly in eastern Europe, had paid out more than $171 million by the end of 2001.

Yet the controversies persist over Holocaust assets, particularly in linking claims on dormant Swiss accounts with additional demands for reparations by Axis and neutral countries for separate wartime actions. Gabriel Schoenfeld, editor of the Jewish American magazine *Commentary*, suggested that some attorneys and activists had taken advantage of the issue for personal gain at the expense of the Swiss, and that some innocent parties had been unfairly attacked during the controversy. For example, as he noted, even banks in Jerusalem held some dormant accounts that might be linked to Holocaust survivors, which were in some cases impossible to trace. Schoenfeld also expressed his fears that the Holocaust itself might be trivialized into a mere matter of money, instead of being presented as a systematic genocide against the Jewish people. For this commentary, however, Schoenfeld received vigorous responses attacking his position, including an acidic letter from Deputy Secretary of the U.S. Treasury, Stuart Eizenstat, who had led the United States' efforts to investigate Holocaust assets in Switzerland and elsewhere. While Eizenstat admitted that the matter of Holocaust assets was by now part of a larger set of issues including stolen artworks, forced labor, and outright slave labor during World War II, he nevertheless upheld the legitimacy of such claims on the Axis nations and, in some cases, the neutral nations that benefited from such acts.

More than 50 years after the end of World War II, issues that were presumed to have been settled were reopened and examined in a post-Cold War climate that questioned the legitimacy of the initial postwar settlement. While the claims on Holocaust assets in Swiss banks slowly came to a conclusion on a case-by-case basis, they remained tied to similar lawsuits over unpaid insurance claims, payment for other stolen assets, and reparations for induced labor. Subsequent events have diminished the impact of the accusations against Switzerland. In such a contentious atmosphere, however, the country will doubtless remain a vital player in the debates over the actions of all neutral nations in wartime and their responsibilities to the victims of war in times of peace.

BIBLIOGRAPHY

Black, Edwin. *IBM and the Holocaust: The Strategic Alliance between Nazi Germany and America's Most Powerful Corporation.* New York: Crown Publishers, 2001.

Bower, Tom. *Nazi Gold: The Full Story of the Fifty-Year Swiss-Nazi Conspiracy to Steal Billions from Europe's Jews and Holocaust Survivors.* New York: HarperCollins, 1997.

Carter, Chelsea J. "Swiss Bank Whistleblower's Uneasy New Life in California," AP Worldstream, March 2, 2001.

Chesnoff, Richard Z. *Pack of Thieves: How Hitler and Europe Plundered the Jews and Committed the Greatest Theft in History.* New York: Doubleday, 1999.

"Clinton Thanks Switzerland for Addressing Holocaust Issues," AP Worldstream, August 22, 2000.

"Don't Exonerate Swiss Banks: Holocaust Victims were Deceived and Looted," editorial, *Miami Herald,* December 13, 1999.

Eizenstat, Stuart. "Holocaust Reparations: Gabriel Schoenfeld and Critics," *Commentary,* January 2001.

Higgins, Alexander G. "Swiss Holocaust Era Accounts," Associated Press, February 5, 2001.

Jelinek, Pauline. "Clinton Working on Holocaust Amends," Associated Press, January 17, 2001.

———. "Holocaust Negotiations Hit Snag," Associated Press, January 17, 2001.

Levin, Itamar. *The Last Deposit: Swiss Banks and the Holocaust Victims' Accounts.* Westport, CT: Praeger Publishers, 1999.

Niewyk, Donald, and Francis Nicosia. *The Columbia Guide to the Holocaust.* New York: Columbia University Press, 2000.

"NY Bill Introduced to Pressure Insurers on Claims by Survivors, Heirs of Holocaust Victims," *Insurance Advocate,* February 14, 1998, p. 34.

"No End in Sight," *The Economist,* August 2, 1997, p. 42.

Olson, Elizabeth. "Swiss Squirm at What Holocaust Payout Implies," *Christian Science Monitor,* August 21, 1998, 5.

Schoenfeld, Garbriel. "Holocaust Reparations—A Growing Scandal," *Commentary,* September 2000.

Stanglin, Douglas, and Richard Z. Chesnoff. "D'Amato: Awash in Secret Documents," *U.S. News and World Report,* April 15, 1996, p. 24.

"Swiss Holocaust Fund Approves Survivors' Last Applications," AP Worldstream, December 14, 2000.

"Swiss Holocaust Fund Expects First Payments in Israel This Month," AP Worldstream, April 13, 2000.

"U.S. Hasn't Fully Paid Debt to Holocaust Victims, Study Finds," *Christian Science Monitor,* January 17, 2001, 4.

Vincent, Isabel. *Hitler's Silent Partners: Swiss Banks, Nazi Gold, and the Pursuit of Justice.* New York: William Morrow and Company, 1997.

Warner, Joan, with John Parry. "Swiss Banks: The Noose Tightens," *Business Week,* July 27, 1998, 1.

Ziegler, Jean. *The Swiss, the Gold, and the Dead: How Swiss Bankers Helped Finance the Nazi War Machine.* New York: Harcourt Brace and Company, 1997.

—*Timothy G. Borden*

THREATS OF TERRORISM IN THE TWENTY-FIRST CENTURY

THE CONFLICT

The ways in which terrorist groups operate have changed significantly in the late 1980s and 1990s, creating new challenges for security agencies in the twenty-first century. Governments must protect their interests against the threat of terrorist attack while safeguarding civil rights and liberties.

Ideological

- Terrorist groups in the early twenty-first century usually form based on shared ideological grounds of politics, religion, or other beliefs and tend to be more loosely organized and less controlled by a central authority than in the past.

- Terrorist attacks, while sometimes less frequent than earlier in the twentieth century, have generally become more deadly, with terrorists focusing on inflicting mass casualties rather than on gaining political support.

Technological

- Globalization has facilitated the easy movement of information, goods, and people, increasing opportunities for terrorists to gain and disseminate information and to penetrate national borders.

- Terrorists increasingly take advantage of high-tech communications, computers, and the Internet to obtain information and organize activities. At the same time, security organizations use these systems to monitor potential terrorists.

- The possibility that terrorists could obtain nuclear, biological, or chemical weapons has increased.

Political

- Efforts to combat terrorism have led to significantly increased international cooperation, and to strict new laws proscribing membership in, or financial support of, organizations defined as terrorist.

- Critics argue that such laws can threaten legitimate political dissent by too broadly defining terrorism and terrorist organizations.

As 1999 drew to a close, cities across the United States prepared gala festivities to celebrate the new millennium. Yet this happy mood was seriously threatened when, on December 14, 1999, an Algerian man who had driven into the United States from Vancouver, Canada, was arrested on suspicion of terrorism. The public soon learned that Ahmed Ressam, whose car contained enough explosives to destroy a large building, was part of a plot by Islamic militants—extremists on the fringe of the Islamic religion and culture—to blow up American landmarks during 2000 celebrations. The country's festive mood turned somber as an accomplice was arrested in Brooklyn, New York, and two others were arrested at the Vermont border. The country braced for the possibility that other accomplices might try to enter the country—or might have already succeeded without detection.

As fears mounted Seattle, Washington, cancelled many of its First Night activities, and other cities increased security measures. Despite security concerns, the White House's "American's Millennium" celebration, which was expected to draw thousands of spectators to the Mall in Washington, DC, went on as planned. New Year's Eve and New Year's Day passed without a terrorist incident. Relieved though the nation was to have avoided violence, the millennium plot emphasized new anxieties and vulnerabilities for a country that has historically felt relatively secure from terrorist attack. Coming as it did on the heels of the Oklahoma City bombing in 1995 and the sarin gas attack on a Tokyo subway, also in 1995, the threats of terrorism in the twenty-first century are very much a personal concern for nations worldwide.

HISTORICAL BACKGROUND

Defining Terrorism

Terrorist acts have occurred throughout history, but the term "terrorism" did not enter the language until the French Revolution (1793–94). A precise definition of the word, however, has been difficult to find. Contemporary attempts by governments to clarify what is meant by terrorism have varied, but definitions generally agree that terrorism is some form of violent struggle intended to bring about a political purpose. Germany's Office for the Protection of the Constitution, for example, defines terrorism as a struggle by means of assault on life and property to attain political goals, particularly crimes such as murder, kidnapping, and arson. The British Prevention of Terrorism Act of 1974 defines the term as "the use of violence for political ends" and includes any violence intended to strike fear in the public. The U.S. State Department considers terrorism to be any politically motivated violence perpetrated by subnational groups or secret state agents that is usually intended to influence an audience. According to U.S. federal law, terrorism is any activity involving criminal violence that seems intended to intimidate civilians or influence the conduct of government by coercion. Recognizing the importance of context in addressing the meaning of terrorism, the Committee of Interior Ministers of the European Union drew up a definition that explicitly excludes traditional warfare. Professor Alex P. Schmid of Leiden University, the Netherlands, suggested that the term should describe, in essence, the "peacetime equivalent of war crimes," or any acts that would be deemed a violation of Geneva Convention rules. What all of these definitions share is the main understanding that terrorism is an act of violence perpetrated by those seeking to achieve their desired goals through coercion and intimidation.

Terrorists choose violence because it draws attention to their cause. Indeed, as Walter Laqueur observed in "Postmodern Terrorism" (*Foreign Affairs*, September-October 1996), "History shows that terrorism more often than not has little political impact, and that when it has an effect it is often the opposite of the one desired." Violent acts may bring attention to the terrorists' cause, but it may also harden public opinion against that cause rather than inspire sympathy for it. The psychological impact of terrorist acts can be overwhelming to both private citizens and governments alike. They can hold the attention of the public, as well as alter the agendas of nations.

The kind of actions usually associated with terrorism include kidnapping and the taking of hostages; hijacking; bombings; arson; and murder of targeted civilians, including journalists, lawyers, and judges. More rarely, terrorists have released, or attempted to release, biological or chemical agents into public food, water, or air supplies. Terrorist acts that involve either the citizens or the territory of more than one country are considered international terrorism. When a terrorist act is committed within one country by its own citizens, it is considered domestic terrorism. According to the U.S. State Department, more than seven thousand terrorist bombings have occurred worldwide since 1968.

Escalating Conflicts Around the World

Though terrorism is not new, its impact in the twentieth century has been especially significant. World War I (1914–18), which ushered in large-scale mechanized warfare resulting in unprecedented destruction, began with a terrorist act: the assassination of Archduke Ferdinand by a Serb militant. After World War II (1939–45) regions that had been colonized by European powers began to demand independence; often, these movements involved terrorist tactics. Terrorist response to British policy in Palestine resulted in three hundred deaths between 1945 and 1947. The war for Algerian independence (1954–62) was marked by atrocities on both sides, with the outlawed Front de Libération Nationale (FLN) responding to savage military suppression by indiscriminate massacres of civilians. Independence movements in Rhodesia, Angola, and Mozambique also involved terrorist bloodshed. In the Philippines the guerrilla Hukbalahap Party (the Huk) engaged in terrorist actions against Filipino peasants, while Chinese communists in Malaysia, frustrated at British reluctance to abdicate power, aimed terrorist attacks at British rubber plantations and murdered plantation owners. Indian independence in 1947 was marred by appalling loss of life—in August and September militant Sikhs intent on their own political agenda massacred between 200,000 and 500,000 Muslim refugees fleeing the Indian-controlled section of east Punjab. Muslims on the Pakistan side also participated in killings.

In the 1970s West Germany's Baader-Meinhof gang, a radical anticapitalist group, engaged in bank robberies, bombings, arson, kidnappings, and assassinations, targeting West German business leaders and U.S. military installations. By the mid-1970s the group had begun to back Palestinian terrorist groups; two of its mem-

SMOKE RISES FROM THE REMAINS OF THE U.S. EMBASSY IN TANZANIA ON AUGUST 7, 1998. THE BOMBING, ALLEGEDLY DIRECTED BY OSAMA BIN LADEN, WAS SEEN AS PART OF A WORLDWIDE CONSPIRACY TO KILL AMERICANS AND DESTROY U.S. PROPERTY. *(AP/Wide World Photos. Reproduced by permission.)*

bers participated in the 1976 Palestinian hijacking of an Air France jetliner, which led to an Israeli rescue mission at Entebbe airport in Uganda. Italy's Red Brigades were also active at this time. The group firebombed factories and warehouses and engaged in kidnappings and murders, most notably of former prime minister Aldo Moro. Basque separatists in Spain and the Irish Republican Army in Northern Ireland sought to advance their causes by bombing public buildings and targeting individuals for assassination. In Peru the extreme leftist group the Shining Path (*Sendero Luminoso*) perpetrated violence and chaos throughout the 1980s. By 1992, when the group's leader, Abimael Guzman, was arrested, the Shining Path had caused approximately 25,000 deaths and seriously damaged the Peruvian economy.

Terrorism also became prominent in the Middle East. The Popular Front for the Liberation of Palestine (PFLP), a militant faction of the Palestine Liberation Organization (PLO) that arose after the Six-Day War of 1967, hijacked 14 airliners within a year of its formation. Palestinian terrorists in Lebanon, often with the financial support and training of pro-Soviet states such as Cuba, East Germany, Syria, Yemen, and Libya, were able to cross into Israel to launch attacks on Israeli civilians. The PFLP also established links with extremist anti-Semitic groups in Italy, Austria, and Germany. In 1972 terrorists calling themselves the Black September group took nine Israeli athletes hostage at the Munich Olympic games. All the hostages, as well as five terrorists, were killed in the ensuing police shootout.

Radical Islam

Political events through the 1980s and 1990s continued to spur terrorist attacks. Developments in the Islamic world threatened escalating violence in several countries, including Afghanistan, Algeria, and the former Yugoslav republic of Bosnia. A coup that replaced Afghanistan's centrist government with a Marxist regime in 1978 led to Muslim protests and insurgencies throughout the country. The new regime was seen as antagonistic to Islam, which prescribes religious law as the foundation of society. When the Soviet Union invaded Afghanistan in 1979 to quell the rebellion, the resolve of the Muslim rebels, or *mujahideen*, grew. As hostilities escalated the Soviets tried to crush the *mujahideen* by launching massive campaigns against Afghan civilians. With the help of weapons from the U.S. Central Intelligence Agency (CIA), the *mujahideen* were able to continue fighting until 1992, when they succeeded in toppling the Soviet puppet government and replaced it with an Islamic republic.

That same year, civil war erupted in Algeria. The Islamic Salvation Front, a radical party intent on bringing strict Muslim law to the country, was on the brink of winning power when the military-led government cancelled parliamentary elections. Protracted guerrilla fighting ensued. By 1999 the death toll reached 100,000—mostly civilians. The Armed Islamic Group (GIA), a guerilla organization engaged in a *jihad*, or holy war, against the Algerian government, is believed to be responsible for most of the deaths. In 1993, when fighting broke out between Serbs and Muslims in Bosnia, the country became a refuge for GIA members, providing them with local passports and weapons and enabling them to maintain close links with factions in Belgium, Britain, France, Italy, Afghanistan, and Turkey.

The uprisings in Afghanistan and Algeria, and the ethnic cleansing campaign in Bosnia, radicalized respective generations of young Muslims who were inspired to fight against oppressive governments and who saw secularization and materialism as concrete threats to religious law. Western democracies, especially the United States, became targets of aggression, as radical religious leaders on the fringe of traditional, peaceful Islam urged their followers to fight against these enemies. Among these leaders was Egyptian sheik Omar Abdel-Rahman, who, according to *New York Times* reporter Richard Bernstein (January 8, 1995) in "On Trial: An Islamic Cleric Rattles Secularism," incited his followers to "hit hard and kill the enemies of God in every spot to rid [the state] of the descendants of apes and pigs fed at the tables of Zionism, Communism, and Imperialism." The sheik also inspired thousands of volunteers from the Islamic world to join the *mujahideen* in Afghanistan. In the late 1980s, he was able to enter the United States when immigration authorities erred in checking a terrorist "watch" list. He settled in New Jersey, where he became the spiritual leader of a fringe group of militant Muslims who went on to commit terrorist acts in the United States.

Terrorism on U.S. Soil

Though increasing numbers of terrorist incidents around the world in the late twentieth century were aimed at U.S. citizens, including the 1983 suicide bombings of U.S. Marine headquarters in Beirut, Lebanon; the 1985 hijacking of the cruise ship *Achille Lauro;* and the bombing of Pan Am Flight 103 over Lockerbie, Scotland, they did not take place within U.S. borders. Troubled as they were by the threat of terrorism abroad, Americans continued to feel relatively safe at home. But when a bomb exploded in the World Trade Center in New York City on February 26, 1993, killing six people and injuring nearly one thousand, Americans could no longer take domestic security for granted. The first major international terrorist campaign in the United States, the World Trade Center bombing was planned and executed by followers of Sheik Omar Abdel-Rahman. Mahmud Abouhalima, an Egyptian native who was convicted of planting the bomb with mastermind Ramzi Yousef, had fought in Afghanistan before coming to the United States. He was caught, tried, found guilty, and sentenced to 240 years in prison for his role in the attack. Yousef, a terrorist who had entered the country with a valid Iraqi passport and applied for political asylum, escaped to Pakistan the night of the explosion. He was arrested there in 1995 and returned to the United States for trial. He too was convicted and sentenced to 240 years in prison.

One of the most disturbing aspects of the bombing was the lack of a clear motive. No evidence or official acknowledgment linked it to a particular American action or policy. When Yousef stood trial in 1997, however, he stated that the attack was meant as retaliation for U.S. support of Israel. According to a November 13, 1997 *New York Times* report on the trial by Benjamin Weiser ("The Trade Center Verdict"), U.S. Secret Service agent Brian G. Parr told the jury that "Mr. Yousef said he had hoped the explosion would topple one tower onto the other, killing tens of thousands of people, to let Americans know they were 'at war.'" Parr added that Yousef has said, "if you could not attack your enemy, you should attack the friend of your enemy." The bombing shocked the country and significantly changed the way American citizens felt about their security.

When the Alfred P. Murrah Federal Building in Oklahoma City, Oklahoma, blew up just after the start of the workday on April 19, 1995, this unprecedented terrorist act further shattered Americans' sense of security. Unlike the World Trade Center bombing, this incident, which killed

CHRONOLOGY

1988 Pan Am Flight 103 is downed over Lockerbie, Scotland; all 259 passengers and crew, as well as 11 residents of Lockerbie, are killed due to the bomb that exploded on board.

1992 Parliamentary elections are cancelled in Algeria, and the Islamic Salvation Front and Armed Islamic Group wage guerrilla war.

1993 The World Trade Center in New York City is bombed; six people are killed and almost 1,000 are injured.

March 1995 Members of the Aum Shinrikyo cult release sarin gas into a Tokyo, Japan, subway during rush hour, killing 12 and injuring thousands.

April 19, 1995 The Arthur P. Murrah federal building in Oklahoma City, Oklahoma, is bombed, killing 169 people; Timothy McVeigh is charged with the crime.

April 24, 1996 U.S. President Bill Clinton signs the new Anti-Terrorism and Effective Death Penalty Act of 1996.

1997 McVeigh is found guilty of masterminding the Oklahoma City bombing and is sentenced to death.

February–May 1998 Osama bin Laden endorses three *fatwas*, or legal decrees, against Americans, encouraging Muslims to wage war against the United States and its allies.

August 7, 1998 U.S. embassies in Kenya and Tanzania are bombed, killing 224 people and wounding more than four thousand; bin Laden is believed responsible.

August 15, 1998 A bomb blast in Omagh, Northern Ireland, kills 29 people and injures 220; it causes the greatest number of deaths of any single act of violence in that country during the history of "The Troubles."

1999 The UN Security Council issues a resolution placing economic sanctions on the Taliban if it continues to harbor bin Laden in Afghanistan. The International Convention for the Suppression of the Financing of Terrorism is adopted by the UN without a vote.

December 1999 Ahmed Ressan, an Algerian terrorist believed to be sponsored by bin Laden, is arrested in Port Angeles, Washington, after entering the United States from Canada in a car filled with explosives. The arrest uncovers a plot to bomb U.S. landmarks on or near January 1, 2000.

October 12, 2000 Suicide bombers attack the USS *Cole*, a navy ship refueling at the harbor in Aden, Yemen; 17 American sailors are killed and 30 are wounded. Osama bin Laden is believed to be responsible for the attack.

January 2001 One of the defendants in the Lockerbie trial is found guilty of murdering 259 passengers and crew and 11 residents of Lockerbie, Scotland.

February 2001 Britain puts a new law into effect that expands the government's power to ban groups and fund-raising campaigns suspected of sponsoring terrorism abroad. The FBI, CIA, and Russia's Federal Security Service (FSB) agree to work together to apprehend bin Laden.

June 2001 Timothy McVeigh is executed for the Oklahoma City bombing.

September 11, 2001 Two hijacked airplanes crash into the World Trade Center in New York City, while a third plane hits the Pentagon in Washington, DC. A fourth plane crashes into a field in Pennsylvania.

169 people—some of them young children in the building's day care center—was the work of an American. Timothy McVeigh, who was found guilty and sentenced to death for setting off the explosion, was not a member of a fanatical religious fringe group, but a seemingly average young man from a middle-class background. Yet he so hated the U.S. government, which he believed was conspiring to deprive individuals of their basic freedoms, that he decided any violence was justified to stop it. Two events in particular inspired McVeigh's rage: the 1992 attack at Ruby Ridge, Idaho, in which the wife of separatist Randy Weaver was shot and killed by an FBI sniper; and federal agents' siege of the Branch Davidian compound in Waco, Texas in April 1993, which ended with a fire that killed more than seventy people. McVeigh timed his Oklahoma City attack to occur on the anniversary of the Waco incident.

The attack in Oklahoma City traumatized the nation. It was the worst terrorist incident to occur in the United States, and it exposed Americans to the disturbing truth that they were vulnerable to domestic terrorism. So outraged was the public that it followed McVeigh's trial with intense interest and emotion. When McVeigh was sentenced to death, some suggested his execution should be televised so that the public could have the satisfaction of watching him die for his crime. McVeigh's execution in June 2001, however, occurred privately.

After the World Trade Center and Oklahoma City bombings, it became clear that U.S. citizens could no longer feel insulated from the threat of terrorist actions. Government response was swift. In 1995 President Bill Clinton (1993–2000) issued a new counterterrorism directive outlining comprehensive strategies to enhance national security and apprehend terrorists. In 1996 Congress passed the Anti-Terrorism and Effective Death Penalty Act. The law gives the federal government a broad range of new investigative, regulatory, and prosecutive powers to prevent and manage terrorist acts. Among its provisions is a ban on the sale of defense materials or services to any foreign country that the president may determine is failing to cooperate with U.S. antiterrorist efforts. The law also expands the government's power to deny political asylum to individuals who belong to any group identified by the secretary of state to be a foreign terrorist organization. In addition, the 1996 law identifies as a crime any transfer of explosives between individuals who know, or should know, that the materials will be used to commit a violent crime; any threat or attempt to develop or use a biological weapon; and any use of chemical weapons either within the United States or against Americans abroad.

Though the millennium terrorists were apprehended in the United States before they were able to execute their plan, their plot showed the critical need to adapt security measures to deal with twenty-first century realities. Antiterrorism policies, experts agree, should include continued attention to "traditional" terrorist threats, as well as measures to deal with new conditions and technologies. At the same time, democracies must balance the need for national security with the need to preserve individual rights.

Globalization

Despite tough new laws and increasing international cooperation, experts agree that terrorism remains a real threat. In 1997 there were 304 international terrorist attacks, 123 of which were against U.S. interests. In 1998 there were 274 international attacks, with 741 persons killed and 5,952 wounded. International attacks totaled 392 in 1999, with 233 persons killed and 706 wounded; 169 of these incidents were directed against U.S. interests. In 2000 international terrorist attacks increased 8 percent, to a total of 423. Casualties

TIMOTHY MCVEIGH

1968–2001 Timothy McVeigh, the central perpetrator in the Oklahoma City bombing, was born in Pendelton, New York, in 1968. He enjoyed a relatively uneventful childhood, and lived with his father after his parents divorced. After failing to find a good job after high school, McVeigh joined the army. He fought in the Persian Gulf War and applied to join the Green Berets, but was turned down. This rejection seems to have been a personal crisis for McVeigh, who took an early discharge and then began drifting from job to job. Around this time, he began to exhibit pronounced far-right beliefs, participating in some right-wing militia activities. He was particularly influenced by Andrew Macdonald's *The Turner Diaries,* a book promoting white supremacist and anti-Semitic beliefs.

Inspired by two federal raids in the early 1990s against separatist groups, the shootout at Ruby Ridge, Idaho, in 1992 and the siege of the Branch Davidian compound in Waco, Texas, the following year, McVeigh planned an act of revenge. With an accomplice, alleged to be Terry Nichols, he obtained seven thousand pounds of explosives which he loaded into a rental truck and then drove to the Murrah Federal Building in Oklahoma City, blowing it up just after the beginning of the workday. McVeigh showed no remorse for the attack. It was reported that, after the blast, McVeigh referred to the children who died as "collateral damage," but admitted that, had he known the building housed a day care center, he might have chosen a different target. He was executed by lethal injection in June 2001 at the Federal Penitentiary at Terre Haute, Indiana.

increased to 405 persons killed and 791 wounded. The number of anti-U.S. attacks also increased to a total of 200.

There is little doubt that one of the most significant trends affecting twenty-first century terrorism is globalization. During the 1990s nations throughout the world moved toward more liberal economies and political structures. New markets opened up for goods and services as free trade expanded; at the same time, business competition increased as companies sought cheap sources of labor in developing countries, where wages remained much lower than in developed countries. Advocates of globalization believe that it is the best way to improve opportunities for workers across the world and to promote economic growth. Critics, however, point out that the globalized economy,

U.S. ARMY SOLDIERS UNDERGO CHEMICAL WARFARE TRAINING IN SAUDI ARABIA IN 1990. ALLIED DOCTORS ADMINISTERED VACCINATIONS AGAINST THREATS SUCH AS BOTULISM, PLAGUE, AND ANTHRAX IN ANTICIPATION OF THE 1991 PERSIAN GULF WAR. *(AP/Wide World Photos. Reproduced by permission.)*

aided by entertainment media, emphasizes Western patterns of consumption, waste, and moral decadence. It has also made it easier for a small minority to amass great wealth; indeed, the gulf between the richest and the poorest has never been greater. Such conditions breed opportunity for some, but resentment among those who are in the lowest economic segments or who reject Western values as secular, individualistic, and exploitative. Such resentments can fuel the kind of loosely-structured and -focused extremist movements that have in fact proliferated in the 1990s.

Global Trends 2015: A Dialogue About the Future with Nongovernment Experts, (National Intelligence Council, 2000) a report prepared for the U.S. National Intelligence Council (NIC), cautions that "regions, countries, and groups feeling left behind will face deepening economic stagnation, political instability, and cultural alienation. They will foster political, ethnic, ideological, and religious extremism, along with the violence that often accompanies it." Globalization facilitates a high degree of movement both within and across borders. Stephen E. Flynn reported in *Foreign Affairs* ("Beyond Border Control," November-December 2000) that, in 1999, some 475 million people entered the United States each year, in addition to 125 million vehicles and 21.4 million import shipments. On one day in February 2000, a record-breaking seven thousand

trucks entered the United States from Canada at the world's busiest commercial land-border crossing, the Ambassador Bridge between Detroit, Michigan, and Windsor, Ontario, Canada. This volume of traffic, in Flynn's words, "expedites passage for terrorists, small arms, drugs, illegal immigrants, and disease." In such conditions governments face increased difficulty in monitoring and maintaining control over information, technology, migrants, arms, and other materials, legal or illegal, that cross their borders. Globalization also encourages urbanization; by 2001 more than half of the population of the developing world lived in cities. Such concentrated population centers give terrorist groups numerous opportunities to recruit new members.

The expansion of information technology and networked systems in a globalized world also facilitates terrorist activity. Computers give terrorists both access to information and the means of disseminating that information to their associates. Belgian police investigating the GIA terrorist group discovered an 8,000-page manual on computer diskette belonging to a GIA member. The document described how to make explosives and employ their use against buildings, bridges, and other potential targets. Other European security agents have found similar documents teaching how to handle high-powered weapons and how to produce toxins.

New Terrorist Trends

Patterns of terrorism through the 1990s suggest several new trends. State-sponsored terrorism has waned significantly, and more countries have agreed to work together to combat terrorist threats. Some countries, however, continue to harbor terrorists or use terrorism as part of state policies. The U.S. State Department's *Patterns of Global Terrorism 2000* (April 2001) lists Iran, Iraq, Syria, Libya, Cuba, North Korea, and Sudan as state sponsors of international terrorism. The report indicates that North Korea and Sudan have begun taking steps to cooperate with global antiterrorist efforts, and the State Department has engaged in discussions with these countries with the goal of seeing them cease all support for terrorist groups.

Terrorist acts by splinter groups and individuals, however, have increased. Readily identifiable terrorist groups of the 1970s and 1980s have been replaced at the turn of the twenty-first century with groups of like-minded individuals who assemble to plan and carry out terrorist attacks. Such groups, like those inspired by Sheik Omar Abdel-Rahman, tend to lack hierarchical structure and are difficult to predict and monitor. The groups of the 1970s and 1980s tended to have larger membership, and ideologies within the group may have varied a bit. For instance, in 1997, after official policies of Sinn Féin, the political wing of the Irish Republican Army (IRA), led to dissent within the IRA, a group of like-minded members left and formed a splinter group called the Real IRA. Smaller, and with a more united ideology, the Real IRA continues its terrorist activities while the Irish Republican Army proceeds to negotiate in a peace process.

Conspiracies that grow out of anger and frustration, according to the National Commission on Terrorism's report *Countering the Changing Threat of International Terrorism,* (June 2000) tend to be more lethal than politically-based attacks: "Religiously motivated terrorist groups . . . represent a growing trend toward hatred of the United States. Other terrorist groups are driven by visions of a post-apocalyptic future of ethnic hatred. Such groups may lack a concrete political goal other than to punish their enemies by killing as many of them as possible, seemingly without concern about alienating sympathizers." Analysts in *Global Trends 2015* write that "Between now and 2015 terrorist tactics will become increasingly sophisticated and designed to achieve mass casualties. We expect the trend toward greater lethality in terrorist attacks to continue." Much of this, they point out, will be directed against the United States and its interest overseas.

Osama bin Laden

The best-known of these loosely affiliated terrorist networks is al-Qaida, headed by Saudi exile Osama bin Laden and believed to be based in Afghanistan, where the Taliban coalition that controls much of the country shelters him and his associates and allows them to operate training camps. Among the major anti-American attacks for which he is believed responsible are the 1998 bombing of U.S. embassies in Kenya and Tanzania, which killed 224 people and wounded more than four thousand; the millennium plot; and the October 12, 2000, bombing of the USS *Cole* navy ship in Aden harbor, Yemen, in which 17 American sailors died and 30 were injured. Bin Laden is suspected of having an extensive network of bank accounts in several countries and of using agricultural, construction, and investment companies as fronts for his terrorist operations. He is also suspected of encouraging violence in and against nations other than the United States and is rumored to have sent fighters to Chechnya to resist Russian troops there.

According to the U.S. State Department, bin Laden endorsed three *fatwas*, a legal opinion by an Islamic leader, against Americans in 1998. Those published on February 23 and May 7, 1998, state that Muslims should kill Americans wherever they are found throughout the world, and declare *jihad*, or holy war, against the United States and its allies. The third *fatwa*, published May 29, stated that Muslims were duty-bound to "terrorize the enemies of God." In light of bin Laden's radical words and extremist actions, he is considered a serious terrorist threat by the United States.

On October 25, 1999, the United Nations (UN) Security Council passed by unanimous vote a resolution demanding that the Taliban stop harboring bin Laden. The resolution also imposed economic sanctions against the Taliban if it did not extradite bin Laden within thirty days. International condemnation of bin Laden has resulted in a high degree of cooperation among nations working to bring him and his associates to justice. In November 2000 Britain and Russia agreed to focus joint efforts on stopping financial support for the Taliban and its support of al-Qaida. In February 2001 the U.S. Federal Bureau of Investigation (FBI) and the CIA announced that they would join forces with Russia's Federal Security Service (FSB) to try to stop bin Laden. In addition, the extradition of several defendants charged in the U.S. embassy bombings in Africa, as well as the guilty verdict against defendants in the Lockerbie trial, are evidence of what the U.S. State Department

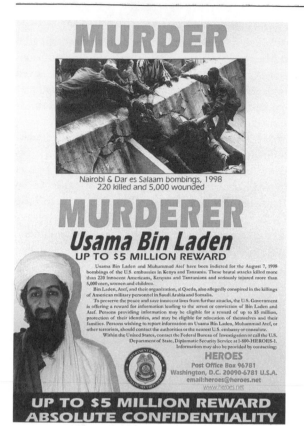

OSAMA BIN LADEN IS WANTED IN CONNECTION WITH THE BOMBINGS OF TWO AMERICAN EMBASSIES IN AFRICA. THE US$5 MILLION REWARD IS THE LARGEST EVER OFFERED FOR A FUGITIVE WANTED BY THE U.S. GOVERNMENT. *(CORBIS CORPORATION (Bellevue). Reproduced by permission.)*

calls a new spirit of "international effort to hold terrorists accountable for their crimes."

"Loose Nukes"

Experts are also concerned about the possibility of terrorists gaining access to nuclear weapons or materials "left over" from the Cold War. According to the *Bulletin of the Atomic Scientists* (November-December 1994) the United States produced approximately seventy thousand nuclear weapons during the Cold War, while the Soviet Union produced approximately fifty-five thousand. After the 1995 Nuclear Non-Proliferation Treaty, the two superpowers agreed to reduce their nuclear arsenals, but some stockpiles remain. What is more, security and safeguards at nuclear storage facilities in the former Soviet Union have eroded, while difficult economic situations in the region make many workers amenable to bribes.

At the same time, Russia's ongoing nuclear energy and missile industry also poses risks. Poor economic conditions in nuclear and missile cities present a security risk to nations worldwide. Workers in these areas are so poorly paid that many could be motivated to sell their skills to the highest bidder. Thousands of people with the skills necessary to design, construct, and launch nuclear warheads, therefore, could be available to terrorist groups or rogue nations.

So concerned is the United States about such scenarios that it has authorized several programs to assist Russia in matters relating to nuclear security. Between 1992 and 1999 the Cooperate Threat Reduction plan appropriated US$3 billion for the safe dismantling of stocks of nuclear, biological, and chemical weapons in the former Soviet Union. The Initiative for Proliferation Prevention, which began in 1994, was designed to create new peacetime economic activities for Russian nuclear scientists. The Nuclear Cities Initiative, created in 1998, was intended to create new jobs for poorly-paid nuclear workers in Russia's ten closed science cities.

Bioterrorism and Chemical Weapons

Another possibility for which governments worldwide must prepare is that terrorists could unleash biological or chemical weapons on unsuspecting populations. As with other kinds of terrorism, the use of biological weapons is not strictly a modern phenomenon. *American Scientist* contributor Steven M. Block explained in a January 2001 article, "The Growing Threat of Biological Weapons," that the ancient Romans are known to have poisoned their enemies' water supplies by throwing dead bodies into wells, and the Tartars in the fourteenth century catapulted the bodies of bubonic plague victims over the walls of the Black Sea port of Kaffa. One of the most horrifying facts of World War I was the use of mustard gas against soldiers—a practice outlawed by the Geneva Protocol of 1925, which also banned "bacteriological methods of warfare." Despite this protocol biological weapons proliferated during World War II. Japanese forces in Manchuria used bioweapons against prisoners of war, using infectious diseases such as cholera, plague, and anthrax. Additionally, Soviet troops during the Battle of Stalingrad may have infected their German opponents with tularemia, a bacterial disease that affects man and animal.

Though the United States officially renounced all biological weapons in 1969 and paved the way for the Biological and Toxin Weapons Convention (BWC) in 1972—which by the end of 2000 had been signed by 160 countries including the United States, Iraq, the Russian Federation, Libya, Iran, and North Korea—the development of biological and chemical weapons was by no means halted. Between 1972 and 1992, the Soviet Union undertook a large bioweapons effort, despite its endorsement of the BWC. This program included research and development not only of conventional biological weapons such as anthrax, glanders, and plague, but also such viruses as smallpox, Marburg, and Ebola. As of 2001 there was no known cure for smallpox, Marburg, or Ebola.

Iraq has also clearly violated the BWC. After the end of the Persian Gulf War (1991), Iraq officially acknowledged that it had conducted research and development on such bacteria as anthrax, botulism, and Clostridium perfringens (which causes gas gangrene), as well as enterovirus 17, rotavirus, and camel pox. Steven Block reported in the *American Scientist* article "The Growing Threat of Biological Weapons," (January 2001) that Iraq grew a total of one half million liters of biological agents during the 1980s and early 1990s. In 1995 the UN ordered that Iraq's bioweapons facilities be destroyed.

The fact that toxic biological and chemical agents have been extensively developed for warfare suggests that they could be an attractive weapon for terrorists. Indeed, this chilling possibility became a reality in March 1995, when members of Japan's Aum Shinrikyo cult released sarin, a nerve gas, in a Tokyo subway during rush hour, killing 12 and injuring thousands. The incident sparked intense fear. These types of attacks may go undetected at first, but within a few days people with unusual symptoms would begin to appear in hospitals. If doctors were not quick to recognize the problem at hand, casualty rates could soar. Many studies, such as the Johns Hopkins Center for Civilian Biodefense Study, have concluded that many hospitals are ill-equipped to handle the effects of a bioweapons attack.

Though the Tokyo attack involved a nerve gas, experts consider the most likely bioterrorist threats to be smallpox, anthrax, and plague. Anthrax itself rarely causes disease in humans, but can form resistant spores that, if introduced to the lungs in high concentrations, lead to an initial phase of relatively mild symptoms, followed days later by severe respiratory distress and shock, which rapidly and almost inevitably leads to death. This can be treated with large doses of antibiotics, but is fatal more than 80 percent of the time if treatment does not commence within a day or so of exposure. Smallpox has no cure, but vaccination can prevent the disease. It is unlikely, however, that present supplies of the vaccine are adequate; furthermore, stocks of the

OSAMA BIN LADEN

1956– Little concrete information has been confirmed about the background of radical Muslim leader Osama bin Laden. He was born in Saudi Arabia around 1956, one of more than 50 children of construction magnate Muhammad bin Ladin. The young bin Laden was considered a quiet and unremarkable boy, who learned the family business and attended university. Various accounts indicate that he was educated in Riyadh, Jeddah, and London, earning a degree in business management or engineering.

By most accounts bin Laden became radicalized when the Soviet Union invaded Afghanistan. He went there in 1980 to fight with the Muslim resistance, and organized thousands of volunteers for the cause from throughout the Arab world. After the Soviet defeat, bin Laden continued his campaign to effect an Islamic revolution. When Saudi Arabia served as a base for U.S. troops in the Gulf War, bin Laden declared a war to "liberate" Muslim holy lands from U.S. dominance. This stance prompted the Saudis to eject him from the country. He fled to Sudan, which also cooperated with U.S. demands not to harbor him, after which he went to Afghanistan, where he presides over a sophisticated network of activities through which he finances and organizes his fringe group of extremists and radical Islamic militancy against the West.

virus are still kept against the necessity of manufacturing new vaccines.

Biological weapons are attractive to terrorists because they can cause massive casualties and fear and are easier to procure and deploy than a nuclear bomb. Yet biological weapons have drawbacks that can deter terrorists. Strict new provisions under the 1996 Anti-Terrorism Act make nearly all steps in developing or acquiring a biological agent for use as a weapon a federal crime. The act criminalizes even threats or attempts to develop or use biological weapons, as well as any use of recombinant DNA technology to create new pathogens (new causes of disease) or more dangerous versions of existing pathogens. It also invests regulating agencies with broad powers to track and monitor biological agents. Another potential deterrent is the problem of deploying biological weapons, which can be difficult to successfully deliver to the intended target.

Indeed, some analysts suggest that, in general, terrorists would not be likely to use bioweapons if they could achieve their purposes with more conventional means such as guns and bombs, which are

DR. WILLIAM PATRICK, FORMER CHIEF OF U.S. OFFENSIVE BIOLOGICAL WEAPONS, ILLUSTRATES IN FRONT OF A CONGRESSIONAL COMMITTEE IN WASHINGTON, DC, HOW EASY IT WOULD BE TO RELEASE BIOLOGICAL AGENTS. *(AP/Wide World Photos. Reproduced by permission.)*

much easier to acquire and use. The National Commission on Terrorism (NCT) noted in *Countering the Changing Threat of International Terrorism* (June 2000), that the Aum Shinrikyo group "used scores of highly skilled technicians and spent tens of millions of dollars developing a chemical attack that killed fewer people than conventional explosives could have. The same group failed totally in a separate attempt to launch an anthrax attack in Tokyo." Others, however, feel that the threat from biological weapons is real and could get worse. The very idea of bioterrorism, moreover, remains chilling. Even a small scale attack can challenge the public's perception of safety, which in itself could be considered a successful attack.

Computer Networks

Troubling as the prospect of bioterrorism is, the possibility of cyberterrorism may pose even greater threats. With communications, transportation, defense, energy, health, financial, and commercial systems increasingly computerized, the entire infrastructure in developed nations is vulnerable to computer attack.

Globalized information technology, according to *Global Trends 2015,*

will significantly increase interaction among terrorists, narcotraffickers, weapons proliferators, and organized criminals, who in a networked world will have greater access to information, to technology, to finance, to sophisticated deception-and-denial techniques and to each other. Such asymmetric approaches—whether undertaken by states or nonstate actors—will become the dominant characteristic of most threats to the U.S. homeland.

Indeed, the threat of cyberterrorism has already driven spending on computer security systems into the billions of dollars.

RECENT HISTORY AND THE FUTURE

Balancing Security and Individual Rights

Experts agree that the best means of dealing with terrorist attacks is prevention. Tougher international standards for airport security have been effected, and advocates have pushed for the adoption of sophisticated tracking systems for freight transportation carriers to enhance border safety without costly and inefficient backups at customs stations. Many governments have instituted strict new laws and policies enabling them to monitor terrorists' activities and deter possible attacks. Both the United States' 1996 Anti-Terrorism Act and Britain's Anti-Terrorism Act of 2000, enacted after a bomb blast in Omagh, Northern Ireland, killed 29 people and injured 220 in 1998, considerably expand such powers. Britain's act created a list of banned organizations and makes it a crime, according to a February 19, 2001 report in *The Times* ("Civil Groups Protest Terror Law") "to be a member of the group, support it financially, display its emblems or share a platform with a member at a meeting of three or more people." The groups proposed for banishment, which as of July 2001 had not yet been voted on by Parliament, include al-Qaida (led by Osama bin Laden), Turkey's Kurdistan People's Party, and the Palestinian Islamic Jihad. As it stands, the list includes the IRA and the Ulster Volunteer Force, among others.

Britain's home secretary insists that the new legislation poses no threat to civil liberties. He pointed to the country's long tradition of allowing freedom of speech and peaceful protest, but added that such individuals are not entitled to engage in violence. Liberal Democrats in the British government worry that the broad definition of terrorism in the act, which also includes those who hack into computers to disrupt government functions or threaten lives, could be used to stifle legitimate protest.

In the United States, government monitoring of political and social groups raises First Amendment issues, specifically the rights to free speech and association. The Supreme Court ruled in *Brandenberg v. Ohio* (1969) that the First Amendment bars criminal penalties on speech "except where such advocacy is directed to inciting or producing *imminent* lawless action and *is likely to* incite or produce such action." Some kinds of investigation, however, are permitted in matters relating to national security. An FBI directive quoted by Philip Heymann in *Terrorism in America* (1998) noted that the FBI has always investigated those "who advocate or threaten to commit serious violations of federal law."

Another area in which security experts and rights advocates have clashed is electronic surveillance. Because high-tech communications systems are attractive tools for terrorists, governments have sought ways to monitor this voluminous flow of information. An automated global interception and relay system run by intelligence agencies in the United States, Britain, Canada, Australia, and New Zealand, known as ECHELON, has been operating since 1971. Though U.S. authorities refuse to acknowledge ECHELON's existence, the governments of Australia and New Zealand have confirmed it. According to the American Civil Liberties Union (ACLU) the system intercepts and processes as many as three billion communications daily, including satellite transmissions, Internet downloads, phone calls, and email messages. The system essentially targets words or phrases most likely to be of interest to intelligence authorities and then tracks their path.

While authorities contend that such monitoring enables them to gather information on terrorists, critics argue that ECHELON is also gathering economic intelligence. The ACLU reports that, in 2000, the French government accused the United States of releasing information from ECHELON to U.S. companies to give them an advantage over the companies' competitors. Critics also contend that information from ECHELON may be used to stifle legitimate political dissent. As of April 2001, the ACLU reported that Russia, Germany, Israel, France, and China run similar surveillance systems. One of the chief purposes of China's system, cited by the ACLU, is to protect China's socialist system from enemy agents, spies, and counterrevolutionary activities.

Crucial as it is for governments to guard against the continued threat of terrorism, it is also essential to protect the principles on which such governments are founded. The NCT warns in *Countering the Changing Threat of International Terrorism* (2000) that

> Terrorist attacks against America threaten more than the tragic loss of individual lives. Some terrorists hope to provoke a response that undermines our Constitutional system of government. So U.S. leaders must find the appropriate balance by adopting counterterrorism policies which are effective but also respect the democratic traditions which are the bedrock of America's strength.

It is possible, many experts believe, to deal effectively with terrorism without resorting to police-state tactics. In the twenty-first century, terrorism will continue to exist, and governments will continue to search for means by which to deal with it effectively. An effective attempt to thwart terrorism must also preserve freedom in an increasingly dangerous society.

Editor's Note: The events of September 11, 2001, in which terrorists hijacked four U.S. airplanes—crashing two into the World Trade Center in New York City and one into the Pentagon in Washington, DC, while the fourth crashed in a Pennsylvania field—occurred while this volume was going to press. The manner of the attacks was unexpected and the casualties, in the thousands, unprecedented. In the immediate aftermath, U.S. President George W. Bush (2001–) declared a "war on terrorism," though how this "war" would manifest itself remained to be seen.

BIBLIOGRAPHY

American Civil Liberties Union, "ECHELON Watch," 2001. Available online at http://www.aclu.org/echelonwatch/index.html (cited July 12, 2001).

Alexander, Yonah. "Commentary: Terrorism in the Twenty-first Century: Threats and Responses," *The World and I*, June 1999.

Bernstein, Richard. "On Trial: An Islamic Cleric Rattles Secularism," *New York Times*, January 8, 1995.

Blanche, Ed. "Targeting bin Laden: The Pitfalls and Perils," *The Middle East*, February 2001, p. 19.

Block, Steven M. "The Growing Threat of Biological Weapons," *American Scientist*, January 2001, p. 28.

Burns, John F. and Craig Pyes. "Radical Islamic Network May Have Come to U.S.," *New York Times*, December 31, 1999.

"Carnegie: Dire Living for Russian Nuke Workers," United Press International, May 2, 2001.

"Civil Groups Protest Terror Laws," *The Times*, February 19, 2001. Available online at http://www.thetimes.co.uk/article/0,,2-87481,00.html (cited July 12, 2001).

"Estimated U.S. and Soviet/Russian Nuclear Stockpiles, 1945–94," *Bulletin of the Atomic Scientists,* November-December 1994.

Evans, Michael. "Grim Prophecy of War on Every Front," *The Times,* February 8, 2001. Available online at http://www.thetimes.co.uk/article/0,,2-80571,00.html (cited July 12, 2001).

Falkenrath, Richard A., Robert D. Newman, and Bradley A. Thayer. *America's Achilles Heel: Nuclear, Biological, and Chemical Terrorism and Covert Attack,* Cambridge, MA: The MIT Press, 1998.

Ferguson, James R., JD. "Biological Weapons and U.S. Law," *Journals of the American Medical Association,* 278 (August 6, 1997):357–60.

Flynn, Stephen E. "Beyond Border Control," *Foreign Affairs,* November-December 2000.

Gannon, John C. "Challenges to U.S. National Security," Speech given at the U.S. Army War College, Carlisle, PA, January 24, 2001. Available online at http://www.cia.gov/cia/public_affairs/speeches/gannon-speech_01242001.html (cited July 12, 2001).

Gordon, Michael R. "The Hidden City: A Special Report: Hard Times for Russia's Nuclear Centers," *New York Times,* November 18, 1998.

Heymann, Philip B. *Terrorism and America: A Commonsense Strategy for a Democratic Society.* Cambridge, MA: The MIT Press, 1998.

Kifner, John. "Terrorists Said to Hide in Canada's Melting Pot," *New York Times,* December 24, 1999.

Laqueur, Walter. "Postmodern Terrorism," *Foreign Affairs,* September-October 1996, p. 24.

National Commission on Terrorism. *Countering the Changing Threat of International Terrorism.* Washington, DC: U.S. Congress, 2000.

National Foreign Intelligence Board. *NIC 2000–02. Global Trends 2015: A Dialogue About the Future with Nongov-*

ernment Experts. Washington, DC: National Intelligence Council, 2000.

National Intelligence Council. "Global Trends 2015: A Dialogue about the Future with Nongovernment Experts," National Foreign Intelligence Board, December 2000.

"Portraits of Osama bin Laden," *Time Daily,* March 4, 1999. Available online at http://www.time.com/time/daily/special/look/0,2633,20894,00.html (cited July 12, 2001).

Reno, Janet. Testimony before the Commerce, Justice and State Subcommittee of the Senate Appropriations Committee on Anti-Terrorism Funds, September 12, 1996.

Tenet, George J. "Worldwide Threat 2001: National Security in a Changing World." Speech delivered to the Senate Select Committee on Intelligence, February 7, 2001. Available online at http://www.cia.gov/cia/public_affairs/speeches/UNCLASWWT_02072001.html (cited July 12, 2001).

U.S. Department of State. "Patterns of Global Terrorism: 1999." Washington, DC: April 2000. Available online at http://www.usis.usemb.se/terror/rpt1999/ (cited July 12, 2001).

U.S. Department of State. "Patterns of Global Terrorism: 2000," Washington, DC: April 2001. Available online at http://www.state.gov/s/ct/rls/pgtrpt/2000/ (cited July 12, 2001).

Vastag, Brian. "Experts Urge Bioterrorism Readiness," *JAMA: The Journal of the American Medical Association,* January 3, 2001.

Weiser, Benjamin. "The Trade Center Verdict: The Overview: 'Mastermind' and Driver Found Guilty in 1993 Plot to Blow Up Trade Center," *New York Times,* November 13, 1997.

—*E.M. Shostak*

TURKEY'S TUG OF WAR: STRADDLING THE DIVIDE BETWEEN EAST AND WEST

On February 19, 2001, Turkey fell into one of its most serious financial crises in years after a contentious meeting of the National Security Council, in which President Ahmet Necdet Sezer accused Prime Minister Bülent Ecevit of moving too slowly in instituting an anti-corruption campaign. By some accounts Sezer literally threw a copy of the constitution at Ecevit, causing the prime minister to storm out of the meeting. By declaring that a crisis existed, Ecevit effectively created one. Investors, already apprehensive over the slow progress of the economy and more than suspicious of Turkey's notoriously shady banking system, quickly began withdrawing funds. As a result, over the next three days, the stock market fell drastically, causing interest rates to soar 5,000 percent and the Turkish lira to drop in value by 30 percent. Although the economy stabilized somewhat in the ensuing months, the crisis highlighted the fragile nature of the economic and political systems in a country that has experienced 11 changes in top governmental leadership in the last ten years.

At stake for the Turks was not just bolstering its debt-burdened economy or accepting the possibility of another transfer of power to still one more ineffective coalition government, the country also faced the time of push-coming-to-shove over finding its place as a full and respected member of the European community, namely by gaining acceptance into the long-coveted position as a member of the European Union (EU). The EU, a coalition of 15 nations, forms the framework for free trade and economic cooperation as well as political unity. The question remains whether Turkey, a nation with one foot in the Middle East and one foot in Europe, can develop an economic, political, and

THE CONFLICT

Turkey, geographically situated with a foothold in both the East and the West, has submitted for membership in the European Union (EU). Before being admitted, Turkey's institutions and practices must meet with EU standards. Previously denied membership in the European Union, many Turks felt that Turkey was being judged on criteria different from other countries that were more firmly established as "Western" nations. There are also groups within Turkey that are anti-Western and assert the country is firmly in the East.

Cultural

- Pro-Islamic groups are against Turkey's bid for membership in the European Union, seeing it as a step away from Turkey's roots in the East and a threat to Turkish culture.

- Turkey sits at the crossroads of the East and the West and shares cultural aspects of both. When the country's first application to the European Union was turned down, many felt it was because the country was judged by different standards from other applicants.

Economic

- Membership in the EU could provide economic benefits to the country, but it must first reform its economic policies and practices.

Political

- Restrictions on freedom of thought and expression, as well as violations of human rights, are some of the issues that remain to be resolved before Turkey can enter the European Union.

MAP OF TURKEY. *(Maryland Cartographics. Reproduced by permission.)*

social plan that meets the expectations of its European peers. Although the EU finally granted Turkey the formal status as a "candidate for membership" in December 1999, Turkey's incorporation into the EU is still not assured. At issue are continuing concerns over economic reform; human rights, particularly in regards to the ethnic Kurdish population in southeastern Turkey; the role of the military and the stability of the democratic structure of the country; Turkey's long-standing problematic relations with Greece, who is already a member of the EU; and the questionable influence of Islamic fundamentalism.

HISTORICAL BACKGROUND

The modern state of Turkey did not come into existence until 1923; however, the corresponding region, a part of Asia Minor, is believed to be one of the oldest continually inhabited areas in the world, beginning with the Hittite empire dating back to the eighteenth century BCE. After being incorporated into the Roman Empire in 50 CE, Constantine I placed his capital in Constantinople (now Istanbul) in 325 CE, which later became the capital of the Byzantine Empire. Arriving from Mongolia in the sixth century CE, the Turks settled in the

region and adopted Islam. By the eleventh century, a group of Islamic Turks succeeded in establishing the Seljuk empire, but it was subsequently destroyed in the thirteenth century by Mongolian invaders. In the aftermath of the empire's disintegration, a leader arose. Osman I formed a new empire, which would become one of the world's greatest. The Ottoman Empire, a name that stems from the Anglicization of Osman's name, reached its peak in the sixteenth century.

The Ottoman Empire steadily declined over the next three centuries. After the death of the last great caliph Suleyman I in 1566, the throne was filled by ineffective and weak rulers. By the beginning of the twentieth century, internal opposition and discord combined with pressure from external forces threatened the empire's continued existence. In 1907 several anti-government factions merged to create the Committee of Union and Progress, also known as the Young Turks, in an effort to bring about a parliamentary government. In 1908 a group of Young Turk army officers in Macedonia revolted. As a result, parliamentary elections were held, and the Young Turks came into power, but the new government was soon weakened by internal dissention and splits. During the ensuing political unrest, foreign powers took advantage of the chaos and attacked: Austria took control of Bosnia and Herzegovina; Bulgaria declared its independence; and Italy seized Libya. By 1912 the Ottoman Empire had lost control of all its European lands, except part of eastern Thrace.

In January 1913 Enver Pasha, a leader of one of the most authoritarian Young Turks factions, staged a successful coup. Although constitutional rule was initially instituted, it was soon replaced by a military dictatorship and power divided among three men: Mehmet Talat Pasha, Ahmet Cemal Pasha, and Enver. As World War I (1914–18) approached, Talat and Cemal advocated a neutral position, but Enver, as minister of war, was determined that the country should align with Germany, and on August 2, 1914, he signed a secret alliance treaty. Two German ships that had been captured when the war broke out in Europe and turned over to the then-neutral Ottoman navy were subsequently staffed with German officers and, flying the Ottoman flag, put to sea to attack Odessa and several other Russian ports. On November 5, 1914, Russia declared war on the Ottoman Empire, followed by Britain and France. Within months, the Ottoman army had some 800,000 forces in the midst of World War I conflicts.

During the winter of 1914–15, Enver ordered the Ottoman invasion of Russia, hoping perhaps to instigate a revolt by Turkish-speaking inhabitants of the region. The results were disastrous; not only did the offensive fail to incite a revolution, but also the Russian counterattack inflicted devastating losses on the Ottoman forces. In eastern Anatolia many Armenians saw the Russians as liberators from Turkish rule and gave aid to the Russian army, and some even joined Russian military units. Consequently, Enver ordered the mass deportation of two million Armenians. Refugees flooded the roads as the crippled and demoralized Ottoman army retreated from the Russian onslaught. Consequently, the deportation soon turned into genocide: Whole Armenian villages were wiped out, and thousands of refugees were murdered along the roadways, with estimates of the killing ranging from 600,000 to more than one million.

Over the next three years the Ottoman army had varying success and failure, but by October 1918, having sustained 325,000 military casualties and with some two million war-related civilian deaths (including the Armenian population), the Ottoman Empire conceded, signing an armistice with the Allied forces on October 30, 1918. The Young Turk leadership trio of Enver, Talat, and Cemal fled to Germany, and the sultan was placed in custody as the Allied powers proceeded to dismantle the Ottoman Empire. Under the Treaty of Sévres, Britain, France, Italy, and Greece each gained control of portions of Ottoman lands. The plans for the dismembering of Turkish-speaking areas, however, stirred considerable dissent and spawned a nationalist movement that would lead to a Turkish war for independence.

Atatürk and Independence

Mustafa Kemal, later known as Kemal Atatürk, emerged as the leader of the nationalist movement. His fervent Turkish nationalism was fueled during his early years at a military academy in Monastir (now in the former Yugoslav republic of Macedonia) during a time when the Ottoman military was in continuous conflict with Macedonian revolutionaries. Upon graduation, he held various posts in Damascus and Thessaloniki, where he became more deeply involved in nationalist activities and helped to form the Young Turks in 1907. He was a successful and highly respected military leader during World War I, and after the armistice, he was appointed to a position within the Ministry of War; however, he was removed to eastern Anatolia after expressing opposition to the Allied occupation. In May 1919, from his post as inspector general in Samsun, Atatürk began to organize a nationalist movement, including a nationalist army.

During 1919 a nationalist congress met twice and adopted the National Pact, which outlined major non-negotiable objectives, the primary objective being the integration of the Turkish Muslim populations into a unified state. When the Ottoman parliament adopted the National Pact in January 1920, the Allied occupation forces, in an effort to quell the opposition movement, seized public buildings, arrested and deported nationalist leaders, and dismissed parliament. In response the nationalists convened the Grand National Assembly in Ankara. Disavowing the Ottoman government, which was now considered a puppet of the Allied forces, the assembly elected Atatürk as president and adopted the Law of Fundamental Organization, also known as the Organic Law, which declared the sovereignty of the nation under the leadership of the Grand National Assembly and Atatürk.

During Turkey's war for independence, nationalist forces engaged Greek forces in Anatolia in 1920, and in 1921, under Atatürk's military leadership, won several important victories, including a 20-day battle with Greek troops outside Ankara in July. The nationalists' military success prompted the Italian and French occupation forces to with-

CHRONOLOGY

1923 The Republic of Turkey is established, and Kemal Atatürk is selected as the country's first president.

1950 The Democrat Party, the first party to compete with Atatürk's Republican People's Party, wins a parliamentary majority. Celal Bayar is elected president, and Adnan Menderes becomes the prime minister.

1959 Turkey first applies for membership into the European Community (later called the European Union).

1960 The Turkish military stages a coup, arrests Bayar, Menderes, and the majority of the Democrat Party members, and charges them with creating a dictatorship and operating outside the constitution.

1961 General elections are held under a new constitution, and civil rule is reinstated.

1963 The EU-Turkey Ankara Agreement is signed, which outlines a path of necessary reforms for Turkey to meet EU membership standards.

1971 The Turkish military stages a second coup. Süleyman Demirel of the Justice Party resigns as prime minister.

1973 General elections are held, and the country is returned to civil rule, although no party wins a majority and the government is run by a series of weak coalitions of competing parties.

1980 The Turkish military stages a third coup, martial law is established, more than 30,000 people are arrested, and numerous political figures are banned

from politics for 10 years. The country comes under severe international scrutiny for reported human rights abuses.

1983 General elections are held, and civil rule is restored under a revised constitution.

1987 Turkey applies for full membership into the European Union.

1989 Turgut Özal of the center-right Motherland Party is elected president. The EU acknowledges Turkey's eligibility, but refuses to consider its application for membership.

1993 Özal dies of a heart attack, and Demirel, now representing the True Path Party, steps into the presidency. Tansu Çiller becomes the first woman to be named prime minister.

1996 Turkey enters into a customs union with the EU.

1997 The EU removes Turkey from its list of candidates being considered for membership, citing the need for further social, political, and economic reforms.

1999 Ahmet Necdet Sezer is elected president. Bülent Ecevit is selected as prime minister.

December 1999 The European Union accepts Turkey as a candidate for full membership.

2001 Turkey announces its National Programme for Adoption of the Acquis, which spells out Turkey's plan to meet EU guidelines for membership. An economic crisis sends inflation rates skyrocketing.

---

draw from Anatolia by October. Before the end of the year Soviet Russia signed a treaty with the nationalists, becoming the first international power to recognize the legitimacy of Atatürk's government. In 1922 the Turkish nationalists launched their last attack to drive out the Greek military. When the offensive threatened to move into regions occupied by the British, the British—who were unwilling to go to war to support Greece—proposed a truce, and the nationalists accepted. With negotiations for extended peace beginning in November 1922, the Treaty of Lausanne was signed in July 1923, which recognized the present-day borders of Turkey. On October 29, 1923, the Republic of Turkey was established by the Grand

National Assembly, and Atatürk became the country's first official president.

Atatürk's Reforms

Although the office of the presidency possessed few constitutional powers, Atatürk left an indelible mark on the formation of the modern Turkish state through his powerful leadership, personal charisma, and penchant for social reform. His avowed goal was the formation of a modern state styled after the countries of Western Europe. To that end, upon assuming office, Atatürk instituted a series of radical reforms. Atatürk's reform program, which became known as Kemalism, consisted of six major tenets: republicanism, nationalism, populism, reformism, etatism, and secularism. These "Six Arrows," considered fundamental and unchangeable, were written into the constitution as the ideological foundation for the development of the country. Republicanism acknowledged that sovereignty is identified with the nation, not an individual ruler. Nationalism was stressed through emphasizing Turkish history and revamping the Turkish language. Populism stressed the national identity as Turkish, regardless of ethnicity. Atatürk made popular the saying *Ne mutlu Turkum diyene* (Happy is he who calls himself a Turk), and previous communal autonomy granted to ethnic groups was eliminated. Reformism simply connoted the ideological justification for the radical changes in social and political processes. Etatism placed the state as a central force in the economic arena, which legitimated the state's control of numerous large enterprises, primarily as a means to avoid the infiltration and influence of foreign investors.

By far the most controversial reform of Kemalism was the declaration of Turkey to be a secular state. The Ottoman Empire had long claimed to be the spiritual leader of Muslims around the globe. For nine centuries Islamic laws, customs, and traditions had been the defining force in the Turkish world. Atatürk abolished the caliphate, closed religious schools, and suppressed Islamic religious orders. The Islamic rule of law, the *seriat*, was replaced with legal codes based on European forms of government. Wearing outward signs of the Islamic tradition was also banned, including the veil for women and the fez for men. Also, as part of his language reform, Atatürk forbid the use of the Arabic script, which had sacred ties to the Koran, and replaced it with a Latinized version of the Turkish alphabet. Of the "Six Arrows," secularism had the most profound and direct effect on the Turkish population, changing the entire social structure of the country, including such socially defined customs as marriage, the role of women, and family relations. Protests arose over this, the most radical of the reforms, but Atatürk tolerated little opposition.

Although the constitution recognized the Grand National Assembly as the representative of the people with the power to elect the president, who in turn appointed a prime minister, Atatürk ruled the country for the remainder of his life essentially as a dictator. He founded the Republican People's Party (Cumhuriyet Halk Partisi; CHP), which served as the country's only political party. Thus he was able to control the assembly, which repeatedly renewed his term as president. Atatürk believed that during the period of reform, an au-

thoritarian government was necessary. When he died in Istanbul on November 10, 1938, the entire population of Turkey went into mourning. In a grand ceremony, Atatürk's body was transported to Ankara and placed in a temporary tomb. In 1953 his remains were moved to a newly built mausoleum, which has since been designated as a national shrine.

After Atatürk

The transfer of power after Atatürk's death was smooth and peaceful. The following day, the Grand National Assembly elected Ismet Inönü, Atatürk's chief lieutenant, as president, and Celal Bayar, the prime minister, remained in that position. As World War II (1939–45) approached, Inönü was committed to keeping Turkey out of the conflict as much as possible by remaining neutral. Only at the very end of the war, when the Allied victory was assured, did Turkey declare war on Germany to fulfill a prerequisite for participating in the Conference on International Organization held in April 1945. The conference created the United Nations, and Turkey became one of its 51 charter members.

After World War II, Inönü opened the door to a more democratic political process by allowing the formation of multiple political parties. In January 1946, two CHP dissidents registered the Democrat Party (DP). In the first contested elections in July 1946, the DP won a modest 62 seats in the 465-seat assembly. In May 1950, however, with an overwhelming 88 percent of the population going to the polls, the DP gained incredible ground, placing 408 members in the assembly. Holding a large majority in the assembly allowed the DP to elect a new president. When the Grand National Assembly selected former Prime Minister Bayar as president, Inönü willingly stepped aside, despite offers from the military to stage a coup. Bayar then named Adnan Menderes as prime minister.

During the 1950s the DP-led government focused on the economy. By reducing state involvement and opening the door to private and foreign investors, Menderes hoped to create an economic environment friendly to the business community. However, political unrest began to develop when the Menderes government imposed restrictions on the press and limited free speech rights. Turmoil also brewed over the perceived corruption and excess of the Menderes administration. When restrictions were placed on public assembly just months before the October 1957 election, public displays of dissent increased. In early 1960, after a series of violent demonstrations, Menderes imposed martial

ONCE BANNED FROM POLITICS, BÜLENT ECEVIT BECAME PRIME MINISTER OF TURKEY IN 1999. *(Bourne Graphics. Reproduced by permission.)*

law and suspended all political activities. In response, on April 28, 1960, students marched in protest in Istanbul. Police fired on the crowd, killing several students. A week later a group of military academy cadets also took to the streets in solidarity with the students.

First Military Intervention

On May 27, 1960, the Turkish military, who considered themselves guardians of the constitution and the ideology of Kemalism, intervened. Under the command of Chief of General Staff, Cemal Gürsel, a group of 38 officers ordered the arrests of Bayar, Menderes, and the majority of DP assembly members on the charges of nullifying the constitution and creating a dictatorship. The coup met with little resistance, and the government was soon functioning under the military administration of the Committee of National Unity, a committee of five officers and three civilians, with Gürsel taking on the roles of president, prime minister, and defense minister. A new constitution was drafted by a constituent assembly and approved by popular vote in July 1961. In October general elections were held to reinstate a civilian government.

Fourteen political parties registered candidates for the 1961 elections, but only four won seats in the now-bicameral legislature. The CHP secured

38 percent of the seats in the 450-member lower house and 24 percent in the 150-member upper house. The Justice Party (Adalet Partisi; AP)—considered the replacement organization of the outlawed DP party—secured 35 percent of the seats in the lower house and 47 percent in the upper house. The remaining 119 and 44 seats in the lower and upper houses, respectively, were divided between the New Turkey Party and the National Action Party (Milliyetçi Haraket Partisi; MHP). The general assembly elected Gürsel as president. Gürsel enlisted 70-year-old former president Inönü as his prime minister.

Because no party had a clear majority, the legislature was unable to agree on who would fill the important cabinet positions, which, although offered by Inönü, required legislative confirmation. The unsuccessful struggle to form coalitions and forge cooperation during the next four years took the country to the brink of another military intervention. In the 1965 general elections, however, the AP won a clear majority in the assembly, and Süleyman Demirel became the prime minister. Demirel pushed to open the economy, and although he did not reject Kemalism, he did change the course of the nation by advocating for the development of a strong privately owned economy that was open to foreign investors. He also eased restrictions on the public expression of Islamic traditions, which gained him and the AP the support of much of the peasantry. He did not garner the trust of the military elite, who considered him and the AP too strongly tied to the former DP party, but he assuaged some fears when he supported General Sunay's bid for the presidency after Gürsel died in office in 1966. Despite the AP's strong majority, the legislative process was slowed by growing factions and divisions within the AP.

In 1966, in an effort to regain political ground, the CHP replaced the elder Inönü with 40-year-old Bülent Ecevit, who moved the party to a left-of-center political orientation that stressed state involvement in the economy, discouraged foreign investment, and pushed for rapid implementation of tax-based public services. Unlike the AP, Ecevit maintained Atatürk's devotion to removing all religious influence from the country's political foundation. Despite Ecevit's successful efforts to broaden the base of support for the CHP, the 1969 election resulted in an increase in the majority of the AP.

As more radical parties began to form and factions broke off from the larger parties, the Turkish democratic process began to falter as coalitions were formed only to be quickly disbanded and reformed, causing unstable alliances. In 1965 right-wing extremist Alparslan Türkes, a former military officer relieved of his duties after the 1960 coup for opposing the return of the country to democratic rule, took leadership of the MHP. After the 1969 elections, the AP began to disintegrate. More conservative AP members broke off to form the short-lived Democratic Party, and more liberal members left the AP to sit as independents. The National Salvation Party (Milli Selamet Partisi; MSP), a coalition of three small right-wing Islamic parties, began to require more compromises for their support than Demirel could offer. As a result, by 1971, Demirel's AP no longer held the majority in the National Grand Assembly. Also, the nation was becoming increasing disrupted by growing acts of violence and terrorism as both left- and right-wing radical groups, including Türkes's MHP, protested the course of the country.

Second Military Intervention

Once again the military stepped in. On March 12, 1971, under the command of General Faruk Gürler, the army forces chiefs demanded that President Sunay install a credible government. Demirel resigned immediately, and Sunay conferred with the military elite regarding the formation of a new government. Nihat Erim, considered a centralist of the CHP, was named prime minister, but the government remained a weak coalition until the 1973 elections. In the presidential election, Gürler was opposed by an AP-nominated candidate, but the assembly deadlocked after seven votes were cast. Subsequently, both candidates withdrew, and the chair of the Senate briefly became acting president after Sunay's term expired on March 28, 1973. Finally, on April 6, after 15 ballots, 70-year-old independent Fahri Korutürk was elected president by the assembly.

The 1973 legislative election results failed to secure a majority for any one party. The CHP, under Ecevit's leadership, regained considerable ground, winning 185 seats in the parliament. On the other hand, the AP declined drastically, retaining only 149 seats. The remaining seats were divided among the pro-Islamic MSP, the Democratic Party, and the Republican Reliance Party (RRP), a new short-lived centralist merger of CHP factions. Because the MSP and the Democratic Party won 48 and 45 seats, respectively, they held enough power to create or destroy a majority coalition. Although Ecevit managed to negotiate an agreement with the MSP leader Necmettin Erbakan, the coalition was short-lived as Erbakan soon withdrew his support. Korutürk

appointed Sadi Irmak as prime minister, but the elderly independent failed to win a vote of confidence, leaving the country without a fully functioning government for much of 1974. In 1975 the AP, MSP, MHP, and RRP joined together to form a conservative coalition as the National Front, under the leadership of Demirel. The National Front, although dependent on the support of independents, eked out a majority for the next two years.

The 1977 elections gave the CHP 213 seats and the AP took 189 seats. Despite the increase in the CHP's popularity, it still did not possess a clear majority. Again Demirel pieced together another right-of-center coalition by forming agreements among AP, MSP, and MHP leadership. With a four-seat majority the three-member coalition proved completely ineffective, and tensions within the country began to rise. The economy had been decimated during the oil crisis of the 1970s and the government could neither redirect the economy nor control the continuing outbreaks of violence and political unrest. Ultimately, more liberal AP members defected to the CHP, and Demirel lost a vote of confidence at the end of 1977. Ecevit was named prime minister, and he managed to patch together a weak four-vote majority that did little to overcome the country's political and economic woes. In December 1978 Ecevit invoked martial law in 13 provinces in response to growing violence, and he resigned the following year after the AP increased its numbers in the legislative elections. Once again Demirel was named prime minister. The country was cast into a full-fledged political crisis when, upon the expiration of Korutürk's presidential term in 1980, parliament could not agree on a new president.

Third Military Intervention

With no elected president, the National Grand Assembly in gridlock, and violence escalating, the military intervened for a third time. On September 12, 1980, the armed forces, under the leadership of General Kenan Evren, peacefully took control of the country. A five-member National Security Council was formed to run the country, and a 160-member assembly was designated to once again redraft the constitution. As its first order of business, the military administration established martial law throughout the country. An estimated 30,000 people were arrested, political parties were abolished, the parliament was dissolved, and its members were banned from political activity for up to 10 years. As a result of the political repression and wide ranging reports of human rights abuses,

KEY POLITICAL FIGURES

Kemal Atatürk. Considering the father of the modern Turkish state, Atatürk led the nationalist war of independence that resulted in the creation of the Republic of Turkey in 1923. He served as president until his death in 1938. His vision of a westernized, secular state remains the ideology of many of Turkey's political elite.

Devlet Bahceli. Leader of the right-wing Nationalist Action Party, Bahceli currently shares control of the government in a three-way coalition.

Celal Bayar. Bayar served as prime minister under Atatürk and, after his death, under President Ismet Inönü. He later helped form the Democrat Party (DP), and was elected president in 1950 when the DP gained a parliamentary majority. His administration was overthrown by a military coup in 1960, and Bayar was placed under arrest.

Tansu Çiller. A member of the True Path Party, Çiller became the first woman prime minister in 1993; however, she was forced to resign in 1995 when her coalition government fell apart.

Süleyman Demirel. Leader of the Justice Party and later the True Path Party, Demirel first became prime minister in 1965. He resigned from office after the 1971 military coup. He was returned to the office of prime minister later, but once again forced from office by the military in 1980 and banned from political activities until 1987. Again elected prime minister in 1991, he became president in 1993 when President Turgut Özal died suddenly. His presidential term expired in 1998.

Bülent Ecevit. Ecevit replaced Ismet Inönü as the leader of the Republican People's Party (CHP) in 1966. His left-of-center ideology stressed state involvement in the economy; he also strongly supported maintaining a secular government. He served as prime minister for several years in the 1970s. He was banned from politics after the 1980 military coup, but came into power again in January 1999 when he was named prime minister, a position he maintained as of 2001.

Ismet Inönü. Atatürk's chief lieutenant, Inönü became Turkey's second president upon Atatürk's death in 1938. Inönü opened up the country's democratic system by allowing the formation of political parties.

Adnan Menderes. Charter member of the Democrat Party (DP), the first party established to challenge Atatürk's Republican People's Party (CHP). He was named prime minister in 1950. His administration was overthrown by a military coup in 1960. Menderes was jailed and later executed for crimes against the state, including the formation of a dictatorship.

Turgut Özal. First serving the administration after the 1980 military coup, Özal became the leader of the right-of-center Motherland Party, and was elected president in 1989. He died of a heart attack while in office in 1993.

Ahmet Necdet Sezer. Formerly the head of the Constitutional Court, Sezer was elected president in 1998 as a compromise among rival political parties. He has become the most popular president since Atatürk. He advocates the westernization of Turkey and strongly supports Turkey's membership in the EU.

Mesut Yilmaz. Yilmaz became the leader of the Motherland Party after Özal's death in 1993. He served as prime minister in 1996, and as of 2001 served as deputy prime minister in a three-way coalition government.

Turkey's reputation within the international community was severely damaged. However, under an economic reform plan fashioned by Turgut Özal, the economy rebounded significantly, but Özal was forced to resign due to political pressure in 1982.

The new constitution was instituted in November 1982, and Evren was selected as president for a seven-year term. Political parties were subject to the approval of the military, and only three received approval: the Motherland Party (Anavatan Partisi; ANAP), which drew support from the right-of-center, was led by Özal; the Populist Party

(Halkçi Partisi; HP), modeled most closely after the CHP, was headed by Necdet Calp; and the Nationalist Democracy Party (Milliyetçi Demokrasi Partisi; MDP), under the leadership of retired general Turgut Sunalp, was the military's choice. In the legislative elections of 1983 the Motherland Party won an absolute majority in the once-again unicameral Grand National Assembly, filling 45 percent of the seats. The Populist Party earned 30 percent, and the Nationalist Democracy, only 23 percent. The following years, several more parties were allowed to form, including the Social Democratic Party (Sosyal Demokrat Parti; Sodep), run by Erdal Inönü, the son of former president; the True Path Party, under the unofficial leadership of Demirel (who remained banned from politics); the Welfare Party (Refah Partisi; RP), which had a religious agenda; and the Democratic Left Party (Demokratik Sol Partisi; DSP), unofficially led by Ecevit (who also remained banned from politics). In 1985 Sodep and the HP merged to create the Social Democratic Populist Party (Sosyal Demokrat Halkçi Parti; SHP).

In the 1987 elections, for the first time since the 1980 coup, all political parties were allowed to participate. Also, the ban on political leaders was lifted by popular referendum. Despite its declining popularity, the Motherland Party continued to run the country, and succeeded in electing Özal as president in 1989. In 1991 Demirel's True Path Party won the most seats in parliament, but failed to gain an absolute majority. Unwilling to cooperate with Özal, Demirel formed a coalition with Inönü's SHP, and 11 years after being ousted by the military, Demirel was once again prime minister. When Özal died unexpectedly in April 1993, Demirel succeeded him as president, and the True Path Party elected former economics minister Tansu Çiller as its new leader, the first woman in Turkish history to serve as prime minister. Çiller was forced to resign in early 1996 after the SHP merged with the re-formed CHP, which withdrew from the coalition. Çiller attempted to form a new coalition with ANAP leader Mesut Yilmaz, but after three months of bickering the alliance failed.

In a move that surprised many, Çiller agreed to an alliance with the Welfare Party, and Erbakan was named prime minister. For the first time, pro-Islamic leadership was a fundamental part of the country's operation. Although not considered another coup, the military, displeased with the Welfare Party's religious emphasis, pressured Erbakan out of office in 1997, and the party was subsequently banned by the Constitutional Court. It has since reappeared as the Virtue Party. Erbakan was replaced as prime minister by Motherland Party's Yilmaz, who served until November 1998, when he lost a parliamentary vote of confidence and stepped down. In January 1999 Ecevit was returned to the office of prime minister, and in April his leadership was confirmed in the national elections as the DSP won the most—albeit not a clear majority—of the seats in the national assembly.

When Demirel's presidential term expired in 1998, Ecevit unsuccessfully lobbied parliament to extend Demirel's term for another seven years. Once again, the numerous parties had difficulty agreeing on a successor. Ultimately, Ahmet Necdet Sezer, the head of the Constitutional Court, was selected as a compromise. The government was then formed around a three-way coalition with Ecevit of the DSP, Yilmaz of the Motherland Party, and Devlet Bahceli of the MHP, a less radical rebirth of Türkes's banned right-wing organization. This coalition currently operates the country. Sezer, chiefly unknown before being elected president, has become the most popular president since Atatürk. Modest and unassuming (his presidential motorcade stops at red lights), Sezer has nonetheless voiced strong opinions on numerous issues, including his commitment to continuing the westernization of Turkey and gaining acceptance into the EU. Whether Sezer can overcome the numerous obstacles that hinder Turkey's progress toward westernization and admission to the European Union remains to be seen.

Turkey and the EU: Background

The European Union, which started out as the European Community in 1958 and transformed into the EU in 1963, has six charter members: Belgium, France, Italy, Luxembourg, the Netherlands, and the Federal Republic of Germany (West Germany). Britain, Denmark, and Ireland joined in 1973; Greece in 1981; Portugal and Spain in 1986; and Austria, Finland, and Sweden in 1995. Turkey first applied for membership in 1959 from which came the Ankara Agreement, reached in September 1963. The Ankara Agreement outlined the progressive steps to be taken that would lead Turkey into full membership, including social, economic, and political reforms. Relations between the EU and Turkey were strained during the military interventions of 1971 and 1980. However, having reestablished the democratic process by 1983, Turkey made the move to request full membership in 1987. Although the EU acknowledged Turkey's eligibility as a European country, it postponed taking further action on the application, citing the need for improvements in Turkey's economic and political arena, including improved treatment of Turkey's Kurdish population. Turkey was further disappointed in 1992 when the EU considered applications from Austria, Finland, Norway, and Sweden, but did not address Turkey's application.

In 1996 Turkey entered into a Customs Union with the EU, the only associate member to obtain this unique status. The customs agreement opened up trade between Turkey and EU member countries, supposedly to help prepare Turkey for full membership. However, at the 1997 meeting of the EU's Association Council, although its eligibility

BÜLENT ECEVIT (FIRST ROW, SECOND FROM LEFT) LEADS THE BID FOR TURKISH MEMBERSHIP IN THE EUROPEAN UNION, WHILE TURKEY ITSELF STRUGGLES TO DETERMINE WHETHER IT IS A PART OF THE EAST OR THE WEST. *(CORBIS CORPORATION (Bellevue). Reproduced by permission.)*

was not questioned, Turkey was effectively removed from the list of prospective full members. Out of 12 other applicants, Turkey was the only country with no definite plan for integration into full membership. Citing the same social and political concerns as in the past, the EU once again outlined changes necessary to improve Turkey's hopes for accession. The rejection was met by bitter disappointment and anger by much of the Turkish population, who believed that Turkey was not being considered on an equal basis with other countries under application. The roller coaster EU-Turkey relationship was finally set on course at the EU meeting in Helsinki in December 1999 at which time Turkey was recognized as a candidate

for full membership. Many questions, however, remain regarding the expectations and timeline for Turkey's ultimate inclusion in the EU.

Obstacles in the Road

One of the major prerequisites outlined in an EU ascension agreement is economic reform, including banking reform, positive steps toward increasing privatization of state-run businesses, and a decrease in the country's debt. With 60 percent of its population of 65 million under the age of 25 and an annual birth rate of 4.8 percent, Turkey, if admitted, would soon be the largest and youngest country among EU members, with an incredible potential for economic growth. In 2000, however, the average per capital income in Turkey was US$3,000, compared to $20,000 in some EU countries. Recent economic difficulties have spooked some EU members, who fear that opening the borders would bring a huge migration of unemployed Turks into the work forces of neighboring countries.

The EU also has expressed repeated concerns regarding Turkey's human rights records. Two human rights monitoring groups, Amnesty International and Helsinki Watch, have reported the ongoing practices of arbitrary arrests, disappearances, killings, torture, and censorship. The problem of human rights abuses is most often focused on Turkey's treatment of its Kurdish population. The Kurdish population inhabits the southeastern region of Turkey, which remains the most underdeveloped area of the country, characterized by endemic poverty, high unemployment, and a severe lack of basic infrastructures such as schools, hospitals, electricity, and sewerage systems. In 1978 Abdullah Ocalan, a Kurdish nationalist, organized the pro-Kurd separatist organization, the Kurdistan Workers' Party (*Partiya Karkere Kurdistan*; PKK), and began a campaign of guerrilla warfare and terrorism in 1984. Although martial law was established and a large number of military and paramilitary units were dispatched to the region, violence continued to escalate through the 1990s. The Turkish military came under severe international scrutiny for allowing widespread human rights abuses against the Kurds during their efforts to quell the violence. Although in 1995 a law that banned the use of the Kurdish language was repealed, it remains illegal to broadcast in the Kurdish language. Turkish suppression of the Kurds was exemplified in 1994 when a pro-Kurdish party was banned and its parliamentarians were jailed. Leyla Zana, one of the imprisoned representatives, was awarded the European Parliament's Sakharov Prize for Peace in 1995, which added fuel to the international outcry against Turkey's treatment of its Kurdish minority. The Kurdish situation has been eased somewhat as PKK activities subsided after Ocalan's capture and arrest in February 1999. Although Ocalan's trial initially sparked an outbreak of violence when he was given the death penalty, the PKK has since called off its 15-year war, and Ocalan remains jailed while his verdict is under appeal.

Another fundamental concern the EU has expressed is the important role that the military continues to play in the country and the overall stability of the Turkish democratic system. In the EU's progress report on Turkey in 1998, the Commission made such statements as "the absence of real civilian control over the army is an anomaly" and "the lack of civilian control of the army gives cause for concern." The military, which remains nearly autonomous from the government, has stepped in to take over the government three times in Turkey's history. In each case, the country was subsequently returned to civilian rule. Some EU members, however, have expressed concern that Turkey is not immune from yet another military takeover as long as the military remains so powerful. Turkey's military elite has not wholeheartedly supported Turkey's bid for acceptance into the EU, which has attached reform requirements on full membership that are undesirable to the military. Such reforms include removing the chief of the general staff, a position that currently ranks directly below the prime minister, from the National Security Council, abolishing all legal barriers to using non-Turkish languages in education and broadcasting (namely, the Kurdish language), and the elimination of the death penalty.

Perhaps the biggest, and most complicated, obstacle in Turkey's road to full membership is the strained relations between Turkey and Greece, who became a member of the EU in 1981. Turkey's problematic relation with Greece is twofold. First at issue is the island of Cyprus. In 1974 Turkey sent troops into northern Cyprus to protect the minority Turkish population who felt threatened by the majority Greek population's push to unite with Greece. Unable to settle the dilemma, the island has since been divided between the Turkish Cypriot and the Greek Cypriot. Turkey is the only country that acknowledges Turkish Cypriot as a legitimate government and maintains 35,000 troops on the island to ensure its protection. Second, Turkey and Greece have an unresolved dispute over territorial rights in the Aegean Sea, which brought them to the brink of war in 1986 and again in 1987. At stake are exploration rights to minerals, especially oil. International law allows countries to explore minerals on their own continental shelf. Whereas Turkey defines the continental shelf as extending out from its shoreline, Greece contends that every one of the thousands of small islands in the Aegean has its own shelf, thus greatly cutting into the region as defined by Turkey. As a member of the EU, Greece has successfully pushed that the resolution of these issues be set as a precondition to Turkey's ascension. Turkey, on the other hand, has strongly objected to the inclusion of such demands, claiming that they have no place within an economic organization.

TURKEY BIDS ON THE 2008 OLYMPICS

Despite consecutive failures to win the bid to host the Olympic Summer Games in 2000 and 2004, Turkey again made the short list of possible locations for the 2008 Olympics. As the time approached for the International Olympic Committee (IOC) to announce its decision, set for July 13, 2001, it appeared, however, that on the list of the five remaining cities under consideration, Istanbul was not considered a favorite to win the bid. The four other cities that continue in contention were Beijing, China; Toronto, Canada; Paris, France; and Osaka, Japan. According to a report released by the IOC on May 15, 2001, Beijing and Toronto had the inside track to being selected, followed by Paris. Istanbul and Osaka were not mentioned among the top contenders.

Turkey has worked hard to persuade IOC officials that Istanbul has much to offer, even bringing veteran politician and ex-president Süleyman Demirel to offer his leadership to the Istanbul Olympic Bidding Committee. Promoting its unique setting as a bridge between Europe and Asia, Turkey hopes to persuade IOC officials that, with its rich culture and historical importance, Istanbul would provide an excellent setting for the Olympics. The cycling road race, for example, would pass through Sultanahmet, the ancient home of Ottoman sultans; and the beach volleyball competition would be held in view of the historic Dolmabahce Palace. Turkish officials also note that a state-of-the-art 80,000-seat stadium for sporting events like soccer and track and field and a new 22,000-seat indoor arena are both nearing completion. Also, it is clear that Istanbul residents would welcome the Olympics, which would bring a great influx of tourism dollars. In a recent poll, some 90 percent of the city residents said they wanted the games to come to Istanbul.

Despite Turkey's enthusiasm, numerous problems stand in the way of securing an Olympic bid. Because Athens, Greece, won the bid for the 2004 Olympics, it seemed unlikely that the IOC would place the games in next-door Turkey just a few years later. Additionally, detractors point to various internal problems within Istanbul and Turkey itself, including traffic congestion, an antiquated public transit system, and ongoing economic instability. Finally, questions have been raised over security issues. Despite the reassurance of Turkish officials, it remains uncertain that such a large event would not attract the terrorist activities of leftist, Islamic, or Kurdish groups. Also working against Istanbul was the strength of the other competing cities. Toronto tops the list for quality and availability of the necessary infrastructure, whereas Beijing holds the politically attractive appeal of bringing the games to the most populous nation in the world. On July 13, the IOC announced that Beijing would host the 2008 Olympic Games. Turkey must wait and try again.

There is also the often unspoken question on the minds of some—both in Turkey and in the EU—of just who is European and who is not. If European identity is based on shared histories in such matters as religion, ethnicity, and intellectual activity, Turkey does not fit the mold in the least. There is a vast cultural gulf between Turkey and the EU countries. Like its Middle Eastern neighbors, Turkey is predominantly Islamic, with its historical roots in the Ottoman Empire. Whereas the majority of the political elite see EU membership as an extremely positive step for Turkey, some openly oppose the attempt to link Turkey with western Europe and advocate for closer relations with the Middle East. The major voice against westernization comes from pro-Islamic groups who desire a return to a government founded on Islamic principles and traditions. In a speech in 1998, pro-Islamic leader Necmettin Erbakan declared that the return to Islamic order in Turkey is inevitable; it only remained to be seen if it would come about with or without violence. The growing popularity of Islamic political groups has given EU members pause, wondering if Turkey can truly fit the definition of being European.

RECENT HISTORY AND THE FUTURE

On March 19, 2001, the Turkish government released the National Programme for Adoption of the Acquis (NPAA). The document lays out Turkey's plans to meet the requirements specified by the EU as conditions for acceptance into full membership. A comprehensive document, the NPAA outlines Turkey's general political and economic targets, including such issues as freedom of thought and expression, combating torture, reduction of regional imbalances, an expressed commitment to a democratic secular society, and Turkish–Greek relations. Touted as a fundamental revision of Turkey's political, economic, social, and administrative structure, the NPAA failed to draw an overwhelmingly positive response from the EU. Although most matters of contention were mentioned, the NPAA lacked the specificity necessary to impress EU members. The language was most likely diluted as a result of compromises necessitated by the three-party coalition. For example, it was largely silent on the expansion of Kurdish language rights, noting that all languages are allowed for private use. Also, vague terms were often employed. Instead of committing to abolishing the death penalty, the document noted the issue "will be taken up by parliament in terms of its shape and scope" and freedom of expression laws would come under "review."

Despite Turkey's hopes that the NPAA would pave the way for speeding up the membership process, it appears that Turkey remains on a slow track for approval. The country has, however, made definite advancements in the recent past. In hopes of restoring confidence in the economy, Turkey's recently appointed economy minister, Kemal Dervis, a highly respected former World Bank executive, released a new economic plan in March 2001 that included promises of revamping the banking system, speeding up the privatization of state-owned Telekom and Turkish Airlines, and stabilizing the rates of interest and foreign exchange. Additionally, hundreds of laws have been rewritten to conform to EU standards. For example, trade unions are now allowed to participate in political activities, and university staff are permitted to join political organizations; the military judge has been replaced by a civilian judge on the State Security Courts, which handles cases of terrorism and activities against the state; and training courses in human rights have been set up for police officers.

Despite political differences, most mainline party leaders agree that EU membership would be an economic, social, and political boom for the country. It becomes a matter of whether the EU is asking for too much too quickly. Does Turkey's odd coalition of leadership have the political will to enact the broad-based changes required by the EU? Will pro-Islamic groups gain the power to turn the Turkish state toward the Middle East and Islamic influence? Can the Turkish government reign in the military, improve human rights, and conduct itself in accordance to Western European standards? For its part, can the EU overcome its underlying fear of allowing a large Muslim country into Europe's inner circle? Is the EU truly willing to associate with a country in which democracy is not yet fully developed? Many questions remain regarding Turkey's long trek toward EU membership and recognition as a full-blooded member of the European community.

BIBLIOGRAPHY

Barkey, Henri J., and Fuller, Graham E. *Turkey's Kurdish Question.* Carnegie Commission on Preventing Deadly Conflict Series. Lanham, MD: Rowman & Littlefield Publishers, 1998.

Bishop, Patrick. "Disastrous Devaluation Leaves Turkey Struggling with Its Identity," *The Daily Telegraph* (London), March 3, 2001, p. 20.

Buzan, Barry, and Thomas Diez. "The European Union and Turkey," *Survival,* (London), vol. 41, Spring 1999: 41–57.

"Charlemagne: Ahmet Necdet Sezer, A Westward-Looking Turk," *The Economist,* vol. 357, November 18, 2000: 64–65.

Govertt, Jon. "A Berlin Wall at the Bosphorus," *Middle East,* vol. 308, January 2001: 38–39.

Kinzer, Stephen. "Turkey Finds European Union Door Slow to Open," *New York Times,* February 23, 1997.

Kirişci, Kemal, and Gareth M. Winrow. *The Kurdish Question and Turkey: An Example of a Trans-state Ethnic Conflict.* London: Frank Cass & Co., 1997.

McCrary, Ernest S. "Drawing the Lines for a European Turkey," *Global Finance,* vol. 14, October 2000: 95–98.

Moore, Molly, and John Anderson. "IMF Rebuffs Plea by Turkey for Aid; Reform Plans Fail to Impress EU Members," *Washington Post,* March 20, 2001, p. A20.

Muftuler-Bac, Meltem. "The Impact of the European Union on Turkish Politics," *East European Quarterly,* vol. 34, Summer 2000: 159–179.

"Relations between Turkey and the European Union," Turkish Ministry of Foreign Affairs. Available online at http://www.mfa.gov.tr (cited May 1, 2001).

Robbins, Gerald. "Turkey in Crisis: The Problem is Egos, Not Economics," *Washington Times,* March 2, 2001, p. A19.

Sanberk, Ozdem. "How to Rescue Turkey," *Newsweek,* March 5, 2001, p. 24.

"Turkey," Library of Congress Federal Research Division, Country Studies. Area Handbook Series. Available online at http://lcweb2.loc.gov/frd/cs/trtoc.html (cited May 1, 2001).

Ugur, Mehmet. *The European Union and Turkey: An Anchor/Credibility Dilemma.* Brookfield, VT: Ashgate Publishing Company, 1999.

—Kari Bethel

DEATH BEFORE DOOMSDAY: CULT MEMBERS FOUND DEAD IN UGANDA

CONFLICT

Religious sects and splinter groups have been multiplying in Uganda since freedom of religion was permitted in 1986. Attention was drawn to the potential danger of such groups in March 2000, when between three hundred and five hundred members of the Movement for the Restoration of the Ten Commandments of God apparently committed mass suicide by locking themselves in a church and setting the building ablaze. Shortly after the fire, hundreds of corpses were found buried in mass graves on land owned by the Ten Commandments Movement.

Political

- For many years, until 1986, the formation of new religious groups was brutally suppressed by the Ugandan government.

- Efforts of the Ugandan government to monitor religious groups have been hampered by the lack of adequate manpower and funds.

Religious

- Many people of faith in Uganda believe that mainstream religions, in particular Roman Catholicism and Anglicanism, have drifted far from their doctrinal roots.

- The inability of established religions to deal with poverty, the rise of AIDS, and other social and economic factors has caused dissatisfaction among the faithful.

- Ugandan regional rivalries are also pervasive in the Catholic Church, giving rise to resentment among both the clergy and laity.

- Cults of the Virgin Mary have been particularly common in Uganda during the 1980s and 1990s.

On March 17, 2000, villagers in Kanungu, Uganda, were startled by an explosion at a settlement that belonged to a local religious group, the Movement for the Restoration of the Ten Commandments. Within moments the building was engulfed in flames. After it was extinguished, villagers were horrified to discover the bones of hundreds of people who had been in the building as it burned. The deaths became sensational news throughout the world. They were seen as a mass suicide by the Ten Commandments Movement, which owned the building and the land around it. Earlier that day the group's followers had filed into the church, which had been stockpiled with large canisters of gasoline.

The death toll was estimated between three hundred and five hundred people. However, so completely had the bodies been consumed by the intense blaze, investigators were unable to determine exactly how many had died in the fire, much less be able to identify the dead. Police believed the group's leaders, Credonia Mwerinde, a bar owner and ex-prostitute, Joseph Kibwetere, an ex-politician, and Dominic Kataribabo, a former Roman Catholic priest, were among the hundreds that had perished. With no apparent survivors, authorities were not confident of uncovering the reason so many would choose to die in such a terrible manner. In the days following the incident, the explanation most frequently offered was that the Movement was a so-called doomsday group—that is, that it preached the apocalyptic dogma that the world would soon undergo cataclysmic destruction at the hands of God, and that only a few faithful would survive. Comparisons were drawn between the Ten Commandments Movement and the mass suicides of groups such as the People's Temple deaths in

Jonestown, Guyana, in 1978 and the Heaven's Gate group in southern California in 1997. Almost immediately the Movement was portrayed as a "cult," with all the sinister overtones connected with the word: the leaders had exercised totalitarian control, members lived a strictly regimented lifestyle, and obeyed unquestioningly.

The story took a more gruesome turn on March 20. Six more bodies were discovered in a septic pit on the Ten Commandments Movement's settlement. The corpses bore signs of foul play; some had crushed skulls, others had been poisoned. These new deaths cast doubt on the fire—perhaps it was not a case of mass suicide but mass murder. These suspicions were strengthened days later when a mass grave, containing more than 150 bodies, was found behind a house that belonged to Father Kataribabo. Signs of murder were unmistakable. Some had ropes still tied around their necks, others had been mutilated with machetes. In the following days more mass grave sites were uncovered by police.

Eventually, as relatives of the dead, former cult members, and villagers who had lived next to the group for years began to talk, police revised their ideas about the leaders. They were believed to have escaped the village just before the fire. The Movement had taught that the end of the world was coming. The Virgin Mary, the main object of the group's worship, would, however, save its members. Consequently, they had been required to give up their possessions—material goods, the leaders explained, would be of no use when the Apocalypse came. Police and the media believed that after deadlines for the end of the world passed in 1992, 1995, and then New Year's Eve 1999, with no Armageddon, dissatisfied cult members began to demand their property back. Credonia Mwerinde was seen increasingly as the mastermind of a remarkably bloodthirsty confidence game, in which the group's leaders bilked followers out of their property, and then, perhaps in desperation, killed them. By the end of March, a warrant had been issued for her arrest, charging her in the murder of hundreds of her followers.

By the beginning of April 2000, the number of dead reached 979, sixty-five more than had died in the Jonestown cult in Guyana in 1978. In the words of the *Montreal Gazette* on April 2, 2000, it was "the deadliest cult tragedy of modern times." Ugandan authorities, overwhelmed by the scale of the incident, gave up the search for new bodies. But unanswered questions remained: How could devout Ugandans, mostly Roman Catholics and Anglicans, fall under the spell of an opportunist like Credonia Mwerinde, who, if reports were to be believed, grew fatter by the day while they subsisted on a starvation diet? If the five hundred in the church had been murdered, why had they gone without protest to their fiery deaths? How had such an event happened in Uganda, a country considered one of the most politically and economically advanced nations in Africa? And was the group really a cult of true believers, in the mold of groups like Jim Jones's People's Temple or that of Heaven's Gate, which believed the Hale-Bopp comet would carry its followers off to heaven after their deaths, or was it simply an elaborate confidence scheme?

HISTORICAL BACKGROUND

Religion in Uganda

By the end of the 1990s, hundreds of fringe religious groups and sects existed in Uganda's capital, Kampala, alone. Uganda presented fertile soil in which groups offering miraculous cures or predicting the imminent destruction of the evil world and the sinners in it—that is, groups sometimes characterized as cults—might take root. Several factors in recent years may have led Ugandans in the Kanungu area to embrace fringe religions in the 1980s and 1990s. One contributing factor is that the region has not shared in the country's general prosperity under the government of President Yoweri Museveni. In addition, a civil war in which brutal guerrilla armies terrorize the countryside, raping, maiming, and murdering innocent villagers, has raged in the area for the better part of fifteen years. The struggle to survive against this backdrop of violence and despair has made the promises of groups such as the Ten Commandments Movement an appealing lure.

Uganda has a reputation for violence, due largely to the regime of President Idi Amin in the 1970s, which murdered some 300,000 of Uganda's 22 million people. Amin was deposed by the military in the late 1970s, and in 1986 a rebel forced led by Museveni seized power. He introduced freedom of press and religion and encouraged foreign investment, which transformed Uganda's economy into the fastest growing in Africa. Those economic changes, however, have meant relatively little to the inhabitants of Uganda's countryside, many of whom scrape out a harsh subsistence living by farming and herding, as they have for centuries. Clean water is in short supply. Few are literate, much less educated. The African AIDS (acquired immunodeficiency syndrome) epidemic has laid waste to the country as well. One out of every ten

CHRONOLOGY

1980s Gauda Kamusha leads an Uganda–wide mission based on a vision of Virgin Mary she experienced.

1986 Yoweri Museveni's rebel group wrests power from the military in Uganda; Museveni establishes freedom of religion.

1986–88 Alice Lakwena's apocalyptic Holy Spirit Movement fights an unsuccessful guerilla war against Yoweri Museveni's regime.

1988–present Joseph Kony's Lord's Resistance Army (LRA) succeeds Lakwena's group as the main anti-government guerilla force. It fights a war of resistance to overthrow Museveni's government and to restore the Ten Commandments as the nation's highest moral and civil law.

1988 Credonia Mwerinde claims to have her first vision of the Virgin Mary, who reportedly tells her to find a man named Joseph to lead a new religion.

1989 Joseph Kibwetere and his wife make first contact with the Marian Workers of Atonement, an apocalyptic Australian religious group.

1992 The leaders of the Ten Commandments Movement tell sect followers that the Virgin Mary has said the world will come to an apocalyptic end this year, and only faithful members of their Movement will be spared destruction. The date passes without event.

1993 The Movement for the Restoration of the Ten Commandments of God registers as a religious group with the Ugandan government.

1995 Again, sect leaders predict the world will end during the coming year, and once again their prophecy does not come to pass.

December 31, 1999 Sect leaders predict the world will experience apocalyptic destruction on New Year's Eve 2000. When this date passes without event, members begin to complain and to demand the return of their money and belongings.

March 17, 2000 The church belonging to the Movement for the Restoration of the Ten Commandments is consumed by fire following a mysterious explosion. The charred remains of three hundred to five hundred sect members are discovered in the building afterwards.

March 20, 2000 The first corpses of murdered sect members are discovered in a septic pit. Over the course of the next week, mass graves are found on other property belonging to the Ten Commandments Movement.

April 2000 Ugandan authorities are completely overwhelmed by the number of dead. Without proper facilities or funds to cope with so large a tragedy the search for other possible grave sites is abandoned.

Early 2001 An official inquiry into the deaths of the Ten Commandments Movement's followers is begun by the Ugandan government, but is hampered by lack of funds.

Ugandans is HIV (human immunodeficiency virus) positive, and the rate is even higher in the southwest where the cult deaths occurred. Father John Mary Waliggo, a Catholic priest, Ugandan human rights commissioner, and a professor of African history, told the *New York Times* on April 9, 2000, that AIDS is the single greatest cause of the rise of religious sects in Uganda. The sects hold out the promise of miraculous AIDS cures or describe an afterlife that offers respite from the constant presence of the disease. Promises of a respite from AIDS played little role in the Ten Commandments Movement, but for other religious sects, the promises are a powerful attraction for followers and offer an alternative to the mainstream religious establishment.

Mainstream churches in Uganda have been unable to deal with the new needs of their faithful, and congregations, primarily Roman Catholic or Anglican, have become increasingly alienated. As their financial resources dwindle, and trained priests become scarcer, churches have become increasingly ineffective in dealing with the pressing problems that beset the country. In the *Los Angeles Times* article "Tracking Multitude of Sects Impossible Task in Uganda" (March 31, 2000), Hubert Van Beek, an executive at the World Council of Churches in Geneva, explained the crisis to Dean Murphy. "Neither the mainstream nor independent churches are able to face the social and economic challenges. You have a situation where people are willing to go for anything if there is a

A CRUCIFIX AND ROSARY ARE REMOVED FROM A ROOM IN THE COMPLEX OF THE MOVEMENT FOR THE RESTORATION OF THE TEN COMMANDMENTS OF GOD, TWO DAYS AFTER A FIRE CLAIMED THE LIVES OF HUNDREDS OF FOLLOWERS. *(CORBIS CORPORATION (Bellevue). Reproduced by permission.)*

promise of a better life." This is where groups such as the Movement for the Restoration of the Ten Commandments of God step in to fill the void. The increase in small religious groups was serious enough by 1994 to be a topic of discussion at a meeting of Roman Catholic bishops in Rome.

Disaffection specifically with the Roman Catholic Church, from which the Ten Command-ments Movement splintered, has its origins in regional and tribal politics. Toward the end of the 1960s, a large Ugandan diocese was divided into three separate dioceses. Bishops were named from outside the affected regions while numerous indigenous clerics were passed over. Regional groups felt that the Church had discriminated against them for no reason. Father Dominic Kataribabo, considered the third in command of the Ten Commandments sect, felt himself the victim of precisely these regional jealousies. After studying theology in the United States, many felt he was qualified for the prestigious and intellectually demanding post of chaplain of Makerere University. Instead he was consigned to a village church to work among illiterate peasants. The posting was viewed by some as a deliberate slap in the face from the Ugandan Catholic hierarchy, dominated by priests from other regions.

Ex-members of the Ten Commandments group admitted later that they had turned to the sect as an alternative to Roman Catholicism. Paul Ikazire, a former Catholic priest who joined the group for a while in the mid-1990s, told the Uganda newspaper *New Vision*, "We joined the movement as a protest against the Catholic Church. . . . The church was backsliding, the priests were covered in scandals and the AIDS scourge was taking its toll on the faithful. The world seemed poised to end." Ikazire left the cult when it seemed to focus more on acquiring its members' property and controlling their daily activities than on faith.

This reaction against the Roman Catholic Church was a common one in Uganda during the 1990s and fueled a boom in Evangelical and Pentecostal churches. Many groups such as the Ten Commandments Movement were said to originally be Pentecostal groups. In fact, many were millenarian churches—they preached that the end of the world as prophesied in the book of Revelation was near. Most shared a charismatic leader and the belief that mainstream churches had strayed from the intent of the Bible. The Movement for the Restoration of the Ten Commandments, for example, demanded that the Roman Catholic Church return to long-abandoned dogmatic roots and preached a life lived in accordance with the Ten Commandments. Ugandan police have maintained the rise of such evangelistic churches is linked to the rise of cults.

Religious Violence in Uganda

Religious violence is just as commonplace in Uganda as unorthodox religious sects. According to Ian Fisher of the *New York Times* (April 9, 2000), in "Uganda's Trauma," at least three Christian rebel groups terrorized the Ugandan countryside during the 1980s and 1990s. In the late 1980s, the Holy Spirit Movement, led by self-styled prophetess Alice Lakwena, waged war against the Museveni government. Lakwena and most of her soldiers were Acholi tribesmen from the north who believed that Museveni's southern-dominated gov-

ernment discriminated against their region. Lakwena—whose name means "messiah"—was raised in the Anglican church, but converted to Roman Catholicism in 1985, after she experienced the Holy Ghost, who instructed her to overthrow the government. "The war is supposed to get rid of all wrong elements in society, so in the end peace is enjoyed by all Ugandans," Lakwena told the *New York Times* in "Ugandan Cult Carrying Out Suicide Raids" (November 5, 1987). Ironically, she was able to legally establish her own religious movement only because Museveni restored freedom of religion when he assumed power in 1986.

Lakwena, like the Ten Commandments Movement, preached an apocalyptic brand of Catholicism. She prophesied a purge of mankind similar to the Great Flood. The doomsday flavor of her Christianity was further spiced with traditional African tribal beliefs. New soldiers were required to undergo an initiation that involved spitting into the mouths of a black chicken, a ram, and a pig. Illness was treated using clay voodoo dolls. Like the Ten Commandments cult, she told her followers that they would be spared in the violence—even the violence she was fomenting. She distributed an oil that she claimed would protect her soldiers from the bullets of their enemies. That promise contributed to her eventual defeat in a battle in the Busoga region. Thousands of Holy Spirit guerrillas, "protected" by Lakwena's magic oil, were shot down by government forces.

Lakwena was forced into exile in 1988. The remnants of the Holy Spirit Movement became the Lord's Resistance Army (LRA). Its leader, Lakwena's cousin Joseph Kony, took righteous Christian violence to a level of brutality that Lakwena had probably never imagined. Kony seems a typical charismatic cult leader, who gave daylong sermons and sometimes spoke in tongues. He mixed Catholic beliefs picked up as an altar boy with African variants, such as a general staff made up of spirits who could turn stones into hand grenades and command invisible jeeps. Like Lakwena, he gave his troops an oil to make them invulnerable to bullets.

Kony also fought to overthrow Yoweri Museveni's government of southerners and to restore the Ten Commandments as the nation's guiding force. In the name of the commandments, Kony waged a war of terror, fought by his Acholi army against other Acholis. Over the course of a decade, his army kidnapped nearly ten thousand children, ages seven and up, from villages throughout Uganda's countryside, frequently torturing or killing parents who resisted. The abducted children were forced to take up arms for the LRA; girls were given to soldiers as wives. Teachers were routinely killed or maimed. There were also occult elements in the group's brutality. People who owned white pigs were slain because white pigs were said to be ghosts in Kony's worldview. People were killed specifically because they were found riding bicycles. An additional political twist to the contradictory story of the LRA—the fundamentalist Christian guerrillas received most of their support from the Muslim government of the Sudan, a sworn enemy of Uganda. Because the LRA can take refuge in bases deep in the Sudan, the Ugandan government has found it difficult to eradicate or control them.

Origins of the Ten Commandments Group

Even after Ugandan police had investigated for weeks the Ten Commandments Movement fire and other killings, a number of questions about the group and its internal dynamics were still unresolved. Was Joseph Kibwetere, nearly seventy years old at the time and reportedly suffering from mental illness, the group's real leader? Or was he merely a figurehead being used by Credonia Mwerinde, a woman portrayed almost universally as a money-hungry ex-prostitute? What kind of members did the Ten Commandments Movement attract? Did members knowingly enter a suicide pact, or were they duped by cult leaders into entering the church, then locked in and murdered? When and why were hundreds killed and buried in the mass graves? Finally, did the leaders survive the fire, and if so, what happened to them? Many of these questions were first addressed with a degree of definitiveness in a report released by Kampala's Makerere University a year after the blaze.

The report maintained that Joseph Kibwetere, Credonia Mwerinde, and Father Dominic Kataribabo were the leaders of the Movement for the Restoration of the Ten Commandments. Kibwetere was a devout Roman Catholic, a former teacher, and a failed politician who was later reduced to running a bar in Kabale. He then began suffering behavioral problems, sometimes described merely as mental illness, other times more specifically as manic depression. The problems were serious enough for Kibwetere to be treated at Butabika Psychiatric Hospital. He claimed that, like Christ, he had died and been resurrected. He also maintained that the Virgin Mary had appeared to him in a vision and instructed him to form a religious movement devoted to the Ten Commandments.

CULT BELIEFS

The following excerpt is a revelation of the final days from *A Timely Message from Heaven, The End of the Present Times*, by the leaders of the Movement for the Restoration of the Ten Commandments of God, quoted in Dean E. Murphy's "Tracking Multitude of Sects Impossible Task in Uganda" (*Los Angeles Times*, March 31, 2000). It illustrates the sect followers' beliefs of what they would experience in the final days preceding the apocalypse.

After all of this came three days of darkness, an event that has never been experienced since the beginning of creation. Those who had repented were told to go in hiding to the houses they had built for this purpose. These houses are called "ark" or "ship." They were ordered to shut all the doors and not to open anything at all. All activities such as eating, praying ... should take place inside for three days.

Anything that remained outside in the dark turned into evil. The devils lamented and cried for three days, after which they were thrown into hell.

The face of the Earth is now as flat as a playground. I saw a new Earth coming down from heaven.... The new Earth is very beautiful and it has plenty of light. Death and the underworld are vanquished, Satan has been put in fetters as well as those who accepted to serve it. The new Earth will be connected to heaven.

Mary later became the central focus of the Ten Commandments Movement's religious life. Mwerinde claimed that in 1984 the Virgin Mary appeared to her, and when she met the Kibweteres she won their trust immediately by telling them that the Virgin Mary had instructed her to search out a man named Joseph. The Movement's compound was named *Ishayuuriro rya Maria*, or "the place Mary comes to the rescue of the spiritually stranded." From the 1970s on, cults of the Virgin were common in Uganda. Visitations at a soccer field in the village of Kibeho were reported regularly. In the 1980s, after Gauda Kamusha saw a rock formation transform itself into the Virgin, she undertook a personal mission to preach repentance and conversion to Christianity. The Kibweteres seem to have first met Mwerinde—who also had a history of mental illness—at one of Kamusha's camp gatherings in 1988.

As reported to Jason Burke in the *Observer* on April 30, 2000 ("Beyond Belief"), Teresa Kibwetere, Joseph's wife, described the state of religious longing she and her husband were in when they met Credonia Mwerinde in the late 1980s:

We used to read in papers (religious pamphlets) of messages from heaven, and we were learning from them what our blessed mother in heaven and our Lord Jesus Christ were saying to the world, and we were sad because it had not happened here. We were good Catholics, as we had been raised to be and had been all our lives. And then something that we thought was a miracle happened. In that year, a woman came to see us who said that she had got messages from heaven. And then she said that our Lady told her that a man called Joseph would come, and that when he came people should follow him to his home. Can you imagine how we felt? Our blessed mother had sent a message with my husband's name. And her name was Credonia, and we believed what she said was true.

The Kibweteres and Mwerinde quickly became close. In 1990, with 27 followers, probably including Credonia Mwerinde, Joseph Kibwetere founded the Movement for the Restoration of the Ten Commandments of God. From that time on, he was addressed by the title of *Omukuru w'entumwa,* meaning "chief apostle and prophet."

Regardless of Kibwetere's status as the founder and elder of the group, Mwerinde seems to have exercised a good deal of control over him and complete control over the Movement. She left her husband in 1989 and moved into the Kibweteres' house. Later she persuaded the couple to give up their home and move with her to her home village, Kanungu. Mwerinde claimed to speak regularly with the Virgin Mary and used her "direct line" to assume control over nearly every aspect of life in the Ten Commandments Movement. No decision could be reached until she had discussed it with Mary. Her word was law, and she came to be known as "The Programmer" among the sect's members. Some investigators later believed that Mwerinde was in fact the true leader of the Ten Commandments Movement, and that Joseph Kibwetere was merely a figurehead used to satisfy their patriarchal Ugandan followers. The true extent of Mwerinde's religious faith and the degree to which she sincerely believed in her visits with the Virgin Mary are further mysteries of the Ten Commandments Movement.

By the time Mwerinde moved into Kibwetere's house, approximately two hundred followers were living there too, most of them women and children. The Movement officially registered as a religious group with the Ugandan government in 1993, and was granted the right to proselytize throughout the country. Around that time Kibwetere moved the sect to Kanungu, where Mwerinde's father donated ten acres of land for a settlement. The Catholic Church opposed the move to Kanungu and worked hard later to draw the sect's leaders back into the fold. After the fire the church unconditionally condemned the cult and its teachings, excommunicated its "obsessed leaders," and denied those who had died in the fire Catholic burial and the prayers of the faithful.

In the late 1980s, Kibwetere and his wife made contact with the Marian Workers of Atonement, an alleged doomsday cult in Australia. The two groups shared a number of beliefs. Like Credonia Mwerinde, William Kamm, the leader of the Marian Workers, claimed to receive messages directly from the Virgin Mary. Both groups believed the Virgin Mary would come to take them to heaven. The Marian Workers also predicted the world would suffer a violent end and that those who were not righteous would be destroyed. The symbol of the Ark held a special place in the minds of both groups as well—it was the special vessel in which the faithful would be protected when Armageddon came.

Mrs. Kibwetere began corresponding with Kamm, who went by the name Little Pebble. "We were interested in visions of His Blessed Mother," Mrs. Kibwetere told Giles Foden of the *Guardian* in "Cult Papers Reveal New Massacre Link" (April 18, 2000). "Little Pebble sent us these papers and I used to write to him. Then he came to Uganda and we went to see him in Kampala." Kamm eventually visited Uganda and held four meetings there in October 1989, just as appearances of the Virgin Mary were most common. Kamm held his meetings on property belonging to the Kampala police, a fact which later raised questions about the relationship of the police with the Ten Commandments group. Those suspicions were bolstered by the fact that at least five former police officers died in the blaze at Kanungu. Critics speculated that alleged government inaction toward the cult was a sign that the authorities were somehow complicit in the deaths.

Everyday Life in the Ten Commandments Sect

Kanungu is an Ugandan village located about 217 miles (135 kilometers) southwest of Kampala, the country's capital. On land contributed by Credonia Mwerinde's family, the Ten Commandments Movement built an impressive compound that included a modern house for the three leaders; two dormitories, one for men and one for women; two guest houses; a kitchen; a primary school; a cemetery; a poultry farm; a dairy farm; and fields of crops. In addition to Kanungu, the group had settlements in at least seven other Ugandan towns, including Kampala. Most members were women

CREDONIA MWERINDE

1952– Credonia Mwerinde, by all accounts the *de facto* leader of the Ten Commandments Movement, is a mysterious figure, and it is difficult to separate fact from legend in the reports of her life. Born in Kanungu, Uganda, to a poor Catholic catechist, Credonia was obsessed with money as a young woman, and she acquired a reputation of being willing to do anything to get it—including granting sexual favors or using violence. She was briefly hospitalized for mental illness in the 1970s. After the fire and the discovery of mass graves connected to the Ten Commandments Movement, stories were told about her seduction, murder, and robbery of a motorist passing through Kanungu; her arson against a local official who rejected her advances; and even the serial murder of her three brothers in order to acquire land for the Movement. The latter claim has been discounted as exaggeration. Mwerinde's parents donated the land after they joined the group.

While in her twenties she married a Kanungu man and they opened a bar together. Although she had not attended church in many years, Mwerinde told her husband in 1988 that she was experiencing visions of the Blessed Virgin. She separated from her husband and returned to her parents' home. She began preaching the word of the Virgin Mary and eventually founded her own religion, the Ten Commandments Movement. Later in 1988, she met Joseph Kibwetere and moved into the Kibweteres' house until the family threw her out.

Joseph Kibwetere accepted Mwerinde's invitation to head the sect. Mwerinde, however, ran the Movement. Father Paul Ikazire, a priest who spent three years in the sect before returning to the Roman Catholic Church, said Mwerinde—allegedly known in the Movement as "The Programmer"—controlled the group with an iron fist. As told to Philip Sherwell in "Heart of Darkness, Sister of Death" in the *Sunday Telegraph* on April 2, 2000, "The meetings were chaired by Sister Credonia, who was the *de facto* head of the cult," Ikazire explained. "Kibwetere was just a figurehead, intended to impose masculine authority over the followers and enhance the cult's public relations."

Reports about Mwerinde's life in the sect vary. According to some, she lived in separate quarters much more comfortable than those used by other sect members. They also said she ate so much that she grew fat while Movement members wasted away on a starvation diet. Others, however, maintain that she fasted regularly, slept on the floor, prayed for hours, and went into mediumistic trances during which she received messages from the Virgin Mary. Her sinful past did not harm Mwerinde's credibility, it helped. She was seen as a kind of Mary Magdalene, a sinner selected by heaven for salvation.

Mwerinde was, at first, believed to have perished in the fire in Kanungu. Others, however, claimed to have seen her driving away from the Movement compound on the morning of March 17, 2000. If so, she vanished without a trace. Authorities believe her to be somewhere in the neighboring Congo.

and children who were previously Protestants, Muslims, and Roman Catholics. Contrary to early reports, members were not only impoverished farmers, but also teachers, carpenters, masons, businessmen, ex-soldiers, and other members of the Ugandan middle class. Members paid a fee when they joined, the equivalent of $2.70 for children, $4.30 for adolescents, and $13.50 for adults. There is evidence that sect members who were able to contribute more received better accommodations.

Life in the sect was difficult and filled with sacrifice. Men and women were separated, and sexual relations were forbidden, even between married couples. Private ownership was also not allowed. When they entered the sect, converts gave up everything they owned, even their clothes. They were issued uniforms, color-coded according to the degree of enlightenment they had attained: new recruits wore black; those who had accepted the Ten Commandments green; and those prepared to die in the Ark wore green and white. Shoes and sandals were not worn.

Daily life in the sect was regulated by a rigid timetable based on prayer and work. On Sundays no work was allowed—indeed, no activity at all except worship. Mondays, Wednesdays, and Fridays were fasting days on which members ate only dinner. On these days they rose at 3 AM and prayed until 5 AM. From 5 AM until 7 AM they were allowed to sleep again. They worked in the fields until 1 PM, when an hour of prayer was held. From

AN UGANDAN SOLDIER VIEWS THE BURNED REMAINS OF CULT FOLLOWERS AND THE CHURCH IN WHICH THEY PERISHED. THE WHEREABOUTS OF THE CULT'S LEADERS ARE UNKNOWN. *(CORBIS CORPORATION (Bellevue). Reproduced by permission.)*

3 PM until 4 PM members could do as they pleased, followed by four more hours of farm work, dinner at 8 PM, and night prayers at 11 PM. Tuesdays, Thursdays, and Saturdays were essentially the same, except members were given breakfast and lunch. Some observers noted that such a regimen—hard work, constant prayer, and little food or sleep—was the classic recipe for brainwashing that the media had come to associate with cult behavior. Others point out that rigid self-denial has been a characteristic of devout religious communities such as monasteries and convents throughout the world.

Members observed absolute silence at all times, none so fervently as sect leader Joseph Kibwetere, who communicated only via sign language and written notes. They were encouraged to spend time studying *A Timely Message from Heaven, the End of the Present Times*, a book written by the sect's leaders and allegedly based on messages they had received from the Virgin Mary and Jesus Christ. Members were promised that if they read the book twenty times, all prayers would be

granted. Early reports maintained that members of the Movement were allowed only the most necessary contact with outsiders. It was later revealed that outside contact was more common than initially presumed. Members frequently worked on local farms, and female members worked as domestics for the district commissioner and other local authorities. Outsiders, however, were not allowed into the compound beyond a so-called visitors' zone. It was also reported that sect members were often moved to settlements far away from their home regions, where they would be less likely to have contact with outsiders. However, according to those same reports, members frequently went door-to-door in the areas they had settled, proselytizing and looking for converts.

Despite its outward profession of Christianity, the Ten Commandments Movement also practiced rituals associated with religions such as voodoo. Rosaries were worn like magic charms, one facing front, one facing back, with another concealed in the clothing. When baptized, members were shaved completely and their nails cut. The trimmed hair and nails were then burnt, and their ashes drunk in tea or water and smeared on a candidate's body.

The Last Days

The Movement for the Restoration of the Ten Commandments was an apocalyptic sect, sometimes sensationally termed a "doomsday sect." It believed in the prophecies of the biblical Book of Revelation: at the end of the world, the earth would experience cataclysmic destruction, when God and his angels came to earth, destroyed all evil and evildoers in a final, bloody battle, and saved the righteous few. From its earliest days, Movement leaders preached that the end of the world was approaching. In keeping with their cult of the Virgin they taught that when the end did come, the Virgin Mary would appear and protect those assembled in the Movement's settlements. Various deadlines for the Apocalypse, however, came and went without event, both in 1992 and 1995. The failure of the prophecies caused some dissatisfaction among members who had surrendered all their worldly possessions on the understanding that they would not be needed in the next life coming. "People started grumbling," Paulina Zikanga, a member who left the sect in 1998 told the *Washington Post* in Karl Vick's "Prophecy's Price" (April 1, 2000). "They were insisting that if the world doesn't end [the cult] should refund their money."

The prophecy was revised. The new date was December 31, 1999, a date with persuasive millennial import: 1999 becoming 2000. Millennial fears raged throughout most of the industrial West, where expectation of worldwide chaos caused by Y2K computer failure fueled the belief among religious and secular groups of all stripes that the end might really be near. That date came and went as well, and the Virgin Mary did not appear in Kanungu to usher believers into heaven. The grumbling increased; the rule of silence was broken. Members demanded their money back, work in the settlements ceased, and members began mixing with outsiders. The iron discipline of camp life disintegrated. To quell the rising tide of dissatisfaction, leaders sent many members back to their old homes and told them they would be notified when to return to the sect. A new date for Mary's coming was announced: March 17, 2000.

The discontent among sect members was established by the Makerere University investigators. They discovered that it was those who complained the most who were asked to put their grievances in writing and afterwards were given private meetings

MASS SUICIDE

Since the Jonestown Massacre in 1978, mass suicide has come to be seen as an inherent part of the cult phenomenon. Remarkably, however, Jonestown was the *first* mass cult suicide of modern times. What's more, the Jonestown suicides were not rooted in religious dogma, like the Ten Commandments Movement's, but in secular ideas. Jim Jones based his suicides on a 1960s Black Panther idea, "revolutionary suicide," which could be used to spark wide-scale revolution in society.

The idea of mass suicide was almost immediately accepted as a characteristic of all cults once Jonestown occurred. Philip Jenkins reported in his book *Mystics and Messiahs* (2000),

> Although this idea was new in 1978, the concept of "cult suicide" was so widely accepted because it so perfectly encapsulated all the images that had been developing over the previous decade: stereotypes of blind obedience, disregard of self and family, violent tendencies, and a preparedness to follow any orders issued by a deranged messiah. The idea became so well established that soon mass suicide seemed a probable outcome of cult extremism.

Links between the belief that the end of the world is imminent, called millenarianism, and mass suicide are equally tenuous. The U.S. government has maintained that the Branch Davidian sect committed mass suicide in Waco, Texas, in 1993, but the claim has been hotly contested by critics who allege that an attack by federal agents was actually responsible for the deaths. Many of the bodies found in the apparent mass suicide of the Solar Temple group in Switzerland and Canada had been bound and beaten, drugged, or shot repeatedly; the group's involvement in international crime and arms trade probably had more to do with those deaths than the belief in Armageddon. Finally, Heaven's Gate, called by Philip Jenkins "the only authenticated case of a cult mass suicide on American soil," based their beliefs on New Age ideas and UFO (unidentified flying object) theories rather than on any religious ideas of the Apocalypse. They believed that they were merely shedding their corporeal bodies so they could be picked up by a UFO behind the Hale-Bopp comet. If the Ten Commandments Movement's fire was a case of mass suicide, it would, according to precedent, be a bizarre exception rather than typical cult behavior.

with the sect's leaders to discuss problems. Most who attended such meetings were never seen again. If inquiries were made, leaders said the members had been moved to another Ten Commandments camp. Their corpses were eventually found in the mass graves. In early March 2000, Father Kataribabo went to the town of Kasese and purchased fifty liters of sulfuric acid, which was used to destroy corpses in some of the graves and to spark the conflagration in the church.

As March 17, 2000 approached, events in Kanungu shifted into high gear. A recruitment drive, complete with radio advertising, was launched in February throughout Uganda. The group sold off everything it owned—livestock, household goods, and clothes—at bargain prices. Members from Movement settlements elsewhere in Uganda traveled to Kanungu a few days before the seventeenth. Authorities in Kanungu were also invited to a party—on March 18, the night after the fire took place. They later termed that invitation a deception to allay suspicions about the preparations for the fire. On March 16 the sect prepared an evening feast, the most elaborate meal members had eaten while in the sect. Three bulls were slaughtered, seventy cases of Coca-Cola were drunk, and everything in the garden was harvested. During the meal Joseph Kibwetere drove to the local police station and turned over titles to the Movement's land.

The next morning members filed into the church for their morning prayers. The doors were locked behind them; the windows had already been nailed shut. The church was their "ark," the vessel in which they would be protected when the Virgin Mary came, clothed in flames, to bear them all to heaven. Investigators could only speculate what happened after everyone entered the church. There was an explosion. It may have been caused by a torch touched to one of several large canisters of gasoline that had been placed throughout the church. It may have ignited by an extremely volatile mixture of water and sulfuric acid. The congregation may even have doused their own clothing in flammable liquid and touched lit candles to themselves. Likely, it was a combination of several factors. Despite the fact that the "ark" had to be prepared at least a day in advance, investigators were not certain how much the congregation knew of their fate when they marched into the church that last morning.

RECENT HISTORY AND THE FUTURE

Government Responses
Following the deaths, the Ugandan government was widely criticized for not monitoring the Ten Commandments Movement more closely and intervening before the mass murder-suicides could occur. Some claimed that authorities never suspected any wrongdoing because the intelligence agencies charged with monitoring fringe religious groups had not worked properly. Others said the responsible agencies were unable to keep up with the workload in cult-rich Uganda because they were under-financed and understaffed. Still others maintained that local authorities were connected with the group and had perhaps been bribed to protect it. Whatever happened, the incident illustrates the difficulties government bodies and police departments face when it comes to regulating fringe religious groups, particularly in a nation that professes freedom of religion.

As Ugandan police searched for other Ten Commandments branches to close down, questions arose over whether the police should have predicted the group's actions. By the time the fire took place, the Ten Commandments Movement had been in existence for almost a decade without incident, and it had been registered with the government for six years. Apparently no criminal complaints were ever filed against the group in that time with local or national authorities and, according to coroner's reports, the murders were committed only a month or so before the fire. Furthermore, the Movement gave no prior sign that it intended to commit mass suicide. On the contrary, the group taught that the world outside the sect would perish in the coming conflagration—members' lives would be saved by the Virgin Mary.

Certainly any government should be committed to preventing murder among its citizenry, but how far can authorities go to control religious groups in the absence of any evidence that laws have been, or might someday be, broken? A group's beliefs may be different, they may appear irrational, silly, heretical, or even dangerous to outsiders, but do such beliefs, in and of themselves, justify suppression, particularly in nations that claim to respect the rights of its citizens to worship as they choose? Indeed the Ten Commandments Movement was not particularly strange as such groups went. For many years the group claimed to be Roman Catholic and maintained it only wanted to return the Church to the true roots of its teachings.

Just being a sect or fringe religion does not suffice to justify suppression. Virtually all of the respected mainstream religions in the Western world—Roman Catholicism, Lutheranism, Episcopalianism, the Mormons, the Quakers, the Baptists, and the Seventh Day Adventists, to name but a few—began as renegade groups that splintered off from older established religions. This knowledge should breed tolerance, or at least a sense of perspective. As Philip Jenkins pointed out in his book *Mystics and Messiahs* (2000), "Presumably no writer would refer to Lutherans or Episcopalians as renegade offshoots of the Roman Catholic Church."

Philosopher of religion William James was quoted in *Mystics and Messiahs* as suggesting that sects and fringe religions may be closer to the sources of genuine religious experience than their mainstream brethren. The one who experiences the first-hand religious experience may become a prophet—perceived by some as a madman—and may gain followers, threatening established religious. James commented that, "the faithful live at second hand exclusively and stone the prophets in their turn." The established religions, he suggested, attempt to stifle new religious spirit, which grew out of the same fount from which they once took their inspiration.

When Yoweri Museveni's new government reversed years of religious oppression in the country and recognized Ugandans' right to religious freedom in 1986, the decree was seen in the West as extraordinarily progressive and a significant move towards democracy in Uganda. At the same time, the decree provided the occasion for the formation of hundreds of fringe religious groups in the country, groups with strange, sometimes threatening beliefs—the Ten Commandments Movement itself formed less than two years after Museveni came to power. By 2000 several hundred church organizations had registered with the government in Kampala alone. For a government with limited resources, it is a difficult task to monitor such a large number of groups—particularly when the overwhelming majority of such groups are harmless. Uganda has made an effort. It has had laws on its books since 1989 that require all church groups to register with the government. Most religious groups in Uganda consider the law an infringement on their freedom of worship. Nonetheless, the Ten Commandments Movement registered as early as 1993 and the authorities were well aware of its existence.

The Ugandan police did not ignore the threat of criminal sects by any means. According to reports made after the Ten Commandments blaze, in 1999 alone police closed down at least four groups in the country. Two of them appeared to be practicing overtly fraudulent behavior: One taught that the more money one contributed to the group the better one's chances of going to heaven. The other

attracted members and money by claiming a God-given ability to cure AIDS. Scams likes these were only a fragment of what was going on in some of the country's numerous religious sects. Monitoring the groups was an overwhelming task for the police.

Cult or Religion?

Doomsday beliefs make it no easier to identify potentially violent fringe religions. The belief that the world will experience a cataclysmic end is fundamental to virtually all branches of Christianity, which has been called " the oldest extant doomsday cult." Apocalyptic scenarios are portrayed in detail in both the Old and New Testaments. Not even an apparent fascination with violence helps identify dangerous religious groups. As Don Lattin, the religion correspondent of the *San Francisco Chronicle* wrote in "Thin Line between Church and Cult" (April 9, 2000) shortly after the Ten Commandment deaths:

> If you think these visions are the exclusive domain of "cultists" and "terrorists," think about this: . . . on April 20, Jews celebrate Passover, which commemorates the story in the Book of Exodus about how God passed over the Israelites when he unleashed a plague that killed all the other first-born children of Egypt. The next day, on Good Friday, Christians gather in church to remember the day when Jesus of Nazareth had nails pounded through his hands and was strung up to die in a slow, tortuous execution.

Unnatural lifestyles also do not help in determining if a group is a potential threat. The Ten Commandments Movement imposed a demanding regimen of work and prayer on its adherents, together with stringent restrictions on how much members ate every day. Some observers called the combination of fasting, hard work, and prayer at Kanungu a classic recipe for brainwashing—using forced physical and psychological hardship to coerce individuals to accept group beliefs. However, religious practices that appear excessive to outsiders—to non-believers—may have real meaning for the spiritual lives of group members. Such practices also have a richly detailed tradition among religious groups throughout the world. What some may perceive as mind control or authoritarianism in the group's leaders, others may see as a lifestyle of discipline and faith. At any rate many experts have come to question whether the idea of "brainwashing," which came into vogue during the 1970s, has any real validity.

Warrants were issued for the arrest of the Ten Commandments Movement leaders. Rewards of Ush2 million (US$1,078) per head were offered for information leading to their capture. More than a year after the Kanungu deaths, however, the whereabouts of the sect's leaders were still unknown. An official government inquiry into the Ten Commandments Movement, the events in Kanungu, and into cults in Uganda in general, was initiated. Hampered by a lack of funding, however, its work had ground to a halt by spring 2001. Because monies had to be spent on upcoming elections, there seemed little chance that the investigation would be continued in the foreseeable future.

The answers to many questions revolving around the Ten Commandments Movement may never be fully resolved. Did the group's followers die willingly in that church, or were they murdered by the sect's leaders? For the Ugandan government, and for governments around the world, the fine line of monitoring fringe religious groups remains—dangerous or peaceable, religion or cult? For the followers of the Movement for the Restoration of the Ten Commandments of God, the answer came too late.

BIBLIOGRAPHY

Barkan, Steven E., and Lynne L. Snowden. *Collective Violence.* Boston, MA: Allyn & Bacon, 2001.

Burke, Jason. "Beyond Belief; How Did a Former Prostitute, a Frustrated Politician and a Failed Priest Lure 1,000 Cult Members to Their Deaths?" *Observer,* April 30, 2000.

Fisher, Ian. "Uganda Cult's Mystique Finally Turned Deadly," *New York Times,* April 2, 2000, sec. 1, p. 14.

———. "Uganda's Trauma; A Deadly Cult Stirs Lively Questions about a Nation's Soul," *New York Times,* April 9, 2000, sec. 4, p. 3.

Foden, Giles. "Cult Papers Reveal New Massacre Link; Documents Show Ugandan Sect Leader 'Inspired by Visits from Australian Doomsday Group," *The Guardian,* April 18, 2000, p. 3.

Handleman, Stephen. "Rescue Saga of Uganda's Girl 'Soldiers,' Rebels Kidnap 8,000 Children in Bush War," *Toronto Star,* December 21, 1997, p. A1.

Jenkins, Philip. *Mystics and Messiahs: Cults and New Religions in American History.* London: Oxford University Press, 2000.

Lattin, Don. "Thin Line between Church and Cult," *San Francisco Chronicle,* April 9, 2000, p. 3.

"'Mary's Flames': The Long Road to Horror in Kanungu," *Africa News Service,* February 8, 2001. Available online at http://www.allafrica.com. (cited April 16, 2001).

Murphy, Dean E. "Tracking Multitude of Sects Impossible Task in Uganda; Africa: Charged with Monitoring 648 Religious Groups, Government Office is Woefully Underfunded, Ill-Equipped," *Los Angeles Times,* March 31, 2000, p. A1.

——— "Ugandan Cult's Deadly Secrets Haunt the Living," *Los Angeles Times,* March 22, 2000, p. A1.

Nelson, Craig. "Followers of Movement Believed Childhood was an Occasion of Sin," *St. Louis Post-Dispatch,* April 3, 2000, p. A6.

———. "'Let Us Go and Burn': Uganda Hunts for Answers to Mass Murder of Cultists," *Montreal Gazette,* April 2, 2000, p. D6.

Onyango-Obbo, Charles. "Kanungu Fire: Why Would 500 Be Burnt to Death for a Prostitute?" *Monitor,* March 22, 2000.

Pavlos, Andrew J. *The Cult Experience.* Westport, CT: Greenwood Press, 1982.

Robbins, Thomas and Dick Anthony. "Religious Movements and the Brainwashing Issue," quoted in Ken Levi, editor, *Violence and Religious Commitment.* University Park, PA: Pennsylvania State University Press, 1982.

Sandars, Richard. "Beyond Belief," *Scotsman,* June 10, 2000, p. 16.

Sherwell, Philip. "Heart of Darkness, Sister of Death," *Sunday Telegraph,* April 02, 2000, p. 29.

"Ugandan Cult Carrying Out Suicide Raids," *New York Times,* November 5, 1987, sec. A, p. 11.

Vick, Karl. "Prophecy's Price; When World Did Not End, Police Say, Ugandan Cult Orchestrated Doomsday," *Washington Post,* April 1, 2000, p. A1.

—Gerald E. Brennan

NEW LABOUR AND THE DEVOLUTION OF POWER IN THE UNITED KINGDOM

July 1, 1999, was a day of grand festivities of historic proportions in Edinburgh, Scotland. That day saw the opening of the first Scottish parliament in nearly three hundred years and marked the beginning of home rule—the "devolution" of power, as it was called—in Scotland. A similar Welsh assembly, the first of its kind ever, had come into being the previous May. On the morning of July 1, Lord Hamilton, the ranking Scottish peer, was driven to Edinburgh palace where he was presented with the Scottish crown. The last time the crown had been used ceremonially was 1651, when Charles II was crowned. After that it was stored away in the palace for safekeeping. Its presence at a new parliament was a mixed symbol for Scots. The crown represented the idea of Scottish sovereignty traceable to the old Scottish kingdom, but also that, in Britain, political power ultimately goes back to the royal family.

Queen Elizabeth II, the ceremonial head of state of the United Kingdom (UK), made her entrance dressed in a simple crimson suit as the Royal Marines played the national anthem, "God Save The Queen." She arrived in an open, horse-drawn carriage with her consort, Prince Philip, and her son, Prince Charles, the heir to the British throne. Nineteen horsemen of the Household Cavalry escorted them along Edinburgh's Royal Mile to the Assembly Hall of the Church of Scotland, which would serve as the temporary home of the new parliament. The Queen was announced by a twenty-one gun salute and greeted by Lord Steel, the former head of the British Liberal Party, and Donald Dewar, the head of the Scottish Labour Party. Dewar accompanied the Royal delegation, along with the Scottish crown on an ornate cushion, into the Assembly Hall.

THE CONFLICT

Ever since England and Scotland joined to form the Kingdom of Great Britain a tension has existed in Scotland, driven by its strong sense of national identity and its pride in its unique national institutions on the one hand, and on the other a sense that it was under the domination of England, its partner to the south. This has led to demands ranging from a greater degree of self-determination to full Scottish independence.

Political

- The Conservative Party opposes devolution, claiming that it would lead to the dissolution of the United Kingdom. The Labour Party favors it, maintaining that more home rule for Scotland and Wales is the only way to defuse nationalist movements and prevent a threat to the UK such as the Provisional IRA in Northern Ireland.

- The Scottish political parties hope to achieve very different ends by means of devolution. For the Labour Party it is a way of maintaining the UK in its fundamental form; for the Liberal Democrats it is a way to transition to a full federal system, with a division of authority between the regions and central government similar to that in the United States; the Scottish National Party sees it as a step to full independence for Scotland.

- The Scottish parliament passes legislation that goes beyond that enacted by the British parliament for the rest of the country. In some cases, as a result, Scots receive benefits not enjoyed by citizens elsewhere in Britain, although the money for them originates with the British parliament in Westminster.

- Based on their populations, both Scotland and Wales are over-represented in the House of Commons compared to England.

- Scotland sends representatives to Westminster and consequently has a say in English affairs; England sends no representatives to Holyrood and has no voice in Scottish affairs.

CHRONOLOGY

1536 Wales and England are unified.

1707 The Act of Union is ratified joining England and Scotland as the Kingdom of Great Britain.

1885 The Scottish Office is created.

1886 Scottish and Welsh home rule is debated in Parliament for the first time.

1926 The position of Scottish secretary is elevated to cabinet rank.

1939 Scottish Office headquarters are moved from London, England, to Edinburgh, Scotland.

1964 The Welsh Office is created.

Late 1960s Rising Scottish nationalism moves the Labour government to propose legislation for home rule in Scotland.

Early 1970s The term "devolution" is coined.

1977 The Scottish-Welsh Bill, a devolution bill, is defeated in the House of Commons.

1979 A devolution referendum on whether regional Scottish and Welsh assemblies should be formed is defeated.

1989 The Scottish Constitutional Convention convenes.

1995 Tony Blair's Labour Party steps up its demands for devolution in Scotland.

May 1, 1997 The Labour Party wins a landslide victory in British national elections. Tony Blair becomes prime minister.

July 1997 The Labour government releases its White Paper, "Scotland's Parliament."

September 11, 1997 A referendum on devolution is held in Scotland.

September 18, 1997 A referendum on devolution is held in Wales.

May 1998 A referendum is held in London to decide if the city is to be led by an elected mayor.

May 9, 1999 Elections for Scottish and Welsh parliaments are held.

July 1, 1999 The new Scottish parliament opens in Edinburgh.

May 4, 2000 The first mayoral elections in its history are held in London.

January 2001 Controversy arises when Scottish ministers refer to Scottish "government," rather than "assembly."

In his opening address, Lord Steel called the new parliament the most important event in Scotland in three hundred years—since the Act of Union in 1707, which unified Scotland and England into a single nation, and the subsequent closing of the last Scottish parliament. The Queen spoke next. She termed the new political order appropriate to the new realities and aspirations in Scotland. Expressing her trust in the will of the Scottish people, she declared their new parliament to be open and presented its officers with a silver scepter, a symbol of the body's legal authority. Dewar accepted the scepter with the hope that the new parliament would fulfill its duties with wisdom, justice, compassion and integrity, and that it would become a voice of the future for Scotland. As the Queen exited, a group of some sixteen hundred Scottish schoolchildren in train, a squadron of planes from the Royal Air Force's Red Arrows flew over head, led by a Concorde supersonic transport.

The Queen's appearance at the opening was deliberately planned to be free of pomp and circumstance. Her appearance was also remarkably well accepted. The Scottish Nationalist Party (SNP), which demanded full independence from English domination for much of the twentieth century, was expected to protest. However, not only did they not denounce the monarch, most of the party was present at the ceremony, albeit with white roses, symbolic of their Scottish patriotism, in their lapels. Most of the British cabinet was also in attendance, along with distinguished guests from Europe and the rest of the world. Conspicuous in his absence was the architect of British devolution, Prime Minister Tony Blair. He had been called suddenly to Northern Ireland to save the fragile peace between Ulster unionists and the Irish Republican Army (IRA).

The formation of the Scottish parliament was the defining gesture in the Blair government's policy of "devolution." Jonathan Bradbury, in *British Regionalism and Devolution,* (1997), defines devolution as "a peculiarly British concept of how power can be divided territorially within a state. . . . devolution creates elected provincial bodies and gives them legislative and/or executive powers derived from the state parliament." Such powers range from the fundamental, such as granting Londoners the power to elect a mayor; to major reforms of the British constitutional system, including the formation of a constituent body in Scotland empowered with limited legislative and fiscal authority. Though a significant development in a parliamentary system like Britain's, such an arrangement is natural in keeping with a federal system where all government powers originate with the nations' regions. For example, in the United States, every U.S. state has an elected legislature empowered to pass laws and levy taxes. Furthermore, under the U.S. constitution, any power not specifically granted to the federal government or prohibited to the states remains with the states. Unlike the United States, where political power flows from the bottom up, in the United Kingdom it circulates from the top down. Historically power rested with the monarch; in modern times it is held by the British parliament, of which the queen is technically still part. Parliament's governmental authority extends right down to regional and local levels, and it has guarded its prerogatives jealously into modern times, even as the complexity of national government increased exponentially after World War II (1939–45).

The term "devolution" was originally coined in the 1970s regarding plans to create an assembly in Scotland which would take over government powers in matters that directly affected Scotland. Since then, it has acquired the more general sense of any delegation of governmental authority to local or regional communities throughout the UK. In the late 1990s, devolution was exercised primarily in Scotland and Wales, which received a new parliament and national assembly respectively, and in the capital London, which was able to elect its first mayor in spring 2000. There has also been discussion of extending devolution to England and its various regions. If approved, these regions would also receive new constituent assemblies.

Devolution inspired profound uneasiness in Britain. The decision to grant Scotland a parliament was a move fraught with anxiety. It certainly did not make it easier that devolution had its origins partly in the popularity of nationalist parties demanding full independence for Scotland, which led some critics to consider devolution as a stepping stone to Scottish independence. The union of England and Scotland has long been considered the glue that holds the United Kingdom together. Give Scotland home rule, devolution critics claimed, and the inevitable result will be independence for Scotland and Wales and the dissolution of the three-hundred-year-old United Kingdom. In fact, two months earlier, as part of the same constitutional reform, Wales had inaugurated its first national assembly. Perhaps the United Kingdom was already breaking apart.

What led Britain to this juncture? Was the nation on the verge of dissolution, as British conservatives claimed? Or was it, on the contrary, essential that the central British government—sometimes referred to as Westminster after the London district in which it is based—loosen its hold on power precisely in order to preserve the United Kingdom?

HISTORICAL BACKGROUND

The British Union and its Aftermath

England traces its history as a nation back to the Norman Conquest of 1066. The creation of the political entity we now know as Great Britain occurred later. After many years of trade and slow assimilation, England and Wales were legally unified in the sixteenth century. England and Scotland united to form Great Britain in 1707, when the Act of Union was ratified. Under the act the royal houses of Scotland and England agreed to merge into a single kingdom. England's Cross of St. George and Scotland's Cross of St. Andrew were combined into the Union Jack, which serves as the flag of the United Kingdom to the present day.

The roots of devolution can be found in this union. When it agreed to the arrangement, Scotland gave up its identity as an independent nation. In return for joining the union, however, it was also granted certain preferential considerations, which distinguished it from other parts of Britain. Scotland retained its own separate system of law and administration; its own educational system, and the Church of Scotland. These Scottish institutions have endured into the twenty-first century and served to foster a sense of Scottish national identity and individuality through the years.

That sense was not only felt by Scots, but also by the British parliament in Westminster. Scotland's system of law, based on different legal principles from England and Wales, necessitated that distinctive, specifically Scottish legislation, be devised by the British parliament. In the 1880s special

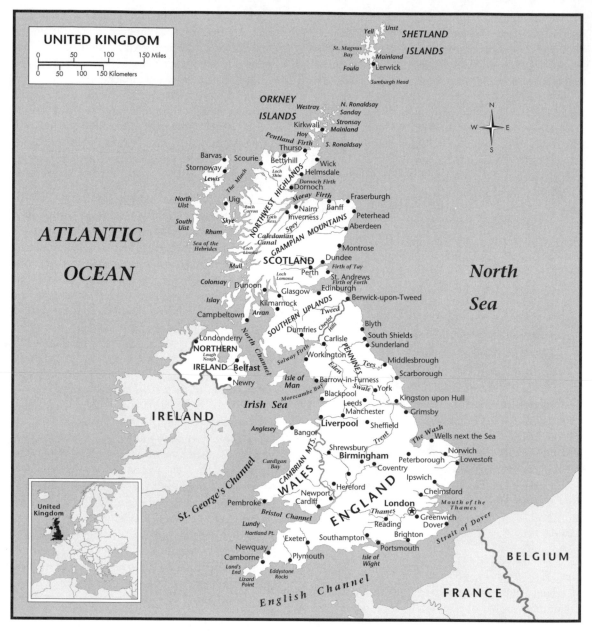

MAP OF THE UNITED KINGDOM. *(Maryland Cartographics. Reproduced by permission.)*

committees were formed in the House of Commons to debate Scottish bills; in 1907 Scottish Grand Committees were created to deal with purely Scottish matters. Scotland's sense of "difference" was also accentuated by the fact that it used its own bank notes and had its own Conservative and Labour political parties independent of the national party hierarchies in London.

The Scottish institutions which had been allowed to survive to make union with England more palatable also nourished Scottish nationalist feelings against alleged English domination through the years, particularly in lean economic times. Scot-

land's agreement to the act of Union was, in the words of Gideon Rachman, an *Economist* editor, quoted in the *Washington Quarterly* article "The Disunited Kingdom" (2000), "essentially an economic bargain." In 1707, the year of the act of Union, England's empire was beginning to expand rapidly, the Industrial Revolution was transforming the nation's manufacturing, and it was very much in Scotland's interest to unite. The economy is a double-edged sword, however. When Britain lost its empire in the twentieth century and went into economic decline, Scots—the nationalist parties in particular—began to ask what the Union had to offer. The economic and political developments of the late twentieth century seemed to support the separatists' case. The creation of the European Union (EU) and the European Monetary Union in the 1990s provided an international framework in which Scotland could survive as an independent state; tourism and North Sea Oil seemed to promise Scotland adequate economic resources.

Scotland was governed until the late nineteenth century by the central British government in Westminster, as was Wales, until the mid-twentieth century. Through the years Scottish separatism had relatively few supporters. Scottish home rule, not to mention devolution in general, was not a particularly burning issue on the British political agenda until late in the twentieth century. However, the first faltering steps toward devolution began in the nineteenth century. Laws passed between 1888–94 formed elected local bodies, county and county borough councils, which then took over administration of services such as housing and education. Around 1886 and 1912, whenever home rule for Ireland was debated in Parliament, devolution for England, Wales, and Scotland was also discussed, as much to justify Irish policy as to respond to any Scottish grievances against Britain. Northern Ireland was given its own assembly in 1920, the year that the Republic of Ireland won its independence from Britain. Early devolution in Ireland, however, was the result of a fiercely active separatist movement in Ireland, which did not exist in Scotland or Wales. As Jonathan Bradbury remarked in *British Regionalism and Devolution* (1997), "Granting of devolution to Northern Ireland between 1921 and 1972 should be seen as a special case determined by sectarian politics of the province and the historical peculiarities of the creation of a separate Irish state." Devolution in Britain was debated once again after World War I (1914–18). It was then seen as a threat to the country's constitutional stability, and no serious steps were taken.

Until the 1980s nearly all British politicians, in particular the two main parties of Conservative and Labour, saw Great Britain as a "union-state" to be governed from Westminster. Despite this image of a centrally governed union-state, there remained a willingness to treat Scotland as a special case, especially when pressure from Scottish nationalists had to be parried. The special treatment had various results.

One of the most significant results was that the Scottish Office, a government department that oversaw Scottish affairs, was created in 1885. Its head, the Scotland secretary, was usually a Scottish member of Parliament (MP) who came to be viewed informally as the Scottish prime minister. The Scotland secretary was elevated to cabinet rank in 1926. By that time the Scottish Office had taken on a wide range of functions, including health, police, prisons, and power to determine the content of specific regional aid bills. The Office moved its headquarters from London to Edinburgh in 1939.

Additionally, in 1922 Scotland was allocated a larger number of seats in the House of Commons than its population entitled it to. By 1974 Scotland was over-represented by 20 percent. And, finally, from the late nineteenth century onward, Scotland received fiscal subsidies from Westminster above and beyond those received by England. At first they were justified as a response to the Scotland secretary's complaints of English subjugation of Scotland; after World War II they were supposed to redress a disproportionate influence of state intervention in Scotland. Opponents to devolution in the 1990s cited advantages such as these as reasons not to grant Scotland home rule.

The Road to Devolution

In the 1960s the Scottish Nationalist Party (SNP) was showing increasing strength among Scotland's voters. By 1974 they garnered 30 percent of Scottish votes and won 11 seats in the House of Commons. Sensing an imminent erosion of the Labour Party's British power base, which was based largely in Scotland, Harold Wilson's Labour government initiated a new public discussion of Scottish home rule. By 1968 both the major parties, the Conservatives and Labour, were formulating plans for devolution in Britain and, in the 1970 election, Labour made devolution one of its campaign planks. It was unsuccessful, and the new Conservative government simply let the question disappear from the political agenda. Labour regained power in 1974, and a combined Scottish-Welsh devolution bill was defeated in 1977. Two years later, however, the voters of Scotland and Wales were able to vote on the question of regional assemblies in a referendum.

One of the reasons the Conservative Party voiced opposition to devolution was the so-called West Lothian Question, first raised by Scottish MP Tom Dalyell and named after his district, West Lothian: Only Scots would be allowed to serve in a Scottish parliament, which would legislate on all Scottish matters. However, Scottish MPs would continue to serve in the British parliament, which makes law for England. If devolution were enacted, Scots would be involved in decision-making that affects England, but the English would have no say in Scottish matters. Labour could offer no satisfying answer to this conundrum. The Labour Party was split on the devolution issue in any case, conflicting as it did with the party's socialist principles, which presumed a strong central government to provide an array of social services. In 1979 the SNP refused to support Labour on devolution, considering it a bad compromise to full independence. Polls at the time, however, showed that despite the SNP's broad support in Scotland, about 65 percent of SNP voters were opposed to full independence. The SNP's opposition to devolution turned into a setback when Conservatives, also known as Tories, won power in 1979 under Margaret Thatcher. The SNP did not recover support for nearly a decade.

With a turnout of 63 percent, Scotland approved the devolution plan by a narrow margin of only 51.6 percent—about 32.8 percent of the entire Scottish electorate voted in favor of the proposed Scottish assembly. In Wales, with 58 percent turnout, a dismal 20.3 percent favored creating a Welsh assembly. The measure was defeated in both regions. "Yes" votes in each region had to equal at least 40 percent of the *total* electorate. A number of reasons for the failure were put forward, including the Labour Party's wavering commitment to the issue, concerted Conservative opposition, and a conviction among the electorate that devolution would hurt both Britain and Scotland economically.

The failed referendum ushered in the election of Margaret Thatcher's Conservative Party, the beginning of seventeen years of Tory rule in Britain. Under the Conservatives', centralization of power with the national government increased. The Tories never had much strength in Scotland. By the end of the 1980s, however, many Scots, including influential groups like labor unions, the Church of Scotland and local governments, had had enough of Scottish affairs being dominated by Westminster. The conviction grew that Scots needed more influence in Parliament than the Scottish Office provided. Urged on by those groups, the Scottish Constitutional Convention (SCC) was formed. It was an alliance of the Scottish Labour and Liberal Democratic Parties, the Scottish women's movement, and Scottish churches. The purpose of the SCC was to formulate plans for Scottish home rule within the United Kingdom, via a Scottish parliament. In essence, it laid the groundwork for devolution. Its reports and proposals, issued up to 1995, became the basis of an influential White Paper, or official statement, on devolution released by the Labour Party in summer 1997. The SCC,

however, did not have the support of all Scottish groups. Most significantly, the Scottish Nationalist Party refused to take part, believing Labour would use its powerful position in the convention to force the SNP to relinquish its demand for full Scottish independence.

By 1995 British Labour, under the leadership of Tony Blair, was stepping up its demands for Scottish home rule. Blair dramatically claimed that if the Conservatives continued to refuse Scotland more control over its own governance, a violent "liberation movement" similar to the Provisional IRA in Northern Ireland would arise. Indeed, around that time so-called Tartan Terrorists sent letter bombs to Blair and George Robertson in Inverness. Robertson was the shadow Scotland secretary in the opposition Labour Party's Shadow Cabinet, whose posts mirrored those in the actual governing cabinet. He helped formulate Labour policy, and advised Blair, the party leader. More Scots were now supporting the SNP. In 1995 polls showed support for it had risen to 26 percent in Scotland, close to its mid-1970s level. A *Glasgow Herald* poll found that 50 percent of Scots favored devolution, while a full 30 percent supported full Scottish independence. Meanwhile, the SNP continued to oppose devolution; its leader Alex Salmond maintained in *Focus Magazin* on March 20, 1995, that "Right now Scotland has no status whatsoever. It would have only second-class status as a devolved region."

The Conservative Party was staunch in its opposition as well, but for different reasons. It argued that devolution would lead to higher taxes in Scotland, which already paid three pence more per pound than the English in income tax. The tax increase would, in turn, cause an economic recession as outside investors fled Scotland. On the other hand, Tories warned, if Labour tried to keep Scottish taxes artificially low, it would face a revolt from taxpayers in England. Conservatives also raised the West Lothian question anew, the situation in which Scots have a say in English affairs but not the other way around. Finally, they maintained that, rather than preserving the Union as Labour hoped it would, devolution presented, in former Prime Minister John Major's words, "an absolute danger to the institutions of the United Kingdom," that would only hasten the breakup of the union.

New Labour and Devolution

By 1996 Tony Blair was well along transforming his party from socialist "old" Labour to "New Labour." Devolution took its place in the debate over broader constitutional change being

TONY BLAIR

1953– Tony Blair was born in Edinburgh, Scotland, in 1953, but he grew up in Durham City in the north of England, where his father Leo Blair worked as a lawyer and university lecturer. When Tony Blair was only ten years old, his father was forced to abandon a run for the House of Commons after suffering a debilitating stroke. Blair later called this the event that spurred him into politics. He attended Fettes College in Edinburgh before entering Oxford University to study law. While in college, Blair was active as an actor and musician, fronting a local rock band called The Ugly Rumors. While practicing as a young lawyer he met Cherie Booth, also a lawyer. They were married in 1980, and by 2001 had four children together.

In 1982 Blair made his first run for a seat in the House of Commons but was defeated. A year later, however, he won election as a Labour candidate. The year 1983 was one in which Labour suffered its worst defeat since 1935 and, witnessing that defeat, Blair began to consider how the Labour Party might be reformed to make it a relevant, vital force in British politics once again. By 1985 Blair had caught the eye of Labour's top leader, Neil Kinnock. Between 1987 and 1992, Blair served as the Labour spokesman on trade and industry with special responsibility for consumer affairs and the city of London; the shadow secretary of state for energy; the shadow secretary of state for employment; and, in 1992, shadow home secretary, one of the leading posts in the Labour ranks. By 1994 Kinnock had been replaced by Scotsman John Smith as the party head. When Smith died unexpectedly in 1994, Tony Blair, at the age of 41, was named to replace him.

As the new leader, Blair set about to bring the Labour Party into modern times. In 1995 the party voted to drop Clause Four of its constitution, which defined its socialist goals of "collective ownership of the means of production, distribution and exchange." Blair also reduced the influence of British labor unions, whose intractable demands in the late 1970s were considered

TONY BLAIR. *(AP/Wide World Photos. Reproduced by permission.)*

partly responsible for the success of Margaret Thatcher. Its leftist past behind, Blair announced that Labour was the party of the radical center, that it advocated—like the Conservatives—fiscal responsibility rather than welfare state spending and taxation. He called his party "New Labour."

In May 1997 Blair led the Labour Party to its biggest victory ever, 419 seats out of 659 in the House of Commons. At 44 he was the youngest man to be named British prime minister since 1812. That decisive mandate from the voters encouraged Blair to push on with his policy of devolution, educational reform, and further reduction of the British welfare state. Tony Blair has advocated British presence in the European Union, although the country has, as of 2001, declined to participate in the European Monetary Union. Tony Blair will undoubtedly go down in history as a visionary politician who transformed the Labour Party and British politics.

advocated by the party. Its program included parliamentary reform, including the revocation of the right to hereditary seats in the House of Lords and a system of proportional representation in the House of Commons, an overhauling of the court system, and a greater emphasis on individual civil rights. The program also included plans for greater self-rule in Wales, and a mayor for the city of London, who for the first time in history would be elected by the city's residents.

On May 1, 1997, Blair's Labour Party won a stunning victory over incumbent Prime Minister John Major and the Conservative Party. Significantly, Scottish Tories did not win a single seat in the House of Commons. The first act of the new

A WORKMAN PUTS UP A LABOUR PARTY POSTER BEFORE THE 1999 EUROPEAN ELECTIONS. THE LABOUR PARTY, LED BY TONY BLAIR (LEFT), WAS A VOCAL PROPONENT FOR THE ESTABLISHMENT OF THE SCOTTISH PARLIAMENT. *(CORBIS CORPORATION (Bellevue). Reproduced by permission.)*

government was to announce that a referendum on devolution would be held in Scotland and Wales in September 1997. It empowered a panel to draw up formal proposals for a devolution plan, which appeared in July 1997 as the government White Paper "Scotland's Parliament." Two separate questions were put before Scottish voters: (1) Should Scotland have its own parliament, with broad powers to legislate in most areas directly affecting Scotland, with the exception of constitutional politics, defense, foreign affairs, social welfare, taxation, and finance policy which were retained by Westminster? (2) Should the new parliament be granted limited powers of taxation, namely to be able to raise or lower tax rates set by the British parliament by 3 percent? Welsh voters were asked only to approve the formation of an assembly—it was specifically not called a parliament—with executive powers only, most notably allocating funds voted to Wales by the British parliament. The assembly could not, however, make law.

Unlike in 1979 a broad political coalition supported devolution in 1997. Each party had its own devolution agenda, however. Labour supported devolution as a way of preserving the political order in the United Kingdom; the Liberal Democrats hoped devolution would lead to a British federal state of more-or- less autonomous political entities, a sort of United States of Britain; the SNP saw it as

a stepping stone to full independence. The Conservatives continued to oppose devolution. Their heavy losses in the 1997 election had left them virtually devoid of support in Scotland, and they could only hope that the differing goals of proponents might foil passage of the referendum.

The Scottish referendum took place on September 11, 1997. More than 60 percent of Scottish residents participated in the referendum, and both Scottish measures passed by large majorities. Nearly 75 percent voted in favor of a Scottish parliament; more than 63 percent supported limited fiscal sovereignty for Scotland. The results were a reversal of those in 1979, because other factors had changed. Unlike 1979, the Scottish Labour Party, labor unions, and even the SNP supported devolution wholeheartedly; in 1979 Scottish voters were indifferent to devolution, but by 1997 the issue had become an important one for them. In 1979 many Scots believed Labour's support of devolution was merely an electoral ploy; by 1997 the less ideological and more pragmatic campaign convinced Scottish voters that their interests would really be represented.

Scottish and Welsh devolution was enacted into law later in 1998. Created by the British parliament, the Scottish parliament could theoretically be done away with again by Westminster if, for example, the Conservatives came to power again. However, the consensus was that once the new parliament had established its sovereignty, it was unlikely to be dismantled without serious domestic strife, particularly since it had received such an overwhelming majority of the Scottish vote.

Unlike the British parliament, the makeup of the new Scottish parliament, was not determined by a simple winner-take-all vote in each district. A proportional system was adopted in which two-thirds of its 129 members were chosen by majority vote in districts. The other one-third were awarded on a proportional basis to every party that got at least 6 percent of the popular vote. The system was a major concession made by the Labour Party to the Liberal Democrats, who were expected to govern in coalition when the first parliament was formed in 2000. It assured representation to all important parties, would foster cooperation rather than the confrontation common in Westminster, and would head off the kind of internal tensions that had wrecked the Unionist-dominated Northern Ireland assembly in 1972. As in Westminster, the leader of the winning party or coalition was seen as the Scottish First Minister. There was talk of abolishing the Scottish Office but it the end it continued in existence, a liaison between Westminster and Holyrood, the Edinburgh district where the Scottish parliament is located.

The Scottish vote may not have marked the end of the United Kingdom, but it certainly might be seen as the death knell for British centralized government. Almost as soon as the votes had been counted, assemblies were proposed for England as a possible solution to the West Lothian problem, as well as for English regions who felt disadvantaged by the new powers of Scotland and Wales.

The elections for the Scottish and Welsh parliaments were held on May 9, 1999. Coinciding with local council elections nationwide and followed by spring elections for the European Parliament, the elections were seen as a referendum on Labour Party policies. The Scottish Labour ticket came out with fifty-six seats. Without a clear majority it formed a coalition government with the Liberal Democrats. Donald Dewar, until then Blair's Scotland Secretary, became the Scottish First Minister As expected, the Conservatives fared badly, and the SNP emerged as the opposition party.

Devolution in Wales

Wales, a large region to the west of England, was slowly absorbed into England in the twelfth and thirteenth centuries, rather than being con-

quered by it. The two were formally joined by an act of union in 1536. When the union took place, Wales integrated English civic and legal institutions. Those facts would make devolution in Wales different in many respects from devolution in Scotland. Prior to its absorption into England, Wales had been a mishmash of principalities controlled by the English and Welsh chieftains under the nominal reign of a Welsh prince. Wales, however, had never existed as a nation with a central government of it own. Unlike Scotland, no Welsh government, legal, religious, or social institutions survived the union with England to underpin a sense of Welsh national identity or to encourage them to regain a lost Welsh government.

Hence, the sense of identity felt by the Welsh is much less political than its counterpart in Scotland. "Welshness," Jonathan Bradbury wrote in *British Regionalism and Devolution: The Challenges of State Reform and European Integration* (1997), "came to be expressed primarily in a cultural sense through religious non-conformism and the Welsh language." Cultural identity has flourished in Wales. Its primary exponent, the Welsh language, is recognized in Wales as the official second language on a par with English; all street signs are written in both languages; Welsh is taught in the schools; and Welsh civil servants are required to be bilingual. Spoken by nearly 20 percent of the population of Wales —compared to about 2 percent for Gaelic in Scotland—Welsh is a living, even thriving, language, and it acts as a powerful anchor for Welsh identity. The Welsh nationalist party Plaid Cymru was originally formed as a cultural defense organization, not as a political group.

Secure in its cultural identity, Wales was quite comfortable in its union with England. It never chafed under rule from Westminster as the Scottish often did. Without separate legal and civic institutions, Wales was closer politically to England than was Scotland. No separate committees were necessary in the House of Commons to draft Welsh legislation. An advisory council for Wales was established in Westminster in 1948, but it was not until 1964 that a Welsh Office, modeled on the Scottish Office, was created. As a result of all these factors, through the years devolution was a far less urgent matter to the Welsh than to the Scots.

Wales occasionally experienced spurts of nationalist activity. In the late 1960s, Plaid Cymru became political in response to what it saw as English neglect of the Welsh economy. In the late 1980s, Wales experienced a short flare of violent nationalism, complete with bomb threats and de-

THE SECOND AGE OF DEMOCRACY

British Prime Minister Tony Blair has often spoken publicly about devolution in the United Kingdom, a process of which he is strongly supportive. In "Democracy's Second Age" (September 14, 1996), *The Economist* relays Blair's words, capturing his vision of devolution and what he believes it will accomplish.

We are now in the Second Age of democracy. It is time to give it a second wind.... Britain is, however, struggling to find its way after the collapse of the grand twentieth century ideologies of left and right. These too often placed ends above means, grand projects of social or economic reconstruction above the democratic requirement for consent, self- government and respect for rights. The result has been eighty years since the first world war of a steady accretion of power to ministers....

Most political decisions of concern to citizens affect their immediate locality. The revival of local government must be the prime means for achieving the second objective of taking government closer to the people. Local government's democratic voice needs strengthening, by establishing a closer engagement between local authorities and their electors. This is why I am so strongly attached to the principle of elected mayors for London and our leading cities—generating local chief executives with a direct mandate, able to mobilise their communities behind urban renewal as mayors across Europe and the United States do....

Strengthening the intermediate tier between London and the localities is also necessary. Here again our agenda is one of sensible, incremental change to meet modern democratic demands. The Scottish Office was established as long ago as 1885 to provide a Scottish dimension to administration north of the border. But it is Westminster-controlled and Westminster-oriented. The Scottish people rightly insist on something more democratic, in the form of a Scottish parliament with legislative powers. The Tories claim that this would threaten the unity of the United Kingdom, yet they rightly consider their proposals for devolved government in Northern Ireland as perfectly compatible with the union. Their opposition to our decentralisation plans ignores the wisdom of the ages, as well as concrete experience in other countries. As William Gladstone, the Victorian prime minister, said: "The concession of local self-government is not the way to sap or impair, but the way to strengthen and consolidate unity."

Precisely this rationale has led every other large European democracy, including France and Spain with centralising traditions as strong as Britain's, to create a regional tier between central government and local authorities. Spain, for example, has met regional aspirations of varying strengths by adopting a rolling programme of devolution, across a lengthy timespan, in line with the flow of popular sentiment.

We are proposing a similarly refined approach for the United Kingdom. Scotland with its distinct national, legal, and cultural institutions is manifestly in a class of its own. Even the current secretary of state for Scotland, Michael Forsyth, concedes that once a Scottish parliament is established, it will be here to stay. In their own separate ways, Wales and London also have powerful claims to—and their people want—their own authorities.

Across the rest of England, popular enthusiasm for a regional political voice varies greatly. Our policy reflects this, allowing greater regional government as people demand it. In the north-east and north-west demand for greater powers is strong. In other places, there is less demand. So be it."

mands for independence. Despite these incidents nationalism never caught on with the Welsh people in general, and even the nationalist Plaid Cymru does not advocate Welsh independence. Welsh home rule was called for regularly over the years, along with Irish and Scottish, but this was more out of the wish to devolve power equally to all British regions rather than to satisfy any broad-based Welsh demands. The 1979 referendum results are indicative of the degree of Welsh interest for the idea of devolution—with voter turnout of about 58 percent, only 20.3 percent supported the formation of a national assembly in Wales.

In recognition, perhaps, of Wales' different political roots, the Labour Party offered Wales a devolution plan very different from its plan for Scotland. While a "parliament" was planned for Scotland, Wales was to get an "assembly." That semantic distinction reflected the significantly different authority each body would have. Scotland's was to be a legislative body that could enact laws and raise taxes for Scotland. The Welsh assembly, on the other hand, would be able to administer grant money for health and education provided by Westminster and to specially tailor laws passed in Westminster for its Welsh constituency. Furthermore, those executive powers would not be exercised by the Welsh assembly as whole, but were to be delegated in an unspecified manner to the first secretary and the cabinet he formed. Three of the four Welsh political parties, Labour, the Liberal Democrats, and Plaid Cymru, supported the devolution plan as presented in the 1997 referendum. The idea was not very popular with the Welsh people though, in part because many Welsh believed the money for such an assembly could be better spent elsewhere. During the campaign leading up to the referendum, several Labour MPs broke ranks and came out against the idea.

The Blair government was nervous that the Welsh would defeat the proposal, so it scheduled their referendum a week after Scotland's in hopes of capitalizing on a bandwagon effect. As returns came in during referendum day, the assembly seemed doomed to defeat. Only a heavy "yes" vote from Carmarthenshire, one of the last Welsh districts to report, gave devolution proponents a victory with the narrowest of majorities, a mere 50.3 percent. The Conservative Party, which had opposed the new assembly, maintained that a majority of 0.6 percent—equivalent to a quarter of the Welsh electorate—was not good enough. Lord Stoddart, a Labourite who opposed the assembly, told the newspaper the *Independent,* (September 20, 1997) "Even the National Union of Mineworkers requires 55 to 45 per cent before going on strike." Nonetheless, legislation for the assembly in Cardiff went forward.

By the end of 1997, British Prime Minister Tony Blair was known as a champion of government decentralization. But following the Welsh referendum, Blair made a tactical error that damaged his reputation and hurt the Welsh Labour Party in the elections for the Wales Assembly. He forced the Welsh Labour Party to accept his unpopular Wales secretary, Alun Michael, as party leader over the more charismatic favorite, Rhodi Morgan. Almost from the start, Michael was rebuked as the puppet of the national party. As a result, when the Wales Assembly was elected in spring 1999, many Labour voters did not go to the polls and the party won only twenty-eight of the sixty seats, forcing it to form an unstable minority government. Michael was forced to be cautious with his issues among the other parties in the assembly, lest he force a vote of no confidence. Lack of support among the Liberal Democrats and Welsh Labour in a debate over the Welsh budget finally forced him to resign in 2000. The Welsh Labour Party subsequently elected Rhodi Morgan as its new party leader.

London Elects a Mayor

Blair's attempts to keep a hand in devolution's results backfired even worse in London's mayoralty election in 2000. Historically the city had been governed by borough or neighborhood councils rather than by an overarching local administration. For a while, London had a general authority, the Greater London Council (GLC), but that body was abolished by Margaret Thatcher's government in the 1980s. In 1997 the new Blair government decided to give London a municipal head of its own. In summer 1997 the government released a White Paper detailing its plans for London: a directly elected mayor with executive powers, along with a small assembly that would oversee the mayor's actions. "We expect the mayor to become a high-profile figure who will speak out on London's behalf and be listened to," the White Paper was noted as stating in *The Economist* (April 29, 2000). "Londoners will all know who their mayor is and have an opinion on how he or she is doing. This will change the face of London politics." Londoners supported Blair's proposals by a margin of almost three to one in a May 1998 referendum on the mayoral question. Almost at once, Jeffrey Archer, a best-selling author and a former Conservative MP, expressed interest in running for the office. Two candidates announced on the Labour side, Oscar-winning actress Glenda Jackson, an MP who has long been active in Labour politics, and Ken Livingstone.

Livingstone was a figure Blair did not want to see as London's new mayor. He represented "Old Labour"—the hardcore socialist wing which, in the view of Blair and his supporters, had destroyed the Labour Party and delivered the country to the Conservatives for 18 years. Livingstone had run the GLC in the mid-1980s, distributing public monies to various far-left causes and constantly taking advantage of his position to criticize the Thatcher government, until the prime minister had finally dissolved the council. Afterwards, Livingstone, by then known as "Red Ken," won a Labour seat in the House of Commons. He was just as outspoken in his criticism of New Labour as he had been of the Conservatives' policies, and he voted regularly against the party line. Unfortunately for the Labour leadership, Livingstone was also extremely popular among Londoners, who remembered his service on the GLC and who sympathized with many of his views, including his opposition to Blair's plan to privatize the London subway system, called the Tube.

Blair made up his mind that Livingstone would not be Labour's candidate for mayor, a decision that threatened to split the Labour Party. Ironically, an aide who served under both men told *The Economist* in "Life Under Ken" (May 6, 2000) that they were "the two most naturally gifted politicians in Britain. . . . both have mastered the crucial art of appearing low-key and likeable on television. Mr. Blair supplements his style with an air of great sincerity; Mr. Livingstone's particular forte is a subversive streak of humour, which simultaneously invites the audience to join him in poking fun at

KEN LIVINGSTONE WON THE MAYOR'S SEAT IN LONDON'S FIRST DIRECT ELECTION TO THAT POSITION. HE RECEIVED A MANDATE WITH 58 PERCENT OF THE VOTE, DESPITE OPPOSITION FROM THE RULING LABOUR PARTY. *(CORBIS CORPORATION (Bellevue). Reproduced by permission.)*

those in authority, and undermines the idea that he is a dangerous radical."

When early polls showed Livingstone far ahead of Jackson, Blair brought in Health Secretary Frank Dobson to run. Stacking the deck against Livingstone, the Labour Party announced that it would establish an "electoral college" to select its mayoral candidate. One-third of the college's votes would be go to London Labour Party members; one-third would be to Labour MPs, nearly all of whom are hardcore Blair supporters; and the other one-third to union members, who were also considered extremely loyal to the prime minister. Under those rules, Livingstone could win the unanimous vote of London Labour and still lose the nomination. Nonetheless, when he continued to lead in the polls, all Labour candidates were required to face a select party committee. Livingstone's interrogation lasted nearly four hours. In the end, Frank Dobson was named the Labour candidate.

The Labour Party was counting on Livingstone to not run as an independent if he failed to win the party's nomination. Livingstone, however, soon entered the race as an independent candidate. Soon he was threatening Labour with a major embarrassment if not an electoral debacle. By December 1999 he was leading the candidates of the three major parties by 38 percent. Because of Blair's machinations, Dobson was seen as a puppet of the central British Labour Party, much like Alun Michael in Wales. To make matters worse, Dobson was running third, behind the Conservative candidate, Steve Norris. Blair went on the attack against Livingstone in a series of meetings in London, but the upstart's strength continued to grow. "Blair's problem is that he has transplanted a clutch of American institutions onto a political culture that finds them alien," wrote Jonathan Freedland in the *New Republic* on January 10, 2000, "so he introduces an office that requires an independent individual—the mayoralty—yet demands that this individual conform to parliamentary-style party discipline." The election began to be as much about Londoners' feelings about the prime minister as it was about who they wanted to govern their city.

CONSTITUTIONAL REFORM

Britain does not have a formal written constitution, like the United States and many other western democracies do. Instead, it is comprised of a combination of custom and law. Unlike the United States, where reforms have to be ratified by each state, most constitutional reforms in the United Kingdom can be effected through the normal parliamentary process. As a result, the process of constitutional reform in Britain is much less arduous than in the United States.

When the British Labour Party formed a government in 1997, its promises for a broad palette of constitutional reforms included far more than its devolution measures. Progress on other reforms during Labour's first four years in office was, however, mixed.

In 1999 it put through its most radical program—reform of the upper house of Parliament, the House of Lords. The origins of the House of Lords extend to the time before the Norman conquest. It is composed of three types of peer: *hereditary peers, life peers,* and *lords spiritual.* Hereditary peers are members of the nobility who pass down their positions from one generation to the next. *Life peers* are nominated by the government on the basis of their contributions to the nation in business, science, culture, and other areas. Their peerages cannot be passed on to their children. The *lords spiritual* are high-ranking clergymen from the Church of England. The Blair government argued that it was an anachronism that seats in a modern parliament would not be elective and would be passed from father to son. A bill abolishing all but 92 of the 750 hereditary peerages passed in November 1999. The 92 remained to assist in the transition to meaningful new structures and functions for the House of Lords, and Labour was criticized for not implementing that additional reform.

During its campaign in 1997, Labour promised to introduce a system of proportional representation (PR) in the House of Commons. Currently MPs are chosen in winner-take-all elections in individual districts. Under a proportional system, districts would continue to elect representatives by majority. In addition, however, every party that won more than 6 percent of the vote nationally would be entitled to a proportionate number of seats in Commons, even if it had won no districts. Proportional representation guarantees that influential smaller parties will be represented in Parliament. Unfortunately, once the Labour Party won in 1997, PR seemed to disappear from its agenda. A number of Labour ministers oppose PR because they believe it would dilute Labour's strength in Commons. A promised referendum on the issue has never taken place. In spring 2001 Blair agreed to review PR for Westminster following the Scottish and Welsh elections in 2003.

In spring 2001 some Labour MPs called on Blair to go radically further with his reforms. This occurred after the daughter-in-law of Queen Elizabeth II, Sophie, Countess of Wessex, made unguarded comments about the Royal Family and leading British politicians, which were recorded by an undercover journalist. The publication of the so-called Sophie tapes followed a string of royal scandals that extend back to the 1960s. It convinced a number of Labour and Liberal Democratic politicians to call on Blair to take steps to overhaul the monarchy or even abolish it completely, perhaps upon the queen's death. Blair's spokespeople maintained he supported the monarchy as an institution. At any rate, it was acknowledged that such a debate would not begin before the parliamentary elections in late 2001.

A week before the election Livingstone had reached an astounding 51 percent in the polls; his nearest rival was Norris with 17 percent. Some observers, like Freedland, believed that Blair would rather see the Tories win the mayoralty than "Red Ken" Livingstone. Just before the election, two newspapers normally loyal to Labour publicly endorsed Norris—he was the only candidate with a shadow of a chance to defeat Red Ken.

On election day, May 4, 2000, Livingstone came away with 58 percent of the vote, giving him by far the largest democratic mandate of any politi-

cian in Britain. This large margin was expected to give Livingstone a good deal of political clout in British politics. At the same time, Labour was not able to win control of the Greater London Assembly, as it had expected. Instead it tied with the Conservatives, giving the control of power in the assembly to the Liberal Democrats and Greens, who had supported Livingstone. In other elections throughout Britain, Labour lost control of 16 local councils to the Tories.

Livingstone made his program clear immediately. He threatened to sue the government if it

What's in a Name? Great Britain, England, and the United Kingdom

In common parlance the terms "Great Britain," "England," and "United Kingdom" are frequently used as if they were interchangeable. Each, however, refers to a distinct geographical and political entity.

The British Isles are comprised primarily of Ireland (the Republic of Ireland and Northern Ireland) and Britain. Britain is comprised of England, Scotland, and Wales. "Great Britain" was formed in 1707 when the nations of England and Scotland were united. England and Wales had by that time already been united by treaties signed in 1536 and 1542.

English control of Ireland dated back to the time of King Henry VIII and earlier. It was not until 1801, however, that Great Britain and Ireland joined to form the United Kingdom, whose full name was originally the United Kingdom of Great Britain and Ireland. When an independent Irish republic was formed in 1921, the UK's full name was changed to United Kingdom of Great Britain and Northern Ireland.

went through with its plans to privatize the London Tube; he announced a plan to levy a surcharge on all drivers entering the center of London, as a way of controlling traffic gridlock there; and he demanded that the government allocate more money for transportation to the city. The election was a bitter personal blow to the prime minister, who made a point of leaving the country for election night. What many observers saw as a vibrant grassroots movement that posed a real radical alternative to New Labour policies, Blair's people considered an unwelcome resurgence of "the worst elements of the extreme Left which it took us 10 years to get rid of," as an unnamed minister told the *Sunday Telegraph* on May 7, 2000, in "The Day Labour Lost to Red Ken."

RECENT HISTORY AND THE FUTURE

In practice, devolution has turned out to be a slightly different beast than the Labour Party predicted during its original campaign for it, particularly in Scotland. Scoffing at the doubtful who felt

the planned Scottish parliament would throw the UK into turmoil, Blair painted a bright picture in which the UK and Scottish parliaments would always be able to cooperate smoothly. As it has worked out, not only have important issues split the two parliaments, they have split the Scottish and British Labour Parties which lead the two bodies. In retrospect, it seems clear that such conflict was inevitable. The Scottish party and parliament serve a different constituency than their British counterparts, and the political realities of Holyrood are far different from Westminster. Blair's Labour Party rules on its own from Westminster; Scottish Labour rules in a coalition with the Liberal Democrats and must compromise on many legislative issues. Blair's opposition in Westminster is the Conservative Party; in Holyrood, Labour faces the SNP, a party with a far different agenda from the Tories. Finally, Blair is the leader of all British Labour politicians, and, in principle, his national party formulates policy for the Scottish party. In the same way, the Scottish parliament is a creature of the British parliament and exists at Westminster's pleasure. Westminster's sovereignty is absolute in Britain; Holyrood's is limited, even within Scotland.

By 2001 the two Labour Parties had already clashed several times. "The problem," as *The Economist* summed it up on May 15, 1999, "is trying to maintain a national system for health and education, while allowing Scots to make their own policies." In general, the defining issue was money—the Scots wanted something different from what Westminster gave the rest of the nation, but it relied on money from Westminster to pay for it. The first split occurred when the Blair government introduced an obligatory £1,000 annual tuition fee for UK university students. Scots felt strongly that university education should be free, and the three parties in the Scottish parliament with Labour, including its coalition partner, the Liberal Democrats, wanted to repeal the tuition fee law. That put the leaders of Scottish Labour in a bind. Should they support the national party line against the rest of Parliament and risk a certain loss, or should they vote for repeal and embarrass and possibly alienate themselves from British Labour? At the last minute, Labour brokered a compromise with the Liberal Democrats that would allow resident Scottish students to defer tuition payments until after they had graduated and begun earning at least £25,000 a year.

A similar confrontation took place over a health care bill. Labour passed a law in Westminster specifying that nursing care for the elderly would be provided free of charge, but not the personal care that elderly shut-ins or invalids might require, such as the preparation of meals and help getting dressed. The government claimed it could not afford anything more. The Scottish Labour Party found itself under tremendous pressure from the Liberal Democrats to provide a complete package of free care for the elderly, and it ultimately supported the bill's passage into law against the wishes of the Blair government. Blair was faced with serious problems. If his government denied the added services to other parts of Britain, how could it justify allocating monies to Scotland for the services, in particular at a time when Scotland was already receiving nearly 20 percent more in pounds per capita from Westminster than England? Conservatives accused Labour, both British and Scottish, of threatening the cohesion of the Union. Labour ministers in Westminster felt not-so-subtle pressure to implement the program in all of Britain. There were other disagreements between Holyrood and Westminster over immigration and gay rights as well.

In short, devolution has caused what the newspaper *Scotland on Sunday* termed "a paradigm shift in Scottish politics." The Scottish parliament has to demonstrate to its constituency that it serves a valuable function in Scotland; Scottish Labour needs to show that it is not a mere extension of the national Labour Party. Thus the political focus in Scotland is on Scotland, more tightly than ever before, rather than on Britain as a whole. That, combined with the considerable influence of the SNP, is combining to make every politician in Scotland focused intensely on Scottish matters. The tendency was strengthened when the original First Minister of the Scottish parliament, Donald Dewar, died suddenly in late 2000. The two men who vied to succeed him, Henry McLeish and Jack McConnel, both staked their claim by hinting that they would strengthen Holyrood and stand up to London for Scottish interests. At the same time, Scottish MPs in Westminster were feeling more and more marginalized by the Scottish parliament.

The matter reached a climax in January 2001, when ministers at Holyrood caused a public uproar by referring to themselves as a "government" rather than an "executive," as specified in the Scotland Act that formed the Scottish authority. The utterance was considered a subtle usurpation of power. The word "government," critics said, could only be used to refer to Westminster. Around the same time, Dewar's successor Henry McLeish expressed the opinion that devolution was a process that could win the Scottish parliament even more powers.

Blair's Scotland Minister Helen Liddell was quick to state publicly that that was out of the question. It was believed that she was taking steps to bring Scottish Labour's platform back in line with British Labour's.

Robert Hazel, a spokesperson for the UK's Constitution Unit, said in the *Irish Times* on December 28, 2000, "This demand for more devolution is the greatest shift in the light of the first year's experience of devolution and the greatest challenge facing the UK government." A poll published in February 2001 by *Scotland on Sunday* showed that two-thirds of Scots favored giving Holyrood full control over taxation in Scotland; however, 75 percent of Scottish voters believed Scotland should remain in the United Kingdom.

Wales has been spared the conflict experienced in Scotland. The Welsh Assembly does not have legislative authority, so it is unable to repeal or alter laws from Westminster. Unlike the SNP in Scotland, the nationalist party in Wales, Plaid Cymru, does not advocate independence from Britain. It does advocate that the Assembly be given the same legislative and tax powers that the Scottish parliament has now. If the Assembly were to get that authority, the same Pandora's box would likely open for the Welsh. Whatever the outcome, Tony Blair's "New Labour" has definitely altered the face of government and the balance of power in the United Kingdom.

BIBLIOGRAPHY

Allerdyce, Jason and Francis Elliott. "Scots Demand Control Over Nation's Taxes," *Scotland on Sunday,* February 18, 2001, p. 1.

Allerdyce, Jason, and Murdo Macleod. "London Steps in after Devolution Shockwave Reaches South," *Scotland on Sunday,* January 28, 2001, p. 12.

"Arise, the Provisional Government of Scotland," *The Scotsman,* January 13, 2001, p. 13.

Barnett, Anthony. "Changing the Rules," *New Statesman & Society,* vol. 9, February 16, 1996, p. 16.

Bell, Alex. "Devolution Debate has Moved to Scots Nats' Ground," *Irish Times,* December 28, 2000, p. 53.

Blair, Tony. "Democracy's Second Age," *The Economist,* September 14, 1996, p. 55.

Bradbury, Jonathan and John Mawson. *British Regionalism and Devolution: The Challenges of State Reform and European Integration.* Regional Policy and Development Series 16, London: Jessica Kingsley Publishers, 1997.

Brand, Jack, and James Mitchell. "Home Rule in Scotland: The Politics and Bases of a Movement," in Bradbury, Jonathan, and John Mawson, *British Regionalism and Devolution: The Challenges of State Reform and Euro-*

pean Integration. Regional Policy and Development Series 16, London: Jessica Kingsley Publishers, 1997.

Brown, Colin. "Wales Decides: 'Yes' by a Whisker. Now the Deals Begin," *The Independent,* September 20, 1997, p. 4.

"The Centre Cannot Hold," *The Economist,* November 6, 1999.

"A City Grows Up," *The Economist,* April 29, 2000.

Dawson, Tim. "SNP Adjusts to Devolution," *New Statesman and Society,* September 29, 1995, p. 7.

"Dividing Lines," *The Economist,* January 8, 2000.

"Ende der Union?," *Focus Magazin,* March 20, 1995, Section: Ausland, no.12, p. 292–93.

Freedland, Jonathan. "Blair Witched," *New Republic,* January 10, 2000, p. 19.

Gaupp, P. "Schottlands Parlament in Edinburgh Eröffnet; Vorrang Volksnaher Festlichkeit vor Monarchischem Pomp," *Neue Zürcher Zeitung,* July 2, 1999, Section: Ausland, p. 1.

Grice, Andrew. "Blair and Kennedy Thrash Out PR Deal," *The Independent,* March 23, 2001, p. 4.

Guttenplan, D.D., and Maria Margaronis. "Letter from London," *The Nation,* 270, no.25 (2000):23.

"In Search of Consensus," *The Economist,* July 3, 1999.

Jones, George. "Hereditaries Go Down Fighting; 'Treason' Protest as Peers Vote to End 600 Years of History," *Daily Telegraph,* October 27, 1999.

"Labour MPs Snap at Ankles of Royals," *News Letter,* April 9, 2001, p. 7.

"Life under King Ken," *The Economist,* May 6, 2000.

Murphy, Joe and David Cracknell. "The Day Labour Lost to Red Ken," *London Sunday Telegraph,* May 7, 2000.

Rachman, Gideon. "The Disunited Kingdom," *Washington Quarterly,* 23, no.2 (2000):25.

"Tuition Fees: An Expensive Lesson," *The Economist,* May 15, 1999.

—Gerald E. Brennan

U.S. MILITARY PRESENCE AT WORLD PORTS: A WELCOME STAY?

Long-simmering feelings of neglect and broken promises felt by the islanders of Vieques, Puerto Rico, came to a climax on April 19, 1999, when a U.S. Navy F-18 fighter pilot dropped two 500-pound bombs nearly a mile off target, killing David Sanes Rodríguez, a Vieques civilian who worked as a security guard at Observation Post-1. Four others were injured. After the accident, which marked the first civilian death linked directly to the military training, the navy suspended all operations on Vieques until an investigation could be completed—but the pot had already boiled over. Within three days numerous Puerto Rican politicians were calling for a permanent end to the bombing, and protesters moved onto the firing range to set up resistance camps. Puerto Ricans quickly mobilized behind a common cause—the removal of the U.S. Navy from Vieques.

More than two years after the incident, tensions on the island have not eased. Although U.S. federal marshals removed protesters from restricted grounds in May 2000, and training maneuvers resumed using inert ordnance (artillery or weapons that will not explode), resistance to the navy's continued presence on Vieques remains strong, and emotions continue to run high. As proposed by the U.S. government under the Bill Clinton administration (1993–2001), Viequenses now wait to vote whether the navy should stay or go. According to the plan, two choices are available. First, Viequenses can choose to allow the navy to stay three more years and practice with inert bombs only. If approved, Vieques would receive US$40 million in economic aid. Second, Viequenses can vote to allow the navy to stay indefinitely and continue to use live bombs, for which Vieques would receive a total of $90 million in economic

THE CONFLICT

On April 19, 1999, a Marine Corps F-18 pilot, on a practice run on the Puerto Rican island of Vieques, misidentified his target and accidentally dropped two 500-pound bombs on Observation Post-1, killing a civilian security guard and injuring four others. The incident sparked large-scale protests against the navy's use of Vieques for live ammunitions training. Protests against U.S. military presence have also occurred in Okinawa and in the Philippines. The United States has tried to negotiate its continued stay at world ports by offering economic incentives, but this may not be enough to staunch the objections.

Health and Ecological
- Civilian health and environmental concerns due to extensive bombings have risen at various sites around U.S. military bases.

Social and Economic
- Nightclubs and prostitution are alleged to follow the establishment of U.S. military bases. These are developments that neighborhoods near the bases do not find desirable.

- Local populations have argued that the presence of the military inhibits tourist trade and other industries that could help the regions economically.

Political
- Puerto Rican Governor Sila Calderín openly opposes the navy's presence on Vieques and has attempted to stop the training maneuvers through court action.

- Dissent from the Philippine people and government resulted in the closing of Subic Naval Station and Clark Air Base, removing the U.S. military presence from the Philippines.

- Residents of Okinawa, Japan, have protested the continued presence of the U.S. military on the island.

- The United States continues to maintain a need for bases around the world, allowing it ready access to potential trouble spots. In return, the United States offers economic incentives to countries voicing opposition, which may provide assurance to the foreign governments, but not necessarily to the local people.

aid. Until the vote is held, scheduled for November 2001, the navy has agreed to reduce the numbers of practice days from 200 to 90 and to use only inert bombs.

Despite the concerns of island residents, the U.S. Navy is both unwilling and unable to move its training location to another site. At the heart of the navy's dilemma is the need to adequately prepare its forces for actual battle. Live ammunition training provides a highly realistic environment that allows military personnel to practice under the stress of combat conditions. Exposure to live ordnance is considered an essential prerequisite to ensure full combat readiness. Also, because the Vieques Inner Range is surrounded by a large area of low traffic airspace and deep-water sea space, it offers a unique and unmatched opportunity for the practice of co-ordinated attacks that can include submarines, surface ships, amphibious landing crafts, and air-planes. The navy argues that no other viable place exists that is adequately suited to provide for such extensive coordinated training and quickly points out that many of the units that took part in the military operations during the Persian Gulf War (1991) and in Kosovo were trained on Vieques.

The situation in Vieques is representative of a new era in U.S. military presence around the world. As the twenty-first century progresses, the U.S. military has encountered increasing pressures to reform its ideology of globally located bases to account for growing concerns over human rights, environmental issues, national sovereignty, and in-creasing disapproval of U.S. interventionism. The resistance and resentment to the presence of the U.S. military baffles many in the United States who view U.S. presence as a benevolent act of protec-tion, one that provides a safe environment for the growth of democracy worldwide. As communities continue to battle against the invasion of their lands by U.S. troops, the U.S. military continues to search for effective methods of training and deploy-ment of its forces.

HISTORICAL BACKGROUND

On January 16, 1893, at the request of the *haoles* (white foreigners), the USS *Boston* sailed into Hawaii, and 150 American soldiers marched to the palace of Queen Liliuokalani. With U.S. Marines in place, the self-appointed civilian "Committee on Public Safety" declared the monarchy dissolved and announced the creation of the Republic of Hawaii. Five years later the United States annexed Hawaii, and the island's newspaper headlined "Hawaii Be-comes the First Outpost of a Greater America."

PROTESTS AGAINST THE PRESENCE OF U.S. MILITARY BASES HAVE INCREASED IN OKINAWA, JAPAN, AND VIEQUES, PUERTO RICO. THE UNITED STATES CLOSED ITS BASES IN THE PHILIPPINES IN 1992. *(AP/Wide World Photos. Reproduced by permission.)*

Also in the Pacific Ocean, Wake and Midway Is-lands, along with American Samoa, became U.S. colonized lands, and helped breach the wide ex-panse of ocean that separated the United States from Asia and Oceania. Other new strategic mili-tary acquisitions came about as the result of the Spanish-American War (1898). The Philippines, Guam, Puerto Rico, and Cuba, all formerly Span-ish colonies, were taken over by the United States during the war. By 1938 the United States had established military bases in Panama, Cuba, Puerto Rico, and the Virgin Islands. The Philippines and Hawaii served as the major naval hubs in the Pa-cific, with smaller outposts at Midway, Wake, and Guam. Prior to World War II (1939–45), how-ever, U.S. overseas military basing did not present a dominating presence around the globe. Japan, Great Britain, France, the Netherlands, Italy, Por-tugal, and Denmark all had a more extensive basing system than did the United States.

World War II Base Expansion

As U.S. involvement in World War II (1939–45) became increasingly likely, the United States stepped up the development of its military bases in the Atlantic, the Caribbean, and South America. In accordance with the 1941 Lend-Lease Accord with Great Britain, the United States traded 50 destroyers for long-term leases in British territories in the Western Hemisphere. As a result, U.S. troops were stationed in Bermuda, the Bahamas, Jamaica, Antigua, St. Lucia, Trinidad, British Guyana, and Newfoundland. The ideology behind the accelerated establishment of bases in these areas was twofold: first, the United States wished to create a defensive barrier against an air or submarine assault by Germany; second, the United States moved into new areas in an attempt to preempt other nations. In other words, the sites were important for the advantages they allowed the United States, and also because U.S. presence denied a potential enemy the opportunity to enjoy those same advantages. As the United States became entrenched in World War II the U.S. basing system grew rapidly and in unprecedented numbers. Having entered the war with less than 100 overseas sites, by the end of World War II the United States' rapidly expanded basing system included more than 2,000 bases located throughout the world, occupying the lands of at least 70 different foreign nations.

Base development during World War II had a significant impact on the American mentality regarding overseas basing. Prior to the war, decisions on base expansion most commonly evolved from one of two viewpoints. First, some strategists objected to building any bases on foreign soil, arguing that doing so not only needlessly aggravated potential enemies but also would very likely pull the United States into unwanted international conflicts. Second, a counter viewpoint suggested that expanding the U.S. military basing system would serve as a preemptive move that would inhibit potential enemies from becoming aggressors against the United States. In both cases the arguments were formed from an isolationist perspective—the best way to keep the United States out of international conflicts.

After World War II the fundamental assumption of isolationism was replaced by a growing trend toward internationalism. Rather than using bases as a method to preclude the United States from involvement in international activities, overseas military basing came to be viewed as an inherent right and responsibility of a superpower nation. By extending its military presence around the world, the United States could determine the course of international events. The dominant view became that planting U.S. military bases on foreign soil was a positive and necessary activity to preserve world peace and to protect the interests of the United States, especially against the perceived imminent threat of Soviet aggression.

The Post-War Years and New Paradigms

Despite the change in ideology, in the postwar years the United States dismantled as many as half of its existing overseas bases. The reasons for the reduction in the number of bases were threefold. Perhaps most importantly, after World War II ended the United States no longer maintained the number of military personnel to staff all of its bases. The demobilization of troops and resources necessitated that priorities be re-established and that base locations no longer deemed of vital importance in peacetime be closed. Additionally, other nations pressured the United States to return bases used during the war. Australia, New Zealand, Iceland, and Denmark all pushed the United States to abandon bases on their lands. The British and French also strongly supported the return of bases built on former colonial areas to their control. Finally, advances in transportation technology made bases used as way stations obsolete. Airplanes and ships could travel farther and faster than ever before; therefore, refueling stations could be fewer and farther between, and strategically, battles could be waged effectively from greater distances.

The trend toward base reduction following World War II was reversed when the United States entered the Korean War (1950–53). During the conflict with Korea in the 1950s and extending into the 1970s during the Vietnam War (1956–75), the U.S. basing system once again expanded, increasing approximately 40 percent, with most of the new bases being built in the Pacific and in Europe (especially in former West Germany). After the United States withdrew from Vietnam, however, the number of bases once again began to decline. The conflicts in Korea and Vietnam did not receive the wholehearted support of the American public, as did World War II, and in the aftermath of the Vietnam War, a general sense of being unwelcome and overly committed began to invade the American psyche. Although the ideology of the United States' legitimate right to a worldwide military presence was not undermined, it did become more acceptable to question the need for wholesale military installations. Also, it was not unexpected that in peacetime questions of cost-effectiveness came more into consideration. The bases that were left intact or expanded to take over functions from

CHRONOLOGY

1893–1938 The United States establishes military bases in Panama, Cuba, Puerto Rico, the Philippines, the Virgin Islands, and Guam, Wake, and Midway islands.

April 26, 1942 The Puerto Rican legislature adopts Law 54, which gives the U.S. Navy the title to 26,000 of Vieques's 33,000 square miles. Vieques residents are relocated to a strip of land in the center of the island.

1945 Despite the end of World War II, the United States maintains its presence on the island of Okinawa, Japan. It later uses Okinawa as a staging base for B-29 bombers during the Korean War.

1947 The Philippines gains its independence and signs an agreement with the United States allowing it 99 years of rent-free use of 16 military installations, as well as the administration of the town of Olongapo.

1950s Farmers in Okinawa protest for the return of lands confiscated by the United States.

1950s–1970s The U.S. basing system expands by about 40 percent, with new bases built in the Pacific and in Europe.

1966 The base agreement between the Philippines and the United States is revised so that sovereignty of the land occupied by U.S. bases reverts to the Philippines. The rent-free stay is reduced to 25 years.

1969 Protests against the U.S. military presence erupt in Okinawa after a B-52 bomber crashes near a densely populated neighborhood on the island.

1971 Widespread protests begin on Culebra, Puerto Rico, calling for the U.S. Navy to withdraw from the island. Culebra was used as a live ammunitions training ground since World War II.

1972 Despite protests, an agreement is signed between the United States and Japan to allow continued U.S. military access to about 20 percent of Okinawa.

June 1974 The United States announces that it will cease weapons training on Culebra by July 1, 1975.

October–December 1983 The United States uses Vieques as the main training location for its invasion of Grenada.

1991 Mount Pinatubo erupts in the Philippines, damaging Clark Air Base. The United States decides to abandon the base rather than restore it.

September 13, 1991 The Philippine Senate rejects the Treaty of Friendship, Peace, and Cooperation, which would have extended the base treaty agreement with the United States by another 10 years.

September 1992 The United States formally turns over Subic Bay Naval Base to the Philippine government.

1994 Governor Rómero files a petition with the U.S. Congress requesting that the navy turn control of 8,000 acres of land over to the Vieques municipal government.

1995 Three U.S. military personnel are accused of abducting and raping a young Okinawan girl. Tensions run high on the island, and the governor of Okinawa announces that he does not support the re-signing of land-lease agreements with the U.S. Navy, set to expire in 1996.

April 19, 1999 One man is killed and four others are injured when the U.S. Navy drops two 500-pound bombs more than one mile off target on Vieques. The incident fuels widespread support for the navy's departure from Vieques; the navy temporarily suspends all maneuvers on the firing range.

May 28, 1999 The navy admits that ammunition tipped with depleted uranium had been deployed on Vieques.

July 4, 1999 Approximately 50,000 people march at Roosevelt Roads Naval Station in Ceiba, Puerto Rico, in protest of the U.S. military's presence.

July 19, 1999 The navy reverses an earlier denial that it used napalm on Vieques in 1993.

December 3, 1999 President Clinton offers $40 million in economic incentives for Puerto Rico and recommends that the navy resume training in Vieques with inert weapons for the next five years.

January 31, 2000 Governor Rosselló announces an agreement between Puerto Rico and the United States, which calls for a referendum vote by Viequenses to determine whether the navy will stay or leave.

February 21, 2000 An estimated 85,000 to 150,000 people march the streets of San Juan, Puerto Rico, to protest the agreement.

April 26, 2001 A federal judge refuses to block the resumption of naval bombing on Vieques, finding insufficient evidence that the planned exercises would cause irreparable harm to citizens.

April 27–May 2, 2001 Protesters storm the gates of the live fire range on Vieques and disrupt training maneuvers; 170 people are arrested.

April 30, 2001 The U.S. Navy transfers 8,000 acres of land over to the Viequenses, the federal government, and conservation groups.

defunct bases were selected on the post-war rationale of the immediate need to control the spread of communism and contain the Soviet Union.

During the last decade of the twentieth century the strategic placement of military bases outside the United States was seriously challenged when the Cold War effectively ended with the dismantling of the Soviet Union. Since World War II, U.S. military strategy had dictated policy aimed at defending against the United States' archenemy, the Soviet Union. When the Soviet Union collapsed it created a new political and military environment around the world that called for new paradigms to be employed. Many coastal communities, usually small and often poor, that played host to the U.S. military for more than 60 years began calling for the United States to vacate. Serious questions of environmental health, toxic contamination, and quality of life began to garner increasing support from politicians and public figures who have the power to bring these issues to the forefront. For example, resistance to U.S. military presence has grown not only on Vieques, but also on the Japanese island of Okinawa and in the Philippines.

Okinawa

Okinawa is an island off the coast of Japan that came under Japanese control in 1871. The island became known to the world in 1944 when Allied forces began their offensive toward mainland Japan, one island at a time. Hoping to buy time, the Japanese attempted to hold Okinawa at all costs, a decision that resulted in the deaths of more than 95,000 Japanese soldiers, 12,500 Allied soldiers, and 150,000 Okinawan civilians—one-fourth of the island's population. Following World War II the United States retained a dominating military force on the island, using it as a staging base for B-29 bombers during the Korean War. As a conquered people, Okinawans had little choice but to accept U.S. military presence. By the 1950s, however, farmers began to protest for the return of their lands confiscated by the United States. In 1969 massive protests erupted after a B-52 bomber crashed on the island, nearly hitting a densely populated housing district and a munitions dump believed to hold nuclear weapons. Although the massive demonstrations resulted in the transfer of Okinawa from U.S. back to Japanese control, the agreement, implemented in 1972, provided for the continued access of the U.S. military to approximately 20 percent of the island.

Discontent resurfaced on Okinawa in 1995 when three U.S. military personnel abducted and raped a 12-year-old Okinawan girl. Although the crime was received with outrage in both Japan and the United States, Okinawans were further incensed by the delay in handing over the three suspects—a navy seaman and two marines—to Japanese authorities. The incident evoked long-held feelings of neglect by the central government in Tokyo and of abuse by the presence of some 30,000 U.S. military personnel, for whom this was not the first crime committed against the Okinawan residents. As a result of increasing tensions the governor of Okinawa announced that, against the wishes of Japan's prime minister, he would not support the re-signing of land-lease agreements with the U.S. Navy that were to expire in 1996.

In 1996 a nonbonding referendum was held on Okinawa regarding the reduction of U.S. forces on the island. According to the results a vast majority of Okinawans favor a gradual reduction of troops, although most favor a continued alliance with the United States. Okinawans, who must contend with the disruptive military exercises, the widespread development of nightclubs, drugs, and prostitution, and the imposition on their land, are simply tired of dealing with the vast U.S. military machine that dominates their island. The hit-and-run death of an 18-year-old Okinawan woman in 1998 by a U.S. Marine, who was charged with drunken driving, leaving the scene of an accident, and professional negligence, added even more public support to a reduction in the U.S. military's presence.

Although the U.S. Department of Defense agreed to scale back its operations somewhat, it has encountered two obstacles. Like Vieques, the military must find alternatives to the present location. The Japanese are adamantly opposed to moving more U.S. troops onto the Japanese mainland. Additionally, U.S. military strategists remain committed to a strong presence in the area. Whereas during the Cold War the placement of troops was primarily to thwart Soviet aggression, in the twenty-first century the U.S. military views Okinawa as a necessary location to keep tabs on the growing military might of China. In the eyes of Okinawans, like the invasion during World War II, the island is a sacrifice the Japanese government is willing to make and is strategically important enough that the United States will retain a continued significant force there into the foreseeable future.

The Philippines

The United States began developing a basing system on the Philippines after wresting control of the islands from Spain in 1898. Subic Naval Station was completed in 1904 and became the U.S. Navy's

DEMONSTRATORS WALK PEACEFULLY TOWARDS THE WHITE HOUSE, PROTESTING THE CONTINUED U.S. MILITARY USE OF BASES LIKE THOSE IN VIEQUES AND OKINAWA. *(AP/Wide World Photos. Reproduced by permission.)*

premiere ship repair and supply station. Although much of the base structure was scuttled by U.S. forces before retreating from the Japanese during World War II, the lands were reclaimed in 1945, and the bases were reactivated. In 1947, a year after the United States granted the Philippines full independence, both countries signed a military bases agreement, which allowed the United States 99 years of rent-free use of 16 military installations, including the administration of the town of Olongapo, which was subsequently turned over to Philippine control in 1959. During the Korean and

Vietnam Wars, Subic Bay and Clark Air Base became major staging areas. The site also became one of the best known locations for entertaining troops. In Olongapo, more than 500 bars, clubs, and bathhouses developed outside the gates of Subic Bay to service the U.S. military men, and prostitution became widespread. Similarly, in Angeles City, another 450 clubs and bars sprang up outside the gates of Clark Air Station.

As discontent with U.S. military presence emerged, the low rumble of resistance was felt in the revision of the base agreement, amended in

VIEQUES VS. THE U.S. NAVY

In some places on Vieques, a small island six miles off the east coast of Puerto Rico, the scenery looks like a picture-postcard of a beautiful Caribbean island—palm trees, pristine beaches, and clear blue water lapping up on shore. Other places look like a war zone. The explosion of bombs and the eruption of heavy artillery and gunfire regularly disrupt the serenity of this Caribbean paradise. Segments of the eastern coast are a wasteland, decimated by 60 years of military assault, and the eastern edge of Vieques has more craters per square mile than the surface of the moon.

On March 17, 1942, the U.S. Navy expropriated two-thirds of the 21-mile by 4-mile island of Vieques to establish a military base and training site linked to the Roosevelt Roads military complex on the mainland of Puerto Rico, which is one of the largest U.S. naval installations in the world. As home to the Atlantic Fleet Weapons Training Facility, the United States military considers Vieques to be vitally important to maintaining battle readiness because it is the only place where U.S. Marines can practice synchronized aerial, offshore, and amphibious attacks. The U.S. military, however, has come under tremendous pressure from Viequenses, Puerto Ricans, and sympathetic U.S. mainlanders to vacate the island.

In 1947 the U.S. Department of Interior released a plan to move all remaining Vieques residents to St. Croix. The plan resurfaced in 1961 when the Department of Defense announced its intentions to abolish the municipality of Vieques and clear the island for the navy. The plan was abandoned after protests supported by the local government, including Puerto Rican Governor Munoz Marín. Again in 1964 the navy attempted to extend its control on the island by taking over the southern coast. The Committee to Defend Vieques, headed by Mayor António Rivera, was established to defeat the plan. Although the navy aborted its efforts to secure the additional lands, its failure to expand the local airport as requested by the Viequenses caused the Woolnor Corporation to abandon its plans to build a $9 million tourist complex on the island. The episode left hard feelings on both sides.

Tensions increased again in April 1989, when the navy evicted a family of squatters from navy-controlled lands. In 1993 the Committee for the Rescue and Development of Vieques was established, working on the goal of four Ds: demilitarization, decontamination, devolution (return of all lands to Viequenses), and economic development. In 1994 Governor Roméro filed petitions in Congress to request that the navy be required to turn over control of the 8,000 acres on the western end of the island to the Vieques municipal government. General feelings of discontent that had long simmered below the surface erupted on April 19, 1999, when civilian David Sanes Rodríguez was accidentally killed during a military drill on the island. For a time, all of Puerto Rico was united behind a common cause—not one more bomb would fall on Vieques.

Although protesters had a single goal, the motivation for removing the U.S. military was mixed. Some objected to the environmental damage inflicted on the island. The consistent bombardment of certain segments of the island has created a virtual wasteland of spent and unspent ordnances and toxic waste. Noting a recent report that the cancer rate on Vieques was 27 percent higher than on mainland Puerto Rico, others claimed that the navy had contaminated the island to such an extent that residents' health was adversely affected. For some, the problems on Vieques were symptomatic of Puerto Rico's ambiguous and imperialist-based relationship with the United States. They saw the removal of the U.S. Navy from Vieques as the first step to Puerto Rican independence from U.S. control. Additionally, there are those who perceived Vieques as a potentially promising location for vacation resorts and tourism, which could only be fully developed if the navy vacates. Human rights advocates cite not only detrimental health effects, but also argue that much of the economic boost provided by the navy has taken the form of nightclubs and widespread prostitution, and thus created an unsafe environment, especially for women. The conflict has also drawn peace protesters from the United States, who view the navy's treatment of Vieques as endemic of the evils of military armament. What gives the protest in Vieques particular punch has been the anti-navy stance openly taken by the Puerto Rican government and the increased support from leaders and members of the mainline churches. Who will win this battle for Vieques remains to be seen.

1966 so that sovereignty of the land occupied by U.S. bases was remitted to the Philippines, and the rent-free stay was reduced to 25 years. Filipino resentment to U.S. military presence stemmed from the degradation of the towns surrounding the bases, the desire for full sovereignty, and the fear of becoming the target of a nuclear attack due to the U.S. housing of nuclear weapons on the islands. In 1987 the Philippines adopted a new constitution that required the removal of all foreign military installations by 1992. Only a new treaty, ratified by the Senate, could overturn the constitutional stipulation.

As 1991 approached it was clear that a vast majority of Filipino senators opposed the continuation of U.S. military presence in the Philippines. Before the matter could be brought before the Senate, however, Mount Pinatubo erupted, heavily damaging Clark Air Base. Buried in ash and mud, the United States decided to abandon Clark rather than commit the estimated $520 million necessary to restore the station. Despite the loss of the air station the U.S. military wanted to maintain Subic Bay because of its unmatched ship repair facilities. Nonetheless, on September 13, 1991, the Philippine Senate rejected the Treaty of Friendship, Peace, and Cooperation, which would have extended the base treaty agreement another 10 years. Consequently, the United States formally turned over Subic Bay Naval Base to the Philippine government in September 1992, and the last U.S. ship departed from the bay the next month. As the U.S. military lamented the loss of a base location considered to be of vital importance, the Philippine government touted the development of private enterprises on the former base a complete success.

Vieques, Culebra, and a Memorandum of Understanding

On March 17, 1942, the U.S. Navy expropriated two-thirds of the 21-mile by 4-mile island of Vieques to establish a military base and training site linked to the Roosevelt Roads military complex on the mainland of Puerto Rico, which is one of the largest U.S. naval installations in the world. The Naval Ammunition Facility was established on 8,000 acres on the western end of the island. On the eastern edge, the navy developed the 11,000-acre Eastern Maneuver Area and the 900-acre Live Impact Area. As a result, approximately 50 percent of the population was forced to relocate. Most moved to a narrow strip in the center of the island; others moved to Puerto Rico, St. Croix, or the United States. The remaining 9,300 residents were

sandwiched between the ammunitions depot and the training grounds.

Though it has received the most recent attention, Vieques is not the first Puerto Rican island to resist the U.S. Navy's presence. In 1971 widespread protests calling for the navy's withdrawal began on Culebra, an island also off Puerto Rico's east coast, north of Vieques, which had been used for live ammunitions training since World War II. The protests on Culebra climaxed after an unscheduled discharge of mortar fire on a beach where children were playing. In June 1974 the U.S. administration announced that the navy would cease weapons training activities on Culebra by July 1, 1975. The shift of training to Vieques that had previously taken place on Culebra sparked organized protests on Vieques. In 1978 fishermen disrupted training maneuvers by crossing into restricted waters, resulting in numerous arrests. In the same year, the governor of Puerto Rico filed a lawsuit requesting a comprehensive injunction against naval training operations, based on claims of ecological damage to the island. The lawsuit failed in U.S. District Court in January 1981. A group of fishermen also filed a lawsuit, arguing that the navy was ruining their livelihood by destroying the fishing environment surrounding the island. The lawsuit was dropped in 1983 when Puerto Rican Governor Carlos Roméro Barceló signed a Memorandum of Understanding (MOU) with U.S. Navy Secretary James Goodrich. In the same year, Vieques was used as the main training location for the U.S. invasion of Grenada.

The MOU focused on four broad areas: community assistance, land use, ordnance delivery in the Inner Range on Vieques, and environmental matters. The intent of the agreement was to acknowledge that the navy's presence could have possible negative implications, and, accordingly, the navy was responsible for providing resources to counter the impact on the community of Vieques. Although the MOU included far-reaching economic development programs, promised increased attention to the concerns of the residents, and improved ecological protection, the agreement generally did not result in any significant change in lifestyle on Vieques. Unfulfilled plans included the development of a jewelry manufacturer's industrial park; a new tourist industry; an herb farm; electronic, printing, and textile factories; and airport expansion. Numerous buildings erected as part of the attempt at economic development have been abandoned and serve as a reminder of the failed plans.

Yet the blame for Vieques's poor economic performance is multifaceted. Issues such as lack of land space and travel distance impede the development of industry, and Vieques's relationship with the navy is further complicated by its relationship with Puerto Rico. The central government in San Juan has repeatedly placed Vieques low on its priority list, and the island's infrastructure of schools, hospitals, and social services is poorly maintained. Although the unemployment rate is officially approximately 27 percent, it realistically runs closer to 50 percent. More than 73 percent of the residents of Vieques live below the poverty line, reflecting a poverty rate almost 15 percent higher than the main island of Puerto Rico. Until recent years, as Vieques has begun receiving national attention regarding its battles with the navy, many Viequenses had the feeling of being a colony of a colony, treated as second-class citizens in Puerto Rico. The matter is further complicated by Puerto Rico's ambiguous relationship with the United States. Although Puerto Ricans were granted U.S. citizenship in 1917 and can be drafted into the U.S. military, they are not afforded the right to vote in U.S. national elections and are represented in Congress only by an elected non-voting resident commissioner.

Official Reports and Ongoing Protests

On May 28, 1999, the navy further hurt its cause when it was forced to admit that 263 uranium-tipped shells were fired on Vieques in February, a charge it had previously denied. The ammunition is illegal, and the navy called the incident an error. Another damaging blow came on July 19, 1999, when the navy reversed its previous denial that it used napalm on the island in 1993. As protesters settled in on the live fire range, determined to stay until forcibly removed, both the Puerto Rican government and the Clinton administration established special commissions to study the problem. Not surprisingly, the two panels drew sharply different conclusions. According to the governor's commission, the navy's presence was the main source of economic stagnation on the island. Lack of access to land and beaches were cited as reasons, as well as the travel time from Vieques to the main island. Although Vieques is six miles, or about 9.5 kilometers, from Puerto Rico, because the entire west end of the island is restricted to naval use, islanders must take a 22-mile, or 35 kilometer, boat ride to get to the nearest town on the main island. Other issues of concern expressed by the Puerto Rican commission included harmful environmental effects, the high rate of health problems, the need for preservation of historic sites, and the noise level, which is often cited by residents as the main irritant. The commission also pronounced the MOU to be ineffective and suggested that it be discarded. Based on its findings, the commission recommended in its July 1999 report that the U.S. Navy abandon all operations in Vieques and return all occupied lands to the Viequenses. Approved by Puerto Rican Governor Pedro Rosselló, the panel's report made the request for the navy's withdrawal the official government policy of Puerto Rico.

Meanwhile, the Special Panel on Military Operations in Vieques, appointed by the secretary of the navy on the request of President Clinton, released its report in October 1999. This study focused on the benefits of live ammunitions training, the lack of any single location that could replace Vieques, and the impact on combat readiness should the training facility be closed. The report also acknowledged the navy's shortcomings in meeting the obligations of the MOU. According to the study, although the navy was initially sincere in its efforts to abide by the MOU, poor planning and execution, coupled with numerous uncontrollable factors, resulted in the failure of most of the navy's initial efforts. The panel also noted that historically the navy has been insensitive to the concerns of the Viequenses, thus contributing to poor relations between the navy and island residents. Nonetheless, because of the island's unique ability to provide comprehensive combined training facilities, the panel recommended that essential tasks, including live fire training, that cannot be completed at other training facilities continue to take place on Vieques for the next five years. Among the 11 recommendations set forth by the panel was the goal of removing the navy from Vieques in five years; the discontinuation of use of the Naval Ammunition Facility and its cleanup and return to the Viequenses; the transfer of 110 acres to the Vieques municipality needed for the expansion of the airport; a reduction in the number of training days per calendar year; a more close monitoring of noise levels; and implementation of numerous ecological, health, and safety plans.

As a result of the secretary of defense's report, President Clinton proposed that the navy resume training for the next five years using only inert ordnance. The plan, however, was rejected outright by the Puerto Rican government. On January 31, 2000, when Governor Rosselló announced his acceptance of Clinton's alternative proposal—three years of training using dummy bombs and the call for a referendum on whether the navy should stay or go—consensus among resistance groups was broken. Many were outraged and felt betrayed by

DEMONSTRATORS BLOCKED THE ENTRY TO THE U.S. MILITARY INSTALLATION ON THE PUERTO RICAN ISLAND OF VIEQUES AND PUT UP SIGNS PROTESTING U.S. MILITARY TRAINING RUNS. *(CORBIS CORPORATION (Bellevue). Reproduced by permission.)*

the governor's acceptance of the compromise. On February 21, 2000, an estimated 85,000 to 150,000 people marched in the streets of San Juan to protest the deal. Following the march, the resistance movement centered on the protest camps that had been continuously occupied since Sanes's death. A wide array of protesters—from the Catholic, Lutheran, and United Methodist Churches to left-wing independistas—maintained constant vigil, serving as human shield against the resumption of the bombing.

The U.S. administration took action to remove the protesters on the base in early May 2000. Three warships, carrying 1,000 marines, arrived off the coast of Vieques, and helicopters hovered over the area. On May 4, 2000, masked federal agents entered the gates at dawn and peacefully arrested 215 protesters after 379 days of occupation. Among those arrested were U.S. Representatives Luis Gutíerrez, a Democrat from Illinois; Nydia Velázquez, a Democrat from New York; New York City councilman José Rivera; and New York state legislator Roberto Ramírez. There were also unsubstantiated reports that some protesters scattered into the brush to avoid arrest and continue the resistance. The arrests, which included two priests and 14 nuns, drew widespread media attention and fueled the fire of continued protests. Between May

and October 2000, more than 800 people were arrested for civil disobedience on Vieques.

RECENT HISTORY AND THE FUTURE

Politically, the tide turned against the navy on Vieques in November 2000, when Puerto Ricans elected Sila Calderón, who garnered much of her support from her promise to rid Vieques of the navy. Upon entering office, Calderón quickly denounced the deal made by Rosselló; however, the U.S. administration still considers the agreement binding and has made plans to hold the referendum in November 2001. Calderón took the navy to court to request an injunction on training maneuvers scheduled for April 2001, but lost her legal battle in U.S. District Court. From April 26 to May 2, scheduled major training operations were interrupted by protesters, who broke through barriers and formed human chains to block the entrance to the bombing range, resulting in 170 arrests. Recently, supporters of the navy's withdrawal pointed to a Portuguese study that linked excessive exposure to low-frequency noise to heart irregularities; the claim has been refuted by the navy, citing a small study done at Johns Hopkins

Medical School that negated the connection between noise and heart disease.

The situation on the island again made headlines in the United States on May 2001, when New York activist Al Sharpton was arrested in Vieques, along with three prominent Puerto Rican politicians from New York—City Councilman Adolfo Carrión, Jr., State Assemblyman José Rivera, and former state legislator Roberto Ramírez. The four, who had traveled to Vieques to participate in the protests, expected to be arrested. A federal judge, however, stunned many when he assessed jail sentences of 40 to 90 days on the politicians—much stiffer penalties than those previously given to protesters, which usually amounted to a fine. Other prominent people still awaiting trial for participating in the protests at the end of April 2001 include actor Edward James Olmos; Representative Luis Gutiérrez, a Democrat from Illinois; and Robert F. Kennedy, Jr., an environmental lawyer. Ruben Berrios, the leader of the Puerto Rican Independence Party, was sentenced on May 16 to four months in jail, based in part on a previous trespassing conviction.

The navy has made attempts to improve public relations and battle the bad publicity surrounding the controversy. On April 30, 2001, the navy transferred the 8,000 acres it occupied on the western end of the island to the Viequenses, the federal government, and conservation groups. The navy has also turned over the 1,100 acres needed to expand the airport. It maintains a Web site dedicated to providing information on the navy's role on Vieques (http://www.navyvieques.navy.mil), noting in particular that, among other benefits, the navy provides the island with civil employment opportunities, protects the waters from drug traffickers, and was instrumental in the disaster relief effort after Hurricane Hugo devastated the region in 1989. Toting the slogan "The Navy Cares," the navy boasts of a strong safety record and its efforts in ecological preservation, and refutes all claims that evidence exists linking the military base to detrimental health effects. Noting that $3 billion has been invested in Vieques's infrastructure, the navy continues to assert the need for adequate training grounds for its forces.

As more governments begin to support the outcries of their citizens to remove U.S. military presence from their soil, the United States will continue to face ongoing problems of finding itself a visitor who has long overstayed its welcome. To combat the attempts to dissolve U.S. bases around the world, the United States has most commonly resorted to offering large economic aid packages for countries to continue to tolerate U.S. military installations. As a result, maintaining foreign bases has become an increasingly expensive endeavor. Whether economic incentives will continue to be sufficient to satisfy host countries remains to be seen. If not, the U.S. military may find itself doing more with less and working harder to appease those concerned with matters of environmental protection, health and safety issues, economic development, and quality-of-life standards. Vieques may prove to be the case-in-point if the Viequenses vote to oust the navy with no concessions.

BIBLIOGRAPHY

Bandow, Doug, and Joseph S. Nye., Jr. "American Military Bases in Japan—Yea or Nay?" *Christian Science Monitor*, February 6, 1998, p. 22.

Blaker, James R. *United States Overseas Basing: An Anatomy of the Dilemma*. New York: Praeger, 1990.

Eldridge, Robert D. "The 1996 Okinawa Referendum on U.S. Base Reduction: One Question, Several Answers," *Asian Survey*, 37 (October 1997): 879–905.

"The Fight Against War Games in Paradise," *Business Week*, May 14, 2001, p. 4.

Gerson, Joseph, and Bruce Birchard, eds. *The Sun Never Sets . . . : Confronting the Network of Foreign U.S. Military Bases*. Boston, MA: South End Press, 1991.

Gregro, A. James, and Virgilio Aganon. *The Philippine Bases: U.S. Security at Risk*. Washington, DC: Ethics and Public Policy Center, 1987.

Grusky, Sara. "The Navy as Social Provider in Vieques, Puerto Rico," *Armed Forces and Society*, 18 (Winter 1992): 215– 30.

Murillo, Mario A. "The Value of Vieques," *NACLA Report on the Americas*, 34 (November 2000): 24.

"Not a Single Bomb More!" *Ecologist*, 30 (July 2000): 62.

Ramirez, Deborah. "Life on Vieques: Defiant Island," *Sun-Sentinel* (Ft. Lauderdale, FL), May 14, 2000, pp. 1G–3G.

"Report to the Secretary of Defense of the Special Panel on Military Operations on Vieques," U.S. Department of Defense, October 18, 1999. Available online at http://www.defenselink.mil/news/Oct1999/viq_101899.html (cited July 19, 2001).

Sarantakes, Nicholas E. *Keyston: The American Occupation of Okinawa and U.S.–Japanese Relations*. College Station, TX: Texas A&M University Press, 2000.

"Secretary of Defense Calls for Continued Dialogue on Vieques," U.S. Department of Defense news release, October 18, 1999. Available online at http://www.defenselink.mil/news/Oct1999/b10181999_bt487-99.html (cited July 19, 2001).

—Kari Bethel

A Democratic Ousting: Yugoslavia Elects a New Leader

The Conflict

The disintegration of Yugoslavia, a multiethnic, multi-religious state held together under centralized communist rule, brought about a resurgence of nationalist tensions that culminated in a series of civil wars in the 1990s, and a leadership that seemed to flourish on conflict. The president of Yugoslavia, Slobodan Milosevic, appeared well-entrenched in his leadership when a newly cooperative opposition challenged him in a round of elections.

Political

- Because of political infighting and personal animosities, those who opposed the leadership of Slobodan Milosevic had a difficult time forming a coalition to oust him at the polls.

- As elections approached in 2000, the opposition came together in an effort to oust Milosevic, supporting candidate Vojislav Kostunica to run against the long-time leader.

- Milosevic controlled much of the nation's media. Despite Milosevic's advantages, the opposition made great gains and ran a close race against him. Kostunica refused to consider a run-off election, insisting he had won the election.

- Protests occurred throughout Yugoslavia in support of Kostunica, though Milosevic refused to step down despite escalating tensions.

Economic

- Yugoslavia may have lost well into the billions of dollars from state corruption under the regime of Slobodan Milosevic. The declining standard of living in Yugoslavia during the 1990s and rampant corruption of officials were two reasons why Milosevic lost most of his political support among Yugoslavia's middle class.

- Milosevic and his family members now face charges in Yugoslavia's courts over the corruption scandals that took place during his years in office.

After suffering through five losing wars, endemic corruption, and constant political repression under the regime of Slobodan Milosevic, Yugoslavia seemed finally ready to oust the man who had ruled for over a decade. The dozens of opposition parties, fragmented by political and personal battles, had united under candidate Vojislav Kostunica, a lawyer with a reputation for putting principle above personal or political gain. In contrast to Milosevic, Kostunica also received the endorsement of the international community for the September 2000 election. Although uncomfortable with his nationalist sentiments, outside observers hoped that Kostunica's election would bring Yugoslavia back into the mainstream of world politics.

While Kostunica had only reluctantly run after being persuaded by the head of the Serbian Democratic Party, Zoran Djindjic, he turned out to be an electrifying candidate. Stressing the themes of personal integrity, economic reform, and stability, Kostunica's speeches contrasted sharply with the bombastic appearances of Milosevic, who controlled most of the media to reiterate the nationalist propaganda that had helped him keep a grip on power for so long. Despite Milosevic's advantage over his challenger, his popularity had declined so precipitously that election observers predicted a landslide victory for the opposition. When the votes were counted, however, Milosevic's election officials declared that Kostunica had failed to win an outright majority of the votes, which forced a run-off election between the two candidates. Declaring that he had won the election outright, Kostunica refused to participate in another election. Instead, the opposition candidate demanded that Milosevic step down, and rallied pro-democracy demonstrations to support his non-violent ouster.

After a series of demonstrations rocked the country, including the torching of the parliament building in the capital, Milosevic did the unthinkable—Bowing to popular protest, the dictator left office on October 7, 2001, and his successor, Vojislav Kostunica, was sworn in as president. Despite stepping down, however, Milosevic remained ensconced in the Presidential Villa with his family for several months. Still a much feared and powerful man, Milosevic surrounded himself with private bodyguards and prepared to make his political comeback. In the meantime, Yugoslav officials prepared to charge the former president on a range of offenses related to the corruption and violence perpetrated under his regime.

On March 31, 2001, a massive raid on the home of Slobodan Milosevic marked the real end of the dictator's grip on power in Yugoslavia. Just a few months after public protests ousted Milosevic from office, federal forces under cover of darkness trapped the former president in his elite Belgrade residence and demanded his surrender. Threatening to kill his entire family and commit suicide, the one-time strong man refused once again to submit to judgment. This time, however, his threats did not work; after 26 hours of intense negotiations, with as many as 1,000 federal guards massing outside his villa, Milosevic gave himself up. The former dictator entered a Belgrade jail to await determination of his legal status, all the while declaring his innocence. In a statement released to the Associated Press, Milosevic claimed that he was merely being "treated like a criminal for doing the best I can for my country" after his political fortunes had turned sour.

That Milosevic was finally toppled in the wake of the federal elections of September 2000 illustrated how weary Serbs were of a seemingly endless round of civil wars and continuing economic gloom. In addition, the leadership skills of his successor to the presidency, Vojislav Kostunica, were crucial to Milosevic's ouster. After a decade of infighting among the many would-be rivals to Milosevic, no serious challenger had managed to unite a significant number of opposition groups until Kostunica agreed to run as a coalition candidate. Running on an essentially non-partisan platform of promising better economic management and a return to more normal and peaceful conditions, Kostunica deftly sidestepped the long-standing and often arcane political arguments that had enervated the opposition and allowed Milosevic to

CHRONOLOGY

1987 Slobodan Milosevic ascends as the leading Serb nationalist politician in Yugoslavia.

May 1989 Milosevic assumes the presidency of the Serbian Republic.

June 1991 Slovenia declares its independence from the Yugoslav federation in the wake of a December 1990 referendum on the issue. A brief war follows, after which Slovenian independence is secured.

1991–92 A war for Croatian independence ends with Croatian sovereignty and territorial gains at Serbia's expense.

1992 A referendum approving Bosnian independence is followed by Serb attacks to prevent secession.

1992–95 Civil war breaks out in Yugoslavia over Bosnian independence. Milosevic turns from war advocate to peacemaker under the Dayton Accords, which recognize the new nation of Bosnia-Herzegovina.

1997–98 Violence grows in the region of Kosovo between Kosovar and Serbian forces. Under Milosevic's leadership, Serb ethnic cleansing in the province is estimated to include at least 250,000 Kosovars removed from their homes.

March 1999 NATO air strikes in Yugoslavia attempt to prevent further Serbian atrocities in Kosovo.

May 1999 Slobodan Milosevic is indicted by the international War Crimes Tribunal in The Hague for actions undertaken in Kosovo.

October 2000 In the wake of federal elections, Milosevic steps down from power after massive public protests in support of opposition candidate Vojislav Kostunica.

April 2001 Milosevic is arrested by the federal government and detained for a one-month period to determine the legal basis for his extradition or prosecution by Yugoslavian courts.

July 2001 Milosevic is handed over for trial by the international war crimes tribunal in The Hague, the Netherlands.

claim a series of electoral victories. In contrast to Milosevic's opportunistic political agenda and personal enrichment during his years in office, Kostunica also ran on his own reputation of absolute integrity and incorruptibility. Kostunica's lack of ties to the ruling Yugoslavian Communist Party and successor Socialist Party further added to his popularity among voters. Although he had led a faction of the opposition Serbian Democratic Party for a decade prior to the election, Kostunica was decidedly outside of the power elite until shortly before his successful presidential campaign.

HISTORICAL BACKGROUND

Serbian Origins

Often described as the crossroads between Europe and the Middle East, the Balkan region of southeastern Europe has incorporated diverse peoples from its earliest recorded times as part of the Roman Empire. Through the fourth century the area was home to Greeks, Dacians, Romans, and other groups, including parties of Goths and Huns that performed raids throughout the Balkans. Beginning in the sixth century, Slavonic-speaking people were added to the ethnic mixture, first as raiders and then as permanent settlers in the regions of Croatia, Serbia, Bulgaria, and elsewhere throughout the region. Although some of the new settlers forcibly took these lands, many of these ancient groups remained in the Balkans, most notably the ancestors of today's Albanians. It was from the mass of Slavic settlers, however, that modern-day Serbs trace their origins.

The first Serbian kingdoms date from medieval times, first under Stefan Vojislav around 1036 and more enduringly under the dynasty founded by Stefan Nemanja after the 1160s. At its height in 1355, medieval Serbia was the dominant power in the Balkans. Shortly thereafter, however, it came into direct conflict with the expanding Ottoman Empire. Refusing to pay tribute and live under Turkish rule, Serbia's leaders committed themselves to war. In 1371 after the Battle of the Martisa River, the Turks controlled most of Bulgaria and Macedonia. Following the devastation of the Battle of Kosovo Polje (Kosovo Plain) in 1389, the Turks ruled Serbia as well. The defeat in Kosovo by the Turks would live on as an enduring historic myth for the Serbs, a loss they vowed to avenge in order to redeem their national sovereignty. Upon the six-hundredth anniversary of the battle, Slobodan Milosevic used its imagery to whip up Serbian nationalist frenzy against Kosovar Albanians.

Modern Serbian Nationalism

The Ottoman Empire continued to expand in the Balkans throughout the early modern period, with many peoples, most notably in Bosnia and Albania, adopting the Islamic religion in the process. Not until the late seventeenth century were Turkish forces pushed back by the armies of the Hapsburg Empire, which established an enduring Military Frontier in the region to secure its reach and prevent any future expansion by the Ottomans, its rival empire. Most of Serbia remained under Ottoman control until 1878, when the Congress of Berlin established the nation's independence while placing the neighboring region of Bosnia-Herzegovina, which included many Serbs, under direct Austro-Hungarian control. Although Serbian nationalists were pleased that this arrangement recognized the end of Ottoman dominance in the Balkans, the fact that many Serbs now lived outside of Serbia in areas controlled by either the Austro-Hungarian or Ottoman Empire remained a source of bitterness. Inspired by nineteenth century Serb politician Ilija Garasanin's call for a territorial entity incorporating all Serbs under one nation, even in regions that encompassed only a minority of Serbs, many Serbs looked forward to the establishment of a Greater Serbia as the dominant country of the Balkans.

The Balkan Wars of 1912–13 added territories in Kosovo and Macedonia to Serbia; yet these gains did not satisfy the ambitions of some nationalist thinkers who resented the continuing Austro-Hungarian presence in the region, particularly in its dependency of Bosnia, where tens of thousands of Serbs resided. The assassination of heir apparent Archduke Franz Ferdinand in Sarajevo in 1914 was accordingly conducted by various secret Serb nationalist societies acting in concert, although most likely without the approval of the Serbian government in Belgrade. When the Serbian government rejected one minor point in Austria-Hungary's ultimatum in response to the assassination, World War I (1914–18) ensued. Within a year, Serbia itself was an occupied territory, its government having fled in October 1915 in a disastrous retreat through Kosovo and Albania to the Mediterranean island of Corfu. Like the Battle of Kosovo, the long retreat became another historical myth that demanded vengeance and redemption, at least in the nationalist rhetoric of future political leaders like Milosevic.

Serbia and Yugoslavia

During the Balkan Wars and World War I, Serbia lost a quarter of its population to war and disease. The nation itself also no longer existed, at least not as an independent Serbian state. Instead, with the encouragement of the victorious Allied Powers, the Kingdom of Slovenes, Croats, and

MAP OF YUGOSLAVIA, WITH SPECIFIC DETAILS OF SERBIA. *(The Gale Group.)*

Serbs, comprised of territory including Slovenia, Croatia, Bosnia-Herzegovina, Serbia, Montenegro, and Macedonia, was declared on December 1, 1918. The newly formed nation of Yugoslavia incorporated such diverse ethnic, religious, and linguistic orders that no single group constituted a majority of the population. Serbs made up the largest group, at almost 39 percent of the total population. Croats were the second-largest population, with almost 24 percent of all citizens. From the beginning, these two ethnic groups competed for supremacy in the new state, with Serbian lead-ership dominating Yugoslavia throughout the 1920s and 1930s. No single political party, however, ever gained a majority of representation during these decades, leading to political inertia that ushered in a royal dictatorship in 1929. Unfortunately, the dictatorship under King Aleksandar failed to stifle the ethnic and religious tensions that fundamentally characterized Yugoslavian politics. Nor did it prevent the economic disaster that began with the global Great Depression that lasted until the eve of World War II (1939–45). After Aleksandar's assassination by an ultra-nationalist

ETHNIC POPULATIONS IN BOSNIA-HERZEGOVINA

as a percentage

	1879	1910	1948	1961	1971	1981	1991
Serbs	42.9	43.5	44.0	42.9	37.2	32.0	31.3
Croats	18.1	22.9	24.0	21.7	20.6	18.4	17.3
Muslims	38.7	32.2	31.0	25.7	39.6	39.5	43.7
Others	0.3	1.4	1.0	9.7	2.6	10.1	7.0

Source: Tim Judah. *The Serbs: History, Myth, and the Destruction of Yugoslavia.* New Haven: Yale University Press, 2000.

ETHNIC SERBS MAINTAIN A STRONG PRESENCE IN OTHER REGIONS OF YUGOSLAVIA, SUCH AS BOSNIA-HERZEGOVINA. *(The Gale Group.)*

Croatian *Ustasha* (or "Rebel") agent in 1934, many feared that the country would dissolve into civil war.

While ethnic and religious tensions most often took the form of infighting between predominately Roman Catholic Croats and Orthodox Serbs, other groups also resented the political power that Serbs held in Yugoslavia during the inter-war period. Slovenes, along with Croats, often viewed Serbia as an eastern-looking and relatively backward region, in contrast to their own closer ties to western Europe. While Serbs argued for a highly centralized state with power concentrated in Belgrade, these groups favored a more decentralized government that allowed more decision making to take place in the republics. Bosnian Muslims, while generally supportive of a unified Yugoslavian state, also resented Serbian domination of federal politics. It was only the onset of World War II and the threat of invasion by Nazi Germany and fascist Italy that forced these groups to put aside their differences and present a unified front to their potential occupiers. In exchange for more guarantees of decentralization in 1939, for example, Croatia agreed to remain part of Yugoslavia and cease making demands for greater autonomy, at least for the moment.

Given Yugoslavia's strategic position in Europe, however, the attempt at forming a Yugoslav federation out of its republics was doomed. By the end of the 1930s the country's economy was tightly bound to Germany, which was its largest trading partner. In addition to this economic tie, Yugoslavia's position as a stepping stone to the resources of southeastern Europe, most importantly the oil fields of Romania, which were within air strike distance of Yugoslavia, meant that Nazi Germany demanded a Yugoslav alliance with the Axis powers soon after the onset of World War II. While the Yugoslav government held out against signing up with Hitler longer than most other countries in the region and most Yugoslavs supported the Allied powers, the country entered the Axis Tripartite Pact on March 27, 1941. Shortly thereafter, the government was overthrown and public protests against the Axis spread across the capital. Fearing immediate invasion, however, the new military government soon reaffirmed its allegiance to the Axis powers. Days later, despite this declaration, the Nazis bombed Belgrade and after eleven days of fighting, Yugoslavia surrendered to Germany on April 17, 1941.

The tragedy of World War II in Yugoslavia revived many of the longstanding ethnic and political feuds that had characterized the nation since its inception, and would set in place the modern forces that would eventually destroy the country in the 1990s. While most of Serbia fell under German occupation for the duration of the war, the Italians set up an Independent State of Croatia under their direct control that comprised all of Croatia and most of Bosnia-Herzegovina. Ethnic cleansing by Croatian *Ustasha* forces against Serbs and Muslims began almost immediately in the fascist puppet state. Reaching an intensity that exceeded the forced removal of 150,000 Serbs that occurred during World War I, *Ustasha* violence introduced more repression, removals, and executions to the region, including willing participation in the Holocaust on Nazi orders. In the areas of the former Yugoslavia under German control, Serb *Chetnik* (or "Unorganized") forces loyal to the government-in-exile actively sought aid from the Allies in their fights against their occupiers, even as they engaged in their own ethnic atrocities against Croats and Muslims.

By 1943 a third group had gained the support of the western Allies for its daring maneuvers against the Axis occupation armies: the Partisans of the National Liberation Movement under Josip Broz Tito. Although the group was a branch of the Communist Party, it managed to put aside ideological differences to form a broad resistance movement throughout the region. In contrast to the counterproductive actions of the Ustasha and Chetniks during World War II, as Branka Prpa-

Jovanovic points out in her essay *The Making of Yugoslavia: 1830–1945,* "It was clear [the Communist Partisans] were alone in maintaining a consistent struggle against the invader. Their appeal to the Yugoslav peoples lay in their patriotic, local, and democratic, rather than ideological, principles." In addition, the Partisans benefited from the inspired and sometimes ruthless leadership of Tito, who was politically astute enough to secure the open support of the Allies for the Partisans. At war's end, he emerged as the unrivaled leader of the newly emergent Yugoslav nation.

Tito and Yugoslavia under the Communists

Born in 1892 of Croatian and Slovenian parentage in the Croatian village of Kumrovec, Josip Broz became universally known by his underground name, Tito. Although participation in Communist Party functions was actively repressed in Yugoslavia through the 1920s and 1930s, Tito embraced Marxism after working in several jobs and workers' organizations. In 1937 Tito chaired the Communist Party of Yugoslavia, a leadership role he would retain until his death in 1980. Tito also embraced the concept of a Yugoslavia that would reestablish the republics under the strong and unifying presence of the ruling Communist Party. Having led the provisional government of Yugoslavia after the collapse of the Axis powers, Tito ensured that the Communists were unchallenged in the first postwar elections in November 1945. Each candidate in the election had first to be approved by the Communists as a suitable nominee for the ballot, and voters were given little choice but to vote for the approved candidate.

Creating a strong centralized state for social and economic planning, Tito's vision of Yugoslavia turned away from its inter-war trend toward federalism. Most Yugoslavs, however, gave Tito their enthusiastic support during the postwar era. Although political repression was a hallmark of Tito's socialist state, the number of imprisonments and executions never reached those of neighboring countries in the Soviet Bloc. Further, the land reforms ushered in by the communists met with approval from formerly landless peasants, who received about half of the nation's land that was not reserved for state enterprises. While the state tried a brief period of collectivization of agriculture in the 1950s, this was a short-lived experiment that ended with most farms returned to private ownership and management. In the industrial sector Tito pushed an extensive and ambitious series of capital-intensive projects that attempted to move Yugosla-

SERBIAN POPULATIONS WITHIN SERBIA AND OUTSIDE OF SERBIA

Serbia total *	9,750,000
Central Serbia	5,850,000
Vojvodina	2,050,000
Kosovo	1,850,000
Bosnia-Herzegovina total**	1,321,000
Croatia total**	532,000
Macedonia total**	44,000
Slovenia total**	42,000
Montenegro total**	19,000

Source: Tim Judah. *The Serbs: History, Myth, and the Destruction of Yugoslavia.* New Haven: Yale University Press, 2000.
* 1988
** 1981

SLOBODAN MILOSEVIC USED APPEALS TO SERB NATIONALISM, AMONG OTHER MEANS, TO GENERATE SUPPORT FOR HIS REGIME. SERBS MAKE UP A LARGE NUMBER OF THE POPULATION ACROSS YUGOSLAVIA. *(The Gale Group.)*

via into the first rank of industrialized nations. The change also increased the number of Yugoslavs living in urban areas; after stagnating through the 1920s and 1930s, the nation's cities once again seemed full of life and relative prosperity, at least in contrast to other Eastern-bloc cities.

Tito also made important changes in Yugoslavia's foreign relations during the immediate postwar era. Adapting the concept of Serbia's role as protector of other Slavic peoples in the region, Tito now envisioned Yugoslavia as the arbiter of the Balkans, a sort of power broker between East and West. This attitude quickly aroused fears by the Soviets that Tito would not heed their directives in diplomatic matters, and Stalin attempted to force Tito into a confederation with Bulgaria to dilute his own power. Counting on the loyalty of his inner circle, as well as genuine public support, Tito boldly broke with the Soviet Union in 1948, and declared Yugoslavia a nonaligned nation, meaning that it was not formally allied with the Western powers led by the United States, nor with the Soviet Union and its Eastern European bloc. At the time, this action was a stunning development, one that threatened once again to bring an invasion upon Yugoslavia. Tito soon enlisted significant foreign aid from the West, however, and by the mid-1950s led an alliance of nonaligned countries that included Egypt, Indonesia, and India. Tito's leadership in the alliance gave Yugoslavia a higher international profile than it had ever enjoyed in the inter-war period, which in turn gave hope that a truly unified Yugoslavian nation might belie the divisions of the past. Throughout the 1950s relations with the Soviet Union remained tense, although a gradual reestablishment of ties took place during the 1960s.

Yugoslavia's economic development during the 1950s was the most rapid of almost any nation. The dominance of central planners far removed from the sites of production, however, meant that investments in manufacturing did not always produce the most efficient or productive results. Although centralized planning was de-emphasized from the mid-1950s onward in favor of more localized decision-making, economic plans were often based on political, not market-based, concerns. In addition, the emphasis on heavy industries produced pollution that poisoned the air and water. Without advanced infrastructure developments to accompany these projects, the destruction of the environment clashed with Tito's plans on industrializing Yugoslavia. Finally, the heavy investment that industrial projects demanded strapped the Yugoslavian economy. It was only with foreign assistance that the country remained solvent during the 1950s, with the West granting aid to cover most of Yugoslavia's trade deficit. To Yugoslavs who looked eastward for comparisons, it seemed that Tito's form of socialism was far outperforming other eastern European countries, especially after planners decided to devote more resources to the production of consumer goods in the 1960s. All the while, however, Yugoslavia's standard of living fell further behind the more efficient, market-based economies of the West. During Tito's rule, up to one-fifth of Yugoslavia's work force was employed as guest workers in other countries, sending much needed cash back to their families.

Although Yugoslavia's socialist dictatorship, with its one-party rule, failed to incorporate the essential components of democracy, Tito allowed a number of liberalizing reforms in the 1960s that seemed to promise greater social and economic freedoms. More decision-making power over cultural, health, and educational matters was sent to local councils, and travel restrictions were eased to allow more Yugoslavs to work abroad. To allay complaints that the wealthier northern regions of the country were subsidizing the economic development of the less prosperous southern areas, investment decisions would increasingly be made in the republics themselves. Significantly, amendments to the constitution in 1971 specified that the federal government would limit its primary functions to defense and foreign policy, trade and monetary policies, civil rights matters, and supervision of the economy. These amendments were retained in the 1974 revised constitution, despite its attempt to strengthen the power of the Party once again by increasing its hold over the Federal Assembly, officials in the republics, and local councils. The 1974 constitution also declared Tito "President-for-Life" of Yugoslavia.

It is not without basis, then, that Tito's rule is called by many the "Golden Age" of modern Yugoslavia. With his death in 1980, however, the fragility of the nation quickly reappeared. As a result of Tito's fear of any rival challenging him for power during his lifetime, the country was burdened with an awkward, rotating presidency among a cabinet made up of representatives from the six republics and two autonomous provinces, Kosovo and Vojvodina. This "collective presidency" made concerted efforts at planning difficult, and a period of political inertia at the national level characterized the decade after Tito's death. In addition to the lack of federal leadership, the redistribution of power to the republics also complicated matters. Along with the traditional battles among the various republics for resources, political infighting now took place between representatives of the republics and federal officials. As a result, an elaborate bureaucracy with conflicting interests made it increasingly difficult to maximize efficiency in the economy.

The decentralization of economic decisions to the republics also had disastrous effects. Because of the intense rivalry generated by the two-tier bureaucracy and among the republics, foreign investment became harder to attract. In the public sector as well, republics were now competing with one another to achieve economic growth; accordingly, each one attempted to retain as much of its resources for its own projects, a strategy that often inefficiently duplicated efforts in other parts of the country. Complicating matters, the global recession of the late 1970s, brought about by surging energy prices, hit Yugoslavia harder than most countries. Dependent on foreign aid and loans to finance its development, the country now found these resources harder to obtain. At one point, the country was forced to reschedule payments on its foreign debt, and at the height of the economic crisis in

1989, inflation hit an annual rate of 2,600 percent. Throughout the 1980s the standard of living for Yugoslavs fell by 40 percent, and by the end of the decade approximately 60 percent of workers failed to achieve the minimum income level guaranteed by the state.

Despite these handicaps, Yugoslavia seemed better positioned than most other eastern European countries to handle the transition into the post-Cold War world of the 1990s. With the decline of the Soviet Union, attempts to democratize political systems and privatize national economies took hold throughout the region. Yugoslavia could claim more experience than its neighbors in both of these areas. Although he had never instituted truly democratic measures, Tito had experimented with various liberalizing measures in his effort to unify the country. And because so many of its citizens had traveled outside the country, Yugoslavs felt that their country was more cosmopolitan than their eastern-bloc neighbors and therefore better able to provide leadership to other transitional countries. In the realm of privatization, Yugoslavia also had begun some steps toward establishing a market-based economy. While public officials were still an intrusive influence throughout the economy, private businesses had always been a presence in Yugoslavia. In 1990 the government began to move to close unprofitable, state-owned enterprises, another step in its efforts to foster private ownership of publicly owned facilities.

Tragically, however, Yugoslavia would turn out to be the exception among transitional eastern European nations, which in most cases embraced democracy without violence. As it had so often in the past, the country was once again plunged into ethnic warfare, with its economy and social fabric ripped apart in the process. Democratization and privatization were both delayed as republics became preoccupied with secession and civil war. The resulting cost in human terms was immeasurable. In the name of various nationalisms, hundreds of thousands of people were killed, forcibly relocated, or caused to abandon their country for good.

The Milosevic Years

Among all participants in this dissolution, Slobodan Milosevic capitalized the most on the chaos of Yugoslavia's transition. A product of Tito's Yugoslavia, Milosevic was born in 1941 in Pozarevac, Serbia, where his parents had settled from Montenegro. Milosevic's childhood was an emotionally difficult one, as his father abandoned the family and returned to Montenegro before Milosevic had turned ten years old. Eventually, his

SERBIA OR YUGOSLAVIA?

The terms *Serbia* and *Yugoslavia* can be confusing for anyone unfamiliar with Balkan history. Specifically, *Yugoslavia* refers to the nation that existed as the Kingdom of the Slovenes, Croats, and Serbs from 1918 to 1941 (officially known as the Kingdom of Yugoslavia after 1929, or simply Yugoslavia) and the Federal Republic of Yugoslavia (FRY) from 1945 onward. FRY consisted of the republics of Slovenia, Croatia, Serbia, Bosnia-Herzegovina, Montenegro, and Macedonia, with the provinces of Kosovo and Vojvodina having autonomous status within Serbia. As a nation, FRY today consists of the republics of Serbia and Montenegro; a referendum on Montenegrin secession is expected to be approved by voters in the summer of 2001.

Serbia itself first existed as a nation in the medieval period around 1036. It expanded its territory until the Turkish conquest in 1459, after which it disappeared from the map. It was revived by the Congress of Berlin in 1878, and existed once again until 1915, when it was occupied by Allied forces in World War I (1914–18). It was subsumed into the newly formed nation of Yugoslavia in 1918. Since that time, *Serbia* refers to the republic of Serbia within FRY.

Because the majority of FRY is today comprised of the republic of Serbia, and a majority of its population is Serbian, many observers use the terms *Yugoslavia* and *Serbia* interchangeably. Adding to the confusion, some authors use the term *FRY* to refer to the "former republics of Yugoslavia."

Serbian or Yugoslavian? As a recognized ethnic group, Serbs are the majority population within the republic of Serbia in FRY. They are also the majority of the population within the Serbian Republic of Bosnia-Herzegovina, established as part of that nation by the Dayton Accords in 1995. The Serbian Republic, or *Republika Srpska*, is not part of Serbia or Yugoslavia, but of Bosnia-Herzegovina. Serbs also reside in the new nations of Croatia, Slovenia, and elsewhere in the region. These Serbs are often referred to as "Croatian Serbs," "Slovenian Serbs," "Bosnian Serbs," and so on.

The term *Yugoslavian* to denote nationality, while fostered by communist officials in FRY to encourage a united identity across ethnic lines, fell into disuse as the country disintegrated.

father committed suicide, a fate his mother would eventually choose as well when Milosevic was an adult. Young Milosevic received another early blow when his beloved uncle, a Partisan war hero and rising official of Tito's Communist Party, com-

AFTER MORE THAN A DECADE IN POWER, PUBLIC PRESSURE FORCED SLOBODAN MILOSEVIC FROM OFFICE IN 2001. *(Archive Photos, Inc. Reproduced by permission.)*

mitted suicide in 1948, possibly as a reaction to Tito's break with the Soviet Union.

Despite the scandal, Milosevic's own devotion to the Yugoslav Communist Party was complete. Although in later years some questioned whether he embraced the Party merely to serve his own ambition rather than out of ideological conviction, his rise through the ranks demonstrated his commitment to party affairs. Milosevic's marriage to Mirjana Markovic, whom he met in Pozarevac while they were students, also aided his political career. Markovic's childhood was as traumatic as her future husband's. Born in 1943 to famous Partisan parents, Markovic never knew her mother, who was arrested by the Germans and eventually assassinated, possibly by the Partisans for revealing information to the Nazis, albeit under torture. In later years, her mother was denounced by the party, despite her father's position as a high-ranking official and associate of Tito. Raised by her maternal grandparents in Pozarevac, Markovic remained estranged from her father and grew up to be a serious and driven individual. Taking on her mother's underground name, Mira, as her own nickname, Markovic seemed determined to redeem her mother's memory through her own devotion to the Communist Party.

Reinforcing each other's ambition, Milosevic and Markovic departed Pozarevac to study together at Belgrade University, where they served as leaders of the local students' Communist Party organization. Milosevic even managed to gain his first paid position with the Party while still a student. Married in 1965, the couple soon had a daughter, Marija; a son, Marko, would follow in 1976 after Markovic had earned a doctorate in sociology from the University of Nis. By that time, Milosevic had taken a series of important positions in the state-managed economy, usually at the behest of his mentor, Ivan Stambolic. In the early 1970s Milosevic gained the directorship of Technogas, a state-run energy company; Stambolic later gave him an appointment as the director of the nation's largest bank, Beobanka. Milosevic's political fortunes paralleled his rise in management. Joining the executive committee of the Serbian Communist Party (SCP) in 1982, within two years Milosevic also chaired its Belgrade operations. When Stambolic became president of Serbia in 1986, Milosevic succeeded his friend as president of the SCP.

While Milosevic sharpened his bureaucratic and political skills during these years, his wife strengthened her ties to Serbia's intellectual establishment through her position as a professor of Marxist sociology at Belgrade University. It was Markovic who helped stifle dissent at Belgrade University, the nation's leading educational establishment, when calls for educational reform threatened her husband's platform. Markovic also proved decisive in Milosevic's ousting of his longtime mentor, Ivan Stambolic, in his move for total domination of the SCP in 1987. In her own right, Markovic led the Yugoslav United Left (YUL) Party, organized in 1990 as a coalition of nationalist and hard-line groups with the goal of keeping communist ideology a driving force in Serbian politics. Markovic also used her column in *Duma* magazine to broadcast Milosevic's opinions while attacking his opponents. Expanding the family's influence on the media, daughter Marija also managed a radio station owned by the YUL. Meanwhile, son Marko, acknowledged to have numerous ties to organized crime, made a fortune from corruption and bribery schemes that exploited his parents' connections. In one instance, Marko was said to have taken over a bakery by pointing a gun at the owner and ordering him to sign over its ownership.

Although the rife corruption and violent repression of Milosevic's regime would eventually turn most Serbs against him, his initial rise to the top was in part based on the genuine popularity of his ultra-nationalist Serbian platform and his skillful manipulation of the media in broadcasting this message. More than any other event, his trip to Kosovo, an autonomous province of the Serbian Republic of Yugoslavia, over Serb charges of ethnic persecution in 1987 was the defining moment of Milosevic's ascent. Ironically, it was Ivan Stambolic who once again assigned this task to Milosevic, whom he trusted enough to serve as his proxy in a difficult situation.

With tensions rife between ethnic Albanians and Serbs in Kosovo, where the Serbs amounted to less than 11 percent of the population in contrast to an estimated 82 percent for Albanians in 1991, the Serbian Academy of Sciences had undertaken a propaganda program to publicize alleged anti-Serbian activities in the province. With this encouragement, Serbians and Montenegrins in Kosovo began to agitate for greater intervention by federal Serbian leadership in Belgrade. SCP President Stambolic, who continued to believe in the future of a united Yugoslavia and wanted to downplay ethnic nationalist issues, was hesitant to endorse such a conflict and decided to send Milosevic to the town of Kosovo Polje in his place to assess the situation and ease some of the tension. Instead, Milosevic seized the opportunity to give a rousing speech in favor of Serbian nationalism. After some Serbs were subdued by the police following a battle that had been set up by Serbian nationalist Miroslav Solevic, Milosevic declared, "No-one should dare to beat you!" Broadcast repeatedly on radio and television from Belgrade, Milosevic's speech was a turning point for Serbian nationalism in Yugoslavian politics. By the end of 1987 he had replaced Stambolic as the leader of the SCP, and he soon moved to consolidate his power over Yugoslavia as well. With Milosevic's skill at stacking the bureaucracy with his supporters and the disarray of power held by the collective presidency in Yugoslavia, Milosevic was in charge of the country by the end of the decade.

Realizing that Milosevic's rise on Serbian nationalist issues would forestall a continuing move toward federalization, leaders in the republics of Slovenia and Croatia began to prepare for secession from Yugoslavia. In Slovenia, the wealthiest and most westward-looking republic, secession was accomplished with relative ease. A referendum was first held on the issue of secession in December 1990, which was approved by voters in the republic. While Milosevic fought a ten-day war to prevent its breakaway, Slovenian independence was secured in July 1991. For the first time in their history, Slovenians had sovereignty over their own nation.

In contrast, the war for Croatian independence involved warfare on a massive scale. After the Serbs blocked the Croatian representative from assuming the head of the collective presidency of Yugoslavia in May 1991, Croatians approved two measures that endorsed secession. Unlike Slovenia, with a much smaller Serbian population, over half a million ethnic Serbs lived in Croatia, and the potential secession of so many Serbs from Yugoslavia threatened Serbian nationalist pretensions. Until a November 1991 UN-cease fire stopped the fighting, about 730,000 people became refugees, and an estimated 10,000 died in the conflict. Because Serbia had retained some Croatian territory for Yugoslavia at the time of the cease-fire, Milosevic claimed a victory. He was also now the unchallenged head of Yugoslavia, which became *de facto* Serbian in terms of its leadership. The victorious gains by Serbs in the Croatian war for independence were short-lived, however, as Croatia regained its territory in a series of military maneuvers in August 1995.

Ironically, the most brutal fighting inspired by Serbian nationalism over independence for Bosnia took place without a direct declaration of involvement by Milosevic. Instead, he used politician Radovan Karadzic and army commander Ratko Mladic as his proxies to carry out a campaign of total warfare against Bosnian Serb's opponents, including mass rapes, executions, and the leveling of civilian targets. After Bosnia voted for independence from Yugoslavia in a referendum boycotted by most Bosnian Serbs in March 1992, Karadzic ordered Serbian forces to besiege the capital city of Sarajevo. With the help of Serbian troops transferred by Milosevic to Mladic's command, a four-year civil war commenced, with an estimated quarter million perishing in the process. Distancing himself from Karadzic as western observers noted the atrocities committed under his watch, Milosevic once again claimed a personal victory as he displaced Karadzic and was recognized as the representative of the Bosnian Serbs at the U.S.-brokered Dayton Peace Accords conference in November 1995. While he was instrumental in ushering in the civil war over Bosnia, Milosevic now claimed to be a peacemaker. For the moment, the acclaim was enough to bolster Milosevic's popularity with nationalists despite the stunning loss to Croatia to regain its territory earlier that year.

Europe's Last Dictator
Through the 1990s, while a series of public protests against his regime occasionally blocked Belgrade's streets, Milosevic's hold on power remained firm. Using his control of the media and

THE PRESIDENTIAL ELECTION IN YUGOSLAVIA WAS A CHANCE FOR THE OPPOSITION TO UNITE BEHIND ONE CANDIDATE AND CAMPAIGN ON HIS BEHALF. *(CORBIS CORPORATION (Bellevue). Reproduced by permission.)*

outright physical repression to block his rivals, Milosevic and his allies held the country under police-state conditions. Milosevic also benefited from the disarray among scattered opposition forces. Although public protests in 1996 and 1997 over fraudulent elections seemed widespread enough to force Milosevic from power, personal infighting among the opposition groups' many leaders doomed their efforts. And, above all else, Milosevic continued to use the theme of Serbian nationalism to his own advantage. Calling for a strong response to attacks made on Serbian police by the Kosovo Liberation Army in February 1998, Milosevic launched military operations against ethnic Albanian villages in the province that quickly turned into another round of ethnic cleansing.

Although he was warned by NATO negotiators against further actions in Kosovo, Milosevic's forces conducted a series of raids that turned an estimated 250,000 to 300,000 ethnic Albanians into refugees. Finally, in response to the discovery of a Serbian massacre of ethnic Albanians in the village of Racak and the continued refusal of Milosevic to negotiate with the West to abate the violence, NATO bombings of Serb military targets began in March 1999. In the hysteria that followed, Milosevic used the excuse of the air strikes to step up efforts to remove ethnic Albanians from Kosovo. By April 1999, it was estimated that some 600,000 refugees had fled the province. While Milosevic was indicted for war crimes by the United Nation's (UN) Hague Tribunal as a result of his actions in Kosovo, he nevertheless restored some of his popularity at home among Serbs who resented NATO's bombing raids as an assault on the Serbian nation.

Looking forward to the next round of federal elections in September 2000, Milosevic seemed assured of another victory based on the fervent devotion of ultra-nationalist Serbs, estimated at about 20 percent of the voters; his party's long-standing fraudulent campaign tactics; and the divided opposition. Under the guidance of Zoran Djindjic, however, an opposition leader of the Serbian Democratic Party, a coalition party formed in the summer of 2000 that quickly capitalized on Milosevic's growing unpopularity with the broad spectrum of Serbs who had suffered devastating

VOJISLAV KOSTUNICA

1944– Vojislav Kostunica, son of a federal judge, was born in Belgrade on March 24, 1944. For speaking out against communist rule in Yugoslavia, his father was removed from the bench. Kostunica inherited his father's principles; after completing his legal studies, he was removed from the law faculty of Belgrade University in the early 1970s for supporting a colleague who voiced criticism of changing Yugoslavia's Constitution according to President Tito's orders.

Taking a job at an academic institute while he finished his doctorate on constitutional law, Kostunica remained involved in politics. He helped to found the Serbian Democratic Party in the wake of Tito's death and went on to head a smaller faction of the party in the 1990s. As a result of his reputation for honesty and absolute incorruptibility, Kostunica was persuaded to run as the opposition candidate for a coalition of eighteen parties against Slobodan Milosevic in the presidential election of 2000. When Milosevic claimed that his opponent failed to receive the necessary majority of votes needed to prevent another run-off election, Kostunica encouraged his supporters to engage in public, nonviolent protests. Within weeks of the contested election, public pressure forced Milosevic out of office, and Kostunica was duly sworn into office in October 2000.

VOJISLAV KOSTUNICA. *(AP/Wide World Photos. Reproduced by permission.)*

personal and economic losses during the warfare and corruption of Milosevic's rule. Uniting under candidate Vojislav Kostunica, the Democratic Opposition Party of Serbia (DOS) held a clear lead in the polls leading up to the election. Milosevic retaliated with the usual nationalist and anti-opposition propaganda, as well as with outright repression and violence. In the most infamous case in the weeks before the election, Milosevic's former mentor Ivan Stambolic disappeared from his Belgrade neighborhood while jogging. It was widely assumed that Milosevic had him assassinated because he feared that Stambolic was preparing to speak out against him and in support of the opposition.

Vojislav Kostunica seemed an unlikely candidate to challenge Europe's most feared dictator, but he had already spent a lifetime in opposition to Yugoslavia's power establishment. Born in Belgrade on March 24, 1944, Kostunica's family opposed Communist rule, which caused his father to lose his judgeship when Kostunica was a child.

Kostunica himself would continue to criticize Tito's regime as an adult, at one point being fired from the faculty of Belgrade University, where he had earned his law degree, for supporting a colleague who had criticized the changes in the 1974 constitution. Earning a living by working at an academic institute, Kostunica turned his attention to more active political involvement after Tito's death in 1980. In 1989 Kostunica helped found the Democratic Party with Zoran Djindjic, although factional battles led Kostunica to form his own party, the Democratic Party of Serbia, shortly thereafter.

While there remained some rivalry between the men, it was Djindjic who later persuaded Kostunica to run as the candidate of the DOS. Djindjic often referred to the task as the hardest one of his life, so hesitant was Kostunica to take up the mantle of the opposition. For years, Yugoslavia's opposition parties had remained too small to mount any serious challenge against Milosevic. Divided by ideological as well as political and personal differences, the parties' lack of experience with consensus-building and compromise—traditionally lacking in Balkan politics—stymied their efforts to build broad-based support. In this environment, Djindjic decided that Kostunica represented their best hope at unifying the fragmented parties that had almost nothing in common besides their opposition to Milosevic. A reserved and thoughtful academic, Kostunica studied issues from every conceivable angle before deciding his position. While this often led him to indecision, it also gained him the respect of his political colleagues for his thoughtfulness. Not so coincidentally, some of these colleagues hoped that the very qualities that made Kostunica a great thinker would keep him from becoming a strong president, allowing them to take up the decision-making duties in the new administration. Djindjic, who had decided not to run as the coalition candidate himself after polls showed that he probably would not win, was rumored to hope for such an outcome.

Although Kostunica differed greatly from Milosevic by earning a well deserved reputation for incorruptibility, he was by no measure any less of a nationalist in terms of his devotion to the idea of a Greater Serbia. He endorsed the Bosnian Serb siege of Sarajevo and visited the troops there to offer his support during the civil war. Kostunica was later quoted in a *Newsweek* profile as referring to the 1995 Serb massacre at Srebrenica, in which 7,000 Muslim men and boys were slaughtered, as "an act of self-defense." And the opposition leader firmly refused to discuss the issue of war-crimes accountability among Serbian leaders, maintaining that because each side had carried out warfare, that each side should account for its own actions. Kostunica doubted at any rate that the legal provisions had been established to extradite any Serb, including Milosevic, for a war crimes hearing by the UN Hague Tribunal, suggesting that he would block any such move.

Denied impartial access to most major media outlets in Yugoslavia, which ran under Milosevic's control, Kostunica ran a populist-style campaign that energized opposition forces. While Milosevic peddled the usual nationalist themes as so often in the past, Kostunica's ran simply as the honest candidate who could "look you in the eyes." Milosevic also used his campaign to slur Kostunica as a "moral degenerate" in its propaganda, although it failed to publicize any charges worse than noting that Kostunica did not have an expansive sense of humor. In contrast, Kostunica asked Yugoslavs to follow their conscience and declare their indepen-

dence from both Milosevic and his western enemies. One of his slogans urged voters to say "No to the White Palace," Milosevic's headquarters, and "No to the White House," a reference to Kostunica's bitterness against the West for its condemnation of Serbs for war crimes.

Despite the reservations over his nationalist stance, western observers endorsed Kostunica's candidacy in the September 2000 election. Then-U.S. Secretary of State Madeleine Albright commented to *Time*, "He wants the Serbian people to be proud, but he is not an ethnic killer. He is not a former communist, and he believes in the rule of law." Kostunica's call for free-market economic reforms and a purging of corruption in Yugoslavia also raised hopes that the massive economic losses of the Milosevic years—estimated in the billions of dollars from corruption alone—would end. Running a vigorous campaign in the face of Milosevic's media-controlled attacks, Kostunica appeared ready to win the election by a landslide. When the votes were counted under Milosevic's bureaucrats after massive numbers went to the polls, however, they announced that the opposition candidate had only barely failed to win an outright majority of the votes. Under electoral rules, a run-off election was in order and was duly scheduled. There was no doubt that Milosevic would use the interim to wage another round of repression to break the opposition and retain office.

Believing that he had actually won a majority of the votes, as independent observers concurred, Kostunica refused to participate in the run-off. Instead, the opposition candidate continued on with his campaign in the hope that growing pro-democracy demonstrations around Yugoslavia would bring a nonviolent ouster of Milosevic. Indeed, in the days following the election, massive numbers of Yugoslavs again took to the streets of Belgrade and other cities. Kostunica himself remained calm, although his dramatic appearance in support of striking miners in the city of Kolubara, who refused to submit to police forces under Milosevic, was one of the most dramatic moments in the days after the election. Once the police backed Kostunica, it was apparent to everyone that the armed forces might not support Milosevic if he called for violent repression against the opposition.

The most decisive actions of Milosevic's exit took place in the capital. While most protesters there heeded Kostunica's call for peaceful demonstrations, a riot in Belgrade culminated with arsonists attacking the Parliament building. While many anticipated that Milosevic would respond with outright violence as he had so many times in the past, the defection of key supporters, particularly in the military, showed how shallow his support had become. Bowing for the first time to public opinion, Milosevic stunned the world by stepping aside. While he withdrew to the White Palace with his family and a retinue of armed guards, his son Marko, perhaps fearing immediate retribution from his organized-crime partners, fled the country to the relative safety of Moscow. Kostunica was sworn in as President of Yugoslavia on October 7, 2000. In keeping with his populist style, he declared that he would continue living with his wife and their two cats in their apartment instead of moving into the presidential residence. For the next six months, Milosevic continued to occupy it.

RECENT HISTORY AND THE FUTURE

Among the list of challenges facing the new leader was the immediate need to revitalize the nation's economy, wrecked by years of warfare, corruption, and state intervention. Although Kostunica received his highest praise from the West for his advocacy of free-market reforms, it remains to be seen how effective his calls will be in a country where the black market economy has become a way of life. In addition to smuggling and producing counterfeit goods, organized crime has also used violence against reformers. Kostunica moved immediately to remove Milosevic's cronies with ties to organized crime, but the power and immense wealth they accumulated in Yugoslavia during his regime remain a potent force.

Kostunica's own nationalist leanings are a paramount obstacle to Yugoslavia's acceptance back into the world community. He has continually resisted cooperation with the United Nations war crimes tribunal, at first refusing to meet with chief prosecutor Carla Del Ponte during her trip to Yugoslavia during the same week that he met with Milosevic. Kostunica questioned on a trip to Bosnia-Herzegovina after his election "Whether it's ethnical or decent to measure the crimes and put them on a scale," as reported by *United Press International*. "There were evils on all sides and I think it is logical that everyone somehow expresses apologies simultaneously and judges their own crimes." With the severity of Serbian war crimes so well documented in Bosnia and other regions, such a statement seemed callous and self-serving.

Serbian nationalism remains a potent force throughout the region and, ironically, Milosevic's ouster has experienced increased demands from Serbs living outside of Yugoslavia for a reestablishment of Greater Serbia. In the Serbian Republic of Bosnia, part of the nation of Bosnia-Herzegovina established by the Dayton Accords in 1995, calls for rejoining with Yugoslavia have become more urgent, despite international opposition to such a change. At times the conflicts have become violent, as demonstrated by rioting in the internationally administered city of Brcko. As Bosnian Serbs comprise about 49 percent of the population and territory of Bosnia-Herzegovina, many feel that their status will be improved by merging with Yugoslavia, where they would be part of the majority ethnic bloc. Similarly, calls for secession from Bosnian Croats in Bosnia-Herzegovina have touched off numerous riots in the southwestern part of the country.

Milosevic is Captured

Once in office Kostunica also refused to order the capture of Milosevic so that he could be brought to trial. Instead, his coalition partner Djindjic ordered the assault in March 2001, without informing the president, who was attending a conference in Geneva. Djindjic realized that without some action on Yugoslavia's part to comply with the UN's demands for a hearing, much of the promised $100 million in U.S. aid would be withdrawn and economic sanctions against Yugoslavia would continue. With foreign aid and debt relief hanging in the balance, Kostunica reluctantly agreed to endorse the raid after it was already underway. With Milosevic under investigation by Yugoslavia on corruption, theft, and murder charges, it still remained unclear whether he would ever face an international tribunal.

The difference in opinion between Kostunica and Djindjic also revealed a rivalry between the two that might bring on the new administration's first political crisis. Rewarded with a position as Prime Minister of Serbia after the elections, Djindjic holds decidedly more pro-western views than Kostunica, who has constantly criticized NATO and UN actions as anti-Serbian. While Djindjic wanted to move against Milosevic to bring him to trial, Kostunica stubbornly refused on both legal and ethical grounds. The president believed that it would not be legally possible to extradite Milosevic to an international court, and commented that the UN War Crimes Tribunal was patently unfair to Serbian war crimes defendants in past cases. After Djindjic ordered the raid by local police, Kostunica at first refused to put federal troops behind the action. He later relented after a tense meeting with

YUGOSLAV VOTERS TURNED OUT ON ELECTION DAY TO VOTE FOR A NEW PRESIDENT. DESPITE POLL RESULTS, SLOBODAN MILOSEVIC REFUSED FOR SEVERAL WEEKS TO ADMIT HIS DEFEAT. *(AP/Wide World Photos. Reproduced by permission.)*

Djindjic, who convinced him that the raid, already underway, was necessary to demonstrate that no one was above the law, not even the former president.

As the Djindjic-Kostunica conflict shows, the nurturing of the very beginning of democratic roots in Yugoslavia remains a challenge for the new president. At no point in the nation's history has it experienced a democratic political system based on consensus or compromise. Indeed, the very nature of Balkan politics has been based on vanquishing competing interests in a winner-take-all game. Even Kostunica's victory over Milosevic carries with it a troubling note. Ironically, while he was no doubt the popular choice of Yugoslavs for the office, final and fair election results have never been certified. In contrast to the peaceful transition of power that is a hallmark of democratic politics, Milosevic was carried out of office by the force of massive numbers of protesters and rioters. In July 2001 Yugoslavia finally did agree to turn Milosevic over to the international war crimes tribunal in the Hague.

BIBLIOGRAPHY

Burg, Steven L., and Paul S. Shoup. *The War in Bosnia-Herzegovina: Ethnic Conflict and International Intervention.* Armonk: M.E. Sharpe, 1999.

Curtis, Glenn E., ed. *Yugoslavia: A Country Study.* Third edition, Washington, DC: Federal Research Division, Library of Congress, 1992.

Doder, Dusko and Louise Branson. *Milosevic: Portrait of a Tyrant*. New York: The Free Press, 1999.

Donia, Robert J., and John V.A. Fine, Jr. *Bosnia and Hercegovina: A Tradition Betrayed*. New York: Columbia University Press, 1994.

Friedman, Francine. *The Bosnian Muslims: Denial of a Nation*. Boulder, CO: Westview Press, 1996.

Glenny, Misha. *The Fall of Yugoslavia: The Third Balkan War*. New York: Penguin Books, 1994.

Judah, Tim. *The Serbs: History, Myth, and the Destruction of Yugoslavia*. New Haven: Yale University Press, 2000.

"Kostunica visits Bosnia-Herzegovina," United Press International. January 19, 2001.

Lampe, John R. *Yugoslavia as History: Twice There Was a Country* Cambridge, MA: Cambridge University Press, 1996.

Malcolm, Noel. *Kosovo: A Short History*. New York: HarperPerrenial, 1999.

"Milosevic Claims His Innocence, Demands Release from Jail," Associated Press Worldstream, April 2, 2001.

Nordland, Rod, and Zoran Cirjakovic. "Try a Little Boredom," *Newsweek*, October 16, 2000.

Ratnesar, Romesh, with Dejan Anastasijevic and Massimo Calabresi. "Man of the Hour," *Time*, October 16, 2000.

Rogel, Carole. *The Breakup of Yugoslavia and the War in Bosnia*. Westport: Greenwood Press, 1998.

Rothschild, Joseph. *Return to Diversity: A Political History of East Central Europe since World War II*. New York: Oxford University Press, 1993.

Silber, Laura and Allan Little. *Yugoslavia: Death of a Nation*. New York: Penguin Books, 1996.

Udovicki, Jasminka and James Ridgeway, eds. *Burn This House: The Making and Unmaking of Yugoslavia*. Durham, NC: Duke University Press, 1997.

West, Rebecca. *Black Lamb and Grey Falcon: A Journey through Yugoslavia*, originally published 1941; reprint, New York: Penguin Books, 1994.

West, Richard. *Tito and the Rise and Fall of Yugoslavia*. New York: Carroll and Graf, 1995.

—*Timothy G. Borden*

CONTRIBUTORS

Gerry Azzata is a former lawyer and law librarian. She has researched and written extensively in the areas of human rights and international law. A freelance writer with the Gale Group and other reference publishers during the past five years, she continues part-time work as a reference librarian. Her specialties are legal issues, biographical material, and bibliographies.

ENTRIES: Female Circumcision: Culture or Cruelty?

Michael P. Belfiore

ENTRIES: Unrest and Assassination in Congo-Kinshasa; Pakistan's Coup: New Regime or Old Tradition?

Linda Benson is a specialist in the modern history of northwestern China and has written numerous articles and several books on the Xinjiang region, the latter including *The Ili Rebellion* (1990) and *China's Last Nomads* (1998). She holds a Master's degree from the University of Hong Kong and a Ph.D. from the University of Leeds, England. Currently she is Professor of History and International Studies at Oakland University, Michigan.

ENTRIES: China's Muslim Challenge: Conflict in Xinjiang

Kari Bethel has a Master of Arts in English and has been a full-time freelance editor and writer since 1997. Prior to that she was employed as an editor and senior editor at the University of Missouri-Columbia for ten years. Ms. Bethel has written for numerous Gale publications and works with several other major publishing companies in the United States. She lives with her husband and three children outside of Columbia, Missouri.

ENTRIES: Fujimori and Montesinos: Power, Politics, and Scandal in Peru; After Somalia's Civil War: Putting the Pieces Back Together Again; Turkey's Tug of War: Straddling the Divide between East and West; U.S. Military Presence at World Ports: A Welcome Stay?

Timothy G. Borden completed his doctorate in history at Indiana University and holds degrees in economics and international relations from Brown University, and in labor history from the University of Toledo. He has worked as a consultant in the areas of international relations and public policy in addition to teaching at Indiana University and the University of Toledo. Dr. Borden's work has appeared in *Labor History, Michigan Historical Review, Polish American Studies, Northwest Ohio Quarterly*, and the *Organization of American Historians Magazine of History*.

ENTRIES: Splitting a Nation: Quebec Separatism in Canada; Currency Exchange: Ecuador Adopts the U.S. Dollar; Opening Europe's Secret Cold War Files; Hong Kong: Walking the Tightrope between Capitalism and Communism; Retained Assets: Swiss Banks Release Previously Held Funds to Holocaust Survivors; A Democratic Ousting: Yugoslavia Elects a New Leader

Ian Boxill teaches sociology at the University of the West Indies, Mona, Jamaica. He has published extensively on development issues in developing countries, including the Caribbean, Asia, and the Pacific region. He is currently involved in a research project in Mexico.

ENTRIES: Haiti's Rocky Road to Democracy; Electing Change in Mexico

Gerald E. Brennan is a freelance writer living in Arcata, California, who writes about a wide variety of subjects. He is currently working on a book about the censorship of Beat literature in the late 1950s.

ENTRIES: Death before Doomsday: Cult Members Found Dead in Uganda; New Labour and the Devolution of Power in the United Kingdom

Gerald W. Fry is currently Professor of International/Intercultural Education and Director of Graduate Studies in the Department of Educational Policy and Administration, University of Minnesota. Previously, he was Director of International Studies, Director of the Center for Asian and Pacific Studies, and Professor of International Studies/Political Science at the University of Oregon. He is a co-founder of the Northwest Regional Consortium for Southeast Asian Studies. He holds a doctorate from Stanford University and a M.P.A. from Princeton University. Professor Fry has been doing work on Southeast Asia for four decades and has spent more than ten years doing field-work in the region, primarily in mainland Southeast Asia. He has spent time in all ten of the Southeast Asian countries and has traveled to Cambodia seven times. In the summer of 1999, he was director of a Fulbright Group Projects Abroad in Cambodia and since 1993 he has co-directed the International Cooperative Learning Project, which involves Cambodia and the Royal University of Phnom Penh. Professor Fry has taught at Mahidol University, Kasetsart University, and the National Institute of Development Administration in Thailand. He was previously a Program Officer for the Ford Foundation's Office for Southeast Asia. Among his many publications are the books *Pacific Basin and Oceania, The International Development Dictionary, Evaluating Primary Education: Qualitative and Quantitative Policy Studies in Thailand,* and *The International Education of Development Consultants: Communicating with Peasants and Princes.*

ENTRIES: Pol Pot and the Prosecution of the Khmer Rouge Leadership in Cambodia

Evelyn Hauser is a researcher, writer, and marketing specialist based in Arcata, California. Her expertise includes historical and trend research in topics such as globalization, emerging industries and lifestyles, future scenarios, biographies, and the history of organizations. She graduated from the College of Economics in Berlin, Germany, and is an active member of the World Future Society. Ms. Hauser has written for several Gale publications, does proprietary research for American and German consulting companies, and writes her own column on future trends in the United States for a German future think tank.

ENTRIES: The Diamond Cartel: Monopolizing an Industry

Wendy Kagan is a freelance writer who travels frequently to Greece. Based in New York's Hudson River Valley, she runs a writing and editing business with her husband and partner, Michael Belfiore. When she is not writing, editing, or traveling, she studies goldsmithing in the Classical Greek, Roman, and Byzantine traditions.

ENTRIES: Whose Marbles Are They? Controversy over the Parthenon Marbles

Jim Nichol is an analyst specializing in the politics of Central Asia and the South Caucasus countries and in Russian affairs at the Congressional Research Service, Library of Congress. He received his Ph.D. from the University of Washington. Publications include *Diplomacy in the Former Soviet Republics* (Praeger, 1996). The views expressed in his articles do not reflect those of any institution.

ENTRIES: Disputed Drilling Rights in the Caspian Sea; Free to Speak? Establishing a Free Press in Russia

Lolly Ockerstrom is a freelance writer in Washington, DC. She is currently working on a book-length collection of creative non-fiction essays. She holds a Ph.D. in English from Northeastern University in Boston, Massachusetts.

ENTRIES: Israel's Assassination of the Opposition

Eugene Ogan, currently located in Honolulu, Hawai'i, is Professor Emeritus of Anthropology at the University of Minnesota. He has carried out anthropological and historical research in the Pacific Islands for almost four decades. His recent publications include "An Anthropology of Colonialism Out of 'The Last Unknown,'" in Machpherson, ed., *Colonial New Guinea* (University of Pittsburgh Press, 2001), and "The Nasioi of New Guinea," in Fitzpatrick, ed., *Endangered Peoples of Oceania* (Greenwood Press, 2001).

ENTRIES: Overthrowing Democracy: Fiji's Coup

E. M. Shostak has taught at Boston University and Northeastern University. She is a contributing editor at the *Boston Book Review.*

ENTRIES: South Africa's Struggle with AIDS; Threats of Terrorism in the Twenty-first Century

Eleanor Stanford served two years in the Peace Corps in the Cape Verde Islands. She is currently a graduate student in English at the University of Wisconsin.

ENTRIES: Economic Sanctions: A Valuable Weapon?; Indonesia: Grappling with Unrest in Aceh and Irian Jaya; Rooting Out Corruption in the Philippines: Impeachment of a President

GENERAL BIBLIOGRAPHY

This bibliography contains a list of sources, primarily books and articles, that will assist the reader in pursuing additional information on the topics contained in this volume.

A

Alexander, Yonah. "Commentary: Terrorism in the Twenty-first Century: Threats and Responses," *The World and I,* June 1999.

Amirahmadi, Hooshang, ed. *The Caspian Region at a Cross-road: Challenges of a New Frontier of Energy and Development.* New York: St. Martin's Press, 1999.

Amstutz, Mark R. *International Conflict and Cooperation: An Introduction to World Politics.* New York: McGraw-Hill Companies, 1998.

Arendt, Hannah. *The Origins of Totalitarianism.* reprint, New York: Harcourt Brace Jovanovich, 1973.

Arrighi, Giovanni. *The Long Twentieth Century.* New York and London: Verso, 1994.

Avruch, Kevin. *Culture and Conflict Resolution.* Washington, DC: U.S. Institute of Peace Press, 1998.

B

Bairoch, Paul. *The Economic Development of the Third World since 1900.* Berkeley, CA: University of California Press, 1975.

Barkan, Steven E., and Lynne L. Snowden. *Collective Violence.* Boston, MA: Allyn and Bacon, 2001.

Bartlett, C. J. *The Global Conflict: The International Rivalry of the Great Powers, 1880–1990.* New York: Addison-Wesley Longman, 1994.

Bercovitch, Jacob and Richard Jackson. *International Conflict: A Chronological Encyclopedia of Conflict Management, 1945–1995.* Washington DC: Congressional Quarterly, 1997.

Blaker, James R. *United States Overseas Basing: An Anatomy of the Dilemma.* New York: Praeger, 1990.

Bradbury, Jonathan and John Mawson. *British Regionalism and Devolution: The Challenges of State Reform and European Integration.* Regional Policy and Development Series 16, London: Jessica Kingsley Publishers, 1997.

Brown, Michael E.. *The International Dimensions of Internal Conflict.* Cambridge, MA: MIT Press, 1997.

C

Collins, Joseph J. and Gabrielle D. Bowdoin. *Beyond Unilateral Economic Sanctions.* Washington, DC: Center for Strategic and International Studies, March 1999.

D

Deudney, Daniel H. and Richard A. Matthew, eds. *Contested Grounds: Security and Conflict in the New Environmental Politics.* Albany, NY: State University of New York Press, 1999.

Diehl, Paul and Nils Gleditsch, eds. *Environmental Conflict.* Boulder, CO: Westview Press, 2000.

Dieter, Fleck, Michael Bothe, and Horst Fischer. *The Handbook of Humanitarian Law in Armed Conflict.* New York and London: Oxford University Press, 2000.

Drezner, Daniel W. *The Sanctions Paradox: Economic Statecraft and International Relations.* Cambridge, MA: Cambridge University Press, 1999.

E

Ebel, Robert and Rajan Menon, eds. *Energy and Conflict in Central Asia and the Caucasus.* Lanham, MD: Rowman & Littlefield Publishers, 2000.

Encyclopedia of World History. New York and London: Oxford University Press, 1999.

Epstein, Edward Jay. *The Rise and Fall of Diamonds: The Shattering of a Brilliant Illusion.* New York: Simon and Schuster, 1982.

F

Fukuyama, Francis. "Rest Easy. It's Not 1914 Anymore," *New York Times,* 9 February 1992.

G

Gall, Susan B., ed. *Worldmark Chronology of the Nations.* Farmington Hills, MI: Gale Group, 2000.

Gall, Timothy L., ed. *Worldmark Encyclopedia of Cultures and Daily Life.* Farmington Hills, MI: Gale Group, 1997.

Ganguly, Rajat and Raymond C. Taras. *Understanding Ethnic Conflict: The International Dimension.* New York: Addison-Wesley Longman, 1998.

Gilpin, Robert and Jean M. Gilpin. *Global Political Economy: Understanding the International Economic Order.* Princeton, NJ: Princeton University Press, 2001.

Goldstone, Jack A., Ted Robert Gurr and Farrakh Mashiri. *Revolutions of the Late Twentieth Century.* Boulder, CO: Westview Press, 1991.

Gottlieb, Gidon. *Nation Against State: A New Approach to Ethnic Conflicts and Sovereignty.* Washington, DC: Council on Foreign Relations Press, 1993.

H

Haass, Richard N. *Conflicts Unending: The United States and Regional Disputes.* New Haven, CT: Yale University Press, 1990.

Haass, Richard N., and Meghan L. O'Sullivan, eds. *Honey and Vinegar: Incentives, Sanctions, and Foreign Policy.* Washington, DC: Brookings Institution, 2000.

Hahnel, Robert. *Panic Rules!: Everything You Need to Know about the Global Political Economy.* Cambridge, MA: South End Press, 1999.

Hodgson, Marshall G. S. "World History and a World Outlook." In *Rethinking World History: Essays on Europe, Islam and World History.* New York: Cambridge University Press, 1993.

Hoffman, Stanley. *World Disorders: Troubled Peace in the Post Cold War Era.* Lanham, MD: Rowman & Littlefield, Publishers, 2000.

Homer-Dixon, Thomas F. *Environment, Scarcity, and Violence.* Princeton, NJ: Princeton University Press, 1999.

Hudson, Christopher, ed. *The China Handbook: Prospects Onto the Twenty-first Century.* Chicago, IL: Glenlake Publishing Company, 2000.

Hunter, Shireen T. *Turkey at the Crossroads: Islamic Past or European Future?* Brussels, Belgium: Centre for European Policy Studies, 1995.

K

Kakar, Sudhir. *The Colors of Violence: Cultural Identities, Religion, and Conflict.* Chicago, IL: University of Chicago Press, 1996.

Kaplan, Robert D. *The Ends of the Earth: From Togo to Turkmenistan, from Iran to Cambodia—A Journey to the Frontiers of Anarchy.* New York: Vintage Books, 1996.

Kanet, Roger E. *Resolving Regional Conflicts.* Urbana, IL: University of Illinois Press, 1998.

Katz, Richard S. *Democracy and Elections.* New York and London: Oxford University Press, 1998.

Keegan, John. *A History of Warfare.* New York: Vintage Books, 1994.

King, Anthony D., ed. *Culture, Globalization and the World-System: Contemporary Conditions for the Representation of Identity.* Minneapolis, MN: University of Minnesota Press, 1997.

Kohn, Hans. "Nationalism," *International Encyclopedia of the Social Sciences,* 11: 63–39.

L

Lal, Brij V., and Kate Fortune, eds. *The Pacific Islands: An Encyclopedia.* Honolulu, Hawai'i: University of Hawai'i Press, 2000.

Lambert, Richard D., Alan W. Heston, and William Zartman. *Resolving Regional Conflicts: International Perspectives.* London: Sage Publications, 1991.

Lawson, Stephanie. *Tradition Versus Democracy in the South Pacific: Fiji, Tonga and Western Samoa* (Cambridge Asia-Pacific Studies). London: Cambridge University Press, April 1996.

M

Mayall, James, ed. *The New Interventionism, 1991–1994: United Nations Experience in Cambodia, Former Yugoslavia, and Somalia.* Cambridge, MA: Cambridge University Press, 1996.

———. *World Politics: Progress and Its Limits (Themes for the 21st Century).* Cambridge, MA: Polity Press, 2001.

McNeill, William H. *Plagues and Peoples.* New York: Anchor Books/Doubleday & Co., Inc., 1998.

McRae, Rob and Don Hubert, eds. *Human Security and the New Diplomacy: Protecting People, Promoting Peace.* Montreal, Canada: McGill-Queen's University Press, 2001.

Miall, Hugh and Tom Woodhouse, et al. *Contemporary Conflict Resolution: The Prevention, Management and Transformations of Deadly Conflict.* Cambridge, MA: Polity Press, 1999.

Mitchell, C. R. *The Structure of International Conflict.* New York: St. Martin's Press, 1990.

N

Nash, Gary B., Charlotte Crabtree, and Ross E. Dunn. "In the Matter of History." In *History on Trial: Culture Wars and the Teaching of the Past.* New York: Alfred A. Knopf, 1998.

National Commission on Terrorism. *Countering the Changing Threat of International Terrorism.* Washington, DC: U.S. Congress, 2000.

Nye, Joseph S. *Understanding International Conflict: An Introduction to Theory and History.* New York: Addison-Welsey Longman, 1999.

O

O'Brien, Patrick K. *Atlas of World History.* New York and London: Oxford University Press, 1999.

Osborne, Milton. *The Mekong: Turbulent Past, Uncertain Future.* New York: Atlantic Monthly Press, 2000.

P

Paris, Erna. *Long Shadows: Truth, Lies, and History.* Bloomsburg, 2001.

Prendergast, John. *Frontline Diplomacy: Humanitarian Aid and Conflict in Africa.* Boulder, CO: Lynne Rienner Publishers, 1996.

R

Ramsbotham, Oliver, Cliver Ramsbotham, and Tom Woodhouse. *Humanitarian Intervention in Contemporary Conflict: A Reconceptualization.* Oxford, England: Blackwell Publishers, 1996.

Ramsbotham, Oliver and Tom Woodhouse. *Encyclopedia of International Peacekeeping Operations.* ABC-CLIO, 1999.

Ratcliffe, Peter. *Race, Ethnicity, and Nation: International Perspectives on Social Conflict.* London: UCL Press, 1994.

Rayner, Caroline, ed. *Encyclopedic World Atlas: A-Z Country-by-Country Coverage.* New York and London: Oxford University Press, 1994.

Reich, Walter, ed. *Origins of Terrorism: Psychologies, Ideologies, Theologies, States of Mind.* Washington, DC: Woodrow Wilson Center Press, 1998.

Rochards, Andrew. "Meaning of 'Genocide'," *Times Literary Supplement,* 15 May 1998.

Rothchild, Donald and David A. Lake, eds. *The International Spread of Ethnic Conflict: Fear, Diffusion, and Escalation.* Princeton, NJ: Princeton University Press, 1998.

S

Sachs, Wolfgang. *Global Ecology: A New Arena of Political Conflict.* London: St. Martin's Press, 1993.

Schlesinger, Arthur Meier. *The Disuniting of America: Reflections on a Multicultural Society.* New York: W.W. Norton, 1998.

Schnaiberg, Allan and Kenneth Alan Gould. *Environment and Society: The Enduring Conflict.* New York: St. Martin's Press, 2000.

Shawcross, William. *Deliver Us from Evil: Peacekeepers, Warlords and a World of Endless Conflict.* New York: Simon and Schuster, 2000.

Simmons, Aan G., and Ian G. Simmons. *Changing the Face of the Earth: Culture, Environment, History.* 2d ed. New York and London: Oxford University Press, 1993.

Smith, David A., Dorothy A. Solinger, and Steven Topik, eds. *States and Sovereignty in the Global Economy.* New York: Routledge, 1999.

Snooks, Graeme Donald. *The Dynamic Society: Exploring the Sources of Global Change.* New York: Routledge, 1996.

Spencer, Metta, ed. *Separatism: Democracy and Disintegration.* Lanham, MD: Rowman & Littlefield Publishers, 1998.

Staub, Ervin. *The Roots of Evil: The Origins of Genocide and Other Group Violence.* Cambridge, MA: Cambridge University Press, 1992.

Stearns, Peter N. "Nationalisms: An Invitation to Contemporary Analysis," *Journal of World History* (Spring 1997): 57–74.

Sulimann, Mohamed. *Ecology, Politics and Violent Conflict.* New York: St. Martin's Press, 1998.

V

Von Hippel, Karin. *Democracy by Force: U.S. Military Intervention in the Post-Cold War World.* Cambridge, MA: Cambridge University Press, 2000.

W

Walter, Barbara F. *Civil Wars, Insecurity, and Intervention.* New York: Columbia University Press, 1999.

Weart, Spencer R. *Never at War: Why Democracies Will Not Fight One Another.* New Haven, CT: Yale University Press, 2000.

Weaver, Frederick Stirton, and Ron Chilcote. *Latin America in the World Economy: Mercantile Colonialism to Global Capitalism.* Boulder, CO: Westview Press, 2000.

Wippman, David, ed. *International Law and Ethnic Conflict.* Ithaca, NY: Cornell University Press, 1998.

Worldmark Encyclopedia of Nations. Farmington Hills, MI: Gale Group, 1998.

Wolfe, Patrick. "Imperialism and History: A Century from Marx to Postcolonialism," *The American Historical Review* 102 (April 1997): 388–420.

Worsley, Peter. *The Three Worlds: Culture and World Development.* Chicago, IL: University of Chicago Press, 1989.

Z

Zhang, Wei-Wei. *Transforming China: Economic Reform and its Political Implications.* New York: St. Martin's Press, 2000.

General Bibliography

INDEX

Page numbers in boldface refer to a topic upon which an essay is based. Page numbers in italics refer to illustrations, figures, and tables. A number followed by a colon refers to the volume containing the given page references.

Index

Index

Index

Index

Index

DATE DUE